AMERICAN LABOR

FROM CONSPIRACY
TO
COLLECTIVE BARGAINING

RELIGION, REFORM, AND REVOLUTION:

Labor Panaceas in the Nineteenth Century

Edited by Leon Stein and Philip Taft

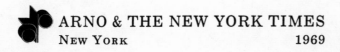

ARNO & THE NEW YORK TIMES
NEW YORK 1969

Library of Congress Catalog Card No. 79–89743

We wish to thank the following libraries for their cooperation
in providing materials for this work:

Columbia University Libraries
The Department of Labor Library
The New York State Library
The State Historical Society of Wisconsin Library
The University of Chicago Library

Manufactured in the United States of America

LIST OF PUBLICATIONS IN THIS VOLUME

INTRODUCTION

Young America created visions of a new kind of citizen—an American, free of inherited bondage, immune to religious prejudice, safe from royal prerogative, and surrounded by the wealth of the frontier. But with the start of the nineteenth century, the realization spread throughout the states that America too was not free of old world burdens. Already tainted by slavery, America entered the new century with tremors of industrial strife.

The Jeffersonian dream of a nation of husbandmen faded out; concern for canals, roads, railroads, factories and tariffs faded in. The American government system of catering to capitalists widened the gap between "producing classes" and "non-producers." Employers knew restraints in hiring, firing, setting wages, and searching out cheap, competing labor. Government felt no obligation to set elementary standards of working and living conditions. Workers witnessed the challenge of inadequate wages, and poverty and sickness testified to the guilt of egalitarianism. Strikes followed; and political action threatened; but no clear voice emerged to speak for the laboring masses. The armies of labor were dispersed, scattered in small shops; coordinated action was difficult, especially in the face of hostile law.

Many a panacea was offered to right the wrongs. Frances Wright (1811–1885) and Robert Dale Owen (1801–1877) joined forces in reform projects and Utopian experiments. Owen established a rural cooperative colony in New Harmony, Indiana, in the hope that nature would free the essential goodness of man. Frances Wright shared that hope; she counted on daring new educational techniques to modify human nature and to bring about a new era of civilization.

Edward Everett (1794–1865), William Ellery Channing (1780–1842), Orestes Brownson (1803–1876), and Calvin Colton (1789–1857) were New England consciences wrestling with the disturbing rise of regional industrialization––wrestling with the New England mills where women and children labored from sunup to sundown.

In the end, conscience deferred to profits. Everett preached the primacy of capital; Channing, with great compassion for the laborer, warned that salvation would come not through struggle, nor through political power, but only through the soul; Brownson, infuriated by failure of reform and religion, preached class struggle, the end of priesthood and banking, and traveled the full route from radicalism to religious fervor. Colton, a preacher and pamphleteer, castigated Brownson as an enemy of Christianity and education, adopted Henry Clay as his hero, and urged high protective tariffs for the benefit of worker and employer.

But for some, soul-searching was not enough. Tobacco-chewing Seth Luther (?–1846), roamed the new nation and returned to New England to work first as a carpenter, denouncing conditions of labor in the mills, then as a forceful pamphleteer, urging workers to organize. Joseph Tuckerman (1778–1840), disdainful of Channing's revolution of the soul—employer's as well as laborer's—called for private efforts to improve the lot of the worker to save the system that produced that lot. In New York Dr. John Hoskins Griscom (1809–1874), former general agent of the commissioners of emigration from 1848 to 1851, pioneered the clinical study of the causes and conditions of poverty. And in Philadelphia Mathew Carey (1760–1839), rich, conservative businessman, perceived the threats of poverty and exploitation to the total society, and issued angry pamphlets filled with statistics and specific details of the sordid results of low wages.

Charles Nordhoff (1830–1901), a printer and sailor, became managing editor of the New York Evening *Post* in 1861 and strongly defended the Union cause as the cause of free labor; Wendell Phillips (1811–1884), used his oratory first to fight black slavery and later to castigate the wage system that made slaves of all workers. He set an example of the kind of political action he favored by running for governor of Massachusetts on the Labor Reform Party ticket in 1870.

The revolutionary movements of Europe found distorted echoes in the United States. Ironically, the first American version of *The Communist Manifesto* by Karl Marx and Friedrich Engels appeared in *Woodhull & Claflin's Weekly,* published by the Woodhull sisters, two friends of Cornelius Vanderbilt who also operated a stock business. Victoria Woodhull had a childhood of family spiritualistic exhibits and fortune telling. She married at 16 and later espoused equal rights for women, free love and socialism of a variety that was condemned in 1872 by Marx's International Working Men's Association.

After the Civil War, Josephine Shaw Lowell (1843–1905) did various charity work and in 1876 she was named a member of the New York State Board of Charities. But in 1889 she resigned to carry on her effective work for the improvement of industrial conditions.

New England had provided leaders who prescribed education, Utopian communities, revolution of the soul, class war for workers. But later in the century, two New Englanders turned from lofty speculations, which did little if anything for the worker in the mill, to campaigns for more mundane, more specific improvements. George Edwin McNeill (1837–1906) was a mill hand; Ira Steward (1831–1883), a machinist. Both believed that the single most important gain for labor would be the shorter work day. McNeill and Steward worked together for the Boston Eight-Hour League. Steward delivered speeches, drew up reports, organized propaganda leagues, lobbied industriously, and was primarily responsible for making the Massachusetts State Legislature outstanding for its labor reform legislation. McNeill, a leader of the Knights of Labor, insisted that progress for the workers would come through economic rather than political organization. He recognized the power of the crafts and in 1886 he left the Knights to found the American Federation of Labor.

For most of the century workers had heard many voices raised in their behalf. As the century entered its last decade, hope rose that the new federation, divested of uplift crusaders and political hopefuls, might achieve some improvement for the worker in the shop by cutting hours, by raising wages, and by winning safeguards for life and limb on the job—all through collective bargainings.

Leon Stein and Philip Taft

RELIGION, REFORM, AND REVOLUTION:

Labor Panaceas in the Nineteenth Century

POPULAR TRACTS.

NO. 3.

CONTAINING

AN

ADDRESS TO THE INDUSTRIOUS CLASSES;

A SKETCH

OF A

SYSTEM OF NATIONAL EDUCATION,

BY FRANCES WRIGHT;

AND

AN ADDRESS TO THE CONDUCTORS OF THE NEW-YORK PERIODICAL PRESS,

BY ROBERT DALE OWEN.

NEW-YORK:

PUBLISHED AT THE OFFICE OF THE FREE ENQUIRER.

1830.

The address to the working classes, by Frances Wright, is from the Free Enquirer of the 5th of December; the subsequent sketch of a system of National Education, is from Frances Wright's lecture on Existing Evil, as delivered in the Arch-street Theatre, Philadelphia; and the address to the conductors of the New-York Press, was first published in the Free Enquirer of November 28th; and was called forth by the repeated efforts made in the principal city papers, to associate heterodoxy in opinion with imprudence in political reform.

*** I sent a copy of the Free Enquirer, containing the article addressed to the conductors of the New-York periodical press, as I promised, to all the principal city papers, who have lately devoted so large a portion of their columns to the abuse of our persons, and misrepresentation (intentional or unintentional) of our principles; yet not one of these papers, so far as I can learn, have copied or in any way adverted to it. It is difficult, with the best desire of judging all things in charity, to suppose purity of motive in conduct like this. But, whatever the motive, it is but just to ourselves and the public, that we employ the only medium now remaining at our command, and give this explanation of our views to the public in pamphlet form.

It merits a careful perusal.

R. D. O.

TO THE

INTELLIGENT AMONG THE WORKING CLASSES,

AND GENERALLY

TO ALL HONEST REFORMERS.

THE industrious classes have been called the bone and marrow of the nation; but they are in fact the nation itself. The fruits of their industry are the nation's wealth; their moral integrity and physical health is the nation's strength; their ease and independence is the nation's prosperity; their intellectual intelligence is the nation's hope. Where the producing laborer and useful artisan eat well, sleep well, live comfortably, think correctly, speak fearlessly, and act uprightly, the nation is happy, free, and wise. Has such a nation ever been? No. Can such a nation ever be? Answer, men of industry of the United States! If such *can* be, it is here. If such *is* to be, it must be your work.

Here the people govern; and *you* are the people,

And you are becoming apprized of this. You are learning your power. In New-York, in Philadelphia, in Boston, in Baltimore, you have looked round and distinguished that all is not well. In Philadelphia you have tried your strength; in New-York you have proved it. In New-York, six thousand votes have appeared at once in the ballot box, on which you had written REFORM.

This has been, indeed, a show of strength, and a sign of determination. As such it has been hailed far and wide, by every friend of human improvement. Through the counties of this powerful state, every mind looks to the metropolis. There *they* have touched the lever who alone can move it. The people have aroused themselves where they are the strongest—in the cities. There at length they have said, "We have the power, and we will use it." Yes, men of industry! you have the power; and it is now with you wisely to steer the vessel of the state into safe harbor, or rashly to peril it in the deeps and shallows of anarchy and stormy contention.

Much, I will not say *all*, depends on your first move. I

will not say *all*, because I believe that, even in spite of errors and blunders, the national institutions, and the good sense which they, in spite of all countervailing influences, have sufficed to generate, would lead you right at last. But *much* depends upon your first move. The honor of the cause depends upon it; the honor of the nation in the eyes of the world depends upon it; the honor of the nation, and your own honor in your own eyes, depend upon it. Move then warily. Take one step at a time, and let that step be always such as you can keep. He who draws back is always weakened; and he who hurries forward with blind speed, must always draw back or stumble. Touch *skilfully* as many minor abuses as circumstances and your own knowledge may permit. Check the banks; limit or repeal charters; tax church property; investigate the nature of its tenure; secure the more immediate interests of the working classes, by procuring the legal acknowledgment of their claims where now they are unheard;— All this will be important, and well, and of immediate utility, if done wisely. But as respects great measures (and all such as above enumerated, are but trifling; are but the lopping off of branches, not the severing of the root)—as respects great measures, attempt but one at a time; speak of but one at a time; if possible, think of but one at a time. Let one, and one *great measure*, alone engross for a long season, your thoughts and unite your efforts. Recall your own youth, and you will understand what that measure ought to be. Look at your children, and you can never forget it. Examine yourselves—weigh your own deficiencies, and you will appreciate all its importance, and its omnipotence.

Pledge yourselves, then, men of industry! pledge yourselves, minds, hearts, and votes, to that one measure—that saving, that regenerating, that omnipotent measure. That one measure, by which alone childhood may find sure protection; by which alone youth may be made wise, industrious, moral, and happy; by which alone the citizens of this land may be made, in very deed, *free and equal*. That measure—you know it. IT IS NATIONAL, RATIONAL, REPUBLICAN EDUCATION; FREE FOR ALL AT THE EXPENSE OF ALL; CONDUCTED UNDER THE GUARDIANSHIP OF THE STATE, AT THE EXPENSE OF THE STATE, AND FOR THE HONOR, THE HAPPINESS, THE VIRTUE, THE SALVATION OF THE STATE.

Until equality be planted in the mind, in the habits, in the manners, in the feelings, think not it can ever be in the condition. Equalize fortunes at this hour, and knavery in one year would have beggared honesty; improvidence would have dissipated its possessions; credulous simplicity would have yielded all to the crafty hypocrite; error would still deceive ignorance, and a ready tongue and a forward spirit, would still banish modest worth to the shade.

But it is not enough to forbear from rash and futile measures; they should not be talked about. Hot heads and hasty spirits will indeed urge to false movements, seek to outstrip time and circumstance, and strain to make effects precede their preparing causes. But a self-respecting people will check the zeal of imprudence, and the intemperate haste of unreasoning or false-reckoning inexperience. They will begin well, that they may end well; they will move slowly and firmly, that they may move unitedly and surely; they will begin with what touches the interests, and may convince the understandings of the great body of the nation, that opposition may be weak and co-operation strong. They will unite on that measure without which every other must be ineffectual, and which must be preparatory to every reform. They will unite on that measure, which, in principle, is so righteous, that the hypocrite dare not openly slander it; so constitutional, that the crooked politician dare not openly oppose it; so universally beneficial, that not one honest man can lift his voice against it.

Unite, then, men of industry! on this measure, and you disarm your enemies; unite on this measure, and all the sound part of the population are your friends. The vote of every righteous parent and every honest man will drop into your ballot box; and your ticket shall carry at the first general struggle, not in your city only, but throughout your state.

Take now then betimes your stand, men of industry! Organize yourselves, prepare your minds, strengthen your numbers, turn a deaf ear to the clamor of enemies; defeat by order, and union, and steady perseverance, the tricks of roguery. Fix your eyes upon the great object—*the salvation and regeneration of human kind, by means of the rational education and protection of youth.* Study this great object in all its bearings; follow it out in all its consequences and effects; digest the means by which it may be secured; let it engage your thoughts and supply your conversations; speak of it at home and abroad; win to it the attention of your wives and of your children themselves; interest all you love, and all you know, and, if possible, all with whom you come in

1*

contact, in weighing its advantages, and advancing its execution!

Bear in mind, men of industry! that *you are the people ;* and that here, by acknowledged right and acknowledged law, *the people govern.* Govern then for yourselves and your children, and for the nation of which you now form the hands, and the feet, and the trunk, and of which you must form *the head* before the head can be in union with the body it regulates. Govern as fathers as well as citizens, as citizens as well as fathers. Bear in mind that the stay and prop of liberty is knowledge ; that the basis of just government is rational education, and, that the life of a republic is equal education. Lay then the true foundation of practical republicanism. Bind all your efforts to the one great measure of a uniform plan of education for all the children and youth of your several states ; and let that plan be in perfect unison with the nature of man, the nature of things, and with the declaration of your country —*all men are free and equal.*   Frances Wright.

Buffalo, November 19, 1829.

SKETCH OF THE PLAN OF NATIONAL EDUCATION.

The measure I am about to suggest, whenever adopted, will in the outset, alleviate those popular distresses whose poignancy and rapid increase weigh on the heart of philanthropy and crush the best hopes of enlightened patriotism. It mus further, when carried into full effect, work the radical cure of every disease which now afflicts the body politic, and build up for this nation a sound constitution, embracing at once, public prosperity, individual integrity, and universal happiness.

This measure, my friends, has been long present to my mind as befitting the adoption of the American people ; as alone calculated to form an enlightened, a virtuous, and a happy community ; as alone capable of supplying a remedy to the evils under which we groan ; as alone commensurate with the interests of the human family, and consistent with the political institutions of this great confederated republic.

I had occasion formerly to observe, in allusion to the efforts already made, and yet making, in the cause of popular instruction, more or less throughout the Union, that as yet, the true principle has not been hit, and that until it be hit, all reform must be slow and inefficient.

The noble example of New-England has been imitated by other states, until all not possessed of common schools blush for the popular remissness. But, after all, how can *common schools*, under their best form, and in fullest supply, effect even the purpose which they have in view?

The object proposed by common schools (if I rightly understand it) is to impart to the whole population those means for the acquirement of knowledge which are in common use: reading and writing. To these are added arithmetic, and, occasionally, perhaps, some imperfect lessons in the simpler sciences. But, I would ask, supposing these institutions should even be made to embrace all the branches of intellectual knowledge, and thus, science offered gratis to all the children of the land, how are the children of the very class, for whom we suppose the schools instituted, to be supplied with food and raiment, or instructed in the trade necessary to their future subsistence, while they are following these studies? How are they, I ask, to be fed and clothed, when, as all facts show, the labor of the parents is often insufficient for their own sustenance, and, almost universally, inadequate to the provision of the family without the united efforts of all its members? In your manufacturing districts you have children worked for twelve hours a day; and, in the rapid and certain progress of the existing system, you will soon have them, as in England, *worked to death*, and yet unable, through the period of their miserable existence, to earn a pittance sufficient to satisfy the cravings of hunger. At this present time, what leisure or what spirit, think you, have the children of the miserable widows of Philadelphia, realizing, according to the most favorable estimate of your city and county committee, sixteen dollars per annum, for food and clothing? What leisure or what spirit may their children find for visiting a school; although the same should be open to them from sunrise to sunset? Or what leisure have usually the children of your most thriving mechanics, after their strength is sufficiently developed to spin, sew, weave, or wield a tool? It seems to me, my friends, that to build school houses now-a-days is something like building churches. When you have them, you need some measure to ensure their being occupied.

I hasten to the rapid development of the system of instruction and protection which has occurred to me as capable, and alone capable, of opening the door to universal reform.

In lieu of all common schools, high schools, colleges, seminaries, houses of refuge, or any other juvenile institution, instructional or protective, let the state. legislatures be directed (after laying off the whole in townships or hundreds) to organize, at suitable distances, and in convenient and healthy situations, establishments for the general reception of all the children resident within the said school district.   These establishments to be devoted, severally, to children between a certain age.   Say, the first to infants between two and four, or two and six, according to the density of the population, and such other local circumstances as might render a greater or less number of establishments necessary or practicable.   The next to receive children from four to eight, or six to twelve years.   The next from twelve to sixteen, or to an older age if found desirable.   Each establishment to be furnished with instructors in every branch of knowledge, intellectual and operative, with all the apparata, land, and conveniences necessary for the best development of all knowledge; the same, whether operative or intellectual, being always calculated to the age and strength of the pupils.

To obviate, in the commencement, every evil result possible from the first mixture of a young population, so variously raised in error or neglect, a due separation should be made in each establishment; by which means those entering with bad habits would be kept apart from the others until corrected.   How rapidly reform may be effected on the plastic disposition of childhood, has been sufficiently proved in your houses of refuge, more especially when such establishments have been under *liberal* superintendance, as was formerly the case in New-York.   Under their orthodox directors, those asylums of youth have been converted into jails.

It will be understood, that, in the proposed establishments, the children would pass from one to the other in regular succession, and that the parents, who would necessarily be resident in their close neighborhood, could visit the children at suitable hours, but, in no case, interfere with or interrupt the rules of the institution.

In the older establishments, the well directed and well protected labor of the pupil would, in time, suffice for, and then exceed, their own support; when the surplus might be devoted to the maintenance of the infant establishments.

In the beginning, and until all debt was cleared off, and so long as the same should be found favorable to the promotion of these best palladiums of a' nation's happiness, a double tax might be at once expedient and politic.

First, a moderate tax per head for every child, to be laid upon its parents conjointly, or divided between them, due attention being always paid to the varying strength of the two sexes, and to the undue depreciation which now rests on female labor. The more effectually to correct the latter injustice, as well as to consult the convenience of the industrious classes generally, this parental tax might be rendered payable either in money, or in labor, produce, or domestic manufactures, and should be continued for each child until the age when juvenile labor should be found, on the average, equivalent to the educational expenses, which, I have reason to believe, would be at twelve years.

This first tax on parents to embrace equally the whole population; as, however moderate, it would inculcate a certain forethought in all the human family; more especially where it is most wanted—in young persons, who, before they assumed the responsibility of parents, would estimate their fitness to meet it.

The second tax to be on property, increasing in per centage with the wealth of the individual. In this manner I conceive the rich would contribute, according to their riches, to the relief of the poor, and to the support of the state, by raising up its best bulwark—an enlightened and united generation.

Preparatory to, or connected with, such measures, a registry should be opened by the state, with offices through all the townships, where on the birth of every child, or within a certain time appointed, the same should be entered, together with the names of its parents. When two years old, the parental tax should be payable, and the juvenile institution open for the child's reception; from which time forward it would be under the protective care and guardianship of the state, while it need never be removed from the daily, weekly, or frequent inspection of the parents.

Orphans, of course, would find here an open asylum. If possessed of property, a contribution would be paid from its revenue to the common educational fund; if unprovided, they would be sustained out of the same.

In these nurseries of a free nation, no inequality must be allowed to enter. Fed at a common board; clothed in a common garb, uniting neatness with simplicity and convenience; raised in the exercise of common duties, in the acquirement of the same knowledge and practice of the same industry, varied only according to individual taste and capabilities; in the exercise of the same virtues, in the enjoyment of the same pleasures; in the study of the same nature; in pursuit of the same object—their own and each other's happiness—say! would not such a race, when arrived at manhood and womanhood, work out the reform of society—perfect the free institutions of America?

TO THE CONDUCTORS OF THE NEW-YORK PERIODICAL PRESS.

During the last three or four weeks, many of you have seen fit to attack myself and my colleagues in terms which I should be sorry either to remember or repeat. I deem it proper, in my turn, to address a few words to you.

The signs of the times are those of much excitement and great enquiry, and they have elicited from you many expressions of alarm. You have prophesied of anarchy and misrule; you have spoken to the fears of the rich and of the timid; painting to the one the violent downfall of a monied aristocracy, and to the other the repetition of scenes similar to those that were once acted by the misguided revolutionists of France. You have spoken to the bigotry of the sectarian by foretelling the decay of religion, and to the apprehensions of the good man by talking of the breaking up of social order and the decline of morality.

I have nothing to do with your motives in sounding this tocsin of alarm. If I cannot believe them honest, I have yet no right to condemn them without full proof. I speak of your conduct, only with reference to its consequences.

There *is* just cause for alarm; not from the people, if they are left to listen to the dictates of their own unheated judgments, and quietly permitted to gain wisdom by experience; for a people—a republican people especially—when they act as a body and are not spurred on by abuse and oppression, seldom persist in violence or injustice, whatever kings and tories may say to the contrary: not, as you idly pretend, from those who never strain their imaginations after other worlds; for it is more especially their interest to preserve the tranquility and secure the peaceful well being of this. But there *is* just cause for alarm—*in the consequences of your own conduct.*

The people have begun to speak and to act for themselves. They are but little accustomed to do so; and it is small wonder, that in so novel an attempt, they should overstep the line of prudence. It was your duty, and (had you but known it) it was your best interest, mildly to remind them, if you saw that they did so; that, perceiving their error, they might remedy it. But what has been your conduct? Most of you have substituted abuse for advice, and violence for argument. One of your number has spoken of the mob, and sneered, even at the noble principle of universal suffrage. You have goaded where you ought to have restrained, and irritated where you might have convinced.

Do you imagine that conduct so unwise shall not produce its effects? Are the people so *very* prudent, so *very* cool-tempered, so philosophically impassive to indignation, that they can sit with quiet pulses and hear themselves thus unworthily abused? If you think they are, you know little of human nature. They will feel—they *have* felt, the stinging injustice of your accusations. And if these should overpower the still small voice of reason within them, and tempt them, against their better judgments, to extravagance somewhat similar to your own, then, perhaps, you will begin to reflect, that, in morals as in physics, the higher the pendulum is raised on one side, the farther it swings to the opposite.

You have accused us as the promoters of anarchy and misrule. Little did you know what leads to anarchy, or, knowing, little did you regard it, when you made the baseless accusation. The best supporters of order are the temperate friends of reform; the most dangerous enemies of a nation, are those who oppose reform and abuse reformers. We, by reason, would effect a quiet and gradual change; you, by ill-timed virulence, may bring about a violent and a dangerous one.

You have told the people that we advocate agrarian laws and arbitrary divisions of property. If you said so with wilful intention to misrepresent, and thereby unfairly to advance the supposed interests of a party, I have no remark to make on your conduct. If you said so, as really believing your own assertion, I request that you will peruse, and afford your readers an opportunity to peruse, the following:

We, the editors of the Free Enquirer, have never directly or indirectly advocated or approved any thing approaching to an agrarian law, any proposal to make a division of lands or property, or any measure tending to weaken that SECURITY to per-

son and property which is indispensable to protect for society the small portion of happiness and tranquillity it now enjoys. We have proposed, and do most earnestly press it on the consideration of all friends to mankind and promoters of human improvement, that EQUAL EDUCATION should be secured to every child born to the republic. What a future generation thus trained up under the common guardianship of the State, to regard each other, not as rich and poor, not as producers and consumers, not as plebeians and patricians, but as friends, companions, and fellow-citizens—what measures they will adopt, or whether they will adopt any, to equalize their possessions— we conceive it neither possible for us now to decide, nor useful for us now to imagine.

I repeat it, we look to NATIONAL EDUCATION ALONE, for national reform. We propose no equalization, but that which equal national education shall gradually effect. Those who say we endeavour to bring about, openly or secretly, any other, say so, either in ignorant presumption of our principles and motives, or because they choose, with their eyes open, to misstate them.

For myself—that I rejoice to see the mechanics and working men awaking to enquiry and to action, that I approve many of the principles they have set forth, that I believe them honestly desirous constitutionally to secure their just rights, and that I wish them, from my soul, success in the attempt, is most true : but that I drew up that set of resolutions which you denominate anarchical, or that I have hesitated, on all fitting occasions, to express my dissent from those among them that set forth equality of *property* as a remedy for evils which I believe equality of *education* only can safely, effectually cure— is most *un*true. The mechanics who drew up the resolutions, and those who afterwards conversed with me on the subject, know that it is ; and cannot put any very charitable construction on your unceasing efforts to persuade your readers to the contrary.

I will forward a copy of the paper containing this article to each of you. I propose but that which is reasonable and just, in requesting those among you who have lately attacked us, to admit into your columns this statement in reply. If you refuse, I cannot but construe the refusal into an evidence that you fear, or at least do not choose to meet, the voice of truth. If you add any comments of your own, have the goodness to send me the papers that contain them ; and if they be brief and to the point, I will, in return, admit them into the Free Enquirer.   ROBERT DALE OWEN.

A

LECTURE

ON THE

WORKING MEN'S PARTY,

FIRST DELIVERED OCTOBER SIXTH,

BEFORE THE CHARLESTOWN LYCEUM,

AND PUBLISHED AT THEIR REQUEST.

=

BY EDWARD EVERETT.

Second Edition.

BOSTON:

PUBLISHED BY GRAY AND BOWEN.

1831.

W. L. Lewis' Print......8, Congress Street.

EVERETT'S

LECTURE

ON THE

WORKING MEN'S PARTY.

MAN is by nature an active being. He is made to labor. His whole organization—mental and physical—is that of a hard-working being. Of his mental powers we have no conception, but as certain capacities of intellectual action. His corporeal faculties are contrived for the same end, with astonishing variety of adaptation.—Who can look only at the muscles of the hand, and doubt that man was made to work? Who can be conscious of judgment, memory, and reflection, and doubt that man was made to act? He requires rest, but it is in order to invigorate him for new efforts;—to recruit his exhausted powers; and as if to show him, by the very nature of rest, that it is Means, not End:— that form of rest, which is most essential and most grateful, sleep, is attended with the temporary suspension of the conscious and active powers. Nature is so ordered as both to require and encourage man to work.—He is created with wants, which cannot be satisfied without labor; at the same time, that ample provision is made by Providence, to satisfy them, with labor.—The plant springs up and grows on the spot, where the seed was cast by accident. It is fed by the moisture, which saturates the earth or is held suspended in the air ; and it brings with it a sufficient covering to protect its delicate internal structure. It toils not, neither doth it spin, for clothing or food.—But man is so created, that, let his wants be as simple as they will, he must labor to supply them. If, as is supposed to have been the case in primitive ages, he lives upon acorns and water, he must draw the water from the spring; and in many places he must dig a well in the soil ; and he must gather the acorns from beneath the oak, and lay up a store of them for winter.—He must, in most climates, contrive himself some kind of clothing of barks or skins; must construct some rude shelter ; prepare some kind of bed, and keep up a fire.—In short, it is well known, that those tribes of our race, which are the least advanced in civilization, and whose wants are the fewest, have to labor the hardest for their support ; but at the same time it is equally true, that in the most civilized countries, by far the greatest amount and variety of work are done; so that the improvement, which takes place in the condition of man, consists, not in diminishing the amount of labor performed, but in enabling men to work more, or more efficiently, in the same time.—A horde of savages will pass a week in the most laborious kinds of hunting ; following the chase day after day; their women, if in company with them, carrying their tents and their infant children on their backs ; and all be worn down by fatigue and famine ; and in the end they will perhaps kill a buffalo. The same number of civilized men and women would probably, on an average, have kept more steadily at work, in their various trades and occupations, but with much less exhaustion ; and the products of their industry would have been vastly greater; or, what is the same thing, much more work would have been done.

It is true, as man rises in improvement, he would be enabled by his arts and machinery, to satisfy the primary wants of life, with less labor ; and this may be thought to show, at first glance, that man was not intended to be a working being ; because, in proportion as he advances in improvement, less work would be required to get a mere livelihood. But here we see a curious provision of nature. In proportion as our bare natural wants are satisfied, artificial wants, or civilized wants, show themselves. And in the very highest state of improvement, it requires as constant an exertion to satisfy the new wants, which grow out of the habits and tastes of civilized life, as it requires in savage life, to satisfy hunger and thirst, and keep from freezing. In other words, the innate desire of improving our condition keeps us all in a state of want. We cannot be so well off that we do not feel obliged to work, either to ensure the continuance of what we now have, or to increase it.—The man, whose honest industry just gives him a competence, exerts himself, that he may have something against a rainy day ;—and how often do we not hear an affectionate father say, he is determined to spare no pains,—to work in season and out of season,—in order that his children may enjoy advantages denied to himself.

In this way, it is pretty plain, that Man, whether viewed in his primitive and savage state, or in a highly improved condition, is a working being. It is his destiny—the law of his nature—to labor. He is made for it,—and he cannot live without it ; and the Apostle Paul summed up the mat-

1 *

ter, with equal correctness and point, when he said, that " if any would not work, neither should he eat."

It is a good test of principles like these, to bring them to the standard of general approbation or disapprobation. There are, in all countries, too many persons, who, from mistaken ideas of the nature of happiness, or other less reputable causes, pass their time in idleness, or in indolent pleasures ; but I believe no state of society ever existed, in which the energy and capacity of labor were not commended and admired, or in which a taste for indolent pleasure was commended or admired by the intelligent part of the community. When we read the lives of distinguished men, in any department, we find them almost always celebrated for the amount of labor they could perform. Demosthenes, Julius Cæsar, Henry the Fourth of France, Lord Bacon, Sir Isaac Newton, Franklin, Washington, Napoleon,—different as they were in their intellectual and moral qualities,—were all renowned as hard-workers. We read how many days they could support the fatigues of a march ; how early they rose, how late they watched ; how many hours they spent in the field, in the cabinet, in the court ; how many secretaries they kept employed ; in short, how hard they worked. But who ever heard of its being said of a man in commendation, that he could sleep fifteen hours out of the twenty-four, that he could eat six meals a day, and that he never got tired of his easy-chair ?

It would be curious to estimate, by any safe standard, the amount in value of the work of all kinds done in a community. This, of course, cannot be done with any great accuracy. The pursuits of men are so various, and the dif-

ferent kinds of labor performed are so different in the value
of their products, that it is scarcely possible to bring the
aggregate to any scale of calculation. If we would form
a kind of general judgment of the value of the labor of a
community, we must look about us. All the improvements,
which we behold, on the face of the earth ; all the buildings
of every kind in town and country ; all the vehicles employed on the land and water ; the roads, the canals, the wharfs,
the bridges ; all the property of all kinds, which is accumulated throughout the world and all that is consumed, from
day to day and from hour to hour, to support those who
live upon it,—all this is the product of labor ; and a proportionate share is the product of the labor of each generation.
—It is plain that this comprehensive view is one, that would
admit of being carried out into an infinity of details, which
would furnish the materials rather for a folio than a lecture.
But as it is the taste of the present day, to bring every thing
down to the standard of figures, I will suggest a calculation,
which will enable us to judge of the value of the labor performed in the community in which we live.—Take the
population of Massachusetts, for the sake of round numbers,
at 600,000 souls. I presume it will not be thought extravagant to assume, that one in six performs every day a good
day's work, or its equivalent. If we allow nothing for the
labor of five out of six, (and this certainly will cover the
cases of those too young and too old to do any work, or
who can do only a part of a day's work,) and if we also allow nothing for those whose time is worth more than that
of the day-laborer, we may safely assume, that the sixth person performs daily a vigorous efficient day's work of body

or mind, by hand or with tools, or partly with each, and that this day's work is worth one dollar. This will give us one hundred thousand dollars a day, as the value of the work done in the state of Massachusetts. I have no doubt that it is a good deal more,—for this would be very little more than it costs the population to support itself, and allows scarce any thing for accumulation, a good deal of which is constantly taking place. It will, however, show sufficiently the great amount of the labor done in this State, to take it as coming up, at least, to one hundred thousand dollars per day.

I have thus far laid down two propositions :—

First, that man is, by his nature, a working being; and second, that the daily value of his work, estimated merely in money, is immensely great, in any civilized community.

I have made these preliminary remarks, as an introduction to some observations, which I propose to submit, in the remainder of this lecture, on the subject of " a working men's party."—Towards the organization of such a party, steps have been taken in various parts of the country. It is probable, that a great diversity of views exists, among those who have occupied themselves upon the subject, in different places. This circumstance, and the novelty of the subject in some of its aspects, and its importance in all, have led me to think, that we might pass an hour profitably, in its contemplation.

I will observe upon it, in the first place, then, that if, as I have endeavored to show, man is by nature a working being, it would follow, that a working men's party is founded in the very principles of our nature.—Most parties may be considered as artificial in their very essence ; many are local, temporary and personal. What will the Adams, or the Jackson, or the Clay party be, a hundred years hence? What are they now, in nine-tenths of the habitable globe? Mere non-entities.—But the working men's party, however organized, is one that must subsist, in every civilized country, to the end of time. In other words, its first principles are laid in our natures.

It secondly follows, from what I have remarked above, that the working men's party concerns a vast amount of property, in which almost every man is interested; and in this respect, it differs from all controversies and parties, which end merely in speculation, or which end in the personal advancement and gratification of a few individuals.

The next question, that presents itself, is, What is the general object of a working men's party? I do not now mean, what are the immediate steps, which such a party proposes to take; but what is the main object and end, which it would secure. To this I suppose I may safely answer, that it is not to carry this or that political election; not to elevate this or that candidate for office, but to promote the prosperity and welfare of working men; that is, to secure to every man disposed to work, the greatest freedom in the choice of his pursuit, the greatest encouragement and aid in pursuing it, the greatest security in enjoying its fruits:—in other words, to make *work*, in the greatest possible degree, produce *happiness*.

The next inquiry seems to be, Who belong to the working men's party? The general answer here is obvious,— All who do the work, or are actually willing and desirous to do it, and prevented only by absolute inability, such as sickness or natural infirmity. Let us try the correctness of this view, by seeing whom it would exclude and whom it would include.

This rule, in the first place, would exclude all bad men; that is, those who may work indeed, but who work for immoral and unlawful ends. This is a very important distinction, and, if practically applied and vigorously enforced, it would make the working men's party the purest society that ever existed since the time of the primitive Christians. It is greatly to be feared, that scarce any of the parties, that divide the community, are sufficiently jealous on this point; and for the natural reason, that it does not lie in the very nature of the parties.—Thus, at the polls, the vote of one man is as good as the vote of another. The vote of the drunkard counts one; the vote of the temperate man counts *but* one. For this reason, the mere party politician, if he can secure the vote, is apt not to be very inquisitive about the temperance of the voter. He may even prefer the intemperate to the temperate; for to persuade the temperate man to vote with him, he must give him a good reason;— the other will do it for a good drink.

But the true principles of the working men's party require, not merely that a man should work, but that he should work in an honest way and for a lawful object. The man, who makes counterfeit money, probably works harder than the honest engraver, who prepares the bills, for those authorized by law to issue them. But he would be repelled with scorn, if he presented himself as a member of the working men's party. The thief, who passes his life, and gains a wretched, precarious subsistence, by midnight trespasses on his neighbor's grounds ; by stealing horses from the stall, and wood from the pile ; by wrenching bars and bolts at night, or picking pockets in a crowd, probably works harder, (taking uncertainty and anxiety into the calculation, and adding, as the usual consequence, four or five years in the compulsory service of the State,) than the average of men pursuing honest industry, even of the most laborious kind : but this hard work would not entitle him to be regarded as a member of the working men's party.

If it be inquired, who is to be the judge, what kind of work is not only no title, but an absolute disqualification for admission to the working men's party, on the score of dishonesty, we answer, that for all practical purposes, this must be left to the law of the land. It is true, that under cover and within the pale of the law, a man may do things morally dishonest, and such as ought to shut him out of the party. But experience has shown, that it is dangerous to institute an inquisition into the motives of individuals ; and so long as a man does nothing which the law forbids,—in a country where the people make the laws,—he ought, if not otherwise disqualified, to be admitted as a member of the party.

There ought, however, perhaps, to be two exceptions to this principle ; one, the case of those who pursue habitually a course of life, which, though contrary to law, is not usually punished by the law, such as persons habitually intemperate. It is plain, that these men ought not to be allowed to act with the party, because they would always be liable, by a very slight temptation, to be made to act in a manner hostile to its interests ; and because they are habitually in a state of incapacity to do any intelligent and ra--tional act.

The other exception ought to be of men who take advantage of the law to subserve their own selfish and malignant passions. This is done in various ways, but I will allude to but one. The law puts it in the power of the creditor, not merely to seize the property of the debtor, in payment of the debt, but to consider every case of inability as a case of fraudulent concealment, and to punish it, as such, by imprisonment. This is often done in a way to inflict the greatest possible pain, and in cases in which not only no advantage but additional cost accrues to the creditor. A man who thus takes the advantage of the law, to wreak upon others his malignant passions, ought to be excluded, not merely from the working men's party, but from the pale of civilized society.

The next question regards idlers. If we exclude from the working men's party all dishonest and immoral workers, what are we to say to the case of the idlers?—In general terms, the answer to this question is plain; they too must be excluded. With what pretence of reason can an idler ask to be admitted into the association of working men, unless he is willing to qualify himself by going to work? and then he ceases to be an idler. In fact, the man who idles away his time, acts against the law of his nature, as a working being. It must be observed, however, that there are few cases where a man is *merely* an idler. In almost every case, he must be something worse,—such as a spendthrift, a gamester, or an intemperate person; a bad son, a bad husband, and a bad father. If there are any persons de-

pendent on him for support; if he idles away the time which
he ought to devote to maintaining his wife, or his children,
or his aged parents, he then becomes a robber; a man that
steals the bread out of the mouths of his own family, and
the clothes off their backs; and he is as much more criminal
than the common highway robber, who takes the stranger's
purse on the turnpike, as the ties of duty to our parents
and children are beyond those of common justice between man
and man. But I suppose it would not require much argument
to show, that the person, who leaves to want those whom
he ought to support, even if he does not pass his idle hours
in any criminal pursuit, has no right to call himself a working man.

There is a third class of men, whose case deserves con
sideration, and who are commonly called busy-bodies.—
They are as different from real working men, as light is
from darkness. They cannot be called idlers, for they are
never at rest; nor yet workers, for they pursue no honest,
creditable employment. So long as they are merely busy-
bodies, and are prompted in their officious, fluttering, unproductive activity, by no bad motive and no malignant passion, they cannot, perhaps, be excluded from the party,
though they have really no claim to be admitted into it.
But here, too, the case of a *mere* busy-body scarce ever
occurs. This character is almost always something more;
a dangerous gossip, a tattling mischief-maker, a propagator,
too frequently an inventor of slander. He repeats at one
fireside, with additions, what he heard at another, under the
implied obligation of confidence; he is commonly in the
front rank of all uneasy and inconsiderate movements, safely

2

entrenched behind his neighbor, whom he pushes into trouble; and he is very fond of writing anonymous libels in the newspapers, on men of whom he knows nothing. Such men—and there are too many of them—ought to be excluded from the party.

Shutting out, then, all who work dishonestly, and all who do not work at all, and admitting the busy-bodies with great caution, the working men's party comprehends all those by whom the work of the community is really done ;—all those who, by any kind of honest industry, employ the talent which their Creator has given them. All these form one great party, one comprehensive society, and this by the very law of our nature. Man is not only, as I observed in the beginning, a working being; but he is a being formed to work in society ; and if the matter be carefully analysed, it will be found, that civilization, that is, the bringing men out of a savage into a cultivated state, consists in multiplying the number of pursuits and occupations : so that the most perfect society is one where the largest number of persons are prosperously employed, in the greatest variety of ways. In such a society, men help each other, instead of standing in each other's way. The farther this division of labor is carried, the more persons must unite, harmoniously, to effect the common ends. The larger the number, on which each depends, the larger the number to which each is useful.

This union of different kinds of workmen in one harmonious society seems to be laid in the very structure and organization of man. Man is a being consisting of a body and a soul. These words are *soon* uttered, and they are so *often* uttered, that the mighty truth, which is embraced in them, scarce ever engages our attention.—But man is composed of body and soul. What is body? It is material substance; it is clay, dust, ashes. Look at it, as you tread it unorganized beneath your feet; contemplate it, when, after having been organized and animated, it is, by a process of corruption, returning to its original state. Matter, in its appearance to us, is an unorganized, inanimate, cold, dull, and barren thing. What it is in its essence, no one but the Being who created it knows. The human mind can conceive of it only as the absolute negation of qualities. And we say, that the body of man is formed of the clay or dust; because these substances seem to us to make the nearest approach to the total privation of all the properties of intellect. Such is the *body* of man.—What is his *soul?*—Its essence is as little known to us as that of body; but its qualities are angelic, divine. It is soul, which thinks, reasons, invents, remembers, hopes, and loves. It is the soul which lives; for when the soul departs from the body, all its vital powers cease; and it is dead;—and what is the body then?

Now the fact, to which I wish to call your attention, is, that these two elements, one of which is akin to the poorest dust on which we tread, and the other of which is of the nature of angelic and even of divine intelligence, are, in every human being, without exception, brought into a most intimate and perfect union. We can conceive, that it might have been different. God could have created matter by itself and mind by itself. We believe in the existence of incorporeal beings of a nature higher than man; and we behold beneath us in brutes, plants, and stones, various orders of material nature, rising, one above another, in organization ; but none of them (as we suppose) possessing mind.—We can imagine a world so constituted, that all the intellect would have been by itself, pure and disembodied ; and all the material substance by itself unmixed with mind ; and acted upon by mind, as inferior beings are supposed to be acted upon by angels. But in constituting our race, it pleased the Creator to bring the two elements into the closest union ; to take the body from the dust ; the soul from the highest heaven ; and mould them into one.

The consequence is, that the humblest laborer, who works with his hands, possesses within him a soul, endowed with precisely the same faculties as those which in Franklin, in Newton, or Shakspeare, have been the light and the wonder of the world ; and on the other hand, the most gifted and ethereal genius, whose mind has fathomed the depths of the heavens and comprehended the whole circle of truth, is enclosed in a body, subject to the same passions, infirmities, and wants, as the man whose life knows no alternation but labor and rest, appetite and indulgence.

Did it stop here, it would be merely an astonishing fact in the constitution of our natures ;—but it does not stop here. In consequence of the union of the two principles in the human frame, every act, that a man performs, requires the agency both of body and mind. His mind cannot see, but through the optic eye-glass ; nor hear till the drum of his ear is affected by the vibrations of the air. If he would speak, he puts in action the complex machinery of the vocal organs ; if he writes, he employs the muscular system of the hands ; nor can he even perform the operations of

pure thought, except in a healthy state of the body. A fit
of the tooth-ache, proceeding from the irritation of a nerve
about as big as a cambric-thread, is enough to drive an understanding, capable of instructing the world, to the verge
of insanity.   On the other hand, there is no operation of
manual labor so simple, so mechanical, which does not require the exercise of perception, reflection, memory, and
judgment; the same intellectual powers, by which the
highest truths of science have been discovered and illustrated.

The degree to which any particular action (or series of
actions united into a pursuit) shall exercise the intellectual
powers, on the one hand, or the mechanical powers on
the other, of course, depends on the nature of that action.
The slave whose life from childhood to the grave is passed
in the field; the New Zealander who goes to war, when he
is hungry, devours his prisoners, and leads a life of cannibal
debauch till he has consumed them all, and then goes to
war again; the Greenlander, who warms himself with the
fragments of wrecks and drift-wood thrown upon the gla-
ciers, and feeds himself with blubber; seem all to lead lives
requiring but little intellectual action; and yet, as I have
remarked, a careful reflection would show that there is not
one, even of them, who does not, every moment of his life,
call into exercise, though in an humble degree, all the powers of the mind.   In like manner, the philosopher who shuts
himself up in his cell, and leads a contemplative existence,
among books or instruments of science, seems to have no
occasion to employ, in their ordinary exercise, many of the
capacities of his nature for physical action;—although he

2 *

also, as I have observed, cannot act, or even think, but with
the aid of his body.

This is unquestionably true. The same Creator who
made man a mixed being, composed of body and soul,
having designed him for such a world as that in which we
live, has so constituted the world, and man who inhabits it,
as to afford scope for great variety of occupations, pursuits,
and conditions, arising from the tastes, characters, habits,
virtues, and even vices, of men and communities.   For the
same reason, that—though all men are alike composed of
body and soul, yet no two men probably are exactly the
same in respect to either ;—so provision has been made, by
the Author of our being, for an infinity of pursuits and employments, calling out, in degrees as various, the peculiar
powers of both principles.

But I have already endeavored to show, that there is no
pursuit and no action that does not require the united operation of both ; and this of itself is a broad natural foundation
for the union into one interest of all, in the same community,
who are employed in honest work of any kind ; viz. that,
however various their occupations, they are all working with
the same instruments ; the organs of the body and the powers of the mind.

But we may go a step farther, to remark the beautiful
process, by which Providence has so interlaced and wrought
up together the pursuits, interests, and wants of our nature,
that the philosopher, whose home seems less on earth than
among the stars, requires, for the prosecution of his studies,
the aid of numerous artificers in various branches of mechanical industry ; and, in return, furnishes the most important

facilities to the humblest branches of manual labor. Let us take, as a single instance, that of astronomical science. It may be safely said, that the wonderful discoveries of modern astronomy, and the philosophical system depending upon them, could not have existed, but for the *telescope*. The want of the telescope kept astronomical science in its infancy among the ancients. Although Pythagoras, one of the earliest Greek philosophers, by a fortunate exercise of sagacity, conceived the elements of the Copernican system, yet we find no general and practical improvement resulting from it. It was only from the period of the discoveries, made by the telescope, that the science advanced, with sure and rapid progress. Now the astronomer does not make telescopes. I presume it would be impossible for a person, who employed in the abstract study of astronomical science time enough to comprehend its profound investigations, to learn and practise the trade of making glass. It is mentioned, as a remarkable versatility of talent in one or two eminent observers, that they have superintended the cutting and polishing of the glasses of their own telescopes. But I presume if there never had been a telescope, till some scientific astronomer had learned to mix, melt, and mould glass, such a thing would never have been heard of. It is not less true, that those employed in making the glass could not, in the nature of things, be expected to acquire the scientific knowledge, requisite for carrying on those arduous calculations, applied to bring into a system the discoveries made by the magnifying power of the telescope. I might extend the same remark to the other materials, of which a telescope consists. It cannot be used to any purpose of

nice observation, without being very carefully mounted, on
a frame of strong metal; which demands the united labors
of the mathematical instrument-maker and the brass-founder.   Here then, in taking but one single step out of the
philosopher's observatory, we find he needs an instrument,
to be produced by the united labors of the mathematical instrument-maker, the brass-founder, the glass-polisher, and
the maker of glass, four trades.*   He must also have an
astronomical clock, and it would be easy to count up half a
dozen trades, which directly or indirectly are connected in
making a clock.   But let us go back to the *object-glass* of
the telescope.   A glass factory requires a building and furnaces.   The man who makes the glass, does not make the
building.   But the stone and brick mason, the carpenter,
and the blacksmith must furnish the greater part of the labor
and skill, required to construct the building.   When it is
built, a large quantity of fuel, wood and wood-coal, or mineral coal of various kinds, or all together, must be provided;
and then the materials of which the glass is made, and with
which it is colored, some of which are furnished by commerce from different and distant regions, and must be brought
in ships across the sea.   We cannot take up any one of
these trades, without immediately finding that it connects itself with numerous others.   Take, for instance, the mason
who builds the furnace.   He does not make his own bricks,
nor burn his own lime; in common cases, the bricks come
from one place, the lime from another, the sand from another.   The brick-maker does not cut down his own wood.

---

* The allusion is here to the simplest form of a telescope.   The illustration would be stronger in the case of a reflector.

It is carted or brought in boats to his yard. The man who carts it does not make his own wagon; nor does the person who brings it in boats, build his own boat. The man who makes the wagon, does not make its tire. The blacksmith, who makes the tire, does not smelt the ore; and the forge-man who smelts the ore, does not build his own furnace, (and there we get back to the point whence we started,) nor dig his own mine. The man who digs the mine, does not make the pick-axe with which he digs it; nor the pump with which he keeps out the water. The man who makes the pump, did not discover the principle of atmospheric pressure, which led to pump-making: that was done by a mathematician at Florence, experimenting in his chamber, on a glass tube. And here we come back again to our glass; and to an instance of the close connexion of scientific research with practical art. It is plain, that this enumeration might be pursued till every art and every science were shown to run into every other. No one can doubt this, who will go over the subject in his own mind, beginning with any one of the processes of mining and working metals, of ship-building, and navigation, and the other branches of art and industry, pursued in civilized communities.

If then, on the one hand, the astronomer depends for his telescope on the ultimate product of so many arts; in return, his observations are the basis of an astronomical system and of calculations of the movements of the heavenly bodies, which furnish the mariner with his best guide across the ocean. The prudent ship-master would no more think of sailing for India, without his Bowditch's *Practical Navigator*,

than he would without his compass; and this Navigator
contains tables, drawn from the highest walks of astronomical science. Every first mate of a vessel, who works a lu-
nar observation, to ascertain the ship's longitude, employs
tables, in which the most wonderful discoveries and calculations of La Place, and Newton, and Bowditch, are interwoven.

I mention this as but one of the cases, in which astronomical science promotes the service and convenience of common life; and perhaps, when we consider the degree to
which the modern extension of navigation connects itself
with industry in all its branches, this may be thought sufficient. I will only add, that the cheap convenience of an almanac, which enters into the comforts of every fireside in
the country, could not be enjoyed, but for the labors and
studies of the profoundest philosophers. Not that great
learning or talent is now required to execute the astronomical calculations of an almanac, although no inconsiderable
share of each is needed for this purpose; but because, even
to perform these calculations requires the aid of tables, which
have been gradually formed on the basis of the profoundest
investigations of the long line of philosophers, who have devoted themselves to this branch of science. For, as we
observed on the mechanical side of the illustration, it was
not one trade alone, which was required to furnish the philosopher with his instrument, but a great variety; so, on the
other hand, it is not the philosopher in one department, who
creates a science out of nothing. The observing astronomer
furnishes materials to the calculating astronomer, and the cal-
culator derives methods from the pure mathematician; and

a long succession of each for ages must unite their labors, in a great result. Without the geometry of the Greeks, and the algebra of the Arabs, the infinitesimal analysis of Newton and Leibnitz would never have been invented.

Examples and illustrations equally instructive might be found in every other branch of industry. The man, who will go into a cotton-mill, and contemplate it from the great water-wheel, that gives the first movement, (and still more from the steam-engine, should that be the moving power,) who will observe the parts of the machinery, and the various processes of the fabric, till he reaches the hy-draulic press, with which it is made into a bale, and the canal or rail-road by which it is sent to market, may find every branch of trade and every department of science lit-erally crossed, intertwined, interwoven with every other, like the woof and the warp of the article manufactured. Not a little of the spinning machinery is constructed on principles drawn from the demonstrations of transcendental mathematics; and the processes of bleaching and dying, now practised, are the results of the most profound re-searches of modern chemistry.——And if this does not satisfy the inquirer, let him trace the cotton to the plantation, where it grew, in Georgia or Alabama; the indigo to Bengal; the oil to the olive-gardens of Italy, or the fishing-grounds of the Pacific Ocean; let him consider Whitney's cotton-gin; Whittemore's carding-machine; the power-loom; and the spinning apparatus; and all the arts, trades, and sciences, directly or indirectly connected with these; and I believe he will soon agree, that one might start from a yard of coarse printed cotton, which costs ten cents, and prove out

of it, as out of a text, that every art and science under
heaven had been concerned in its fabric.

I ought here to allude, also, to some of those pursuits
which require the ability to exercise, at the same time, on
the part of the same individual, the faculties, both of the intellectual and physical nature,—or which unite very high
and low degrees of mental power. I have no doubt, that
the talent for drawing and painting, possessed by some men
to such an admirable degree, depends partly on a peculiar
organic structure of the eye, and of the muscles of the hand,
which gives them their more delicate perceptions of color
and their greater skill in delineation. These, no doubt, are
possessed by many individuals, who want the intellectual
talent,—the poetic fire,—required for a great painter. On
the other hand, I can conceive of a man's possessing the
invention and imagination of a painter, without the eye
and the hand required to embody on the canvass the ideas
and images in his mind. When the two unite, they make
a Raphael or a Titian; a Martin or an Allston. An accomplished statuary, such as Canova or Chantrey, must, on the
one hand, possess a soul filled with all grand and lovely
images, and have a living conception of ideal beauty; and
on the other hand, he must be a good stone-cutter, and able
to take a hammer and a chisel in his hand, and go to work
on a block of marble, and chip it down to the lip of Apollo
or the eyelid of Venus.—The architect must be practically
acquainted with all the materials of building, wood, brick,
mortar, and stone; he must have the courage and skill to
plant his moles against the heaving ocean, and to hang his
ponderous domes and gigantic arches in the air; while he

must have taste to combine the rough and scattered blocks of the quarry into beautiful and majestic structures; and discern clearly in his mind's eye, before a sledge-hammer has been lifted, the elevation and proportions of the temple. The poet must know, with a schoolmaster's precision, the weight of every word, and what vowel follows most smoothly, on what consonant; at the same time, that his soul must be stored with images, feelings, and thoughts, beyond the power of the boldest and most glowing language, to do more than faintly shadow out. The surgeon must, at once, have a mind naturally gifted and diligently trained, to penetrate the dark recesses of organic life; and a nerve and tact, which will enable him to guide his knife among veins and arteries, out of sight, in the living body of an agonizing, shrieking fellow creature, or to take a lancet in his left hand, and cut into the apple of the eye. The lawyer must be able to reason from the noblest principles of human duty and the most generous feelings of human nature; he must fully comprehend the mighty maze of the social relations; he must carry about with him a stock of learning almost boundless; he must be a sort of god to men and communities, who look up to him, in the hour of the dearest peril of their lives and fortunes; and he must at the same time be conversant with a tissue of the most senseless fictions and arbitrary technology, that ever disgraced a liberal science. The merchant must be able to look, at the same moment, at the markets and exchanges of distant countries and other hemispheres, and combine considerations of the political condition, the natural wants, the tastes and habits of different parts of the world; and he must be expert at figures

3

—understand book-keeping by double entry,—and know as well how to take care of a quarter chest of tea as a cargo of specie. The general-in-chief must be capable of calculating for a twelvemonth in advance the result of a contest, in which all the power, resource, and spirit of two great empires enter and struggle, on land and by sea; and he must have an eye, that can tell at a glance, and on the responsibility of his life, how the stone walls, and trenched meadows, the barns, and the woods, and the cross-roads of a neighborhood, will favor or resist the motions of a hundred thousand men, scattered over a space of five miles, in the fury of the advance, the storm of battle, the agony of flight, covered with smoke, dust, and blood.*

It was my intention to subject the art of printing to an analysis of the trades, arts and sciences connected with it; but I have not time to do it full justice, and the bare general idea need not be repeated. I will only say that, beginning with the invention, which bears in popular tradition the name of Cadmus, I mean the invention of alphabetical signs to express sounds, and proceeding to the discovery of convenient materials for writing, and the idea of written discourse; thence to the preparation of manuscript books; and thence to the fabric, on a large scale, of linen and cotton paper, the invention of moveable types, and the printing press, the art of engraving on metal, of stereotype printing, and of the power press,—we have a series of discoveries, branching out into others in every department of human pursuit; connecting the highest philosophical principles with

* This paragraph is taken, with some alterations, from an Essay, published by the author some years ago in a Periodical Journal.

the results of mere manual labor, and producing, in the end, that system of diffusing and multiplying the expression of thought, which is, perhaps, the glory of our human nature. Pliny said, that the Egyptian reed was the support on which the immortal fame of man rested. He referred to its use in the manufacture of paper. We may with greater justice say as much of the manufacture of paper from rags, and of the printing press, neither of which was known to Pliny.— But with all the splendor of modern discoveries and improvements in science and art, I cannot but think that he, who, in the morning of the world, first conceived the idea of representing sounds by visible signs, took the most important step in the march of improvement. This sublime conception was struck out in the infancy of mankind. The name of its author, his native country, and the time when he lived, are known only by very uncertain tradition; but though all the intelligence of ancient and modern times, and in the most improved countries, has been concentred into a focus, burning and blazing upon this one spot, it has never been able to reduce it to any simpler elements, nor to improve, in the slightest degree, upon the original suggestion of Cadmus.

In what I have thus far submitted to you, you will probably have remarked, that I have illustrated chiefly the connexion with each other of the various branches of science and art; of the intellectual and physical principles. I have not distinctly shown the connexion of the moral principle, in all its great branches, with both. This subject would well form the matter of a separate essay. But its elementary ideas are few and plain. The arts and sciences, whose connexion we have pointed out, it is plain, require for their cultivation a civilized state of society. They cannot thrive in a community which is not in a state of regular political organization, under an orderly system of government, uniform administration of laws, and a general observance of the dictates of public and social morality. Farther, such a community cannot exist without institutions of various kinds for elementary, professional, and moral education; and connected with these, are required the services of a large class of individuals, employed in various ways, in the business of instruction; from the meritorious schoolmaster, who teaches the little child its A, B, C, to the moralist, who lays down the great principles of social duty for men and nations, and the minister of divine truth, who inculcates those sanctions, by which God himself enforces the laws of reason. There must also be a class of men competent by their ability, education, and experience, to engage in the duty of making and administering the law, for in a lawless society it is impossible that any improvement should be permanent. There must be another class competent to afford relief to the sick, and thus protect our frail natures from the power of the numerous foes that assail them.

It needs no words to show, that all these pursuits are in reality connected with the ordinary work of society, as directly as the mechanical trades, by which it is carried on.— For instance, nothing would so seriously impair the prosperity of a community, as an unsound and uncertain administration of justice. This is the last and most fatal symptom of decline in a state. A community can bear a very considerable degree of political despotism, if justice is duly administered between man and man. But where a man has no security, that the law will protect him in the enjoyment of his property; where he cannot promise himself a righteous judgment in the event of a controversy with his neighbor; where he is not sure, when he lies down at night, that his slumbers are safe, there he loses the great motives to industry and probity; credit is shaken; enterprise disheartened, and the State declines.—The profession, therefore, which is devoted to the administration of justice, renders a service to every citizen of the community, as important as to those whose immediate affairs require the aid of counsel.

In a very improved and civilized community, there are also numerous individuals, who, without being employed in any of the common branches of industry or of professional pursuit, connect themselves, nevertheless, with the prosperity and happiness of the public, and fill a useful and honorable place in its service.   Take, for instance, a man like Sir Walter Scott, who probably never did a day's work, in his life, in the ordinary acceptation of the term, and who has for some years retired from the subordinate station he filled in the profession of the law, as sheriff of the county and clerk of the Court.   He has written and published at least two hundred volumes of wide circulation.   What a vast amount of the industry of the community is thereby put in motion!—The booksellers, printers, paper-makers, press-makers, type-makers, book-binders, leather-dressers, ink-makers, and various other artisans required to print, publish, and circulate the hundreds and thousands of volumes, of the different works, which he has written, must be almost numberless.   I have not the least doubt, that, since the series of his publications began, if all whose industry,—directly

3 *

or remotely,—has been concerned in them, not only in Great Britain, but in America, and on the Continent of Europe, could be brought together and stationed side by side, as the inhabitants of the same place, they would form *a very considerable town.* Such a person may fairly be ranked as a working man.

And yet I take this to be the least of Sir Walter Scott's deserts. I have said nothing of the service rendered to every class, and to every individual in every class, by the writer, who beguiles of their tediousness the dull hours of life ; who animates the principle of goodness within us, by glowing pictures of struggling virtue ; who furnishes our young men and women with books, which they may read with interest, and not have their morals poisoned as they read them. Our habits, our principles, our characters,—whatever may be our pursuit in life,—depend very much on the nature of our youthful pleasures, and on the mode in which we learn to pass our leisure hours. And he who, with the blessing of Providence, has been able, by his mental efforts, to present virtue in her strong attractions, and vice in her native deformity, to the rising generation, has rendered a service to the public, greater even than his, who invented the steam-engine, or the mariner's compass.

I have thus endeavored to show, in a plain manner, that there is a close and cordial union between the various pursuits and occupations, which receive the attention of men in a civilized community :—That they are links of the same chain, every one of which is essential to its strength.

It will follow, as a necessary consequence ; as the dictate of reason and as the law of nature ;—that every man in so-

ciety, whatever his pursuit, who devotes himself to it, with
an honest purpose, and in the fulfilment of the social duty
which Providence devolves upon him, is entitled to the good
fellowship of each and every other member of the community;—that all are the parts of one whole; and that between those parts, as there is but one interest, so there
should be but one feeling.

Before I close this lecture, permit me to dwell for a short
time on the principle, which I have had occasion to advance
above, that the immortal element in our nature—the reasoning soul—is the inheritance of all our race. As it is
this which makes man superior to the beasts that perish;
so it is this, which, in its moral and intellectual endowments,
is the sole foundation for the only distinctions between man
and man, which have any real value. This consideration
shows the value of institutions for education and for the diffusion of knowledge. It was no magic, no miracle, which
made Newton, and Franklin, and Fulton. It was the patient, judicious, long-continued cultivation of powers of the
understanding, eminent, no doubt, in degree, but not differing in kind, from those which are possessed by every individual in this assembly.

Let every one then reflect, especially every person not
yet passed the forming period of his life, that he carries
about in his frame as in a casket, the most glorious thing,
which, this side heaven, God has been pleased to create, an
intelligent spirit. To describe its nature, to enumerate its
faculties, to set forth what it has done, to estimate what it can
do, would require the labor of a life devoted to the history
of Man. It would be vain, on this occasion and in these

limits, to attempt it. But let any man compare his own nature with that of a plant, of a brute beast, of an idiot, of a savage ; and then consider that it is in mind alone, and the degree to which he improves it, that he differs essentially from any of them.

And let no one think he wants opportunity, encouragement or means.—I would not undervalue these, any or all of them, but compared with what the man does for himself, they are of little account. Industry, temperance, and perseverance are worth more than all the patrons, that ever lived in all the Augustan ages. It is these, that create patronage and opportunity. The cases of our Franklin and Fulton are too familiar to bear repetition. Consider that of Sir Humphrey Davy, who died last year, and who was in many departments of science, the first philosopher of the age.*—He was born at Penzance in Cornwall, one of the darkest corners of England ; his father was a carver of wooden images for signs, and figure-heads, and chimney-pieces. He himself was apprenticed to an apothecary, and made his first experiments in chemistry with his master's phials and gallipots, aided by an old syringe, which had been given him by the surgeon of a French vessel, wrecked on the Land's End. From the shop of the apothecary, he was transferred to the office of a surgeon ; and never appears to have had any other education, than that of a Cornish school, in his boyhood. Such was the beginning of the career of the man, who, at the age of twenty-two, was selected, by our own countryman, Count Rumford,

* The sketch of Sir Humphrey Davy which follows, to the end of the lecture, is abridged from the article in the Annual Biography for 1830.

(himself a self-taught benefactor of mankind,) to fill the chair of Chemistry at the Royal Institution, in London, such was the origin and education of the man, who discovered the metallic basis of the alkalis and the earths; invented the safety-lamp; and placed himself, in a few years, in the chair of the Royal Society of London, and at the head of the chemists of Europe. Sir Humphrey Davy's most brilliant discoveries were effected by his skilful application of the Galvanic Electricity, a principle, whose existence had been detected, a few years before, by an Italian philosopher, from noticing the contractions of a frog's limb suspended on an iron hook, a fact which shows how near us, in every direction, the most curious facts lie scattered by nature. With an apparatus, contrived by himself to collect and condense this powerful agent, Sir Humphrey succeeded in decomposing the earths and the alkalis; and in extracting from common potash, the metal (before unknown) of which it consists;—possessing at 70° of the thermometer the lustre and general appearance of mercury, at 50°, the appearance of polished silver and the softness of wax; so light that it swims in water; and so inflammable that it takes fire, when thrown on ice.

These are perhaps but brilliant novelties; though connected, no doubt, in the great chain of cause and effect, with principles of art and science, conducive to the service of man. But the invention of the safety-lamp, which enables the miner to walk unharmed through an atmosphere of explosive gas, and has already saved the lives of hundreds of human beings, is a title to glory and the gratitude of his fellow men, which the most renowned destroyer of his race might envy.

The counsels of such a man, in his retirement and meditation, are worth listening to. I am sure you will think I bring this lecture to the best conclusion, by repeating a sentence from one of his moral works :—

"I envy," says he, "no quality of the mind or intellect in others; not genius, power, wit or fancy; but if I could choose what would be most delightful, and I believe most useful to me, I should prefer A FIRM RELIGIOUS BELIEF to every other blessing."

PRIZE ESSAY.

AN

ESSAY

ON

THE WAGES PAID TO FEMALES

FOR THEIR LABOUR;

IN THE

FORM OF A LETTER,

FROM A GENTLEMAN IN BOSTON TO HIS FRIEND IN PHILADELPHIA.

BY JOSEPH TUCKERMAN.

Philadelphia:

FOR SALE BY CAREY & HART, JOHN GRIGG, AND TOWAR & HOGAN
IN BOSTON, BY CARTER & HENDEE, AND CUMMINGS &
HILLYARD; IN NEW YORK, BY COLLINS & HANAY;
AND, IN BALTIMORE, BY E. J. COALE.

March 25, 1830.

EXTRACT FROM THE GAZETTE OF THE UNITED
STATES, July 15, 1829.

PREMIUM.

"The editor of this paper, is authorized to offer (and pledges himself for the performance) a gold medal with a suitable inscription, value one hundred dollars, or a piece of plate of equal value, for the best essay (its merits to be decided on by competent and impartial judges,) on the inadequacy of the wages generally paid to seamstresses, spoolers, spinners, shoebinders, &c. to procure food, raiment, and lodging; on the effects of that inadequacy upon the happiness and morals of those females, and their families, when they have any; and on the probability that those low wages frequently force poor women to the choice between dishonour and absolute want of common necessaries. The whole, as far as the nature of the case will admit, to be corroborated by facts, and to embrace an inquiry whether those evils are susceptible of remedy or alleviation; and if so, by what means."

The various essays offered in consequence of the above advertisement, having been carefully examined by the Committee appointed to decide on their relative merits, the prize has been awarded to the Rev. Joseph Tuckerman, of Boston.

Philadelphia, February 1, 1830.

GRIGGS & DICKINSON, PRINTERS.

PREFATORY NOTE.

DURING the last summer, the author of the following Essay, saw, in the United States' Gazette, a proposition for essays, "on the inadequacy of the wages given to poor females, for their labour; and upon the effects of their low wages on their happiness and morals." He had before thought upon this subject, and was therefore induced to bring into some order the views he had taken of it. The form of a letter was adopted, because it seemed to him, that he might thus accomplish his task with greater ease to himself. And the letter is supposed to be addressed to a gentleman, who was designated, in a printed address to the public of Philadelphia, within the past summer, as a suitable person for the office of a minister to the poor in that city, because, it was supposed by the writer, that if the Essay should be successful, and should therefore be printed, it might thus in some degree be made subservient to the cause of this ministry, in the city in which the letter would in that case, be published. The writer, however, then knew not, that the premium offered for the best Essay on this subject, was wholly the contribution of an individual; although he was aware, that there was an individual in Philadelphia, who had felt and written much, upon the inadequacy of the wages of poor females. This individual is as well known for his enlarged philanthropy, as he is for the extensive business in which he has been engaged. To him, therefore,

MATHEW CAREY, Esq.,

This Essay is respectfully presented, by

JOSEPH TUCKERMAN.

Boston, February, 1830.

REV. THOMAS ALLEN.

Boston, September 29th, 1829.

My dear Sir,

I thank you for your letter of the 9th instant, and I greatly rejoice that your attention is directed, with so much earnestness, to the condition of the poor, and to the means of their improvement and happiness. You have but just begun, you say, to cultivate an acquaintance with them, and have much to learn upon the important question, of the best means of doing them good. I, too, am but a learner upon this question. But I have the advantage of the experience of a few years in the service of the poor; and I shall be glad and grateful indeed, if, by giving you the results of this experience, I may, in any degree, assist you in the course of benevolent exertion, to which you have devoted yourself.

Let me, however, frankly state to you, that I know little of poverty, or of the poor, except as I have seen them in Boston. You will perhaps say, that there is but little difference in the condition of this class of our fellow beings, in any large city. In some respects, without doubt, this is true. But in others, I apprehend, it is not true. In some of our large cities, there has been a much greater influx of poor foreigners, even in proportion to the native population, than in others. And not only is the amount of poverty thus increased, and of course, its necessary sufferings; but there is also, probably, more than a proportionate increase of vice, and

1 *

of the miseries of vice. In some cities, also, trade and commerce are for a time more active, than in others; and the demand for labour there, is consequently greater. The industrious poor can, therefore, more easily obtain support for themselves, and for their families. And, besides these causes, there are others, which may occasion great suffering for a few weeks, or a few months; and may make the city in which they occur, for a while, to be a scene of greater distress, than may be felt in others, and perhaps not very distant cities, in the same season. I refer to the circumstances, for example, that, for a considerable time, rents, and certain articles of food, may be held at the prices of a time of prosperity, while the demand for labour is so much lessened, that a very large part even of the virtuous poor may not be able to obtain the employment, by which they can pay for a home, and subsistence for their families. This, in truth, is at this very time a fact in Boston. I think that it is not so, or at least, not in an equal degree, in Philadelphia. And I know that every one in Cincinnati, who is disposed to work, may even now not only support his family, but that there is a demand there for labourers, beyond the supply of them. The circumstances, however, in which one or two cities differ, in respect to the condition of the poor, are, without doubt, of much less importance, than those in which they resemble each other. You, will, I am sure, be able to give me much and important instruction, by your observations on the state of the poor, in your own city. And I shall be happy if I can throw any light upon your path, by any suggestions I may offer in regard to those, by whom I am myself surrounded.

You have confined the inquiries in your letter to two topics. The first is, " The inadequacy of the wages generally paid to seamstresses, spoolers, spinners, shoe binders, &c. to pay rent, and to purchase food and clothing." The second is, " The effects of these inadequate wages upon the happiness and morals, not merely of those females, but of their families, when they have any; and the probability that these low wages frequently force poor women to the choice between dishonour, and the absolute want of common necessaries."—To arrive at any satisfactory results on these topics, we must, however, look beyond them, to the elementary principles of wages; and to the connected circumstances, physical and moral, which have an important bearing upon the wants, the virtue and vice, and, therefore, upon the happiness and misery of the poor.

In the first place, then, let us consider the doctrine of wages in its more extended application. By following it back into its principles, we shall understand more clearly, not only how far the sins and sufferings of the poor, at any time, are to be ascribed principally to the inadequacy of their wages to the support of their families; but, how far it is even practicable at any time, to accomplish an important change in the rate of their wages. And in this course of inquiry, we shall best ascertain what are the true means, and the only true means, of doing for them, and to them, the greatest, the most extensive, and the most permanent good. I am aware that I have thus brought you to the verge of a wide field of observation. But be not discouraged, for I have no thought of attempting thoroughly to explore it. I shall but direct your attention to some of the objects in it, of which, as I have thought much, I must speak in the language of conviction respecting them.

Let me then remind you, that the classes are very numerous, of those who are wholly dependent upon wages. They would, indeed, be numerous, if we looked for them among those only who have no trade, and who are generally distinguished alone, as labouring men. This large division includes shop, market, and other porters; carmen; those who are employed in lading, and unlading vessels; wood-sawyers; hod-carriers; house servants; those employed by mechanics in a single branch of their business; and multitudes, who are men and women of any work, occasionally required in families, as washing, scouring, &c.; or on the wharves, or in the streets of the city. Besides these, the number is great of those, who are journeymen, and many of whom will never be any thing but journeymen, in the various mechanic arts; and considerable numbers are also employed in the different departments of large manufactories, who possess no capital; and who know, and will continue to know, little or nothing in any other department of these establishments, except that in which they are themselves employed. All these, in the strictest sense, and in the common acceptation of the term, are dependent on the wages which they can obtain for their services. But even this view of the subject does not comprehend the whole of it. Let us then change our position for a moment, and look at it in its more extended relations.

Wages are defined to be " the hire paid for time, talents and labour, employed in the creation of a product of industry."* In this view of it, the term comprehends *salaries;* and extends to the hire that is paid for every service, that is performed for a stated price. The terms, *interest, rent,* and *wages,* express receipts in the various forms in which returns are made, or income is produced, by *industry,* by *land,* and by *capital.* All income, therefore, which is independent of land, or of capital possessed, or improved, in the sense in which the political economist views it, is *wages.* This view of the subject is important. For although the principles by which wages are graduated, or affected, admit of some modifications: for example, in the services in which rare and distinguished talents are wanted, and in which they cannot be increased according to the demand there may be for them;—yet, with these exceptions, the principles which affect wages in one class, must, and will, more or less, affect them in all the other classes of a community. They who are hired, and receive wages, in the service of government, and are appointed to offices which involve, or are supposed to involve, great and peculiar responsibility; and they too, who receive wages as the ministers of religion; and some others, who act as the agents of great establishments, which require peculiar intelligence, skill, or tried uprightness, as well as time, may not suffer, and generally do not suffer, in the temporary checks and changes of commerce, trade, manufactures, and agriculture, as others suffer, for whose services there is a demand exactly proportioned to the state of trade and commerce, of manufactures, and of agriculture; and of whom there is always a very speedy sup-

* Say's Catechism of Political Economy, Chap. Wages.

ply, equal at least to the demand, and generally beyond it. Besides, the salaries, or wages, which are
given to those who act in these offices, do not depend
on the interest, or the will, of a single individual.
Men in these departments of labour, are generally appointed by large numbers; or, if by a few, it is by
those who feel that great interests are concerned in the
question, of the change of a labourer, to whom a large
hire is given. But so it is not with a labourer of more
common talents, who is hired by an individual, and
who is employed in a work for which another may easily be substituted. He, whether he be a clerk or a
porter, a journeyman, or a scavenger, must work for the
wages that he can get; and these will be proportioned
to the existing demand for his service. He may even
be obliged to live without work, because he may not
be able to obtain the work that he can do. This is not
theory, but simple fact. And we must look at facts
as they are on all subjects, if we would rightly comprehend, and act wisely in regard to them.

The principles which determine the rate of wages,
and the ease or difficulty of obtaining them, may be
reduced to two. The first is, the proportion which
the supply of labourers bears to the existing demand
for them. The second is, the price of rent, and of
food and clothing; or, in other words, of the means of
subsistence.

These, however, are general principles, and they
are derived only from general facts. It is, indeed,
with general principles, and general facts alone, that
the political economist concerns himself. "The price
of labour," says Malthus,* "when left to find its na-

* Essay on Population, vol. ii. pp. 155—157.

tural level, is a most important political barometer, expressing the relation between the price of provisions,
and the demand for them; between the quantity to be
consumed, and the number of consumers; and, taken
in the average, independently of accidental circumstances, it further expresses clearly the wants of the
society respecting population." But it is one thing to
arrive at correct *general principles*, on this great subject, so intimately affecting the condition and happiness of many ten thousands of our fellow beings; and
it is quite another thing to settle the principles,
which are applicable to those " accidental circumstances," which are of frequent occurrence; and which
sometimes occasion a most serious temporary depression of wages, and even *an utter inability to obtain labour, while the price both of rent, and of provisions, is
long kept above the level of the price of labour.* There
are times, indeed, when the hire of labour finds its natural level, or its fair proportion to the prices of rent,
and of provisions. But, suppose the case, that it
should fall below this level. Suppose even, that by
any peculiar combination of causes, extending their
depressing influence at once, to commerce and trade,
to agriculture, and to manufactures, many thousands
should be thrown out of employment, or should find it
impracticable to obtain the employment, by which they
might pay their rent, and feed, and clothe their families. Or, suppose, even still further, that under this
general depression, there should be in a large city, at
once double the number of labourers required for its
services, while the price of rent continued to be, what
it was in the most prosperous times; and, while
butchers' meat, and some other articles of food, were

at best reduced but little below their old prices. It requires no prophet's eye to see, that here must necessarily be a greatly increased amount of suffering. The political economist looks upon the checks and embarrassments, which produced this suffering, as " accidental circumstances;" and speaks of this suffering, as " a transient evil."* But in truth, it sometimes comprehends more than any language can describe. Nor is it a mere vagary of the imagination, that such a state of things may exist. I have said, that I know little of poverty, and of the poor, but as I have seen, and as I daily see them, in Boston. But that which exists here, may also, and probably will, in a greater or less degree, sometimes at least, be found elsewhere. Let us then bring before us the facts on the subject, as they are to be seen within this narrow circle. In other words, the present state of wages, and the present condition of the poor, in Boston,—what are they?

We are now suffering greatly, from the checks which have been given to our trade and commerce, and from the failure of some of our large manufacturing establishments. We deplore this state of things, in view of the losses it has occasioned to some of our capitalists; the utter ruin of some, who, a short time since, thought themselves secure in the possession of an ample fortune; the difficulties and embarrassments of many of our men in trade; and of many, too, of our enterprising mechanics. But, should we forget the number, ten times larger, of those who have no capital but time and industry; who have no resource for self-support, but their daily labour; and who, in a failure of

* Say's Political Economy, B. 1, Chap. 7, p. 31.

demand for their services, are at once brought to great, and perhaps, to utter want? To every friend of the order and security of society, be he a Christian, or an infidel, it is a question of deep import, what are the best means of meeting the exigencies of great and peculiar suffering among the poor? To the philanthropist, and the Christian, it involves still higher interests; and, as he dwells upon it, he will find that it calls him to still higher duties, and to more solemn responsibilities. In regard to those who have lost much, but who still retain much, the real evil of their condition, with respect to their losses, may not in fact be great. The remedy of their difficulties, is also within their own reach; for their very sufferings, if wisely improved by them, or, in other words, if they shall be excitements to greater prudence and activity, and to a wiser economy, may even be means of securing them a greater abundance, than they possessed before they met with these losses. But I believe that I may state with confidence, that in consequence of the improved machinery, which is now used in printing, and by the substitution of boys and girls, for men, in the work of printing offices, there are at this time, or within the past summer there have been, in our city, *between two and three hundred journeymen printers, who have been able at best, to obtain but occasional employment in the occupation, in which they have been educated.* I am assured, too, that *there are as many as two hundred journeymen carpenters, and in all, not less than a thousand journeymen mechanics, in the same condition.* And of day labourers, in all the departments of their service, the supply is at least twice beyond the demand. Nor is the difficulty less, nor the distress, which is expe-

2

rienced by the very large class of females, comprehending some hundreds, who have families depending
on them; and who themselves depend for their own,
and the support of their families, either upon their needle, or some other daily labour. I have recently been
told, by a very respectable keeper of a slop-shop, that
he has for some time past, had fifty applications a day
from females, for work with which he could not supply them; and *the work sought by them, is, coarse
shirts, to be made at ten, eight, or even six and a quarter cents each; or labourers' frocks, or duck pantaloons,
at the same prices.* Now let it be considered, that there
are among us hundreds of these poor females, mothers,
and widows, who are deeply anxious to support their
families, by their own exertions; but who, even while
their families are in health, and when employment can
be obtained for every hour in every day, can at best,
earn but a dollar, or a dollar and a quarter in a week;
who yet, however, are sometimes taken off from their
labours by their own, or the sickness of their children;
and often, even when they are all in health, cannot obtain more than two or three days work in a week. In
this state of things, the prices of rent, of food and
of clothing, ought to come down to the level of wages;
or, if the price of day wages has not yet essentially lessened, to the level of the difficulty of obtaining employment, and thus of obtaining wages. And so they
will, if this state of things shall be of long continuance.* Nor have we reason to complain, even as far

---

* Wages, in some departments of labour, have in some measure been lessened. The pressure, however, has not yet continued long enough, to bring them down generally to the level of

as the poor are concerned, of the price of clothing, and of some important articles of food. But while the rents of such houses as are occupied by the rich, and by the middling classes of society, of which we have in fact more than are sufficient to meet demands for them, have come down in some proportion to the general depression of trade and commerce, the rents of the poor continue to be as high, as they have been for some years past; for the very plain reason, that houses of the kind, rented by the poor, are rather below, than above, the demand for them. It is not easy to obtain a room, either in a garret or cellar, and however small, inconvenient, and unfit to live in, at fifty cents per week. Nor are there many to be had for sixty-two and a half, or seventy-five cents a week.* The common price of a room is a dollar a week; of a room and bed-room, a dollar and twenty-five cents; and, where larger accommodations are required, and sometimes, at least, they seem to be absolutely required, the rent is proportionally higher. It is also an important circumstance in this connexion, that the houses which are occupied by this class of our population, to a considerable extent, are not let to them by their owners. An owner lets his house to one, who becomes responsible for the whole rent; and who, it may be, retains certain rooms

demand. They are kept up, in part, by the high price of rent; and quite as much, or more, by the liberal spirit of employers. A considerable number of those who depend on wages for their support, have, also, within a short time, left the city; by which the poor who remain are in some measure benefited, a greater number of them being thus enabled to find employment.

* The case is not quite so bad in Philadelphia. None of our poor pay more than fifty cents per week.—EDITOR.

in it for his own family. The object in taking the whole house, in this case, is, to obtain his own lodgings, at the smallest possible price. Aware, therefore, as the renter is, that he may lose by some of his tenants, he requires the highest price from each, that he may be as secure as possible against ultimate loss. And these rents are generally demanded at the end of every week, and sometimes in advance, as the only condition of obtaining a room. Under this system, rent is obtained, if an amount equal to it can be earned in the week. There are, without doubt, cases in which a considerable amount of rent is lost. But, as a general fact, it is paid, not only when it absorbs every cent that is earned, but often by the sale of one and another article of furniture, that can possibly be spared, and without the sacrifice of which, a home could not be retained. There are great numbers of mothers, widows, who would now, if they could, go into service in families. But they must hire a room, because they must provide a home for their children.—Let us then look at these facts, in view of the questions, what is the tendency, and what are the dangers, of a time of peculiar distress among the poor? And, what are the best provisions that can be made for the remedy, or relief of the evils, to which they, and society around them, are thus exposed?

First, what is the tendency, and what are the dangers, of a time of peculiar distress among the poor?

Among the poor, there is all the diversity of character, which is to be found in the other classes of society; and, I am happy in being able to bear my testimony to the fact, that there are those among them, who, under all the depression, the discouragements, and sufferings of their condition, have a strength of religious principle, a purity of religious sentiment, and a consequent energy and fortitude, which would do honour to those in the most favoured conditions of human life. As far as respects *them*, the tendency and the danger of a time of peculiar want and distress excites no very strong feeling of alarm, in the minds of those who know them. But this is not a very large class. There are far more of those, who are to be recognised as virtuous poor, and who are not only honest, temperate, and industrious, but to an important extent, pious, who yet have not very great strength of character; and, who are not *safe* in the day of very great trial. They are able, and willing to work; and, while the employment can be obtained, by which they may pay their rent, and get food and clothing for themselves and their children, they not only would not ask for charity, but many of them would prefer not to receive it. But if, by their best exertions, they cannot pay their rent; or, if their wages will not enable them to provide for their absolute necessities, or for those of their children, the sentiments of piety, which they thought were deeply laid in their hearts, are shaken. They look about them for the causes of their sufferings; and some will trace the evil to its true causes. But some, too, will think that they find them, in the insensibility of the rich, to the wants and sufferings of the poor. Discontent, envy, jealousy and resentment are awakened. And feeling, as they do, that they cannot obtain redress from those, from whom they think that the injury proceeds, they seek their satisfaction, in the secret indulgence of their irritated feelings; and, in the expression of these feelings, when

2 *

they have an opportunity to express them. Does this seem to any one to be mere theory, or a creation of fancy? Here is a wife, whose husband, very feeble in health, under the best circumstances can earn but little; and often, for successive days, can absolutely earn nothing. She has two, or three, or four young children, and she supported them comfortably, while she could find employment. But she cannot now find it more' than two or three days in a week. Again: Here is a widow, she has three, or four, or five children. She goes from one to another of the slop-shops to seek for work, and from day to day cannot obtain it. Or, she occasionally gets a dozen shirts, or a dozen pair of pantaloons, or a dozen of truckmen's frocks to make; and the highest price to be received for her labour, the very hard labour of a week,—and with some it is the labour of ten or twelve days,—is a dollar and twenty cents. Here is one more tried, more unhappy than a widow. She has an intemperate husband; the whole charge of supporting her family is upon her; and yet, with the best dispositions to industry, and the best efforts for employment, she cannot earn more than half of what is required, to secure a home and food for those who are dependent on her. And, here is another, with an honest and temperate, but inefficient husband; of whom it is very doubtful whether he earns sufficient for his own sustenance. She, too, is struggling with the same embarrassments; and enduring all a mother's sufferings, who would, but cannot, provide for the wants of her children. And, even again: Here are a husband and wife, whose united efforts,— and neither of them fail in effort,—are often insufficient for the support of their family during the passing week, because they cannot procure employment in the only services of which they are capable. These, I repeat, with the exception of the intemperate husband to whom I have referred, in an important sense are *virtuous poor*. And they are the representatives of many. Nor have I at all exaggerated their embarrassments, and sufferings. And who will say that ordinary virtue, or even that virtue in which he might confide under happier circumstances, is secure amidst such difficulties, and such temptations? How many of those, who have no mean opinion of their own virtue, may be confident that they would themselves retain all the heroism of their own resolution in duty, if, through successive weeks, or successive months, they should be dependent on daily labour for daily bread, and often be unable to find the service, by which bread could be obtained for their children; if often, for weeks and months they had but the choice, for the subsistence of their families, to beg, to borrow, or to steal? And if, in addition to these sufferings of many virtuous poor, we consider the wants and distresses which they experience, either when they are themselves confined by sickness, or when their children are sick, and requiring all their time, and thought, and care, it will be felt, I think, that the exposures of their virtue are neither few nor small;—that, in truth, they demand the most solemn regard of those, who know any thing of human weakness, or propensity to evil, and who have any interest in the cause of human virtue, salvation and happiness.

From these turn your attention to another class. Of the intemperate, there are very many who depend, for themselves and their families, upon daily wages. And

there are very many too, who are not confirmedly intemperate, who are even regarded as sober men,
who consider themselves, and are considered, as honest men; and who have no means of support except
their daily earnings. Suppose these earnings, then, to
fail them. The journeyman mechanic, or the hand-
cartman, or the day-labourer, traverses the streets and
wharves for work, and from day to day returns home
as empty-handed as when he left it, because he could
find no work to do; and, at the end of the week or
month, cannot pay his rent, or the debt which has been
incurred at the grocer's. Is his moral condition a safe
one? Is it not rather full of danger? Is not the man,
who would have revolted at the thought that he would
ever have become a drunkard, most alarmingly exposed to the sin and misery of living, and dying a drunkard? And ought it to surprise us, if the honesty of many
of these men, who have been very partially educated; the
best security of whose uprightness, perhaps, has been
in the maxim, that honesty is the best policy; and who,
it may be, have overcome some small temptations to
benefit themselves by the injury of others, and have thus
gathered some strength to their virtue in the days of
abundant labour; ought it to surprise us, if in these circumstances, the honesty of many of this class should fail
them; and if, in a time of adversity, of perplexity, of great
embarrassment and want, and when they know not where
to look for employment, or for provision for their families, they should be driven by their wants to crime?
I would not, under any circumstances, be the apolo-
gist of crime. But it will not require a long acquaintance with the poor, in a time of prevailing distress,
to know that what I have here stated is fact. The

want of employment brings those who would otherwise be industrious, to association with the idle and dissipated.   Excited by embarrassments abroad, and by
trouble at home, they seek oblivion of their sufferings
in that, which seems to them, for the time, to be the
smaller evil,—I mean, intoxication.   And, when once
thus given up to intemperance, what evils may not be
dreaded? Prosperity, without doubt, is attended with
many and great exposures of virtue.   But great and
pressing want, for which not even the best dispositions
to labour can secure a provision, may drive him, or
her, who suffers it, to the greatest sins; and expose
society to all that is to be feared, from an unbridled license in crime.

Nor are these the only evils to be apprehended in a
time of great and extensive suffering among the poor.
The number is always considerable, in this class of the
population of a large city, of those who maintain little or no discipline at home; and whose children, in
consequence either of the gross negligence of parents,
or their excessive fondness, or their equally excessive
severity, are exposed to all that is to be dreaded in a
life of ungoverned passion, and of vice.   There are
many, too, the children of widows, who rejecting maternal control, and becoming early the associates of
idlers and vagrants, at ten and twelve years of age,
are profane, false, and dishonest; who have already begun to love ardent spirits, and can talk flippantly of
the lewdness, of which it would be thought that they
could yet hardly form a conception.   And there are
children, who have faithful mothers,—mothers who
are at least anxious to do what they can for their children's virtue,—but whose fathers are not to them *as fa-*

thers; and who are even more rapidly carried on in the career of sin, from which maternal influence is insufficient to restrain them, by the daily example of a profane and intemperate parent. Among all the objects of a philanthropist, no one has stronger claims, than the salvation of these children. Even in a time of prosperity, the number of girls, as well as of boys, who are thus constantly exposed to moral ruin, is alarmingly great. And if we add to these, who are living with their parents, the large number of boys, who, while they can only, and very imperfectly read and write, and have not begun to cipher, are taken from school to be placed in shops and offices, not as apprentices, but as errand boys, and who will therefore grow up in ignorance, and probably be alone the associates of vicious boys; and of girls who are put to service at twelve, and fourteen years of age, in families in which their education and their virtue are unregarded;—the number of children of the poor, in a large city, demanding the most solemn interest in their dangers, and the most earnest efforts for their rescue, will be considerably enlarged. Some of the children to whom I refer, are truants from our schools. Some are kept at home by their parents, either to gather chips, or to beg, or to be market boys. And some are suffered by their parents to live where they will, and as they will, provided only that they occasion to them as little inconvenience as may be. What, then, in these various families, must be the effects on children, of a time of great and pressing want, when it shall scarcely be practicable, by any honest occupation, to obtain the means of subsistence ? Can it be doubted, whether the number of young vagrants, in such a time, will be

greatly increased ? Or, is it doubted, whether they will
be proportionally more dishonest, or more reckless in
the sins to which they have become accustomed ? This,
to my mind, is one of the most affecting of the aspects
of a time of great distress among the poor; and unless,
at such a time, some strong means shall be used to
prevent the evil, it will be found that a few months
only of peculiar want and difficulty will be sufficient,
to .add a large per centage to the amount of future
crime, and wretchedness.

There is a view of this subject, which, if it could
be brought distinctly before the public, could hardly
fail, I think, at once to make a deep and strong impression of the moral dangers of a large class of children in our cities, now but too little regarded by us;
and to excite an active sympathy for the families to
which they belong. I refer to the disclosures which
might be obtained, of the causes of crime, by a careful
examination and comparison of the cases of juvenile offences, which are brought before our Police Courts.
Ask the magistrates of these courts, from whence come
the children who are arraigned before them for pilfering,
and whom they are every week sending to the Refuge,
or to Prison ? They will tell you, that three fourths of
them are from families, which have looked to these
children *for a part of their means of support.* And if
they have looked into these cases, they will tell you
also, that some of these children have been kept from
school, that they might beg; and others, that by any
service they might earn a dollar a week, to be appropriated for the payment of rent, or for the purchase of
necessary food. Is it asked, from whence arises the dependence of these parents upon their children ? I an-

swer, often, without doubt, from the idleness and intemperance of the parents. But not always. There are
cases, and very affecting cases, in which poor mothers,
widows, who have three, four, or five children, who must
be sheltered, and fed, and clothed, and warmed; and
for whom they cannot, by their best labours, provide a
home, and the absolute necessaries of existence. These
children, to a considerable extent, form a distinct class.
They have other associations with life, and form other
habits, than the children who are in a regular course of
education at school: They have much time, every day,
which they know not how to appropriate to any useful
purpose; and they are every day at once surrounded
by temptations to dishonesty, while passion, and appetite, and all the lower propensities of our nature are
developing within them, and maturing under the influences, which are most suited to make them the governing principles in the mind.—I pity the man who
can look upon all this evil, and say that these parents
alone are accountable for it. No: there is not an individual in society, who can minister to the removal,
or to the melioration of it, who has not a share of ac-
countableness for it. If there are families who thus
give up their children to moral ruin, while yet they
are able to educate and to provide for them, there
should be an authority in society, which may compel
the parent to do his duty. And if there are parents,
—and I know that there are such,—who are honest,
temperate and industrious, but who are either unable
to find the work by which they may support their children, or who cannot, even by constant labour, feed,
and clothe, and educate them, these parents and their
children, as far as it is necessary for these objects,

should be assisted by others. For the present, I leave the question, what is the provision which should be made for them? Let us first look at facts, and then seek for the principles to which they should lead us.

You ask me, whether the wages given to poor females do not often force them to the choice between dishonour, and the absolute want of common necessaries? I have no doubt but this is one of the causes, by which some of the daughters of poor parents are brought to ruin. There are, however, other causes of the crimes and miseries of the poor, which lie far deeper than the question of the effects of high, or of low wages, upon their condition and character. The truth is, that the moral and religious instruction of this class of the population of cities has hardly, till within a short time, engaged even the smallest interest; and even now there is not a city in Christendom, in which it has obtained the attention which it claims. The poor, therefore, have lived, and to a great extent are living, as *a caste,*—cut off from those in more favoured circumstances; and doomed to find their pleasures, and sympathy in their sufferings, alone among themselves.

But although, of the large number of most melancholy cases of female depravity, which have fallen under my notice, I cannot say with confidence of any one, that I should ascribe it *principally* to the difficulty of obtaining a subsistence by honest industry; yet I would ask any one to go into the families of forty, or fifty of those, who depend upon their daily labour for their daily bread; and to hear there of the applications which are sometimes made for work, which they cannot obtain; and of the wants, and sufferings which are

3

felt, even when, by the unremitted toil of a week, they
have earned a dollar, or at most, a dollar and a half.
They owe a few dollars of rent, which they cannot
pay. Their clothing is hardly sufficient for warmth
in the cold of autumn, and how much less in that of
winter? And they know not how, or where, to obtain
more. Their food is often scanty, as well as of the
coarsest kind. They are dunned, and threatened, and
harassed; and now appease a creditor by the sale of
one article of their poor furniture, and now of another.
They pass a few months in one place, and then are
compelled to seek a shelter elsewhere. Is not such a
situation too perilous for human virtue? And here are
female children, some of whose parents would be
thought respectable, if they were not so very poor,
living in the very neighbourhood of all that is unprincipled, and profligate; daily exposed to the gaze, and
to the address, of the lowest and basest of our race.
Would it not then be passing strange, if some of them,
by what they see and hear abroad, and by what they
suffer at home, should not be seduced, and betrayed to
their ruin? I have said, that there are those among
the poor, who have an energy, a fortitude, a resolution
in virtue, which do honour to our nature. And many
children,—many suffering daughters of greatly distressed mothers, furnish noble examples of all that is
excellent in filial, and in Christian piety. But there
are weak children,—intellectually and morally weak,
I mean,—wayward and passionate children, impatient
of restraint; and vain, giddy, and light-minded children,
even in the families of the pious poor. Pinched, then,
pious as they sometimes are, by want at home, and seeing others whom they have known to be as destitute as

themselves, abundantly provided with the gratification which they most want, they overlook,—they wish not to know, the degradation and misery which are concealed under the appearance of comparative abundance, and happiness. They are offered the wages of guilt, and they accept them.—Who can doubt whether some, if not many, might have been saved from the ruin into which they have thus fallen, if they could have found regular employment with their parents at home; and if the united labours of the parents and children could have secured to them a comfortable subsistence? On this question, at least, I have no doubt. The heart of one parent sinks and sickens under the discouragements of want, while that of another is exasperated and made desperate. And the children, unless more happily constituted than children generally are, will be given up to the influence of their own prevailing passions. Under such circumstances, if assailed by strong temptation, what is their security? Or, will it be wonderful if they are lost?

I cannot, however, confine my views to a single aspect of this subject. The opportunity is a favourable one, and I will not lose it, to speak freely to you of the prevailing licentiousness of our cities. The cases are not few,—and I have come to the knowledge of too many of them, in which young women, who come from the country for service in the city, and who bring here all the truth and artlessness of a virtuous country life, are seduced, despoiled, destroyed, by profligate and base young men, who yet call themselves *gentlemen!* These young women come here in the simple attire, and with the simple manners, of the country. But they soon learn, that, to be the companions of their

equals, they must in dress be the rivals of their mis-
tresses. Their taste, therefore, is first corrupted, and
then, their manners. They attract the attention of the
prowlers who are seeking for them. They are offered the
bribe of dishonour, and are the victims of reckless perfidy
and lust. I would that these base, these unprincipled
destroyers of innocence, and that every votary of licentious pleasure, could see, as I have seen, the deep, the
hopeless depravity, to which they have brought the victims of their passions; and whose ruin, in the books of
heaven, is already charged upon *their* souls. I would
that they could see, as I have seen, the unutterable
wretchedness of her, who, in the feeling that she has
lost all by which the confidence of the world is to be
obtained, knows not where to look for support; while
under the upbraidings of an awakened conscience,
she revolts with horror from the thought of returning
to her guilty course. What shall she do ? Where shall
she go ? How dreadful the conflict within her! How
agonizing her condition! Would that every young
man, when he is tempted to enter the haunts of guilty
pleasure, could see, as I have *seen*, the anguish of a
father, seeking the recovery of a guilty son; and witness the writhings of a mother's heart, while she is
imploring the sympathy and assistance of a stranger,
for the salvation of him, whom she has nursed at her
bosom, and for whose salvation she would gladly give
up her own life! O, would that the destroyer of a
daughter's virtue could see, as I have *seen*, a mother
seeking for her lost, her prostituted child! Would that
he could feel, but for one hour, the desolation of that
mother's soul! He may now be heedless of the misery
he has occasioned; of the ruin he has accomplished.

But, if he shall ever regain his lost conscience, be it here, or hereafter, he will find within himself a hell, the agonies of which, had he but understood them, he would not have incurred, even for ten thousand lives of unchecked profligacy.

But there are still other causes which minister to this guilt and misery. From the tavern bar, from the tippling shop, and the gambling house, the passage is short, and always open, which leads to the deepest sinks of human infamy. At the tavern bar, in the tippling shop, and in the gambling house, to which young men are allured; where their basest passions are excited, and where the restraints of domestic discipline, and the pleasures of domestic affection and virtue are lost; where parental solicitude, and interest, and love are forgotten, or are remembered but to be shaken from the mind as an incumbrance, which vice cannot support; where debt is incurred, for relief from which, the resort is dishonesty; and where a desperation of mind is produced, under the influence of which it is felt, that the most effectual refuge from the misery of crime is, to go as deeply into crime, as they may with hope of safety;—here it is that many, who might have been the unspeakable treasure and joy of the hearts of their parents; who might have been respectable and respected, useful and prosperous, beloved and happy, and the honour and strength of those with whom God has connected them, have been and are deluded, and corrupted; have been made the murderers of their fathers' and mothers' peace, the bane of the community in which they live, and the destroyers of their own, and of the souls of their depraved associates. Here it is that they are prepared for those pits of destruction, the receptacles

3 *

of prostituted females. Nor among the most zealous
to do good in this world, is there more watchfulness and
effort employed for the prevention of evil, than is maintained by the keepers and inmates of these houses of
abandoned women, to beguile to them young men,
whom they may bring to their own measure of crime
and degradation.—I wish to write calmly, dispassion-
ately of these great evils, difficult as it is to repress
the indignation which they awaken; for I would address myself to the intelligent, to the discriminating,
to the virtuous, who will look at the whole subject
with a calm and steady eye; and who will bring their
best judgment to bear upon the question, how may we
most extensively, and most effectually check, if we
may not completely remedy, this worst of all the evils
of cities? They ought to be understood, as they are
not, by every inhabitant of cities. And the combined
intelligence and virtue of every parent, and of every
friend to virtue in a city, be he young or old, be he a
parent, or childless, ought to be arrayed against them.

I have referred to the agency of the female keepers,
and of the inmates, of houses of bad fame, in seducing
young *men* to a life of profligacy, and, I believe that,
to this same agency, may immediately be attributed
the seduction of far the greatest numbers of the prostituted of their own sex. At least, this is the cause
to which the largest number of these unhappy beings,
whom I have known, have ascribed their ruin. Of all
God's creation of which I have any knowledge, I have
met with no being of any comparative hardihood, or of
any comparative capacity in guilt, with that of an
abandoned woman. These keepers walk our streets
in the dress of ladies; and, if in want of "boarders,"

for so the inmates of their houses are called,—they will ask a poor girl whom they meet, if she *wants a place?* And, if she answers that she does, the unsuspecting victim is directed to the abode of sin, where, if it shall be possible, her destruction will be accomplished. I have known a girl who was sent to our House of Correction, when she was only fifteen years old, who had thus been inveigled; and who was almost at once transferred from the pandemonium to which a base woman had directed her for service, to the prison in which I met with her. And the inmates of these houses invite there those with whom they are acquainted, holding out to them all the attractions of society and liberty. God help the poor girl, who at once finds it difficult, or impracticable, to support herself by her labours, who is but feebly established in principle, and is exposed to an acquaintance with any of the abandoned of her own sex. If she shall but be brought into the connexion of an hour with one of these female fiends, who are going about seeking the ruin of such as she is, her danger of irretrievable destruction is most imminent. I have but recently attended upon the sick bed of one of the poor girls, who has thus been deluded, and lost. She is twenty-four years old; a child of respectable parents in the country, and she came to this city, " to learn the trade of a milliner." While working in a milliner's shop, she became acquainted with a young woman, who frequently went there for articles of dress; with whom, after a time, she would occasionally walk; and by whom, at length, she was conducted to the " boarding-house," of her companion. From that day, virtue and peace were lost. After about three years of progress in sin, she is now on the verge of the grave, into which she will very soon fall, to appear before her final Judge; where she will meet her who first beguiled, and soon also, him who despoiled her. I asked her, 'where now is she who led you astray?' Her reply was, 'she is dead.' 'And have many,' I asked, 'of those with whom you have lived in transgression, also died young?' 'Yes,' was her answer; 'they die very soon.' It was thought expedient to remove this young woman into the country. I asked her, if she would be carried home? 'O, no,' she said; 'I have not seen my mother these two years, and I could not now bear to see her.'—In a manner not very dissimilar, I doubt not that many poor girls in this city, and in all our cities, are every year immolated, and lost among us.

In following back the seduction, the dishonour and ruin, both of young men, and young women, to their causes, it is not to be forgotten, and it ought to be known to those to whom it is not known, that every lure of which profligacy can avail itself, is employed, to give attraction to the first scenes and circumstances of that course of life, which is soon to end in the deepest degradation and wretchedness. Outward appearances alone being regarded, there is not a stronger contrast exhibited in human life, than in the condition of her, who is brought into the highest class of profligates, and who is receiving the most ample hire of prostitution; and of her, the same individual,—who has descended step by step into the poor, filthy residences, where the lowest of her own sex, with scarcely garments to cover them, the wretched victims of loathsome disease, are daily deadening more and more the little sensibility which remains to them, by intemperance, profaneness and riot;—and are there the companions of men, as lost to virtue, to shame, and to all that is human, as themselves. From these most miserable abodes, and these most degraded of human beings, there seems indeed little to be apprehended in respect to the virtuously educated among the young. There is nothing conceivable more disgusting, more revolting, than is to be seen there. But there are resorts of impurity, as well for the rich as for the poor; for him or her who is taking the first step in this way to death, as well as for the worn and hardy sensualist, who is brought as near as man can be, to the extinction of all the principles of his moral nature. I know, indeed, that there are some, who pass at once,—or seemingly pass at once, into the lowest recesses of pollution and crime. But, for the most part, at least, they have been familiar with the language and spectacle of crime, even from their childhood. They have lived in the neighbourhood, and have breathed the air of guilt, and have perhaps been fed with its earnings, before they ever heard there was such a thing as virtue. There are, however, other and very different habitations of abandoned women. There are houses of ill fame, which cannot be supported but at a great expense; and which, yet, are from year to year supported in all our cities; and with equal prodigality in a time of great and general depression, as in seasons of the greatest prosperity. There are houses, in which abandoned women are living in comparative luxury, and splendor; living apparently at their ease, and possessed of abundant means to gratify their tastes and humours; and where young men and young women, of whom better things might have been hoped, are allured to the wreck of their virtue and their souls. And from whence come these attractions to sin, these re-

wards of prostitution? How are these houses supported? And how are their inmates,—" the boarders"
there, enabled to indulge in all the extravagancies of
dress, which dazzle and bewilder those, who, when
they can obtain employment, can earn but a dollar, or
a dollar and a half in a week; and who sometimes are
in want of the apparel, which is important for their
comfort, or at least for that which they consider as a
decent appearance, because they cannot find employment? Here, here is a sin, which cries to heaven,—I
will not say for vengeance, but, for a most fearful retribution; and as surely as God is a moral Governor,
the day of retribution for this sin will come upon the
guilty. And who, I ask again, are the guilty? They
are, not less the keepers, and the inmates of these
houses, than their SUPPORTERS. They are the young
men and the men of every age, the single and the married men, who at once furnish the means of this guilty
luxury; and who are, in the sight of God, the destroyers of the bodies and the souls of those, to whose corruption they are the ministers. I speak plainly on
this subject, because it demands plainness. I know that
some of the sons of men of fortune here basely squan-
der the treasure, which their fathers' industry and enterprise have accumulated; and that young men who
cannot avail themselves of their fathers' property, for
the support of all this sin, are gratifying their base propensities by the robbery of their masters, and by overwhelming themselves with debt.—I cannot enlarge
on this topic. I would only show, that the evil is various in its causes, and that great numbers are concerned in these causes. And this view of the subject

is important, because, in a more partial consideration
of it, we shall not arrive at the most effectual means
of resisting, and of checking the evil; and why should
we look at the evil at all, if nothing is to be attempted
for its remedy?

Unprepared, therefore, as I am to speak with confidence of the extent of the influence of the low wages,
for which females are often compelled to work, and of
the difficulty which they often find of obtaining work,
even at the small prices which are given for it, in leading them to dishonour and crime, I have yet no
doubt that this is one of the causes, by which several are
brought to debasement and ruin. I would to God, indeed, that it were the children of the poor only, or that
it were those of the rich alone, who are thus falling
into the deepest depravity! But, in truth, the contagion spreads to not a few of all classes. My attention,
however, is called peculiarly to the moral exposures of
the poor; to the exposures to crime and misery, which
are incidental to poverty. In view of the remedy of
the evil, let it then be our first inquiry, may any means
be devised of raising the wages of the poor, and thus
of improving their condition, by enabling them more
entirely to provide for their own support?

To this question, I think, every political economist
would unhesitatingly say, no. For, if the proportion
which the supply of labourers whether male or female,
bears to the existing demand for them, be small, wages
will be high. If, on the other hand, the number of labourers be essentially greater than the demand for
them, wages will be low. These are elementary principles; and, considered as general principles, we cannot

reverse them.* The change from low to high, or from high to low wages, will not always be very exactly graduated by the supply of labour to the demand for it.

* The doctrine here held by the reverend writer, although generally correct, must be read with some considerable qualification. If carried to the full extent, it would be in the power of employers, when there was a great superabundance of persons wanting work, to reduce the wages of a week to what would be necessary for the support of a single day—as the applicants for employment would, perhaps, think it better to work for even that pittance, than have no employment. And it approaches to this point, when shirts are made for ten, and six cents, as we are told is sometimes the case. On this subject, the following observations from a recent publication, on this very important subject, are submitted to public consideration.—EDITOR.

"I freely admit, that there may be cases in which even liberal men may find a change impracticable—cases in which competition may have so far reduced the price of the manufactured article, as to render a rise in the price of the labour employed on it, incompatible with that due degree of profit on capital to which it has a fair claim. In all such cases the evil is without remedy, and must be submitted to. But this is by no means the case generally. There are numbers of men who make large fortunes by the labours of this class, and who might afford, and might not be unwilling to afford, to the humble ministers of their wealth, wherewith to support themselves without the degradation of soliciting charity, or the risk of being driven to a course of wickedness, resulting in misery here and perhaps hereafter. And surely any man duly impressed with the duties of morals and religion, would rather spend ten or twenty years in making a fortune, while he was dispensing the means of happiness among his dependents, and earning their heartfelt blessings, than wring it in half the time out of the sweat and blood of those dependents, while he was entitling himself to their, ' curses, not loud but deep. ' "

But there will, and necessarily must be, a constant tendency, and approximation towards it. New works may indeed be projected, for the employment of the supernumerary labourers of a city. But if, by the products of the industry thus directed, there should be a supply of these products above the demand for them, the sufferings of the poor would be deferred, by the employment thus given to them, only to be increased at a future time; for it is the very circumstance, which has thrown them out of employment, that the products to be obtained by their services are not *wanted*. The truth is, and it is not to be forgotten, that the poor do not, and never can, suffer alone. They suffer, because those who have been their employers, cannot find a market for the productions of their labour; and, in this depression of the market, or of the business which gives employment to the poor, their employers *cannot afford* to give the wages, which they can afford to give in a time of prosperity, and when there is a demand for these products of industry. I am aware, that there is in many a disposition to grind the poor; to get out of them all that they can, and to give as little for their service as they can. But, after all, the rate of wages

" It would be easy to prove, from a comparison of the prices charged to the public for the work done by the class in question, with the wages they receive, that a rise in the rate of those wages might be made, consistently with a due regard to self-interest. A few cents added to the price of making a shirt, a vest, or a pair of pantaloons, would be but a trifling deduction from the profits of the employer—but, to the employed, make all the difference between comfort and misery: what an irresistible appeal to every bosom in which exists a scintilla of justice or humanity!"—EDITOR.

does not depend on this class of employers.* It does, and it must depend, principally, upon the want of the products of the labour of the poor, and upon the proportion of the supply of labour to the demand for it. In anticipation of a winter, like that which is now before us, the tailors of our city, in order to give employment to poor females, might have a very large portion of their summer work done during the winter months. And this, without doubt, would give immediate relief to many. But it would cause a great increase of suffering through the next summer. And the results would necessarily be similar, whatever supply of work could be obtained, above the demand for it. I could not, therefore, look to any such expedients for the relief of the poor. Still, however, I would not despair of the practicability of keeping up wages, in a time of peculiar suffering, somewhat above the demand for the service of the poor. But I know of only one way in which it can be done, with any real advantage to them.

It is practicable, I doubt not, to a certain extent, to quicken the consciences of the employers of the poor

---

* These views are to be received *cum grano salis.* When the number of work-people greatly exceeds the demand for their labour, the persons to whom allusion is made in the text, have unfortunately great influence in lowering the rate of wages. Those who seek for employment and find great difficulty in procuring it, very frequently underbid each other. The persons alluded to avail themselves of this disposition, and reduce the rates below the usual standard. The example is followed by others, who would never have originally made any reduction. And to this case the *facilis descensus Averni,* of Virgil, fully applies. To reduce prices in such cases, is easy—to raise them extremely difficult.—EDITOR.

and thus to secure, on their part, a willingness to sacrifice some of their own gains, to the great objects, at
once, of the virtue, and comfort of those who labour for
them. I believe, indeed, that there are many, who
need only to understand how great is the suffering,
which is endured by the virtuous poor, at a time when
they can obtain but occasional employment, and when
their wages are generally reduced in inverse proportion
to the demand for their work, to be willing and more
than willing, to keep the hire of those who labour for
them as high as it may be, consistently with any fair
profits to themselves from these labours. Nothing,
more, indeed, would be necessary to secure this good
to the poor, in a society of Christians, than an appeal
to their sense of *justice*. It is clearly required by the
elementary principle of our religion, that we do to
others, as we would, in a change of circumstances, that
they should do to us. Let this single principle be
faithfully applied, and there not only would be no oppression, but there would always be *a generous consideration of the hireling in his wages*. I know a partner in a house, which has not unfrequently given employment to eight or nine hundred women, in the coarse
work of a large tailoring establishment; and I am informed by this individual, that, during the business
year of 1828, this house employed, on an average,
three hundred females every day; but that now, and
for some months past, they have not had work for more
than an average of a hundred and seventy. Within a
year, however, this house has paid fifteen hundred dollars in extra wages to poor females; that is, in wages
above the sum, at which they might have had the work
done by the females whom they have employed, and

which has been given by many others for similar work. This house has acted upon the principle, that they ought willingly to submit to a reduction of their own profits, when such large numbers, as those whom they have employed, have found it difficult, by their own industry, to find the means even of subsistence. And, so, I think, every true Christian will act, in similar circumstances. This house has thus virtually given fifteen hundred dollars to the poor, during the past year, in the most judicious manner in which it could possibly have been given to them. Without overstocking the market, it has encouraged industry by the same means, by which it has relieved want.

The best charity which can be exercised towards those who are capable of labour, is to give them, as far as possible, the labour by which they may earn the means of their subsistence; and, whenever they are employed, amply to remunerate them for their services. And this is a charity, which might be exercised far more extensively than it is, without any interference with the general principles which regulate wages. Even in a time of great general embarrassment, there are some families among the poor, who are constantly supplied with work, and who receive a generous compensation for it. They are connected with families, which have sympathy with the condition and necessities of the poor; with families which feel that, if retrenchment be necessary, it should be begun with the expenses of the table, of dress and fashion; and, to whatever extent it is carried, and to whatever objects it is directed, that, its last application should be to the employment, and wages of those, who, by their most constant labours, can but earn the means of their support; and with whom the fai-

lure of work, or the curtailment of wages, is inevitable
want, and bitter suffering, and perhaps exposure to debasement and crime. Nor are these, let me say, always, or peculiarly, the families of the rich. I have
heard, indeed, very much said of retrenchment, and
of economy, in rich families, where I could not trace
any associations with the terms, in the minds of those
who employed them, beyond the very circumstances
and services, on which the poor depend for their daily
bread! And I have earnestly wished that some of
those, who are living in the midst of abundance, and
are endeavouring to spare and save the few shillings,
which have been paid to the washerwoman, or the
laundress, or the seamstress, or the scourer, or the labourer of a y description whom they once readily employed, and for whom they had been accustomed very
easily to find something to do, would but go with me,
while they are forming their plans of economy, into
the families of those, who ask only to obtain any work,
by which they may be saved from dependence and beggary. Economy, rightly understood, rises to the character of a Christian virtue. But what is economy?
And what are its proper objects? I hold him to be an
economist, in the highest sense of the term, who saves
in those things in which he ought to save, that he may
expend liberally in those in which he ought, according
to his means, to be liberal. his is Christian economy. Let it be understood, and practised, and comparatively few of the poor will want employment. Or,
whatever may be the number who would, but cannot
earn the means of their subsistence, none will then
suffer unheeded, or be tempted by their wants to degradation and sin.

4 *

To other means, then, of giving relief to the suffering poor, let us direct our attention. And we shall
think more clearly, and justly on this subject, if we
separate the poor into classes. It is not necessary, indeed, for our present purpose, to enter into all the
particulars of an exact classification of them. A few
large and general divisions are all that will be required
to illustrate the principles, which I think have a very
important bearing upon the question, of the best means
of providing for the poor of cities?

A word, however, in the first place, respecting these
principles. They are:

1st, That it is God's will that all, as far as they
have capacity for labour, should provide for their own
support.

2dy, That it is equally God's will, if any cannot
from physical disability, or other insuperable difficulties, provide for themselves, that they should be provided for by those whose means enable them to contribute to their relief.

And, 3dly, That while it is the duty of all, whom
God has placed in more favoured conditions of life, to
minister to the *temporal wants* of their suffering fellow
creatures, it is yet never to be forgotten by any who
can serve them, that the most effectual means by
which we may improve their condition is, *by improving
their characters.* In other words, we shall most effectually relieve, and comfort, and bless the poor, by the
means by which we recover them from vice, or sin,
and advance them in moral and religious principles; in
the sentiments and habits of piety and virtue.

In view of these principles, I would divide the poor
who ought not to be left at large, from those who ought

not to be sent either to a work-house, or to a house of public charity.

Of these two great divisions, the first comprehends four classes: 1st, the proper subjects of an alms-house; 2d, the proper subjects of a work-house; 3d, orphan children, who, however, are not vicious; 4th, vicious children, who cannot be controlled by parents or guardians.—I am fully aware of the difficulty of making the provision, which I feel persuaded should be made, for these classes of the poor. But we must first distinctly understand what should be done, and then calmly, but resolutely, seek its accomplishment. In proportion as we can separate those who belong to these classes, from the mass of society, we shall greatly facilitate the work of provision for those who will still remain, to a very considerable extent, dependent on private or on public bounty.

First, them, who are the proper subjects of an *Alms-House?*

It will be observed, that I speak of an alms-house, as a distinct institution from a work-house. And it should so far at least be made a distinct institution, that no one, and especially no *man*, who is capable of any labour, should be sent to an alms-house. I would have an alms-house to be, what its name imports that it should be, a refuge for those *who cannot contribute to their own support*. And although I would not send all of this class to such a house, I would have none sent to it, except those who belong to this class. The moral evil is very great, of forming one society, in a large establishment, of those who might be made to support themselves, and of those who are incapable of labour. If an alms-house pauper should regain the strength, with which he may be enabled to work, and cannot be trusted abroad, he should be transferred to a work-house.

Even in the most prosperous circumstances of a large city, there are not a few in it, who, from age, from bodily debility, from disease, or mental imbecility, cannot provide for their own wants; and who have no friends peculiarly interested in them, who are able, or, if able, are disposed, to support them. Among them may be some, who are virtuous, and proper objects of a strong and affectionate interest. And they should be the objects of such an interest. But no private means that could be employed for their comfort would be so effectual, as well as so economical, as a well regulated alms-house.—To an alms-house, also, should be sent all those who are separated from their families and friends by their vices, and who are incapable of self-support, while yet they are not held by the laws to be criminals. And here, also, should be sent the young children, those, for example, under ten years of age,—of parents, who, by vagrancy or crime, are separated from their families; and orphan children of the poor, for whom no other provision can be made. Colquhoun, in his Police of London, says, that one-fifth of the gross number in a London work-house is composed of " Infant Poor," who, by extreme indigence, or the death of their parents, have been cast upon the public for support. In our House of Industry,* there are now 184 such children. It would be

* Our " House of Industry" is designed to combine in one institution, an Alms-House, and a work-house. The average number of its inmates in summer is about 400; and in winter about 500. It now contains about 500: of these, 184 are children. The children regularly attend school, and, at a suitable age, are

impracticable to provide for so many, beside those who are in our asylums, (and especially for the number of such children who require some specific provision should be made for them,) by any efforts of private benevolence; I would therefore send them to an Alms-House. But in this house, they should be as entirely as possible *separated from its adult inmates.* The city to which they belong should become their parent, and, as far as possible, should discharge a parent's duty towards them.

Secondly. There is another class, who are the proper subjects of *a work-house:* who are they?

I wish to be explicit on this subject, not alone because I think that great pecuniary interests are concerned, but because I am persuaded, that very great moral benefits are in this way only to be secured to very many of the poor, and great evils to be averted

indented to farmers and mechanics in the country. The expenses of the institution, during the past year, with the exception of those incurred for permanent objects, was 13,903 dollars. Its income from the farm, from picking oakum, &c. was 4,432 dollars. The discipline is as good as it can be, under the embarrassment of the impracticability of a proper classification of its subjects. But, to my mind, the evil is most obvious, of a union of those who are, with those who are not, capable of labour. Far less work is in this case done by those, who are able to work, than might otherwise be obtained from them. Beside, public sentiment is not now what it should be, on the subject of sending able-bodied vagrants and beggars to a work-house; and what it would be, if we had a well-regulated work-house, in which this class of paupers could at once be made to support themselves, and in some measure, at least, recovered to virtue, by the very course adopted to save the public from the burden of supporting them.

both from them, and from society. Nay, I think it to be incomparably better for the interests of virtue, and ultimately, even for the pecuniary interests of the public, that a small loss should be occasionally incurred, by keeping those employed, who are dependent on public charity, and who are able to work, than that an alms-house should be, to any one who has strength to labour, a life of easy idleness. I would, therefore, that all who are able to work, and either unable, from inefficiency of character, to provide for themselves, or who, if left at large, *will not* support themselves by their own industry, and who have no friends who will take the charge of them, should be sent to a work-house. If they will go there at the bidding of an overseer of the poor, it is well. If they refuse to go, an authority should be vested somewhere, which can compel them.

A vagrant, however dependent and miserable, and unfit for self-direction, must now be left free, while he chooses to be at large, till he has committed some *crime;* and he is then sent to prison for one, or two, or three, or six months, again to be sent forth, more expert in knavery, but not more inclined to labour, though perhaps physically more capable than before. To me, indeed, it seems most absurd, to talk of the personal rights, and of the constitutionally guarantied freedom of those who not only have nothing, and who, though able, will do nothing, for self-support, but whose example is every day extending corruption to those around them. They are, indeed, sent to prison, when they are found in a state of brutal drunkenness. But instead of this, there should be as well defined an authority to send them to a work-house, even when

they are not intoxicated, or if they do not reduce themselves to the debasement of great intoxication, as there
is to send a thief to a jail. *There*, they not only might
do much for self-support, and many of them, even more
than would be required for their support, but they
might, and should, be treated as moral and immortal
beings, who are to be instructed, and *reclaimed*, and
saved. It is a most palpable injustice, a crying wickedness, to commit a man for intemperance to the same
prison, to which men are sent for theft, and forgery,
and counterfeiting, and other equally heinous civil offences. Let this principle be adopted, and faithfully
acted upon, with a judicious classification of the subjects, and the number will be considerably lessened of
the inmates of our prisons. Nor would there then be the
attraction there is now in alms-houses, to the idle, the
able-bodied beggar. Nor is this all the good that would
be so obtained. The demand for charity in this city would
then be much less than it now is; the facilities for supplying the wants of the better classes of the poor would
be greatly increased—the vice of the city would be
greatly reduced in its amount; and, by the Christian
discipline of the house, some at least of these poor vagrants, all of whom would otherwise die as miserably
as they have lived, would be made to live virtuously,
and to die happily.

The third class named, was that of *orphan children
who are not vicious.*

These, as far as provision can be so made for them,
are the proper subjects for male and female orphan
asylums; and where they cannot be so provided for,
they should be sent to an Alms-House. With us, occasionally, children are received into these asylums,

who are not orphans. But it is only in cases in which the parent, or parents, either from extreme and hopeless poverty, or by moral incapacity, are unfitted to retain the charge of their children. The children in these asylums are instructed in the free schools of our city; and they have other important advantages over those, who are in our alms-house. But it will be difficult to make this provision for half the poor children in a city, who must be supported either by private, or by public benevolence.

The fourth class, in this division of the poor, are vicious children, who cannot be controlled by their parents, or guardians.

For these children, we have an institution called "The School of Reformation." In this school children are reclaimed from vice, and qualified for usefulness You have one for the same objects, called "The Refuge." These institutions I consider as second to none, except our public schools and our churches, for the prevention of pauperism, and crime, and misery. They are, however, of so recent a date every where, that much is to be learned by the public, as well concerning the proper subjects for them, as the immense moral benefits to which they may be conducive; and by their directors and superintendants, respecting the true mode of conducting them. I would, however, lay it down as a principle, that every boy and every girl, under fifteen or sixteen years of age, who can neither be kept at school, nor at any regular and useful employment, and who is beyond parental control, who has begun to be a nuisance, and who, if left to go on, must and will fall into crime, should, if possible, before the guilt of crime has been incurred, be sent to this Refuge

or School. And there let them be committed to the care
of those, who, like Mr. Wells, the excellent Superin-
tendant of our School, "have no hesitation in saying,
that every boy under the age of fifteen years, and somewhat older, however bad he may have been, CAN BE RE-
FORMED;" and we shall find these schools to be immediate, and great blessings, in the relief and comfort
which they will bring to poor and greatly distressed
parents. I know how great is this relief, for I have
had opportunities of witnessing it. And I have had
the happiness, too, of seeing children, whom I have
been instrumental in placing there, and who had
seemed to be past recovery, restored to virtue and usefulness, and giving unspeakable joy to the hearts of
parents, whom they had most deeply distressed by their
departures from virtue. In a few years, we shall see
the effects of these institutions, in the diminished numbers of our street vagrants, and of the inmates of our
prisons. The interest of the whole community should
be enlisted in favour of these schools; and a minister
of the poor may do much, both to enlighten the public
judgment respecting them, and to assist the parents of
disobedient children, in securing this provision for
their salvation and happiness. These institutions furnish, to my mind, one of the noblest triumphs which our
religion has obtained over sin. If established as extensively as they should be, and supported by public
favour as they deserve to be, they will be for temporal
and spiritual salvation to many ten thousands.

From these let us turn to the second great division
which we have made of the poor. I mean to *those who
ought not to be sent either to a work-house, or to an
alms-house.*

5

Take from society at large all the classes of the poor who ought to be separated from it, and there will still remain a very large class of those who will be occasionally dependent on charity, and some who will even be wholly dependent on the care and benevolence of others, who yet ought to be aided *at home.* There are virtuous poor, who have seen better days, who have been reduced, if not from affluence, yet from a comfortable competency of the good things of life, to want, and some to great want. There are many also who have been dependent all their lives upon their daily labours, and who have lived respectably, and have been respected by all around them, but by infirmity or age are able to make but little provision, and some of them can make no provision, for the absolute necessaries of existence. And there are others who are always ready to do what they can for their own wants, but who are sometimes taken off from their work by sickness, and sometimes are greatly embarrassed and distressed by a failure of demand for their labours. There are cases, as I have said, and they are numerous, in which mothers are doing all that they can for the education of their children, who yet obtain but little assistance from their husbands, and who must be assisted to feed and clothe their children, and with fuel in the winter, and sometimes even in the payment of their rent, towards whom it would not only be unjust, but also injurious to society, to send them to an alms-house, or to a work-house. All these, and some not as deserving as these, but who are striving for self-support, and on whom moral influences may be successfully exerted at home, should be left principally to *private charity.* This I hold to be a position of great importance. It is clearly the dictate of the spirit of our religion. And if we can only bring the more favoured classes of society to understand their true interests, in regard to these classes of the poor, which are in truth no other than their Christian duties towards them, there would be no difficulty in providing for every suffering family among us.

Our overseers of the poor are empowered, to a certain extent, to supply the very poor with the necessaries of life, *at their own homes.* The amount thus expended in the year 1828, was 8473 dollars. This is right; but there is still left a great amount of want, which must be met by private charity. The great question on this subject is, how is this charity to be excited, and exercised? Would that I had a voice, or a pen, by which I might rightly affect the public mind on this great question! I should then have done a good, by which my life would indeed have been made a blessing, as well to the rich, as to the poor. But I shall not have laboured in vain, if I can persuade even a few to their duty.

Let me say, then, that my principal dependence for this division of the poor would neither be upon benevolent societies, useful as they are when wisely directed; nor upon the contributions of the city overseers of the poor. Nor, if they would, can they meet, all or nearly all, the strongly pressing, and greatly distressing wants, of very many of the indigent. Nor is it desirable that these agents of others should, even if they could, have the exclusive care of the poor. Those in the more favoured classes of society are indeed but too slow to learn the duties, which grow out of the relation they sustain to the humbler classes of their fellow creatures, as beings of a common nature with themselves; although, from the exercise of Christian benevolence towards them, they would receive, in their own moral improvement, and in all that will exalt them in the view of God and angels, quite as great a good as they will ever be able to impart. The lesson should indeed be repeated often, and strongly, and with a distinctness not to be misunderstood, from every pulpit, and in every family, that the poor are our fellow immortals; who are to be rescued from their dangers, comforted in their troubles, and relieved in their necessities, not merely by a few agents sent to them as the representatives of the kindly feelings, and the Christian sympathy of their fellow beings around them; but, *by the personal cares and efforts of all, who have the means, and opportunities of doing them good.* Our great want is, and I believe that it is the great want, with respect to the poor, in all the cities in Christendom, not so much of benevolent societies, as of *a more widely diffused spirit of personal interest in the work of improving their condition, by improving their characters.* Awaken this spirit, and bring it into action, and an incalculable sum of vice and misery will be prevented.

The questions arise, what is the good which is thus to be done? and, how are we to qualify ourselves to perform it? To one proposing these inquiries, I would reply, let your first care be for those, who belong to your own house. And never flatter yourself with the delusion, that you are exercising Christian benevolence, when that which you bestow in charity is fairly the property of your creditor. Are you willing, however, to do what you can for others? Begin with your domestics, to whom you not only owe something, but

much more, than the payment of their wages. You
may do much to improve their moral and their religious character; and, perhaps, to save some of them
from the most terrible ruin.—You have also *beggars,*
who come to your houses for food. Do you know who
they are, and whether you are doing good, or evil, by
what you may there bestow upon them? Or, have you a
right to refuse them your kindness, merely because you
know not whether they may not abuse it? Or, is it too
much to ask of you, to learn of them where they live,
and to avail yourself of an hour of leisure to visit them?
Or, do you feel too little concern about them, to care
who they are, or whether their wants are supplied; or
whether they are worthy, or not, of your bounty?
Who has made you to differ from these beggars? To
whom do you owe all that you have yourself received?
And is it too much to ask of you, as a return for God's
goodness to yourself, that you will personally acquaint
yourself with the condition, and do something for the
improvement, of a few of those poor among your fellow creatures? In aiding a poor parent in keeping her
children at school; in teaching a filthy family to become cleanly; in exciting an idle family to industry;
in providing work for a family, which knows not where
to obtain it; or by obtaining a place in the country for
a boy, or a girl, who, if left with its parents, would
soon fall into vagrancy and vice; or by one or another of many offices of kindness, which will cost but little either of time or money, you may gradually, but
greatly advance the virtue and happiness of a family.
You may save a poor boy from dishonesty, from intemperance, from a life of guilt and wretchedness; or a
poor girl from dishonesty, pollution, and utter ruin.

5 *

And will not one such good obtained, be to you an ample recompense for all the care that you can give to the improvement and happiness of many families? It is a poor excuse for the neglect of this duty, "I have not leisure for it." Look back, at the close of any week, upon the wasted hours of it which you may call to remembrance, and ask yourself,—deliberately, and seriously, I mean,—how you would feel in a review of these hours, if you had given them to faithful endeavours to relieve, and bless some of those, who greatly need your kindness? Or, I will say to you, on the first day of a week, determine that you will find half a dozen hours in it, or at least half an hour in each day in which you will faithfully visit some poor families, for the purpose of doing all the good,—I mean the moral good,—that you shall be able to do in them; and when you are resting yourself from your labours, or are lying upon your pillow, on Saturday night; look back to the hours which have been so spent, and say, if you have suffered in your business by the appropriation you have made of them? Or, have they subtracted any thing from the amount of your happiness? Or, have they spread any gloom over the future, either with respect to this life or the life to come? Or, can you give the leisure of Sunday to a holier employment, than that of thus visiting the poor! Here, my dear sir, is the true ground on which to take our stand, for obtaining the greatest, the most effectual, and the most permanent good, for the poor.

And here I would take my stand, in answering the question, how may we most effectually meet, and resist. that secret and open licentiousness, that profligate violation, not of good morals only, but of decency,

that abandonment of multitudes to vice, and even to
the grossest vices, which has too long been considered
as an evil, necessarily incidental to large cities; and
therefore to be first silently endured,—and then, as it
is in some of the cities of the old world, authorized by
law; and, even made a source of the public revenue?
This false and base doctrine, as low in the sources
from which it springs, as the causes are vile which produce and nourish all this evil, ought to be fully exposed,—brought to the light in which it shall be seen
in its true character, and consequences. Do you ask
me, then, how we may resist, and how we may hope
to check this tendency in cities to deep and radical
corruption? I reply, that something may be done by
wise legal enactments; and much might be done by
these means, if the efforts of wise legislators were
seconded by a strong accordant moral sentiment in
the community. The true difficulty, however, is, that
moral sentiment is not strong enough to demand the
requisite laws; or, if a few shall demand them, this
sentiment is not extensive enough to secure their execution. Let us then fairly meet this difficulty at once,
and direct our whole attention to it. Public sentiment
must be enlightened on the great topics, of the evils incidental to cities, of the causes of these evils; and of
their actual character and influences. Men of intellect,
and of moral energy, must feel strongly, that they are
responsible for the good which they can do, in enlight-
ening and directing public opinion and judgment; and
they must be aroused to a sense of this responsibility.
The public newspapers must speak plainly upon these
great interests. They must be made the subjects of
conversation; and in essays level with common compre-

hension, they must be brought before all our families. The characters of restorateurs, of taverns, and of all places of resort, should be as freely discussed, and as openly talked of, as the most ordinary questions of the day. And a house known to be vile, to be a trap for the young, and a haunt of the abandoned, should be as publicly designated, as a pest house would be in a city. Yes, and all who are known to be supporters of such a house, be they young or old, married or single, the sons of merchants, of mechanics, or of the poor, should be branded by public sentiment as INFAMOUS; and so they will be, when public sentiment shall be as enlightened and as active as it should be. But if a profligate can pass one evening with gamblers, or prostitutes, and be welcomed on the next in the splendid drawing room, and treated as if he were as highly estimated, and perhaps even more so, than are the modest, the virtuous; if it be thought that a young gentleman is indulging in a very natural, and not very reprehensible love of pleasure, who is known to be fond of a fashionable eating house, and sometimes to go to a brothel, while yet, in that which is called good society, he maintains the decencies of life; or, if it be thought not very disreputable to be occasionally intemperate, if general indications are in favour of sobriety; and not a very crying sin to be a seducer, if the victim of his licentiousness has been a child of poverty;— then, law is a dead letter. The contagion will spread. Cities will become more and more sinks of depravity. Fathers and mothers, in increasing numbers, as a city increases in its inhabitants, will have to mourn over their blasted hopes, and our cities, like the worst of those of the old world, will by and by be rotten to the very heart, and ready for destruction. May God avert from us this awful condition! But, my friend, that he may, we have ourselves something, and much to do in the work. A new interest, I think, is excited on this subject. May it spread and strengthen, till the moral sense of the community, in its collected power, shall make our cities, in purity, and righteousness, models for the cities of the world!

To you, my dear sir, who have dedicated yourself to the office of a minister of the poor, I need only add, that you may, and I doubt not that you will, do much for the virtue and piety, and thus for the best relief and comfort of many hundreds of your suffering fellow creatures. It will be well for you if the affluent shall enable you to contribute something for the supply of the distressing want, which you will sometimes be called to witness. You may also be greatly useful in directing the charity at once of individuals, and of societies. And, if your office shall be rightly appreciated, you will be enabled to connect intelligent and virtuous individuals in the more favoured classes of society, with families of the poor, to whom they may be the best possible benefactors—instruments of their moral redemption. In discharging the duties of your office, you will find much to try, and to depress,—I will not say to discourage, you. But there is no office sustained by man which will give a larger compensation for its cares, and pains, and sorrows. I rejoice in the truly liberal principles, in which its establishment has been begun in your city. You have only to act upon these principles, and the good that will result from your efforts will be certain and great. A ministry exclusively for the poor, by which Christian instruction, and consolation, and encouragement, will be carried, as widely as possible, to every habitation of the destitute; by which the poor, as far as it shall be found practicable, shall be persuaded, following their own convictions of duty, to unite themselves with the Christian societies around them; and by which they will obtain a friend, an adviser in all their difficulties; one to aid them in the charge of their children; one to whom they may speak with confidence of all their sufferings, and all their interests; and who will prove himself worthy of this confidence: the establishment of this ministry will be an era in the history of your city. We have now four ministers who are so employed in Boston. God grant that, with you, and with us, this ministry may be as permanent, and an object of as deep interest, as that of our churches! And may you so accomplish your work in it, as to obtain the acceptance and reward of a faithful servant.

Yours, very faithfully,

J. T.

THE END.

A N

ADDRESS

TO THE

WORKING-MEN OF NEW-ENGLAND,

ON THE

STATE OF EDUCATION,

AND

ON THE CONDITION OF THE PRODUCING CLASSES

IN

EUROPE AND AMERICA.

WITH PARTICULAR REFERENCE TO THE EFFECT OF MANUFAC-
TURING, (AS NOW CONDUCTED,) ON THE HEALTH
AND HAPPINESS OF THE POOR,

AND

ON THE SAFETY OF OUR REPUBLIC.

DELIVERED

IN BOSTON, CHARLESTOWN, CAMBRIDGEPORT, WALTHAM, DOR-
CHESTER, MASS., PORTLAND, SACO, ME., AND DOVER, N. H.

By SETH LUTHER.

' Who has not been delighted with the clock-work movements of a large cotton manufactory.'
Hon. H. Clay, Speech in Senate.
' They (Cotton Mills) are the principalities of the destitute, the palaces of the poor.'
Hon. John Q. Adams, Report on Manufactures.
' The *poor* must work or *starve*, the *rich* will take care of themselves.'
Hon. John Whipple, Answer to Interrogatories from Secretary of Treasury.
' Witness the SPLENDID EXAMPLE of England.'
Hon. A. H. Everett, Report on Manufactures for N. Y. Central Committee.

' Tis yours to judge how wide the limits stand
Between a splendid and a happy land.' — *Goldsmith.*

BOSTON:
PUBLISHED BY THE AUTHOR.
1 8 3 2.

The following letter was received from the Chairman of a meeting of the Working-men of Boston, assembled at Chauncy Hall, on Friday evening, July 6, 1832.

BOSTON, JULY 10, 1832.

MR SETH LUTHER,

SIR,

Several gentlemen interested in the cause of the Producing Classes of our country, after hearing your appropriate and animated Address on Friday evening last, appointed a committee to request of you a copy for publication. It is with pleasure I communicate that request.

REPLY.

BOSTON, SEPTEMBER 15, 1832.

MR CHAIRMAN,

SIR,

On the reception of your note of the 10th July, I informed you that however gratifying the request of gentlemen might be as approbatory of sentiments expressed in my address; there were certain reasons, which, if known to the committee, would excuse me from complying *at that time* with their request. Those reasons no longer stand in the way. Not only so, circumstances have occurred which render it necessary in justice to our cause, and to myself, that this performance, however imperfect, should be laid more fully before the public. Misrepresentation and slander have been extremely active in endeavors to injure our cause; and persons interested in continuing present abuses, *are now* and probably will *always* be *determined* to crush *me*. ' Apostle of Sedition,' ' Disturber of the Peace,' ' Disorganizer,' ' Agitator,' ' Spy,' ' Hunt,' ' Cobbet,' &c, are terms freely applied to me by some Manufacturers and their minions, because I have advocated the cause of the POOR and NEEDY, and in some *slight degree* exposed the unrighteous conduct of those who officially declare ' that the poor must work or starve, and the rich will take care of themselves;' and who import FOREIGN wool to reduce the price of wool raised by OUR OWN FARMERS; — FOREIGN workmen to cut down the wages of American Citizens, — and FOREIGN *Machinery* to throw *our own Machinists* out of employ, — and *this* for the purpose of supporting AMERICAN Industry. I have been told, Sir, by the Agent of the York Manufacturing Company, at Saco, Me, that I was lowering the *standard* of *Morality* by delivering this address. I could heartily wish that my life had been as free from stain as is this address of immoral tendency. I shall however leave the Public to judge respecting the correctness of the principles here laid down. It is but of little consequence to me what my fate is, provided the FRIENDS of HUMANITY will demand that the SLAVERY in American Manufactories shall cease FOREVER.

I am with respect, yours, &c,

SETH LUTHER.

N. B. You will observe, Sir, that I have embodied some important information in this copy which was not contained in the address as delivered in Boston.

Yours,   S. L.

REFERENCE

ERRATA.

In page 17 this mark ‡ refers to Appendix E.
Same page, this mark * refers to note †.
    Do   this mark † refers to note ‡.

ADDRESS.

MR. CHAIRMAN AND GENTLEMEN,

You will not expect from the speaker an Address, such as you sometimes hear from men of liberal education ; being a practical mechanic, and having had but few advantages, he *could not*, if he *would*, amuse you with well turned and polished periods, or surprise you with impassioned eloquence. Our business is with facts. Indisputable *facts*. Facts of the highest moment to us as individuals, and as citizens of a *nominally* free country ; for we cannot admit that any country *is*, or any people *can* be free, where distinctions in society exist, in opposition to that ' self-evident truth, — ALL MEN ARE CREATED EQUAL..' The speaker will endeavour, in the course of this address, to call things by their right names, and while he *solemnly* and *sincerely* disavows all *party* views, with reference to the great political questions which agitate our nation, he intends ' to hew to the line, and let the chips fly in whose eyes they may.' Tyranny, cruelty, and oppression, of whatever kind, coming within the range of our observation, shall be pointed out and exposed, let it be found where it may. We do not come here this evening with views hostile to any body, or profession of men, as *such*, for we believe the interests of all classes are involved in the *intelligence* and *welfare* of those who labour — those who produce *all* the wealth and enjoy so *small* a portion of it themselves. Hence we are induced to assume and express a decided hostility to *principles* and *practices*, which will, if not immediately eradicated and forsaken, destroy all the rights, benefits, and privileges intended for our enjoyment, as a free people : And these principles and practices are found among all parties.

When abuses exist, however *great*, and however *hard* they may bear on any portion of the community, he who raises his voice for ' reform,' is sure to meet with deadly hatred, and bitter, untiring, and remorseless persecution from interested persons. *Ridicule, slander, threats*, and *abuse* is his *sure, certain*, and inevitable reward. Hence men bear *much* before they are willing to encounter such a *mass* of difficulties in an attempt

2

to improve their condition. Notwithstanding *this*, and notwithstanding the speaker has received a due share of this sure reward, we dare not withhold our voice, when we reflect on the present state of things in our beloved country as touching the producing classes. When we reflect on the sufferings and privations of our fathers in the days of our Revolution, while we see so many proofs of their *firmness* and *wisdom ;* when we read of their undying zeal, and untiring efforts in the war of Liberty ; when we look towards that *Holy Hill* where Warren fell, and where blood flowed like water from the hearts of Freemen, we feel it incumbent upon us, to sound an *alarm* when our rights are not only *endangered*, but some of them already wrested from us, by the powerful and inhuman grasp of monopolized wealth.

In pursuing the proposed subject, on the state of education and condition of the Producing Classes in Europe and America, we assume the following positions, viz. ' In a free government, education, which elevates the mind, diffuses intelligence, and leads to virtue, is the *only sure foundation* of freedom and public safety. Without education, a portion of the community is cast into the shade, and oftentimes intellect of the first order is lost to its possessor and to the world. Children of the poor, as well as the rich, ought to be instructed both in letters and morals, and NO STATE OF SOCIETY CAN EXCUSE THE NEGLECT OF IT. If we wish to live in a community, peaceably, orderly, free from excess, outrage and crime, we must use our exertions for the general diffusion of education, of intelligence, among every class of our citizens. In this course we shall find our interest and happiness. In looking over the catalogue of offenders, we shall find, that vice of every kind and degree most generally springs from ignorance. The want of learning and moral instruction leads to idleness, dissipation and crime, and often ends in ruin.'*

On these plain, simple principles, we ' take post,' and fortify our position by the history of all time, all nations, and all people. We now are prepared to show that a spirit of monopoly exists in this country as well as in Europe, which is sapping and mining the VERY FOUNDATIONS of our free institutions. A ' STATE of SOCIETY ' exists in this country, which prevents the producing classes from a participation in the fountains of knowledge, and the benefits equally designed for all. This state of things is produced and sustained by *Avarice*. Whether avarice is or is not, in part or as a whole a natural or acquired vice, we shall not at this time pretend to decide. We are, however, inclined to think that be it natural or acquired, it is nurtured and fostered by a defective edu-

* General Brigham, Mayor of Providence. See Appendix A.

cation. Be this as it may, we witness daily the dreadful effects of this evil passion. It hardens the heart, sears the conscience, and deafens the ear to the cry of suffering humanity. It nerves the arm of the midnight assassin as he plunges the deadly steel into the heart of his sleeping and unconscious victim : It urges the worse than midnight assassin to slander those who are contending against its unhallowed influence. Avarice manufactures drunkards, chains and lashes the slave, and crowds down and oppresses the poor, the friendless, and the destitute : it is the father of *all crime*, from the days of Adam until the present time. This *fiend* induced Judas to betray his master, and Benedict Arnold to make an attempt to sell his country. It induced a certain rich man to throw a poor sick slave into the sea from a slave ship, and *Avarice* afterwards placed *that man* in high office in his own country. Under the influence of this principle, the IMMORTAL and detestable Combination of Merchants in Boston, pledged themselves, on the 18th of May last, to drive to starvation or submission, the Shipwrights, Caulkers and Gravers of that City.† That *dignified body*, composing a part of the HIGHER ORDERS, issued another UKASE on the 20th of July last, in which, and by which, they AUTHORIZED the masters to ALLOW their journeymen time to escape the Cholera.* Urged on by the cursed hell-born principle of Avarice, men stake every thing for GOLD. Any, every means, and all kinds of *meanness* are used to get rich. No matter what are the immediate or more remote consequences; the widow weeps, the fatherless starve, blood flows, hearts are broken, characters destroyed, suicide is committed, gray hairs brought down with sorrow to the grave, and the world is filled with ignorance, vice and misery, that men may gorge, *if possible*, an insatiate appetite for gold. For gold Guatamozin was broiled by Cortez on a bed of live coals, and the Spaniards in Mexico and elsewhere, hunted the poor Indians with *bloodhounds*, carrying devastation, by fire and sword among defenceless men, women, and children, wherever their unhallowed feet polluted the soil of the New World. For a moment we will notice the effects of this *lust* of possession in other countries, and then enquire if the same causes, or *some* of them at *least*, are not in active operation in our own, ' our native land,' which have destroyed the happiness of the MANY, that the FEW may roll and riot in splendid luxury. We must for want of time pass over poor degraded Spain, whose Monarch expends much of his royal time in *manufacturing* embroidered petticoats for the virgin Mary ; Portugal, the playthings of whose Sovereign are gibbets, halters, dungeons, and poisons, and

* See the Ukase in Appendix B.
† $20,000 were subscribed for this purpose.

whose only amusements appear to be the groans, struggles, and dying agonies of his miserable subjects. France, unhappy France, drenched with the blood of millions of human victims to remorseless ambition. Russia, governed by an Emperor to whom the *very name* of Freedom is hateful, and who has rendered the name of ' Nicholas ' the scorn of countless ages by his former and recent conduct towards *bleeding, degraded, murdered* POLAND.

Passing over these countries with a brief notice we fix our eyes on England from whence came our fathers. We are induced to do so because we are called upon by a body of Monopolists alias Manufacturers, to ' WITNESS the SPLENDID *Example* of *England.*' See what manufactures have done for her. (This call is contained in a report written by a gentleman whose name will be seen on the title page of this address). He is supported by a Senator from Rhode Island who says ' if all the gold and diamonds and precious stones in the world, were implanted in the soil of Great Britain, it would be *nothing* compared to the *mine of wealth* she has found in the protecting policy.'* Although we are, and ever have been friendly to all that promised happiness to our Country, we now wish to be *expressly understood*, as being a decided enemy to all Systems the tendency of which is to prevent the diffusion of intelligence. We think we shall be able to prove that ' all the gold and diamonds and precious stones in the world' would not pay for *one half* of the misery of the producing classes in England. We shall also show that a great proportion of the misery and degradation of the starving population of that country is in a great degree produced *directly* by manufacturing operations, which have made England a ' *Splendid Example*' for our imitation. Perhaps some one will say ' what have we to do with this subject ?' ' Let Cotton mills take care of themselves.' We wish they might, (if they will abuse the power given by the people) and if they always had taken care of themselves the country would not now be distracted and shaken from the extremities to the centre by the PROTECTION given to men who are oppressing the poor by and with the power obtained from the people through the Government. We hope to be able however to answer the proposed query satisfactorily to all *humane* men. It has always been the policy in Imperial and Kingly governments, to talk much about *National* glory, *National* wealth, and *National* improvement.

The splendid victories, high titles and refinement of the ' HIGHER ORDERS,' are sounded forth by the governments and their parasites ; this is answered by the degraded subject, who, while he cries *vive le roi*, ' long live the king', knows not why he does so,

---

* Here is a direct appeal to the passion of AVARICE.

and for the most part is at a loss for bread for his hungry family. Under such governments the subjects are amused with carnivals, masquerades, military parades, imposing and splendid religious ceremonies, and national songs. This course is pursued by men in power, to keep the 'common people' the 'LOWER ORDERS' from *thinking*, from *reasoning*, from watching the movements of Emperors, Kings, Dukes, Lords, and other villains, who are fleecing the poor. We shall find, notwithstanding all our *boasted liberty* and *freedom*, that there are many men in *our own* country, who in *their way*, are pursuing the same course. In viewing ' the *Splendid Example* of England,' we are not to look at present on the dazzling lustre of her national glory ; for we do know that in the exact ratio of the increase of the power and wealth and glory of all *nations* as such, so is the *misery* of the *poor* increased. We propose to draw aside the veil. We propose to make an attempt to dissipate the enchantment which distance lends to the view : We leave the crown, the coronet, the palaces, and *all* the *glittering mockery* which hides the rottenness within her borders, from the view of men who are ' hankering after the fleshpots of despotic power.' We leave such things for the contemplation of those who ' sigh for butter in a lordly dish.' We will go where the poor are '*steeped* to the *lips*' in filth and wretchedness, and deep degradation. We shall produce a picture, which ought to make any man *blush* to be the author of that sentence — ' *Witness* the *Splendid Example* of *England*,' unless his heart were adamant, and his face *case-hardened steel*. As a general remark, we observe that for a long series of years, 40 per cent, or nearly one half of the population of England and Wales, (6,000,000) have been without the means of a mere subsistence, and have been humbled to the condition of *paupers*, during some portion of the year, suing for relief from those who hold the property of the kingdom. *Three millions* of Englishmen are, throughout the year, relieved in the work-houses, or from the poor rates.* Ireland, bleeding at every pore, under the weight of this *Splendid Example*, is not included in this statement. Again; in London there are about 2500 persons committed for trial yearly. Amount of annual depredations, £ 2,100,000 ; 18 prisons ; 5204 Alehouses ; annual amount of counterfeit coin, £ 200,000, 3000 receivers of stolen goods, 50,000 prostitutes, 10,000 servants at all times out of employ ; 10,000 rise every morning, without knowing how they are to subsist through the day. This is a small part of the Splendid Example of England.† In a report

* Hon. John Bell's Speech.
† We make these statements merely to show how men thirsting for

in the House of Commons it was stated, that out of 1500 families of poor, in the neighbourhood of Spitalfields, a manufacturing district in London, there were 300 cases of abject poverty and destitution, and at least 100 of *literal starvation.* They were at the moment pressed by the landlord, baker, and tax-gatherer : had pawned and sold every thing that would bring money, and were absolutely without a *morsel of bread,* for themselves or families. These persons are represented to be worthy, honest, and industrious, by the report of the House of Commons.

We shall proceed to show that misery in horrid forms exists, particularly in the manufacturing districts of England. We shall produce indisputable evidence from the testimony of English and American authorities, which will show conclusively that this misery is directly produced by manufacturing operations. Having done so, we shall show that we are, in these United States, following with fearful rapidity the '*Splendid Example of England.*' An English writer says, the Factory System is a system of most horrible abuse of the noble animal and intellectual nature which God has given to the human species. In one factory, where 475 children are employed, 235 are between *nine* and *twelve,* 199 between *twelve* and *fifteen,* and 50 between *fifteen* and *eighteen* years of age. They are superintended by 15 men, and are compelled to come to their daily *drudgery* every month in the year at 6 o'clock in the morning, and to remain in the factory until 7 in the evening, and sometimes until eight or nine, making 14 or 15 hours of labour in a day, with an intermission of but a half an hour for meals, rest, and recreation. The consequence of this excess of toil is, that the growth of the body is checked, and the limbs become weak, and sometimes horribly distorted. These little slaves of the factory often fall asleep, and, in this state of listlessness, their fingers and hands get involved in the machinery. They are often frightfully mangled, and are then sent to the hospital. Dr Smith, of the Leeds' Infirmary, says his attention was first drawn to this subject TWELVE YEARS since, in consequence of the unusual number of cases of deformity of the lower extremities, sent from a neighbouring MANUFACTURING TOWN. He says his surprise ceased, when he ascertained the number of hours they were compelled to labour. Another English writer says that it is proved, on undoubted au-

National Glory, will lose sight (purposely) of all the misery and vice, found among a people, when their eyes are dazzled with the ' Splendid Example' of a nation whose government is grinding its subjects to powder, to support the worse than useless splendour of national glory, and national wealth, while starvation is tearing the very vitals of hundreds of thousands of the miserable poor of England, Ireland, and Wales.

thority, that children of very tender ages are compelled to work in mills from 12 to 15 hours, with only 30 minutes for all meals. They are employed in a heated and vitiated atmosphere during this time; and children of six years old are compelled to labor longer than a negro slave,* or even an adult convict, whose hours of labour cannot by law exceed TEN. Richard Oastler, Esq., in a speech made in Manchester or Leeds, England, said, ' In my opinion the Factory System has caused a great deal of the distress and immorality of the present time, and a great deal of the weakness of men's constitutions of the present time. When I contemplate the life of a factory child, my heart is filled with *horror* to think that human nature can be *so* corrupt ; that one individual, calling himself a man, could live for a *single day* under the load of guilt, which he must feel *as* a man, who is causing such dreadful misery.' He gives us an example of one little child, ' for,' said he, ' the *whole mass* of *factory woes* would *cloud your understandings*, and make you like myself — *mad*. I will not present fiction to you, but tell you what I have seen. Take a little child ; she shall rise from her bed at 4 in the morning, of a cold winter's day — before that time she awakes perhaps half a dozen times, and says, " father is it time? — father is it time?" When she gets up, she feels about for her little bits of rags, her clothes, and puts them on to her weary limbs, and trudges onward to the mill, through rain or snow, 1 or 2 miles, and there she works from 13, and even to 18 hours, with only 30 minutes interval. Homewards again at night she would go when she was able, but many a time she hid herself in the wool in the mill, not being able to reach home ; — at last she sunk under these cruelties, into the grave.' Mr Oastler said he could bring *hundreds* of *instances* of this kind, with the difference, that they worked 15, instead of 18 hours. If these children were a moment behind the time to go into the mill, there stood a monster, in human form, and as they passed, he lashed them. One boy, for an absence of half an hour, was stripped and gagged, and flogged with a hazel stick until the skin was flayed off from his neck to his hips.

A member of parliament stated, that it rarely happened that persons brought up in factories lived over the age of 40 years ; consequently the manufacturing districts were filled with orphans. The labour of children was so severe, that even adults must sink under its inhuman pressure. *The hours of labour had from time to time increased*, until *no constitution*, however robust, could withstand its *inhuman pressure*. The mortality among children,

* By a law of parliament, the *negro* slaves in the West Indies, cannot be made to labor more than *nine* hours per day.

thus employed, exceeds by far that among others. The average longevity in a worsted mill, employing over four hundred females, does not exceed 13 years. A surgeon, who travelled in Manchester, found in one mill, 167 children, and, out of that number, 47 were deformed from excessive labour. The demand for steel machines to prop up bent limbs, beautifully formed by nature, was so great, that one dispensary was obliged to refuse orders for them until the parish paid half the cost. If children are idle in the mills, they are beaten with a leathern strap, or belt, of well-seasoned leather.

What think you, Mr Chairman and gentlemen, these miserable beings care about the 'Splendid Example of England?' Just as much as some of our statesmen and monopolists care about their misery, when they call on us to witness this example.

The Hon. Z. Allen, of Providence, (R. I.) has lately published 'The PRACTICAL TOURIST,' from notes taken in Europe. He says, 'that the most highly-coloured sketches of the moral depravity of many of the manufacturing population of Manchester, England, fall short of the reality. A stranger, if he walk the streets on pleasant evenings, is frequently addressed by abandoned females. Unless, indeed, peremptorily refused, they assume assurance, and press their importunities with a shamelessness, that can only be the result of long-practised habits of vice. Here the virtuous and vicious females are brought into communion, without inquiry and without reproach;' and '*the passing traveller is induced to pause at the sight, and denounce* such sources of present WEALTH, however overflowing and abundant.' 'While the *enriching stream** is *undermining* and *contaminating* the *best interest* of man,* — God forbid,' says Mr Allen, 'that there ever should be a Manchester in the New World.' This is the testimony of an *American* manufacturer, a gentleman of great wealth, respectable scientific and literary attainments, and much practical knowledge. Yet we hear other gentlemen exultingly call LOWELL the *Manchester* of America. Are gentlemen willing to carry out the parallel according to the testimony of Mr Allen ? We hope not, at present, but we fear for the future. Already, at Lowell, 'a disturbance of the peace is of almost nightly occurrence,'† and a riot is no strange thing.

What kind of population does the manufacturing districts in England produce and foster ? We give in answer the testimony of Mr Hewitt, Agent for the American Temperance Society, who has lately returned from Europe. He says, 'the LOWER ORDERS

* This *enriching stream* is the manufacturing system.
† Report of Selectmen of Lowell.

in Europe are as stupid as our slaves. Of this class is the Spitalfields weavers, EIGHTY THOUSAND in number, who are precisely
like Southern slaves, except in color ; and have the appearance
of SAVAGES and BARBARIANS. All Europe, he continues, seems
to be struggling to throw off the chains of a *thousand years*, but
every effort seems to bind them faster. The reason is the *common people* cannot govern themselves, and without the assistance
of the *common people*, a FREE GOVERNMENT CANNOT EXIST.' A
most precious confession, and *most noble* truth. Mr Hewitt does
not give us a satisfactory reason *why* they cannot govern themselves, or *how* they became so degraded. The reason, and the
only one which can be given, is that they are *buried in ignorance*.
But how did this happen ? How became they so ignorant, so
degraded in a land famed for its colleges, philosophers and statesmen ? Let us examine, and if we can answer these queries with
reference to England, to which Mr Hewitt more particularly refers, it will throw much light on our subject. Dr James Phillips
Kay, of Manchester, England, treats this subject in a masterly
manner ; he gives us cause and effect in such a plain style, that
those who are not wilfully blind *must see* the direful effects of a
system so much extolled by men who care for nothing but *cent
per cent*. He says the people employed in mills are crowded
together in one *dense mass** in cottages separated by narrow, un-
paved, and almost pestilential streets, in an atmosphere loaded
with the smoke and exhalations of a large manufacturing city.
These operatives are engaged during TWELVE HOURS in a day,
(Gentlemen will please remember that, as we shall refer to it
again) in a heated and enervating atmosphere which is frequently loaded with dust and filaments of cotton, and consequently
extremely unhealthy. They are engaged in an employment which
absorbs their attention, and unremittingly employs their physical
energies. They are DRUDGES, who watch the movements, and
assist the operations of a mighty material force, which toils, ever
unconscious of fatigue. The labor of the operative must rival
the mathematical precision, the incessant motion and exhaustless

* It is evident to all acquainted with cotton mills in the United States,
that in many places the population engaged in and about mills is crowded
already in ' one dense mass.' At Lowell 72 persons (Irish) were found
' in one half of a *small house*.' This is directly chargeable on the present mode of conducting manufactures in this country. It is the effect
of a cause, and that cause is in its turn the effect of the mode of conducting the Manufacturing System. Were it not for inducements held out
by manufacturers and owners, our country would not now be deluged by
the hundreds of thousands of the miserable and degraded population of
Europe.

power of the machine.* Hence, beside the *negative* results, a total abstraction from every moral and intellectual stimulus, the absence of variety, banishment from the grateful air, and the cheering influence of light. The physical energies are exhausted by incessant labor, and imperfect nutrition. Having been subjected to the prolonged labor of an animal, his physical energies wasted, his mind in supine action, the operative has neither moral dignity, nor intellectual nor organic strength to resist the seductions of his appetite. His wife and children, too, frequently subjected to the same process, are unable to cheer his moments of leisure. Domestic economy is unknown. Meals are prepared and *devoured with heedless haste*. Home has no other relation to him than as a shelter. It chiefly presents him with a scene of physical exhaustion, from which he is glad to escape. Himself impotent of all the distinguishing aims of his species, he sinks into sensual sloth, or revels in more degraded licentiousness. His house is ill furnished and uncleanly, frequently damp. His food meagre and innutritious ; he is debilitated and hypochondriacal, and he falls the victim of dissipation.' Here, then, are the causes which render the ' common people' unfit to govern themselves. Here we see the result of the operations of the Factory System in producing ignorance, vice and misery. Here also is an answer to those who say that ' the majority of the laboring classes in the United States would be dissipated and drunken' if not chained to the plough, the anvil, the broad axe, the work-bench, or the *cotton mill.* Here is a looking glass for those who out of *pure benevolence* keep their mills running at ' 4 per cent profit,'† that the free citizens of this Republic may not be *permitted* to commit depredations on the HIGHER ORDERS. Such imputations we repel with indignation and despise alike the statements and their authors. Dr Thackrah, an eminent surgeon in Leeds, England, says ' that chiidren who work in factories are stunted, the vital principle suffers. Such persons are more liable to acute diseases. In a word, the factory system tends to produce a weak, stunted, and short lived race.' He concludes by saying that the proposed measure before parliament for reducing the hours of labor to TEN, is recommended alike by PATRIOTISM, JUSTICE, and HUMANITY. We have now witnessed the ' SPLENDID EXAMPLE of ENGLAND,' and what do we discover? We find evils enough in the review to send the blood burning through our veins with indignation, or

* Any person who cannot see a Cotton Mill in this picture must be *blinded* by *Avarice.*

† Hon. John Whipple, in answer to the question from the General Government, What are the profits on Manufactures?

15

chilling with the recital of cruelties almost too horrid to name. We pity the man who, knowing 'these facts, would not feel his blood boil in his veins at the recital. A human being who could see and know these things, as they exist in Europe, and call upon us to witness the ' *Splendid Example* of *England*,' cannot, in our opinion, have the soul of a man. Perhaps it would not be too much to say that those who are so eager after National glory, ought to be condemned to travel eternally over mountains of *gunpowder*, shod with *fire brands;* exhibiting to all creation a *Splendid Example* of punishment justly awarded to those who wish and *probably* then would have a high elevation above the vulgar Farmer, Mechanic and Laborer.

Well might the Hon. Daniel Webster exclaim, in 1824, ' He saw nothing in a manufacturing population *elsewhere* to recommend it to us.' He thought THEN there were great evils in it. He thought THEN that a population of that description ought not to be purchased at so much cost. He thought THEN manufacturing was an employment which tended to make the poor both more numerous and more poor, and the rich fewer in number, and perhaps more rich. What he thinks *now* we cannot tell.* In our review we have seen a large body of human beings *ruined* by a neglect of education, rendered miserable in the extreme, and incapable of self government ; and this by the grinding of the rich on the faces of the poor, through the operation of cotton and other machinery. Have we nct reason to exclaim in the language of Goldsmith, when he says,

> ' Ye Friends to truth, ye Statesmen who survey
> The *rich* man's joy *increase* the *poor's decay*,
> Tis your's to judge how wide the limits stand,
> Between a SPLENDID and a HAPPY land.'†

We now turn to our own country ; and would to God we could find no resemblance between the two nations relative to this subject; would we could find nothing under the broad folds of the 'Star-spangled Banner' resembling the cruelties practised, and the ignorance prevalent in England. We observed that it is becoming fashionable in our country to cry out about *National* glory, *National* wealth, march of Improvement, march of Intellect. We have pointed out to you the reason why the Monopolists of Europe raise this cry, and you will, ere long, probably, discover the same design in our own country ; to wit, to prevent the ' common people,' the LOWER ORDERS, by which our HIGHER

* See Appendix, C.
† See Appendix, D.

ORDERS mean farmers, mechanics and laborers, from *thinking*, *reasoning*, and watching the movements of these same HIGHER ORDERS.

Some of our statesmen, capitalists, and monopolists take very broad and lofty views of these subjects. They *appear* not to *trouble* themselves about the miseries of the poor. It seems

> ' The widows grief, the orphan's nakedness,
> The poor man's woe,
> These they *can never* see ;
> And their dull ear
> Can never catch the wailing wretchedness
> Wrung from the lowly lived.
> The bitter tears that sickness or misfortune
> Cause to flow, ne'er warmed the *ice*
> Of their *obdurate* hearts.'

We have shown how great a mass of human misery is hidden in England, under the glare of *National* wealth, and the splendor of National glory. You have visited the thick and crowded *manufacturing town*,

> ' Where avarice plucks the staff away,
> Whereon the weary lean,
> And vice reels o'er the midnight bowl,
> With song, and jest, obscene.'

To hide existing, or anticipated and *inevitable* evils, of the like kind, resulting from like causes, our ears are constantly filled with the cry of *National* wealth, National glory, *American* System, and American industry. We are told that operatives are happy in our mills, and that they want no change in the regulations,* and that they are getting great wages, saving 25 per cent† over and above their living. This stuff is retailed by owners, and agents, and sold wholesale at the rate of eight dollars for a day's work of four hours in the capital at Washington. This cry is kept up by men who are endeavouring *by all the means in their power* to cut down the wages of *our own people*, and who send agents to *Europe*, to induce *foreigners* to come here, to underwork *American* citizens, to support *American* industry, and the *American* system.

The whole concern, (as now conducted) is as great a humbug

* So say the owners of slaves in all countries where human flesh and blood is bought and sold to pamper the luxury of ' *we the people*' alias *we* who wield might for right.

† See Cozzens' Report on the Manufactures of Rhode Island.

as ever deceived any people. We see the system of manufacturing lauded to the skies; senators, representatives, owners,
and agents of cotton mills using all means to keep out of sight
the evils growing up under it. Cotton mills where cruelties
are practised, excessive labour required, education neglected, and
vice, as a matter of course, on the increase, are denominated
' the‡ principalities of the destitute, the palaces of the poor.'
We do not pretend to say that this description applies in all its
parts, to all mills alike — but we do say, that most of the causes
described by Dr Kay of Manchester are in active operation in
New England, and as sure as effect follows cause, the result must
be the same. A member of the United States Senate seems to be
extremely pleased with cotton mills ; he says in the senate, ' Who
has not been delighted with the clockwork movements of a large
cotton manufactory, he had visited them often, and *always* with
increased delight.'* He says the women work in large airy†
apartments well warmed, they are neatly dressed, with ruddy
complexions, and happy countenances ; they mend the broken
threads and replace the exhausted balls or broaches, and at stated
periods they go to and return from their meals with light and
cheerful step. (While on a visit to that pink of perfection, Waltham, I remarked that the females moved with a very light step,
and well they might, for the bell rung for them to return to the
mill from their homes in 19 minutes after it had rung for them to go
to breakfast : some of these females boarded the largest part of a
half a mile from the mill). And the grand climax is, that at the end
of the week, after working like slaves for 13 or 14 hours every day,
' they enter the temples of God on the Sabbath, and thank him for
all his benefits' — and the *American System* above all requires a
peculiar outpouring of gratitude. We remark, that whatever

* See Appendix E.

† We imagine he never worked in one 13 or 14 hours per day.

‡ So far from this, in some establishments the windows have been
nailed down, and the females deprived of even fresh air, in order to support the ' *American System.*'

An actual rebellion took place not long since, in consequence of this
high-handed and tyrannical measure, among the 1000 females in a vast
overgrown establishment. We learn that frequently the females have
become entirely unmanageable in consequence of various cruelties practised on them at that place. We learn that not long since the agent
newly appointed, made a rule that ' all who were not within the gates at
the last stroke of the bell, was to pay a fine of 12½ cents,' whereupon
the girls rose en masse. The confusion was great and the order revoked.
How delightful to live in ' a principality of the destitute, a palace of the
poor.'

girls or others may do west of the Alleghany mountains, we do not believe there can be a *single person found* east of those mountains, who ever *thanked God* for *permission* to work in a *cotton mill.*

Without being obliged to attribute wrong or mercenary motives to the Hon. Senator (*whose talents certainly must command respect from all,* let their views in other respects be what they may), we remark, that we think he was most grossly deceived by the circumstances of his visit. We will give our *reasons,* in a few words spoken (in part) on a former occasion, on this subject. It is well known to all that when *Honourables* travel, that timely notice is given of their arrival and departure in places of note. Here we have a case — the Honourable Senator from Kentucky is about to visit a *cotton mill* — due notice is given ; the men, girls, and boys, are ordered to array themselves in their best apparel. Flowers of every hue are brought to decorate the mill, and enwreath the brows of the fair sex. If nature will not furnish the materials from the lap of summer, art supplies the deficiency. Evergreens mingle with the roses, the jasmine, and the hyacinth, to honour the *illustrious* visitor, the champion, the very Goliah of the American System. He enters! Smiles are on every brow. No *cow-hide,* or *rod,* or '*well seasoned strap*' is suffered to be seen by the Honourable senator, or permitted to disturb the enviable happiness of the inmates of this almost *celestial* habitation. The Hon. Gentleman views with keen eye the ' clock work.' He sees the rosy faces of the Houries* inhabiting this palace of beauty ; he is in ecstasy — he is almost *dumfounded* — he enjoys the enchanting scene with the most intense delight. For an hour or more (not 14 hours) he seems to be in the regions described in Oriental song, his feelings are overpowered, and he retires, almost unconscious of the cheers which follow his steps ; or if he hears the ringing shout, 'tis but to convince him, that he is in a land of reality, and not of fiction. His mind being filled with sensations, which, from their novelty, are without a name, he exclaims, 'tis a paradise ; and we reply, if a Cotton Mill is a ' paradise,' it is ' *Paradise Lost.*'

If we might be permitted to use a yankee privilege, and *guess* what would be the *drift* of the meditations of a person so happily wrought up, we might suppose he would *think poetically* as follows :

> I've seen them elegantly move
> Where shuttles swiftly slide,

* Fabled beauties of the Mahometan paradise.

Methinks the ' *Clock-work*' I do love,
O'er which their fingers glide.

' Their auburn tresses carelessly
O'erhang a neck of snow,
And dazzlingly they glitter
In sunset's crimson glow.'

' They are more fair to look upon
Than sylph or fairy thing,'
More pleasant to enraptured eyes
Than budding flowers of spring.

We believe there are *many* beautiful and virtuous ladies employed in cotton mills, but we do know, notwithstanding this, that the
wives and *daughters* of the *rich* manufacturers would no more
associate with a '*factory girl*,' than they would with a *negro
slave.* So much for equality in a *republican* country.

We would respectfully advise the honourable senator to travel
incognito, when he visits Cotton Mills. If he wishes to come at
the *truth*, he must not be known. Let him put on a *short jacket
and trowsers*, and join the LOWER ORDERS' for a short time ;
then let him go into a factory counting room, and pull off his hat,
which he will be told to do in some of our ' *Republican Institutions*'* called Cotton Mills ; then let him attempt to get work for
75 cents, or 100 for 14 hours per day instead of *eight* dollars for
four hours, and he will then discover some of the *intrinsic beauties* of factory 'clockwoik.' In that case we could show him in
some of the prisons in New England, called cotton mills, instead
of rosy cheeks, the *pale, sickly, haggard* countenance of the
ragged child. Haggard from the *worse* than *slavish* confinement
in the cotton mill. He might see that child driven up to the
' clockwork' by the cowskin, in some cases ; he might see in some
instances, the child taken from his bed at four in the morning, and
plunged into cold water to drive away his slumbers, and prepare
him for the labors in the mill. After all this he might see that
child *robbed*, yes, *robbed* of a part of his time allowed for meals
by moving the hands of the clock backwards, or forwards, as
would best accomplish that purpose. We could show him 'clockwork' with a peculiar escapement, having power to move a whole
factory village from three to six hundred miles east or west (from
any other place, no *matter where*), by calculation of longitude.
In one case we find Exeter N. H. 600 miles west of Boston, by

* John Q. Adams' Report on Manufactures.

the operation of this factory '*clockwork*.' The honorable gentleman might see *patent lever* '*clockwork*' of the *first quality* running on *diamonds*, which never was *guilty* of keeping the *true*
time, while in the atmosphere of a manufacturing village, or in
the pocket of an agent, overseer, or owner of a cotton mill. He
might see in some, and not unfrequent instances, the child, and
the female child too, driven up to the clockwork with the cow-
hide, or well seasoned strap of 'AMERICAN MANUFACTURE.'
We could show him *many* females who have had corporeal punishment inflicted upon them ; one girl eleven years of age who
had her leg broken with a billet of wood ; another, who had a
board split over her head by a heartless monster in the shape of
an overseer of a cotton mill ' paradise.' *

We, shall for want of time, (not stock) omit entering more
largely into detail for the present, respecting the cruelties practised in some of the American mills. Our wish is to show that
education is neglected, and that as a matter of course, because
if 13 hours actual labour, is required each day, it is *impossible*
to attend to education among children, or improvement among
adults. With regard to hours of labour in cotton mills, there is
a difference here as well as in England. In Manchester 12
hours *only* is the rule, while in some other towns in England
many more are required.† The mills *generally* in New England,
run 13 hours the year round, that is, actual labour for all hands ;
to which add one hour for two meals, making 14 hours actual
labour — for a man, or woman, or child, must labour hard to go a
quarter, and sometimes half a mile, and eat his dinner or breakfast in 30 minutes and get back to the mill. At the Eagle mills,
Griswold, Connecticut, 15 hours and 10 minutes actual labour in
the mill are required ; at another mill in the vicinity, 14 hours
of actual labour are required. It needs no argument, to prove
that education *must* be, and is almost entirely neglected. Facts

* We do not pretend to say that all overseers are thus cruel, but we
do say, that foreign overseers are frequently placed over American women and children, and, we are sorry to add, that sometimes foreigners in
this country have employed American overseers to carry into effect their
tyrannical rules in these mills.

† In the cotton mills in France, ' during the longest days in summer,
the help commence work at 6 o'clock A. M., work till nine, when *one
hour* is allowed for breakfast, and another hour at dinner between 2 and
3 P. M., and the daily labour of 12 hours is finished about sunset.' —
Allen's Practical Tourist. It appears, that the ' help' in Free America,
are driven harder than they are in Europe. American Citizens ! will
you longer submit to worse tyranny than your enslaved brethren in the
old world ? or the slaves, in the southern parts of your own country.

21

speak in a voice not to be misunderstood, or misinterpreted. In 8 mills all on one stream, within a distance of two miles, we have 168 persons who can neither read nor write. This is in Rhode Island. A committee of working men in Providence, report 'that in Pautucket there are at least *five hundred children*, who scarcely know what a school is. These facts, say they, are adduced to show the blighting influence of the manufacturing system as at present conducted, on the progress of education; and to add to the darkness of the picture, if blacker shades are necessary to rouse the spirit of indignation, which should glow within our breasts at such disclosures, in all the mills which the enquiries of the committee have been able to reach, books, pamphlets, and newspapers are *absolutely prohibited.* This may serve as a tolerable example for every manufacturing village in Rhode Island.' In 12 of the United States, there are 57,000 persons, male and female, employed in cotton and woollen mills, and other establishments connected with them; about two-fifths of this number, or 31,044 are under 16 years of age, and 6000 are under the age of 12 years. Of this 31,044, there are in Rhode Island *alone,* 3,472 under 16 years of age. The school fund is, in that State, raised in considerable part by lottery. Now we all know, that the poor are generally the persons who support this legalized gambling; for the rich as a general rule, seldom buy tickets. This fund then, said to be raised by the rich, for the education of the poor, is actually drawn from the pockets of the *poor*, to be expended by the rich,* on *their own children,* while this large number of children, (3,472), are entirely, and totally deprived of all benefit of the school fund, by what is *called* the *American System.* Actually *robbed* of what is *emphatically* their own, by being *compelled* to labour in these '*principalities of the destitute*' and these '*palaces of the poor,*' for 13 hours per diem, the year round. *What must be* the result of this state of things? 'We cannot regard even in anticipation, the contamination of moral and political degradation spreading its baleful influence throughout the community, through the medium of the uneducated part of the present generation, promulgated and enhanced in the future, by the increase of posterity, without starting with horror from the scene, as from the clankings of a TYRANT's chain. † Perhaps,

* By the *rich*, we here mean those, who are able to educate their own children, without resorting to the school fund. Among them will be found owners, agents, and overseers, who, many of them, take good care that their own children are educated, while the really poor children must remain ignorant, from the nature of the case.

† Memorial to Congress, from the Providence and Pautucket Association of Working Men.

4

some may (as they have done) ask why do so many go to these mills, if they are such evil places. We answer, that the public are entirely deceived, as to the facts of the case. We have endeavoured to expose that deception; and further, we are authorized to say to *any man*, be he who he may, who represents the population employed in cotton mills, to be a happy and contented people, and who wish no amelioration in their condition, that the statements to that effect are FALSE. We appeal to the tens of thousands, under the *tyrannical government* of the mills, to support us in that assertion. Not only so, those who misrepresent the population thus employed, *know their own statements to be false.* It cannot be otherwise.* We have said the public are deceived; we have shown in part how they are deceived; we will give more evidence to that point. If *one girl* in a mill, earns, by extra exertion, $4 per week, it is blazed abroad, from Maine to Mexico, that the *girls* in that mill earn from one to four dollars per week; if an overseer gets 43 dollars per month, and the men under him from 10 to 20 clear of board, it is proclaimed that the men get from 10 to 43 dollars per month, ' according to their strength.' This is the same as saying, that all the officers of the United States, get from $300 to $25,000 per annum, according to their strength; and there is as much sense in one as the other, and one proves as much as the other.† These factory owners are very fond of using the rule of AVERAGE, and they prove everything by that rule. One of them who said, 'the poor must work or starve,' used this rule to prove that the profit on manufacturing, was but 4 per cent. He said one factory commenced operation in 1806, and by 'judicious management,' cleared $300,000; another commencing at the same time, sunk $150,000 by 'careless and injudicious management.' Now, strike an average on this loss on one hand, and gain on the other, and the profit on Cotton mills is four per cent ;‡ only give us this rule of average, and let us use it in this way, and we will prove that Washington and Arnold were both traitors, or patriots, which you please; because we will *average* the TREASON of one, with the PURE PATRIOTISM of the other, and the sum is done. By

* See Appendix F.
† A letter from Waltham to the author, says, that of all the hands there, only one gets 43 dollars per month, and that is the overseer of the machine shop ; and many do not get 10 dollars per month. But a writer in the Concord paper says, they get from 10 to 43 dollars per month, *according to their strength.* We should think the Agent must be a powerful strong man, for we believe he gets 12 or 1500 dollars per year.
‡ See answer to Interrogatories by Hon. John Whipple.

such means are the public deceived. Again, people are induced to go into mills to work, by a direct and false appeal to the passion of avarice; but why do they not leave, when they find they are deceived? We will give some of the reasons. In many mills, the overseers are ordered by the agents, to tell the help, that if they leave that establishment, the agents will write to all the other Factories, and tell their agents not to employ them. At Dover this has been done, and we know of other places where the same thing is practised. Other means are practised. If a girl is discharged from the service of the Company for any fault, and the agent is the judge in all cases, she cannot get her pay short of two weeks; so that if she has two or three dollars due, and belongs 100 or more miles from home, she must wait on that MAMMOTH COMPANY a fortnight for her pay; by this time, she is in debt for her board, and she must either go to the agent, and *humbly* ask him to give her employment, or starve. He, knowing that 'the poor must work or starve, and that the rich will take care of themselves,' *humanely* takes her into the cotton mill 'palace' on his own terms. We do not say that this is the exact mode of procedure; but we do say, that it is a natural consequence of that one-sided and arbitrary rule. The hands are compelled to work for 'such wages as the Company sees fit to pay,'* to pay all fines assessed, without knowing what the prices or fines may be. Hands are liable to be discharged at any moment, but they cannot discharge themselves, short of a fortnight's notice. Cotton mills are called 'Republican Institutions.' At Dover, we understand, when any of the workmen go into the '*presence*' in the counting-room, they are told to pull off their hats: one man who entered the '*presence chamber*' did not do this, and gave as his reason, that no person was in when he entered; therefore, he did not conceive it necessary. He was told, 'I will let you know, you must take off your hat to respect the 'Office!'†

We must here give one more proof of the *Republican* nature of these institutions. Mr F.‡ a machinist of Dover, was a candidate for the Legislature of New Hampshire, set up by the Working Men. On the day of election, he was asked by S., foreman of the Company's Machine shop, if he meant to stand as a candidate. F. replied, you have had conversation enough with me to know my opin-

* See Appendix G.

† It is customary in London, to bow to a nobleman's carriage as it passes, whether empty or not.

‡ The names of Parties are in possession of the Author of this address, and can be known at any time.

ion on that subject. S. said I am authorized to say to you, that if you do stand or are elected, you will be *discharged*, and that *to-morrow morning*. F. said, if you say positively I shall be discharged, I shall not take myself out of the way on any consideration whatever. S. faltered a little, and said, I will not say positively, but probably. F. said to S., if you think I will be deprived of my rights by such threats, you dont know me. Am I to be deprived of my rights? my citizenship by a *Manufacturing Company*? On this they separated. F. was not discharged the next day, because the supposition is, the Company had no excuse which would satisfy the public. Mr F. was elected, and attended the session of the legislature. On his return he called on the Agent, who told him he had no more work for him, and said F. had broken his contract. He asked, what is the contract? You agreed to work for a year. You are mistaken, I am under no such contract. The agent said, I directed Mr S., an officer under me, to make such a contract with all who would do so. Now said F. I can tell you to what time you allude. At that time there was a considerable complaint of low wages. Mr S. came into the shop, and said, to all those who were satisfied with the wages, that would or should be the standard for the year. I said for one I shall be satisfied. Now suppose I had gone to see my friends three or four weeks, would you have discharged me? No, said the Agent. If I had been unwell, or about street, or any where *else*, except at the Legislature, would you have discharged me? No, said the Agent. I am informed that this Mr F. bears a character without reproach, and was before on friendly terms with S. During the conversation on election day, F. said to S., It has always been said, that Manufacturing Corporations are aristocratical, and although they deny it in all cases, this proves the allegation to a demonstration.* But how does this affect the persons who are not employed in the mills? what have we to do with this tyranny in the mills? We answer, that the owners of mills oppose all reduction in the hours of labour, for the purposes of mental culture. Not that they care about hours of labour in *Cities*, but they fear the ' contagion' will reach their SLAVE MILLS.† Hence they go into the shop of the Carpenter, and others who carry on business, and actually *forbid* them to employ what they sneeringly call ' *ten hour* men.'

---

* Mr W. G. of Lowell, we understand, was discharged from employ, for attending a Convention of Working men, in Providence, Rhode Island, December 5, 1831. In retaliation for this violation of all right principle, the Working men of Lowell turned Mr K. B. (Agent at Lowell) out of the Legislature of Massachusetts, and put Mr W. G. in his place.

† See Appendix H.

Telling the employers, you shall not have our work unless you do
as WE say. We have appealed to their sense of justice, their
sense of humanity, their love of country, to consider the evils they
are bringing on the poor, through ignorance. What has been the
reply? one says ' if a man offers to work for me ten hours, I will
kick him off my premises ;' another says, I will shut down my
gates, and you will starve in a week, and rather than do *that*, you
will work on our terms. Another says, ' O, they can't stand it
more than a day or two, and they will soon come back and BEG
to go to work.' While the official* organ of Rhode Island Manufacturers gravely asserts, that these same people are saving 25
per cent of their wages, clear gain, and a Rhode Island Representative is telling us how much better we are situated than *southern* slaves.† Now when these same men want the votes of the
Working men, they will say, ' in strains as sweet as angels use,'
Fellow Citizens, we want you assistance, give us ' your voices,
your voices, your *sweet* voices.' But if you want time to improve
your minds, take care of your families, and educate your children,
you are called ' *Disturbers of the peace*,' ' Agitators,' ' An unholy
alliance,' Disorganizers, a ' Dangerous Combination' against the
higher ORDERS. Such, Fellow Citizens of New England, is the
language used to you and respecting you. While these men are
boasting that they ' can take care of themselves ;' while they are dependent on you every moment for the protection of that property,
which they have obtained from your *bones*, and *sinews*, and *hearts-
blood*, they are using it in an attempt to starve you into submission. This is no fiction ; the speaker has heard merchants
say, in a public room, in a public Hotel in Boston, that 'the Shipwrights, Caulkers and Gravers, had given up, and thrown themselves entirely on our mercy.' ' OUR MERCY !' are we ready for
that word ? Does not your hearts throb with one pulsation as
you answer No ! Is not that reply echoed from old Bunker's
Height, where *Freemen* stood and *Freemen* fell *rejecting* the mercy, and *scorning* the *power* of TYRANTS.
  Are not our feelings the same in this case ? If they are not,
we may well ask ourselves, as we falter from our duty to ourselves and country,

> ' Where shall we bury our shame?
>   Where, in what desolate place,
>   Hide the last wreck of a name,
>   Thus broken and stained by disgrace?

* Benjamin Cozzens.　　　† See Appendix I.

' Was it for *this* we sent out
Liberty's cry from our shore?
Was it for *this*, that her shout
Thrilled through the world's *very core?*'

But, No! we ask for mercy from no being, but the merciful
God; and we hold in *utter scorn, any* man that would offer or
receive *mercy* in such a case; and we announce, with unfeigned
pleasure, that the Boston shipwrights, caulkers and gravers, never
have asked or received, nor never *will* ask or receive *mercy* from
aristocrats, be they merchants, manufacturers, or any other *Republican* TYRANTS.

As we have adverted to Bunker Hill, we remark, in passing,
that the unfinished monument is a most excellent emblem of our
unfinished independence. There let it *stand* unfinished, until the
time passes away when aristocrats talk about *mercy* to mechanics
and laborers. There let it *stand* unfinished until our rights are
acknowledged, and we, as workingmen, will carry it to its destined
height without screwing a *five-dollar-bill* out of the hard earnings
of the poor man, or appealing to our fair countrywomen to replace money, which we believe has been expended — *extrava-
gantly;* leaving, after all, that structure a monument of disgrace
to this age and this nation, and a *deeper, blacker* disgrace to *some*
of its managers, who, while they are calling on us for money to
raise a monument to *national glory*, are using their influence to
prevent us from improving our condition in any way whatever.
One of these PATRIOTS signed the UKASE, issued in Boston last
May, not by the emperor of Russia, but by men *pretending* to be
American citizens.

We wish to remark on the words — combinations and excitements. Combinations are good, or evil, according to their objects.
The combination to murder Captain White, in Salem, was an evil
and a wicked combination; but the combination to detect and
punish the murderers was useful, necessary, and just. So, it
seems, the *word* is not so *terrible*, in *itself* considered. Men of
property find no fault with combinations to extinguish *fires* and
protect their *precious persons* from danger. But if *poor men* ask
JUSTICE, it is a most HORRIBLE COMBINATION. The Declaration
of Independence was the work of a combination, and was as hateful to the TRAITORS and TORIES of those days, as combinations
among working men are now to the *avaricious* MONOPOLIST and
purse-proud ARISTOCRAT.

Think you, Mr Chairman and gentlemen, there was no com-

bination, when some of the inhabitants of Providence *commenced**
the revolution, in 1772, by burning the British tender Gaspee, in
Providence River? Was there no combination, when the leather
apron of the farmer and mechanic were seen mingling with the
shining uniform of the 'British Regulars,' and when that class, who
are *now* so much *despised* by the HIGHER ORDERS, achieved our
'independence?' Was there no combination, when Bostonians, in
the disguise of Mohawk Indians, made a dish of TEA at the expense
of *King George* the *Third*, using Boston harbour for a tea-pot?
When the IMMORTAL and ILLUSTRIOUS WASHINGTON took York
Town by storm, *there* was a combination of *red-hot cannon balls*
and *bombshells*, (from a combination of American and French
forces,) for three days and three nights in succession, pouring in
on a haughty foe, to the tune of Yankee-doodle. No doubt Lord
Cornwallis was a great enemy to COMBINATIONS.

When monopolists, and others, belonging to the HIGHER OR-
DERS, wish to carry any of *their* measures into effect, they *can*
and *do* form ' *combinations ;*' they *can* and *do* talk of supporting
their views at the point of the *bayonet*, and of exterminating such
citizens of this FREE COUNTRY as oppose *their* views. This has
been threatened by H. Niles, in his Register, during the last session of Congress. Manufacturers assembled at Concord, Massachusetts, in June last, and passed a solemn resolve, that they had
rather have *this Union dissolved*, than to have the ' protecting
policy given up.' Who ever heard of farmers, mechanics, and
labourers, forming such a 'combination' as this? Who ever heard
of working men assembling on the soil once *wet* with *blood* to
cement this Union, and passing *such* a resolve as this? But RICH
men can do this, and then denominate that *accursed* resolve, the
'Voice of Middlesex.' For our part, we had rather see our
country transformed into one *wide, desolate,* and *smouldering
ruin,* than to *even think* of dissolving this Union.

So much for combinations. Now for ' *excitements.*' Tyrants,
in all countries, are always alarmed at ' *excitements.*' The ' *excitement*' which existed in Poland, troubled ' We, Nicholas,' emperor of all the Russias, extremely; and when the flame of
LIBERTY was, for a time, smothered by an overwhelming force,
the minions of the Autocrat proclaimed, that ' ORDER is restored
at Warsaw.' Any excitement among working-men troubles We,
the Aristocracy, very much in the same way. And when they
partially succeed in bearing down the exertions of the poor, by
the overwhelming weight of WEALTH, they proclaim that *order* is
restored in Boston, Providence, Lowell, and elsewhere. Martin

* The first blood shed in the revolutionary war, was on board the
Gaspee in Providence River.

Luther was cautioned by the Pope of Rome, not to make an 'excitement;' but Luther had found that the pope, (in his opinion at least,) was not the ' Vicegerent of God on earth,' and he did not feel disposed to kiss the GREAT TOE of ' HIS HOLINESS' in token of reverence, although it was done *every day* by emperors and kings, cardinals and bishops, and perchance by monks, friars, and pilgrims, if they could *get money* to PAY for the *glorious privilege.*

The situation of the producing classes in New England is at present very unfavorable to the acquisition of mental improvement. That ' the manufacturing establishments are extinguishing the flame of knowledge,' we think has been abundantly proved. It is true there is a great cry about the schools and lyceums, and books of ' *sentiment,* and *taste,* and *science,*' *especially* at WALTHAM.* But of what use is it to be like Tantalus, up to the chin in water, if we cannot drink. The Waltham people seem to be much in the situation of the horse whose master was asked if he ever fed him. ' Feed him ?' replied he, ' now that's a good un, why he's got a bushel and a half of oats at home, *only he aint got no time to eat 'em.*' One evil attached to some mills we have not as yet noted. It is this. At Waltham it is or has been the case that all who go to work there are obliged to pay for the support of the minister employed by the Corporation, and then we hear the Corporation boasting of supporting Religious Worship. This is or has been the case at Leicester, Massachusetts, and at Saxonville, in Framingham. So that liberty of conscience is infringed in direct violation of the law of the land. At York Company Mills, in Saco, Maine, all who are employed are compelled to go to meeting, so that a Catholic must violate his conscience by attending on a Protestant meeting, or the reverse, and so with all other denominations who do not happen to have a meeting of their own kind at Saco. This is palpable injustice. It seems the owners of Mills wish to control their men in all things. To enslave their bodies and souls, make them think, act, vote, preach, pray, and worship, as it may suit ' We the Owners.' That the influence of Manufacturing (as now conducted) is detrimental to the public is beyond dispute. The whole system of labor in New England, *more especially in cotton mills*, is a cruel system of exaction on the bodies and minds of the producing classes, destroying the energies of both, and for no other object than to enable the ' rich' to 'take care of themselves,' while ' the poor must work or starve.' The rich *do* take care of themselves, in one sense, both in this country and Europe. While the daughters of these Nabobs are ' taking care of themselves,'

* See Appendix J.

while they are gracefully sitting at their harp or piano in their splendid dwellings, while music floats from quivering strings through perfumed and adorned apartments, and dies with gentle cadence on the delicate ear of the rich, the nerves of the poor woman and child, in the cotton mill, are quivering with almost dying agony, from excessive labor, to support this splendor ; and after all this, if that woman or child should lose five minutes time out of 13 hours, she is docked a quarter of a day. In one mill we learn that a little girl was cut off in time, one and a quarter days for 25 minutes, that is, one quarter for five minutes for five days in succession. We believe this is a part of what is called 'judicious management.' If these things are so, and we challenge contradiction, are we not justified in making an ' excitement,' and in forming a ' combination,' to check these growing evils ? Unless these evils can be remedied, are we not justified in ' denouncing these sources of present wealth, however overflowing and abundant, while the enriching stream is undermining and contaminating the best interests of man.' ' If education and intelligence is the *only sure* FOUNDATION of public safety,' and if we are convinced that there are causes in active operation sapping and mining that foundation, can any man say, ' It is nothing to me ?' ' If the children of the poor ought to be instructed as well as the rich,' ought we not to see that it is done ? If it depends on education whether we ' live in a peaceable, orderly community, free from excess, outrage and crime, can we say it is nothing to us ?' Who knows but in the course of events his son or daughter, or sister or brother, will not be driven into a cotton mill by the hard hand of adverse fortune, and be made to suffer the evils we have described. If ' without the assistance of the common people a free government cannot exist,' and we find that the capability to govern depends on intelligence and learning ; is it not a fearful reflection that so many thousands of children are deprived of education, and so many adults of every opportunity for mental improvement ? Let us no longer be deceived. Let us not think we are free until working-men no longer trust their affairs in the hands of designing demagogues. But some manufacturers say, it is not so bad as it is in England yet, and when it is, it will be time enough to mend. That man must have a *very benevolent* heart who can say such things. As well might he say the Cholera is not so severe in Boston yet as it has been in New York, so it is of no use to take any measures to prevent its spread. We are told, that we are not yet so poor as they are in England. We do not yet have to exist on oatmeal and potatoes, and therefore we ought not to complain. This is the same as saying, We will cut off one of your arms to support *American* Industry, and you must not complain, for in other countries they

5

cut off *both* arms.   Witness the ' Splendid Example of England.'
The Manufacture of Cotton, to advantage, as it is called, commenced in deception and fraud.   In 1775* Richard Arkwright
the barber, became Hon. Sir Richard Arkwright, for becoming a
thief; for ' he stole the invention of spinning cotton from an unsuspecting friend, a turner by trade,' and after his exaltation to
his ' blushing honours,' he turned his wife out of doors, and would
live with her no longer, for the reason that she, poor, weak
woman, could not understand his factory ' *clockwork.*'   So that
the woman, whom he took for better or worse, and who married
him in his character of Dick Arkwright, the barber, was forsaken
by him in his character of Sir Richard.   At the period mentioned, 57 years ago, Sir Richard commenced spinning ' good round
yarn ;' and from that time the *abject misery* of the poor, in England, has increased with a fearful rapidity.   Forty-two years
since (1790) the first cotton mill was erected in Pawtucket, (R. I.)
It was hailed as a happy era in our history ; so was the same thing
hailed in England.   It has made England *great* and splendid and
rich ; and as degraded and as miserable as *great* and *rich* and
splendid.   One of the authorities we have produced, says, that
the hours of labour has from time to time increased in England,
until ' *no constitution* can withstand its inhuman pressure.'   Such
has been the case during 42 years *we* have had cotton mills ; and
the constitutions of the operatives in this country are sinking, at
this moment, under its ' *inhuman pressure.*'   We have seen *one
thousand* girls pour out, at noon, of *one* establishment alone, and
most of them bore the marks of sickly debility.   Will this be denied ?   If so, be it known, that these females pay out of their wages
ten hundred and *forty* dollars *per annum ;*   and that sum, we are
told, is used for MEDICINE alone.   We are informed, that this
fund frequently falls short.   Now, what must become of these
persons, when they shall become unable to work ?   Will owners
support them ?   No !   ' They have not even the assurance of the
most wretched cornfield negro in Virginia, who, when his stiffened
limbs can no longer bend to the lash,' must be supported by his
owner.   But those who work in cotton-mills, after all their energies are destroyed by the same causes so definitely described by
Dr Kay, of Manchester, must be supported in some way.   Then
the burden will fall on the public where the persons belong ; after
they have amassed immense wealth, not for themselves, but owners, they will be thrown on the public resources, and drag out a
miserable existence in a poor-house.

It has been said, that the speaker is opposed to *the* American

* See History of Stocking Weaving.

System. It turns on one single point, — If these abuses are *the* American System, he is opposed. But let him see *an* American System, where education and intelligence is generally diffused, and the enjoyment of *life* and *liberty* secured to all; he then is ready to support *such* a system. But so long as our government secures exclusive privileges to a *very small part of the community*, and leaves the majority the '*lawful prey*' to avarice — so long does he contend against *any* 'System' so exceedingly unjust and unequal in its operation.* He knows, that we must have manufactures. It is impossible to do without them; but he is yet to learn that it is necessary, or just, that manufactures must be sustained by injustice, cruelty, ignorance, vice, and misery; which is now the fact to a startling degree. If what we have stated be true, and we challenge denial, what must be done? Must we fold our arms and say, It always was so, and always will be. If we did so, would it not almost rouse from their graves the heroes of our revolution? Would not the cold marble, representing our beloved Washington, start into *life*, and reproach us for our *cowardice?* Let the word be — Onward! onward! We know the difficulties are great, and the obstacles many; but, as yet, we 'know our rights, and knowing, dare maintain.' We wish to injure no man, and we are determined not to be injured as we have been; we wish nothing, but those equal rights, which were designed for us all. And although wealth, and prejudice, and slander, and abuse, are all brought to bear on us, we have one consolation — '*We are the Majority.*'

One difficulty is a want of information among our own class, and the HIGHER ORDERS reproach us for our ignorance; but, thank God, we have enough of intelligence among us yet, to show the world that all is not lost.

Another difficulty among us is — the Press has been almost wholly, and is now in a great degree closed upon us.† We venture to assert, that the press is *bribed* by *gold* in many instances; and we believe, that if *law* had done what *gold* has accomplished, our country would, before this time, have been deluged with blood. But working-men's papers are multiplying; and we shall soon, by the diffusion of intelligence, be enabled to form a *front*, which will show all *monopolists*, and all TYRANTS, that we are not only determined to have the name of freemen, but that we will LIVE FREEMEN and DIE FREEMEN.

Fellow-citizens of New England, farmers, mechanics, and labourers, we have borne these evils by far too long; we have been deceived by all parties; we must take our own business into our

* See Appendix K.   † See Appendix L.

own hands. Let us awake. Our cause is the cause of truth — of justice and humanity. *It must prevail.* Let us be determined no longer to be deceived by the cry of those who produce *nothing* and who enjoy *all,* and who *insultingly* term us — the *farmers, the mechanics and labourers,* the LOWER ORDERS — and *exultingly* claim our homage for themselves, as the

Higher ORDERS —

While the DECLARATION OF INDEPENDENCE asserts that

'ALL MEN ARE CREATED EQUAL.'

THE LITTLE FACTORY GIRL TO A MORE FORTUNATE PLAYMATE.

AUTHOR UNKNOWN.

I often think how once we used in summer fields to play,
And run about and breathe the air that made us glad and gay;
We used to gather buttercups and chase the butterfly —
I loved to feel the light breeze lift my hair as it went by!

Do *you* still play in those bright fields? and are the flowers still there?
There are no fields where *I* live *now* — no flowers any where!
But day by day I go and turn a dull and tedious wheel;
You cannot think how sad, and tired, and faint I often feel.

I hurry home to snatch the meal my mother can supply,
Then back I hasten to the task — that not to hate I try.
At night my mother kisses me, when she has combed my hair,
And laid me in my little bed, but — *I'm not happy there.*

I dream about the factory, the fines that on us wait —
I start and ask my father if — I have not lain too late?
And once I heard him sob and say — ' Oh better were a grave,
Than such a life as this for thee, thou little sinless slave!'

I wonder if I ever shall obtain a holiday?
Oh if I do, I'll go to you and spend it all in play!
And then I'll bring some flowers home, if *you* will give me some,
And at my work I'll think of them and holidays to come!

APPENDIX.

Appendix A.

Lyttleton Bulwer stated in the British House of Commons, that out of 128 persons in Berkshire, committed for incendiarism, only 25 could write, and only 37 could read. In Abington, out of 30 prisoners, only 6 could read or write ; of fifty prisoners tried at Lewes, *one only* could read or write. The same connexion existed in France, between crime and ignorance. In 1820, in the French Court of Assize, there were 6,962 persons accused ; out of this number, 4,519 were ignorant of writing and reading, and only 129 persons, about a 57th part, had received a superior education.

Appendix B.

The caption of this Immortal document was affixed to it by a Mechanic in Boston, that the Ukase might be promulgated in due form.

UKASE.

[We, the Merchants of Boston, by the Grace of God, and power of Gold, masters of all the Mechanics in this our City, have issued this our Ukase, to make known to our subjects, our will and pleasure. *Hear* and *Obey.*]

Copy of the Ukase, from the Merchants of Boston, to the Master Carpenters and Caulkers, *most graciously* communicated to Messrs Leach Harris & Son.

Boston, July 20th, 1832.

Gentlemen : — At a meeting of the Merchants held last evening at the Exchange Coffee House, the following Resolution was passed.

It being understood that the journeymen Carpenters and Caulkers,

5

have abandoned their Combination to control the liberty of individuals, in the hours of Labour, and considering the extreme warmth of the weather, and the fear of Pestilence that pervades the community, it is the sense of this meeting that the Master Carpenters and Caulkers be AUTHORISED to allow to their journeymen, two hours intermission at noon during the present month and August. It being *expressly understood* that they SHALL commence the day's work at sunrise, and terminate it at sunset.

WILLIAM GODDARD,
JOHN BROWN,
HENRY WILLIAMS,
J. L. DIMMOCK,   } *Committee.*
THOMAS B. CURTIS,
B. A. GOULD,

To Messrs LEACH HARRIS & SON.

Here is assumption of power without precedent in our country. Here is the ' *Republicanism* ' of the Dark Ages. The *fact is*, the journeymen Carpenters and Caulkers had taken the ' two hours ' at noon, (and they begun at five in the morning, and quit at seven at night, and on Saturday at six) five or six weeks before this *notable* document was concocted from the *brains* of these NOBLEMEN.

APPENDIX C.

It certainly seems that some of our Statesmen are in the situation of Jeptha, without his distress. He in a moment of exultation, had made a vow to sacrifice the first living thing which should meet him at his door, on his return from victory, and when his lovely daughter met his view, he lifted his robe* to hide her from his sight, still determined on the sacrifice. So with Statesmen, exulting at what they think will produce NATIONAL GLORY, they vow to sacrifice every thing to that end. But when they see *tens* of *thousands* of children ready for their inevitable doom, they lift the robe of office and popularity, to hide from their eyes the dreadful sight, still determined on the sacrifice.

We are justified in this supposition, for we never heard the most *ardent* and *strenuous* advocate of the ' *American System*,' in Congress or out, say *one word* in favour of *protecting* the operatives in our ' *Clockwork* ' *Cotton Mill* ' *Palaces of the poor*.' On the contrary, they say Congress has no right to do so.

* See Augurs' beautiful Marble group, representing this Event.

APPENDIX D.

It is a singular fact, that while Manufacturers on one hand, are telling their help they must support *the* System, or they will all be paupers as people are in *England* ; on the other, they are calling on this nation ' to witness ' and follow the ' *Splendid Example of England.*'

APPENDIX E.

If the gentleman who penned this sentence had told us, in the same style, what these Mills were to the middling and *higher orders*, he would probably have said, ' they are the Lighthouses of the skies ' to the middling classes, and the ' heaven of heavens ' to the rich. We like to see parallels carried out to their legitimate conclusion.

APPENDIX F.

We refer particularly to those who live in the vicinity of manufacturing establishments ; persons at a distance no doubt are deceived, and led to say things, about which they know nothing. The speaker has for years lived among Cotton mills, worked in them, travelled among them, and is extensively acquainted with them, and with persons who are engaged in them, and they will *all* with one united voice, support the assertions here made. The speaker has examined this subject for years, and he pledges himself to prove all the allegations here made, and as much more as they wish of the same kind, if the owners of Cotton-mills will place it in his power to compel the attendance of witnesses.

Not only so, we assert that the great body of the inhabitants of New England, look upon employment in a cotton mill with horror and detestation, and would think it as great a misfortune as could possibly befall them, to be driven by any circumstances, to labour in these ' palaces of the poor,' as now conducted. So detestable is work in a mill to children, that in one case, both parents have been seen, before sunrise, each with a stick, driving their child from the house to the mill. If such a statement will rouse the indignation of the friends of children, what will be thought of the following:

A boy twelve years old, the son of Joseph Buxton, of Mendon, had been worked for some time in a cotton mill in that town. The confinement was irksome to the boy, who was inclined to work upon a farm, and he was heard to say, that he had rather die than work in a cotton mill. No heed was paid to the child's suffering or complaint, and late in August last, he drowned himself in the pond adjoining the factory. — Thank God ! the blood of that poor little innocent is not upon my head.

It may not be out of place here to remark, that in this same town of Mendon, a factory agent shut down the gates, and marched ninety workmen up to the polls, who established a road, and sent a representative to General Court, in defiance of the inhabitants. The owners, all of them, lived in another state. Here is a sample of independent voters ? Think you, our fathers would have submitted to such a gross violation of their rights ? No, they would sooner have driven these political hirelings from the polls at the point of their bayonets.

Appendix G.

*Conditions on which Help is hired by the Cocheco Manufacturing Company, Dover, N. H.

We, the subscribers, do hereby agree to enter the service of the *Cocheco Manufacturing Company*, and conform, in all respects, to the Regulations which are now, or may hereafter be adopted, for the good government of the Institution.

☞ We further agree, *to work for such wages per week, and prices by the Job, as the Company may see fit to pay,* AND BE SUBJECT TO THE FINES, as well as entitled to the premiums paid by the Company.

We further agree to allow two cents each week, to be deducted from our wages, for the benefit of the SICK FUND.

We also agree not to leave the service of the Company, without giving two weeks notice of our intention, without permission of an agent ; and if we do, we agree to forfeit to the use of the Company, two weeks' pay.

We also agree not to be engaged in any combination, whereby the work may be impeded, or the Company's interest in any work injured; if we do, we agree to forfeit to the use of the Company, the amount of wages that may be due to us at the time.

We also agree that in case we are discharged from the service of the Company for any fault, we will not consider ourselves entitled to be settled with, in less than two weeks from the time of such discharge.

Payments for labour performed are to be made monthly.

---

* These Conditions are much like the handle of a jug, all on one side. They are certainly not binding in law; for there is no obligation in them, on the part of the Company; and any agreement is null and void for that reason. It is, by law, impossible to make a person agree to something, of which he is ignorant. See first and second rules. If we are compelled or induced, by any means, to swear an oath to keep a secret before we know what the secret is, the oath is not binding on us, legally or morally.

APPENDIX H.

This is, we learn, one reason given by some of the Merchants in Boston, who are also largely concerned in manufacturing, why they opposed the reduction of the hours of labour in Boston. ' It wont do, said they, if hours are reduced here, our " *help* " in the mills will hear of it, and it will make them uneasy.' Manufacturers in Providence pursued a similar course.

For the information of ' *our help* ' the speaker observes, that the reduction of the hours of labour has taken place in Boston, among Shipwrights, Caulkers and Gravers, some Founders, as Algers and Ashcrofts, also in Utica and Buffalo, New York, Detroit, Michigan, and partially in New Bedford. The cause is daily gaining ground among the friends of ' *Humanity.*' We trust the day is not far distant, when the 20th March 1832, will become as important in the History of our Country, as the 4th of July, 1776. For it will be the anniversary of the downfall of tyranny and oppression at home, and that day is the anniversary of the downfall of Foreign Tyranny and Oppression.

APPENDIX I.

The speaker cannot but feel as every man ought to feel, indignant at such language as this. Has it come to this, that we must be told we ought to be content, because we are not yet actually in chains of iron. We happen to know something about southern slavery, having resided in a slave country at various periods, and we know that children born in slavery do not work one *half* the hours, nor perform one *quarter* of the labour that the white children do in Cotton mills, in free New England. It is nearly so with adult slaves. If the children in Mills in New England are almost entirely deprived of education, will the gentleman show us the great advantage *they* possess over *slave* children ? Further, we do know that the slaves in the South enjoy privileges, which are not enjoyed in some of our Cotton mills. At Dover, N. H. we understand, no operative is allowed to keep a pig or a cow, because it would take a few minutes time to feed the pig and milk the cow. We learn also it is now, or has been the case, that that ' Republican Institution ' even monopolized the *milk business*, kept cows themselves, and compelled their ' help ' to buy milk of them. This we suppose was to give a *market* to the *Farmer*, of which we hear so much.

APPENDIX J.

A writer, calling himself 'A Factory Hand,' in the Yeoman's Gazette, Concord, September 1, 1832, tells a fine story about the advantages at Waltham, ' the flowers of taste and sentiment' and feeling, and the ' hardy plants of the understanding,' and ' all that sort of thing ;' but, after all, he says, ' *with particular reference to our situation in the Cotton Mills*, (mark that,) it would not do to reduce the hours of labour; for more harm would be done by the *vicious*, than good by the virtuous, if THUS *let loose* on the community.' Surely *this* indicates an *extremely great* degree of cultivation of ' the flowers of *taste* and *sentiment*' and ' *refinement*' and ' *understanding* with particular reference to our situation in the cotton-mills' at Waltham. It wont do to ' LET US LOOSE on the community.' This is *highly* complimentary to the *lower orders* employed at Waltham. This is ' taste' and ' sentiment' and ' refinement' and ' understanding,' with a *vengeance*. Why, this is the *very reason* that people are shut up in the STATE PRISON. It will not answer to ' *let them loose* on the community.' If the work-people in Waltham can bear this, we are mistaken in them. If they will be *insulted* in this way, and not resent it, they are certainly to be pitied.

Another, or the same writer, signing ' An Operative,' with reference to the author of this address, says, ' Our reformer may congratulate himself in not receiving a flagellation, or a ducking, while at Waltham.' Now, we suppose this is a specimen of the ' *flowers of feeling, taste, and sentiment,*' and ' *moral principle and religious sentiment*' ' *cultivated with fatherly care at Waltham.*'

Perhaps the author owes his safety to the fact, that the Company did not ' let loose' the vicious characters in Waltham ; for the large Hall where he lectured was filled to overflowing with an attentive and civil audience, for which he returns to them his thanks. We have never said or written a word against the morality of the Waltham people; but these *astonishing writers*, these defenders of ' the higher classes,' make them a savage and vicious people; so much so, that, according to them, it will not do to ' let them loose on the community.' We learn for the first time, from these writers, that Waltham owners are the jail-keepers of the vicious and outrageous part of the community, and merely run their mills to keep them in prison for the public safety. *How very benevolent!*

If cotton-mill owners cannot EMPLOY better defenders than these sapient writers are, they had better have none. But this is as much as they can expect for 70 cents per day for 13 hours work in the mill, the scribbling thrown in gratis.

Appendix K.

We insist upon it, that the power of the Constitution ' to provide for the common defence,' shall be exerted to provide safeguards against the dreadful evils which manufacturers are bringing upon us. For we insist, that if Congress have power to protect the owners against foreign competition in the shape of goods, they have the same right to protect the operative from foreign competition in the shape of importation of foreign mechanics and labourers, to cut down wages of our own citizens. We call upon manufacturers to do justice to the operative, and warn them to remember that working-men, the farmer, mechanic, and labourer, are the majority, and are determined to be gulled no longer by the specious and deceptive cry of American Industry, while they are ground down into the dust by importation of foreign machinery, foreign workmen, and foreign wool; and deprived of improvement for themselves and an opportunity to educate their children, merely to enable ' the rich to take care of themselves;' while the poor must work for such prices as manufacturers ' see fit to give,' or starve, as a reward for votes given for their oppressors.

Appendix L.

Editors of papers, in the interest of manufacturers, can publish accounts of the sufferings of children and others in *England,* in cotton and woollen mills, and apparently shed tears enough to *operate* a *small* cotton-mill ' palace of the poor ;' but, if we ask them to publish well authenticated accounts of sufferings in *American* mills, they refuse; and so far as *tears* are concerned, their eyes are as dry as the crater of a volcano.

APPEAL

TO

THE WEALTHY OF THE LAND,

LADIES AS WELL AS GENTLEMEN,

ON THE

CHARACTER, CONDUCT, SITUATION, AND PROSPECTS

OF

THOSE WHOSE SOLE DEPENDENCE FOR SUBSISTENCE IS ON THE LABOUR OF THEIR HANDS.

———

BY M. CAREY,

AUTHOR OF ' VINDICIÆ HIBERNICÆ,' ' THE OLIVE BRANCH,' ' ESSAYS ON POLITICAL ECONOMY,' ETC. ETC.

———

" See them look o'er
" The labour past, and toils to come explore—
" See them alternate suns and show'rs engage,
" And hoard up aches and anguish for their age."

On turnpikes and canals " Their steps pursue,
'· When their warm pores imbibe the evening dew :
" Then own, that labour may as fatal be,
" To these, thy slaves, as thine excess to thee." CRABBE.

* * * " Dejected widows with unheeded tears,
" And crippled age, with more than childish fears." IDEM.

" What mean ye * * that ye *grind the faces of the poor*, saith the Lord God of Hosts ?"
ISAIAH iii. 15.

" We ought never to forget, that in alleviating the immediate sufferings of the poor [women], we
" are only *palliating*, not *eradicating* the evils of poverty. We must never forget that the LOW
" RATE OF WAGES IS THE ROOT OF THE MISCHIEF, and that unless we can succeed in
" raising the price of [their] labour, *our utmost efforts will do little towards effectually bettering their*
" *condition.* The distribution of alms, &c., may be useful in their way ; but *they do not reach the*
" *source of the evil.*"—BARTON.

" The interests of the poorer classes of society are so interwoven with those of every part of the
" community, that there is no subject more deserving of general attention, nor any knowledge more
" entitled to the exalted name of science, than that, in which their well-being is concerned ; than
" that, the tendency of which is *to carry domestic comfort into the recesses of every habitation, and*
" *to add to the virtue and morality of a nation, by increasing its happiness.* The noblest and most
" elevated employments of the human mind lose their importance, when placed in competition with
" researches ON WHICH THE WELFARE AND GOOD CONDUCT OF MILLIONS MAY DEPEND, AND THE
" RESULT WHEREOF MAY ADD AS MUCH TO NATIONAL PROSPERITY AS TO INDIVIDUAL HAPPINESS."
SIR THOMAS BERNARD.

———

SECOND EDITION, IMPROVED.

———

PHILADELPHIA:

STEREOTYPED BY L. JOHNSON, No. 6 GEORGE STREET.

July, 1833.
[*For gratuitous distribution.*]

TO THE

IMPARTIAL HUMANE SOCIETY

OF

BALTIMORE,

AND

THE FEMALE HOSPITABLE SOCIETY

OF

PHILADELPHIA,

(WHOSE NOBLE EXAMPLES OUGHT TO BE FOLLOWED IN EVERY CITY AND TOWN IN THE U. STATES)

THIS PAMPHLET IS RESPECTFULLY DEDICATED,

AS

A SMALL MARK OF APPROBATION, OF THEIR

LIBERALITY, HUMANITY, AND FOSTERING CARE,

DIRECTED TOWARDS THE RELIEF OF

A LARGE, OPPRESSED, AND SUFFERING

CLASS OF FEMALES,

WHOSE CASE OFTEN PRESENTS SCENES OF DISTRESS, TO WHICH NOTHING

BUT OCULAR DEMONSTRATION COULD SECURE CREDIT,

IN A

COUNTRY FAR MORE PROSPEROUS

THAN ANY OTHER PORTION OF THE HABITABLE GLOBE.

BY THE AUTHOR.

Philadelphia, June 24, 1833.

PREFACE.

THE subject of the following essays is deeply interesting to a large portion of the human race, much of whose happiness, morals, and manners depends on its being correctly understood, and rightly acted on. It therefore demands the most serious reflection of the wise, and the good, and the liberal.

Some of the most material of the opinions herein contained, are in direct hostility with those generally prevalent on the same subject, and even by some highly enlightened citizens. But few can be ignorant that the most enlightened and profound men, may be radically and fatuitously in error on particular points. Bacon believed in astrology; Johnson in the Cocklane ghost—and the great Judge Hale in witchcraft. He sentenced a miserable wretch to death, for that imaginary crime. Need I add a word to prove the folly of placing implicit credit, without due examination, on opinions sanctioned by great names, or regarded as venerable from their antiquity.

All I ask for such opinions as at the first view may appear heterodoxical, is a fair, and candid, and repeated examination. Let them not be cast aside with scorn, as mankind are too apt to do, because they coincide not with preconceived views. If they cannot pass this ordeal, let them perish. If otherwise, I hope they will meet with that attention, and produce those practical results, which the importance of the subject demands.

Should it appear, as it probably will, to some of my readers, that I have expressed myself with too much warmth, in discussing the sufferings of the seamstresses, &c. let it be borne in mind, that I have been pleading the cause of probably 12,000 women in Boston, New York, Philadelphia, and Baltimore, (with souls as precious in the eye of heaven as the most exalted females that ever trod the earth—as a Maria Theresa, a Princess Victoria, a Mrs. Washington, a Mrs. Madison, or a Mrs. Monroe,) who are grievously oppressed and reduced to the utmost penury, in a land literally flowing with milk and honey, while many of those for whom they toil, make immense fortunes, by their labours.

We are assured, as I have stated,* by ladies fully competent to judge on the subject, that nine cotton shirts a week are as much as the great mass of seamstresses can make. Those shirts are frequently made for 6, 8, and 10 cents, leaving 54 a 72 a 90 cents a week for the incessant application of a human being, during thirteen or fourteen hours a day, for the payment of rent, the purchase of food, clothes, drink, soap, candles and fuel!!!!!!!!!!!!!!!!!!

Deplorable as is the condition of the poor in the crowded cities of Europe, there are few females there who earn much less than this—and therefore, it must follow, that there is frequently as intense a degree of distress suffered here, as in London or Paris. The principal difference is not in the *intensity*, but in the *extent* of the distress. Compared with London or Paris, there are few who suffer in this way here. But it is no alleviation of the misery of an unfortunate female in Philadelphia or Boston, who makes shirts for six or eight cents, or even ten, that is to say, who earns from nine to fifteen cents per day, that there are fewer similarly circumstanced here than in those cities.

It is often triumphantly asked, respecting the case of the women who are so very inadequately remunerated for their labours, What remedy can be applied to such an inveterate evil? Does not the proportion between supply and demand, in this, as in all other cases, regulate prices? And while there

---

* Page 13.

3

is such an over-proportion of labour in the market, must not competition reduce prices, as it has done, to the lowest grade, even below the minimum necessary to support existence?

I am well aware of the superabundance of female labour—of the direful effects of over-driven competition, not only on the comfort and happiness, but on the morals of the labouring classes of society, in every quarter of the globe. But I contend for it, that every principle of honour, justice, and generosity, forbids the employer to take advantage of the distress and wretchedness of those he employs, and cut down their wages below the minimum necessary to procure a sufficiency of plain food and of clothes to guard against the inclemency of the weather. Whoever passes this line of demarcation, is guilty of the heinous offence of "*grinding the faces of the poor.*" The labour of every human being ought to insure this remuneration at least. And I am persuaded that there are thousands of honourable men who give inadequate wages. to males as well as females, merely because they have never thought sufficiently on the subject; and who, therefore, have no idea of the real state of the case. They would scorn to give the wages they do at present, were they aware of the distress and misery thus entailed on those by whose labours, I emphatically repeat, they not only enjoy all the comforts and luxuries of life, but many of them make immense fortunes. My object is to induce upright men thus circumstanced, to scrutinize the affair, and obey the dictates of their better feelings as soon as they have ascertained the truth. Of the honourable issue I cannot entertain a doubt.

Let me most earnestly, but most respectfully, conjure the ladies, into whose hands these lines may come, to ponder deeply, and frequently, and lastingly, on the deplorable condition of so many of their sex, who are ground to the earth by an inadequate remuneration for their painful labours. Let them raise their voices, and exert their influence in their defence, and urge their male friends to enter the lists in the holy cause of suffering humanity. I am not so enthusiastic or deluded as to suppose that a complete remedy can be applied to so enormous and so inveterate an evil—an evil, the remedy of which requires more generosity and disinterestedness than usually fall to the lot of mankind. But by proper efforts, the oppression of the mass of the sufferers may at least be *mitigated*, and no inconsiderable portion of them may be completely relieved.

The ladies will, I hope, pardon me for an observation which applies to some of them, but I hope to only a few. I have known a lady expend a hundred dollars on a party; pay thirty or forty dollars for a bonnet, and fifty for a shawl; and yet make a hard bargain with a seamstress or washerwoman,* who had to work at her needle or at the washing-tub for thirteen or fourteen hours a day, to make a bare livelihood for herself and a numerous family of small children! This is "a sore oppression under the sun," and ought to be eschewed by every honourable mind. "Let it be reformed altogether."

Philadelphia, June 18, 1833.

* *Extract of a letter from the Rev. Mr. Dupuy.*

Philadelphia, April 13*th.*

DEAR SIR,—As you are desirous of ascertaining the average amount of wages paid to some of the poor, I send you an individual whose case is peculiarly hard. I know the woman to be a person who would on no account deviate from the truth. She gets $10 per quarter for washing, and frequently washes eight dozen of clothes per week—she finding soap, starch, fuel, &c. This is about ten cents per dozen. Your obedient servant,

MR. M. CAREY.   CHARLES M. DUPUY.

APPEAL TO THE WEALTHY, &c

ESSAY I.

I PROPOSE in these essays to consider, and attempt to refute, certain pernicious errors which too generally prevail respecting the situation, the conduct, the characters, and the prospects of those whose sole dependence is on the labour of their hands—who comprise, throughout the world, two-thirds, perhaps three-fourths, of the human race—and on whose services the other third or fourth depend for their necessaries, their comforts, their enjoyments, and their luxuries.

According to these calculations, the number of persons in the United States depending on wages for their support must be eight or nine millions. This is a deeply interesting view of the subject, and fully proves its immense importance; and how solicitous we should be to guard against errors in discussing it—errors which may perniciously affect the interests and happiness of so large a portion of the human family. Whatever concerns their comfort or happiness—whatever tends to increase or decrease their comforts—to improve or deteriorate their morals, demands the most serious attention of the friends of humanity, of all whose views extend beyond their own narrow selfish concerns, and who, without the services of this class, would be forlorn and helpless.

The class in question is susceptible of two great subdivisions—those who are so well remunerated for their labours, as to be able, not merely to provide, when employed, for seasons of stagnation and sickness, but by industry, prudence, and economy, to save enough in the course of a few years, to commence business on a small scale on their own account. With this fortunate description, which is numerous and respectable, I have no concern at present. My object is to consider the case of those whose services are so inadequately remunerated, owing to the excess of labour beyond the demand for it, that they can barely support themselves while in good health and fully employed; and, of course, when sick or unemployed, must perish, unless relieved by charitable individuals, benevolent societies, or the guardians of the poor. I use the word "*perish*" with due deliberation, and a full conviction of its appropriate application to the case, however revolting it may seem to the reader; for as these people depend for daily support on their daily or weekly wages, they are, when those wages are stopped by whatever means, utterly destitute of wherewith to support their existence, and actually become paupers, and therefore, without the aid above stated, would, I repeat, "*perish*" of want.

The crisis of suffering through which this class about three years since passed here and elsewhere, and the occurrence of similar suffering in all hard winters (and, in other seasons, from sickness and destitution of employment), often without receiving that extra aid which such a state of things loudly demands, appears to require a sober and serious investigation, in order to probe to the bottom so deplorable a state of things, whereby the comfort and happiness of such a large portion of human beings are so cruelly shipwrecked, and to ascertain what are the causes of the evil, and whether it be susceptible of any remedy.

The erroneous opinions to which I have alluded are—

1. That every man, woman, and grown child, able and willing to work may find employment.

5

2. That the poor, by industry, prudence, and economy, may at all times support themselves comfortably, without depending on eleemosynary aid—and, as a corollary from these positions,

3. That their sufferings and distresses chiefly, if not wholly, arise from their idleness, their dissipation, and their extravagance.

4. That taxes for the support of the poor, and aid afforded them by charitable individuals, or benevolent societies, are pernicious, as, by encouraging the poor to depend on them, they foster their idleness and improvidence, and thus produce, or at least increase, the poverty and distress they are intended to relieve.

These opinions, so far as they have operated—and, through the mischievous zeal and industry of the school of political economists by which they have been promulgated, they have spread widely—have been pernicious to the rich and the poor. They tend to harden the hearts of the former against the sufferings and distresses of the latter,—and of course prolong those sufferings and distresses.

"Posterity will scarcely credit the extent to which the popular feeling has been *worked upon and warped by the ravings of some of our modern economists.* They, truly, have done all that in them lay, TO EXTINGUISH IN THE BOSOMS OF THE MORE OPULENT CLASSES, EVERY SPARK OF GENEROUS AND BENEVOLENT FEELING TOWARDS THE DESTITUTE AND NEEDY PAUPER. *In their eyes, pauperism is a crime, for which nothing short of absolute starvation can form an adequate punishment.*"—London Quarterly Review, July, 1828.

Many wealthy individuals, benevolent and liberal, apprehensive lest by charitable aid to persons in distress, they might produce evil to society, are, by these pernicious and cold-blooded doctrines, prevented from indulging the feelings of their hearts, and employing a portion of their superfluous wealth for the best purpose to which it can be appropriated—that purpose which, at the hour of death, will afford the most solid comfort on retrospection—that is, " to feed the hungry ; to give drink to the thirsty ; to clothe the naked ; to comfort the comfortless."* The economists in question, when they are implored by the starving poor for " bread," tender them " a stone." To the unfeeling and uncharitable of the rich (and such unhappily there are), these doctrines afford a plausible pretext, of which they are not slow to avail themselves, for withholding their aid from the poor. They have moreover tended to attach a sort of disrepute to those admirable associations of ladies and gentlemen, for the relief of the poor, on which Heaven looks down with complacence, and which form a delightful oasis in the midst of the arid deserts of sordid selfishness which on all sides present themselves to the afflicted view of the contemplative observer.

In entering on this discussion, it is necessary to consider the character and conduct of the classes whose case I have undertaken to review. Both are, I am persuaded, greatly and perniciously mistaken.

There is scarcely any propensity more universal among mankind, than the tendency to generalize from inadequate particulars. From the good or the bad qualities of half a dozen persons or things, most people are disposed to draw general conclusions affecting the whole species or genus to which the half dozen belong. It is not therefore wonderful, although greatly to be regretted, that on beholding a number of worthless poor, so many superficial

---

* How transcendently superior are those who, like Mr. Perkins and Mr. Philips of Boston, Mr. Brown of Rhode Island, Mr. Oliver of Baltimore, Mr. Rutgers of New York, Mr. Ralston, Mr. Henry, and Mrs. Stott of Philadelphia, &c., *bestow* thousands and tens of thousands on public charities or other benevolent objects, to those who retain their millions to the last moment of their existence ! Ten thousand dollars *bestowed* during life have more real merit than a million *bequeathed* at the last gasp, when it can be no longer grasped.

persons feel disposed to set down the mass as worthless. A little reflection will prove the folly and injustice of this procedure. The estimable part of the poor, who struggle with their poverty, who resist the temptations to fraud and transgressions of every kind, are generally in the back-ground—they escape notice. Hundreds of them may be within a few squares of us, and never attract our attention. Let us suppose a case. A man has, in the course of a year, dealings with five hundred of those persons who depend on their labour for support: among this large number, he discovers ten or a dozen tricky and worthless, who are on the watch to cheat and deceive him. Will he not, in his conversation about his affairs (and how many are there who have no other subject of conversation?) dwell more on the frauds and tricks of these, than on the correct conduct of the four hundred and eighty or four hundred and ninety? And will not superficial persons be disposed to generalize and stigmatize the whole from his statements?

Far from being surprised that among the poor there are to be found many worthless persons, it appears, that the surprise, all things considered, ought to be, that there are so few. In the first place, it is well known that we are the creatures of education and example; and how lamentably deficient the mass of the poor are in point of education and example, we all know. No small proportion have had no education; others only a mere smattering: and the examples which they are to copy, are, alas! too generally ill qualified to form them as useful or estimable members of society.

The higher orders of society have generally enjoyed the advantages of a good education and good examples: the censorial eye of the public is on them, and serves as a curb to restrain them from guilt: regard to character has a powerful operation. Nevertheless, do we not unfortunately see considerable numbers of them who lapse from the paths of rectitude? How powerfully do such lapses tend to extenuate those of the poor, who are under no such controlling or restraining circumstances, and have so much stronger incentives to aberration!

The population of Philadelphia is about 160,000 souls, of whom about 100,000 depend on the labour of their hands; 40,000 are probably labourers, hodmen, seamstresses, families of workmen on the canals and rail-roads. The utmost industry and economy they can employ will scarcely suffice to sustain them, if not unremittingly employed; and few of them are so fortunate as to be employed through the year. These last descriptions of persons are those whose case I have undertaken to consider.

Philadelphia, June 20, 1833.

ESSAY II.

The first position on which I propose to animadvert is—

" That every man, woman, and child, able and willing to work, may find employment."

So far is this from being true, that a very cursory reflection would satisfy any candid person, that in the most prosperous times and countries, there are certain occupations, which, by the influence of fashion or other causes, suffer occasional stagnations. There are other occupations, at which employment is at all times precarious—and others, again, which furnish little or no employment at certain seasons of the year.

To the first class belong all those who minister to the fanciful wants of society—wants contracted or expanded by the whim or caprice of fashion. For instance, the Prince of Wales having, some years since, laid aside his

shoe-buckles, and supplied their place with ribands, shoe-buckles became un-
fashionable, and the journeymen buckle-makers were reduced to a state approaching to starvation. Cases of this kind occur occasionally, in this country, though not by any means to the same extent, nor arising exactly from the
same causes. But, whatever may be the cause, the effect is equally oppressive to the sufferer, deprived of his usual sources of support. Three instances
occur to my mind at this moment. The custom of cropping the hair threw
half of our hair-dressers out of employment. The general use of lamps produced a similar effect on the chandlers. And the introduction of marble cutting in the New York prisons operated perniciously on the stone-cutters of
that state, particularly in the metropolis.

In the second class, the most conspicuous are the shoe-binders, the spoolers, and seamstresses employed on coarse work, who, being far more numerous than the demand for their service requires, a portion of them are at all
times but partially employed.

In the third class may be enumerated labourers on canals and turnpike roads,
hod-carriers, wood-sawyers, wood-pilers, &c. &c.

Instances repeatedly occur in our cities of decent men, with the most satisfactory recommendations, seeking employment in vain for months, as porters. There is at all times a superabundance of clerks. An advertisement
for a clerk will, in an hour or two, produce a dozen or two of applications.
I have known persons of this class, burdened with families, obliged to descend to menial and degrading employments for support.

It is frequently said, as a panacea for the distresses of those people—"Let
them go into the country; there they will find employment enough." To
say nothing of the utter unfitness of most of those persons for country labour,
this is taking for granted what remains to be proved. The country rarely
affords employment for extra hands, except for a few weeks in harvest time.
Farmers are generally supplied with steady hands at all other seasons. But
were it otherwise, take the case of a man of a delicate constitution, with a
wife and three or four small children; what a miserable chance would he
stand of support by country labour!

So far as regards seamstresses and spoolers, the employment of the two
classes, through the year, does not average above 40 a 45 weeks. One thousand of the former have been employed by the Provident Society in this city,
during a winter, who could procure only four shirts per week, for which they
received but fifty cents! Some of them, living two miles from the office, had
to travel that distance for this paltry pittance—and above half of them had no
other dependence. In the absence of all other evidence, this would be abundantly sufficient to establish the cruelty and injustice of the accusations brought
against this ill-fated and oppressed class, when they are involved in the general censure passed on the poor for idleness and improvidence.

The second position which I propose to controvert is—

"That the poor, by industry, prudence, and economy, may at all times support themselves
comfortably, without depending on eleemosynary aid: and, as a corollary from this,
"That their sufferings and distresses chiefly, if not wholly, arise from their idleness, their
dissipation, and their extravagance."

A primary element in this discussion is a consideration of the wages ordinarily paid to the class of persons whose case I attempt to develope, and whose
cause I have undertaken to plead—and first, of the very numerous class,
labourers on canals and turnpikes.

By the annexed letter from JOSEPH M'ILVAINE, Esq., formerly secretary of
the board of canal commissioners, it appears that the average wages of this
class, in common times, are from ten to twelve dollars per month and found;

that in winter they may be had for five dollars; and that sometimes, in that season, when labour is scarce, they work for their board alone.

DEAR SIR,   *Philadelphia, Feb. 14th,* 1831.
It is difficult to answer with precision your inquiry as to the *average wages* of canal labourers. They vary with the seasons, and are still more dependent upon the proportion of labourers to the work required to be done. *In the winter season men can be had at $5 a month and found. In some cases I have known them to work a whole winter for merely their food.* On the contrary, at the busier periods of the year, $15 to $20 a month have been given when hands were scarce. I incline to think, however, that $10 to $12 a month and found might be taken as a pretty fair average. Contractors, in making their calculations, set down 70 to 75 cents a day for each man employed, including wages and food. This would give about $12 a month as the average of wages.   Very respectfully, &c.
                                                          JOS. M'ILVAINE.
M. CAREY, Esq.

It is important to observe, that in this and similar cases, averages do not afford a fair criterion for a correct decision. This may at first glance appear unsound doctrine, but a very slight reflection will remove all doubt on the subject. Suppose A and B to work, the former at seven dollars, and the latter at ten—the average would be eight and a half. But would it be fair to calculate the capacity of A to support his family by this average? Surely not. The calculation must be made on his actual wages: I will therefore assume ten dollars for ten months, and five dollars for two—and take the case of a labourer with a wife and two children. Many of them have three or four.

10 months at 10 dollars, - - - - - - -	$100 00
2 months at 5 dollars, - - - - - - -	10 00
Suppose the wife to earn half a dollar per week, - - -	26 00
Total, - - - - - -	136 00

I now submit a calculation of the expenses of such a family, every item of which is at a low rate.

Shoes and clothes for self and wife, each 12 dollars, - -	$24 00
Washing at the canal, 6¼ cents per week, - - - -	3 25
Shoes and clothes for two children, each 8 dollars, - - -	16 00
Rent, 50 cents per week, - - - - - - -	26 00
Soap, candles, &c. 6 cents per week, - - - - -	3 12
Fuel, at 12 cents per week, - - - - - - -	6 24
Meat, drink, vegetables, &c. &c. 8 cents per day, each, for wife and children, - - - - - - - - - - - }	87 60
	$166 21*
Deficit, - - - - - - - - -	$30 21

This is one of a large class, whom some of our political economists of the new school are not ashamed to stigmatize as worthless and improvident, because they do not, forsooth, save enough out of their miserable wages, to support themselves and families, in times of scarcity, without the aid of benevolent societies; whereas it appears that their wages are inadequate to their support, even when fully employed.

* Statement in detail of the expenses of such a family per week, exclusive of clothes and rent, which, I trust, will be found moderate.

Bread, - - - -	$0.62½	Salt, pepper, and vinegar, -	$0.07
Meat, - - - -	20	Fuel, soap, candles, &c. -	21
Potatoes, - - - -	15		
Butter, - - - -	15	Per week, - - - -	$1.69½
Tea, - - - -	10		
Sugar, - - - -	12	Per day, about - - -	.24½
Milk, - - - - -	7		

B

Here let it be observed, there is no allowance for a single day in the whole year, lost by accident, by sickness, or by want of employment—no allowance for expense arising from sickness of wife or children—no allowance for the contingency stated by Mr. M'Ilvaine, of working, during the winter months, for board alone. It is assumed that no unfavourable circumstance has taken place—that every thing has " run on with a smooth current ;" and yet the man's earnings and those of his wife fall short of their support $30.21 !

But we will present the case in another point of view. Suppose him to have $12 per month for ten months ; and $5 for two ; that his wife earns half a dollar per week ; and let us see the result.

10 months, at $12 each, - - - - - - -	$120
2 do. at $5 - - - - - - - -	10
Wife's earnings per week, 50 cents, - - - - -	26*
	$156
Expenditure as before, - - - - - - -	$166.21

Even on this supposition he falls short about ten dollars a year of a meagre support, without, let me repeat, the loss of a single hour in the year by sickness or want of employment. What a hideous view of the situation of an industrious man, burdened with a family, and contributing largely to advance the best interests of society ! what an overwhelming commentary on the idle and vapid declamations against the improvidence of the poor ! and what an irresistible argument in favour of benevolent societies ! †

The allowance for food and drink is probably too low. The rations in prisons and almshouses are from 5 to 8 cents per day. In those cases, the supplies are furnished by contract, under the influence of eager competition. The articles are all purchased by wholesale, and on a large scale. How immense the difference between this case and that of the poor, who purchase all in the small way, and generally on credit, at a price enhanced by the risk incurred by the sellers. The difference in the price of wood may afford a tolerable specimen of the disadvantage under which the poor labour in their purchases. By the measurement of some wood recently purchased on a small scale, it appears that oak wood, sold out by three or four cents worth at a time (the mode in which it is too generally purchased by the poor), produced about ten dollars per cord, when the price at the wharf was only five or six dollars !

Philadelphia, June 24, 1833.

—•••◉◉•••—

ESSAY III.

I HAVE too good an opinion of human nature, although by no means a believer in its perfection or perfectibility, to doubt that those speculative citizens, who have for years employed their time and their talents in denouncing the idle-

---

* Although I have allowed 50 cents per week for the earnings of a wife, it must be obvious that a woman with two or three small children to attend, and making shirts for 6, 8, 10, or even 12½ cents each, can contribute little to the support of a family.

† So far as regards canal labourers, the sickness and mortality among them form a painful drawback on the benefits mankind derive from their labours. It is not at all improbable, indeed it is almost certain, that among the whole number employed, five per cent. return to their families in the winter, with broken constitutions, by fevers and agues, one half of whom are carried off to an untimely grave. Those that escape this state often linger for years in a state of debility, subject to occasional returns of their painful and enervating disorder.

ness, the worthlessness, and the improvidence of the poor, will, on a cool examination of the subject here presented to view, be filled with astonishment and deep regret at the infatuation, whereby they have attempted to dry up the sources of charity and benevolence in the breasts of the rich, and, as far as in them lay, doomed the poor to remediless pauperism—an unholy and ungodly employment. To superior beings, looking down on human affairs, nothing can be a more just subject of amazement than a wealthy man, with an income of 5, 6, or 7000 dollars a year, enjoying not only all the comforts but all the luxuries of life, and laying the four quarters of the globe under contribution for his raiment and the gratification of his appetites, who denies occasional relief to persons circumstanced as I have stated in the case cited, from a conscientious apprehension of injuring society by affording encouragement to idleness and improvidence! and nothing can be a more genuine subject of holy indignation, than a wealthy person, not labouring under such a delusion, and yet refusing to aid in cases of distress and wretchedness.

Calculations respecting city labourers, hod-men, wood-pilers, scavengers, and various other classes, whose sole dependence is on the casual employment of their hands, are attended with considerable difficulty. I have made inquiries of different persons, particularly of master-builders, as regards labourers and hod-men. Their statements vary extremely. One eminent builder, who employs a number of hands, states, that allowing for occasional heavy rains, in spring, summer, and fall, and the partial suspension of building in winter, those persons are not sure of employment more than 200 days in the year. This appears to be quite too low. Another, who states that wages vary from 25 to 37½ cents per day in winter, and from 62½, 75, 87½ to 100 cents, in spring, summer, and fall, assumes an average of 60 cents per day throughout the year. This again is apparently too low. Be this as it may, whatever the wages assumed, of the various estimates, it will be manifest from the preceding statements, that the most rigid economy will not secure persons with families, of the description in question, from occasional distress, in the event of any of the calamities to which they are subject, that is, accidents, sickness, want of employment, &c.

I do not pretend my calculations are strictly accurate. They are, however, a sufficiently near approximation, to satisfy every candid mind of the enormous and pernicious errors which prevail on this subject. When a labourer has a wife and only one child, or neither one nor the other, he undoubtedly fares well, and does not fall within the scope of this essay. When, on the other hand, he has a sickly wife and three or four or five children, and is himself occasionally sick, his case is truly deplorable; and many of them have four, five, and six children. Their children are, I believe, generally more numerous than those of the rich.*

I might extend these views to a greater length, and embrace various other occupations, which stand on nearly the same ground as those I have specified: but I presume it cannot be necessary; and hope I have established a point of infinite importance to the poor, and highly interesting to the rich—that is, that even among the occupations of males, there are some which are so indiffer-

---

* I submit a story, recorded, I believe, by Montaigne. A lady who had been long married, and never had a child, paid a visit to one of her tenants who had ten or eleven. The farmer's wife was complaining to the lady how hard she found it to provide for her numerous family; the lady soothingly said, "*Be comforted, good woman; when God sends mouths, he always sends meat.*" "*Yes, truly, my dear Madam; but unfortunately he sends the meat to you, and the mouths to me.*" Such is the case with many of our wealthy men, who are blessed with a superabundance of all the good things of this world, with few or no children—while many of our weavers and labourers, who have half a dozen or a dozen, have not means to afford them proper nourishment.

ently remunerated, that no industry, no economy, no providence, in times when the parties are fully employed, will enable them to save wherewith to support themselves and families in times of stagnation, and during severe seasons; and that of course they must rely, on those occasions, upon the overseers of the poor, or benevolent societies, or charitable individuals, or on such extraordinary aid, as, to the honour of our citizens, the late (1830) distressing scenes called forth. If I succeed in deeply imprinting this important truth on the public mind, so that it may produce the proper effect, by removing the injurious prejudices that prevail on the conduct and character of the labouring poor, on the effects of benevolent societies, and on the claims of those societies for extensive support, I shall regard myself as signally fortunate.

There is one idea on the subject of benevolent societies which deserves serious consideration, and appeals not merely to our charity and beneficence, but to our selfishness. It often happens that individuals who have for a long time struggled with distress and difficulties, and with a laudable spirit of pride and self-respect, which cannot be too carefully cherished, shrunk from the degradation of a dependence on the guardians of the poor, are on the point of giving way in a time of severe pressure, but, being then temporarily relieved by a benevolent society, are rescued from this painful necessity. Whereas they might otherwise sink into permanent paupers, and ultimately cost the public ten times as much as the amount which rescued them from this degradation.

Let it not be for a moment supposed, that I carry my defence of the poor to such an extravagant and ill-judged length, as to contend that all their distresses and sufferings arise from inadequate wages, or that they are all faultless: far from it. I know there are among them, as among all other classes, worthless persons—and some supremely worthless. Among the heavy sins of this class are intemperance, and desertion by some of them, of their wives and children, or, what is at least as bad, living in a state of idleness on the earnings of their wives. Indeed, so far as regards their ill-fated partners, the latter course is the worse. In the one case, the husband only withdraws his aid: in the other, he not only commits that offence, but adds to the burdens of his wife.

As regards the sexes, there are, among the poor, twice as many worthless males as females—idle, dissipated, and intemperate. The females are, with few exceptions, orderly, regular, and industrious, and husband their slender means with exemplary economy—an economy without which they would frequently undergo intense suffering from hunger.

But while I freely admit that there are among the poor many worthless, I am fully satisfied, from the most attentive examination of the subject, that the worthless of both sexes bear but a very small proportion to those who are industrious and meritorious. Unfortunately, the worthless occupy a more prominent space in the public eye, and with many are unceasing objects of animadversion and reprobation; their numbers and their follies and vices are magnified: whereas the industrious and meritorious are, I repeat, generally in the background, out of view.*

*Extract from a Report of the Managers of the Female Hospitable Society.

"The Managers of the Female Hospitable Society state, that in their opinion, a very large "proportion of the distress among the industrious poor originates in the low prices of "women's wages, and the uncertainty of constant employment.

"This society has never been able to give work to one fourth of those who apply, even in "the most flourishing state of its funds: now not more than one in ten receives any!

"MARY A. SNYDER, Governess F. H. Society.
"MARGARET SILVER, Secretary."

The industry and virtue of the labouring poor appear undeniable, from the fact, that there is no occupation, however deleterious or disgraceful, at which there is any difficulty in procuring labourers, even at the most inadequate wages. The labour on canals in marshy situations, in atmospheres replete with pestilential miasmata, is full proof on this point. Although the almost certain consequence of labouring in such situations is a prostration of health, and danger of life; and that no small portion of the labourers, as I have already stated, return to their families in the fall or winter with health and vigour destroyed, and labouring under protracted fevers and agues, which in many cases undermine their constitutions, and return in after-years, and too often hurry them prematurely into eternity: their places are readily supplied by other victims who offer themselves upon the altars of industry.

This is one of those decisive facts which ought to silence cavil for ever on this important subject.

Philadelphia, June 26, 1833.

—◦◉◦—

ESSAY IV.

LET us now turn to the appalling case of seamstresses, employed on coarse work, and to that of spoolers: and here " I will a tale unfold, to harrow up the soul" of all those endowed with feelings of humanity.

Coarse shirts and duck pantaloons are frequently made for 8 and 10 cents. The highest rate in the United States, with two highly honourable exceptions, which I shall notice presently, is 12½ cents. Women free from the incumbrance of children, in perfect health, and with constant, uninterrupted employment, cannot, by the testimony of ladies of the first respectability, who have fully scrutinized the affair, make more than nine shirts per week, working from twelve to fifteen hours per day, and possessing considerable expertness.*

Extract of a letter from J. W. Wyman, a New York Police Magistrate.

" *New York, Jan.* 25, 1830.

" It is most undoubtedly true, that the compensation which poor women with small chil-" dren obtain for their labour, is so scanty that the least interruption in their accustomed em-" ployment occasions a corresponding diminution in their receipts, and they are at once (for " they literally live from hand to mouth), compelled to raise the means in some other way, and " none so ready or convenient, probably, as to send some article of wearing apparel as a pledge " for the sum required. Every casualty in such a family will subject them to a similar incon-" venience, until every article in their possession has disappeared, and *they are left to starve,* " *unless the hand of charity is extended for their relief.*

" The evils arising from the inadequate compensation given for most kinds of female " labour, are by no means confined to their poverty. It is frequently the case, and my own " experience enables me to speak with confidence, that women of this description are obliged " to keep their children in the streets, either to beg, or by some light employment to earn a " penny through the day; this leads to bad associations, and frequently to crime. *Of the* " *children brought before me for pilfering, nine out of ten are those whose fathers are dead,* " *and who live with their mothers, and are employed in this way.* The petty plunder obtained " in this way finds a ready market at some old junk shop, and the avails are in part carried " home as the earnings of honest labour."

---

* *Copy of a statement signed by thirty Philadelphia ladies of respectability, intelligence, and competence to decide on the subject.*

" *Philadelphia, June 5th,* 1830.

" The undersigned, having seriously considered the case of those seamstresses who work " in their own lodgings, and whose dependence is on their needles, are convinced that the

The Boston Society for the employment of seamstresses, of which I know not the exact title, pays, as I am credibly informed, but *ten cents for those shirts*, thus limiting the ill-fated women to 90 cents per week, if fully employed, which is seldom the case. Rent of rooms in Boston is higher than here : but suppose it the same, there remain for food, drink, clothes, fuel, soap, candles, &c. 40 cents per week, or less than 6 rents per day !

" prices they receive for their work are inadequate for their support ; that expert seamstresses, " if fully employed, and unincumbered with children, cannot make more, working early and " late, than eight or nine shirts, or duck pantaloons, per week ; that the highest price paid " here for those articles is 12½ cents each ; which amounts only to one dollar twelve and a " half cents per week : that the women in question almost universally pay 50 cents per week " for their lodgings, which leaves but 62½ cents per week, or 9 cents per day, for meat, drink, " clothing, fuel, &c., *for an expert woman, constantly employed, and without children !* that " cases very frequently occur, of the above articles being made for 10, and even for 8, and " sometimes for 6 cents ; that these women are frequently unemployed ; that many of them " are widows, who formerly lived in affluence ; that no small number are aged and infirm, and " unfit for any other occupation ; that the occasional want of employment, and sickness, make " a serious drawback on their slender means of support ; that many of them, *but for the* " *assistance they receive from charitable individuals and benevolent societies, would not only* " *be unable to pay their rent, but be often sorely distressed for want of the common neces-* " *saries of life !* Taking the whole of these afflicting circumstances under consideration, " they strongly recommmend their case to the consideration of the public at large, but more " particularly to that of those by whom they are employed, in the hope that some alleviation " of the sufferings of this numerous class may be devised and effected.

" Various other species of female labour are equally ill paid, particularly those of spoolers " and winders of thread ; but they have not judged it necessary to go into more particulars."†

Philadelphia, *May* 24th, 1830.

☞ The ladies' names are omitted from motives of delicacy.

Testimony of leading citizens of Philadelphia, on the subject of the above certificate.

" It is impossible to peruse this statement without extreme regret and surprise, that such a " state of things should have existed in this flourishing city, wholly unknown, as it must have " been, to the mass of our citizens. That the case of the unfortunate women referred to calls " loudly for a remedy, so far as may be practicable, cannot for a moment be doubted. That a " complete and radical remedy is practicable, we do not flatter ourselves, *while the demand* " *for employment so far exceeds the demand for that species of labour.* And we regret to " say, that there are cases in which *the competition among the sellers of the articles produced* " *by those women, may have so far reduced their prices as to render it impossible for the em-* " *ployers to raise the wages without injustice to themselves.* Yet we fondly hope there are " very many cases in which the employers may be able to reconcile more liberal wages, with " a due regard to their own interest. And when the extent and intensity of the suffering that " must inevitably arise from the present low rate of wages are duly considered, we rely that " every man of generous and liberal feeling, who can afford to raise the compensation for the " labours of those women, will cheerfully obey the dictates of humanity and justice.

" CADWALADER EVANS,	" PAUL BECK, Jun.
" MATTHEW L. BEVAN,	" HENRY TROTH,
" SAMUEL RICHARDS,	" J. K. MITCHELL, M. D.
" HENRY KUHL,	" SAMUEL HILDEBURN,
" THOMAS LATIMER,	" BENJAMIN TUCKER,
" ROBERT RALSTON,	" JAMES GRAY,
" WILLIAM MEREDITH,	" PETER HILL,
" ALEXANDER HENRY,	" L. P. GEBHARD, M. D.
" Rev. G. R. LIVINGSTON,	" SAMUEL D. BREED,
" SOLOMON ALLEN,	" W. GARRIGUES, Jun.
" JAMES TAYLOR,	" CHARLES D. MEIGS, M. D.
" COLEMAN SELLERS,	" MATHEW CAREY.
" ANDREW BAYARD,	" *Philadelphia, June* 10, 1830."

† A similar statement has been signed by a number of ladies in New York and Baltimore

Those incumbered with children, or in indifferent health, or inexpert, cannot make more than six or seven. They are, moreover, as I have already stated, very partially employed. But laying aside all the various disadvantages and drawbacks, and placing the circumstances in the most favourable point of light, let us consider the case of a woman in perfect health, without children, and with uninterrupted employment; and see the result of her painful labours, and how little attention is paid to the awful denunciation against those that " *grind the faces of the poor.*" Allowing nine shirts per week, at 12¼ cents, and constant, uninterrupted employment, let us view the appalling result.

9 shirts per week = 1.12¼. - - - Per annum, -		$58 50
Rent at 50 cents, - - - - - - - -	26 00	
Shoes and clothes, suppose, - - - - - -	10 00	
Fuel per week, say 15 cents, - - - - -	7 80	
Soap, candles, &c., 8 cents, - - - - -	4 16	
Remain for food and drink 20 cents per week, or about 2¾ cents per day!!!!!! - - - - - - -	10 54	
		——— $58 50

But suppose the woman to have one or two children; to work for ten cents, which is not below the usual average; to be a part of her time unemployed, say one day in each week; and to make, of course, six, but say seven shirts.

7 shirts, or 70 cents per week, is, per annum, - - -		$36 40
Rent, fuel, soap, candles, &c. as before, - - -	$47 96	
Deficit, - - - - - - - - -	11 56	
		——— $36 40

Here is no declamation; no pathetic appeal; no solemn invocation, to arouse the dormant feelings of humanity. It is all a plain statement of harrowing facts, that defy the severest scrutiny. It exhibits a state of suffering which, I had almost said, cries to heaven for vengeance.

In speaking of the effect on some of the unfortunate seamstresses, to drive them to licentious courses, I ought to use the strongest language the subject would admit of, in order to make a deep impression on the reader, somewhat commensurate with the magnitude of the evil, and the enormity of the oppression under which they groan. A due consideration of their actual situation, and the gloomy prospects before them, would lead, *a priori*, to anticipate such a deplorable and fatal result. Beset on one side by poverty and wretchedness, with scanty and poor fare, miserable lodgings, clothing inferior in quality and often inadequate in quantity, without the most distant hope of a melioration of condition, by a course of honest and unremitting industry; and on the other side, tempted by the allurements of present enjoyment, comfortable apartments, fine dress, with a round of pleasures : all these held out by vice and crime to entice them from the paths of virtue, is it wonderful that many of them fall victims, and enter on the " broad path that leads to destruction?" Is not the trial almost too severe for poor human nature? Let those who pass a heavy censure on them, and are ready exultingly to cry out, with the Pharisee in the gospel, "Thank God, we are not like one of these," ponder well what might have been their conduct in similar circumstances.

But that this is too often the result does not depend on an elaborate process of reasoning, which, notwithstanding its plausibility, might lead to erroneous conclusions. We have the evidence of various citizens, whose opportunities duly qualify them to decide the question by the infallible test of facts.*

* *Extract of a letter from Dr. Van Renssellaer, of New York.*
" My profession affords me many and unpleasant opportunities of knowing the wants of " those unfortunate females, who try to earn an honest subsistence by the needle, and to wit-

Such is the hideous, the deplorable state of a numerous and interesting portion of the population of our cities in the most prosperous country in the world! And be it noted, to the discredit of the wealthy portion of the nation, of both sexes, particularly the ladies, that this subject has for five years been pressed on the public attention, in almost every shape and form, without exciting a single efficient effort in Boston, New York, or Philadelphia—I will not say to remedy or alleviate this horrible state of things—but even to inquire into it, and ascertain whether it be or be not remediless! It is impossible to regard this apathy without exciting the utmost astonishment.

I have not lightly thrown a higher degree of censure on the ladies in this case, than on the gentlemen. It is peculiarly the cause of the former. Their sex are "ground to the earth," and it is the proper duty and province of the ladies to stand forth in their defence. In such a holy cause of humanity, their efforts could not have failed of success. They might readily have stimulated their fathers, brothers, husbands, and cousins, to meet and devise some plan to mitigate sufferings, which drive numbers of unfortunate women to DESTRUCTION—to ruin here, and perhaps hereafter. Half the zeal, the effort that they make in other causes, not calling so loudly for their interference, would have sufficed to render the defence of those oppressed women fashionable. But they have looked on with calm indifference. Application on the subject has been made in Philadelphia and New York, personally or by letter, to above fifty ladies in each city; and every one of them expressed deep sympathy for the sufferers, but the sympathy has been barren and unproductive.

I will now take the case of a city labourer, whose wages average about 75 cents per day through the year, when employed; and suppose him to lose only eight weeks in the year by sickness and want of employment. Let

---

"ness the struggles often made by honest pride and destitution. *I could cite many instances* "*of young, and even middle-aged women, who have been 'lost to virtue,' apparently by no* "*other cause than the lowness of wages, and* THE ABSOLUTE IMPOSSIBILITY OF PROCURING "THE NECESSARIES OF LIFE BY HONEST INDUSTRY."

"MY DEAR SIR,   *New York, 5th April,* 1830.

'The subject of conversation at our last interview is one of great importance in every "well-regulated community, and cannot fail to interest every benevolent mind. I mean the "inadequate price usually paid for female labour, particularly to poor widows who are bur- "dened with small children. It is a subject which ought to arouse the feelings of every phi- "lanthropist: for I have no hesitation in saying, from my own observation, as one of the "acting magistrates of this city, that *no inconsiderable portion of female distress and* FEMALE "DEPRAVITY is to be attributed to the very scanty remuneration they receive for honest in- "dustry. I hope, therefore, most sincerely, that your unceasing efforts in the cause you have "so disinterestedly espoused, will be crowned with ultimate success.

"Yours, sincerely,
"MR. CAREY.   "JOHN W. WYMAN."

Extract of a letter from the Rev. Ezra Stiles Ely, D. D.

"From intimate acquaintance with many of the industrious poor, for eighteen years past, "both in New York and in this city, I am constrained to say, that your remarks concerning "the inadequate payment which females receive for their labour, are just, and ought deeply "to affect every benevolent person, who has any wish to do justly, and see honest industry "suitably rewarded. *A common slave, in the states of Virginia, Tennessee, and Kentucky,* "*is much better compensated for his labour, by his necessary food, clothing, lodging, and* "*medicines, than many respectable mothers and daughters in this city, who apply themselves* "*diligently to their work, two hours for every one occupied by the negro in his master's* "*service.* Your remarks will apply to the folding and stitching of books, to the sewing of "carpet rags, to the binding of shoes,   *   *   *   no less than to the work done for "the army and navy."

us see the result, and how far he is from being able to save wherewith to meet the casualties of sickness and want of employment.

44 weeks, at $4.50, - - - - - - - -	$198 00
Shoes and clothing for self and wife, - - - -	24 00
For two children, at $8 each, - - - - -	16 00
Rent, 50 cents per week, - - - - - -	26 00
Soap, candles, &c. at 8 cents per week, - - -	4 16
Fuel, at 15 cents per week, - - - -	7 80
Bread, meat, drink, vegetables, &c. for self, wife, and two } children, at 8 cents each per day, - - - - }	116 68
	$194 64

This is a sample of a large class, whom citizens, wallowing in wealth and enjoying all the luxuries of life, vituperate for not saving enough when employed, wherewith to support themselves during hard winters and times of sickness!!! And let it be observed, that this calculation is for two children, whereas some of those persons have four or five.

There are, I believe, some journeymen in Philadelphia whose wages do not much, if any thing, exceed four dollars and a half a week.

Philadelphia, June 28, 1833.

ESSAY V.

BUT we are gravely told, that some of the seamstresses ought to go to service—that servants are scarce; if they would condescend to fill that station, they might have comfortable homes, abundance of good food, light labour, and high wages.

That there may be found some individuals among those oppressed women who might go to service, and whom a false pride prevents from taking that course, I admit. But on a careful inquiry of the Matron of the Provident Society, and of the Managers of the Female Hospitable Society, I am persuaded the number is small, and bears but a slight proportion to the whole number of the seamstresses. There is among them a large proportion of aged widows, who are wholly unfit for service, and many young widows, with two or three small children, who are as dear to them, as theirs are to the rich; whom, of course, they cannot bear to part with; and whom their wages, as servants, would not support at nurse.

Extract of a letter from Mrs. Margaret Silver, Secretary of the Female Hospitable Society.
" Philadelphia, Jan. 5, 1832.

" On consulting with the Managers of the Female Hospitable Society, we have concluded " from the experience which twenty-three years have given us, to return the following answers " to your queries:—

" 1. The number of women who apply for work in the winter season, is, on an average, " five hundred.

" 2. As to persons among them fit for house-maids, or service in families, not one in fifty.

" 3. As to the number of widows, the proportion is as seventy-five to an hundred; the " remainder, chiefly wives deserted by their husbands, or whose husbands do nothing for the " maintenance of their children, who are too young to do any thing for themselves.

" 4. As to aged females, one half are of that class, and one fifth of the whole infirm.

" Yours, &c.
" MR. M. CAREY.   " MARGARET SILVER, *Secretary."*

Extract of a letter from Mrs. Queen, Matron of the Philadelphia Provident Society.

" SIR,—As far as I can judge, from what the women told me last winter, I should think " that *at least six hundred of them were widows. At least two thirds of them said they had*

C

"*children to support.* The recompense they received averaged about fifty cents per week, "while they took out work. Few of them lived in the city. *The greater part of them* "*came from Kensington, Northern Liberties, and Southwark.* "Mr. M. Carey."

The pernicious consequences of the inadequate wages paid the women of the classes in question, is strikingly displayed by the state of the out-door paupers in the city of Philadelphia, in 1830. Of 498 females, there are,

Seamstresses, - - 142
Washerwomen, - - 62
Spoolers, - - - 28
Shoe-binders, - - 10
—— 242

Being nearly one half of the whole number. There are 406 widows.

It may excite wonder how the seamstresses, spoolers, &c., are able to support human nature, as their rent absorbs above two-fifths of their miserable earnings. The fact is, they generally contrive to raise their rent by begging from benevolent citizens, and of course their paltry earnings go to furnish food and clothing.

I stated that there are two honourable exceptions to the low rate of wages paid to seamstresses. They are entitled to a high degree of applause, and are worthy examples, which ought to be generally followed. The one is "the Female Hospitable Society of Philadelphia," the other "the Impartial Humane Society of Baltimore." The former, although its resources are very slender, too slender considering its usefulness, has uniformly paid 18¾ cents for making shirts and duck pantaloons, and in the same proportion for other articles. The scale of prices of the latter is as follows:

	cents.		cents.
Linen shirts, - - -	75 to 87½	Gentlemen's shams, - -	18¾ to 50
Gentlemen's pantaloons, -	62½ to 75	Children's suits of clothes,	50 to 87½
Roundabouts, - - - -	75	Do. cloaks, - - -	62½
Linen collars, - - - -	10	Do. mittens, - -	10 to 12½
Unbleached cotton shirts, large, -	25	Women and children's aprons,	6¼ to 31¼
Do. do. small,	12½ to 18¾	Women's plain dresses, -	43¾ to 50
Bleached do. large, -	31¼	Bonnets, - - - -	25 to 75
Do. do. small, -	25	*All other articles in proportion.*	

It is deeply to be regretted that in such a wealthy and public-spirited city as Baltimore, this institution has but three hundred subscribers,* although the subscription is but one dollar per annum ; whereas for so glorious an object as rescuing such numbers of interesting females from penury and distress, and all their demoralizing consequences, had the annual subscription been five dollars, there ought to have been one thousand subscribers.

The following is tne list of prices paid by the Female Hospitable Society of Philadelphia :†

* This fact must excite a high degree of astonishment and regret. There are in Baltimore citizens whose liberality may, in some cases, vie with the illustrious examples set in Boston, which stands pre-eminent above any other city in the world (London perhaps excepted) for displays of munificence on the most magnificent scale. That citizens of such a calibre should overlook the claims of this noble institution—should not make a liberal provision for it, so as to place it on high ground, and to enable it to extend its usefulness to a degree commensurate with the demand upon it, can only arise from its merits not having attracted a due degree of attention. I venture to hope that this state of things will not be allowed to exist much longer, and that the institution will have in future that degree of support to which it is fairly entitled.

† The observations made in the preceding note respecting the Impartial Hospitable Society of Baltimore apply with equal force to this Society. Its objects, and views, and merits, are the same. Too much praise cannot be awarded to Mrs. Snyder and Mrs. Silver, who have devoted many years to this institution, and contributed largely to its success.

	cents.		cents.
Fine linen shirts, - - -	50	Drawers and duck pantaloons, -	$18\frac{3}{4}$
Next quality do. - - -	40	Check shirts, - - - -	16
Fine muslin do. - - -	40	Flannel, do. - - - -	14
Next quality do. - - -	$37\frac{1}{2}$	Collars, separate from the shirt, $6\frac{1}{4}$, 8, $12\frac{1}{2}$	
Next quality do. - - -	$31\frac{1}{4}$	Quilting, - - - - .75 to 1.25	
Common muslin shirts, - -	25	Comfortables, according to the size, from	
Coarse unbleached do. - -	$18\frac{3}{4}$	$2 to 2.50 and $3.	
Boys' shirts, - - - -	$18\frac{3}{4}$	Bed-quilts, do. do.	

The case of the spoolers is at least as hard, and their sufferings as great, as those of the seamstresses. By no degree of industry and skill can they earn in summer more than a dollar and a quarter, or a dollar in winter; and during the latter season, they are, for the most part, employed but half their time.

Philadelphia, July 1, 1833.

ESSAY VI.

IV. The fourth position which I undertook to controvert, is, that

"Taxes for the support of the poor, and aid afforded them by benevolent societies and "charitable individuals, are pernicious; as, by encouraging the poor to depend on them, they " foster their idleness and improvidence, and thus produce, or at least increase, the poverty " and distress they are intended to relieve."

If I have proved, as I hope I have, satisfactorily, that there are classes of people, male and female, whose dependence is on their hands for support, and whose wages, when fully employed, are not more than sufficient for that purpose ; that when unemployed, they must be reduced to penury and want; and that there are classes of females, whose wages are inadequate for their support, even when constantly employed; it follows, of course, that the poor rates, the aid of benevolent societies, &c., far from producing the pernicious effects ascribed to them, are imperiously necessary, and that without them, numbers would, as I have stated, actually perish of want, or would have recourse to mendicity; and mendicants impose a far heavier tax on a community than the same number of paupers supported by poor rates. The support of 549 out-door paupers of Philadelphia, in 1830, averaged $46\frac{1}{4}$ cents per week—or less than 7 cents per day. Some of them received only a quarter of a dollar a week. I submit a statement of the whole number, with the pittance they respectively received :—

42	a	25 cents.
2	a	$31\frac{1}{4}$
186	a	$37\frac{1}{2}$
259	a	50
17	a	$62\frac{1}{2}$
42	a	75
1	a	100

549

If these had been strolling mendicants, as, by the abrogation of the poor laws, and the annihilation of benevolent societies, they would have become, the average, instead of seven cents per day, would more probably have been 25 or 30 cents ; thus increasing the burdens on the community three or four fold. Many of them, with a woe-begone appearance, whether real or fictitious, calculated to excite sympathy, would probably have realized 50 cents, and often a dollar a day.

Those of our fellow-citizens who complain of the oppression of our poor laws, will learn with surprise, that of the 549 out-door paupers, there were no less than 390 above 60 years of age, and 6 above 100. Almost all of these were in a state of superannuation, 50 of them were blind, and 406 of the whole number, as I have already stated, were widows. I annex a statement of their respective ages.

Between 10 and 20	4
20 and 30	26
30 and 40	42
40 and 50	40
50 and 60	47
	——159
60 and 70	154
70 and 80	161
80 and 90	60
90 and 100	9
Upwards of 100	6
	——390
	——549*

Of the whole number, 381 had 935 children, of whom 372 were at home with their parents. I have been unable to procure a statement of the ages or characters of the tenants of our alms-house—but presume that they were somewhat similar to those of the out-door paupers.†

Philadelphia, July 4, 1833.

—••◉◉••—

ESSAY VII.

THE question of the most eligible mode of supporting the poor, whether by statutory provision, or by voluntary contributions of individuals, has created a great diversity of opinions in Great Britain—opinions advocated with the utmost zeal and ardour, and with considerable talents, on both sides. On one side, a powerful party, at the head of which at present are the editors of the Edinburgh Review (formerly Mr. Malthus), is in favour of a total abolition, as speedily as possible, of the system of statutory provision. The other party, headed by the editors of the Quarterly Review, maintains, that all the evils of which the complaints are so loud and general, are the result of the abuse of the system. The subject is deeply interesting, both as regards the

* Hazard's Register of Pennsylvania, vol. vi. p. 266.

† The following extract from the presentment of the Grand Jury of the Mayor's Court for the June session for 1833, exhibits a degree of wretchedness of which few of our citizens have any idea. It fully establishes the necessity of the interference of benevolent associations and charitable individuals, to relieve such severe suffering, and ought to make those persons blush, who, enjoying the good things of the world, involve the poor in an indiscriminate mass of obloquy; unjustly charge all their misery to intemperance and other vices; and, decrying those associations, avert, as far as in them lies, the current of charity in its course to their support. Think of the miseries of six families in one small house, destitute of the most essential conveniences! Let it be eternally borne in mind, that if intemperance and other vices produce poverty on the one hand—poverty, degrading and remediless poverty on the other, as often produces recklessness, intemperance, and their baleful concomitants.

"3d. The block of buildings bounded by Vine and Sassafras and Water and Front streets, "the Inquest are of opinion, presents a nuisance of a very serious nature, and which may "prove detrimental to the public health. *There are in this block* 29 *houses or tenements,* "*containing* 94 *families, consisting of* 472 *individuals.* These houses generally cover all "the ground belonging to the premises : in many of them are residing six families each! "and they have not the convenience of a privy, nor a situation in which one could be "placed ! they are almost without ventilation : the tenants are compelled to use vessels of "various kinds, which are emptied either into the streets and gutters, or into the neighbour-"ing docks !"

payers and the recipients, and demands to be soberly and calmly and candidly discussed, uninfluenced by the names or standing of the advocates, or by previous prejudices, however great.

The investigation may at present be prosecuted with more advantage than at any former period. The British parliament some time since appointed a commission, composed of the Bishop of London, the Bishop of Chester, Messrs. W. J. Bourne, Nassau W. Senior, Henry Bishop, Henry Gawler, and W. Coulson, to investigate the subject thoroughly. They addressed pertinent queries to the different overseers of the poor, and the magistrates throughout the kingdom; the responses to which shed a flood of light on the subject, and dispelled the clouds of darkness and delusion under which it has been obscured.

Copies of a digest of the information thus collected, published so late as last March, have been forwarded to this country to different individuals, for the purpose of ascertaining the nature of our system for the support of the poor. Of this publication, the most authentic and conclusive that has appeared on the subject, I shall principally avail myself in the following view of it.

The law of the 43d Elizabeth, the result of the collected wisdom of the great statesmen by whom that queen was surrounded, was framed after various experiments. It ordered that " competent sums should be raised" [by the overseers of the poor] " for the necessary relief of the lame, impotent, " old, blind, and such other among them being poor and unable to work;" and that the able-bodied, idle vagrants should be compelled to labour for their support. This law, which is marked by the strongest features of enlightened humanity and sound policy, has been in operation above two hundred years, and has undergone various alterations—some, obvious improvements—others, deteriorations; but the frame-work of it remains as originally enacted. I will state the main objections alleged against such a system. It is asserted by the editors of the Edinburgh Review—

1. That the necessary and inevitable consequence of a statutory provision for the poor, is, to increase regularly and oppressively the amount of the burdens, as has been the case for some years in England.

2. That it encourages imprudent and improvident marriages, and of course produces the distress it professes to relieve, and multiplies a pauper population.

3. That it destroys, or at least impairs, the stimulus to industry, by insuring a support to the idle and vicious, equal to what honest industry can acquire by useful labour.

Were these objections well founded, they would unquestionably give irresistible force to the loud call that prevails for the abolition of a system pregnant with such baleful consequences. But I hope to prove, by the most unquestionable evidence, that the evils complained of are solely the result of the most flagrant, barefaced, and corrupt abuses, such as are perhaps without parallel in any other country in the world. Let it be observed, that I should not here trespass on the public with this subject, but that the opinions of the Edinburgh Review are spreading in this country, and are advocated by some of our best citizens. The Rev. Mr. Tuckerman, author of a Report to the Legislature of Massachusetts, and W. M. Meredith, Esq., author of an elaborate one to the Legislature of Pennsylvania on this subject, both decidedly concur in ascribing the worst consequences to a legal provision for the poor, and deprecate its continuance. These opinions are gaining ground, and therefore it is highly proper to bring them to the test of the talisman of truth and fact, so as not only to enable those who *may* be called to legislate on this subject, to act understandingly, but to enable the public at large to decide between the conflicting opinions.   I premise the exact words of the first objection.

"After the principle of a legal assessment has begun to be acted upon, there is no one "expedient within the reach of human skill, by which the progress and increase of pauperism "can be arrested."—*E. R.** vol. xxix. 279.

This is a strong, unqualified assertion ; let us see how it is borne out by facts.   The earliest accounts of the amount of the English poor rates that we have, date in 1673, when they amounted to £840,000 ;† whereas in 1750, after a lapse of 77 years, they were reduced to about £700,000,‡ being a reduction of 16 per cent., notwithstanding the intervention of the sanguinary and expensive wars of William III., Queen Anne, George I., and part of those of George II.

On these simple facts the question might be confidently rested, so far as regards the first and most important allegation, the regular and progressive increase of pauperism, and consequently of poor rates.   But we must not rely wholly on these facts ; others of equal force remain, drawn, *mirabile dictu!* from the same Edinburgh Review.

"From the period [1601] when the act of the 43d of Elizabeth, the foundation of the ex-"isting code of poor laws, was promulgated, to the commencement of the late war, there had "been scarcely any increase of pauperism : and FEW OR NONE OF THOSE PERNICIOUS CONSE-"SEQUENCES HAD ACTUALLY RESULTED from their operation, which we are naturally led, "looking only to the principles they involve, to *suppose* they must produce."—*E. R.* vol. xlvii. p. 304.

Thus, after assuring us that "there is no expedient within the reach of human skill to prevent the progress and increase of pauperism," in the case of "a legal establishment for the support of the poor," we are gravely informed that "scarcely any increase" took place for 190 years under that system ! ! May we not say "ex ore tuo" to the oracle which pronounced the former dictum? And does not this strong contrast warn us against surrendering our judgment to those self-installed judges of literature, politics, and government?   Again :

"According to the official accounts, it appears that the total sum raised by assessment un-"der the name of poor rates, in England and Wales, during the three years ending with "1750, amounted at an average to £730,135 a year, of which £689,971 were expended on "the poor, being A MERE TRIFLE MORE THAN THE SUM EXPENDED ON THEM AT THE REVO-"LUTION, *and about £300,000 less than the sum supposed to have been expended at the* "*commencement of the century !*"—*Idem*, p. 307.

"During the period between the termination of the American war and the commencement "of the late French war, the rates were again considerably reduced."—*E. R.* vol. lii. p. 351.

Let us go on, and "make assurance doubly sure."

"It may safely be concluded, that the *rates were considerably lower in* 1793 *than in* 1785. "How much this reduction might amount to, it is impossible accurately to conjecture, but at "the commencement of the late war, they could hardly, one should think, exceed £1,400,000 "or £1,500,000 a year."—*E. R.* vol. xlvii. p. 318.

"*The poor rates gradually diminished during the three years ending* March 25, 1821 ; "*and that year were nearly one eighth, or one million less, than in the year* 1818."—*Q. R.* vol. xxviii. p. 357.

"Sums expended for relief of the poor; 1817, 1818, £7,890,148 : 1820, 1821, £6,958,445. "Total population in England and Wales:—1811, 10,502,500 : 1821, 12,218,500."— *Ibid, note.*

The Edinburgh Review, among other evils, ascribed to the operation of the poor laws, has asserted that their tendency is to increase a pauper population.   Let us hear it again on the other side of the question.

"It is established by evidence which it seems to be impossible to controvert, how much soever

---

* *E. R.* refers to the Edinburgh Review, and *Q. R.* to the London Quarterly Review.
† Eden on the Poor Laws, vol. i. p. 189.   ‡ Idem, p. 249.

" the conclusion may be at variance with the opinions that have recently been current on the
" subject, that from *their institution down to a late period, the effect of the poor-laws was*
" *not to increase, but to diminish population!!!"—E. R.* vol. xlvii. p. 314.

Here are most palpable contradictions! " Who shall decide," not " when
doctors disagree," but when the doctor disagrees with himself?

Having fairly stated the contradictory opinions of the leading journal hostile to the poor-laws, it is but right to state the views of their advocate.

" The experience of more than two centuries has only confirmed the wisdom of the mea-
" sure. *The evils that have been attributed to the poor-law are justly chargeable only to*
" *the abuses that have been locally permitted to creep into its administration.* There are
" few, if any persons, practically acquainted with the subject, that do not now recognise this
" truth."—*Q. R.* vol. xliv. 512.

" The mischief which the poor-laws produce has arisen wholly from their mal-administra-
" tion or perversion. The system itself *is humane, just, necessary, befitting a Christian*
" *state, and honourable to the English nation."—Q. R.* vol. xxxvii. p. 540.

" Reflection and experience have produced a general conviction, that the principles of the poor-
" law of Elizabeth are consistent with the sound policy of that important reign, and cannot
" in the present state of things be safely departed from : and that a compulsory provision
" for the poor—as it originated not in abstract theory and speculation, but was resorted to from
" necessity, and after other measures had been repeatedly tried in vain—continues to be an
" indispensable obligation upon such a system of government as ours."—*Q. R.* vol. xxviii.
p. 349.

It is incredible, but nevertheless true, that the Edinburgh Review, after
having distinctly admitted that for 190 years the poor-laws had not " increased
pauperism, or population, or the poor rates," to any perceivable extent, has
carried its blind opposition to them to such an extreme length as to advocate
the substitution of mendicity, with all its immoralities, its frauds, its impositions, its degradation! So much for a bigoted devotion to theory, in utter disregard of fact or experience.

" Those who are destitute must be relieved somehow, and must have some way of making
" their wants known : and therefore we see no alternative between *the allowance of mendicity,*
" *under some modification* or other, and the establishment of the very system which is now
" bearing so oppressively down upon the country. And we do confess, that rather than have such
" a system, *we would sit down under mendicity in its very worst form!* we would let it roam
" unrestricted and at large, as it does in France !!! We would suffer it to rise, without any con-
" trol, to the height of unlicensed vagrancy, and are most thoroughly persuaded that even
" under such an economy, the whole poverty of the land would be disposed of at less expense
" to the higher orders, and with vastly less both of suffering and depravity to the lower or-
" ders of society !"—*E. R.* vol. xxix. p. 286.

What! mendicity with all its loathsomeness, and depravity, and corruption, preferable for " *the lame, the impotent, the old, the blind, and the poor*
unable to work," to having them comfortably supported at a moderate expense in poor-houses!! What next?

Philadelphia, July 8, 1833.

—◆◉◆—

ESSAY VIII.

I TRUST that it fully appears from the above evidence, even that of the
Edinburgh Review, the great opponent of the poor-laws of England, that those
laws, so generally reprobated at present, were not for 190 years attended with
any of the oppressive and disastrous consequences which have of late years
attended their administration. The cause of those evils must then be sought
for in something extraneous to the laws themselves, some essential difference
in the mode of administration, which I shall endeavour to point out. The
evils may be traced to three sources.

1. The dishonest system pursued by the manufacturers and agriculturists, whereby they *combine to reduce wages below the minimum necessary for the support of those they employ*, and force the overseers to make up the difference.

2. The support, by a regular weekly stipend, of masses of able-bodied men, without exacting any labour in return, and without regard to character or conduct; whereby thieves, rogues, and pickpockets are enabled to live in idleness, and enjoy in many instances more of the necessaries of life than the honest and industrious poor; thus destroying all stimuli to industry or regard to character.

3. Supporting at a heavy expense the mothers of hosts of illegitimate children; thus offering a premium to lewdness.

Of each in turn: and first, of the dishonest combination to reduce wages.

" A practice had obtained, of labourers being engaged at half or even one-third of the usual " rate of wages, upon an understanding with their employers, that *the difference would be* " *made up to them from the parochial funds.*"—*Information received from his Majesty's Commissioners, as to the Administration of the Poor-laws*, p. 163.

" The elders [a self-elected body of magistrates] of Hartland, in Devonshire, meet once in " the beginning of the month, and dine at the parish expense, asking friends to dine with " them. Some time after dinner, the paupers who cannot get work are brought in one by " one, *are put up to auction*, and the elders bid according to the value they fix upon them; " *the difference with what is necessary for their subsistence being made up from the* " *rates.*"—*Idem*, p. 166.

" *By combining together, as they almost uniformly do*, the farmers in agricultural parishes " can *reduce the rate of wages to any limit they please.* They are enabled to do this, be- " cause the parish, by granting such a supplementary allowance to the labourer as will sup- " port him and his family, prevents him from emigrating to another district, as he would most " certainly do, were his employers to attempt artificially to depress his wages in a country un- " fettered by this system."—*E. R.* vol. xlvii. p. 322.

" Its effect is to force the occupiers of villas, as well as shopkeepers, tradesmen, &c., or " those who do not employ labourers, *to pay a portion of the wages of those who do :* and " thus to place every farmer, who might be disposed to act on a more liberal system, in a rela- " tively disadvantageous situation !   The farmers are in this way led to encourage a system " which *fraudulently imposes a heavy burden upon others.*"—*Ibid.*

" Instead of securing a refuge for the really destitute, the poor-laws have been perverted in " the southern counties to the very worst purposes: they have been made a means of *re-* " *ducing wages to the lowest level, of pauperising the whole population, and of throwing a* " *large proportion of the expense of labour upon those who do not employ a single labourer.* " *This perversion began in* 1795."—*E. R.* vol. liii. p. 46.

" Persons who have no need of farm labour *are obliged to contribute to the payment of* " *work done for others.* This must be the case wherever the labourers, necessarily employed " by the farmers, receive from the parish any part of the wages, which, if not so paid, would " be paid by the farmers themselves."—*E. R.* vol. liii. p. 50.

" And for what object are three fourths of mankind thus degraded and kept down ?   The " immediate gain is the master's; but that is only a temporary advantage, followed by a train " of bad consequences, from which the masters and the whole community suffer."—*E. R.* vol. xxii. p. 198.

" We have had silk-masters who have made rapid fortunes by giving their men low wages, " and *driving them on the parish for the rest of their means of subsistence.*"—*Commissioners' Report on the Poor-laws*, p. 277.

" Wherever this pernicious system has been fully matured, it has, as might have been an- " ticipated, produced an entire revolution in the manners and habits of the working classes. " Every incentive to individual exertion it has abolished; every motive of sobriety, steadiness, " honesty, it has utterly destroyed.   Among them exists no longer any anxiety about the in- " terests of their employer, or any regard for their own character: for what motive is there to " induce a labourer to work hard, when he is aware that he will be paid, not in proportion to " the quantity of work done by him, but according to a general standard established in the " parish ?"—*Q. R.* vol. xxxiii. p. 449.

Next, of the support by the overseers of the idle, the lazy, the worthless, of thieves, and able-bodied rogues and vagabonds.

" The assistant-overseer and the other parish officer, allowed, that *no attention whatever*
" *was ever paid to character;* but that the most notorious drunkards, swearers, and thieves,
" with wives and families, were all duly relieved by the arithmetic of the magistrates' scale. I
" asked them, if they never took these men before the bench for punishment. Their answer
" was, that they had so often been reprimanded, and triumphed over, (to use their own ex-
" pression), that they had given it up in despair, and *relieved all alike, bad and good, meri-*
" *torious and profligate."—Commissioners' Report*, p. 108.

" The *greatest thief in the parish has the magistrate's allowance; the honest but unfor-*
" *tunate, get nothing more."—Idem*, p. 9

" Being secure of good wages for mere nominal work, the ill-disposed and idle *throw them-*
" *selves wilfully on the parish;* the effect is most ruinous on the small householders, who,
" being already on the verge of pauperism, may be converted, by a slight addition to their
" burden, from payers to receivers of rates."—*Idem*, p. 15.

" In the month of December, 1832, four healthy young men, receiving from 12*s.* to 14*s.*
" per week from the parish, refused to work at thrashing for a farmer, at 2*s.* 6*d.* and a quart
" of ale per day ; and the only punishment inflicted on them by the parish officers, *was taking*
" *off half a day's pay*, 1*s.*!! at the same time, *a poor widow, aged* 75, *could obtain but* 1*s.*
" *per week for her support from the vestry !!"—Idem*, p. 16.

" Out-door paupers have nearly the same amount of wages allowed them *without work,*
" *that could have been obtained by independent labourers by hard work;* the pauper hav-
" ing in addition to the money payments, *frequent allowances of clothes* from the parish, and
" payments on account of rent, and ' other advantages!' "—*Idem*, p. 218.

" A man lately married a girl, who left her place for that purpose on Wednesday. They
" applied for relief on the Saturday. It will appear from the scale, that, *on marriage there*
" *is an immediate increase of* 3*s. per week."—Idem*, p. 3.

" There is a butcher who occupies, I think, 20 acres of land, who has five or six cows and
" a horse. A son of this butcher, an able-bodied man, is constantly on the parish."—*Idem*,
p. 84.

" So long as this continues a parish of its present *small extent, with its present number of*
" *poor,* the property must be *an encumbrance to the proprietor ;* for he can expect no rent,
" *the rates assessed upon the land far exceeding its value,* amounting, as they last year have
" done, to *more than* 32*s. in the pound at rack rent."—Idem*, p. 88.

" Of this population [6468] there were 430 able-bodied persons receiving relief, 360 were
" regular, and 60 casual. A short time since, 1000 *persons were receiving relief."—Idem*,
p. 186.

" The English peasant no longer looks on parish relief as a degradation: such a feeling is
" extinct."—*Idem*, p. 200.

" Mr. Cliff, the assistant-overseer of Burghfield parish, stated : ' Whilst the allowance sys-
" tem went on, it was a common thing for young people to come to me for parish relief two
" or three days after they were married : nay, *I have had them come to me just as they came*
" *out of the church, and apply to me for a loaf of bread to eat, and for a bed to lie on*
" *that night !!"—Idem*, p. 236.

" A woman says she was not bred up to work, and *won't work;* she does not even choose
" to knit ; and during the last month she received 6*s.,* 4*s.,* 4*s.,* and 3*s.* in the four weeks,
" week by week."—*Idem*, p. 121.

" Those labourers who have families, say, ' We can get 10*s.* or 12*s.* per week from the
" parish ; why should we slave ourselves for this sum ?"—*Idem*, p. 123.

" This system secures subsistence to all ; to the idle as well as to the industrious; to the
" profligate as well as to the sober ; and, *as far as human interests are concerned, all*
" *inducements to obtain a good character are taken away."—E. R.* vol. xlvii. p. 321.

Under the third head, the encouragement afforded to the mothers of illegitimate children, the following disgusting facts are abundantly sufficient.*

" A woman of Swaffham was reproached by the magistrate with the burdens that she had

---

* I had strong doubts about the propriety of publishing the odious, offensive, and immoral
statements under this head ; and should have pretermitted them, but that it would be doing
manifest injustice to the argument. The clamour against the poor laws arises wholly from a
want of discrimination between their proper administration and their abuse. It is therefore
imperiously necessary to display, in their utter deformity, the monstrous abuses by which a
charitable, benevolent, and sagacious system has, after a period of 190 years' admirable administration, been degraded, dishonoured, and rendered so unpopular as to create a loud outcry
for its abolition.

" brought upon the parish, upon the occasion of her appearing before him to present the
" parish with *her seventh bastard!* She replied, ' I am not going to be disappointed in my
" company with men to save the parish.' This woman *now receives* 14s. *a week for her
" seven bastards, being two shillings a head for each.* Mr. Sewell informed me that had
" she been a widow, with seven legitimate children, she would not have received so much by
" 4s. or 5s. a week, according to their scale of allowance to widows. *A bastard child is thus
" about twenty-five per cent. more valuable to a parent than a legitimate one ! ! !"—Commissioners' Report,* p. 393.

" One woman named Smith has three children by three different fathers. She has never
" been punished, and the parish allows her 6s. per week. Women are very rarely punished ;
" has only known one or two instances in his memory of the parish. *Bastards very
" common."—Idem,* p. 394.

" An unmarried girl, upon leaving the workhouse after her fourth confinement, said to the
" master, ' Well, if I have the good luck to have another child, I shall draw a good sum from
" the parish, and with what I can earn myself, will be better off than any married woman in
" the parish."—*Idem,* p. 395.

" Bastardy is very much increasing in Badford; believes that one third of all the number
" applying to the parish, old and young, are bastards."—*Idem,* p. 396.

" Is bastardy pretty much the same in your parish as in the rest of the county ?—Yes ;
" very bad. *There are two women who have four children each, and each by three different
" fathers.* The order on the father varies, from 1s. 6d. to 3s. 6d., according to his circum-
" stances. *But the women extort money by threatening to swear the child first to one, then
" to another."—Idem,* p. 385.

" In the first place, I appeal to the experience of all overseers in rural districts, whether
" the *instances of marriages taking place among the labouring classes, without previous
" pregnancy, are not so very rare as to constitute no exception to the general assertion,* that
" PREGNANCY PRECEDES *marriage."—Idem,* p. 392.

" There are twenty-five bastards supported by the parish at 1s. 6d. per week."—*Idem,*
p. 105.

" There are at the present time eleven bastards on the weekly list. The parish receives
" for two only.

" It is well known that for from £3 to £4, and a treat, many men consent to be sworn to as
" the fathers of illegitimate children, knowing that the parish *cannot enforce payment against
" them,* and that, generally speaking, *it will not be attempted."—Idem,* p. 122.

" Nine out of ten of the orders of removal which the parish receives, are cases of bastardy.
" Mr. Barnet knows whole families in the town which are bastards from generation to genera-
" tion. He has observed that magistrates generally favour the mothers of bastards in their
" complaints against overseers."—*Idem,* p. 397.

" The English law has abolished female chastity, self-respect, proper pride, and all the
" charities of domestic life, derived from and connected with its existence. It has destroyed,
" likewise, the beneficial influence which this virtue in women reflects on the character of
" men."—*Idem,* p. 399.

" In referring to the printed lists, it will be observed, that out of sixty illegitimate children,
" the allowance from the father is only recovered for twelve."—*Idem,* p. 403.

" A woman has brought three illegitimate children on the parish, and for the last she was
" committed to prison for three weeks. She told the vestry that she would, if put to jail
" again, *swear the child to the overseer :* she is now pregnant a fourth time. This same in-
" dividual says openly to the vestry, ' If you don't give me some relief (enough, in fact, to
" support her in idleness), *I will bring you some more bastards to keep.' "—Idem,* p. 122.

Philadelphia, *July* 10, 1833.

—₪₪₪€ ❀ ❀₪₪₪—

ESSAY IX.

Is it wonderful that pauperism, profligacy, and other evils, together with
poor rates, have rapidly increased under such a hideous system of mismanagement! And is it not unaccountable that such an enlightened nation as England should have for nearly forty years submitted to it without serious and
decisive efforts to free themselves from it, before it had arisen to its present
alarming and oppressive height ?

It remains to ascertain whether or not the evils are remediless, and if not, what are the remedies? Fortunately, on this important point we are not left to mere speculation or theory. The experiment has been tried in several parishes in England, and found completely successful : and it is unnecessary to observe, that a remedy found effectual in one disorder, bids fair to be equally so in all disorders of an exactly similar type. The remedy is an asylum, where *labour will be found for the able-bodied, and support refused but in return for labour.* This has in many parishes diminished the applications for relief, and the poor rates 20, 30, 40, and in some, 50 per cent.

The principal means of effecting the reformation has been the abolition of the interference of the magistrates, who, strange to say, in almost every instance when the paupers appealed from the overseers, decided in favour of the appellants, although in most instances wholly unacquainted with the merits or demerits of the case, which the overseers had properly investigated. This shocking procedure was so uniform, that the overseers found themselves generally forced to comply with the demands of the paupers, often obstreperously and impudently preferred. Select vestries with final jurisdiction have been appointed in many of the parishes, and have in every instance produced the most salutary reformation.

" Some time ago, for instance, we had a lot of granite broken : there were not above 20 " per cent. of the men who began the work, who remained to work at all ; there were not " above 2 per cent. who remained the whole of the time during which the work lasted ! !"— *Report of Commissioners on Poor-laws*, p. 209.

" In June, 1821, a select vestry was formed : and although they had to clear off a debt of " £300, they speedily effected a great reduction of the rates. The cases were all investigated " respectively, and the relief adjusted by judgment of the vestry. *The expenditure, which,* " *according to the parliamentary returns, was £720 in 1819–20, was reduced to £347 in* " *1822–23, and to £216 in 1828–29.*"—*Idem*, p. 369.

" In Swallowfield, where it was partially effected, the rates were reduced from 9s. and 10s. " in the pound to 5s. 8d., and during the last year to 3s. 8d. in the pound."—*Idem*, p. 337.

" The able-bodied applicants for parochial relief increased in such numbers, that it has " recently been found necessary to recur to the use of the stone-yard to stem the influx : 900 " *of the applicants for relief were set to work ; only 85 have continued at work !!!*"—*Idem*, p. 210.

" He cited the cases of nine families who had applied for relief, but had refused it when " they were told they would be removed" [to the workhouse.] ' Six of these families,' he " said, ' had not only been saved from pauperism, but they were now *in a better situation* " *than he had ever before known them to be in.*' "—*Idem*, p. 208.

" The interference of the magistrates is unknown. The present acting guardian took on " himself the management in 1815. In four years *he reduced the expenditure* £2,600 ; and " though the population has nearly doubled since that period, the rates have never exceeded " what they were after that reduction."—*Idem*, p. 106.

" The parish officers of St. James's, Westminster, state, that ' on one occasion, in the " month of November last, upwards of 50 paupers were offered admission into the work- " house, in lieu of giving them out-door relief ; and that of that number *only four accepted* " *the offer ;*' and that ' since then, the same system has been pursued in a number of in- " stances, and *attended with a similar result.*' "—*Idem*, p. 214.

" All the lazy, profligate, and disorderly part of the community, necessarily entertain the " greatest possible disinclination to the hard labour and severe discipline enforced in every " well-conducted workhouse."—*E. R.* vol. xlvii. p. 308.

" The real use of a workhouse, is to be an asylum for the able-bodied poor ; for the maimed " and impotent poor may, speaking generally, be more advantageously provided for else- " where ; but it ought to be such an asylum as will not be resorted to, except by those who " have no other resource, and who are wholly without the means of supporting themselves." —*Ibid.*

" From the year 1821 to 1826, the average assessment was £3500 per annum ; from 1826 " to 1831, the average has been £1800. The population in 1821 was 5317 ; in 1831 it had " increased to 6341 ; thus exhibiting decreasing rates with an increasing population."— *Commissioners' Report*, p. 189.

" Previous to the establishment of this house, the average rates of the parish of Shardlow " were £570 ; since that period they have been reduced full one third. In the year ending

"1832 they were £344. 2s. The population in 1811 was 750; in 1831, 1091."—*Idem*, p. 193.

"Have you refused applicants relief unless they went into the house?—Yes; and a large "portion decline going into it, *and we get rid of them.*"—*Idem*, p. 205.

"The old system attracted vagabonds to the parish who have now left us, and kept many "in idleness, which led to pilfering. Some of these people I now see at work in the parish. "*The change, I am sure, has benefited the people themselves,* for they would commonly spend "two or three hours to get a sixpence in charity, rather than give an hour's labour to obtain "the same sixpence."—*Idem*, p. 268.

"What number of undeserving cases did you get rid of, in consequence of this alteration "and of your investigations? About 150 as an immediate consequence of this alteration; "but, all together, including the clearing of the workhouse (with which the magistrates had "nothing to do), *we got rid of about* 500 *in the course of two years.*"—*Ibid.*

"Very great numbers of lazy people, rather than submit to the confinement and labour of "the workhouse, are content to throw off the mask, and *maintain themselves by their own* "*industry.* And this was so remarkable here, at Maidstone, that when our workhouse was "finished, and public notice given that all who came to demand their weekly pay should be "immediately sent thither, *little more than half the poor upon the list came to the overseers* "*to receive their allowance.*"—*Idem*, p. 328.

"About ten or eleven years since, the officers of the town of Maidstone were induced, from "the great cost of the poor (which had increased, I think, to 7s. or 8s. per week each), to "set on foot some inquiries. The result was, that the officers reduced the diet: and after "enforcing the alteration for about two months, they contracted with a person to keep the "poor for about 3s. 3d. per head. They have continued the contracting system ever since." —*Idem*, p. 329.

"In the instances of individuals, as well as in several whole parishes, wherever the influ-"ence of the present system has been removed, the rise of the condition of the people has "been proportionate to the removal of that influence, or their previous depression. In Cook-"ham, where the change was most extensive, the parochial expenditure was reduced from "£3133 to £1155, and *the general condition of the labouring classes improved.*"—*Idem*, p. 337.

———————●❀●———————

Have I not produced a superabundance of proofs, that for 190 years the ope-ration of the poor-laws in England was beneficent and salutary; that the most enormous abuses have prevailed in their administration for nearly 40 years; that those abuses satisfactorily account for a large and oppressive increase of the poor rates; and that a universal rule to afford no relief to able-bodied men but for labour performed, the more severe the better, would apply a remedy to the great mass of the abuses? When men who do not employ labourers, are obliged to pay a portion of the earnings of those employed by their neighbours —when thieves and robbers are supported at the public expense—when pros-titutes with illegitimate children receive larger allowance from the overseers of the poor than honest widows with their legitimate offspring—when able-bodied men, refusing to work, are supported with weekly stipends, equal to the wages of honest industry, can we be surprised at the enormous increase of the poor rates? Can any thing be more unfair or illogical than to charge these hideous abuses of the laws to the laws themselves? And is it not cer-tain, that the introduction into every parish in the kingdom of such reforms as have taken place in Maidstone, Cookham, &c. &c., (whereby the rates were reduced 30, 40, and in some cases 60 per cent., although the population had increased, and the condition of the •poorer classes was improved,) would produce a great reduction of the rates, and a melioration of the state of society throughout the kingdom?

Philadelphia, July 13, 183?

ESSAY X.

It is to be observed, that a cause has been steadily and powerfully operating to increase the poor rates, wholly independent of the multifarious abuses above specified. I mean the rapid and oppressive reduction of wages, consequent on the wonderful improvements in machinery. Manual labour succumbs in the conflict with steam and water power: and as three-fourths of mankind depend on the labour of their hands for a support; and further, as at the best of times there is always a superabundance of labour in the market, every thing that supersedes the demand for that labour must increase competition; lower wages; produce distress; and, to the same extent, increase the poor rates.

Mr. Brougham has published an elaborate work on the advantages of the improvement of machinery.* But unhappily for his argument, he introduces in the very first page a powerful fact which fully proves that the advantages, admitting them to the full extent that he contends for, are accompanied by a mass of suffering that fully counterbalances all the good with which they are pregnant. He states that a certain Jos. Foster, a working weaver of Glasgow, being examined on the subject of wages, in 1827, by a committee of the British House of Commons, declared :

" That he and many others, who had formed themselves into a society, were in great dis-
" tress ; that numbers of them worked at the hand-loom FROM EIGHTEEN TO NINETEEN HOURS
" A DAY; that THEIR EARNINGS, AT THE UTMOST, DID NOT AMOUNT TO MORE THAN
" SEVEN SHILLINGS A WEEK; and that sometimes *they were as low as four shillings.* That
" twenty years before that time, *they could readily earn a pound a week* by the same indus-
" try: and that as *power-loom weaving had increased, the distress of the hand-weavers had*
" *also increased in the same proportion.*"

Here is an overwhelming fact on this subject, which must puzzle the Malthuses, the Seniors, the Editors of the Edinburgh Review, and all those who so loudly declaim against poor rates.

A large body of men, earning, as Foster says, twenty shillings a week in 1807, and gradually reduced to seven, six, or four shillings, in 20 years, might in the early period have been not only able to support themselves comfortably, but to save, in a few years, money enough to commence business on a small scale : whereas in process of time they would be reduced, step by step, to absolute pauperism, unable to support their families, and obliged to rely on eleemosynary aid, public or private. And let it be observed, that this is not a solitary case. The reduction has extended, in a greater or less degree, to almost every branch into which machinery has been introduced.†

* " The notion, that it can be nationally profitable to save the employment of labour by
" improvements in machinery, when *those whose labour is thus supplanted, must be supported*
" *in idleness, at the public expense,* is as irrational as it would be for the owner of a pair of
" carriage-horses, who is obliged by law, or the will under which he inherits, to keep them
" on good provender in his stable, *to attempt to save money by setting up a steam coach.*"—
Q. R. vol. xliii. p. 257.

† The effect of machinery to increase the poor rates is obvious from the following tables, by which it appears that the latter have increased, *pari passu,* with the increase of the former.

The spinning Jenny was invented by Hargreaves, in	1767
Arkwright's machine, worked by horse power, was invented in	1769
put in motion by water, in	1771
The mule Jenny, worked by hand, was invented by Crompton in	1775
Wm. Kelly applied machinery to it in	1792

It is obvious that the war of machinery upon manual labour was not confined to the cotton

" The hand-loom weavers are very numerous [in Burnley.] They weave coatse calicoes, " and *are not able to earn more than five shillings per week.*"—*Report of Commissioners* on the *Poor-laws*, p. 368.

" The wages of the manufacturing people were necessarily so low that *from the most labo-* " *rious exertions they could hardly procure a subsistence ; between six and seven shillings* " *being the extreme weekly earnings of an industrious man ; and he must work fourteen* " *hours a day to get that sum.* Mr. May, a master manufacturer, stated that he had known " the time when a stockinger could earn one pound sterling per week."—*Idem*, p. 185.

" The price of wheat, according to the account kept at Eton College, during the first men- " tioned years, (1767, 1768, 1770,) was 51s. a quarter ; and during 1810, 1811, its price was " 110s., being a rise of 115 per cent: and Mr. Young estimates that butchers' meat had " in the same period risen 146, butter 140, and cheese 153 per cent: being on an average, a " rise of 138½ per cent: so that wages, as compared with these articles, had DECLINED in the " interval considerably more than one *third*, or 38½ per cent. And if the increased cost of " tea, sugar, beer, leather, &c., besides the house-duty and window-tax, had been taken into " account, the diminished power of the labourer over the necessaries and comforts of life, " would have appeared still greater."—*E. R.* vol. xxxiii. p. 173.

" How then can we be surprised at the excess of poverty and misery which has been ex- " perienced since the peace ?"—*Ibid.*

" The poor rates have existed more than two centuries, and they incontestibly prove " the condition of the day labourer to be worse at present than at any former time during " that period. This, too, should be remembered, that the condition of the middle ranks has " been materially improved meanwhile : their comforts, their luxuries, their importance have " been augmented ten-fold : their intellectual enjoyments have been enlarged and multiplied ; " the situation of the poor would be relatively worse, if they had only remained stationary, " without receiving a proportional increase of comforts: but this has not been the case,—it " is absolutely worse. *The same quantity of labour will no longer procure the same quantity* " *of the necessaries of life.*"—*Q. R.* vol. xv. p. 195.

" In many parishes of Kent, Suffolk, Bedford, Essex, Norfolk, &c. wages were in 1824 as " low as 6d. a day, or 3s. a week : in others they amounted to 4s. and 5s.: in others again " to 6s., and in some they rose as high as 9s., which was the maximum."—*Ibid.*

" Mr. Mahony asserts, as the result of an extensive experience in the south and west of " Ireland, that the receipts of a day labourer throughout the year average but 5d. per diem. " The payment for a day's work is generally from 8d. to 10d., but deducting Sundays, saints' " days, bad weather, and occasional loss of time, the receipts average but half that sum."— Q. R. vol. xliv. 542.

" In the year 1786 the wages for spinning No. 100 cotton yarn was 10s. per pound ; in " 1790 they were reduced to 4s. ; and in a few years fell to 8d.:" that is to say, one fifteenth of the wages in 1786.—*Encyclopædia Britannica*, vol. xxiv. p. 397.

It would appear that the facts above adduced are abundantly sufficient to put down for ever the chief ground on which the opposition to the poor-laws rests ; that is, their assumed inevitable tendency to a ruinous and oppressive increase of poor rates. But unfortunately theorists blindly shut their eyes to opposing facts, and view with microscopic eye all those that appear to lend sanction to

and woollen branches, although more severely felt in these than in others. It went on in every other branch to which machinery was applicable.

Years.	Poor taxes. £	Population.	Poor rates per head.
1673	840,000*		3s. 4d.
1750	700,000†	6,467,000‡	2s. 2d.
1770	1,306,000†	7,428,000‡	3s. 5d.
1780	1,774,000†	7,953,000†	4s. 4d.
1790	2,569,009†	8,675,000†	5s. 11
1800	3,861,000†	9,168,000‡	8s. 5d.
1810	5,407,000†	10,502,500‡	10s. 3d.
1820	6,680,000†	11,977,663‡	11s.

    * F. M. Eden's State of the Poor, vol. i. p. 189.
    † Lowe on the Present State of England, pp. 185, 186.
    ‡ Statistical Tables, page 3.

their theories. The facts here stated are clear, decisive, and irrefragable ; and it is astonishing how those enlightened men, who have so long and so zealously trumpeted forth the supposed unavoidable evils of this system, should be so blind to their force as not to seek some other cause to account for its oppressive results.

It is believed that the poor are supported in Scotland by voluntary subscriptions, and that assessments for the support of the poor, and mendicity, are unknown. Both assertions appear to be egregiously erroneous, as may be seen by the annexed extracts. But even were they literally correct, it does not thence follow that the same reasoning would apply in England. The Scotch are a peculiar people. They are brought up with more advantages than most other people in Europe; their education is better attended to; their habits are more orderly. But with all these advantages, which are immensely valuable, they are obliged to have recourse to assessments for the support of the poor; and are moreover plagued with the heavy curse of mendicity.

" If the case of the poor in Scotland and Ireland be produced as a proof, that leaving them " to private charity would have a better effect than the rates of England, the answer is ob- " vious—that in Scotland they are not left to private charity in their principal cities, but are " admitted to a provision out of the funds of the general session of those cities."—*Ruggles's History of the Poor,* vol. ii. p. 78.

" Notwithstanding all the eulogiums which have been passed on the manner in which the " poor of Scotland are maintained, we find, that even at this moment, vagrant mendicity is " nearly universal in that country. Scotland possesses a series of very severe laws for the " suppression of vagrancy; and resolutions have been recently entered into, by more than " one county, to carry their provisions into effect."—*Q. R.* vol. xxxviii. p. 74.

" But these resolutions have hitherto proved unavailing, in consequence of the extreme " humanity of parishioners, who cannot resist listening to the plea of apparent distress, and " bestowing alms. It is indeed computed that the stranger poor carry away, in the shape of " alms, from the parish, more in value each year than would support comfortably the whole " poor on the parish-roll : and a general belief prevails, that the practice is attended with " many most hurtful effects, both to the best interests of the public, and to the morals of the " mendicant. They (i. e. the Committee of the Assembly) consider begging as a violation " of the whole provision, purposes, and spirit of our poor-laws; as a heavy loss to the com- " munity, of productive labour, from the wandering and idle habits of beggary; as encourag- " ing the vices of those who are professionally pilfering vagrants ; and as habituating, generally, " the pauper to duplicity, falsehood, improvidence, and dissipation."—*Minutes and Report of the Committee of the General Assembly,* 1818, p. 14.

But even if sufficient sums could be raised by voluntary contributions, there would be strong objections to this mode, as the burden would fall very unequally.

" By statutory provision the burden is equally laid upon persons of property, according to " their ability; while *in voluntary contributions, the richest are not always found the most* " *charitable.*"—*Q. R.* vol. xxviii. p. 354.

Philadelphia, July 16, 1833.

—●◉●—

ESSAY XI.

It now remains to consider the case of those countries where there are no taxes raised for the support of the poor, whose support is extorted by mendicity, and how far the plan of tolerating that abominable nuisance as a substitute, recommended by the Edinburgh Review, would be preferable to a statutory provision. This comparison affords the best, indeed the only correct criterion of the merits of the respective modes of providing for the poor.

In a publication issued at Paris about the close of the last century, say 1795, the latest account I have been able to procure, it is stated that there were then in that country 300,000 able-bodied beggars, who occasioned a loss to the state of 125,000,000 livres, equal to about $20,000,000. It is presumable that each ' able-bodied beggar,' on an average, had dependent on him at least two persons, a wife and a child.   Here is an aggregate of nearly a million of souls in a state of beggary, prowling abroad, and preying on the public to an enormous amount, levied merely on the charitable ; whereas, had the same sum been levied by law, it would have probably far more than supported all the paupers whose age and infirmity rendered them entitled to public aid, and been borne in somewhat like equitable proportions by the whole community.   To aggravate the evil, these beggars are " considered as the great nursery of all the robbers and assassins that infest the country."— *Q. R.* vol. xxxviii. p. 74.

" The population of Paris in 1823 was 713,966 souls, of whom 61,500 were entirely supported in hospitals and other charitable institutions, and 64,000 at their own houses."— *Idem,* p. 73.

" Notwithstanding this oppressive provision, *' her streets, her quays, and all her public places, are filled with mendicants !' "—Ibid.*

" The patrimony of the poor," says a report of the bureaux de charité, " was sufficient to support one fourth of the inhabitants, and yet the poor were in want."—*Q. R.* vol. xxxviii. p. 74.

" Naples is crowded with beggars, whose number defies all calculation.   I feel it indeed a " fruitless task for my pen to attempt a description of the scenes I have witnessed, and I lay " it down in despair—But no ! what I can tell is as much as need be known of human " misery.   As we step out of our house, twenty hats and open hands are stretched out to- " wards us.   We cannot take ten steps without meeting with a beggar, who crosses our path, " and with groans and piteous exclamations solicits our mite.   Women, often dressed in black " silk, and veiled, intrude themselves impudently upon us.   Cripples of all sorts hold up their " stump of a leg or an arm close to our eyes : noseless faces, devoured by disease, grin at us; " children quite naked, nay, even men, are to be seen lying and moaning in the dirt.   A drop- " sical man sits by the wall, and shows us his monstrous belly.   Consumptive mothers lie by " the road-side with naked children on their laps, who are compelled to be continually crying " aloud.   If we go to church, we must pass through a dozen such deplorable objects at the " door ; and when we enter, as many fall down on their knees before us.   Even in our dwell- " ings, we are not free from the painful spectacle."—*Kotzebue's Travels through Italy,* vol. i. pp. 251, 252.

" In large cities, in coming out of one house, you are fairly hunted till you get into an- " other ; the fraternity, however, appear to have this point of etiquette, that only one hunts " you at a time : but before you are out of sight of the former beggar, whom you have re- " lieved, you are considered fair game for the rest of the pack."—*Q. R.* vol. xxxviii. p. 73.

" If the whole sum which is paid in *misapplied* alms by the farmers and peasantry were " estimated, it would amount to a very heavy poor-tax !"—*Idem,* p. 530.

" Mr. B. Bryan calculates that there are half a million of houses in Ireland of the farming " class, each of which contributes in this way, on an average, a ton of potatoes a year towards " the support of the poor: *the value of this alone would be near two million of money."—Ibid.*

" In the kingdom of the Netherlands, Sweden, Norway, and Switzerland, the poor are pro- " vided for on a plan which does not essentially differ from our own, at a cost to the com- " munity, which, when compared with the wealth of each country, equals, at least, the highest " expense which has been found to attend the English system.   *Over all the remainder of* " *the continent, the mendicant system—the delight of the Malthusians—prevails in all its* " *vigour : but the intolerable burden of this system can only be conceived by those who have* " *witnessed its pressure."—Q. R.* vol. xxxviii. p. 72.

The worthlessness, the improvidence, the dissipation of the labouring classes are fertile themes of declamation with the new school of political economists. To those who cling to their wealth with the tenacity of " grim death," it is delightful to descant on these topics, as they regard them as a full justification of their invariable rejection of the claims of the poor.   But I have one strong fact in proof of the providence of a large portion of that class, which outweighs a volume of frothy declamation on the opposite side of the question.

" In 1815, there were no fewer than 925,439 individuals in England and Wales, being " about *one eleventh* of the then existing population, members of friendly societies, formed " for the express purpose of affording protection to the members during sickness and old age, " and *enabling them to subsist without resorting to the parish funds."—E. R.* vol. xlvii. p. 304.

It is highly probable that these were generally heads of families ; but say that only two-thirds were of that description, and that each of them averaged two in family besides himself, it would make an aggregate of about 2,150,000 souls of the labouring population, who do not look to the poor rates in times of sickness or want of employment. The population of England was at that time about 10,000,000 ; of course, the above number constituted a fifth of the whole. What a triumphant fact in favour of the providence of the labouring classes in England and Wales, notwithstanding the various circumstances connected with their situation, tending to degrade and render them reckless ! How complete a refutation of the unceasing vituperation under which they labour ! The importance of this fact is greatly enhanced by the consideration of the paltry wages the mass of the labouring classes receive ; and how ill they can spare any part of it to make such provident provision for future distress.

A feature in the connexion between the manufacturers and the operatives in England, which has a tendency to degrade and pauperize the latter, and, of course, to increase the poor rates, deserves to be noticed. When work is slack, the former combine to lower wages : this they can effect without any difficulty, their numbers being small ; of course they can readily co-operate in any plans they may form : and the necessities of the operatives, who depend on their weekly wages for their weekly support, oblige them to submit. But when the demand for goods is brisk, the rise of wages must be either voluntary on the part of the employers, which rarely takes place, or by an association among the operatives, which, considering their numbers, is not easily effected ; and which, moreover, if attempted to be enforced upon those who cannot or will not voluntarily acquiesce in the arrangement, is, by law, a criminal offence, subjecting the parties to fine and imprisonment. It is obvious, therefore, that the war is carried on between the manufacturers and their journeymen upon very unequal terms, to the great disadvantage of the latter.

Philadelphia, July 19, 1833.

—»•◉•«—

ESSAY XII.

It is frequently asked—what remedy can be found for the enormous and cruel oppression experienced by females employed as seamstresses on coarse work, spoolers, &c. ? While these classes are so much more numerous than the demand for their services requires, a complete remedy for the evil is, I am afraid, impracticable. I venture to suggest a few palliatives.

1. Public opinion, a powerful instrument, ought to be brought to bear on this subject. All honourable members of society, male and female, ought to unite in denouncing those who 'grind the faces of the poor,' by taking female labour without a compensation at least adequate for the support of human existence. The pulpit ought to unite in this crusade against a crying injustice, productive of such distressing consequences.

2. Let the employments of females be multiplied as much as possible. They are admirably calculated for various occupations from which they are at present in a great degree excluded, more especially shop-keeping in retail stores.

3. The poorer class ought to have exclusively the business of white-washing and other low employments, now in a great degree monopolized by men.

4. Let the Provident Societies, intended to furnish employment for women in winter, be munificently supported ; and let those Societies give fair and

E

liberal wages, following the laudable example of the Impartial Humane Society of Baltimore, and the Female Hospitable Society of Philadelphia.

5. Let the ladies have some of the poor women, who are half starved, making coarse shirts at 6, 8, and 10 cents each, taught fine needle-work, mantua-making, millinery, clear starching, quilting, &c. There is always a great want of women in these branches.

6. Let schools be opened for instructing poor women in cooking. Good cooks are always scarce.

7. Schools for young ladies, and infant schools, ought, with few exceptions, to be taught by females, who should be regularly educated for those important branches, which are peculiarly calculated for their sex, and which would afford excellent occupation for the daughters of reduced families.

8. Ladies who can afford it, ought to give out their sewing and washing, and pay fair prices. Let them display their economy in any other department than in one which has a tendency to distress and pauperize deserving persons of their own sex.

9. In the towns in the interior of the state, and in those in the western states, there is generally a want of females as domestics, seamstresses, &c. &c. ; and in factories, as spoolers, spinners, and weavers. It would be a most meritorious appropriation of a part of the superfluous wealth of the rich, to provide for sending some of the superabundant poor females of our cities to those places.

10. To crown the whole, let ladies who lead the fashion, take up the cause of these poor women, *con amore.* It is a holy cause. They may, with moderate exertions, render it fashionable to endeavour to rescue from unmerited and cruel sufferings, oppressed, forlorn, and neglected classes, as precious, I emphatically repeat, in the eye of Heaven, as the most exalted and high-minded among themselves.

Other palliatives might be devised, were public attention directed to the subject in any degree proportioned to its importance.

———◦❀◦———

I conclude these essays, by stating, in brief, the points which I undertook to prove, and which, I flatter myself, I have fully proved :

1. That the wages of seamstresses, employed on common work, of spoolers, &c. &c., are inadequate for their support, even if fully employed, and unincumbered with children.

2. That of course, when not fully employed, or when burdened with children, they must necessarily be in a state of constant pauperism.

3. That such a state of things in a prosperous country—" a land flowing with milk and honey"—is a national disgrace, and calls loudly for a remedy, at least for some mitigation of the evil.

4. That the wages of labourers on canals and turnpikes, of hod-men, &c., &c., are barely sufficient, if they have families (as the greater number of them have), to support them, when fully employed; and that, therefore, in case of sickness, or want of employment, they must depend in a greater or less degree on public or private aid.

5. That the operation of the poor-laws in England from 1601, when the system was enacted, till 1795, when the flood-gates of abuse and corruption were thrown wide open, was benignant and salutary.

6. That the exorbitant increase of the poor rates in England is chiefly owing to the enormous abuses in the administration of the poor-laws, but partly to the oppressive reduction of the price of labour, resulting from the great improvements in machinery.

7. That the countries which have no poor-laws, are subject to oppressive burdens, probably not inferior to those of the English, but in another form, that is, by mendicity.

8. That mendicants generally levy contributions on the humane and charitable, to three or four times the amount that would support an equal number of paupers, either in alms-houses or at their own dwellings.

How far I have succeeded in the establishment of these positions, must rest with the public at large, from whose decision there is no appeal. But be that decision what it may, it cannot deprive me of the gratification of having, at the expense of no small portion of obloquy from those with whose personal interests some of my doctrines interfere, pleaded as holy a cause as any of those which for years past have been presented at the bar of the public.

Philadelphia, July 20, 1833.

APPENDIX.

The following observations on the situation of the poor, on mendicity, and on poor-laws, by C. D. Colden, Esq., formerly Mayor of the city of New York, who had the best opportunity of judging on those important points, are so pertinent and so conclusive in favour of the doctrines advocated in this pamphlet, that I earnestly recommend them to the consideration of the public.

" A sentiment is very prevalent, that *our various charitable societies and our public esta-* " *blishment for the poor have a pernicious tendency.* We are called upon to look at Eng- " land, and to observe how she is burdened with paupers, and oppressed by her poor rates. " It is supposed that the increase of paupers among us is owing to our following her exam- " ple ; and that we are precipitating ourselves into the same embarrassments.

" I think *there is as little justice as humanity, in censuring our charitable establishments.* " I do not believe they augment the number of the poor. Paupers come here to avail them- " selves of the benevolence of our citizens ; but if these charities did not exist, the metropolis " would still be the natural resort in the winter, of all the destitute who could reach it. In- " stead of relieving them through the instrumentality of societies, we should meet them in " the street, and could not resist their appeals to our individual charity.

" I have read much of what has been written respecting the establishment of poor-houses, " and have paid attention to various plans which have been proposed for dispensing with " them ; but I never yet met with the suggestion of any plan which appeared to me to be " practicable, or which I thought would be endured in this country.

" In our own alms-house there were, when I last visited it, about 1600 paupers. I had " often heard it said that *many found shelter there who did not require or deserve an asy-* " *lum of that description.* I endeavoured to satisfy myself how far this suggestion was " founded in fact. After having seen every individual under the poor-house roof, and con- " versed with a great proportion of them, *I left the establishment with a conviction that none* " *were there as paupers who could with any humanity be turned out. We have been fre-* " *quently told that the poor and indigent should be left to rely on the charity of individuals.* " Let us suppose that the 1600 unfortunate people I have mentioned, were cast out, and told " they must beg. *I fear death would as often relieve them from misery, as charity.* But " suppose it were otherwise : would we, in this community, *endure the sight of the aged, the* " *infirm, and the cripple, asking alms of every passenger ? Would we endure to see our* " *fellow-creatures perishing in the streets ?* Such objects are presented in many of the cities " of Europe. In Naples, they are every-day occurrences. *It is not uncommon to see a* " *human being dying on the steps of a palace.* Here, I am certain, such scenes would not " be tolerated, though the expense of our public charities should be tenfold. But if we have " not these establishments, how are the poor to obtain relief, but by becoming mendicants ? " and when their physical powers are prostrated by age, sickness, or accident, what shall be " done with them ? Humanity forbids us to answer—*let them linger and die like beasts* " *upon our pavements.* An asylum must be provided for them ; and our charitable institu- " tions are no more than a compliance with this moral obligation. *If there be abuses, cor-* " *rect them ;* but do not let the abuses, if they exist, or pecuniary considerations, so far harden

"our hearts, or blind our judgments, as to induce us to abandon the poor to the precarious-
"ness of the individual charity they may chance to meet.

"As to the example of England, which we are called upon to regard with so much terror,
"I think it yet remains to be proved, that the multiplication of her paupers, or the pressure
"of her poor-laws on her wealthy citizens, *are justly to be imputed to either her public or*
"*private charities.* We are told that the facility with which alms may be obtained, sinks
"the independent spirit of the needy, and paralyzes a disposition to struggle for their own
"support. I do not believe the pride of man is so easily overcome, or that a mere invitation
"to dependence, is sufficient to induce him to accept it. We know that in England, the
"reduction of great naval and military establishments, * * * * and the astonishing
"operations of her labour-saving machines, have left millions of her citizens unemployed.

"There are so many to labour, and so little labour to be done, that many must be idle:
"or, if employed, it is for wages that will not enable them to provide the necessaries of life
"*If the manufacturer does not afford his workmen sufficient to support himself and his*
"*family, the deficiency must be, and is in England, drawn from the abundance of the*
"*wealthy.* It is in this way that one class of the population in England becomes necessarily
"dependent on the other.

"The rich are not only obliged to maintain the helpless, but their wealth must contribute to
"the support of their unemployed or pinched manufacturers. If the master manufacturer
"cannot afford to pay, or does not pay his workman but half what is necessary for his sub-
"sistence, the other half must be paid by poor rates, and the rich are in truth merely paying
"to support the manufactories, or for the labour from which the manufacturer derives his
"profits. Suppose there are five millions in England who cannot find employment; or that
"if they do, their wages will not purchase half what is necessary to sustain life; they must
"be maintained, in whole or in part, by the public. *Can it be right to charge this necessity*
"*to their charitable institutions? Suppose these were abolished; how would the condition*
"*of the one class or the other, of the poor or the rich, be meliorated?*

"The labourer could no more command work than he can now, and the rich would have to
"support him; if not by legal contributions, he would be compelled to do it by that force
"which no human laws are sufficient to restrain, when its exertions are the only means of
"preservation. *It does, therefore, appear to me unreasonable and unfounded, to impute the*
"*increase of paupers in England, and the consequent augmentation of her poor-rates, to*
"*the superabundance of her charity.*

"Our situation is not, and cannot be for ages, similar to that of England. While we have
"so many millions of acres of uncultivated land, it is impossible that any portion of our popu-
"lation should want employment.

"It is true, that just now, [1819] our cities are overwhelmed with deluded and destitute
"foreigners; but this is an evil which will in a little while cure itself, and the recurrence
"of which we must prevent by appropriate laws. But do not let us, from the vain dread of
"the evils of which England so loudly complains, *discourage charitable institutions, which,*
"*when duly regulated, are the highest ornaments of civilization.*

"There is one marked difference between our situation and that of England, which, I think,
"deserves to be noticed. The evils of want and poverty extend themselves to every part of
"her dominions. Indeed it is her land-holders and farmers, who most loudly complain of
"the oppression of her poor laws.

"With us, *the cause of complaint is entirely confined to our maritime cities. I do not*
"*believe there is a town in the state, in which the poor-rates amount to a mill, or a thou-*
"*sandth part upon the dollar.* This seems to me to show that the pauperism of our cities, is
"owing to adventitious circumstances; and that we have no reason to dread that we are
"extending a charity to the poor, which will bring upon us the calamities so much deplored
"in England.

"*We must always be content to bear with our due proportion of poor, as we must to*
"*share all other evils incident to humanity.* But in estimating what proportion we are to
"expect, and in comparing our own condition in this respect, with that of other countries, I
"think we ought not to forget, that while there are some circumstances peculiar to us which
"are favourable, there are others calculated to produce pauperism. Among these I would
"enumerate the following:

"The common drink of the poorer classes of our people is ardent spirits; and I cannot but
"think it unfortunate that this is so cheap, that a man can purchase as much as will make
"him drunk, for no more than would pay for a pot of porter in England.

"We have no standing army, or navy, that take off so many thousand idlers in other coun-
"tries. We have, to be sure, both an army and a navy; but they are on so small a scale,
"that their effects on society in this respect, are not felt. We have no transportation laws
"for crimes."

LECTURES

ON

THE ELEVATION

OF THE

LABOURING PORTION

OF THE

COMMUNITY.

BY WILLIAM E. CHANNING.

MANCHESTER:

ABEL HEYWOOD, 56 AND 60, OLDHAM STREET,

1840.

MANCHESTER
PRINTED BY A. HEYWOOD, 56 AND 60, OLDHAM-STREET.

INTRODUCTORY REMARKS.

THE following Lectures were prepared for two meetings of Mechanics, one of them consisting of Apprentices, the other of adults. For want of strength they were delivered only to the former, though in preparing them, I had kept the latter also in view. " The Mechanic Apprentices' Library Association," at whose request the Lectures are published, is an institution of much promise, not only furnishing considerable means of intellectual improvement, but increasing the self-respect and conducing to the moral safety of the members.

When I entered on this task, I thought of preparing only one lecture of the usual length. But I soon found, that I could not do justice to my veiws in so narrow a compass. I therefore determined to write at large, and to communicate through the press the results of my labour, if they should be thought worthy of publication. With this purpose, I introduced topics which I did not deliver, and which I thought might be usefully presented to some who might not hear me. I make this statement to prevent the objection, that the Lectures are not, in all things, adapted to those to whom they were delivered. Whilst written chiefly for a class, they were also intended for the community.

As the same general subject is discussed in these Lectures, as in the " Lecture on Self Culture," published last winter, there will, of course, be found in them that coincidence of thoughts, which always take place in the writings of a man, who has the inculcation of certain great principles much at heart. Still, the point of view, the mode of discussion, and the choice of topics differ much in the two productions ; so that my state of mind would be given very imperfectly were the present Lectures withheld.

This is, probably, the last opportunity I shall have for communicating with the labouring classes through the press. I may, therefore, be allowed to express my earnest wishes for their happiness, and my strong hope that they will justify the confidence of their friends, and will prove by their example the possibility of joining with labour all the improvements which do honour to our nature.

W. E. C.

BOSTON, FEB. 11, 1840.

LECTURE I.

It is with no common pleasure that I take part in the present course of lectures. Such a course is a sign of the times, and very interesting to all who are interested in the progress of their fellow creatures. We hear much of the improvements of our age. The wonders achieved by machinery are the common talk of every circle; but I confess that, to me, this gathering of mechanics' apprentices, whose chief bond of union is a library, and who come together weekly to refresh and improve themselves by the best instruction which the state of society places within their reach, is more encouraging than all the miracles of the machinist. In this meeting I see, what I desire most to see, that the mass of the people are beginning to comprehend themselves and their true happiness; that they are catching glimpses of the great work and vocation of human beings, and are rising to their true place in the social state. The present meeting indicates a far more radical, more important change in the world, than the steam engine, or the navigation of the Atlantic in a fortnight. That members of the labouring class, at the close of a day's work, should assemble in such a hall as this, to hear lectures on science, history, ethics, and the most stirring topics of the day, from men whose education is thought to fit them for the highest offices, is a proof of a social revolution, to which no bounds can be set, and from which too much cannot be hoped. I see in it a repeal of the sentence of degradation passed by ages on the mass of mankind. I see in it the dawn of a new era, in which it will be understood, that the first object of society is to give incitements and means of progress to all its members. I see in it the sign of the approaching triumph of men's spiritual over their outward and material interests. In the hunger and thirst for knowledge and for refined pleasures, which this course of lectures indicates in those who labour, I see that the spirit of man is not always to be weighed down by toils for animal life and by the appetite for animal indulgences. I do attach great importance to this meeting, not for its own sake or its immediate benefits, but as a token and pledge of a new impulse given to society through all its conditions. On this account I take more pleasure in speaking here, than I should feel in being summoned to pronounce a show-oration before all the kings and nobles on earth. In truth, it is time to have done with shows. The age is too stirring, we are pressed on by too solemn interests, to he justified in making speeches for self-display or mere amusement. He who cannot say something in sympathy with, or in aid of, the great movements of humanity, might as well hold his peace.

With these feelings and convictions, I am naturally, almost necessarily, led to address you on a topic, which must ensure the attention of such an audience, namely, the elevation of that portion of the community who subsist by the labour of the hands. This work, I have said, is going on. I may add, that it is advancing no where so rapidly as in this city. I do not believe that, on the face of the earth, the spirit of improvement has anywhere seized so strongly on those who live by the sweat of the brow, as among ourselves. Here it is nothing rare to meet the union of intellectual culture and self-respect with hard work. Here the prejudice against labour as degrading has very much given way. This, then, is the place where the subject, which I have proposed, should be discussed. We ought to consider, in what the true elevation of the labouring portion consists, how far it is practicable, and how it may be helped onward. The subject, I am aware, is surrounded with much prejudice and error. Great principles need to be brought out and their application plainly stated. There are serious objections to be met, fears to be disarmed, and rash hopes to be crushed. I do not profess to have mastered the topic. But I can claim one merit, that of coming to the discussion with a feeling of its importance, and with a deep interest in the class of people whom it concerns. I trust

6

that this expression of interest will not be set down as mere words, or as meant to answer any selfish purpose. A politician, who professes attachment to the people, is suspected to love them for their votes; but a man, who neither seeks nor would accept any place within their gift, may hope to be listened to as their friend. As a friend, I would speak plainly. I cannot flatter. I see defects in the labouring classes. I think, that as yet the greater part of them have made little progress; that the prejudices and passions, the sensuality and selfishness of multitudes among them, are formidable barriers to improvement; that multitudes have not waked as yet even to a dim conception of the end for which they are to struggle. My hopes do not blind me to what exists; and, with this clear sense of the deficiencies of the multitude of men, I cannot, without guilt, minister to their vanity. Not that they alone are to be charged with deficiencies. Look where we may, we shall discern in all classes ground for condemnation; and whoever would do good ought to speak the truth of all, only remembering that he is to speak with sympathy, and with a consciousness of his own fallibleness and infirmity.

In giving my views of the elevation of the labouring multitude, I wish that it may be understood, that I shall often speak prospectively, or of changes and improvements, which are not to be expected immediately, or soon; and this I say that I may not be set down as a dreamer, expecting to regenerate the world in a day. I fear, however, that this explanation will not shield me from this and like reproaches. There are men, who, in the face of all history, of the great changes wrought in men's condition, and of the new principles which are now acting on society, maintain that the future is to be a copy of the past, and probably a faded rather than a bright copy. From such I differ, and did I not differ I would not stand here. Did I expect nothing better from human nature than I see, I should have no heart for the present effort, poor as it may be. I see the signs of a better futurity, and especially signs that the large class, by whose toil we all live, are rising from the dust; and this faith is my only motive to what I now offer.

The elevation of the labouring portion of society: this is our subject. I shall first consider, in what this consists. I shall then consider some objections to its practicableness, and to this point shall devote no small part of the discussion; and shall close the subject with giving some grounds of my faith and hope, in regard to the most numerous class of our fellow-beings,

What is to be understood by the elevation of the labouring class? This is our first topic. To prevent misapprehension, I will begin with stating what is not meant by it, in what it does not consist. I say, then, that by the elevation of the labourer, I do not understand that he is to be raised above the need of labour. I do not expect a series of improvements, by which he is to be released from his daily work. Still more, I have no desire to dismiss him from his workshop and farm, to take the spade and axe from his hand, and to make his life a long holiday. I have faith in labour, and I see the goodness of God in placing us in a world where labour alone can keep us alive. I would not change, if I could, our subjection to physical laws, our exposure to hunger and cold, and the necessity of constant conflicts with the material world. I would not, if I could, so temper the elements, that they should infuse into us only grateful sensations, that they should make vegetation so exuberant as to anticipate every want, and the minerals so ductile as to offer no resistance to our strength or skill. Such a world would make a contemptible race. Man owes his growth, his energy, chiefly to that striving of the will, that conflict with difficulty, which we call effort. Easy, pleasant work does not make robust minds, does not give men a consciousness of their powers, does not train them to endurance, to perseverance, to steady force of will; that force without which all other acquisitions avail nothing. Manual labour is a school, in which men are placed to get energy of purpose and character, a vastly more important endowment than all the learning of all other schools. They are placed, indeed, under hard masters, physical sufferings and wants, the power of fearful elements, and the vicissitudes of all human things; but these stern teachers do a work which no compassionate, indulgent friend could do for us; and true wisdom will bless Providence for their sharp ministry. I have great faith in hard work. The material world does much for the mind by its beauty and order; but it does more for our minds by the pains it inflicts, by its obstinate resistance, which nothing but patient toil can overcome, by its vast forces, which nothing but unremitting skill and effort can turn to our use, by its perils, which demand continual vigilance, and by its tendencies to decay. I believe that difficuties are more important to the human mind than what we call assistances. Work we all must, if we mean to bring out and perfect our nature. Even if we do not work with the hands, we must undergo equivalent toil in some other direction. No business or study which does not present obstacles, tasking to the full the intellect and the will, is worthy of a man. In science, he who does not grapple with hard questions, who does not concentrate his whole intellect in vigorous attention, who does not aim to penetrate what at first repels him, will never attain to mental force. The uses of toil reach beyond the present world. The capacity of steady, earnest labour is I apprehend, one of our great preparations for another state of being. When I see the vast amount of toil required of men, I feel that it must have important connections with their future existence, and that he who has met this discipline manfully, has laid one essential foundation of improvement, exertion, and happiness in the world to come. You will here see that to me labour has great dignity. It is not merely the grand instrument by which the earth is overspread with fruitfulness and beauty, and the ocean subdued, and matter wrought into innumerable forms for comfort and ornament: it has a far higher function, which is, to give force to the will, efficiency, courage, the capacity of endurance, and of persevering devotion to far-reaching plans. Alas, for the man who has not learned to work! He is a poor creature. He does not know himself. He depends on others, with no capacity of making returns for the support they give; and let him not fancy that he has a monopoly of enjoyment. Ease, rest owes its deliciousness to toil; and no toil is so burdensome as the rest of him who has nothing to task and quicken his powers.

I do not, then, desire to release the labourer from toil. This is not the elevation to be sought for him. Manual labour is a great good; but in so saying I must be understood to speak of labour in its just proportions. In excess it does great harm. It is not a good, when made the sole work of life. It must be joined with higher means of improvement, or it degrades instead of exalting. Man has a various nature, which requires a variety of occupation and discipline for its growth. Study, meditation, society, and relaxation should be mixed up with his physical toils. He has intellect, heart, imagination, taste, as well as bones and muscles; and he is grievously wronged, when compelled to exclusive drudgery for bodily subsistence. Life should be an alternation of employments, so diversified as to call the whole man into action. Unhappily our present civilization is far from realizing this idea. It tends to increase the amount of manual toil, at the very time that it renders this toil less favourable to the culture of the mind. The division of labour, which distinguishes civilized from savage life, and to which we owe chiefly the perfection of the arts, tends to dwarf the intellectual powers, by confining the activity of the individual to a narrow range, to a few details, perhaps to the heading of pins, the pointing of nails, or the tying together of broken strings; so that while the savage has his faculties sharpened by various occupations, and by exposure to various perils, the civilized man treads a monotonous, stupifying round of unthinking toil. This cannot, must not always be. Variety of action, corresponding to the variety of human powers, and fitted to develope all, is the most important element of human civilization. It should be the aim of the philanthropist. In proportion as Christianity shall spread the spirit of brotherhood, there will and must be a more equal distribution of toils and means of improvement. That system of labour which saps the health, and shortens life, and famishes intellect, needs, and must receive, great modification. Still, labour in due proportion is an important part of our present toil. It is the condition of all outward comforts and improvements, whilst, at the same time, it conspires with higher means and influences in ministering to the vigour and growth of the soul. Let us not fight against it. We need this admonition, because, at the present moment, there is a general disposition to shun labour; and this ought to be regarded as a bad sign of our times. The city is thronged with adventurers from the country, and the liberal professions are overstocked, in the hope of escaping the primeval sentence of living by the sweat of the brow; and to this crowding of men into trade we owe not only the neglect of agriculture, but what is far worse, the demoralization of the community. It generates excessive competition, which of necessity generates fraud. Trade is turned to gambling; and a spirit of mad speculation exposes public and private interest to a disastrous instability. It is, then, no part of the philanthropy which would elevate the labouring body, to exempt them from manual toil. In truth, a wise philanthropy would, if possible, persuade all men of all conditions to mix up a measure of this toil with their other pursuits. The body as well as the mind needs vigorous exertion, and even the studious would be happier were they trained to labour as well as thought. Let us learn to regard manual toil as the true discipline of man. Not a few of the wisest, grandest spirits have toiled at the work-bench and the plough.

I have said that, by the elevation of the labouring mass, I do not mean that they are to be released from labour. I add in the next place, that this elevation is not to be gained by efforts to force themselves into what are called the upper ranks of society. I wish them to rise, but I have no desire to transform them into gentlemen or ladies, according to the common acceptation of these terms. I desire for them not an outward and showy, but and inward and real change; not to give thom new titles and an artificial rank, but substantial improvements and real claims to respect. I have no wish to dress them from a Parisian tailor's shop, or to teach them manners from a dancing school. I have no desire to see them, at the end of the day, doff their working dress, that they may play a part in richly attired circles. I have no desire that they should be admitted to luxurious feasts, or should get a taste for gorgeous upholstery. There is nothing cruel in the necessity which sentences the multitude of men to eat, dress, and lodge plainly and simply, especially where the sentence is executed so mildly as in this country. In this country, where the demand for labour is seldom interrupted, and the openings for enterprise are numerous beyond precedent, the labouring class, with few exceptions, may well be satisfied with their accommodations. Very many of them need nothing but a higher taste for beauty, order, and neatness, to give an air of refinement and grace as well as comfort to their establishments. In this country the mass of labourers have their share of outward good. Their food, abundant and healthful, seasoned with the appetite which labour gives, is, on the whole, sweeter, as well as healthier, than the elaborate luxuries of the prosperous; and their sleep is sounder and more refreshing than falls to the lot of the less employed. Were it a possible thing, I should be sorry to see them turned into men and women of fashion. Fashion is a poor vocation. Its creed, that idleness is a privilege, and work a disgrace, is among the deadliest errors. Without depth of thought, or earnestness of feeling, or strength of purpose, living an unreal life, sacrificing substance to show, substituting the factitious for the natural, mistaking a crowd for society, finding its chief pleasure in ridicule, and exhausting its ingenuity in expedients for killing time, fashion is among the last influences under which a human being, who respects himself or who comprehends the great end of life, would desire to be placed. I use strong language, because I would combat the disposition, too common in the labouring mass, to regard what is called the upper class with envy or admiration. This disposition manifests itself among them in various forms. Thus, when one of their number prospers, he is apt to forget his old acquaintance, and to work his way, if possible, into a more fashionable caste. As far, indeed, as he extends his acquaintance among the intelligent, refined, generous, and truly honourable, he makes a substantial improvement of his condition; but if, as is too often the case, he is admitted by way of favour into a circle which has few claims, beyond those of greater luxury and show, and which bestows on him a patronizing condescending notice, in exchange for his old, honourable influence among his original associates, he does any thing but rise. Such is not the elevation I desire for the labourer. I do not desire him to struggle into another rank. Let him not be a servile copyist of other classes, but aim at something higher than has yet been realized in any body of men. Let him not associate the idea of dignity or honour with certain modes of living, or certain outward connections. I would have every man stand on his own ground, and take his place among men according to personal endowments and worth, and not according to outward appendages; and I would have every member of the community furnished with such means of improvement, that, if faithful to himself, he may need no outward appendage to attract the respect of all around him.

I have said that the people are not to be elevated by escaping labour or by pressing into a different rank. Once more, I do not mean by the elevation of the people, that they should become self-important politicians; that, as individuals or a class, they should seize on political power; that by uniting their votes they should triumph over the more prosperous; or that they should succeed in bending the administration of government to their particular interests. An individual is not elevated by figuring in public affairs, or even by getting into office. He needs previous elevation, to save him from disgrace in his public relations. To govern one's self, not others, is true glory. To serve through love, not to rule, is Christian greatness. Office is not dignity. The lowest men, because most faithless to principle, most servile to opinion, are to be •found in office. I am sorry to say it, but the truth should be spoken, that, at the present moment, political action in this country does little to lift up any who are concerned in it. It stands in opposition to a high morality. Politics, indeed, regarded as the study and pursuit of the true, enduring good of a community, as the application of great unchangeable principles to public affairs, is a noble sphere of thought and action; but politics, in its common sense, or considered as the invention of temporary shifts, as the playing of a subtle game, as the tactics of party for gaining power and the spoils of office, and for elevating one set of men above another, is a paltry and debasing concern. The labouring class are sometimes stimulated to seek power as a class, and this it is thought will raise them. But no class as such should bear rule among us. All conditions of society should be represented in the government, and alike protected by it; nor can any thing be expected but disgrace to the individual and the country, from the success of any class in grasping at a monopoly of political power. I would by no means discourage the attention of the people to politics. They ought to study in earnest the interest of the country, the principles of our institutions, the tendencies of public measures. But the unhappiness is, they do not *study ;* and, until they do, they cannot rise by political action. A great amount of time, which, if well used, would form an enlightened population, is now wasted on newspapers and conversations, which inflame the passions, which, unscrupulously, distort the truth, which denounce moral independence as treachery to one's party, which agitate the country for no higher end than a triumph over opponents ; and thus multitudes are degraded into men-worshippers or men-haters, into the dupes of the ambitious, or the slaves of a faction. To rise, the people must substitute reflection for passion. There is no other way. By these remarks, I do not mean to charge on the labouring class all the passionateness of the country. All classes partake of the madness, and all are debased by it. The fiery spirits are not confined to one portion of the community. The men, whose ravings resound through the hall of Congress, and are then circulated through the country as eloquence, are not taken from among those who toil. Party prejudices break out as fiercely on the exchange, and even in the saloon, as in the workshop. The disease has spread everywhere. Yet it does not dishearten me, for I see that it admits of mitigation, if not of cure. I trust, that these lectures and other sources of intellectual enjoyment now opening to the public, will abate the fever of political excitement, by giving better occupation to the mind. Much, too, may be hoped from the growing self-respect of the people, which will make them shrink indignantly from the disgrace of being used as blinded partizans and unreflecting tools. Much also is to be hoped from the discovery, which must sooner or later be made, that the importance of government is enormously overrated, that it does not deserve all this stir, that there are vastly more effectual means of human happiness. Political institutions are to be less and less deified, and to shrink into a narrow space ; and just in proportion as a wiser estimate of government prevails, the present phrenzy of political excitement will be discovered and put to shame.

B

I have now said what I do not mean by the elevation of the labouring classes. It is not an outward change of condition. It is not release from labour. It is not struggling for another rank. It is not political power. I understand something deeper. I know but one elevation of a human being, and that is elevation of soul. Without this, it matters nothing where a man stands or what he possesses ; and with it, he towers, he is one of God's nobility, no matter what place he holds in the social scale. There is but one elevation for a labourer, and for all other men. There are not different kinds of dignity for different orders of men, but one and the same to all. The only elevation of a human being, consists in the exercise, growth, energy of the higher principles, and powers of his soul. A bird may be shot upwards to the skies by a foreign force ; but it rises, in the true sense of the word, only when it spreads its own wings and soars by its own living power. So a man may be thrust upward into a conspicuous place by outward accidents ; but he rises, only in so far as he exerts himself, and expands his best faculties, and ascends by a free effort to a nobler region of thought and action. Such is the elevation I desire for the labourer, and I desire no other. This elevation is indeed to be aided by an improvement of his outward condition, and, in turn, greatly improves his outward lot; and thus connected, outward good is real and great ; but supposing it to exist in separation from inward growth and life, it would be nothing worth, nor would I raise a finger to promote it.

I know it will be said that such elevation as I have spoken of, is not and cannot be within the reach of the labouring multitude, and of consequence they ought not to be tantalized with dreams of its attainment. It will be said that the principal part of men, are plainly designed to work on matter for the acquisition of material and corporeal good, and that, in such, the spirit is of necessity too wedded to matter to rise above it. This objection will be considered by and by ; but I would just observe, in passing, that the objector must have studied very carelessly the material world, if he suppose that it is meant to be the grave of the minds of most of those who occupy it. Matter was made for spirit, body for mind. The mind, the spirit, is the end of this living organization of flesh and bones, of nerves and muscles ; and the end of this vast system of sea and land, and air and skies. This unbounded creation of sun and moon, and stars, and clouds, and seasons was not ordained merely to feed and clothe the body, but first and supremely to awaken, nourish, and expand the soul, to be the school of the intellect, the nurse of thought and imagination, the field for the active powers, a revelation of the Creator, and a bond of social union. We were placed in the material creation, not to be its slaves, but to master it, and to make it a minister to our highest powers. It is interesting to observe, how much the material world does for the mind. Most of the sciences, arts, professions, and occupations of life, grow out of our connexion with matter. The natural philosopher, the physician, the lawyer, the artist, and the legislator, find the objects, or occasions, of their researches in matter. The poet borrows his beautiful imagery from matter. The sculptor and painter express their noble 'conceptions through matter. Material wants rouse the world to activity. The material organs of sense, especially the eye, wake up infinite thoughts in the mind. To maintain, then, that the mass of men are and must be so immersed in matter, that their souls cannot rise, is to contradict the great end of their connexion with matter. I maintain, that the philosophy which does not see in the laws and phenomena of outward nature, the means of awakening mind, is lamentably shortsighted; and that a state of society, which leaves the mass of men to be crushed and famished in soul by excessive toils on matter, is at war with God's designs, and turns into means of bondage what was meant to free and expand the soul.

Elevation of soul, this is to be desired for the labourer as for every human being, and what does this mean? The phrase, I am aware, is vague, and often serves for mere declamation. Let me strive convey some precise ideas of it; and, in doing this, I can use no language which will save the hearer from the necessity of thought. The subject is a spiritual one. It carries us into the depth of our own nature, and I can say nothing about it worth saying, without tasking your powers of attention, without demanding some mental toil. I know that these lectures are meant for entertainment rather than mental labour; but, as I have told you, I have great faith in labour, and I feel that I cannot be more useful than in exciting the hearer to some vigorous action of mind.

Elevation of soul, in what does this consist? Without aiming at philosophical exactness I shall convey a sufficiently precise idea of it, by saying that it consists, first, in force of thought exerted for the acquisition of truth, secondly, in force of pure and generous feeling, thirdly, in force of moral purpose. Each of these topics needs a lecture for its development. I must confine myself to the first; from which, however, you may learn in a measure my views of the other two. Before entering on this topic, let me offer one

preliminary remark. To every man who would rise in dignity as a man, be he rich or poor, ignorant or instructed, there is one essential condition, one effort, one purpose, without which not a step can be taken. He must resolutely purpose and labour to free himself from whatever he knows to be wrong in his motives and life. He who habitually allows himself in any known crime or wrong doing, effectually bars his progress towards a higher intellectual and moral life. On this point every man should deal honestly with himself. If he will not listen to his conscience, 'rebuking him for violations of plain duty, let him not dream of self-elevation. The foundation is wanting. He will build, if at all, in sand.

I now proceed to my main subject. I have said that the elevation of a man is to be sought, or rather consists, first, in force of thought exerted for the acquisition of truth; and to this I ask your serious attention. Thought is the fundamental distinction of mind, and the great work of life. All that a man does outwardly is but the expression and completion of his inward thought. To work effectually, he must think clearly: to act nobly, he must think nobly. Intellectual force is a principal element of the soul's life, and should be proposed by every man as a principal end of his being. It is common to distinguish between the intellect and the conscience, between the power of thought and virtue, or holiness, and to say that virtuous action is worth more than strong thinking. But we mutilate our nature by thus drawing lines between actions or energies of the soul, which are intimately, indissolubly bound together. The head and the heart are not more vitally connected than thought and virtue. What is conscience, but the highest act of the intellect? Do we not degrade it by making it a mere feeling? Is it not something more? Is it not a wise discernment of the right, the holy, the good? Take away thought from virtue, and what remains worthy of a man? Is not high virtue more than blind instinct? Is it not founded on, and does it not include clear, bright perceptions of what is lovely and grand in character and action? Without power of thought, what we call conscientiousness, or a desire to do right, shoots out into illusion, exaggeration, pernicious excess. The most cruel deeds on earth have been perpetrated in the name of conscience. Men have hated and murdered one another from a sense of duty. The worst frauds have taken the name of pious. Thought, intelligence, is the dignity of a man, and no man is rising but in proportion as he is learning to think clearly and forcibly, or directing the energy of his mind to the acquisition of truth. Every man, in whatsoever condition, is to be a student. No matter what other vocation he may have, his chief vocation is to think. I say every man is to be a student, a thinker. This does not mean, that he is to shut himself within four walls and bend body and mind over books. Men thought before books were written, and some of the greatest thinkers never entered what we call a study. Nature, scripture, society, and life present perpetual subjects for thought; and the man who collects, concentrates, employs his faculties on any of these subjects for the purpose of getting the truth, is so far a student, a thinker, a philosopher, and is rising to the dignity of a man. It is time that we should cease to limit to professed scholars the titles of thinkers, philosophers. Whoever seeks truth with an earnest mind, no matter when or how, belongs to the school of intellectual men.

In a loose sense of the word, all men may be said to think; that is, a succession of ideas, notions, passes through their minds from morning to night; but, in as far as this succession is passive, undirected, or governed only by accident and outward impulse, it has little more claim to dignity than the experience of the brute, who receives, with like passiveness, sensations from abroad through his working hours. Such thought, if thought it may be called, having no aim, is as useless, as the vision of an eye, which rests on nothing, which flies without pause over earth and sky, and of consequence receives no distinct image. Thought, in its true sense, is an energy of intellect. In thought, the mind not only receives impressions or suggestions from without or within, but re-acts upon them, collects its attention, concentrates its forces upon them, breaks them up and analyzes them, like a living laboratory, and then combines them anew, traces their connexions, and thus impresses itself on all the objects which engage it.

The universe in which we live was plainly meant by God to stir up such thought as has now been described. It is full of difficulty and mystery, and can only be penetrated and unravelled by the concentration of the intellect. Every object, even the simplest in nature and society, every event of life, is made up of various elements subtly bound together; so that to understand any thing, we must reduce it from its complexity to its parts and principles, and examine their relations to one another. Nor is this all. Every thing which enters the mind, not only contains a depth of mystery in itself, but is connected by a thousand ties with all other things. The universe is not a disorderly, disconnected heap, but a beautiful whole, stamped through-

out with unity, so as to be an image of the One Infinite Spirit. Nothing stands alone: all things are knit together, each existing for all, and all for each. The humblest object has infinite connexions. The vegetable which you saw on your table to-day, came to you from the first plant which God made to grow on the earth, and was the product of the rains and sunshine of six thousand years. Such a universe demands thought to be understood; and we are placed in it to think, to put forth the power within, to look beneath the surface of things, to look beyond particular facts and events to their causes and effects, to their reasons and ends, their mutual influences, their diversities and resemblances, their proportions and harmonies, and the general laws which bind them together. This is what I mean by thinking; and by such thought the mind rises to a dignity, which humbly represents the greatness of the Divine intellect; that is, it rises more and more to consistency of views, to broad general principles, to universal truths, to glimpses of the order and harmony and infinity of the Divine system, and thus to a deep, enlightened veneration of the Infinite Father. Do not be startled, as if I were holding out an elevation of mind utterly to be despaired of; for all thinking, which aims honestly and earnestly to see things as they are, to see them in their connexions, and to bring the loose, conflicting ideas of the mind into consistency and harmony, all such thinking, no matter in what sphere, is an approach to the dignity of which I speak. You are all capable of the thinking which I recommend: you have all practised it in a degree. The child who casts an inquiring eye on a new toy, and breaks it to pieces that he may discover the mysterious cause of its movements, has begun the work of which I speak, has begun to be a philosopher, has begun to penetrate the unknown, to seek consistency and harmony of thought; and let him go on as he has begun, and make it one great business of life to inquire into the elements, connexions, and reasons of whatever he witnesses in his own breast, or in society, or in outward nature, and, be his condition what it may, he will rise by degrees to a freedom and force of thought, to a breadth and unity of views, which will be to him an inward revelation and promise of the intellectual greatness for which he was created.

You will observe, that in speaking of force of thought as the elevation of the labourer and of every human being, I have continually supposed this force to be exerted for the purpose of acquiring truth. I beg you never to lose sight of this motive, for it is essential to intellectual dignity. Force of thought may be put forth for other purposes, to amass wealth for selfish gratification, to give the individual power over others, to blind others, to weave a web of sophistry, to cast a deceitful lustre on vice, to make the worse appear the better cause. But energy of thought, so employed, is suicidal. The intellect, in becoming a pander to vice, a tool of the passions, an advocate of lies, becomes not only degraded, but diseased. It loses the capacity of distinguishing truth from falsehood, good from evil, right from wrong; it becomes as worthless as an eye, which cannot distinguish between colours or forms. Woe to that mind which wants the love of truth! For want of this, genius has become a scourge to the world, its breath a poisonous exhalation, its brightness a seducer into paths of pestilence and death. Truth is the light of the Infinite Mind, and the image of God in his creatures. Nothing endures but truth. The dreams, fictions, theories which men would substitute for it, soon die. Without its guidance effort is vain, and hope baseless. Accordingly, the love of truth, a deep thirst for it, a deliberate purpose to seek it and hold it fast, may be considered as the very foundation of human culture and dignity. Precious as thought is, the love of truth is still more precious; for without it, thought wanders and wastes itself, and precipitates men into guilt and misery. There is no greater defect in education and the pulpit, than that they inculcate so little an impartial, earnest, reverential love of truth, a readiness to toil, to live, and die for it. Let the labouring man be imbued in a measure with this spirit; let him learn to regard himself as endowed with the power of thought for the very end of acquiring truth; let him learn to regard truth as more precious than his daily bread; and the spring of true and perpetual elevation is touched within him. He has begun to be a man; he becomes one of the elect of his race. Nor do I despair of this elevation of the labourer. Unhappily, little, almost nothing, has been done as yet, to inspire either rich or poor with the love of truth for its own sake, or for the life, and inspiration, and dignity it gives to the soul. The prosperous have as little of it as the labouring mass. I think, indeed, that the spirit of luxurious, fashionable life is more hostile to it than the hardships of the poor. Under a wise culture, this spirit may be awakened in all classes, and wherever awakened, it will form philosophers, successful and noble thinkers. These remarks seem to me particularly important, as showing how intimate a union subsists between the moral and intellectual nature, and how both must work together from the beginning. All human culture rests on a moral foundation, on

an impartial, disinterested spirit, on a willingness to make sacrifices to the truth. Without this moral power, mere force of thought avails nothing towards our elevation.

I am aware that I shall be told that the work of thought which I have insisted on is difficult, that to collect and concentrate the mind for the truth is harder than to toil with the hands. Be it so. But are we weak enough to hope to rise without toil? Does any man, labourer or not, expect to invigorate body or mind without strenuous effort? Does not the child grow and get strength by throwing a degree of hardship, and vehemence, and conflict into his very sports? Does not life without difficulty become insipid and joyless? Cannot a strong interest turn difficulty into pleasure? Let the love of truth, of which I have spoken, be awakened, and obstacles in the way to it will whet, not discourage, the mind, and inspire a new delight into its acquisition.

I have hitherto spoken of force of thought in general. My views will be given more completely and distinctly, by considering, next, the objects on which this force is to be exerted. These may be reduced to two classes, Matter and Mind; the physical world which falls under our eyes, and the spiritual world. The working man is particularly called to make matter his study, because his business is to work on it, and he works more wisely, effectually, cheerfully and honourably, in proportion as he knows what he acts upon, knows the laws and forces of which he avails himself, understands the reason of what he does, and can explain the changes, which fall under his eye. Labour becomes a new thing, when thought is thrown into it, when the mind keeps pace with the hands. Every farmer should study chemistry. so as to understand the elements or ingredients, which enter into soils, vegetation, and manures, and the laws according to which they combine with and are loosened from one another. So the mechanic should understand the mechanic powers, the laws of motion, and the history and composition of the various substances which he works on. Let me add, that the farmer and the mechanic should cultivate the perception of beauty. What a charm and new value might the farmer add to his grounds and cottage, were he a man of taste? The product of the mechanic, be it great or small, a house or a shoe, is worth more, some times much more, if he can succeed in giving it the grace of proportion. In France, it is not uncommon to teach drawing to mechanics, that they may get a quick eye and a sure hand, and may communicate to their works the attraction of beauty. Every man should aim to impart this perfection to his labours. The more of mind we carry into toil, the better. Without a habit of thought, a man works more like a brute or machine, than like a man. With it his soul is kept alive amidst his toils. He learns to fix an observing eye on the processes of his trade, catches hints which abridge labour, gets glimpses of important discoveries, and is sometimes able to perfect his art. Even now, after all the miracles of invention which honour our age, we little suspect what improvements of machinery are to spring from spreading intelligence and natural science among workmen.

But I do not stop here. Nature is to engage our force of thought, not simply for the aid which the knowledge of it gives in working, but for a higher end. Nature should be studied for its own sake, because so wonderful a work of God, because impressed with his perfection, because radiant with beauty, and grandeur, and wisdom and beneficence. A labourer like every other man is to be liberally educated, i. e. he is to get knowledge not only for his bodily subsistence, but for the life and growth and elevation of his mind. Am I asked, whether I expect the labourer to traverse the whole circle of the physical sciences? Certainly not; nor do I expect the merchant, or the lawyer, or preacher to do it. Nor is this at all necessary to elevation of soul. The truths of physical science, which give greatest dignity to the mind, are those general laws of the creation, which it has required ages to unfold, but which an active mind, bent on self-enlargement, may so far study and comprehend, as to interpret the changes of nature perpetually taking place around us, as to see in all the forces of the universe the workings of one Infinite Power, and in all its arrangements the manifestation of one unsearchable wisdom.

And this leads me to observe the second great object on which force of thought is to be exerted, and that is mind, spirit, comprehending under this word, God and all his intelligent offspring. This is the subject of what are called the metaphysical and moral sciences. This is the grand field for thought; for the outward, material world is the shadow of the spiritual, and made to minister to it. This study is of vast extent. It comprehends theology, metaphysics, moral philosophy, political science, history, literature. This is a formidable list, and it may seem to include a vast amount of knowledge, which is necessarily placed beyond the reach of the labourer. But it is an interesting thought, that the key to these various sciences is given to every human being in his own nature, so that they are peculiarly accessible to him. How is it that I get my ideas of God, of my fellow

creatures, of the deeds, suffering, motives, which make up universal history? I comprehend all these from the consciousness of what passes in my own soul. The mind within me is a type, representative of. all others, and therefore I can understand all. Whence come my conceptions of the intelligence, and justice, and goodness, and power of God? It is because my own spirit contains the germs of these attributes. The ideas of them are first derived from my own nature, and therefore I comprehend them in other beings. Thus the foundation of all the sciences, which treat of mind, is laid in every man's breast. The good man is exercising in his business and family, faculties and affections, which bear a likeness to the attributes of the Divinity, and to the energies which have made the greatest men illustrious; so that in studying himself, in learning the highest principles and laws of his own soul, he is in truth studying God, studying all human history, studying the philosophy which has immortalized the sages of ancient and modern times. In every man's mind and life all other minds and lives are more or less represented and wrapped up. To study other things, I must go into the outward world and perhaps go far. To study the science of spirit, I must come home and enter my own soul. The profoundest books that have ever been written, do nothing more than bring out, place in clear light, what is passing in each of your minds. So near you, so within you is the grandest truth.

I have indeed no expectation, that the labourer is to understand in detail the various sciences which relate to mind. Few men in any vocation do so understand them. Nor is it necessary; though, where time can be commanded, the thorough study of some particular branch, in which the individual has a special interest, will be found of great utility. What is needed to elevate the soul is, not that a man should know all that has been thought and written in regard to the spiritual nature, not that a man should become an Encyclopedia, but that the great ideas, in which all discoveries terminate, which sum up all sciences, which the philosopher extracts from infinite details, may be comprehended and felt. It is not the quantity, but the quality of knowledge, which determines the mind's dignity. A man of immense information may, through the want of large and comprehensive ideas, be far inferior in intellect to a labourer, who, with little knowledge, has yet seized on great truths. For example, I do not expect the labourer to study theology in the ancient languages, in the writings of the Fathers, in the history of sects, &c. &c., nor is this needful. All theology, scattered as it is through countless volumes, is summed up in the idea of God; and let this idea shine bright and clear in the labourer's soul, and he has the essence of theological libraries, and a far higher light than has visited thousands of renowned divines. A great mind is formed by a few great ideas, not by an infinity of loose details. I have known very learned men, who seemed to me very poor in intellect, because they had no grand thoughts. What avails it, that a man has studied ever so minutely the histories of Greece and Rome, if the great ideas of freedom, and beauty, and valour, and spiritual energy have not been kindled by these records into living fires in his soul. The illumination of an age does not consist in the amount of its knowledge, but in the broad and noble principles, of which that knowledge is the foundation and inspirer. The truth is, that the most laborious and successful student is confined in his researches to a very few of God's works; but this limited knowledge of things may still suggest universal laws, broad principles, grand ideas, and these elevate the mind. There are certain thoughts, principles, ideas, which by their nature, rule over all knowledge, which are intrinsically glorious, quickening, all-comprehending, eternal, and with these I desire to enrich the mind of the labourer and of every human being.

To illustrate my meaning, let me give a few examples of the great ideas which belong to the study or science of mind. Of course, the first of these, the grandest, the most comprehensive, is the idea of God, the Parent Mind, the Primitive and Infinite Intelligence. Every man's elevation is to be measured first and chiefly by his conception of this Great Being; and to attain a just, and bright, and quickening knowledge of Him, is the highest aim of thought. In truth, the great end of the universe, of revelation, of life, is to develop in us the idea of God. Much earnest, patient, laborious thought is required to see this Infinite Being as he is, to rise above the low, gross notions of the Divinity which rush in upon us from our passions, from our selfish partialities, and from the low-minded world around us. There is one view of God particularly suited to elevate us. I mean the view of him as the "Father of our spirits;" as having created us with great powers to grow up to perfection; as having ordained all outward things, to minister to the progress of the soul; as always present to inspire and strengthen us, to wake us up to inward life, and to judge and rebuke our wrong doing; as looking with parental joy on our resistance of evil; as desiring to communicate himself to our minds forever. This one idea, expanded

in the breast of the labourer, is a germ of elevation, more fruitful than all science, no matter how extensive or profound, which treats only of outward finite things. It places him in the first rank of human beings. You hear of great theologians. He only deserves the name, be his condition what it may, who has by thought, and obedience, purified and enlarged his conception of God.

From the idea of God, I proceed to another grand one, that of man, of human nature; and this should be the object of serious, intense thought. Few men know as yet what a man is. They know his clothes, his complexion, his property, his rank, his follies and his outward life. But the thought of his inward being, his proper humanity, has hardly dawned on multitudes; and yet who can live a man's life, that does not know what is the distinctive worth of a human being? It is interesting to observe, how faithful men generally are to their idea of a man; how they act up to it. Spread the notion, that courage is true manhood, and how many will die rather than fall short of that standard; and hence, the true idea of a man, brought out in the labourer's mind, elevates him above every other class who may want it. Am I asked for my conception of the dignity of a human being? I should say, that it consists, first, in that spiritual principle, called sometimes the reason, sometimes the conscience, which rising above what is local and temporary, discerns immutable truth, and everlasting right; which in the midst of imperfect things, conceives of perfection; which is universal and impartial, standing in direct opposition to the partial, selfish principles of human nature; which says to me with authority, that my neighbour is as precious as myself and his rights as sacred as my own; which commands me to receive all truth however it may war with my pride, and to do all justice however it may conflict with my interest; and which calls me to rejoice with love in all that is beautiful, good, holy, happy in whatever being these attributes may be found. This principle is a ray of Divinity in man. We do not know what man is, till something of the celestial grandeur of this principle in the soul be discerned. There is another grand view of man, included indeed in the former, yet deserving distinct notice. He is a free being; created to act from a spring in his own breast, to form himself and to decide his own destiny; connected intimately with nature, but not enslaved to it; connected still more strongly with God, yet not enslaved even to the Divinity, but having power to render or withold the service due to his Creator; encompassed by a thousand warring forces, by physical elements which inflict pleasure and pain, by dangers seen and unseen, by the influences of a tempting, sinful world, yet endued by God with power to contend with all, to perfect himself by conflict with the very forces which threaten to overwhelm him. Such is the idea of a man. Happy is he in whom it is unfolded by earnest thought.

Had I time I should be glad to speak of other great ideas belonging to the science of mind, and which sum up and give us, in one bright expression, the speculations of ages. The idea of human life, of its true end and greatness; the idea of virtue, as the absolute and ultimate good; the idea of liberty, which is the highest thought of political science, and which, by its intimate presence to the minds of the people, is the chief spring of our country's life and greatness,—all these might be enlarged on; and I might show how these may be awakened in the labourer, and may give him an elevation which many who are above labour want. But, leaving all these, I will only refer to another, one of the most important results of the science of mind, and which the labourer, in common with every man, may and should receive, and should strengthen by patient thought. It is the idea of his importance as an individual. He is to understand that he has a value, not as belonging to a community, and contributing to a general good which is distinct from himself, but on his own account. He is not a mere part of a machine. In a machine the parts are useless, but as conducing to the end of the whole, for which alone they subsist. Not so a man. He is not simply a means, but an end, and exists for his own sake, for the unfolding of his nature, for his own virtue and happiness. True, he is to work for others, but not survilely, not with a broken spirit, not so as to degrade himself; he is to work for others from a wise self-regard, from principles of justice and benevolence, and in the exercise of a free will and intelligence, by which his own character is perfected. His individual dignity, not derived from birth, from success, from wealth, from outward show, but consisting in the indestructible principles of his soul, this ought to enter into his habitual consciousness. I do not speak rhetorically or use the cant of rhapsodists, but I utter my calm, deliberate conviction, when I say that the labourer ought to regard himself with a self-respect, unknown to the proudest monarch who rests on outward rank.

I have now illustrated what I mean by the great ideas which exalt the mind. Their worth and power cannot be exaggerated. They are the mightiest influences on earth. One great thought breathed into a man may regenerate him. The idea of freedom in ancient and modern republics, the idea of inspiration in various religious sects, the idea of immortality, how have these triumphed over worldly interests! How many heroes and martyrs have they formed! Great ideas are mightier than the passions. To awaken them is the highest office of education. As yet it has been little thought of. The education of the mass of the people has consisted in giving them mechanical habits, in breaking them to current usages and modes of thinking, in teaching religion and morality as traditions. It is time that a rational culture should take place of the mechanical; that men should learn to act more from ideas and principles, and less from blind impulse and undiscerning imitation.

Am I met here by the constantly recurring objections, that such great thoughts as have now been treated of, are not to be expected in the multitude of men, whose means of culture are so confined. To this difficulty I shall reply in the next lecture; but I wish to state a fact, or law of our nature, very cheering to those who, with few means, still pant for generous improvement. It is this, that great ideas come to us less from outward, direct, laborious teaching, than from indirect influences, and from the native working of our own minds; so that those, who want the outward apparatus for extensive learning, are not cut off from them. Thus laborious teachers may instruct us for years in God, and virtue, and the soul, and we may remain nearly as ignorant of them as at the beginning; whilst a look, a tone, an act of a fellow creature, who is kindled by a grand thought, and who is thrown in our path at some susceptible season of life, will do much to awaken and expand this thought within us. It is a matter of experience, that the greatest ideas often come to us, when right-minded, we know not how. They flash on us as lights from heaven. A man seriously given to the culture of his mind in virtue and truth, finds himself under better teaching than that of man. Revelations of his own soul, of God's intimate presence, of the grandeur of the creation, of the glory of disinterestedness, of the deformity of wrong doing, of the dignity of universal justice, of the might of moral principle, of the immutableness of truth, of immortality, and of the inward sources of happiness; these revelations, awakening a thirst for something higher than he is or has, come of themselves to an humble self-improving man. Sometimes a common scene in nature, one of the common relations of life, will open itself to us with a brightness and pregnancy of meaning unknown before. Sometimes a thought of this kind forms an era in life. It changes the whole future course. It is a new creation. And these great ideas are not confined to men of any class. They are communications of the Infinite Mind to all minds which are open to their reception; and labour is a far better condition for their reception than luxurious or fashionable life. It is even better than a studious life, when this fosters vanity, pride, and the spirit of jealous competition. A child-like simplicity attracts these revelations more than a selfish culture of intellect, however far extended.—Perhaps a caution should be added to these suggestions. In speaking of great ideas, as sometimes springing up of themselves, as sudden illuminations, I have no thought of teaching that we are to wait for them passively, or to give up our minds unthinkingly to their control. We must prepare ourselves for them by faithfulness to our own powers, by availing ourselves of all means of culture within our reach; and what is more, these illuminations, if they come, are not distinct, complete, perfect views, but glimpses, suggestions, flashes, given us, like all notices and impressions from the outward world, to be thought upon, to be made subjects of patient reflection, to be brought by our own intellect and activity into their true connection with all our other thoughts. A great idea, without reflection, may dazzle and bewilder, may destroy the balance and proportion of the mind, and impel to dangerous excess. It is to awaken the free, earnest exertion of our powers, to rouse us from passiveness to activity and life, that inward inspirations, and the teachings of outward nature, are accorded to the mind.

I have thus spoken at large of that force of thought which the labourer is to seek as his true elevation; and I will close the subject with observing, that on whatever objects, or for whatever purposes this force may be exerted, one purpose should be habitually predominant, and that is, to gain a larger, clearer comprehension of all the duties of life. Thought cannot take too wide a range; but its chief aim should be to acquire juster and brighter perceptions of the right and the good, in every relation and condition in which we may be placed. Do not imagine, that I am here talking professionally, or sliding unconsciously, by the force of habit, into the tone of the pulpit. The subject of Duty belongs equally to all professions and all conditions. It were as wise to think of living without breath or of seeing without light, as

to exclude moral and religious principle from the work of self-elevation. And I say this, because you are in danger of mistaking mere knowledge for improvement. Knowledge fails of its best end, when it does not minister to a high virtue. I do not say that we are never to think, read, or study but for the express purpose of learning our duties. The mind must not be tied down by rigid rules. Curiosity, amusement, natural tastes may innocently direct reading and study to a certain extent. Even in these cases, however, we are bound to improve ourselves morally as well as intellectually, by seeking truth and rejecting falsehood, and by watching against the taint which inheres in almost all human productions. What avails intellectual without moral power? How little does it avail us to study the outward world, if its greatness inspire no reverence of its Author, if its beneficence awaken no kindred love towards our fellow creatures? How little does it avail us to study history, if the past do not help us to comprehend the dangers and duties of the present; if from the sufferings of those who have gone before us we do not learn how to suffer, and from their great and good deeds how to act nobly; if the development of the human heart, in different ages and countries, do not give us a better knowledge of ourselves? How little does literature benefit us, if the sketches of life and character, the generous sentiments, the testimonies to disinterestedness and rectitude, with which it abounds, do not incite and guide us to wiser, purer, and more graceful action? How little substantial good do we derive from poetry and the fine arts, if the beauty, which delights the imagination, do not warm and refine the heart, and raise us to the love and admiration of what is fair, and perfect, and lofty in character and life? Let our studies be as wide as our condition will allow; but let this be their highest aim, to instruct us in our duty and happiness, in the perfection of our nature, in the true use of life, in the best direction of our powers. Then is the culture of intellect an unmixed good, when it is sacredly used to enlighten the conscience, to feed the flame of generous sentiment, to perfect us in our common employments, to throw a grace over our common actions, to make us sources of innocent cheerfulness and centres of holy influence, and to give us courage, strength, stability amidst the sudden changes and sore temptations and trials of life.

LECTURE II.

In my last lecture, I invited your attention to a subject of great interest, the elevation of the labouring portion of the community. I proposed to consider, first, in what this elevation consists; secondly, the objections which may be made to its practicableness; thirdly, the circumstances which now favour it, and give us hope that it will be more and more accomplished. In considering the first head, I began with stating in what the elevation of the labouring class does not consist, and then proceeded to show positively what it is, what it does consist in. I want time to trace the ground over which we then travelled. I must trust to your memories. I was obliged by my narrow limits to confine myself chiefly to the consideration of the intellectual elevation which the labourer is to propose; though in treating this topic, I showed the moral, religious, social, improvements which enter into his true dignity. I observed, that the labourer was to be a student, a thinker, an intellectual man as well as a labourer; and suggested the qualifications of this truth which are required by his peculiar employment, by his daily engagements in manual toil. I now come to consider the objections which spring up in many minds, when such views of the labourer's destiny are given. This is our second head.

First, it will be objected, that the labouring multitude cannot command a variety of books, or spend much time in reading; and how, then, can they gain the force of thought, and the great ideas, which were treated of in the former lecture? This objection grows out of the prevalent disposition to confound intellectual improvement with book-learning. Some seem to think, that there is a kind of magic in a printed page, that types give a higher knowledge than can be gained from other sources. Reading is considered as the royal road to intellectual eminence. This prejudice I have virtually set aside in my previous remarks; but it has taken so strong a hold of many as to need some consideration. I shall not attempt to repel the objection by decrying good books. Truly good books are more

c

than mines to those who can understand them. They are the breathings of the great souls of past times. Genius is not embalmed in them, as is sometimes said, but *lives* in them perpetually. But we need not many books to answer the great ends of reading. A few are better than many, and a little time given to a faithful study of the few will be enough to quicken thought and enrich the mind. The greatest men have not been book-men. Washington, it has often been said, was no great reader. The learning commonly gathered from books is of less worth than the truths we gain from experience and reflection. Indeed, most of the knowledge from reading in these days, being acquired with little mental action, and seldom or never reflected on and turned to use, is very much a vain show. Events stirring the mind to earnest thought and vigorous application of its resources, do vastly more to elevate the mind, than most of our studies at the present time. Few of the books, read among us, deserve to be read. Most of them have no principle of life, as is proved by the fact, that they die the year of their birth. They do not come from thinkers, and how can they awaken thought? A great proportion of the reading of this city is useless, I had almost said pernicious. I should be sorry to see our labourers exchanging their toils for the reading of many of our young ladies and young gentlemen, who look on the intellect as given them for amusement; who read, as they visit, for amusement; who discuss no great truths and put forth no energy of thought on the topics which fly through their minds. With this insensibility to the dignity of the intellect, and this frittering away of the mind on superficial reading, I see not with what face they can claim superiority to the labouring mass, who certainly understand one thing thoroughly, that is, their own business, and who are doing something useful for themselves and their fellow creatures. The great use of books is to rouse us to thought; to turn us to questions which great men have been working on for ages; to furnish us with materials for the exercise of judgment, imagination, and moral feeling; to breathe into us a moral life from higher spirits than our own; and this benefit of books may be enjoyed by those who have not much time for retired study.

It must not be forgotten, by those who despair of the labouring classes because they cannot live in libraries, that the highest sources of truth, light, and elevation of mind, are not libraries, but our inward and outward experience. Human life, with its joys and sorrows, its burdens and alleviations, its crimes and virtues, its deep wants, its solemn changes, and its retributions always pressing on us; what a library is this? and who may not study it? Every human being is a volume, worthy to be studied. The books which circulate most freely through the community, are those which give us pictures of human life. How much more improving is the original, did we know how to read it? The labourer has this page always open before him; and, still more, the labourer is every day writing a volume more full of instruction than all human productions; I mean his own life. No work of the most exalted genius can teach us so much as the revelation of human nature in the secrets of our own souls, in the workings of our own passions, in the operations of our own intelligence, in the retributions which follow our own good and evil deeds, in the dissatisfaction with the present, in the spontaneous thoughts and aspirations, which form part of every man's biography. The study of our own history from childhood, of all the stages of our development, of the good and bad influences which have beset us, of our mutations of feeling and purpose, and of the great current which is setting us towards future happiness or woe; this is a study to make us nobly wise; and who of us has not access to this fountain of eternal truth? May not the labourer study and understand the pages which he is writing in his own breast?

In these remarks I have aimed to remove the false notion into which labourers themselves fall, that they can do little towards acquiring force and fulness of thought, because in want of books. I shall next turn to prejudices more confined to other classes. A very common one is, that the many are not to be called to think, study, improve their minds, because a privileged few are intended by God to do their thinking for them. "Providence," it is said, "raises up superior minds, whose office it is to discover truth for the rest of the race. Thinking and manual toil are not meant to go together. The division of labour is a great law of nature. One man is to serve society by his head, another by his hands. Let each class keep to his proper work." These doctrines I protest against. I deny to any individual or class this monopoly of thought. Who, among men, can show God's commission to think for his brethren, to shape passively the intellect of the mass, to stamp his own image on them as if they were wax? As well might a few claim a monopoly of light and air, of seeing and breathing as of thought. Is not the intellect as universal a gift as the organs of sight and respiration? Is not truth as freely spread abroad as the atmosphere or the sun's rays? Can we imagine that God's highest gifts of intelligence, imagination, and moral power, were bestowed to provide only for animal wants? to be denied the natural means of growth, which is action? to be starved by drudgery? Were the mass of men made to be monsters? to grow only in a few organs and faculties, and to pine away and shrivel in others? or were they made to put forth all the powers of men, especially the best and most distinguishing? No man, not the lowest, is all hands, all bones and muscles. The mind is more essential to human nature, and more enduring than the limbs, and was this made to lie dead? Is not thought the right and duty of all? Is not truth alike precious to all? Is not truth the natural aliment of the mind as plainly as the wholesome grain is of the body? Is not the mind adapted to thought, as plainly as the eye to light, the ear to sound? Who dares to withhold it from its natural action, its natural element and joy? Undoubtedly some men are more gifted than others, and are marked out for more studious lives. But the work of such men is not to do others' thinking for them, but to help them to think more vigorously and effectually. Great minds are to make others great. Their superiority is to be used, not to break the multitude into intellectual vassalage, not to establish over them a spiritual tyranny, but to rouse them from lethargy and to aid them to judge for themselves. The light and life which spring up in one soul are to be spread far and wide. Of all treasons against humanity, there is no one worse than his who employs great intellectual force to keep down the intellect of his less favoured brother.

It is sometimes urged by those who consider the multitude as not intended to think, that at best they can learn but little, and that this is likely to harm rather than to do them good. "A little learning," we are told "is a dangerous thing." "Shallow draughts" of knowledge are worse than ignorance. The mass of the people, it is said, can go to the bottom of nothing; and the result of stimulating them to thought, will be the formation of a dangerous set of half thinkers. To this argument I reply, first, that it has the inconvenience of proving too much; for, if valid, it shows that none of any class ought to think. For who, I would ask, can go to the bottom of any thing? Whose "learning" is not "little?" Whose "draughts" of knowledge are not "shallow?" Who of us has fathomed the depths of a single product of nature or a single event in history. Who of us is not baffled by the mysteries in a grain of sand? How contracted the range of the wisest intellect? But is our knowledge, because so little, of no worth? Are we to despise the lessons which are taught us in this nook of creation, in this narrow round of human experience, because an infinite universe stretches around us, which we have no means of exploring, and in which the earth, and sun, and planets, dwindle to a point? We should remember, that the known, however little it may be, is in harmony with the boundless unknown and a step towards it. We should remember too, that the gravest truths may be gathered from a very narrow compass of information. God is revealed in his smallest work as truly as in his greatest. The principles of human nature may be studied better in a family than in the history of the world. The finite is a manifestation of the infinite. The great ideas, of which I have formerly spoken, are within the reach of every man, who thirsts for truth and seeks it with singleness of mind. I will only add that the labouring are not now condemned to draughts of knowledge so shallow as to merit scorn. Many of them know more of the outward world than all the philosophers of antiquity; and Christianity has opened to them mysteries of the spiritual world, which kings and prophets were not privileged to understand. And are they, then, to be doomed to spiritual inaction, as incapable of useful thought?

It is sometimes said that the multitude may think on the common business of life, but not on higher subjects, and especially on religion. This, it is said, must be received on authority: on this, men in general can form no judgment of their own. But this is the last subject on which the individual should be willing to surrender himself to others' dictation. In nothing has he so strong an interest. In nothing is it so important that his mind and heart should be alive and engaged. In nothing has he readier means of judging for himself. In nothing, as history shows, is he more likely to be led astray by such as assume the office of thinking for him. Religion is a subject open to all minds. Its great truths have their foundation in the soul itself, and their proofs surround us on all sides. God has not shut up the evidence of his being in a few books, written in a foreign language, and locked up in the libraries of colleges and philosophers; but has written his name on the heavens and on the earth, and even on the minutest animal and plant; and his word, taught by Jesus Christ, was not given to scribes and lawyers, but taught to the poor, to the mass of men, on mountains, in streets, and on the seashore. Let me not be told that the multitude do actually receive religion on authority, or on the word of others. I reply, that a faith so received seems to me of little worth. The precious, the living, the effectual part of a poor man's faith, is that, of which he sees the reasonableness and excellence; that which approves itself to his intelligence, his conscience, his heart; that which answers the deep wants in his own soul, and of which he has the witness in his own inward and outward experience. All other parts of his belief, those which he takes on blind trust, and in which he sees no marks of truth and divinity, do him little or no good. Too often they do him harm, by perplexing his simple reason, by substituting the fictions and artificial systems of theologians for the plain precepts of love, and justice, and humility, and filial trust in God. As long as it was supposed, that religion is to benefit the world by laying restraints, awakening fears, and acting as a part of the system of police, so long it was natural to rely on authority and tradition as the means of its propagation; so long it was desirable to stifle thought and inquiry on the subject. But now that we have learnt that the true office of religion is to awaken pure and lofty sentiments, and to unite man to God by rational homage and enlightened love, there is something monstrous in placing religion beyond the thought and the study of the mass of human race.

I proceed to another prejudice. It is objected, that this distinction of ranks is essential to social order, and that this will be swept away by calling forth energy of thought in all men. This objection, indeed, though exceedingly insisted on in Europe, has nearly died out here; but still enough of it lingers among us to deserve consideration. I reply, then, that it is a libel on social order to suppose that it requires for its support the reduction of the multitude of human beings to ignorance and servility; and that it is a libel on the Creator to suppose that he requires, as the foundation of communities, the systematic depression of the majority of his intelligent offspring. The supposition is too grossly unreasonable, too monstrous, to require laboured refutation. I see no need of ranks either for social order or for any other purpose. A great variety of pursuits and conditions is indeed to be desired. Men ought to follow their genius, and to put forth their powers in every useful and lawful way. I do not ask for a monotonous world. We are far too monotonous now. The vassalage of fashion, which is a part of rank, prevents continually the free expansion of men's powers. Let us have the greatest diversity of occupations. But this does not imply that there is a need of splitting society into castes or ranks, or that a certain number should arrogate superiority, and stand apart from the rest of men as a separate race. Men may work in different departments of life, and yet recognise their brotherly relation, and honour one another, and hold friendly communion with one another. Undoubtedly, men will prefer as friends and common associates, those with whom they sympathise most. But this is not to form a rank or caste. For example, the intelligent seek out the intelligent; the pious, those who reverence God. But suppose the intellectual and the religious to cut themselves off by some broad, visible distinction from the rest of society, to form a clan of their own, to refuse admission into their houses to people of inferior knowledge and virtue, and to diminish as far as possible the occasions of intercourse with them; would not society rise up as one man, against this arrogant exclusiveness? And if intelligence and piety may not be the foundations of a caste, on what ground shall they, who have no distinction but wealth, superior costume, richer equipages, finer houses, draw lines around themselves and constitute themselves a higher class? That some should be richer than others is natural, and is necessary, and could only be prevented by gross violations of right. Leave men to the free use of their powers, and some will accumulate more than their neighbours. But, to be prosperous is not to be superior, and should form no barrier between men. Wealth ought not to secure to the prosperous the slightest consideration. The only distinctions which should be recognised are those of the soul, of strong principle, of incorruptible integrity, of usefulness, of cultivated intellect, of fidelity in seeking for truth. A man, in proportion as he has these claims, should be honoured and welcomed everywhere. I see not why such a man, however coarsely if neatly dressed, should not be a respected guest in the most splendid mansions, and at the most brilliant meetings. A man is worth infinitely more than the saloons, and the costumes, and the show of the universe. He was made to tread all these beneath his feet. What an insult to humanity is the present de-

ference to dress and upholstery, as if silk-worms, and looms, and scissors, and needles could produce something nobler than man. Every good man should protest against a caste founded on outward prosperity, because it exalts the outward above the inward, the material above the spiritual; because it springs from and cherishes a contemptible pride in superficial and transitory distinctions; because it alienates man from his brother, breaks the tie of common humanity, and breeds jealousy, scorn, and mutual ill will. Can this be needed to social order?

It is true that in countries, where the mass of the people are ignorant and servile, the existence of a higher and a worshipped rank tends to keep them from outrage. It infuses a sentiment of awe, which prevents more or less the need of force and punishment. But it is worthy of remark, that the means of keeping order in one state of society, may become the chief excitement of discontent and disorder in another, and this is peculiarly true of aristocracy or high rank. In rude ages, this keeps the people down; but when the people by degrees have risen to some consciousness of their rights and essential equality with the rest of the race, the awe of rank naturally subsides, and passes into suspicion, jealousy, and sense of injury, and a disposition to resist. The very institution which once restrained, now provokes. Through this process the old world is now passing. The strange illusion that a man, because he wears a garter or a ribbon, or was born to a title, belongs to another race, is fading away; and society must pass through a series of revolutions, silent or bloody, until a more natural order takes place of distinctions which grew orignally out of force. Thus aristocracy instead of giving order to society, now convulses it. So impossible is it for arbitrary human ordinations permanently to degrade human nature, or subvert the principles of justice and freedom.

I am aware that it will be said, " that the want of refinement of manners and taste in the lower classes will necessarily keep them an inferior caste, even though all political inequalities be removed." I acknowledge this defect of manners in the multitude, and grant that it is an obstacle to intercourse with the more improved, though often exaggerated. But this is a barrier which must and will yield to the means of culture spread through our community. This evil is not necessarily associated with any condition of human life. An intelligent traveller [*], tells us that in Norway, a country wanting many of our advantages, good manners and polite-

* See Laing's Travels in Norway.

ness are spread through all conditions; and that the "rough way of talking to and living with each other, characteristic of the lower classes of society in England, is not found there." Not many centuries ago, the intercourse of the highest orders in Europe was sullied by indelicacy and fierceness; but time has worn out these stains, and the same cause is now removing what is repulsive among those who toil with their hands. I cannot believe that coarse manners, boisterous conversation, slovenly negligences, filthy customs, surliness, indecency, are to descend by necessity from generation to generation in any portion of the community. I do not see why neatness, courtesy, delicacy, ease and defference to other's feelings, may not be made the habits of the labouring multitude. A change is certainly going on among them in respect to manners. Let us hope that it will be a change for the better; that they will not adopt false notions of refinement; that they will escape the servile imitation of what is hollow and insincere, and the substitution of outward shows for genuine natural courtesy. Unhappily they have but imperfect models on which to form themselves. It is not one class alone which needs reform in manners. We all need a new social intercourse, which shall breathe genuine refinement; which shall unite the two great elements of politeness, self-respect and a delicate regard to the rights and feelings of others; which shall be free without rudeness, and earnest without positiveness; which shall be graceful yet warm-hearted; and in which communication shall be frank, unlaboured, overflowing, through the absence of all assumption and pretence, and through the consciousness of being safe from heartless ridicule. This grand reform, which I trust is to come, will bring with it a happiness little known in social life; and whence shall it come? The wise and disinterested of all conditions must contribute to it; and I see not why the labouring classes may not take part in the work. Indeed, when I consider the greater simplicity of their lives and their greater openness to the spirit of Christianity, I am not sure, but that the "golden age" of manners is to begin among those, who are now despaired of for their want of refinement.

In these remarks, I have given the name of "prejudices" to the old opinions respecting rank, and respecting the need of keeping the people from much thought. But allow these opinions to have a foundation in truth; suppose high fences of rank to be necessary to refinement of manners; suppose that the happiest of all ages were the feudal, when aristocracy was in its flower and glory, when the noble, superior to the laws, committed more murders in one year, than the multitude in twenty. Suppose it best for the labourer to live and die in thoughtless ignorance. Allow all this, and that we have reason to look with envy on the past; one thing is plain; the past is gone, the feudal castle is dismantled, the distance between classes greatly reduced. Unfortunate as it may be, the people have begun to think, to ask reasons for what they do and suffer and believe, and to call the past to account. Old spells are broken, old reliances gone. Men can no longer be kept down by pageantry, state robes, forms and shows. Allowing it to be best, that society should rest on the depression of the multitude, the multitude will no longer be quiet when they are trodden under foot, but ask impatiently for a reason why they too may not have a share in social blessings. Such is the state of things, and we must make the best of what we cannot prevent. Right or wrong, the people will think; and is it not important that they should think justly? that they should be inspired with the love of truth, and instructed how to seek it? that they should be established by wise culture in the great principles on which religion and society rest, and be protected from scepticism and wild speculation by intercourse with enlightened and virtuous men? It is plain, that in the actual state of the world, nothing can avail us, but a real improvement of the mass of the people. No stable foundation can be laid for us but in men's minds. Alarming as the truth is, it should be told, that outward institutions cannot now secure us. Mightier powers than institutions have come into play among us, the judgment, the opinions, the feelings of the many; and all hopes of stability, which do not rest on the progress of the many, must perish.

But a more serious objection, than any yet considered, to the intellectual elevation of the labouring class, remains to be stated. It is said "that the labourer can gain subsistence for himself and his family, only by a degree of labour which forbids the use of means of improvement. His necessary toils leave no time or strength for thought. Political economy, by showing that population outstrips the means of improvement, passes an irrepealable sentence of ignorance and degradation on the labourer. He can live but for one end, which is to keep himself alive. He cannot give time and strength to intellectual, social, and moral culture, without starving his family, and impoverishing the community. Nature has laid this heavy law on the mass of the people, and it is idle to set up our theories and dreams of improvement against nature."

This objection applies with great force to Europe, and is not without weight here. But it does not discourage me. I reply, first, to this objection, that it generally comes from a suspicious source. It comes generally from men who abound, and are at ease; who think more of property than of any other human interest; who have little concern for the mass of their fellow creatures; who are willing, that others should bear all the burdens of life, and that any social order should continue which secures to themselves personal comfort or gratification. The selfish epicure and the thriving man of business easily discover a natural necessity for that state of things, which accumulates on themselves all the blessings, and on their neighbour all the evils of life. But no man can judge what is good or necessary for the multitude, but he who feels for them, and whose equity and benevolence are shocked by the thought, that all advantages are to be monopolised by one set of men, and all disadvantages by another. I wait for the judgment of profound thinkers and earnest philanthropists on this point, a judgment formed after patient study of political economy and human nature and human history; nor even on such authority shall I readily despair of the multitude of my race.

In the next place, the objection under consideration is very much a repetition of the old doctrine, that what has been must be; that the future is always to repeat the past, and society to tread for ever the beaten path. But, can anything be plainer, than that the present condition of the world is peculiar, unprecedented? that new powers and new principles are at work? that the application of science to art is accomplishing a stupendous revolution? that the condition of the labourer is in many places greatly improved, and his intellectual aids increased? that abuses, once thought essential to society, and which seemed entwined with all its fibres, have been removed? Do the mass of men stand where they did a few centuries ago? And do not new circumstances, if they make us fearful, at the same time keep us from despair? The future, be it what it may, will not resemble the past. The present has new elements, which must work out weal or woe. We have no right then, on the ground of the immutableness of human affairs, to quench, as far as we have power, the hope of social progress.

Another consideration in reply to the objection, that the necessary toils of life exclude improvement, may be drawn not only from general history, but from the experience of this country in particular. The working classes here have risen and are still rising intellectually, and yet there are no signs of starvation, nor are we becoming the poorest people on earth. By far the most interesting view of this country is the condition of the working multitude. Nothing among us deserves the attention of the traveller so much, as the force of thought and character, and the self-respect awakened by our history and institutions in the mass of the people. Our prosperous classes are much like the same classes abroad, though, as we hope, of purer morals; but the great working multitude leave far behind them the labourers of other countries. No man of observation and benevolence can converse with them, without being struck and delighted with the signs they give of strong and sound intellect and manly principle. And who is authorised to set bounds to this progress? In improvement the first steps are the hardest. The difficulty is to wake up men's souls, not to continue their action. Every accession of light and strength is a help to new acquisitions.

Another consideration in reply to the objection is, that as yet no community has seriously set itself to the work of improving all its members, so that what is possible remains to be ascertained. No experiment has been made to determine, how far liberal provision can be made at once for the body and mind of the labourer. The highest social art is yet in its infancy. Great minds have nowhere solemnly, earnestly undertaken to resolve the problem, how the multitude of men may be elevated. The trial is to come. Still more, the multitude have nowhere comprehended distinctly the true idea of progress, and resolved deliberately and solemnly to reduce it to reality. This great thought, however, is gradually opening on them, and it is destined to work wonders. From themselves their salvation must chiefly come. Little can be done for them by others, till a spring is touched in their own breasts; and this being done, they cannot fail. The people, as history shows us, can accomplish miracles nder the power of a great idea. How muchu have they often done and suffered, in critical moments, for country, for religion! The great idea of their own elevation is only beginning to unfold itself within them, and its energy is not to be foretold. A lofty conception of this kind, were it once distinctly seized, would be a new life breathed into them. Under this impulse they would create time and strength for their high calling, and would not only regenerate themselves but the community.

Again, I am not discouraged by the objection that the labourer, if encouraged to give time and strength to the elevation of his mind, will starve himself and impoverish the country, when I consider the energy and efficiency of mind. The highest force in the universe is mind. This created the heavens and earth. This has changed the wilderness into fruitfulness, and linked distant countries in a beneficent ministry to one another's wants. It is not to brute force, to physical strength, so much as to art, to skill, to intellectual and moral energy, that men owe their mastery over the world. It is mind which has conquered matter. To fear, then, that by calling forth a people's mind, we shall impoverish and starve them, is to be frightened at a shadow. I believe that, with the growth of intellectual and moral power in the community, its productive power will increase, that industry will become more efficient, that a wiser economy will accumulate wealth, that unimagined resources of art and nature will be discovered. I believe that the means of living will grow easier, in proportion as the people shall become enlightened, self-respecting, resolute, and just. Bodily or material forces can be measured, but not the forces of the soul, nor can the results of increased mental energy be foretold. Such a community will tread down obstacles now deemed invincible, and turn them into helps. The inward moulds the outward. The power of a people lies in the mind; and this mind, if fortified and enlarged, will bring external things into harmony with itself: it will create a new world around it corresponding to itself. If, however, I err in this belief; if, by securing time and means for improvement to the multitude, industry and capital should become less productive; I still say, sacrifice the wealth and not the mind of a people. Nor do I believe that the physical good of a community would in this way be impaired. The diminution of a country's wealth occasioned by general attention to intellectual and moral culture, would be followed by very different effects from those, which would attend an equal diminution brought about by sloth, intemperance, and ignorance. There would, indeed, be less production in such a country; but the character and spirit of the people would effect a much more equal distribution of what would be produced; and the happiness of a community depends vastly more on the distribution than on the amount of its wealth. In thus speaking of the future, I do not claim any special prophetical gift. As a general rule, no man is able to foretell distinctly the ultimate, permanent results of any great social change. But as to the case before us, we ought not to doubt. It is a part of religion to believe, that by nothing can a country so effectually gain happiness and lasting prosperity, as by the elevation of all classes of its citizens. To question this seems an approach to crime.

―――― " If this fail,
The pillared firmament is rottenness,
And earth's base built on stubble."

I am aware that, in reply to all that has been said in favour of the possibility of uniting self-improvement with labour, discouraging facts may be brought forward from our daily experience. It may be said, that in this country, under advantages unknown in other lands, there is a considerable number, on whom the burden of toil presses very heavily, who can scarcely live with all their efforts, and who are cut off by their hard condition from the means of intellectual culture; and if this take place now, what are we to expect hereafter in a more crowded population? I acknowledge, that we have a number of depressed labourers, whose state is exceedingly upropitious to the education of the mind; but this argument will lose much of its power, when we inquire into the causes of this evil. We shall then see that it comes not from outward necessity, not from irresistible obstacles abroad, but chiefly from the fault or ignorance of the sufferers themselves; so that the elevation of the mind and character of the labourer tends directly to reduce, if not remove, the evil. Of consequence, this elevation finds support in what is urged against it. In confirmation of these views, allow me just to hint at the causes of that depression of many labourers, which is said to show that labour and self-improvement cannot go on together.

First, how much of this depression is to be traced to intemperance? What a great amount of time, and strength, and money might multitudes gain for self-improvement, by a strict sobriety! That cheap remedy, pure water, would cure the chief evils in very many families of the ignorant and poor. Were the sums, which are still lavished on ardent spirits, appropriated wisely to the elevation of the people, what a new world we should live in! Intemperance not only wastes the earnings, but the health and the minds of men. How many, were they to exchange what they call moderate drinking for water, would be surprised to learn, that they had been living under a cloud, in half-stupefaction, and would become conscious of an intellectual energy of which they had not before dreamed! Their labours would exhaust them less, and less labour would be needed for their support; and thus their inability to cultivate their high nature would, in a great measure, be removed. The working class, above all men, have an interest in the cause of temperance, and they ought to look on the individual, who lives by scattering the means and excitements of drunkeness, not only as the general enemy of his race, but as their own worst foe.

In the next place, how much of the depression of labourers may be traced to the want of a strict economy. The prosperity of this country has produced a wastefulness, that has extended to the labouring multitude. A man here turns with scorn from fare that, in many countries, would be termed luxurious. It is, indeed, important that the standard of living in all classes should be high; that is, it should include the comforts of life, the means of neatness and order in our dwellings, and such supplies of our wants as are fitted to secure vigorous health. But how many waste their earnings on indulgences which may be spared, and thus have no resource for a dark day, and are always trembling on the brink of pauperism? Needless expenses keep many too poor for self-improvement. And here let me say, that expensive habits among the more prosperous labourers, often interfere with the mental culture of themselves and their families. How many among them sacrifice improvement to appetite! How many sacrifice it to the love of show, to the desire of outstripping others, and to habits of expense which grow out of this insatiable passion! In a country so thriving and luxurious as ours, the labourer is in danger of contracting artificial wants and diseased tastes; and, to gratify these, he gives himself wholly to accumulation, and sells his mind for gain. Our unparalleled prosperity has not been an unmixed good. It has inflamed cupidity, has diseased the imagination with dreams of boundless success, and plunged a vast multitude into excessive toils, feverish competitions, and exhausting cares. A labourer, having secured a neat home and a wholesome fable, should ask nothing more for the senses; but should consecrate his leisure, and what may be spared of his earnings, to the culture of himself and his family, to the best books, to the best teaching, to pleasant and profitable intercourse, to sympathy and the offices of humanity, and to the enjoyment of the beautiful in nature and art. Unhappily, the labourer, if prosperous, is anxious to ape the rich man, instead of trying to rise above him, as he often may, by noble acquisitions. The young in particular, the apprentice, and the female domestic, catch a taste for fashion, and on this altar sacrifice too often their uprightness, and almost always the spirit of improvement, dooming themselves to ignorance, if not to vice, for a vain show. Is this evil without remedy? Is human nature always to be sacrificed to outward decoration? Is the outward always to triumph over the inward

man? Is nobleness of sentiment never to spring up among us? May not a reform in this particular begin in the labouring class, since it seems so desperate among the more prosperous? Cannot the labourer, whose condition calls him so loudly to simplicity of tastes and habits, take his stand against that love of dress, which dissipates and corrupts so many minds among the opulent? Cannot the labouring class refuse to measure men by outward success, and pour utter scorn on all pretensions founded on outward show or condition? Sure I am, that were they to study plainness of dress and simplicity of living, for the purpose of their own true elevation, they would surpass in intellect, in taste, in honourable qualities, and in present enjoyment, that great proportion of the prosperous who are softened into indulgence or enslaved to empty show. By such self-denial, how might the burden of labour be lightened, and time and strength redeemed for improvement!

Another cause of the depressed condition of not a few labourers, as I believe, is their ignorance on the subject of health. Health is the working-man's fortune, and he ought to watch over it, more than the capitalist over his largest investments. Health lightens the efforts of body and mind. It enables a man to crowd much work into a narrow compass. Without it little can be earned, and that little by slow, exhausting toil. For these reasons I cannot but look on it as a good omen, that the press is circulating among us cheap works, in which much useful knowledge is given of the structure, and functions and laws of the human body. It is in no small measure through our own imprudence that disease and debility are incurred, and one remedy is to be found in knowledge. Once let the mass of the people be instructed in their own frames; let them understand clearly that disease is not an accident, but has fixed causes, many of which they can avert, and a great amount of suffering, want, and consequent intellectual depression, will be removed. I hope I shall not be thought to digress too far, when I add, that were the mass of the community more enlightened on these points, they would apply their knowledge, not only to their private habits, but to the government of the city, and would insist on municipal regulations favouring general health. This they owe to themselves. They ought to require a system of measures for effectually cleansing the city; for supplying it with pure water, either at public expense or by a private corporation; and for prohibiting the erection or the letting of such buildings as must generate disease. What a sad thought is it, that in this metropolis, the blessings which God pours forth profusely on bird and beast, the blessings of air, and light, and water, should, in the case of many families, be so stinted, or so mixed with impurities, as to injure instead of invigorating the frame? With what face can the great cities of Europe and America boast of their civilization, when within their limits thousands and ten thousands perish for want of God's freest, most lavish gifts? Can we expect improvement among the people who are cut off from nature's common bounties, and want those cheering influences of the elements which even savages enjoy? In this city, how much health, how many lives are sacrificed to the practice of letting cellars and rooms which cannot be ventilated, which want the benefits of light, free air, and pure water, and the means of removing filth? We forbid by law the selling of putrid meat in the market: why do we not forbid the renting of rooms, in which putrid, damp, and noisome vapours are working as sure destruction as the worst food? Did people understand that they are as truly poisoned in such dens, as by tainted meat and decaying vegetables, would they not appoint commissioners for houses as truly as commissioners for markets? Ought not the renting of untenantable rooms and the crowding of such numbers into a single room as must breed disease, and may infect a neighbourhood, to be as much forbidden as the importation of a pestilence? I have enlarged on this point, because I am persuaded that the morals, manners, decencies, self-respect, and intellectual improvement, as well as the health and physical comforts of a people depend on no outward circumstances more than on the quality of the houses in which they live. The remedy of the grievance now stated lies with the people themselves. The labouring people must require that the health of the city shall be a leading object of the municipal administration, and in so doing they will promote at once the body and the mind.

I will mention one more cause of the depressed condition of many labourers, and that is sloth, "the sin which doth most easily beset us." How many are there who, working languidly and reluctantly, bring little to pass, spread the work of one hour over many, shrink from difficulties which ought to excite them, keep themselves poor, and thus doom their families to ignorance as well as to want.

In these remarks I have endeavoured to show that the great obstacles to the improvement of the labouring classes are in themselves, and may therefore be overcome. They want nothing but the will. Outward difficulty will shrink and vanish before them, just as far as they are bent on progress, just

D

as far as the great idea of their own elevation shall take possession of their minds. I know that many will smile at the suggestion, that the labourer may be brought to practice thrift and self-denial, for the purpose of becoming a nobler being. But such sceptics, having never experienced the power of a grand thought or generous purpose, are no judges of others. They may be assured, however, that enthusiasm is not wholly a dream, and that it is not wholly unnatural for individuals or bodies to get the idea of something higher and more inspiring than their past attainments.

Having now treated of the elevation of the labourer, and examined the objections to it, I proceed, in the last place, to consider some of the circumstances of the times which encourage hopes of the progress of the mass of the people. My limits oblige me to confine myself to very few. And, first, it is an encouraging circumstance, that the respect for labour is increasing, or rther, that the old prejudices against manual toil as degrading a man, or putting him in a lower sphere, are wearing away; and the cause of this change is full of promise; for it is to be found in the progress of intelligence, Christianity, and freedom, all of which cry aloud against the old barriers created between the different classes, and challenge especial sympathy and regard for those who bear the heaviest burdens, and create most of the comforts of social life. The contempt of labour, of which I have spoken, is a relic of the old aristocratic prejudices, which formerly proscribed trade as unworthy of a gentleman, and must die out with other prejudices of the same low origin. And the result must be happy. It is hard for a class of men to respect themselves, who are denied respect by all around them. A vocation, looked on as degrading, will have a tendency to degrade those who follow it. Away then, with the idea of something low in manual labour! There is something shocking to a religious man in the thought, that the employment which God has ordained for the vast majority of the human race, should be unworthy of any man, even the highest. If, indeed, there were an employment, which could not be dispensed with, and which yet tended to degrade such as might be devoted to it, I should say that it ought to be shared by the whole race, and thus neutralized by extreme division, instead of being laid, as the sole vocation, on one man or a few. Let no human being be broken in spirit, or trodden under foot, for the outward prosperity of the state! So far is manual labour from meriting contempt or slight, that it will probably be found, when united with true means of spiritual culture, to foster a sounder judgment, a keener observation, a more creative imagination, and a purer taste than any other vocation. Man thinks of the few, God of the many; and the many will be found at length to have within their reach the most effectual means of progress.

Another encouraging circumstance of the times is, the creation of a popular literature, which puts within the reach of the labouring class the means of knowledge in whatever branch they wish to cultivate. Amidst the worthless volumes which are every day sent from the press for mere amusement, there are books of great value, in all departments, published for the benefit of the mass of readers. Mines of inestimable truth are thus open to all who are resolved to think and learn. Literature is now adapting itself to all wants; and I have little doubt, that a new form of it will soon appear for the special benefit of the labouring class. This will have for its object, to show the progress of the various useful arts, and to preserve the memory of the founders, and of men who have laid the world under obligation by great inventions. Every trade has distinguished names in its history. Some trades can number, among those who have followed them, philosophers, poets, men of true genius. I would suggest to the members of the association, whether a course of lectures, intended to illustrate the history of the more important trades, and of the great blessings they have conferred on society, and of the eminent individuals who have practised them, might not do much to instruct, and at the same time to elevate them. Such a course would carry them far into the past, would open to them much interesting information, and at the same time introduce them to men whom they may well make their models. I would go farther: I should be pleased to see the members of an important trade setting apart an anniversary for the commemoration of those who have shed lustre on it by their virtues, their discoveries, their genius. It is time that honour should be awarded on higher principles than have governed the judgment of past ages. Surely the inventor of the press, the discoverer of the compass, the men who have applied the power of steam to machinery, have brought the human race more largely into their debt, than the bloody race of conquerors, and even than many beneficent princes. Antiquity exalted into Divinities the first cultivators of wheat and the useful plants, and the first forgers of metals; and we, in these maturer ages of the world, have still greater names to boast in the records of useful arts. Let their memory be preserved to kindle a generous emulation in those who have entered into their labours.

Another circumstance, encouraging the hope of progress in the labouring class, is to be found in the juster views they are beginning to adopt in regard to the education of their children. On this foundation, indeed, our hope for all classes must chiefly rest. All are to rise chiefly by the care bestowed on the young. Not that I would say, as is sometimes rashly said, that none but the young can improve. I give up no age as desperate. Men who have lived thirty, or fifty years are not to feel as if the door were shut upon them. Every man who thirsts to become something better, has in that desire a pledge, that his labour will not be in vain. None are too old to learn. The world, from our first to our last hour, is our school, and the whole of life has but one great purpose, education. Still, the child uncorrupted, unhardened, is the most hopeful subject; and vastly more I believe is hereafter to be done for children, than ever before, by the gradual spread of a simple truth, almost too simple, one would think, to need exposition, yet up to this day wilfully neglected, namely, that education is a sham, a cheat, unless carried on by able, accomplished teachers. The dignity of the vocation of a teacher is beginning to be understood. The idea is dawning on us, that no office can compare in solemnity and importance with that of training the child; that skill to form the young to energy, truth and virtue is worth more than the knowledge of all other arts and sciences, and that of consequence the encouragement of excellent teachers, is the first duty which a community owes to itself, I say the truth is dawning; and it must make its way. The instruction of the children of all classes, especially of the labouring class, has as yet been too generally committed to unprepared, unskilful hands, and of course the school is in general little more than a name. The whole worth of a school lies in the teacher. You may accumulate the most expensive apparatus for instruction; but without an intellectual, gifted teacher, it is little better than rubbish; and such a teacher, without apparatus, may effect the happiest results. Our university boasts, and with justice, of its library, cabinets, and philosophical instruments; but these are lifeless, profitless, except as made effectual by the men who use them. A few eminent men, skilled to understand, reach and quicken the minds of the pupils, are worth all these helps. And I say this, because it is commonly thought, that the children of the labouring class cannot be advanced, in consequence of the inability of parents to furnish a variety of books and other apparatus. But in education, various books and implements are not the great requisites, but a high order of teachers. In truth, a few books do better than many. The object of education is not so much to give a certain amount of knowledge, as to awaken the faculties, and give the pupil the use of his own mind; and one book, taught by a man who knows how to accomplish these ends, is worth more than libraries as usually read. It is not necessary, that much should be taught in youth, but that a little should be taught philosophically, profoundly, livingly. For example, it is not necessary, that the pupil be carried over the history of the world from the deluge to the present day. Let him be helped to read a single history wisely, to apply the principles of historical evidence to its statements, to trace the causes and effects of events, to penetrate into the motives of actions, to observe the workings of human nature in what is done and suffered, to judge impartially of action and character, to sympathize with what is noble, to detect the spirit of an age in different forms from our own, to seize the great truths which are wrapped up in details, and to discern a moral Providence, a retribution, amidst all corruptions and changes; let him learn to read a single history thus, and he has learned to read all histories; he is prepared to study, as he may have time in future life, the whole course of human events; he is better educated by this one book, than he would be by all the histories in all languges as commonly taught. The education of the labourer's children need never stop for want of books and apparatus. More of them would do good, but enough may be easily obtained. What we want is, a race of teachers acquainted with the philosophy of the mind, gifted men and women, who shall respect human nature in the child, and strive to touch and gently bring out his best powers and sympathies; and who shall devote themselves to this as the great end of life. This good I trust is to come, but it comes slowly. The establishment of normal shools, shows that the want of it begins to be felt. This good requires, that education shall be recognized by the community, as its highest interest and duty. It requires, that the instructors of youth shall take precedence of the money getting classes, and that the women of fashion shall fall behind the female teacher. It requires, that parents shall sacrifice show and pleasure to the acquisition of the best possible helps and guides for their children. Not that a great pecuniary compensation is to create good teachers; these must be formed by individual impulse, by a genuine interest in education; but good impulse must be seconded by outward circumstances; and the means of education will always bear a proportion to the respect in which the office of teacher is held in the community.

Happily in this country the true idea of education, of its nature and supreme importance, is silently working and gains ground. Those of us, who look back on half a century, see a real, great improvement in schools and in the standard of instruction. What should encourage this movement in this country is, that nothing is wanting here to the intellectual elevation of the labouring class, but that a spring should be given to the child, and that the art of thinking justly and strongly should be formed in early life; for, this preparation being made, the circumstances of future life, will almost of themselves carry on the work of improvement. It is one of the inestimable benefits of free institutions, that they are constant stimulants to the intellect; that they furnish, in rapid succession, quickening subjects of thought and discussion. A whole people at the same moment are moved to reflect, reason, judge and act on matters of deep and universal concern; and where the capacity of thought has received wise culture, the intellect unconsciously by an almost irresistible sympathy, is kept perpetually alive. The mind, like the body, depends on the climate it lives in, on the air it breathes; and the air of freedom is bracing, exhiliarating, expanding, to a degree not dreamed of under a despotism. This stimulus of liberty, however, avails little, except where the mind has been learned to think for the acquisition of truth. The unthinking and passionate are hurried by it into ruinous excess.

The last ground of hope for the elevation of the labourer, and the chief and the most sustaining, is the clearer development of the principles of Christianity. The future influences of this religion are not to be judged from the past. Up to this time it has been made a political engine, and in other ways perverted. But its true spirit, the spirit of brotherhood and freedom, is beginning to be understood, and this will undo the work which opposite principles have been carrying on for ages. Christianity is the only effectual remedy for the fearful evils of modern civilization; a system which teaches its members to grasp at everything, and to rise above everybody, as the great aims of life. Of such a civilization, the natural fruits are contempt of others' rights, fraud, oppression, a gambling spirit in trade, reckless adventure, and commercial convulsions, all tending to impoverish the labourer and to render every condition insecure. Relief is to come, and can only come from the new application of Christian principles, of universal justice, and universal love, to social institutions, to commerce, to business, to active life. This application has begun, and the labourer, above all men, is to feel its happy and exalting influences.

Such are some of the circumstances which inspire hopes of the elevation of the labouring classes. To these might be added other strong grounds of encouragement, to be found in the principles of human nature, in the perfections and providence of God, and in the prophetic intimations of his word. But these I pass over. From all, I derive strong hopes for the mass of men. I do not, cannot see, why manual toil and self-improvement may not go on in friendly union. I do not see, why the labourer may not attain to refined habits and manners as truly as other men. I do not see, why conversation under his humble roof may not be cheered by wit and exalted by intelligence. I do not see, why amidst his toils he may not cast his eye around him on God's glorious creation, and be strengthened and refreshed by the sight. I do not see, why the great ideas which exalt humanity, those of the Infinite Father, of Perfection, of our nearness to God, and of the purpose of our being, may not grow bright and strong in the labourer's mind. Society, I trust, is tending towards a condition, in which it will look back with astonishment at the present neglect or perversion of human powers. In the development of a more enlarged philanthropy, in the diffusion of the Christian spirit of brotherhood, in the recognition of the equal rights of every human being, we have the dawn and promise of a better age, when no man will he deprived of the means of elevation but by this own fault; when the evil doctrine, worthy of the arch-fiend, that social order demands the depression of the mass of men, will be rejected with horror and scorn ; when the great object of the community will be to accumulate means and influences for awakening and expanding the best powers of all classes ; when far less will be expended on the body and far more on the mind: when men of uncommon gifts for the instruction of their race, will be sent forth to carry light and strength into every sphere of human life ; when spacious libraries, collections of the fine arts, cabinets of natural history, and all the institutions by which the people may be refined and ennobled, will be formed and thrown open to all; and when the toils of life, by a wise intermixture of these higher influences, will be made the instruments of human elevation.

Such are my hopes of the intellectual, moral, religious, social elevation of the labouring class. I should not, however, be true to myself, did I not add, that I have fears as well as hopes. Time is not left me to enlarge on this point, but without a reference to it, I should not give you the whole truth. I would not disguise from myself or others the true character of the world we live in. Human imperfection throws an uncertainty over the future. Society, like the natural world, holds in its bosom fearful elements. Who can hope, that the storms, which have howled over past ages, have spent all their force ? It is possible, that the labouring classes, by their recklessness, their passionateness, their jealousies of the more prosperous, and their subserviency to parties and political leaders, may turn all their bright prospects into darkness, may blight the hopes which philanthropy now cherishes of a happier and holier social state. It is also possible, in this mysterious state of things, that evil may come to them from causes, which are thought to promise them nothing but good. The present anxiety and universal desire is to make the country rich, and it is taken for granted that its growing wealth is necessarily to benefit all conditions. But is this consequence sure ? May not a country be rich, and yet great numbers of the people be wofully depressed ? In England, the richest nation under heaven, how sad, how degraded the state of the agricultural and manufacturing classes ! It is thought, that the institutions of this country give an assurance, that growing wealth will here equally benefit and carry forward all portions of the community. I hope so ; but I am not sure. At the present time a momentous change is taking place in our condition. The improvement in steam navigation has half annihilated the space between Europe and America, and by the progress of invention the two continents are to be more and more placed side by side. We hail this triumph of the arts with exultation. We look forward to the approaching spring, when this metropolis is to be linked with England by a line of steamboats, as a proud era in our history. That a great temporary excitement will be given to industry, and that our wealth and numbers will increase, admits no dispute ; but this is a small matter. The great question is, will the mass of the people be permanently advanced in the comforts of life, and still more, in intelligence and character, in the culture of their highest powers and affections ? It is not enough to grow, if our growth is to resemble that of other populous places. Better continue as we are, better even decline, than tread in the steps of any great city, whether of past or present times. I doubt not, that under God's providence, the approximation of Europe and America is ultimately to be a blessing to both; but, without our vigilance, the nearer effects may be more or less disastrous. It cannot be doubted that, for a time, many among us, especially in the prosperous classes, will be more and more infected from abroad, will sympathise more with the institutions, and catch more the spirit and manners of the old world. As a people we want moral independence. We bow to 'the great' of other countries, and we shall become for a time more and more servile in our imitation. But this, though bad, may not be the worst result. I would ask, what is to be the effect of bringing the labouring classes of Europe twice as near us as they now are? Is there no danger of a competition that is to depress the labouring classes here? Can the workman here stand his ground against the half famished, ignorant workmen of Europe, who will toil for any wages and who never think of redeeming an hour for personal improvement? Is there no danger, that with increasing intercourse with Europe, we shall import the striking, fearful contrasts, which there divide one people into separate nations? Sooner than that our labouring class should become a European populace, a good man would almost wish, that perpetual hurricanes, driving every ship from the ocean, should sever wholly the two hemispheres from each other. Heaven preserve us from the anticipated benefits of nearer connexion with Europe, if with these must come the degradation, which we see or read of among the squalid poor of her great cities, among the overworked operatives of her manufactories, among her ignorant and half brutalized peasants. Any thing, every thing should be done to save us from the social evils which deform the old world, and to build up here an intelligent, right-minded, self-respecting population. If this end should require us to change our present modes of life, to narrow our foreign connexions, to desist from the race of commercial and manufacturing competition with Europe; if it should require, that our great cities should cease to grow, and that a large portion of our trading populatian should return to labour, these requisitions ought to be obeyed. One thing is plain, that our present civilization contains strong tendencies to the intellectual and moral depression of a large portion of the community; and this influence ought to be thought of, studied, watched, withstood, with a stern, solemn purpose of withholding no sacrifice by which it may be counteracted.

Perhaps the fears now expressed may be groundless. I do not ask you to adopt them.

My end will be gained, if I can lead you to study, habitually and zealously, the influence of changes and measures on the character and condition of the labouring class. There is no subject, on which your thoughts should turn more frequently, than on this. Many of you busy yourselves with other questions, such as the probable result of the next election of President, or the prospects of this or that party. But these are insignificant, compared with the great question, whether the labouring classes here are destined to the ignorance and depression of the lower ranks of Europe, or whether they can secure to themselves the means of intellectual and moral progress. You are cheated, you are false to yourselves, when you suffer politicians to absorb you in their selfish purposes, and to draw you away from this great question. Give the first place in your thoughts to this. Carry it away with you from the present lecture; discuss it together; study it when alone; let your best heads work on it; resolve that nothing shall be wanting on your part, to secure the means of intellectual and moral wellbeing to yourselves, and to those who may come after you.

In these lectures, I have expressed a strong interest in the labouring portion of the community; but I have no partiality to them considered merely as labourers. My mind is attracted to them, because they constitute the majority of the human race. My great interest is in human nature, and in the working classes as its most numerous representative. To those who look on this nature with contempt or utter distrust, such language may seem a mere form, or may be construed as a sign of the predominance of imagination, and feeling over the judgment. No matter. The pity of these sceptics I can return. Their wonder at my credulity cannot surpass the sorrowful astonishment with which I look on their indifference to the fortunes of their race. In spite of all their doubts and scoffs, human nature is still most dear to me. When I behold it manifested in its perfect proportion in Jesus Christ, I cannot but revere it as the true temple of the divinity. When I see it as revealed in the great and good of all times, I bless God for these multiplied and growing proofs of its high destiny. When I see it bruised, beaten down, stifled, by ignorance and vice, by oppression, injustice and grinding toil, I weep for it, and feel that every man should be ready to suffer for its redemption. I do and must hope for its progress. But in saying this, I am not blind to its immediate dangers. I am not sure, that dark clouds and desolating storms are not even now gathering over the world. When we look back on the mysterious history of the human race, we see that Providence has made use of fearful revolutions as the means of sweeping away the abuses of ages, and of bringing forward mankind to their present improvement. Whether such revolutions may not be in store for our own times, I know not. The present civilization of the Christian world presents much to awaken doubt and apprehension. It stands in direct hostility to the great ideas of Christianity. It is selfish, mercenary, sensual. Such a civilization cannot, must not endure for ever. How it is to be supplanted, I know not. I hope, however, that it is not doomed, like the old Roman civilization, to be quenched in blood. I trust, that the works of ages, are not to be laid low by violence, rapine and the all devouring sword. I trust, that the existing social state contains in its bosom something better than it has yet unfolded. I trust, that a brighter future is to come, not from the desolation, but from gradual, meliorating changes of the present. Among the changes, to which I look for the salvation of the modern world, one of the chief is, the intellectual and moral elevation of the labouring class. The impulses which are to reform and quicken society, are probably to come, not from its more conspicuous, but from its obscure divisions; and among these, I see with joy new wants, principles and aspirations, beginning to unfold themselves. Let what is already won, give us courage. Let faith in a parental Providence give us courage; and if we are to be disappointed in the present, let us never doubt, that the great interests of human nature are still secure under the eye and care of its Almighty Friend.

THE END.

A. HEYWOOD, PRINTER, OLDHAM-STREET, MANCHESTER.

THE

LABORING CLASSES,

AN

ARTICLE

FROM THE

BOSTON QUARTERLY REVIEW

BY O. A. BROWNSON

THIRD EDITION.

BOSTON:
BENJAMIN H. GREENE,
1840.

PREFATORY NOTE.

The following article is republished from the Boston Quarterly Review to meet the pressing demand for it, which a needless excitement about it has produced.

The writer of the article makes it his duty to read all that he can find written against either him or his doctrines; but he feels under no obligations to reply. The doctrines of the article in question have been objected to, but he will now enter into no defence of them. He will only say that he has seen no criticism upon them, that indicates that the critic had even the most distant conception of the thought of his author. The majority of those who object to the article, are respectfully commended to the care of the instructors in our primary schools; for if they could read they would find that the article itself refutes most of the objections they urge.

In regard to what is said of the hereditary descent of property, it may be well for readers to bear in mind that the article contains but a brief statement of a doctrine without any explanations or details; and also that in proposing the abolition of hereditary property, it merely does it as a prospective measure, as a measure which will ultimately be found necessary to the complete enfranchisement of the proletary. The writer of the article recognises in its fullest extent man's natural right to property, and he would be the last to suffer the legislature to interfere with any of the natural rights of man. He advocates no wild scheme of a community of goods; he holds to individual property. Within the limits of the moral law, he would leave every man free to do what he will with his own. But it is an admitted principle, that a man's natural right to property ceases when he ceases to exist. In other words, man can own property only during his life. It is also an admitted principle, that it is not by virtue of a natural right that the child inherits from the father. Consequently, the right by which a man disposes of his property by a will effective after his death, and by which a child succeeds to the paternal estate, is not a natural right, but a legal right. It exists by virtue of positive law, which society has enacted. Now, the writer of the article in question objects to this law, and contends that another and better law regulating the descent of property from one generation to another, may be devised, and must be before the true elevation and independence of the laboring classes can be effected. This point he will make good hereafter. All that he would say now is that he makes no attack on the right of property, that he proposes to disturb no man in his possessions, nor to plunder any man of aught he has. He simply contends that in the future progress of the race it will be necessary to change the mode by which property descends. The change he contends for is precisely the same in principle with that by which primogeniture and entail were abolished. By contending that property should go to the state at a man's decease, he by no means intends to convey the idea, that the private property of a man on his decease becomes public property, and may therefore go into the public treasury, or be used for public purposes. It goes to the state in point of fact no more than now. All the writer means is, that the state so far takes the control of the matter, as by a uniform and equitable law, to say how what has ceased to be one man's property shall be reappropriated, or become the property of another. This would in reality give the state no more control over property than it now in theory claims and is admitted to have.

But however this all may be, no one can read the article without perceiving that the writer would by no means propose this as a measure for the immediate action of the community. There is a time for all things. The time for discussion is whenever the public can be interested in the subject discussed. The time for carrying a measure into execution is only when the public very generally demand it, when the public conscience cannot do without it, and when it can be introduced with some prospect of its being permanent and effective. But the writer is pleased that he has alarmed our staunch conservatives. It will do them good, and compel them by and by to set their faces towards the future.

Boston, July 23, 1840.   O. A. B.

THE LABORING CLASSES.

THOMAS CARLYLE * unquestionably ranks among the ablest writers of the day. His acquaintance with literature seems to be almost universal, and there is apparently no art or science with which he is not familiar. He possesses an unrivalled mastery over the resources of the English tongue, a remarkably keen insight into the mysteries of human nature, and a large share of genuine poetic feeling. His works are characterized by freshness and power, as well as by strangeness and singularity, and must be read with interest, even when they cannot be with approbation.

The little work, named at the head of this article, is a fair sample of his peculiar excellencies, and also of his peculiar defects. As a work intended to excite attention and lead the mind to an investigation of a great subject, it possesses no ordinary value; but as a work intended to throw light on a difficult question, and to afford some positive directions to to the statesman and the philanthropist, it is not worth much. Carlyle, like his imitators in this country, though he declaims against the destructives, possesses in no sense a constructive genius. He is good as a demolisher, but pitiable enough as a builder. No man sees more clearly that the present is defective and unworthy to be retained; he is a brave and successful warrior against it, whether reference be had to its literature, its politics, its philosophy, or its religion; but when the question comes up concerning what ought to be, what should take the place of what is, we regret to say, he affords us no essential aid, scarcely a useful hint. He has fine spiritual instincts, has outgrown materialism, loathes skepticism, sees clearly the absolute necessity of faith in both God and man, and insists upon it with due sincerity and earnestness; but with feelings very nearly akin to despair. He does not appear to have found as yet a faith for himself, and his writings have almost invariably a skeptical tendency. He has doubtless a sort of faith in God, or an overwhelming Necessity, but we cannot perceive that he has any faith in man or in man's efforts. Society is wrong, but he mocks at our sincerest and best directed efforts to right it. It cannot subsist as it is; that is clear: but what shall be done to make it what it ought to be, that he saith not. Of all writers we are acquainted with, he is the least satisfactory. He is dissatisfied with every thing himself, and he leaves his readers dissatisfied with everything. Hopeless himself, he makes them also hopeless, especially if they have strong social tendencies, and are hungering and thirsting to work out the regeneration of their race.

Mr. Carlyle's admirers, we presume, will demur to this criticism. We

* Chartism. By Thomas Carlyle.

have heard some of them speak of him as a sort of soul-quickener, and profess to derive from his writings fresh life and courage. We know not how this may be. It may be that they derive advantage from him on the homœopathic principle, and that he cures their diseases by exaggerating them ; but for ourselves we must say, that we have found him anything but a skilful physician. He disheartens and enfeebles us ; and while he emancipates us from the errors of tradition, he leaves us without strength or courage to engage in the inquiry after truth. We rise from his writings with the weariness and exhaustion one does from the embraces of the Witch Mara. It is but slowly that our blood begins to circulate again, and it is long before we recover the use of our powers. Whether his writings produce this effect on others or not, we are unable to say ; but this effect they do produce on us. We almost dread to encounter them.

Mr. Carlyle would seem to have great sympathy with man. He certainly is not wanting in the sentiment of Humanity ; nor is he deceived by external position, or dazzled by factitious glare. He can see worth in the socially low as well as in the socially high ; in the artisan as well as the noble. This is something, but no great merit in one who can read the New Testament. Still it is something, and we are glad to meet it. But after all, he has no true reverence for Humanity. He may offer incense to a Goethe, a Jean Paul, a Mirabeau, a Danton, a Napoleon, but he nevertheless looks down upon his fellows, and sneers at the mass. He looks down upon man as one of his admirers has said, " as if man were a mouse." But we do not wish to look upon man in that light. We would look upon him as a brother, an equal, entitled to our love and sympathy. We would feel ourselves neither above him nor below him, but standing up by his side, with our feet on the same level with his. We would also love and respect the commonplace mass, not merely heroes and sages, prophets and priests.

We are moreover no warm admirers of Carlyle's style of writing. We acknowledge his command over the resources of our language, and we enjoy the freshness, and occasional strength, beauty, and felicity of his style and expression, but he does not satisfy us. He wants clearness and precision, and that too when writing on topics where clearness and precision are all but indispensable. We have no patience with his mistiness, vagueness, and singularity. If a man must needs write and publish his thoughts to the world, let him do it in as clear and as intelligible langague as possible. We are not aware of any subject worth writing on at all, that is already so plain that it needs to be rendered obscure. Carlyle can write well if he chooses ; no man better. He is not necessarily misty, vague, nor fantastic. The antic tricks he has been latterly playing do not spring from the constitution of his mind, and we must say do by no means become him. We are disposed ourselves to assume considerable latitude in both thought and expression ; but we believe every scholar should aim to keep within the general current of his language. Every language receives certain laws from the genius of the people who use it, and it is no mark of wisdom to transgress them ; nor is genuine literary excellence to be attained but by obeying them. An Englishman, if he would profit Englishmen, must write English, not French nor German. If he wishes his writings to become an integral part of the literature of his language, he must keep within the steady current of what has ever been regarded as classical English style, and deny himself the momentary eclat he might gain by affectation and singularity.

We can, however, pardon Carlyle altogether more easily than we can his American imitators. Notwithstanding his manner of writing, when continued for any considerable length, becomes monotonous and wearisome, as in his History of the French Revolution,—a work which, with all its brilliant wit, inimitable humor, deep pathos, and graphic skill, can scarcely be read without yawning,—yet in his case it is redeemed by rare beauties, and marks a mind of the highest order, and of vast attainments. But in the hands of his American imitators, it becomes puerile and disgusting; and what is worthy of note is, that it is adopted and most servilely followed by the men among us who are loudest in their boasts of originality, and the most intolerant to its absence. But enough of this. For our consolation, the race of imitators is feeble and shortlived.

The subject of the little work before us, is one of the weightiest which can engage the attention of the statesman or the philanthropist. It is indeed, here, discussed only in relation to the working classes of England, but it in reality involves the condition of the working classes throughout the world,— a great subject, and one never yet worthily treated. Chartism, properly speaking is no local or temporary phenomenon. Its germ may be found in every nation in Christendom ; indeed wherever man has approximated a state of civilization, wherever there is inequality in social condition, and in the distribution of the products of industry. And where does not this inequality obtain ? Where is the spot on earth, in which the actual producer of wealth is not one of the lower class, shut out from what are looked upon as the main advantages of the social state ?

Mr. Carlyle, though he gives us few facts, yet shows us that the condition of the workingmen in England is deplorable, and every day growing worse. It has already become intolerable, and hence the outbreak of the Chartists. Chartism is the protest of the working classes against the injustice of the present social organization of the British community, and a loud demand for a new organization which shall respect the rights and well-being of the laborer.

The movements of the Chartists have excited considerable alarm in the higher classes of English society, and some hope in the friends of Humanity among ourselves. We do not feel competent to speak with any decision on the extent or importance of these movements. If our voice could reach the Chartists we would bid them be bold and determined ; we would bid them persevere even unto death ; for their cause is that of justice, and in fighting for it they will be fighting the battles of God and man. But we look for no important results from their movements. We have little faith in a John Bull mob. It will bluster, and swagger, and threaten much ; but give it plenty of porter and roast-beef, and it will sink back to its kennel, as quiet and as harmless as a lamb. The lower classes in England have made many a move since the days of Wat Tyler for the betterment of their condition, but we cannot perceive that they have ever effected much. They are doubtles nearer the day of their emancipation, than they were, but their actual condition is scarcely superior to what it was in the days of Richard the Second.

There is no country in Europe, in which the condition of the laboring classes seems to us so hopeless as in that of England. This is not owing to the fact, that the aristocracy is less enlightened, more powerful, or more oppressive in England than elsewhere. The English laborer does not find his worst enemy in the nobility, but in the middling class. The middle class is much more numerous and powerful in England than in any other European country, and is of a higher character. It has always been powerful ; for by means of the Norman Conquest it received large accessions from the old Saxon nobility. The Conquest established a new aristocracy, and degraded eht old to the condition of Commoners. The superiority of the English Commons is, we suppose, chiefly owing to this fact.

The middle class is always a firm champion of equality, when it concerns humbling a class above it; but it is its inveterate foe, when it concerns elevating a class below it. Manfully have the British Commoners struggled against the old feudal aristocracy, and so successfully that they now constitute the dominant power in the state. To their struggles against the throne and the nobility is the English nation indebted for the liberty it so loudly boasts, and which, during the last half of the last century, so enraptured the friends of Humanity throughout Europe.

But this class has done nothing for the laboring population, the real *proletarii*. It has humbled the aristocracy; it has raised itself to dominion, and it is now conservative, — conservative in fact, whether it call itself Whig or Radical. From its near relation to the workingmen, its kindred pursuits with them, it is altogether more hostile to them than the nobility ever were or ever can be. This was seen in the conduct of England towards the French Revolution. So long as that Revolution was in the hands of the middle class, and threatened merely to humble monarchy and nobility, the English nation applauded it; but as soon as it descended to the mass of the people, and promised to elevate the laboring classes, so soon as the starving workman began to flatter himself, that there was to be a revolution for him too as well as for his employer, the English nation armed itself and poured out its blood and treasure to suppress it. Every body knows that Great Britain, boasting of her freedom and of her love of freedom, was the life and soul of the opposition to the French Revolution; and on her head almost alone should fall the curses of Humanity for the sad failure of that glorious uprising of the people in behalf of their imprescriptible, and inalienable rights. Yet it was not the English monarchy, nor the English nobility, that was alone in fault. Monarchy and nobility would have been powerless, had they not had with them the great body of the English Commoners. England fought in the ranks, nay, at the head of the allies, not for monarchy, not for nobility, nor yet for religion; but for trade and manufactures, for her middle class, against the rights and well-being of the workingman; and her strength and efficiency consisted in the strength and efficiency of this class.

Now this middle class, which was strong enough to defeat nearly all the practical benefit of the French Revolution, is the natural enemy of the Chartists. It will unite with the monarchy and nobility against them; and spare neither blood nor treasure to defeat them. Our despair for the poor Chartists arises from the number and power of the middle class. We dread for them neither monarchy nor nobility. Nor should they. Their only real enemy is in the employer. In all countries is it the same. The only enemy of the laborer is your employer, whether appearing in the shape of the master mechanic, or in the owner of a factory. A Duke of Wellington is much more likely to vindicate the rights of labor than an Abbot Lawrence, although the latter may be a very kind-hearted man, and liberal citizen, as we always find Blackwood's Magazine more true to the interests of the poor, than we do the Edinburgh Review, or even the London and Westminster.

Mr. Carlyle, contrary to his wont, in the pamphlet we have named, commends two projects for the relief of the workingmen, which he finds others have suggested, — universal education, and general emigration. Universal education we shall not be thought likely to depreciate; but we confess that we are unable to see in it that sovereign remedy for the evils of the social state as it is, which some of our friends do, or say they do. We have little faith in the power of education to elevate a people compelled to labor from twelve to sixteen hours a day, and to experience for no mean portion of the time a paucity of even the necessaries of life, let alone its comforts. Give your starving boy a breakfast before you send him to school, and your tattered beggar a cloak before you attempt his moral and intellectual elevation. A swarm of naked and starving urchins crowded into a school-room will make little proficiency in the " Humanities." Indeed, it seems to us most bitter mockery for the well-dressed, and well-fed to send the schoolmaster and priest to the wretched hovels of squalid poverty, — a mockery at which devils may laugh, but over which angels must weep. Educate the working classes of England ; and what then ? Will they require less food and less clothing when educated than they do now ? Will they be more contented or more happy in their condition ? For God's sake beware how you kindle within them the intellectual spark, and make them aware that they too are men, with powers of thought and feeling which ally them by the bonds of brotherhood to their betters. If you will doom them to the external condition of brutes, do in common charity keep their minds and hearts brutish. Render them as insensible as possible, that they may feel the less acutely their degradation, and see the less clearly the monstrous injustice which is done them.

General emigration can at best afford only a temporary relief, for the colony will soon become an empire, and reproduce all the injustice and wretchedness of the mother country. Nor is general emigration necessary. England, if she would be just, could support a larger population than she now numbers. The evil is not from over population, but from the unequal repartition of the fruits of industry. She suffers from over production, and from over production, because her workmen produce not for themselves but for their employers. What then is the remedy ? As it concerns England, we shall leave the English statesman to answer. Be it what it may, it will not be obtained without war and bloodshed. It will be found only at the end of one of the longest and severest struggles the human race has ever been engaged in, only by that most dreaded of all wars, the war of the poor against the rich, a war which, however long it may be delayed, will come, and come with all its horrors. The day of vengeance is sure ; for the world after all is under the dominion of a Just Providence.

No one can observe the signs of the times with much care, without perceiving that a crisis as to the relation of wealth and labor is approaching. It is useless to shut our eyes to the fact, and like the ostrich fancy ourselves secure because we have so concealed our heads that we see not the danger. We or our children will have to meet this crisis. The old war between the King and the Barons is well nigh ended, and so is that between the Barons and the Merchants and Manufacturers, — landed capital and commercial capital. The business man has become the peer of my Lord. And now commences the new struggle between the operative and his employer, between wealth and labor. Every day does this struggle extend further and wax stronger and fiercer ; what or when the end will be God only knows.

In this coming contest there is a deeper question at issue than is commonly imagined ; a question which is but remotely touched in your controversies about United States Banks and Sub Treasuries, chartered Banking and free Banking, free trade and corporations, although these controversies may be paving the way for it to come up. We have discovered no presentiment of it in any king's or queen's speech, nor in any president's message. It is embraced in no popular political creed of the day, whether christened Whig or Tory, *Juste-milieu* or Democratic. No popular senator, or deputy, or peer seems to have any glimpse of it; but it is working in the hearts of the million, is struggling to shape itself, and one day it will be uttered, and in thunder tones. Well will it be for him, who, on that day, shall be found ready to answer it.

What we would ask is, throughout the Christian world, the actual condition of the laboring classes, viewed simply and exclusively in their capacity of laborers? They constitute at least a moiety of the human race. We exclude the nobility, we exclude also the middle class, and include only actual laborers, who are laborers and not proprietors, owners of none of the funds of production, neither houses, shops, nor lands, nor implements of labor, being therefore solely dependent on their hands. We have no means of ascertaining their precise proportion to the whole number of the race; but we think we may estimate them at one half. In any contest they will be as two to one, because the large class of proprietors who are not employers, but laborers on their own lands or in their own shops will make common cause with them.

Now we will not so belie our acquaintance with political economy, as to allege that these alone perform all that is necessary to the production of wealth. We are not ignorant of the fact, that the merchant, who is literally the common carrier and exchange dealer, performs a useful service, and is therefore entitled to a portion of the proceeds of labor. But make all necessary deductions on his account, and then ask what portion of the remainder is retained, either in kind or in its equivalent, in the hands of the original producer, the workingman? All over the world this fact stares us in the face, the workingman is poor and depressed, while a large portion of the non-workingmen, in the sense we now use the term, are wealthy. It may be laid down as a general rule, with but few exceptions, that men are rewarded in an inverse ratio to the amount of actual service they perform. Under every government on earth the largest salaries are annexed to those offices, which demand of their incumbents the least amount of actual labor either mental or manual. And this is in perfect harmony with the whole system of repartition of the fruits of industry, which obtains in every department of society. Now here is the system which prevails, and here is its result. The whole class of simple laborers are poor, and in general unable to procure any thing beyond the bare necessaries of life.

In regard to labor two systems obtain; one that of slave labor, the other that of free labor. Of the two, the first is, in our judgement, except so far as the feelings are concerned, decidedly the least oppressive. If the slave has never been a free man, we think, as a general rule, his sufferings are less than those of the free laborer at wages. As to actual freedom one has just about as much as the other. The laborer at wages has all the disadvantages of freedom and none of its blessings, while the slave, if denied the blessings, is freed from the disadvantages. We are no advocates of slavery, we are as heartily opposed to it as any modern abolitionist can be; but we say frankly that, if there must always be a laboring population distinct from proprietors and employers, we regard the slave system as decidedly preferable to the system at wages. It is no pleasant thing to go days without food, to lie idle for weeks, seeking work and finding none, to rise in the morning with a wife and children you love, and know not where to procure them a breakfast, and to see constantly before you no brighter prospect than the almshouse. Yet these are no unfrequent incidents in the lives of our laboring population. Even in seasons of general prosperity, when there was only the ordinary cry of "hard times," we have seen hundreds of people in a no very populous village, in a wealthy portion of our common country, suffering for the want of the necessaries of life, willing to work, and yet finding no work to do. Many and many is the application of a poor man for work, merely for his food, we have seen rejected. These things are little thought of, for the applicants are poor; they fill no conspicuous place in society, and they have no biographers. But their wrongs are chronicled in heaven. It is said there is no want in this country. There may be less than in some other countries. But death by actual starvation in this country is we apprehend no uncommon occurrence. The sufferings of a quiet, unassuming but useful class of females in our cities, in general sempstresses, too proud to beg or to apply to the alms-house, are not easily told. They are industrious; they do all that they can find to do; but yet the little there is for them to do, and the miserable pittance they receive for it, is hardly sufficient to keep soul and body together. And yet there is a man who employs them to make shirts, trousers, &c., and grows rich on their labors. He is one of our respectable citizens, perhaps is praised in the newspapers for his liberal donations to some charitable institution. He passes among us as a pattern of morality, and is honored as a worthy Christian. And why should he not be, since our *Christian* community is made up of such as he, and since our clergy would not dare question his piety, lest they should incur the reproach of infidelity, and lose their standing, and their salaries? Nay, since our clergy are raised up, educated, fashioned, and sustained by such as he? Not a few of our churches rest on Mammon for their foundation. The basement is a trader's shop.

We pass through our manufacturing villages; most of them appear neat and flourishing. The operatives are well dressed, and we are told, well paid. They are said to be healthy, contented, and happy. This is the fair side of the picture; the side exhibited to distinguished visitors. There is a dark side, moral as well as physical. Of the common operatives, few, if any, by their wages, acquire a competence. A few of what Carlyle terms not inaptly the *body-servants* are well paid, and now and then an agent or an overseer rides in his coach. But the great mass wear out their health, spirits, and morals, without becoming one whit better off than when they commenced labor. The bills of mortality in these factory villages are not striking, we admit, for the poor girls when they can toil no longer go home to die. The average life, working life we mean, of the girls that come to Lowell, for instance, from Maine, New Hampshire, and Vermont, we have been assured, is only about three years. What becomes of them then? Few of them ever marry; fewer still ever return to their native places with reputations unimpaired. "She has worked in a Factory," is almost enough to damn to infamy the most worthy and virtuous girl. We know no sadder sight on earth than one of our factory villages presents, when the bell at break of day, or at the hour of breakfast, or dinner, calls out its hundreds or thousands of operatives. We stand and look at these hard working men and women hurrying in all directions, and ask ourselves, where go the proceeds of their labors? The man who employs them, and for whom they are toiling as so many slaves, is one of our city nabobs, revelling in luxury; or he is a member of our legislature, enacting laws to put money in his own pocket; or he is a member of Congress, contending for a high Tariff to tax the poor for the benefit of the rich; or in these times he is shedding crocodile tears over the deplorable condition of the poor laborer, while he docks his wages twenty-five per cent.; building miniature log cabins, shouting Harrison and "hard cider." And this man too would fain pass for a Christian and a republican. He shouts for liberty, stickles for equality, and is horrified at a Southern planter who keeps slaves.

One thing is certain ; that of the amount actually produced by the operative, he retains a less proportion than it costs the master to feed, clothe, and lodge his slave. Wages is a cunning device of the devil, for the benefit of tender consciences, who would retain all the advantages of the slave system, without the expense, trouble, and odium of being slave-holders.

Messrs. Thorne and Kimball, in their account of the emancipation of slavery in the West Indies, establish the fact that the employer may have the same amount of labor done 25 per ct. cheaper than the master. What does this fact prove, if not that wages is a more successful method of taxing labor than slavery ? We really believe our Northern system of labor is more oppressive, and even more mischievous to morals, than the Southern. We, however, war against both. We have no toleration for either system. We would see a slave a man, but a free man, not a mere operative at wages. This he would not be were he now emancipated. Could the abolitionists effect all they propose, they would do the slave no service. Should emancipation work as well as they say, still it would do the slave no good. He would be a slave still, although with the title and cares of a freeman. If then we had no constitutional objections to abolitionism, we could not, for the reason here implied, be abolitionists.

The slave system, however, in name and form, is gradually disappearing from Christendom. It will not subsist much longer. But its place is taken by the system of labor at wages, and this system, we hold, is no improvement upon the one it supplants. Nevertheless the system of wages will triumph. It is the system which in name sounds honester than slavery, and in substance is more profitable to the master. It yields the wages of iniquity, without its opprobium. It will therefore supplant slavery, and be sustained— for a time.

Now, what is the prospect of those who fall under the operation of this system ? We ask, is there a reasonable chance that any considerable portion of the present generation of laborers, shall ever become owners of a sufficient portion of the funds of production, to be able to sustain themselves by laboring on their own capital, that is, as independent laborers? We need not ask this question, for everybody knows there is not. Well, is the condition of a laborer at wages the best that the great mass of the working people ought to be able to aspire to ? Is it a condition,—nay can it be made a condition,—with which a man should be satisfied ; in which he should be contented to live and die ?

In our own country this condition has existed under its most favorable aspects, and has been made as good as it can be. It has reached all the excellence of which it is susceptible. It is now not improving but growing worse. The actual condition of the working-man to-day, viewed in all its bearings, is not so good as it was fifty years ago. If we have not been altogether misinformed, fifty years ago, health and industrious habits, constituted no mean stock in trade, and with them almost any man might aspire to competence and independence. But it is so no longer. The wilderness has receded, and already the new lands are beyond the reach of the mere laborer, and the employer has him at his mercy. If the present relation subsist, we see nothing better for him in reserve than what he now possesses, but something altogether worse.

We are not ignorant of the fact that men born poor become wealthy, and that men born to wealth become poor ; but this fact does not necessarily diminish the numbers of the poor, nor augment the numbers of the rich. The relative numbers of the two classes remain, or may remain, the same. But be this as it may; one fact is certain, no man born poor has ever by his wages, as a simple operative, risen to the class of the wealthy. Rich he may have become, but it has not been by his own manual labor. He has in some way contrived to tax for his benefit the labor of others. He may have accumulated a few dollars which he has placed at usury, or invested in trade; or he may, as a master workman, obtain a premium on his journeymen; or he may have from a clerk passed to a partner, or from a workman to an overseer. The simple market wages for ordinary labor, has never been adequate to raise him from poverty to wealth. This fact is decisive of the whole controversy, and proves that the system of wages must be supplanted by some other system, or else one half of the human race must forever be the virtual slaves of the other.

Now the great work for this age and the coming, is to raise up the laborer, and to realize in our own social arrangements and in the ac ual condition of all men, that equality between man and man, which God has established between the rights of one and those of another. In other words, our business is to emancipate the proletaries, as the past has emancipated the slaves. This is our work. There must be no class of our fellow men doomed to toil through life as mere workmen at wages. If wages are tolerated it must be, in the case of the individual operative, only under such conditions that by the time he is of a proper age to settle in life, he shall have accumulated enough to be an independent laborer on his own capital,—on his own farm, or in his own shop. Here is our work. How is it to be done?

Reformers in general answer this question, or what they deem its equivalent, in a manner which we cannot but regard as very unsatisfactory. They would have all men wise, good, and happy; but in order to make them so, they tell us that we want not external changes, but internal; and therefore instead of declaiming against society and seeking to disturb existing social arrangements, we should confine ourselves to the individual reason and conscience; seek merely to lead the individual to repentance, and to reformation of life; make the individual a practical, a truly religious man, and all evils will either disappear, or be sanctified to the spiritual growth of the soul.

This is doubtless a capital theory, and has the advantage that kings, hierarchies, nobilities,—in a word, all who fatten on the toil and blood of their fellows, will feel no difficulty in supporting it. Nicholas of Russia, the Grand Turk, his Holiness the Pope, will hold us their especial friends for advocating a theory, which secures to them the odor of sanctity even while they are sustaining by their anathemas or their armed legions, a system of things of which the great mass are and must be the victims. If you will only allow me to keep thousands toiling for my pleasure or my profit, I will even aid you in your pious efforts to convert their souls. I am not cruel; I do not wish either to cause, or to see suffering; I am therefore disposed to encourage your labors for the souls of the workingman, providing you will secure to me the products of his bodily toil. So far as the salvation of his soul will not interfere with my income, I hold it worthy of being sought; and if a few thousand dollars will aid you, Mr. Priest, in reconciling him to God, and making fair weather for him hereafter, they are at your service. I shall not want him to work for me in the world to come, and I can indemnify myself for what your salary costs me, by paying him less wages. A capital theory this, which one may advocate without incurring the reproach of a disorganizer, a jacobin, a leveller, and without losing the friendship of the rankest aristocrat in the land.

This theory, however, is exposed to one slight objection, that of being condemned by something like six thousand years' experience. For six thousand years its beauty has been extolled, its praises sung and its blessings sought, under every advantage which learning, fashion, wealth, and power can secure; and yet under its practical operations, we are assured, that mankind, though totally depraved at first, have been growing worse and worse ever since.

For our part, we yield to none in our reverence for science and religion; but we confess that we look not for the regeneration of the race from priests and pedagogues. They have had a fair trial. They cannot construct the temple of God. They cannot conceive its plan, and they know not how to build. They daub with untempered mortar, and the walls they erect tumble down if so much as a fox attempt to go up thereon. In a word they always league with the people's masters, and seek to reform without disturbing the social arrangements which render reform necessary. They would change the consequents without changing the antecedents, secure to men the rewards of holiness, while they continue their allegiance to the devil. We have no faith in priests and pedagogues. They merely cry peace, peace, and that too when there is no peace, and can be none.

We admit the importance of what Dr Channing in his lectures on the subject we are treating recommends as " self-culture." Self-culture is a good thing, but it cannot abolish inequality, nor restore men to their rights. As a means of quickening moral and intellectual energy, exalting the sentiments, and preparing the laborer to contend manfully for his rights, we admit its importance, and insist as strenuously as any one on making it as universal as possible; but as constituting in itself a remedy for the vices of the social state, we have no faith init. As a means it is well, as the end it is nothing.

The truth is, the evil we have pointed out is not merely individual in its character. It is not, in the case of any single individual, of any one man's procuring, nor can the efforts of any one man, directed solely to his own moral and religious perfection, do aught to remove it. What is purely individual in its nature, efforts of individuals to perfect themselves, may remove. But the evil we speak of is inherent in all our social arrangements, and cannot be cured without a radical change of those arrangements. Could we convert all men to Christianity in both theory and practice, as held by the most enlightened sect of Christians among us, the evils of the social state would remain untouched. Continue our present system of trade, and all its present evil consequences will follow, whether it be carried on by your best men or your worst. Put your best men, your wisest, most moral, and most religious men, at the head of your paper money banks, and the evils of the present banking system will remain scarcely diminished. The only way to get rid of its evils is to change the system, not its managers. The evils of slavery do not result from the personal characters of slave masters. They are inseperable from the system, let who will be masters. Make all your rich men good Christians, and you have lessened not the evils of existing inequality in wealth. The mischievous effects of this inequality do not result from the personal characters of either rich or poor, but from itself, and they will continue, just so long as there are rich men and poor men in the same community. You must abolish the system or accept its consequences. No man can serve both God and Mammon. If you will serve the devil, you must look to the devil for your wages, we know no other way.

Let us not be misinterpreted. We deny not the power of Christianity. Should all men become good Christians, we deny not that all social evils would be cured. But we deny in the outset that a man, who seeks merely to save his own soul, merely to perfect his own individual nature, can be a good Christian. The Christian forgets himself, buckles on his armor, and goes forth to war against principalities and powers, and against spiritual wickedness in high places. No man can be a Christian who does not begin his career by making war on the mischievous social arrangements from which his brethren suffer. He who thinks he can be a Christian and save his soul, without seeking their radical change, has no reason to applaud himself for his proficiency in Christian science, nor for his progress towards the kingdom of God. Understand Christianity, and we will admit, that should all men become good Christians, there would be nothing to complain of. But one might as well undertake to dip the ocean dry with a clam-shell, as to undertake to cure the evils of the social state by converting men to the Christianity of the Church.

The evil we have pointed out, we have said, is not of individual creation, and it is not to be removed by individual effort, saving so far as individual effort induces the combined effort of the mass. But whence has this evil originated? How comes it that all over the world the working classes are depressed, are the low and vulgar, and virtually the slaves of the non-working classes? This is an inquiry which has not yet received the attention it deserves. It is not enough to answer, that it has originated entirely in the inferiority by nature of the working classes; that they have less skill and foresight, and are less able than the upper classes, to provide for themselves, or less susceptible of the highest moral and intellectual cultivation. Nor is it sufficient for our purpose to be told, that Providence has decreed that some shall be poor and wretched, ignorant and vulgar; and that others shall be rich and vicious, learned and polite, oppressive and miserable. We do not choose to charge this matter to the will of God. "The foolishness of man perverteth his way, and his heart fretteth against the Lord." God has made of one blood all the nations of men to dwell on all the face of the earth, and to dwell there as brothers, as members of one and the same family; and although he has made them with a diversity of powers, it would perhaps, after all, be a bold assertion to say that he has made them with an inequality of powers. There is nothing in the actual difference of the powers of individuals, which accounts for the striking inequalities we everywhere discover in their condition. The child of the plebeian, if placed early in the proper circumstances, grows up not less beautiful, active, intelligent, and refined, than the child of the patrician; and the child of the patrician may become as coarse, as brutish as the child of any slave. So far as observation on the original capacities of individuals goes, nothing is discovered to throw much light on social inequalities.

The cause of the inequality, we speak of, must be sought in history, and be regarded as having its root in Providence, or in human nature, only in that sense in which all historical facts have their origin in these. We may perhaps trace it in the first instance to conquest, but not to conquest as the ultimate cause. The Romans in conquering Italy no doubt reduced many to the condition of slaves, but they also found the great mass of the laboring population already slaves. There is every where a class distinct from the reigning class, bearing the same relation to it, that the Gibbeonites did to the Jews. They are principally *colons*, the cultivators for foreign masters, of a soil of which they seemed to have been dispossessed. Who has dispossessed them? Who has reduced them to their present condition,—a condition which under the Roman dominion is perhaps even ameliorated? Who were this race? Whence came they? They appear to be distinct from the reigning race, as were the Helotæ from the Doric-Spartan. Were they the aborigines of the territory? Had they once been free? By what concurrence of events have they been reduced to their present condition? By a prior conquest? But mere conquest does not so reduce a population. It may make slaves of the prisoners taken in actual combat, and reduce the whole to tributaries, but it leaves the mass of the population free, except in its political relations. Were they originally savages, subjugated by a civilized tribe? Savages may be exterminated, but they never, so far as we can ascertain, become to any considerable extent " the hewers of wood and drawers of water " to their conquerors. For our part we are disposed to seek the cause of the inequality of conditions of which we speak, in religion, and to charge it to the priesthood. And we are confirmed in this, by what appears to be the instinctive tendency of every, or almost every, social reformer. Men's instincts, in a matter of this kind, are worthier of reliance than their reasonings. Rarely do we find in any age or country, a man feeling himself commissioned to labor for a social reform, who does not feel that he must begin it by making war upon the priesthood. This was the case with the old Hebrew reformers, who are to us the prophets of God? with Jesus, the Apostles, and the early Fathers of the Church? with the French democrats of the last century; and is the case with the Young Germans, and the Socialists, as they call themselves in England, at the present moment. Indeed it is felt at once that no reform can be effected without resisting the priests and emancipating the people from their power.

Historical research, we apprehend, will be found to justify this instinct, and to authorize the eternal hostility of the reformer, the advocate of social progress, to the priesthood. How is it we ask, that man comes out of the savage state? In the savage state, properly so called, there is no inequality of the kind of which we speak. The individual system obtains there. Each man is his own centre, and is a whole in himself. There is no community, there are no members of society; for society is not. This individuality, which, if combined with the highest possible moral and intellectual cultivation, would be the perfection of man's earthly condition, must be broken down before the human race can enter into the path of civilization, or commence its career of progress. But it cannot be broken down by material force. It resists by its own nature the combination of individuals necessary to subdue it. It can be successfully attacked only by a spiritual power, and subjugated only by the representatives of that power, that is say, the priests.

Man is naturally a religious being, and disposed to stand in awe of invisible powers. This makes, undoubtedly, under certain relations, his glory; but when coupled with his ignorance, it becomes the chief source of his degradation and misery. He feels within the workings of a mysterious nature, and is conscious that hidden and superior powers are at work all around him, and perpetually influencing his destiny; now wafting him onward with a prosperous gale, or now resisting his course, driving him back, defeating his plans, blasting his hopes, and wounding his heart. What are his relations to these hidden, mysterious, and yet all-influencing forces? Can their anger be appeased? Can their favor be secured? Thus he asks himself. Unable to answer, he goes to the more aged and experienced of his tribe, and asks them the same questions. They answer as best they can. What is done by one is done by another, and what is done once is done again. The necessity of instruction, which each one feels in consequence of his own feebleness and inexperience, renders the recurrence to those best capable of giving it, or supposed to be the best capable of giving it, frequent and uniform. Hence the priest. He who is consulted prepares himself to answer, and therefore devotes himself to the study of man's relations to these invisible powers, and the nature of these invisible powers themselves. Hence religion becomes a special object of study, and the study of it a profession. Individuals whom a thunder-storm, an earthquake, an eruption of a volcano, an eclipse of the sun or moon, any unusual appearance in the heavens or earth, has frightened, or whom some unforseen disaster has afflicted, go to the wise-man for explanation, to know what it means, or what they shall do in order to appease the offended powers. When reassured they naturally feel grateful to this wise-man; they load him with honors, and in the access of their gratitude raise him far above the common level, and spare him the common burdens of life. Once thus distinguished, he becomes an object of envy. His condition is looked upon as superior to that of the mass. Hence a multitude aspire to possess themselves of it. When once the class has become somewhat numerous, it labors to secure to itself the distinction it has received, its honors and its emoluments, and to increase them. Hence the establishment of priesthoods or sacerdotal corporations, such as the Egyptian, the Braminical, the Ethiopian, the Jewish, the Scandinavian, the Druidical, the Mexican, and Peruvian.

The germ of these sacerdotal corporations is found in the savage state, and exists there in that formidable personage called a *jongleur*, juggler, or conjurer. But as the tribe or people advances, the juggler becomes a priest and the member of a corporation. These sacerdotal corporations are variously organized, but everywhere organized for the purpose, as that arch rebel, Thomas Paine, says, " of monopolizing power and profit." The effort is unceasing to elevate them as far above the people as possible, to enable them to exert the greatest possible control over the people, and to derive the greatest possible profit from the people.

Now if we glance over the history of the world, we shall find, that at the epoch of coming out of the savage state, these corporations are universally instituted. We find them among every people; and among every people, at this epoch, they are the dominant power, ruling with an iron despotism. The real idea at the bottom of these institutions, is the control of individual freedom by moral laws, the assertion of the supremacy of moral power over physical force,—a great truth, and one which can never be too strenuously insisted on; but a truth which at this epoch can only enslave the mass of the people to its professed representatives, the priests. Through awe of the gods, through fear of divine displeasure, and dread of the unforseen chastisements that displeasure may inflict, and by pretending, honestly or not, to possess the secret of averting it, and of rendering the gods propitious, the priests are able to reduce the people to the most wretched subjection, and to keep them there; at least for a time.

But these institutions must naturally be jealous of power and ambitious of confining it to as few hands as possible. If the sacerdotal corporations were thrown open to all the world, all the world would rush into them, and then there would be no advantage in being a priest. Hence the number who may be priests must be limited. Hence again a distinction of clean and unclean is introduced. Men can be admitted into these corporations only as they descend from the priestly race. As in India, no man can aspire to the priesthood unless of Braminical descent, and among the Jews unless he be of the tribe of Levi. The priestly race was the ruling race; it dealt with science, it held communion with the Gods, and therefore was the purer race. The races excluded from the priesthood were not only regarded as inferior, but as unclean. The Gibeonite to a Jew was both an inferior and an impure. The operation of the principles involved in these considerations, has, in our judgment, begun and effected the slavery of the great mass of the people. It has introduced distinctions of blood or race, founded privileged orders, and secured the rewards of industry to the few, while it has reduced the mass to the most degrading and hopeless bondage.

Now the great mass enslaved by the sacerdotal corporations are not emancipated by the victories which follow by the warrior caste, even when those victories are said to be in behalf of freedom. The military order succeeds the priestly; but in establishing, as it does in Greece and Rome, the supremacy of the state over the church, it leaves the great mass in the bondage in which it finds them. The Normans conquer England, but they scarcely touch the condition of the old Saxon bondmen. The Polish serf lost his freedom, before began the Russian dominion, and he would have recovered none of it, had Poland regained, in her late struggle, her former political independence. The subjection of a nation is in general merely depriving one class of its population of its exclusive right to enslave the people; and the recovery of political independence, is little else than the recovery of this right. The Germans call their rising against Napoleon a rising for liberty, and so it was, liberty for German princes and German nobles; but the German people were more free under Napoleon's supremacy than they are now, or will be very soon. Conquest may undoubtedly increase the number of slaves; but in general it merely adds to the number and power of the middle class. It institutes a new nobility, and degrades the old to the rank of commoners. This is its general effect. We cannot therefore ascribe to conquest, as we did in a former number of this journal, the condition in which the working classes are universally found. They have been reduced to their condition by the priest, not by the military chieftain.

Mankind came out of the savage state by means of the priests. Priests are the first civilizers of the race. For the wild freedom of the savage, they substitute the iron despotism of the theocrat. This is the first step in civilization, in man's career of progress. It is not strange then that some should prefer the savage state to the civilized. Who would not rather roam the forest with a free step and unshackled limb, though exposed to hunger, cold, and nakedness, than crouch an abject slave beneath the whip of the master? As yet civilization has done little but break and subdue man's natural love of freedom; but tame his wild and eagle spirit. In what a world does man even now find himself, when he first awakes and feels some of the workings of his manly nature? He is in a cold, damp, dark dungeon, and loaded all over with chains, with the iron entering into his very soul. He cannot make one single free movement. The priest holds his conscience, fashion controls his tastes, and society with her forces invades the very sanctuary of his heart, and takes command of his love, that which is purest and best in his nature, which alone gives reality to his existence, and from which proceeds the only ray which pierces the gloom of his prison-house. Even that he cannot enjoy in peace and quietness, nor scarcely at all. He is wounded on every side, in every part of his being, in every relation in life, in every idea of his mind, in every sentiment of his heart. O, it is a sad world, a sad world to the young soul just awakening to its diviner instincts! A sad world to him who is not gifted with the only blessing which seems compatible with life as it is—

absolute insensibility. But no matter. A wise man never murmurs. He never kicks against the pricks. What is is, and there is an end of it ; what can be may be, and we will do what we can to make life what it ought to be. Though man's first step in civilization is slavery, his last step shall be freedom. The free soul can never be wholly subdued ; the etherial fire in man's nature may be smothered, but it cannot be extinguished. Down, down deep in the centre of his heart it burns inextinguishable and forever, glowing intenser with the accumulating heat of centuries ; and one day the whole mass of Humanity shall become ignited, and be full of fire within and all over, as a live coal ; and then—slavery, and whatever is foreign to the soul itself, shall be consumed.

But, having traced the inequality we complain of to its origin, we proceed to ask again what is the remedy? The remedy is first to be sought in the destruction of the priest. We are not mere destructives. We delight not in pulling down ; but the bad must be removed before the good can be introduced. Conviction and repentance precede regeneration. Moreover we are Christians, and it is only by following out the Christian law, and the example of the early Christians, that we can hope to effect anything. Christianity is the sublimest protest against the priesthood ever uttered, and a protest uttered by both God and man ; for he who uttered it was God-Man. In the person of Jesus both God and Man protest against the priesthood. What was the mission of Jesus but a solemn summons of every priesthood on earth to judgment, and of the human race to freedom ? He discomfited the learned doctors, and with whips of small cords drove the priests, degenerated into mere money changers, from the temple of God. He instituted himself no priesthood, no form of religious worship. He recognized no priest but a holy life, and commanded the construction of no temple but that of the pure heart. He preached no formal religion, enjoined no creed, set apart no day for religious worship. He preached fraternal love, peace on earth, and good will to men. He came to the soul enslaved, "cabined, cribbed, confined," to the poor child of mortality, bound hand and foot, unable to move, and said in the tones of a God, " Be free; be enlarged; be there room for thee to grow, expand, and overflow with the love thou wast made to overflow with."

In the name of Jesus we admit there has been a priesthood instituted, and considering how the world went, a priesthood could not but be instituted ; but the religion of Jesus repudiates it. It recognizes no mediator between God and man but him who dies on the cross to redeem man ; no propitiation for sin but a pure love, which rises in a living flame to all that is beautiful and good, and spreads out in light and warmth for all the chilled and benighted sons of mortality. In calling every man to be a priest, it virtually condemns every possible priesthood, and in recognising the religion of the new covenant, the religion written on the heart, of a law put within the soul, it abolishes all formal worship.

The priest is universally a tyrant, universally the enslaver of his brethren, and therefore it is Christianity condemns him. It could not prevent the reestablishment of a hierarchy, but it prepared for its ultimate destruction, by denying the inequality of blood, by representing all men as equal before God, and by insisting on the celibacy of the clergy. The best feature of the Church was in its denial to the clergy of the right to marry. By this it prevented the new hierarchy from becoming hereditary, as were the old sacerdotal corporations of India and Judea.

We object to no religious instruction ; we object not to the gathering together of the people on one day in seven, to sing and pray, and listen to a

discourse from a religious teacher ; but we object to every thing like an outward, visible church ; to everything that in the remotest degree partakes of
the priest. A priest is one who stands as a sort of mediator between God
and man ; but we have one mediator, Jesus Christ, who gave himself a ran-
som for all, and that is enough. It may be supposed that we, protestants,
have no priests ; but for ourselves we know no fundamental difference between a catholic priest and a protestant clergyman, as we know no difference
of any magnitude, in relation to the principles on which they are based, between a protestant church and the catholic church. Both are based on the
principle of authority ; both deny in fact, however it may be in manner, the
authority of reason, and war against freedom of mind ; both substitute dead
works for true righteousness, a vain show for the reality of piety, and are
sustained as the means of reconciling us to God without requiring us to become godlike. Both therefore ought to go by the board.

We may offend in what we say, but we cannot help that. We insist upon
it, that the complete and final destruction of the priestly order, in every
practical sense of the word priest, is the first step to be taken towards elevating the laboring classes. Priests are, in their capacity of priests, necessarily enemies to freedom and equality. All reasoning demonstrates this,
and all history proves it. There must be no class of men set apart and authorized, either by law or fashion, to speak to us in the name of God, or to
be the interpreters of the word of God. The word of God never drops
from the priest's lips. He who redeemed man did not spring from the
priestly class, for it is evident that our Lord sprang out of Judea, of which
tribe Moses spake nothing concerning the priesthood. Who in fact were
the authors of the Bible, the book which Christendom professes to receive
as the word of God ? The priests ? Nay, they were the inveterate foes of
the priests. No man ever berated the priests more soundly than did Jere-
miah and Ezekiel. And who were they who heard Jesus the most gladly ?
The priests ? The chief priests were at the head of those who demanded
his crucifixion. In every age the priests, the authorized teachers of religion,
are the first to oppose the true prophet of God, and to condemn his prophe-
cies as blasphemies. They are always a let and a hindrance to the spread
of truth. Why then retain them ? Why not abolish the priestly office ?
Why continue to sustain what the whole history of man condemns as the
greatest of all obstacles to intellectual and social progress.

We say again, we have no objection to teachers of religion, as such ; but
let us have no class of men whose profession it is to minister at the altar.
Let us leave this matter to Providence. When God raises up a prophet, let
that prophet prophesy as God gives him utterance. Let every man speak
out of his own full heart, as he is moved by the Holy Ghost, but let us have
none to prophesy for hire, to make preaching a profession, a means of gaining a livelihood. Whoever has a word pressing upon his heart for utterance,
let him utter it, in the stable, the market-place, the street, in the grove, under the open canopy of heaven, in the lowly cottage, or the lordly hall. No
matter who or what he is, whether a graduate of a college, a shepherd from
the hill sides, or a rustic from the plough. If he feels himself called to go
forth in the name of God, he will speak words of truth and power, for
which Humanity shall fare the better. But none of your hireling priests,
your " dumb dogs " that will not bark. What are the priests of Christendom as they now are ? Miserable panders to the prejudices of the age, loud
in condemning sins nobody is guilty of, but silent as the grave when it concerns the crying sin of the times ; bold as bold can be when there is no dan-

ger, but miserable cowards when it is necessary to speak out for God and outraged Humanity. As a body they never preach a truth till there is none whom it will indict. Never do they as a body venture to condemn sin in the concrete, and make each sinner feel "thou art the man." When the prophets of God have risen up and proclaimed the word of God, and, after persecution and death, led the people to acknowledge it to be the word of God, then your drivelling priest comes forward, and owns it to be a truth, and cries. "cursed of God and man is he who believes it not." But enough. The imbecility of an organized priesthood, of a hireling clergy, for all good, and its power only to demoralize the people and misdirect their energies, is beginning to be seen, and will one day be acknowledged. Men are beginning to speak out on this subject, and the day of reckoning is approaching. The people are rising up and asking of these priests whom they have fed, clothed, honored, and followed, What have ye done for the poor and friendless, to destroy oppression, and establish the kingdom of God on earth? A fearful question for you, O ye priests, which we leave you to answer as best ye may.

The next step in this work of elevating the working classes will be to resuscitate the Christianity of Christ. The Christianity of the Church has done its work. We have had enough of that Christianity. It is powerless for good, but by no means powerless for evil. It now unmans us and hinders the growth of God's kingdom. The moral energy which is awakened it misdirects, and makes its deluded disciples believe that they have done their duty to God when they have joined the church, offered a prayer, sung a psalm, and contributed of their means to send out a missionary to preach unintelligible dogmas to the poor heathen, who, God knows, have unintelligible dogmas enough already, and more than enough. All this must be abandoned, and Christianity, as it came from Christ, be taken up, and preached, and preached in simplicity and in power.

According to the Christianity of Christ no man can enter the kingdom of God, who does not labor with all zeal and diligence to establish the kingdom of God on the earth; who does not labor to bring down the high, and bring up the low; to break the fetters of the bound and set the captive free; to destroy all oppression, establish the reign of justice, which is the reign of equality, between man and man; to introduce new heavens and a new earth, wherein dwelleth righteousness, wherein all shall be as brothers, loving one another, and no one possessing what another lacketh. No man can be a Christian who does not labor to reform society, to mould it according to the will of God and the nature of man; so that free scope shall be given to every man to unfold himself in all beauty and power, and to grow up into the stature of a perfect man in Christ Jesus. No man can be a Christian who does not refrain from all practices by which the rich grow richer and the poor poorer, and who does not do all in his power to elevate the laboring classes, so that one man shall not be doomed to toil while another enjoys the fruits; so that each man shall be free and independent, sitting under "his own vine and figtree with none to molest or to make afraid." We grant the power of Christianity in working out the reform we demand; we agree that one of the most efficient means of elevating the workingmen is to christianize the community. But you must christianize it. It is the gospel of Jesus you must preach, and not the gospel of the priests. Preach the Gospel of Jesus, and that will turn every man's attention to the crying evil we have designated, and will arm every Christian with power to effect those changes in social arrangements, which shall secure to all men the equality of position and condition, which it is already acknowledged they possess in relation to their rights. But let it be the genuine Gospel that you preach, and not that pseudo-gospel, which lulls the conscience asleep, and permits men to feel that they may be servants of God while they are slaves to the world, the flesh, and the devil; and while they ride roughshod over the hearts of their prostrate brethren. We must preach no Gospel that permits men to feel that they are honorable men and good Christians, although rich and with eyes standing out with fatness, while the great mass of their brethren are suffering from iniquitous laws, from mischievous social arrangements, and pining away for the want of the refinements and even the necessaries of life.

We speak strongly and pointedly on this subject, because we are desirous of arresting attention. We would draw the public attention to the striking contrast which actually exists between the Christianity of Christ, and the Christianity of the Church. That moral and intellectual energy which exists in our country, indeed throughout Christendom, and which would, if rightly directed transform this wilderness world into a blooming paradise of God, is now by the pseudo-gospel, which is preached, rendered wholly inefficient, by being wasted on that which, even if effected, would leave all the crying evils of the times untouched. Under the influence of the Church, our efforts are not directed to the reorganization of society, to the introduction of equality between man and man, to the removal of the corruptions of the rich, and the wretchedness of the poor. We think only of saving our own souls, as if a man must not put himself so out of the case, as to be willing to be damned before he can be saved. Paul was willing to be accursed from Christ, to save his brethren from the vengeance which hung over them. But nevertheless we think only of saving our own souls; or if perchance our benevolence is awakened, and we think it desirable to labor for the salvation of others, it is merely to save them from imaginary sins and the tortures of an imaginary hell. The redemption of the world is understood to mean simply the restoration of mankind to the favor of God in the world to come. Their redemption from the evils of inequality, of factitious distinctions, and iniquitous social institutions, counts for nothing in the eyes of the Church. And this is its condemnation.

We cannot proceed a single step, with the least safety, in the great work of elevating the laboring classes, without the exaltation of sentiment, the generous sympathy and the moral courage which Christianity alone is fitted to produce or quicken. But it is lamentable to see how, by means of the mistakes of the Church, the moral courage, the generous sympathy, the exaltation of sentiment, Christianity does actually produce or quicken, is perverted, and made efficient only in producing evil, or hindering the growth of good. Here is wherefore it is necessary on the one hand to condemn in the most pointed terms the Christianity of the Church, and to bring out on the other hand in all its clearness, brilliancy, and glory the Christianity of Christ.

Having, by breaking down the power of the priesthood and the Christianity of the priests, obtained an open field and freedom for our operations, and by preaching the true Gospel of Jesus, directed all minds to the great social reform needed, and quickened in all souls the moral power to live for it or to die for it; our next resort must be to government, to legislative enactments. Government is instituted to be the agent of society, or more properly the organ through which society may perform its legitimate functions. It is not the master of society; its business is not to control society, but to be the organ through which society effects its will. Society has never to petition government; government is its servant, and subject to its commands.

Now the evils of which we have complained are of a social nature. That is, they have their root in the constitution of society as it is, and they have attained to their present growth by means of social influences, the action of government, of laws, and of systems and institutions upheld by society, and of which individuals are the slaves. This being the case, it is evident that they are to be removed only by the action of society, that is, by government, for the action of society is government.

But what shall government do? Its first doing must be an *undoing*. There has been thus far quite too much government, as well as government of the wrong kind. The first act of government we want, is a still further limitation of itself. It must begin by circumscribing within narrower limits its powers. And then it must proceed to repeal all laws which bear against the laboring classes, and then to enact such laws as are necessary to enable them to maintain their equality. We have no faith in those systems of elevating the working classes, which propose to elevate them without calling in the aid of government. We must have government, and legislation expressly directed to this end.

But again what legislation do we want so far as this country is concerned? We want first the legislation which shall free the government, whether State or Federal, from the control of the Banks. The Banks represent the interest of the employer, and therefore of necessity interests adverse to those of the employed; that is, they represent the interests of the business community in opposition to the laboring community. So long as the government remains under the control of the Banks, so long it must be in the hands of the natural enemies of the laboring classes, and may be made, nay, will be made, an instrument of depressing them yet lower. It is obvious then that, if our object be the elevation of the laboring classes, we must destroy the power of the Banks over the government, and place the government in the hands of the laboring classes themselves, or in the hands of those, if such there be, who have an identity of interest with them. But this cannot be done so long as the Banks exist. Such is the subtle influence of credit, and such the power of capital, that a banking system like ours, if sustained, necessarily and inevitably becomes the real and efficient government of the country. We have been struggling for ten years in this country against the power of the banks, struggling to free merely the Federal government from their grasp, but with humiliating success. At this moment, the contest is almost doubtful,— not indeed in our mind, but in the minds of no small portion of our countrymen. The partizans of the Banks count on certain victory. The Banks discount freely to build "log cabins," to purchase "hard cider," and to defray the expense of manufacturing enthusiasm for a cause which is at war with the interests of the people. That they will succeed, we do not for one moment believe; but that they could maintain the struggle so long, and be as strong as they now are, at the end of ten years constant hostility, proves but all too well the power of the Banks, and their fatal influence on the political action of the community. The present character, standing, and resources of the Bank party, prove to a demonstration that the Banks must be destroyed, or the laborer not elevated. Uncompromising hostility to the whole banking system should therefore be the motto of every working man, and of every friend of humanity. The system must be destroyed. On this point there must be no misgiving, no subterfuge, no paliation. The system is at war with the rights and interest of labor, and it must go. Every friend of the system must be marked as an enemy to his race, to his country, and especially to the laborer. No matter who he is, in what party he is found, or what name he bears, he is, in our judgment, no true democrat, as he can be no true Christian.

Following the destruction of the Banks, must come that of all monopolies, of all PRIVILEGE. There are many of these. We cannot specify them all; we therefore select only one, the greatest of them all, the privilege which some have of being born rich while others are born poor. It will be seen at once that we allude to the hereditary descent of property, an anomaly in our American system, which must be removed, or the system itself will be destroyed. We cannot now go into a discussion of this subject, but we promise to resume it at our earliest opportunity. We only say now, that as we have abolished hereditary monarchy and hereditary nobility, we must complete the work by abolishing hereditary property. A man shall have all he honestly acquires, so long as he himself belongs to the world in which he acquires it. But his power over his property must cease with his life, and his property must then become the property of the state, to be disposed of by some equitable law for the use of the generation which takes his place. Here is the principle without any of its details, and this is the grand legislative measure to which we look forward. We see no means of elevating the laboring-classes which can be effectual without this And is this a measure to be easily carried? Not at all. It will cost infinitely more than it cost to abolish either hereditary monarchy or hereditary nobility. It is a great measure, and a startling. The rich, the business community, will never voluntarily consent to it, and we think we know too much of human nature to believe that it will ever be effected peaceably. It will be effected only by the strong arm of physical force. It will come, if it ever come at all, only at the conclusion of war, the like of which the world as yet has never witnessed, and from which, however inevitable it may seem to the eye of philosophy, the heart of Humanity recoils with horror.

We are not ready for this measure yet. There is much previous work to be done, and we should be the last to bring it before the legislature. The time, however, has come for its free and full discussion. It must be canvassed in the public mind, and society prepared for acting on it. No doubt they who broach it, and especially they who support it, will experience a due share of contumely and abuse. They will be regarded by the part of the community they oppose, or may be thought to oppose, as "graceless varlets," against whom every man of substance should set his face. But this is not, after all, a thing to disturb a wise man, nor to deter a true man from telling his whole thought. He who is worthy of the name of man, speaks what he honestly believes the interests of his race demand, and seldom disquiets himself about what may be the consequences to himself. Men have, for what they believed the cause of God or man, endured the dungeon, the scaffold, the stake, the cross, and they can do it again, if need be. This subject must be freely, boldly, and fully discussed, whatever may be the fate of those who discuss it.   EDITOR.

THE

SANITARY CONDITION

OF

THE LABORING POPULATION

OF

NEW YORK.

WITH SUGGESTIONS FOR ITS IMPROVEMENT.

A DISCOURSE

(WITH ADDITIONS)

DELIVERED ON THE 30TH DECEMBER, 1844, AT THE REPOSITORY OF THE
AMERICAN INSTITUTE.

BY

JOHN H. GRISCOM, M. D.

FELLOW OF THE COLLEGE OF PHYSICIANS AND SURGEONS; PHYSICIAN OF THE
NEW YORK HOSPITAL; LATE PHYSICIAN OF THE CITY AND
EASTERN DISPENSARIES.

NEW YORK:

HARPER & BROTHERS, 82 CLIFF-STREET.

1845.

PREFACE.

THE subject matter of the following pages was originally addressed, in the form of a letter, to the Chief Magistrate of the city. Its preparation was undertaken, principally with a view to an exposition of the true principles which should regulate the action of public bodies, in matters relating to the health of cities, in a knowledge of, or concern for, which, recent events had shown our own municipal legislature, to be somewhat deficient. Appreciating fully the importance of its facts and suggestions, the Mayor transmitted the communication to a co-ordinate branch of the City Government, recommending it to their serious attention. After several weeks' deliberation upon it, the committee to whom it was referred arrived at the conclusion, embodied in the following language quoted from their report: " Your committee do not profess to be judges of the subject, or in other words, they do not think it proper at this time, to go into such a measure," and they recommended that the paper be returned to its author. Under these circumstances no other course remained, in order to obtain for the subject its merited attention, than to lay the communication before the public, as was done in a free lecture.

The writer embraces this occasion to acknowledge his obligations to the several professional gentlemen, and Tract agents, who have so kindly aided him in preparing this exposé of the sanitary condition and wants of this city ;—to Hon. James Harper, for his complimentary though un-availing recommendation of the paper to the Common Council, as well as to him and to Hugh Maxwell, Andrew Boardman, Gen. James Tall-madge, Wm. B. Crosby, Peter Cooper, Horatio Allen, T. G. Mower, M. D. U. S. A., James J. Mapes, Hon. Wm. T. McCoun, J. L. Mott, Wm. Shotwell, Josiah Rich, and Wager Hull, for the voluntary and libe-ral assistance rendered by them, in bringing it before the public, in its present form. Thanks are due also to the American Institute for the ree use of their Repository, for the delivery of the discourse.

272 *East Broadway, January*, 1845.

CONTENTS.

SANITARY CONDITION

OF THE

LABORING POPULATION OF NEW YORK.

No duty can engage the attention of the magistracy of a city or state, more dignified in itself, more beneficial to the present generation, or more likely to prove useful to their descendants, than that of procuring and maintaining a sound state of the public health.

Of the three objects contemplated in the Declaration of Independence as necessary to be secured by government, the first named is " Life." Higher purposes cannot be conceived for which governments should be instituted.

As upon the condition of health of an individual are based his physical and mental strength, his ability for self-maintenance, his personal happiness, and that of others dependent on him, and also his usefulness to his family, to the community and his country ; and as the community depends for its prosperity upon the performances of its members, individually and collectively, in the measure of influence committed to them respectively, so does the health of the people affect the capacity and interests of the state.

As upon the individual, when sick, falls an increased pecuniary burden, with (in general) a suspension of income, so upon the state or city, must rest, not only the expenses of removing an unsound condition of public health, but also, from the attendant loss of character, a diminution of its resources.

When individuals of the pauper class are ill, their entire support, and perchance that of the whole family, falls upon the community. From a low state of general health, whether in an individual or in numbers, proceed diminished energy of body and of mind, and a vitiated moral perception, the frequent precursor of habits and deeds, which give employment to the officers of police, and the ministers of justice.

These, among other considerations, together with the recent expression by the chief magistrate of the city of his interest in the sanitary condition of his constituency, by the recommendation to the Common Council of a measure of no ordinary importance to their welfare

1

and comfort,* induce me to urge attention to a measure of improvement which has long impressed my mind, as one, above all others, demanding the action of the City Government.

When it was my pleasure, as it was my duty, in 1842 and '43, to devote my small energies to the sanitary improvement of my native city, stimulated by the consciousness of being engaged in a work heretofore untried in any systematic form, and promising results of the highest and most enduring interests to my fellow citizens, I seized the occasion to recommend to the Common Council the adoption of a measure of Health Police, which I thought of serious necessity. It was the last effort I was enabled to make upon the subject, before I was again consigned to the private ranks, by removal from office. I then hoped to see the small beginning I had made, grow into shape and usefulness under the fostering hands of whoever might be my successors. But, in common with all who had the subject so much at heart, I have been disappointed; for not only was it untouched, but the seeds which I had planted were neglected, and suffered to rot in the ground. Another political revolution brought with it the hope, strengthened by loud professions of municipal reform, that at last the day was certain and at hand, when this subject would be no longer allowed to slumber, but would be regarded as one of the most urgent, and among the first, of the objects of attention by the new Common Council. The expectations of the public could not be mistaken; but an erroneous appreciation, or an entire misconception, in some quarter, of the duties and requisite qualifications of an officer of health, has deferred the hopes entertained of the further prosecution of this interesting, and vitally important, sanitary reform.

The desire which stimulated me in former days was, however, not suffered to sleep in my bosom; a year's reflection, and daily and more extended observation, have not only confirmed my confidence in the feasibility, but increased the conviction of the necessity, of the measure I had proposed, and they have enabled me to modify, enlarge, and illustrate the plan, while the determination displayed by the new chief magistrate to do *his* share of the reforms promised, has inspired me afresh with the hope that the present might be a favourable time for a renewed presentation of my favourite design.

It is a measure of SANITARY REFORM. It is designed to relieve the city of a part of the heavy burden of sickness and mortality, which now oppresses its population, more especially that portion least able to relieve themselves, and most requiring the interposition and protection of Law. It will be seen to be a measure of humanity, of justice to the poor, of safety to the whole people, and of economy to the public treasury.

The objects of this communication, briefly stated, are these ;—1st, to show that there is an immense amount of sickness, physical disability, and premature mortality, among the poorer classes ;—2d, that these are, to a large extent, unnecessary, being in a great degree the results

* Public Baths.

of causes which are removeable ;—3d, that these physical evils are productive of moral evils of great magnitude and number, and which, if considered only in a pecuniary point of view, should arouse the government and individuals to a consideration of the best means for their relief and prevention ; and 4th, to suggest the means of alleviating these evils and preventing their recurrence to so great an extent.

Before proceeding to the explanation of the subject, it is necessary to understand the distinction between *Public Health* and *Individual Health*. In some senses these are different, in others they are similar, and have an intimate connexion. The difference depends chiefly on the cause being *personal* or *general*. Thus an individual may be made sick by causes which affect no one else, as in Dyspepsia, Ophthalmia, Rheumatism, &c., and yet even these diseases, personal and peculiar as they seem to be, will sometimes be found dependent upon causes which affect large numbers at the same time. For instance, the well water, which we have heretofore been obliged to drink, was the frequent cause of Dyspepsia, and some other complaints. Ophthalmia sometimes prevails extensively in asylums and hospitals, and at the Long Island farms it has several times proved a scourge, while both it and Rheumatism are frequent among the residents of damp and dark cellars.

Consumption is an instance of a disease of individual character, but which is, to a very considerable extent, in its commencement and progress, influenced by the circumstances surrounding the patient. The same may be said of Scrofula especially, of which, indeed, many other diseases are only accompaniments or symptoms.

While there is scarcely a disease which may not at times become epidemic or endemic, there are some more strikingly and uniformly so ; ex. gr. : Fevers of various kinds, as Yellow, Typhus, Intermittent, and likewise Small Pox, Scarlatina, Cholera, Measles, &c.

Summer is the season generally deemed most prolific in diseases ; the cause usually assigned for this is the heat of the weather acting upon animal and vegetable matter, producing more extensive and rapid decomposition, the gases from which are generally imagined to be so destructive to health and life. It is true that certain diseases prevail mostly during the hot months—these are Yellow Fever, Cholera Infantum, and the like, while Typhoid and Bilious diseases are frequent in autumn, the latter also attributable to the same causes. The quantity of these offensive vegetable and animal materials is, therefore, among other things, supposed to be, in a considerable degree, the generator, and regulator of the intensity, of these diseases. But this is not by any means the whole of this subject. By a reference to some of the Annual Mortality Reports, it will be seen that sometimes as great a number of deaths occurs during the cold months as during the hot. These are mostly of those affections attributable to the influence of cold and of increased moisture, principally diseases of the Lungs. To a certain degree this view of causes is correct, but in both cases, a well-directed inquiry into the condition in which people live, the position and arrangement of their working and lodging rooms, the character of their food, their habits of dress and cleanliness, the well or ill ventilated rooms they occupy by day and by night, would, in this city, as it has done in other places, develope an amount of ignorance and inattention to the laws of life which would astound the most credulous, and fully account for the great and premature mortality of our citizens.

At all seasons of the year, there is an amount of sickness and death in this, as in all large cities, far beyond those of less densely peopled, more airy and open places, such as country residences. Even in villages of small size, there is an observable difference over the isolated country dwelling, in the proportionate amount of disease prevailing; proving conclusively that the congregation of animal and vegetable matters, with their constant effluvia, which has less chance of escape from the premises, in proportion to the absence of free circulation of air, is detrimental to the health of the inhabitants.

These circumstances have never yet been investigated in this city, as they should be. Our people, especially the more destitute, have been allowed to live out their brief lives in tainted and unwholesome atmospheres, and be subject to the silent and invisible encroachments of destructive agencies from every direction, without one warning voice being raised to point to them their danger, and without an effort to rescue them from their impending fate. Fathers are taken from their children, husbands from their wives, " ere they have lived out half their days,"—the widows and orphans are thrown upon public or private charity for support, and the money which is expended to save them from starvation, to educate them in the public schools, or, perchance, to maintain them in the work-house or the prison, if judiciously spent in improving the sanitary arrangements of the city, and instilling into the population a knowledge of the means by which their health might be protected, and their lives prolonged and made happy, would have been not only saved, but returned to the treasury in the increased health of the population, a much better state of public morals, and, by consequence, a more easily governed and respectable community.

It is of course among the poorer laboring classes that such knowledge is most wanted. The rich, though they may be equally ignorant of the laws of life, and of the best means of its preservation, live in larger houses, with freer ventilation, and upon food better adapted to support health and life. Their means of obtaining greater comforts and more luxuries, are to them, though perhaps unconsciously, the very reason of their prolonged lives. Besides this, they are less harassed by the fears and uncertainty of obtaining for themselves and families a sufficiency of food and clothing. They are thus relieved of some of the most depressing influences, which tend to reduce the energy of mind and body in the poor, and render the latter more susceptible to the inroads of disease.

Sanitary regulations affect the pauper class of the population more directly than any other, because they live in situations and circumstances which expose them more to attacks of disease. They are more crowded, they live more in cellars, their apartments are less ventilated, and more

exposed to vapors and other emanations, &c., hence, ventilation, sewerage, and all other sanitary regulations, are more necessary for them,
and would produce a greater comparative change in their condition.
The influence of drainage upon the health and lives of the population,
is too well known to require, at this day, any argument. Almost every
one has heard of the effects of marshy soil, in country situations, producing Intermittent Fever, or Fever and Ague, and of the entire disap-
pearance of the disease, simply by draining off the water, and permitting the ground to become dry. Its results in populous cities are
equally well marked. The last instance which has come to my knowledge is one stated by Professor Buckland, that in St. Margaret, Leicester, England, containing 22,000 inhabitants, it appeared that one portion
of it was effectually drained, some parts but partially so, and others not
at all. In the latter, the average duration of life is *thirteen years and a
half*, while in the same parish, where the drainage is better, though
only partial, the average is *twenty-two years and a half*, showing the
frightful effects of a bad atmosphere. It were easy to quote several
instances, some important ones, from London statistics, but it is unnecessary, as I presume the fact will not be disputed, that sewerage and
its kindred measures, exert a striking influence over the condition and
duration of human life.

The investigations to which I have briefly alluded, as so necessary
and desirable for this city, have been carried on in other countries, with
a degree of enthusiasm, sustained by talent and learning, which does
honor to Philanthropy. No one can rise from the perusal of the works
of Edwin Chadwick of London, or of Parent Du Chatelet of Paris, or
of many others who have labored in this field of humanity, without
feeling a portion of the ardor which inspires them, and wishing he had
been thrown into the same pursuit, that some of the leaves of the same
laurel might encircle his own brow. It is the cause of Humanity, of
the poor, the destitute, the degraded, of the virtuous made vicious by the
force of circumstances, which they are now investigating, and exposing
to the knowledge of others.

It is often said that " one half the world does not know how the
other half lives." The labor of raising the veil which now separates
the two halves, by which the misery and degradation of the one, have
been concealed from the view of the other, has been theirs and their
associates. Howard, called by distinction *the Philanthropist*, revealed
to the gaze of the astonished multitude the interior of the prisons of
England, and straightway the process of reform commenced in them,
and continued until the prison system of the present day, has become
one of the most striking examples of the spirit of the times. But Chadwick and Du Chatelet, especially the former, are diving still deeper into
the subject of moral and physical reform. They are probing to the
bottom the foul ulcers upon the body of society, and endeavoring to
discover the causes of so much wretchedness and vice, which fill the
prisons and work-houses. Howard's labors tended to *cure* the disease,
Chadwick's to *prevent* it. These operations constitute a highly important part of the great work of melioration and improvement, in the con-

dition of mankind, now going on, in nearly all civilized countries, and which characterize the present age.

If not on a par, in importance, with the improvement in education, which has of late made such rapid strides, it certainly is second only to it, and indeed it may well be questioned, whether improvement in the physical condition of the lower stratum of society, is not a necessary precedent, in order that education of the mind may exercise its full and proper influence over the general well-being. Teach them how to live, so as to avoid diseases and be more comfortable, and then their school education will have a redoubled effect, in mending their morals, and rendering them intelligent and happy. But without sound bodies, when surrounded with dirt, foul air, and all manner of filthy associations, it is vain to expect even the child of education, to be better than his ignorant companions, if indeed you do not, by educating him, give him an additional weapon, by which he may prey more successfully upon his fellows.

This country, and especially this city, it is hoped, will not much longer be behind others in this cause of the suffering poor and depressed humanity. Some movements, promoting this investigation, have recently been commenced, but much is yet to be done. The path has been pointed out to us by pioneers across the Atlantic ; there is abundant disposition to pursue the object, which only requires to be sought out, and put to work by the authorities, to procure all the desirable results of such labours.

The system of tenantage to which large numbers of the poor are subject, I think, must be regarded as one of the principal causes, of the helpless and noisome manner in which they live. The basis of these evils is the subjection of the tenantry, to the merciless inflictions and extortions of the *sub-landlord*. A house, or a row, or court of houses, is hired by some person of the owner, on a lease of several years, for a sum which will yield a fair interest on the cost. The *owner* is thus relieved of the great trouble incident to the changes of tenants, and the collection of rents. His income is sure from one individual, and obtained without annoyance or oppression on his part. It then becomes the object of the lessee, to make and save as much as possible, with his adventure, sufficient sometimes to enable him to purchase the property in a short time.

The tenements, in order to admit a greater number of families, are divided into small apartments, as numerous as decency will admit. Regard to comfort, convenience, and health, is the last motive ; indeed, the great ignorance of this class of speculators (who are very frequently foreigners and keep a grog shop on the premises) would prevent a proper observance of these, had they the desire. These closets, for they deserve no other name, are then rented to the poor, from week to week, or month to month, the rent being almost invariably required in advance, at least for the first few terms. The families moving in first, after the house is built, find it clean, but the lessee has no supervision over their habits, and however filthy the tenement may become, he cares not, so that he receives his rent. He and his family are often found steeped as low in depravity and discomforts, as any of his tenants, being above them only in the possession of money, and doubtless often beneath them in moral worth and sensibility.

It is very frequently the case that families, after occupying rooms a few weeks, will change their location, leaving behind them all the dirt which their residence has occasioned. Upon this the next comers will sit down, being so much occupied with the hurry of moving, and with the necessity of placing their furniture immediately in order, that attention to cleansing the apartment is out of the question, until they are " settled," and then, if done at all, it is in the most careless and inefficient manner. Very often, perhaps in a majority of the cases in the class of which I now speak, no cleaning other than washing the floor, is ever attempted, and that but seldom. Whitewashing, cleaning of furniture, of bedding, or persons, in many cases is *never* attempted. Some have old pieces of carpet, which are never shaken, (they would not bear it,) and are used to hide the filth on the floor. Every corner of the room, of the cupboards, of the entries and stairways, is piled up with dirt. The walls and ceilings, with the plaster broken off in many places, exposing the lath and beams, and leaving openings for the escape from within of the effluvia of vermin, dead and alive, are smeared with the blood of unmentionable insects, and dirt of all indescribable colours. The low rooms are diminished in their areas by the necessary encroachments of the roof, or the stairs leading to the rooms above ; and behind and under them is a hole, into which the light of day never enters, and where a small bed is often pushed in, upon which the luckless and degraded tenants pass their nights, weary and comfortless.

In these places, the filth is allowed to accumulate to an extent almost incredible. Hiring their rooms for short periods only, it is very common to find the poor tenants moving from place to place, every few weeks. By this practice they avoid the trouble of cleansing their rooms, as they can leave behind them the dirt which they have made. The same room, being occupied in rapid succession, by tenant after tenant, it will easily be seen how the walls and windows will become broken, the doors and floors become injured, the chimneys filled with soot, the whole premises populated thickly with vermin, the stairways, the common passage of several families, the receptacle for all things noxious, and whatever of self-respect the family might have had, be crushed under the pressure of the degrading circumstances by which they are surrounded.

Another very important particular in the arrangements of these tenements must here be noticed. By the mode in which the rooms are planned, *ventilation is entirely prevented.* It would seem as if most of these places were built expressly for this purpose. They have one or two windows, and a door at one side of the room, but no opening anywhere else. A draught of air *through,* is therefore an utter impossibility. The confined position of the dwelling itself, generally, prevents the access of the external currents of air, even to the outside, to any considerable extent. The window sashes, in addition, perhaps are so arranged, that the upper one (if there are two) cannot be let down, being permanently fastened up ; hence the external air, poor as it is, cannot visit the upper section of the room, unless by opening the door, by which the interior of the room is exposed to view. If there is a sleeping apartment, it is placed at the extremity of the room farthest from the windows, is generally but little larger than sufficient to hold a bedstead, and its area is reduced, for air, by the bed furniture, trunks, boxes, &c. and having no windows, fresh air and sun light are entire strangers to its walls. In this dark hole there is, of course, a concentrated accumulation of the effluviæ of the bodies and breaths of the persons sleeping in it, (frequently the whole family, several in number,) and this accumulation goes on from night to night, without relief, until it can easily be believed the smell becomes intolerable, and its atmosphere productive of the most offensive and malignant diseases. There is no exaggeration in this description. I cannot too highly color the picture, if I would. What, then, will be thought of the condition of thousands of our fellow-citizens in the *winter season*, when every crevice is closed to keep out the cold air, and when I state, that what I have described, I have repeatedly seen and felt in the *summer*, when the windows and doors are opened to the fullest extent, day and night, admitting all the ventilation possible, small as it is.

I have had recent occasion to visit several of these pestiferous places, and I pen these paragraphs in the month of August, with their sight and smell fresh upon my senses.

The almost entire absence of household conveniences, contributes much to the prostration of comfort and self-respect of these wretched people. The deficiency of water, and the want of a convenient place for washing, with no other place for drying clothes than the common sitting and bed room, are very serious impediments in the way of their improvement. Without any convenient or safe place to deposit wood, or coal, or food in large quantities, all their purchases are by " the small," from the neighboring grocer, (who is perhaps the landlord,) at prices from 10 to 50 per cent. above the rates at which they might be obtained, under better circumstances.

But the most offensive of all places for residence are the *cellars*. It is almost impossible, when contemplating the circumstances and condition of the poor beings who inhabit these holes, to maintain the proper degree of calmness requisite for a thorough inspection, and the exercise of a sound judgment, respecting them. You must descend to them ; you must feel the blast of foul air as it meets your face on opening the door ; you must grope in the dark, or hesitate until your eye becomes accustomed to the gloomy place, to enable you to find your way through the entry, over a broken floor, the boards of which are protected from your tread by a half inch of hard dirt ; you must inhale the suffocating vapor of the sitting and sleeping rooms ; and in the dark, damp recess, endeavor to find the inmates by the sound of their voices, or chance to see their figures moving between you and the flickering blaze of a shaving burning on the hearth, or the misty light of a window coated with dirt and festooned with cobwebs—or if in search of an invalid, take care that you do not fall full length upon the bed with her, by stumbling against the bundle of rags and straw, dignified by that name, lying on the floor, under the window, if window there is ;—all this, and much more, beyond the reach of my pen, must be felt and seen, ere you can appreciate in its full force the mournful and disgusting condition, in which many thousands of the subjects of our government pass their lives.

" There vapors, with malignant breath
Rise thick, and scatter midnight death."

There are two features of a cellar residence which more especially render them objectionable; 1st, the dampness, and 2d, the more incomplete ventilation. In *any* cellar the impossibility of access for the heat of the sun to the parts of the soil adjacent to the floor and walls, and the absence of currents of air through the room, keep it much more damp than rooms above ground, where the heat and air have freer access. This is emphatically the case with *inhabited* cellars, inasmuch as the inmates are careful to exclude the external air, by closing all the avenues of its approach, in order to preserve the temperature high in winter and low in summer. The moisture, whose escape is thus prevented, is in itself a very prolific source of disease, and combined with the darkness and impure air of these places, is actually productive of a great amount of sickness. Could the sun and air be made to reach them, and were it possible to establish a sufficient ventilation through them, much of their noxiousness would be relieved ; but under no circumstances can they be made fit for the residence of *living* beings ; they are properly adapted only as receptacles for the dead.

In addition to these impediments to the drying of these places, they are very often so situated, that the surface water finds its way into them at every rain storm. It may be remembered that in the summer of 1843 all the underground apartments in many sections of the city were completely flooded by a deluge of rain. In the eastern part of the city, in Delancy, Rivington, Stanton, and many other of the neighbouring streets, almost every cellar (and great numbers of them are inhabited) were half filled with water. This evil will not recur to so great an extent, in the neighborhood alluded to, sewers having been built in some of the streets. But in other sections, indeed in every section, where the position of the basement is unaltered, and sewers are not constructed, the nuisance must be suffered at every rain storm. In some courts to which I can point, *the surface is below the level of the street*, and at every rain, the water being unable to run off into the street, is all discharged down into the adjacent areas and cellars, keeping them almost constantly wet. It was but a short time ago I met with the case of a woman, the wife of a tailor living in a noted court in Walker-street, and occupying partly a basement, in which she was compelled to pass much of her time. She has lived there six months, four of which she has been sick with rheumatism, and on that account, unable to work. Otherwise she would be able to earn considerable by assisting her husband. They have four children depending upon them, and are obliged to seek assistance from the public, in consequence of this sickness. She attributes her disease to the water in the cellar, which runs in, and obliges her to bale out, and wipe up, at every storm. The money expended upon them in charity, would have rectified all this

2

difficulty, have preserved the health and strength of the family, and saved all parties much trouble and suffering.

Another case is that of a woman with two children—her husband a labourer—living in a cellar in Lewis-street, two months. Before moving to this place, she lived in an upper room in Spring-street, and was there always well, *but has been sick ever since she went to live in the cellar.*

Another applied for medical aid who lives in a cellar, *immediately adjoining which, is the vault of a church-yard, the moisture from which comes through into the apartment, to such an extent, as obliged them to move the bed away from the wall.*

It is not a difficult matter for the Dispensary Physician, while receiving applications for medical aid at the office, to distinguish, in a majority of cases, the cellar residents from all others, without asking a question. If the whitened and cadaverous countenance should be an insufficient guide, *the odor of the person* will remove all doubt; a musty smell, which a damp cellar only can impart, pervades every article of dress, the woolens more particularly, as well as the hair and skin.

At No. 50 Pike-street is a cellar about ten feet square, and seven feet high, having only one very small window, and the old fashioned, inclined cellar door. In this small place, were lately residing *two families consisting of ten persons,* of all ages.

Dr. Reid, the ventilator of the new houses of parliament, places the quantity of air necessary for the perfect, free, and wholesome respiration of each adult person at ten cubic feet per minute.* Others before him have estimated it as low as two cubic feet. I coincide with Dr. Reid in his statement of the amount necessary for the attainment and preservation of *perfect health ;* but the latter estimate is entirely too low. If we take the average of these two extremes, (six feet,) we shall find that the ten persons in the cellar of 50 Pike-street would render its 700 feet of air, unfit for the support of health, *in less than fifteen minutes.* Now, suppose them to retire and close the door and window at ten o'clock at night, what must be the condition of the air of the room, when they rise at five the next morning ?

Is it astonishing that the Dispensary is called upon, very frequently, to extend its aid to these inmates ? and should there not be some remedy for this dreadful state of things ? The whole of these premises, besides the cellar, is in a condition unfit for human habitation, and yet crowded to a melancholy degree. A sanitary law that would reach this case, and

* " If we look to the fact that less than half a cubic foot of air passes through the lungs of an adult in a minute, this estimate may at first appear excessive, but if we remember, that at each expiration, a quantity of air is emitted, which mingles with an additional portion of air largely exceeding its own bulk, and that there are twenty such expirations in a minute, while provision is likewise required for the air that affects the surface of the body, and for the endless variety of minor effects produced by furniture, lighting, heating, refreshments, &c: ; where no peculiar adaptation for these purposes have been introduced beyond those usually observed, it will be seen that the estimate is by no means immoderate. *The real question is not, what the constitution can bear, but* that amount which is conveniently accessible in ordinary habitations, *and which is essential for the wants of the system.*"—ILLUSTRATIONS OF THE THEORY AND PRACTICE OF VENTILATION, BY DAVID BOSWELL REID, M. D.

be well applied, would save a large amount of life, health, money, and morals. The same may be said of hundreds of other places, of which this is a fair average sample. There are many places still worse.

An inquiry into the amount of air allowed to children in schools, to the inmates of prisons, and to laborers in work-shops, will exhibit a degree of neglect, or ignorance, in relation to this vitally important subject, in individuals having the training and guardianship of these classes, truly lamentable, as well as surprising. For examples.

One of the Public Infant Schools of this city, having an average attendance the year round, of 200 children, was for a long time, and until recently, kept in the basement of a church, the dimensions of which were 46 × 30 × 8½ feet, equal to 11730 cubic feet. The proximity of the adjoining buildings rendered it so dark in a sunny day, it was difficult to see to write on a slate a short distance from the windows. A large stove warmed the room in winter. These children had about sixty cubic feet each, for the six school hours, equal to ten cubic feet per hour, when each child should have ten cubic feet per minute. *Ventilation was unthought of,* until recently, and now in consequence of the position and arrangement of the building, it is very imperfect.

The dormitories of the House of Refuge have each an area of less than 200 cubic feet. When the door is closed on the inmate, his bed, which is about eighteen inches from the floor, is extended nearly across the cell, diminishing by so much its atmospheric area, and intercepting almost wholly the communication between a very small opening at the bottom, and another at the top, and one in the middle, of the door. Those openings were intended, but are wholly inadequate, for ventilation, even if no bed were there. For the perfect decarbonization of the blood, the air in each dormitory, at the lowest proper estimate, will remain sufficiently pure for the space of thirty minutes only, yet the youthful inmates are locked in from 8 P. M. till 5 A. M. *nine hours, with no other ventilation than what I have described.* Their work-shops cannot be said to be much better supplied with air. The effects of this privation are plainly marked upon the countenances, and general physical development, of the children.

The general arrangement of the cells in the City Prison is but little if any better. Besides the small window near the ceiling on one side, air is admitted only through *five auger holes in the door* on the opposite side, and these latter are of no service at night, when the inner door is closed.

We now naturally come, in the course of this inquiry, to two important questions, preparatory to the suggestion I intend to make, of a remedy for these evils.

1st. What is the effect of this degraded and filthy manner of life upon the health of the individuals, and the duration of their lives?

2d. What is its influence upon their morals, their self-respect, and appreciation of virtue?

The answers to these queries must have an important bearing upon the moral obligations, the pecuniary expenses, and the order and character of the City Government. If it can be shown that much sickness and many premature deaths are results of these residences, it will be evident that the care of the sick, and the support of the widows and orphans, must add greatly to the expenses of the city ; and if it can be proved that degraded habits, bad associations, and immoral practises (though the results only of circumstances, and not of education) are their consequences, it will be equally apparent, there will thus be continued, a class in the community more difficult to govern, more disposed to robbery, mobs, and other lawless acts, and less accessible to the influences of religious and moral instruction.

With regard to the first question, an argument can hardly be necessary. Almost every one can recall to mind, some proof of the effects of nauseous odors, of the inhalation of foul air, or of sleeping in a small confined apartment, upon his own health and feelings. These effects may have been only temporary, but they will serve to show that a prolonged continuance of them, must, in reason, produce permanently bad results upon the mental and corporeal powers. If the inhaled air (one great source of the life, health, and vigor of the animal structure) is deteriorated in quality, or diminished in quantity, below the standards necessary for a perfect decarbonization of the blood in the lungs, the blood necessarily becomes burdened with impurities, and fails to impart to the system the qualities demanded by nature for the due maintenance of health and strength. Every city resident who takes a stroll into the country, can testify to the difference between the atmospheres of the two situations :—the contrast of our out-door (to say nothing of the in-door) atmosphere, loaded with the animal and vegetable exhalations of our streets, yards, sinks, and cellars—and the air of the mountains, rivers, and grassy plains, needs no epicurean lungs to detect it. The superior corporeal activity, and the mental exhilaration imparted by it, are the prima facie proofs of its superiority. Compare the pale face of the city belle, or matron, after the long confinement of the winter and spring, with the same countenance in the fall, upon her return from a few weeks tour to the Springs and Niagara, and observe whether the return of the long absent rose upon the cheek, is not accompanied with a greater elasticity of frame, and a happier and stronger tone of mind.

Descend a few steps further, from the airy and well-lighted chamber and parlor, to the confined apartments of the pent-up court, and the damp, secluded cellar ; draw a contrast between the gay inhabitant of the former, and the attenuated tenant of the latter, and we may then judge of the influences of the air, which they respectively respire.

Observe, further, the vast difference in the development of frame, healthiness of countenance, and power of endurance, between the children of the farmer, and the offspring of the city resident.

A highly respected friend, a distinguished advocate, informed me, lately, that some of his children had not had a day's illness during the two years they had been at school in the country, while the others, residing at home, though in a comparatively salubrious position in the city, cost him from twenty to thirty dollars each, per annum, for medicine and medical attendance.

The following facts show, by figures, the sad condition in which a very large number of our people may be said, barely to exist.

As a great part of the population of these places are destitute of the means of paying for medical assistance, the duty of ministering to them in hours of sickness, falls upon the Dispensary Physicians. I find, upon examining the records of their labors, the reports of the three medical charities, for the year ending March, 1844, there were prescribed for at the offices, and the homes of the poor, at the

Northern   Dispensary, 13,317 Patients,
Eastern   "   17,107   "
New York   "   23,858   "

Total,   54,282

From this number a deduction is to be made of those vaccinated, being 4505. In visiting the sick poor at their homes, however, it happens very frequently that some are prescribed for, whose names are neglected to be entered, so that it is perfectly safe to estimate the number of sick persons who received aid from these charities, to be *over* 50,000 *in one year*. In the corresponding year there were admitted into the Alms House Hospital 2332 patients, and into the City Hospital, about 1000, exclusive of seamen, making a total of over 53,000, without enumerating the sick poor attended by private charity.

This is truly an appalling statement. Those unacquainted with the number and character of the poor, would scarcely believe so great a number actually existed in this city, destitute of means, and there might arise an inclination to suspect an exaggeration of the statements, were not the names and residences entered at length on the registers.

Does it not become the duty of the magistrate and the philanthropist upon the presentation of such a statement as this, of the waste and havoc of the life, health, and strength of the people, to institute an inquiry into the causes of so great an amount of sickness, and to use every possible means to alleviate them?

Another fact developed by these reports is conclusive as to the influence of the causes to which I have alluded, of this great amount of sickness.

If the habitation of damp, dark cellars, and of narrow alleys and courts, and the breathing of a vitiated atmosphere, are *rightly* asserted to be promotive of disease, then those most subject to these causes should be sick in the greatest numbers. Now the *male* part of this class breathe a totally different air through the day, at their labors in the streets, along the rivers, or upon buildings, and *only at night* are they subject to the worse atmosphere. Thus more than half their hours are passed under more healthful circumstances. Even the boys who spend several hours at play, or even in a partially ventilated school-house, follow an improved regimen in this particular. On the other hand, *the females, both night and day*, inhale the polluted atmosphere of the dwellings, and are more continually under all the other bad influences of their unfortunate situations.

Do the official results correspond with these premises?

It will be seen upon examining the Dispensary returns, that in some years the proportion of females to males, prescribed for at the Dispensaries, has been as 12 to 10½—in others, 12 to 8½, and in one instance as 19 to 11. This comparison is rendered more striking when we take into account the greater amount of intemperance among the males.

The Annual Reports of the City Inspector show that nearly one-half the deaths by consumption are of the *foreign part of the population*, and that more than *one-third* the whole number of deaths are of foreigners. Such an immense disproportion can only be accounted for on the supposition that some extraordinary causes of death prevail among the strangers who come to reside among us. Now it is a pretty well ascertained fact, that a large majority of the cellar and court population of this city consists of persons of foreign birth and their children. Of the Dispensary patients, about 60 *per cent.* are natives of other countries, and if it were possible to ascertain the parentage of the children receiving aid from these institutions, we should find a larger proportion than this directly dependent upon foreigners. There is no doubt that 75 per cent. of them are either immigrants, or the children of such. Put these facts, then, side by side, and we are confirmed in the conclusion that the domiciliary condition of these poor beings, the confined spaces in which they dwell, the unwholesome air they breathe, and their filth and degradation, are prolific sources of an immense amount of distress and sickness, which in their turn, serve, by the loss of time, of wages, and of strength, to aggravate the miserableness of their condition, to increase the danger to the public health, and the burden of public and private charity.

The evils thus resulting are occasionally exhibited in an endemic form, i. e., some disease of a marked character will break out and attack a considerable number of persons in the same neighborhood, the extent of its prevalence depending upon the extent of the cause, or the facilities for its propagation. Thus a fever may commence in a certain place inhabited mostly by the destitute and filthy :—if the adjoining tenements are occupied by the same class of persons, and kept in the same dirty and ill-ventilated condition, the tenants of the latter will be very liable to attacks of the same disorder. The disease will often be observed to pass by houses in a better condition, and re-appear at a distance, where similar causes prevail.

Frequently, too, the prevailing disorder, though perhaps covering a large district, will be seen only in certain parts of houses, as the cellars. Several instances of this have occurred in New York, one of which was the memorable Banker (now Madison) Street fever of 1820. 562 blacks inhabited the infected district, of whom 119 lived in cellars ; of these 119, 54 were sick of the prevailing fever, and 24 died. Of the remaining 443, who lived above ground, 101 were sick, and 46 died. Out of 48 blacks in 10 cellars, 33 were sick, of whom 14 died, while out of 120 whites, living immediately over their heads, in the same houses, not one even had the fever. Numerous other instances have occurred, which have attracted less attention, probably because of their frequency rendering them less notorious. But there is, as is well known to the physicians who move among these haunts of wretchedness, a silent agency continually at work, destroying annually the health and lives of hundreds of our fellow-citizens, and entirely within the power of the city government to control or subdue, but which, by a strange neglect, appears to have been hitherto allowed to work out destruction unopposed.

I am enabled, by the kindness of some of my medical friends, to present a history of some of the endemic diseases which prevail in the precincts to which I have alluded. The following communications contain the testimony of gentlemen thoroughly acquainted with the character of these places, and the condition of their inmates, and whose opinions are entitled to the most weighty consideration.

I will only add to their views, that disorders arising and fostered in these low places, will sometimes become so virulent as to extend among and jeopard the lives of better classes of citizens ; while on the occurrence of general epidemics, these localities constitute minor streams, whose poisonous waters, as they mingle with the great river of disease, give additional impetus to its destructive current.

From John A Swett, M. D. one of the Attending Physicians of the City Hospital.

New York, August 12th, 1844.

DEAR DOCTOR.—The epidemic continued fever, about which we had some conversation a few days ago, occurred during the summer and autumn of 1837, at the time I was physician to the N. Y. Dispensary, and had charge of a district, embracing a part of the 6th, 10th, and 14th wards, being bounded on the north and south by Walker and Chatham-streets, and extending east and west, from Allen to Mott-streets. The first cases occurred, I think, in July, and the disease continued to prevail in the latter part of September, at which time I ceased to observe it, being myself attacked with the same disease, which confined me until the cold weather in December, at which time the disease had disappeared in the district.

The epidemic interesting me very much, the cases were carefully observed, and in many instances full notes were taken of their history. The number of cases which fell under my observation was probably about thirty—it is very possible it exceeded this. They resembled each other very much in their history, and the more so, probably, from the fact that they were subjected to a very simple and uniform treatment. The organs principally affected were the brain, and those of the abdomen. Delirium and stupor, with tympanitis, and abdominal tenderness, were very commonly noticed, and often in a very marked degree, although vomiting and diarrhœa were seldom urgent, and always easily controlled. The tongue always became dry as the disease advanced, and typhoid symptoms, although not in an aggravated form, usually appeared before the termination. I remember the frequent occurrence of rose colored spots over the abdomen, and that in some instances, they were so large and numerous as to constitute one of the most marked symptoms, resembling rather the eruption of roseola, than the trifling eruption we frequently notice in fever. Nearly all the cases recovered. I do not remember more than one or two that terminated fatally, and in these no post mortem examination was allowed. The treatment pursued was very simple, and consisted chiefly in attention to cleanliness, and to ventilation; the patients being allowed the free use of simple beverage, with the occasional administration of mild purgatives in some instances, and small doses of morphine in others; indeed fresh air, as far as it could be had, and cold water, were the principal agents to which I trusted for the restoration of my patients, and I had seldom reason to regret my reliance on this simple means. The benefit of this mode of treating these cases appeared to me particularly marked during the convalescence, which was surprisingly rapid, and almost invariably commenced on or near the fourteenth day after the attack.

The poor population of this district was principally Irish and German, whose habits, as you know, are more or less filthy, and who lived crowded together, with a family in every room in the house, and sometimes more. I did not observe, however, that the disease was decidedly more prevalent in those parts of the district which were most filthy and crowded, at least so far as individual houses were concerned, although if the district be divided into two equal parts by the Bowery, it is a remarkable fact that *all the cases*, I think without an exception, occurred to the west of this great thoroughfare, and it is quite certain, also, that the poor population is more crowded in this western division where the fever prevailed, than in the eastern where it did not exist at all.

The most striking circumstance that I noticed in this fever was, that in every instance (save one which I regard as a doubtful case) the disease existed *either in basements, or the first floor of houses that had neither basements nor cellars under them.* This circumstance early attracted my attention, and constant inquiry never enabled me to find any cases in the upper stories of those houses in which the disease was prevailing in the basement rooms, and yet these upper rooms were as full of people and as filthy as those below, and a more or less frequent communication existed between them. As a matter of course these basements were less exposed to ventilation than the rooms above, but this was not always the case. I remember, in particular, one old wooden house at the corner of two streets, without cellar or basement, in which the disease prevailed on the ground floor where the ventilation was excellent, and where filthy habits were certainly not observed. Indeed, it has always been my opinion that the cause of this fever was an emanation from the ground on which the dwellings in which it occurred were standing, and the principal reasons for this opinion I have already stated, viz. the abrupt and complete limitation of the disease in one direction at least, by the Bowery, and its occurrence only in the lowest rooms.   I remain truly yours,

JOHN A. SWETT.

From Stephen Wood, M. D. Physician to the Eastern Dispensary.

211 Madison-street, 8th Mo. 17th, 1844.

DEAR DOCTOR.—Agreeably to thy request, I have drawn up the following sketch of some cases, (which have occurred in my practice as one of the physicians of the E. Dispensary,) illustrating in some measure, the influence of locality and mode of life on health and diseases, which thou art at liberty to use in such manner as thou may think proper.

Some time during the Autumn of last year I attended at No. 249 Stanton-street, Charles Peterson, aged about forty-five years, of intemperate habits. He had Pneumonia, followed by Typhus symptoms, and lived but two or three days after my first visiting him. He had been sick for several days previously, and without medical attendance. At No. 96 Sheriff-street, and in the immediate neighborhood of this case, and at nearly the same time, I had another of like character, of about the same age, and of similar habits. This case likewise terminated fatally in the course of a few days.

In one of these cases the pulse was full and strong, so that I thought it best to bleed. The bleeding was followed by blisters, &c. ; but it soon became necessary to resort to stimulants, and other supporting measures. In the other case bleeding was not practised ; but a blister was applied to the chest, expectorants, stimulants, &c., administered, although with but temporary relief.

Both of these men, with their families, were wretchedly poor, living in cellar rooms, some six feet below the street, dark and damp, with very scanty ventilation, and ceilings, or rather beams so low, that I could not stand erect between them. The apartments at my first visit were filthy and offensive in the extreme ; yet some improvement became evident afterwards, as I generally in this class of patients, find it necessary in the first place, to lecture them on the importance of cleanliness, ventilation, temperance, &c.

I attribute the result of these cases, mainly to the situation, manner of living, and habits of the subjects. This at least was the conclusion I recollect I came to at the time ; my attention having being arrested at the fatality of cases which at first appeared likely to have a successful issue, as I had often had others of a like nature, terminate well under more favorable circumstances.

The widow of the patient, at 96 Sheriff-street, died last spring, with fever of a low form in the same miserable house. *Subsequently at this house a quantity of water was found under the flooring.* Lodgers were taken in there, and on one occasion, I found the owner, a colored woman, intoxicated.

Since her death, between one and two months ago, I attended a man of similar habits with the two cases above described, in an upper room of the same house with the two last, small, dirty, and badly ventilated. This also was a case of Pneumonia Typhoides, and ended in death.

I have had other cases in these premises at different times, and some of them have been attended, (indeed I may say *most,*) with symptoms indicating a low state of the vital forces, and they have been generally slow in convalescing.

All these cases occurred in colored persons. The building in which they were is only occupied by persons of this class ; and most of them

3

appear to be intemperate, and of the very lowest grade—" the offscouring of all things."

On the premises, and in the vicinity, are a number of vile grog-shops, at which these poor creatures obtain the means of their physical sufferings, and intellectual, moral, and religious degradation, and too often, it is to be feared, their final and lasting ruin.

I rejoice however in stating, that within a few months a visible improvement has taken place in these abodes of misery, and in some of their occupants. This has been effected mainly by the Health Warden and Street Inspecter of the ward (eleventh.) One of the groceries through their interference has been shut up, some of the worst of the rooms closed, and the inmates sent to Blackwell's Island.

In the course of my practice, I have had many forms of disease apparently caused and kept up by residence in low, dark, damp, and insufficiently ventilated apartments. Yet I would not exclude the influence of other sources of the " ills which flesh is heir to," particularly of deficient or improper nourishment and bad nursing ; and frequently no nursing at all, especially among Dispensary patients.

The condition of the dwellings of many of the poor of our city, is a subject much needing the careful attention of the philanthropist, if not of our municipal authorities, who, it appears to me, ought to have a more watchful supervision of the tenements of this portion of our population.   Respectfully thy Friend,
                                        STEPHEN WOOD.

From B. W. McCready, M. D. late Physician to the City Dispensary, and City Prison.

Wednesday, September 3d, 1844.

MY DEAR SIR—If I apprehend aright the purport of your queries, you wish to know of me whether I have met with any cases of infectious diseases occurring among the poor, which might have been prevented by proper sanitary regulations. In the summer of '42, a number of cases of Typhus fever, of a very severe type, occurred in a building in the rear of No. 49 Elizabeth street, under circumstances which left no doubt as to its local origin. The front building, a small two story frame house, was partly occupied by the proprietor, or lessee, of the building, as a liquor store, and partly sub-let to several Irish families. A covered alley-way led to the rear building. This was a double frame house, three stories in height. It stood in the centre of the yard. Ranged next the fence, where a number of pig styes and stables, which surrounded the yard on three sides. From the quantity of filth, liquid and otherwise, thus caused, the ground, I suppose, had been rendered almost impassable, and to remedy this, the yard had been completely boarded over, so that the earth could nowhere be seen. These boards were partially decayed, and by a little pressure, even in dry weather, a thick greenish fluid could be forced up through their crevices. The central building was inhabited wholly by negroes. In this building there occurred, in the course of six weeks, nine cases of Typhus fever. The two first taken, resided on the ground floor, and both died. The others residing on the second and third floors, finally recovered. Two other cases at least, occurred among those who were temporarily in the house as nurses, or visitors, but as they were all at their own houses, these patients did not come under my own observation. The disease would undoubtedly have spread farther, but the inhabitants took the alarm, and the house for a time was deserted. At my solicitation the Alderman of the ward visited the building, the number of pigs about the establishment was reduced to that allowed by law, and chloride of lime, white-washing, &c., liberally, and assiduously employed.

I had three cases of Typhus in a back cellar, in the rear, I think, of 16 Marion Street, though it may have been 12 or 14. The cellar was ten or twelve feet under ground, the first floor of the house being a little elevated above the level of the yard, and dimly lighted (not ventilated) by one small window. It either had no communication whatever with the front cellar, or the communication was completely blocked up. A child was in the first place seized by the disease, then its mother, then a lodger who lived with them. They all recovered, but how, it would be hard to tell. No one appeared to come near them, save the visitor from the almshouse, and myself.

That Typhus fever, generated in the first place under particular circumstances, may become highly contagious, is now, I believe, the general opinion of the best informed of the profession. A very striking illustration of this occurred in my practice. A young Irish woman who had come to this country with her husband and child, was taken with Typhus at the house of her father, just after she had been landed from an emigrant ship. The family, at that time, resided in Madison Street. She had a very severe attack, and came near dying. Next, her father, who had been many years in this country, was seized. Then the child. The family now removed from Madison Street to Elizabeth Street. The greatest care was taken to preserve proper ventilation, cleanliness, &c. In despite of this, the disease sucessively attacked two younger brothers, the mother, two grown sisters, and an elder brother. I was in attendance in the family from Christmas, at which time I found the young woman who was first attacked, almost in articulo mortis, till May, when the disease, after having successively visited every member of the family, finally disappeared.

Yours, sincerely,
B. W. McCready.

Among the diseases most frequently resulting from an imperfection in the means of life, is *scrofula*, in its Protean forms. Dr. Watson, of London, the latest authority in the Practice of Medicine, in speaking of the general causes of this disease, enumerates as the most prominent, " Insufficient nutriment, exposure to wet and cold, impurity of atmosphere, want of natural exercise, and mental disquietude. To estimate the separate effect of each of these causes, may be difficult, but their combined influence is unquestionable." After a considerable experience in Dispensary and Hospital practice, I hesitate not to declare, and believe I shall be supported in the opinion by my colleagues in the institutions with which I have been and am now connected, that *this disease is the great scourge of the pauper population.* It exhibits itself in the skin, in the eyes, the viscera of the abdomen and of the chest, in the muscles, and in the bones; in fact, every organ of the body, which is dependent for its healthy condition upon a sound state of the blood, (and there is no exception,) may and does give evidence, differing in each case, of the influence of this degeneration, and the great prevalence of its producing causes.

The question will very naturally arise in the reader's mind, whether much of the ills to which the poor are heir, is not produced by the necessarily restricted quantity, and impure quality, of their food. To this I reply, that food in the varied imperfections of quality and amount, unquestionably constitutes one of the most frequent and powerful of the causes of human diseases generally. It is under some of the circumstances of animal organization, no less important to the maintenance of life and sound health, than air, with, however, this great and essential difference, viz. that an individual may exist several days without any additional food, but not three minutes without air. Further, if he is deprived of but one of the ingredients of the atmosphere, oxygen, instant death is the consequence.

I believe, however, it will be found, in a vast majority of cases, where food is properly accounted a cause of illness, this is produced by *too great a quantity being eaten,* or by an alteration of its properties by the refinements of cookery, and the addition of stimulating condiments. Plethora, and its long train of ills, are the results of over feeding, and over stimulation, but these are not the diseases of the poor. Among them we rather find, Cachexia,* Scrofula, and all the consequences of debility and vitiation, which are far more attributable to an imperfection and paucity in the necessaries of life, more especially of air, clothing, and cleanliness. Dyspepsia, almost wholly the effect of improper dieting, is scarcely ever found in Dispensary practice, while no disease is more common with the wealthier classes. All the ills for which the poor seek advice, whether peculiar to them or not, are aggravated, and altered in character, not by the food they eat, so much as by the air they breathe, and their other depraved physical circumstances of life. The sin of intemperance in eating cannot be laid at the doors of the cellars, and the entrances of the alleys and courts, while that of intemperance in drinking, though a dreadful addition to the horrors of his already too degraded physical and moral condition, is, with the ignorant and poverty-stricken troglodyte, a venial fault, in comparison with the pampered luxuriousness and equally injurious and intemperate, though more refined indulgences of his wealthier and more responsible neighbor.

I conclude this part of my subject, by calling attention to a few facts, illustrating the relative duration of life, of different classes of population; premising that, in consequence of the imperfection of our means in obtaining the statistics of vitality and mortality of our own

---

* A bad habit of body, known by a depraved or vitiated state of the solids and fluids.

population, it will be necessary to go abroad for some of the facts which bear upon this important inquiry.

It is ascertained that in civilized communities, one-fourth part of all the human race who are born, die before attaining their first year; more than one-third before arriving at five years of age, and before the age of twenty, one half the human race, it is supposed, cease to exist. On referring to the last two annual reports of the mortality of this city, I observe that of the persons who *have died*, about the same proportion as is above stated, of all who are *born*, that is, about one-fourth died in the first year, about one-third before five years, *but more than one half* before twenty years of age.

No facts could speak in louder tones of the injurious operations of the circumstances of civilized life. That one-half should die before arriving fairly upon the broad platform of strength, usefulness, and hope in the world, is the significant finger pointing with unerring certainty to the sins of ignorance, and abuse of the bountiful and unfailing means of life and comfort lavished upon us by Providence, which lie at our doors. Can this ignorance of the laws of health be excused, or can this abuse of Heaven's bounties be defended? There can be no justification for either in the eye of the Creator and Giver of all things.

The savages who live in the caves of the earth, because they have neither the knowledge, nor means, to build houses, are pardonable; yet their natural instincts teach them the uses and necessity of fresh air and exercise. Yet we, who claim to be intelligent and civilized, who are taught the minutest particulars of nature's laws, suffer our numbers and strength, the bones, and sinews, and hearts of our people, to waste and die away in narrow and gloomy caverns of our own construction, with a rapidity surpassing that of the combined torrents of pestilence and war. Our sin is the greater that we permit these things in the midst of the light of science, and under the inspiring dictates of a religion, whose most prominent features are charity and love.

In the celebrated report of the Sanitary Condition of the Laboring Population of Great Britain, Mr. Chadwick gives the following, among other instances, of the comparative chances of life, in different classes of the community.

Truro.

No. of Deaths.		Aver. age of Dec'd.
33	Professional persons, or gentry and their families,	40 years.
138	Persons engaged in trade, or similarly circumstanced, and their families,	33 "
447	Laborers, Artisans, and their families,	28 "

Bolton Union (manufacturing district.)

103	Gentlemen, professional persons, and their families,	34 "
381	Tradesmen, and their families,	23 "
2232	Mechanics, servants, laborers, and their families,	18 "

Bethnal Green (manufacturing, chiefly domestic.)

101	Gentlemen, and persons engaged in Professions, and their families,	45 "
273	Tradesmen and their families,	26 "
1258	Mechanics, servants, laborers, and their families,	16 "

In Liverpool, a commercial, and not a manufacturing town, where, according to the report of Dr. Duncan, 40,000 people live in cellars, and where one in twenty-five of the population are annually attacked with fever, the mean chances of life appear to be still lower, than in Manchester, Leeds, or among the silk weavers of Bethnal Green. In size and character Liverpool is somewhat allied to New York, hence its vital statistics are more particularly interesting to us, as more likely to approach ours in similarity.

Liverpool, 1840.

No. of Deaths.		Aver. age of Dec'd.
137	Gentry, Professional persons, &c.	35 years.
1738	Tradesmen, and their families,	22 "
5597	Laborers, Mechanics, Servants, &c.	15 "

The following shows the difference in the average duration of life, between the inhabitants of a manufacturing and of an agricultural place, and it will be observed that the *laborers of the latter, attain to an age equal to the professional people, and gentry, of the former.*

	Average age of Death in Manchester,	in Rutlandshire.
Professional persons, and gentry and their families,	38 years.	52 years.
Tradesmen and their families, (Farmers and Graziers included with Shopkeepers, in Rutlandshire,)	20 "	41 "
Mechanics, laborers and their families,	17 "	38 "

This comparison exhibits very clearly the advantages of a pure atmosphere, out-door occupation, domiciliary cleanliness, and above ground residence, Rutlandshire being distinguished for all these, and as a consequence, for a more orderly, steady, and respectable population.

The influence of degraded associations, of habitual neglect of cleanliness, and prostration of health by impure living, upon the moral habits of the people, and as impediments to their social and political improvement, is a question with which I propose now to occupy the reader's attention, for a brief space, in the hope, that if it can be shown that these are probable causes of misery and crime, there will be found herein an additional reason for the action of the City government upon the measures, I, or others may suggest, for the melioration of the condition of those classes of the community more exposed to their influences.

Let any one ask himself the question, whether his own self-respect, his carefulness to avoid improprieties of conduct, and to maintain cleanliness of house and person, are not greatly enhanced by the examples of those around him. I believe it will not be disputed that the practices of those with whom we associate, by choice or compulsion, possess a decided influence over not only our own acts and habits, but over our thoughts and even our judgments. Circumstances govern our lives, and precepts for good are feeble, unless accompanied by the strong arm of example. " Example is better than precept," was the lesson taught us daily in our school exercises in penmanship. All society regulates the conduct of its members, and its phases of character are marked by their deportment and opinions. The "outcasts of society" constituting a very numerous tribe, form societies of their own, and stamp, in a degree, the character of the community of which they are a part. We have, as have all large cities, numbers of them with us, but they should be regarded, not as such by choice, so much as by *compulsion*—as the creatures of circumstances beyond their control.

The tide of emigration which now sets so strongly towards our shores, cannot be turned back. We *must* receive the poor, the ignorant, and the oppressed from other lands, and it would be better to consider them as coming filled with the energy of hope for happier days, and more useful labors, than they found at home. No one, I presume, seriously believes they come with bad intentions, and then whose fault is it that they live here in cellars more filthy than the cabins of whose wretchedness we hear so much, and for whose existence, half the blame is thrown upon the government they have left.

Let us first cast the beam from our own eye. *We are parties to their degradation, inasmuch as we permit the inhabitation of places, from which it is not possible improvement in condition or habits can come. We suffer* the sub-landlord to stow them, like cattle, in pens, and to compel them to swallow poison with every breath. They are *allowed*, may it not be said *required*, to live in dirt, when the reverse, rather, should be enforced.

This depressed physical condition, and bad moral and social habits and propensities, to my mind, have an intimate relation to each other— they stand clearly in the attitudes of cause and effect. For instance, how often do we find poverty to be the instigator of theft, and immoral indulgences the results of certain circumstances in life.

Men's passions are kept in check by the restrictions of the society in which they live. Remove those checks—take from the individuals the moral atmosphere in which they move, and their evil passions will rise.

In a family composed of several persons of both sexes, in circumstances admitting of their living in separate apartments, the restraints of the circle of which they are a part, compel an observance of the separation of the sexes, and other social proprieties. They grow up habituated to correct deportment and moral restraints, which accompany them into all their relations of life. But confine that same family to one room, compel them to perform all their personal and domestic duties in view of each other, to sleep, dress, and undress in each other's presence, and can it be doubted that the nice moral distinctions so necessary to a life of virtue, will be gradually subdued, or overthrown, the heart be hardened against the teachings of the moralist, and the wave of lustful passion become of increased power? Yet this is the condition of hundreds of families, who would gladly escape the Maelstrom of morals which threatens to engulf them. And this is undoubtedly a principal source of the dreadful amount of licentiousness infesting this city.

As breathing an impure atmosphere will produce a depressed tone of bodily feeling and positive physical disease, so will a vitiated moral atmosphere, induce a relaxed state of moral feeling, and positively licentious habits.

Whence issue, in times of riot and tumult, the disturbers of the peace, but from the cellars and alleys, where they have never been taught to respect themselves, much less others.

If a family of good disposition be reduced by force of circumstances to occupy the same premises with numbers of others of a different character, it will be next to impossible to maintain their former tone of morals, or domiciliary cleanliness and order, and they must soon lapse into the same habits and feelings as their neighbors, adding thus their numbers to those who before swelled the list of the profane and evil disposed.

I have remarked upon the influence of the impure atmosphere, the damp and crowded apartments, and other circumstances, upon the health of the poorer residents of New York:—the following extract from an able writer* must commend itself, in this connection, to the judgment of every right thinking man.

" Although it is most true that the calamity of sickness, or even of death itself, is nothing compared with crime, yet it is also true, that sickness induces poverty, which is one of the tempters to crime, and that a deranged condition of the physical system, often urges to vicious and destructive indulgences by the unnatural appetites which it creates, and thus ill health becomes the parent of guilt as well as of bodily pains. It exercises a powerful influence over feelings, temper, and disposition, aud through these upon moral character."

It follows, therefore, that a correction of the physical, will tend to abate the moral, evils of the community.

It is well known there has existed in this city for a series of years, an organization denominated the City Tract Society, which supports a number of Tract Missionaries, whose time is devoted to visiting the abodes of the humble and destitute, wherever the way may open, and carrying to them the words of moral and religious instruction—endeavoring to instil into their minds ideas of self-respect, and self-dependence, preaching to them temperance and virtue, enticing children to the Sabbath and public schools, relieving with what means they may possess, the physical necessities of the poor, and performing all other deeds which a mind actuated by benevolence and Christian love may do. Many of these gentlemen have been a long time engaged in this work, and probably no body of men possesses more thorough knowledge of the localities of this city, of the condition of its inhabitants, of the influence of circumstances upon the tone of morals in all classes, drawn from actual observation, or of the alterations and additions required in the police and sanitary codes, for the improvement of the city at large, and in its various particulars.

To these gentlemen I have applied for their opinions, and such illustrations, bearing upon this topic, as their prolonged and valuable experience may be supposed to have furnished them. I addressed to them

---

* Hon. Horace Mann.

the following queries—the subjoined responses, selected from among a number, must carry conviction to the minds of all who read them, that an effort is demanded of government, benevolence and wealth, to remove the impediments now lying in the way of the physical and moral improvement of the destitute classes of this city.

Queries addressed to the Tract Missionaries.

1st. To what extent does the congregation of different sexes, and various ages of the same family of the poor, in one apartment, influence their morals, and do they, or do they not, seem to place a lower estimate on moral character, (though free from actual vice,) than others, a grade above them in physical condition? In other words, have you observed an appreciation of morals and character, graduated according to the circumstances and condition of life?

2d. Have you found physical distress to present a bar to your moral and religious instructions, and do you think relief from their bodily ailments would enable you to be of greater service to the poor in your calling?

3d. Have you observed that personal and domiciliary negligence and filthiness tend to depress still more the moral sensibility, and make the poor more reckless of character—and do you believe, that domiciliary and personal cleanliness, though combined with an equal degree of poverty, give to the individual or family, more self-respect, more aptitude to receive instruction, and more happiness?

4th. If constrained by law to keep themselves, their furniture, clothing and dwellings, more clean, by frequent use of water and lime, do you think there would be a greater inclination to improve their associations, and obtain a better state of moral and social feeling?

5th. In your opinion would regular domiciliary visits by an officer of health, empowered to enforce a law to promote the cleanliness of house and persons, have any influence in raising the tone of feeling among the poor, as well as relieving sickness and prolonging life?

6th. Are there not many who would be pleased to be aided and instructed in the best mode of improving the condition of their dwellings, and be glad to receive the visits of such an officer?

7th. Can you relate any instances bearing on the subject, or applicable as illustrations to either of the queries?

From Rev. George Hatt, Missionary of 1st and 2d Wards.

Answer 1st. It is impossible to state to what extent a bad influence is produced by the congregation of different sexes in one apartment, but that it tends to debase the mind, and more especially in the female, prevents the development of that sensitive modesty which is her greatest charm, and her surest protection, I think no one can doubt. Still in my opinion, it is unfair and incorrect to measure appreciation of character by outward circumstances, or condition of life. The many offices to which the one apartment must be converted, produces a want of neatness, and personal cleanliness. A single fact will show some of the

4

evils of the one room system. As a Tract visiter knocked at the door of a room, he was invited in; he opened the door and entered, when, to his astonishment, he found a man entirely naked, sitting with his wife and children; the former was washing the shirt which the man had taken off. This was on a Sabbath day.

Answer 2d. Physical distress often prevents the poor, or indeed any class, from being benefited by religious instruction. But on the other hand, it often softens and prepares the mind for its more ready reception; I believe the possession of the ability, judiciously to relieve the pressing wants of the poor, and to alleviate their bodily ailments, would be of great service in the attempt to elevate their moral and social condition.

Answer 3d. I should presume that recklessness of character *generally* precedes negligence and filthiness—for instance, I have known a man who had a happy home to become a drunkard; this vice soon reduced him from an industrious, cleanly man, to a reckless, loathsome being. His wife, too, having become discouraged, falls into the snare. Now the once happy home is a scene of filth and confusion. Go to work with that family, become instrumental in restoring them to sobriety and in- dustry, and the change will be as apparent in the second instance as it was in the first.

As it respects the latter part of this question, I would add, that much, very much, depends upon the manner in which individuals are brought up. Some families will with six dollars per week, appear more respecta- ble, and possess more self-respect than others with ten dollars, with an equal number in the family. The difficulty in most cases is in the training. Hence the importance of educating the young.

Answer 4th. In my opinion constraint by law ought to be on the landlord. No landlord ought to be allowed to let a place which is known to be unhealthy under a heavy penalty. There are thousands in this city who are pent up in cellars, with ground for the floor, into which I would not put a hog, if I wanted him to thrive. Last winter I visited a place in Washington-street, where in one such hole, thirteen persons were staying, four adults, and nine children. At times the tide came in; it was always damp, and there was a woman sick with Pleurisy.

Answer 5th. Then in reference to the fifth question, I would say, that the health officer should be empowered to levy the fine upon landlords who transgressed the law. The officer should be empowered also to remove the family into some healthy abode, taking care that the fine be enough to cover expenses, and that having done so, the unhealthy place should be locked up, and the key kept by the officer, until a guarantee be given, that, if possible, the place be rendered habitable.

Answer 6th. I would recommend that the corporation build, and en- courage the building of houses suitable for the poor, so constructed that each family may have at least two rooms; do this, and many of those evils which now exist will be done away, and the blessing of many who are now ready to perish, will come upon them.

From J. B. Horton, Missionary of the 7th Ward.

New York August 23d, 1844.

DR. GRISCOM.—DEAR SIR—Your *questions* in relation to the demoralizing influences resulting from the *unhappy physical condition* of a multitude of families in this city—both as it regards the numbers of all ages and each sex, *jammed into one apartment*—that with some miserable additions to its list of uses reminds us of the poor cobbler's stall in the song, which " He us'd for kitchen, for parlor, for hall,"—and the negligence of personal and domiciliary cleanliness ; with others concerning the best means of obviating those evils, requesting me to give such answers to each and all, as my judgment and experience shall dictate, with such illustration of facts, as my Missionary labors in this city for ten years past may have furnished, are before me, and shall receive due attention.

For I hail with joy any feasible project, or attempt, to meliorate the *natural* or *moral condition* of man, and especially of that class of my own fellow-citizens, who so far from reposing on beds of roses or down, seem doomed to endless toil by day—and by night to lie down, perhaps in a crowded, uncleanly, and unventilated apartment, where before their slumbers are ended, the air has been so often inhaled, that it would need but little farther diminution of its vital qualities, to become *so foul* as to cause them " *to sleep, to wake no more.*"   And I rejoice, sir, that *you* have undertaken the task of presenting to the authorities of this city and the public, such views of the physical and moral condition of our city, and the appropriate means of improving it in both respects, as will, I trust, not only do honor to your head and heart, but lead ultimately to such sanitary regulations, as shall make this great emporium of the commerce of the Western world, not only as renowned for *natural and moral purity*, as for the amount of her wealth and the extent of her commercial enterprise, but as the exuberant goodness of God in bestowing on her naturally a pure air, and civilly and artificially the free use of the Holy Bible and Croton water, has given her the means to be.

I now proceed to answer the questions propounded.   And first, you inquire, " To what extent does the congregation of different sexes, and various ages of the same family of the poor, in *one apartment*, influence their morals, and do they, or do they not, seem to place a lower estimate on moral character, than others placed a grade above them in physical condition ?"   As it regards the *extent* of the evil influence on morals, arising from such herding together, of all ages and both sexes, it is impossible for me to determine, but that it is of most pernicious tendency, no one who has the slightest acquaintance with poor human nature, can, for a moment, entertain a doubt.   Under such circumstances, it is impossible from the nature of things to prevent the instinctive modesty of youth from receiving a mortal wound, by a constant familiarity with scenes and sounds fit only for the greatest privacy—" For (truly) nature's blush by custom is wiped off."

And thus one of the greatest barriers and defences of chastity, is in the very morning of life overturned and destroyed ; that jewel of such inestimable value, that the means of its preservation is worthy of the most profound consideration of the statesman and philanthropist. That the physical condition of an individual or a family, has a powerful and important bearing on the moral character, for weal or woe, needs no labor to prove; although neither of us has any idea of embracing Fourierism—the main doctrine of which, I believe, is, that most of the ills of life, as now experienced in the world, flow not from the moral obliquity of human nature, but from the *wrong, civil, and physical* position of men. " Poverty and riches are both severe temptations," the latter, however, by far more dangerous, at least to the final and eternal interests of men. For though abject poverty may lead to brutal degradation, placing families even in Christian communities in circumstances as unfavorable to chastity, and the common decencies of life, as the Sandwich Islanders were previous to the introduction of Christianity among them by American Missionaries—when they slept in their *one apartment*, men, women and children, *with their hogs*, " cheek by jowl !" Yet riches foster appetites and passions still more hostile to virtue and religion ; hence it was averred by the Maker and Savior of men, that " it is easier for a camel to go through a needle's eye than for a rich man to enter the kingdom of God." Extremes meet—therefore I have made some of the foregoing observations, to show that every gradation in the circumstances of an individual or a family, from abject poverty to " *a happy mediocrity*," defined exactly in Agur's prayer, " Neither poverty nor riches," (which even the insensate infidel Tom Paine, had not the moral hardihood to deny as replete with true wisdom,) will have a good influence on their morals, but not beyond that point.

I have farther to say in relation to this question, that though I have not the shadow of a doubt resting on my mind, as to the deteriorating moral effect of a large family embracing both sexes and all ages, being pent up in one apartment, where *all things* must be done *in common*, yet I have no striking facts as an illustration in proof to give, but have a distinct impression that where I have met with families so circumstanced, or among the abject poor, their moral sensibilities in some respects were very obtuse, and in nothing that I recollect more often manifested than the shameful nudities of children.

In regardt o your second question, " Have you found physical distress to present a bar to your moral and religious instructions, and do you think their relief from bodily ailments would enable you to be of greater service to the poor in your calling ?" I answer, that I have often found persons and families, in such circumstances of distress, from want of food and raiment, or by excruciating bodily pain, I thought it would be preposterous and vain to say much to them on the subject of religion, until their minds and bodies were somewhat relieved and disenthraled from the absorbing power of want and pain by physical appliances. And always under such circumstances, I have gone to work to procure food and clothing, or a physician and medicine ! to prepare the way for moral and religious culture. And happy should I be if the facility for ministering to the poor and suffering were many fold increased, as it regards giving the worthy poor both food and physic ; thereby increasing our prospect of being useful to them in religious matters.   And I rejoice in the society recently organized in this city, by a truly intelligent and philanthropic class of our wealthy citizens, for " the improvement of the condition of the poor," who have already prepared the way for the Tract Missionary to exert the happiest influence on hundreds of families.

As proof that physical distress and bodily ailments present a bar to moral and religious culture, I have only to assure you, that the common answer given to Missionaries by persons in such circumstances, when asked if they wish to seek religion, or avail themselves of the means of grace by attending church, or of Sabbath and public school instruction for their children, is this, " Oh, we are so poor—we have such trouble to get our daily bread, so destitute of comfortable and decent apparel, that we have no time to think about religion—cannot go decently to church, nor send our children to Sabbath or public schools."

In answer to your third question, viz.   " Have you observed that personal and domiciliary negligence and filthiness tend to depress still more the moral sensibilities, and make the poor still more reckless of character ; and do you believe that domiciliary and personal cleanliness, though combined with equal poverty, give the individual or family more self-respect, more aptitude to receive instruction, and more happiness ?"   I reply, that I have observed those families and persons who live habitually in squalid filth, negligent of personal and domiciliary cleanliness, like wicked men and seducers, wax morally worse and worse.   And were it proper, I should like to introduce you to two such families, who are now prominently before my mind, for whom I have long labored, but apparently in vain, as it regards their moral reformation, while on the other hand I could introduce you to those who, though equally poor, yet careful about their persons and places, have received instruction gladly, and as we trust with lasting profit—and none can doubt for a moment that the latter class are by far more happy ; though through a perverted taste, it may be possible for a savage " to glory in the deepest jet."

Your fourth and fifth questions involve so nearly the same thing—a mere requisition of my opinion, " Whether the interference of municipal authority—constraining by law, and law officers—the dirty and negligent, to take better care of their persons, furniture, and apartments, would subserve any valuable purpose, or raise a better tone of moral and social feeling ?"—for brevity's sake, I shall consider and answer them as one, by saying that I can see no good reason why a State and City that have *legislated so immensely*, and sacrificed so much public and private property to establish and execute Quarantine Laws, (many of them of more than doubtful utility,) to prevent the importation of Yellow Fever, Cholera, and the Plague, into our populous city, should by any means judge it absurd or unnecessary, to enact a few laws, and appoint a few officers to inspect certain persons and places within the city, (with power to remove) where and by whom all those infectious and contagious maladies may be *manufactured*, and of such a quality, too, as to be perhaps more dangerous than those of foreign growth.

In regard to your 6th question, " Whether there are not many families that would like to be aided and instructed in the best mode of improving the condition of their dwellings, and would be glad to receive the visits of such an officer ?" I answer, that the feeling with which such an officer would be received, must materially depend on the ability and tact with which he would discharge a duty so delicate—for delicate indeed it must be to interfere with the private concerns of any individual, however poor he may be—that claims to be *one* of the *independent citizens of the United States—one* of the *sovereign people !* However, I do not believe, though the task should be arduous, but that some such regulations might be introduced into our city, with the happiest results. Yet I should perfectly despair of the success of any such sanitary measures if adopted, should those who have the power of appointing the necessary officers, manifest the same reckless indifference to their talents and attainments in medical skill and science, as we have sometimes heretofore had the misfortune to see manifested in the appointment of health officers.

I have now gone through with your questions, dear sir, and answered them according to my best ability, and the limited time allotted me ; but not perhaps in a way that will be satisfactory to yourself, or available for the public good. You will, however, I have no doubt, in your kindness, take " the will (in this instance) to serve," for the deed.

But before I close this already long communication, I beg leave to suggest to you one thing to be brought forward in some part of your work, viz. to show the far greater propriety and necessity of having an Inspector General, with plenty of sub-officers, who shall determine *where,* and *what kind* of a *house* shall be built for a human being, or a family to inhabit ; and how much room—and how many rooms, shall be rented to families consisting of so many persons, and such sexes, than an inspector general and his posse, to examine dead beef and pork, flour, tobacco, &c., that nobody is forced to buy or use if bad, while the poor are literally forced by poverty and griping landlords, to live in dens and holes, where immorality and death are speedily engendered. Yet still farther and *above all,* do, my dear sir, bring out most prominently the absolute futility of any sanitary measures, for the health, or morals of this city as a whole, until that *curse* of *all curses* most direful, that most prolific source of *poverty, crime, disease,* and *death,* " Intoxicating *drink,*" be considered and treated legislatively and judiciously as a most dangerous, deleterious, and deadly poison, and those who make and sell the same as a beverage for gain, as unworthy, not only of the name of Christian but of man, and should henceforth be ranked with fiends—and those who drink it as such—as maniacs, and fools, and treated accordingly.   With much respect, yours,

J. B. HORTON.

From Samuel Russell, Jr., Missionary of the 8th Ward.

New York, Aug. 26th, 1844.

DR. GRISCOM—DEAR SIR—Whether the sentiment of the great Teacher, " The poor ye have always," is the mere record of an important *fact* or a *prediction,* I shall not stop to inquire ; one thing, however, is certain, it ever has been, and is now, a sentiment of *truth ;* and a true disciple of that teacher, will rejoice in any efforts of others, and contribute his own, for the well-being of that large class of the community.

Having been engaged for several years in labors for the benefit of the poor, the following opinions have been formed, and are submitted in reply to your series of questions ; hoping that they may, in some humble measure, subserve the best interests of that class whose servant 1 am, and hope to be, during the remainder of my life.

1st. The instances are many, in which one or more families, of from three to seven or more members, of all ages, and both sexes, are congregated in a single, and often contracted apartment. Here they eat, drink, sleep, wash, dress and undress, without the possibility of that privacy which an innate modesty imperatively demands ; in sickness or health it is the same. What is the consequence ? The sense of shame, that greatest, surest safeguard to virtue, except the grace of God, is gradually blunted, ruined, and finally destroyed. Now scenes are witnessed and participated in, with a countenance of brass, the very *thought* of which, once would have filled the sensitive heart of modesty with pain, and covered its cheek with burning blushes. The mind of one thus brought in daily and nightly contact with such scenes, must become greatly debased, and its fall before the assaults of vice rendered almost certain.

In reply to the latter part of the question, allow me to say that neither extreme of society is favourable to the highest appreciation of morality. The rich man who delights in sinful indulgence, and retains his position in society by his gold, places really no higher estimate upon virtue for its *own sake*, than the veriest wretch, who in the eye of day, wallows in the very mire of moral pollution. From such a one, to him who retains his place among his fellows by his *virtues*, there is, doubtless, a regular gradation in the appreciation of morals and character.

2d. Physical distress often introduces me to the acquaintance of families, when if they were in other circumstances, access to them might not be obtained ; yet before any moral or spiritual instruction will be regarded, the wants and ailments of body must first be cared for.

Before the formation of the " Society for the improvement of the condition of the poor," my usefulness was greatly curtailed from the impossibility of ministering to the physical wants of the poor ; now it is otherwise, thanks to the noble men comprising that society.

3d. This question, I answer unhesitatingly, in the affirmative.

4th. The law of kindness in the heart, and the words of sympathy upon the lips, afford the surest avenue to the confidence of the poor, and will succeed when legal coercion will utterly fail. Use the former when you *can*, the latter when you *must*.

5th. The success or failure of such visitation would depend very much, if not entirely, upon the character of the officer, and his manner of performing such visitation. If possessed of a kind and affable manner, and if a desire for the comfort and permanent good of the poor were discernible in all his deportment, he would hardly be regarded as an officer of law, but as a friend to be confided in, and his instructions appreciated and followed—if otherwise, he would be looked upon with mistrust, and probably resisted.

6th. This question I answer in the affirmative, provided the officer possess the qualifications named in the reply to the fifth query; and also provided the expense be borne by the landlord, or the public—otherwise, in the negative.

7th. A multiplicity of cases bearing on this whole subject have led me to the conclusion to which I have come, and expressed above; but no particular one now occurs to my mind, of sufficient interest, to warrant being repeated here.

The published reports of the " City Tract Society," in numerous instances, show what means *have* resulted in the *elevation of the poor,* and to those documents I would beg leave respectfully to refer you.

Yours, &c.   SAMUEL RUSSELL, JR.

Missionary, 8th Ward.

From Jno. H. Bulen, Missionary of the 13th Ward.

New York, August 20th, 1844.

DEAR SIR—The subject of your recent note, making certain inquiries, is one of no ordinary interest to any one who is endeavoring, in a sphere however circumscribed, or by means however humble, to be instrumental in elevating the moral condition of man.

The intimate relation of the moral to the physical condition, may not be so easily and precisely defined, as practically understood; and perhaps your end will be as fully attained by eliciting the results of experience, as by any fine wrought, philosophical disquisition of that relation. I am truly glad you have taken the subject in hand. I have long wished that some one, able to make his voice heard by the community, would speak out in language to be understood. Should you succeed in awakening an interest in the community, which shall result in the domiciliary renovation at which you aim, you will need no reward but the rich consciousness of having rendered valuable aid to the philanthropic enterprises of the day.

Nearly ten years' constant intercourse with the poor of this city, has fully convinced me that no greater obstacle is presented to their moral elevation, than that want of self-respect, and recklessness of character, induced by associations almost impossible to avoid, under existing arrangements, when very much reduced in pecuniary circumstances.

Suppose a respectable mechanic or merchant reduced by unavoidable misfortune to penury. He must leave his comfortable home. Accustomed to fulfil his promises, the least possible promise for rent will, in his opinion, be the best arrangement for the present; and, however the hearts of those accustomed to domiciliary cleanliness and comfort, may sicken as they enter where twenty or more families are domiciled on the same lot, with passage and yard conveniences common to all, yet they will make a virtue of necessity—it is a shelter—its walls encircle all now dear to their hearts—and most prized of all, perhaps, because it hides them from their acquaintances of more prosperous days. They, of course, purify their narrow home, and, as far as may be, make it comfortable. When weary nature must have rest, their one room, which has served both as kitchen and parlor, must also be their place of retirement.

What modesty would recently have shrunk from, must now be submitted to, and once submitted to, is ever after less and less painful. Then commences a deterioration of moral perception. It is impossible for one, of so many families, to keep the places common to all, clean and orderly; and what is habitually witnessed in the halls and the apartments of neighbors, will soon be permitted, for the present, in their own, especially as none accustomed to other appearances will probably be their visitors.

This downward course is so rapid, and the result so certain, that few will fail to discern the cause. Yet as the influence of this physical and mental condition upon the moral susceptibilities, may not be so apparent, there may be a necessity for saying, in answer to your first inquiry—that I have observed a depreciation of susceptibility of moral and religious teachings, towards either extreme of society; but as the poor are more accessible, my opportunities have been almost exclusively confined to that extreme. With this explanation, I answer, unhesitatingly, that I have observed, with, perhaps, no more than the usual exceptions to a general rule, a graduation of appreciation of morals and character, according to physical condition. And in answer to your second, that I have often found an obtuseness of perception induced by physical condition, an insuperable bar to moral and religious instruction. And to your third—that I have no doubt that domiciliary and personal cleanliness would increase self-respect, and an aptitude to receive moral and religious instruction, while their negligence would diminish them.

To your fourth and fifth inquiries, I may be allowed to answer, that compulsory measures in relation to domiciliary arrangements are ordinarily, peculiarly unwelcome, especially to the poor, who are usually jealous over what they conceive to be their now too circumscribed rights. And yet so little of the responsibility of the accumulated impurities of their crowded habitations rests on a single family, that I think I may say in answer to your sixth inquiry, that the majority of them would be glad to receive official aid and instruction. There are, probably, but very few who do not think they would be glad to live more cleanly, if their neighbors would render it possible by doing so too. Any improvement, although constrained, would undoubtedly increase their relf-respect, and, of course, their happiness, and facilitate the efforts of those who are endeavoring to advance their spiritual interests.

Most of the cases of which I have kept any record, would rather illustrate the influence of improved morals on physical condition. And yet there is no doubt of their reciprocal influence. Not unfrequently, the commencement of the elevating process is the relief of some physical distress, such as feeding the hungry, clothing the naked, or healing the sick, by the use of such means as the benevolent supply; always

5

endeavoring to keep before the mind those great truths on which we rely, through the efficient agency of the Spirit, for moral renovation.

As an illustration of the depreciating process alluded to in your first inquiry, I recollect a case in point, although not recorded. An intimate friend of mine was acquainted with a young lady, about thirty years ago, then moving in good society, with moral susceptibilities, and a refined, discriminating sense of propriety, somewhat above mediocrity. At about the age of twenty-two, she married, as was thought, respectably. A few years proved that the husband's morals and habits were not such as to secure respect or independence; and they gradually sunk, and my friend lost sight of them.

About six years since, a child was brought by a Tract visitor, from a filthy cellar, and put into the Sabbath school class of my friend, who, upon learning the name of the child, visited the mother, and found her to be the same person known years ago as a young lady of refinement. She had now lost all ambition ; her husband was a worthless inebriate ; her children, with countenances of promise, were, like their mother, completely at home in their most miserable apartment, rendered exceedingly so by neglect. Her moral susceptibilities were as entirely changed as her physical condition. Religious truth seemed to make no impression upon her mind—her heart seemed callous. Speak of her early life, and the fountain of feeling seemed to break up, and the tears would flow. A deep impression rests upon my mind, that lost as she was, if she could have been placed in circumstances of comfort and cleanliness approximating to those of her youth, the probabilities would have been in favor of her moral renovation. As this was beyond my reach, attention was turned to more hopeful cases, alas! in too many instances to meet the same disappointment from the same cause, and she was again lost sight of.   Truly, yours,

J. H. BULEN.

From Rev. Isaac Orchard, Missionary of the 15th Ward.

Bedford Street, August 20th, 1844.

DR. GRISCOM,—DEAR SIR—In relation to the questions you have proposed, I would group together the 1st, 2d, and 3d, as relating to a prevalent evil, and the 4th, 5th, and 6th, as relating to a proposed remedy; and this I do the more readily, because the points suggested under the former class, appear to me to be almost self-evident, and the remarks I may make upon the latter class, may be more conveniently made upon the three questions collectively, than singly.

1st, 2d, and 3d. The extent, concerning which the first question inquires, is, I fear, very great, and frequently leads to actual evil. To the points suggested in these questions, I would give an affirmative answer, regarding them all as general rules, liable to some exception. Thus a person of coarse mind and manners may be found associating with the refined and polite, or a refined and polite person with the ill-behaved and uncouth ; but it is not there we would seek for them. Applying whatever experience I have obtained on this subject, I am induced to regard it as a general law of our nature, that minds and manners should take an impress from those with which they associate ; and this is painfnlly evident in many cases, where we observe those who have fallen from opulence, fashion, and high standing, into poverty. Suppose a lady, accustomed to luxury and elegant society, so reduced that she has to earn her living by labor, and necessarily to mingle amongst the poor. You may see traces of her former condition, yet they will be but little more than traces. Compelled to bring her mind to her circumstances, to associate with, and perhaps receive instruction from, persons whom she once would have avoided, she must either be solitary in her manners, or despised as seeking pre-eminence, or she must come down to the standard of those around her, aud the last of these will be, in most cases, preferred, although it will involve a great diminution of self-respect. When independent in fortune, that person felt independent in mind, and abhorred any thing mean—but when reduced to dependence upon another for bread, or even for labor, and seeing that the most obsequious obtain the most smiles, then the cravings of want will humble the high spirit, and self-interest will induce that per- son to submit to the meanness of obsequiousness, although subjecting herself, at the same time, to the most painful feelings and self-reproach. It is evidently very difficult, almost impossible, for persons in general to avoid the influence of physical condition upon mind. Thus it is with those who have sunk from an elevated position, and it will be the same with those who have sunk from an humble position to one still lower. Perhaps the majority of charity seeking persons amongst us, may be of this class ; they were never rich, but perhaps were quite above want ; now they have sunk in circumstances from some cause, and the associates with whom they mingle are of a lower grade than in former days. This they do not know how to avoid, for these are now their neighbors. To keep on good terms with them, they mingle in their company, unite in their sentiments, and associate in their vices.

To some passer-by, it appears strange that in the block standing south of the Catholic Cathedral, and other places contiguous, there are so many gin-shops ; and they ask where are the customers to support these shops? They cannot be in the neighboring houses, for there also customers are wanted—the bottles are exhibited in house after house, and I have known two such shops in one house ;—whence came the customers? Now this is a question that the licensing power might have asked before they granted their license to sell, and there would have been nothing ultra in it, however ultra might have been the question, whether or not such sale should be licensed at all? But in the multiplicity of cases, it is evident the good fathers of the city forgot to ask the question. Is it possible that a Catholic Cathedral, like a theatre, can be the attractor of a circle of gin-shops? No ! no ! to suppose that these shops are sustained by the worshippers at St. Patrick's, when going to, or returning from church, would be very unkind, and perhaps very unjust ; for I have discovered that those houses contain, to a considerable extent, *their own customers*. It is unquestionably true, that when persons sink into poverty, they do not like to be scowled upon—they feel it even more than in better days—yet people will scowl upon them; their old friends and acquaintances will avoid them, lest they should want something. Landlords will be more particular than ever as to their rent, and when they have got it, not be respectful, and scarcely civil. Some benevolent person calls to inquire as to a poor family needing aid—the landlord says nothing that will help them, and the room appears (in the estimation of some short-sighted philanthropists) too good for a family receiving charity, and besides there are several articles of decent furniture—the visitor is dissatisfied, and leaves, but leaves no aid behind. The broken down spirit is prostrated—hope is blasted—in a little while the few decent articles are gone that food may be obtained, and the poor, dispirited castaways seek a refuge where all, being poor, will sympathize with each other, and where the landlord, even if he charge higher rent than they gave before, will speak soothingly, and though he advise them to drown their cares in whiskey, will be very faithful in giving them an excellent character to all inquirers. Lodgings for such persons, on such terms, may be found in the houses I have described. These houses contain, I say, to a large extent, their own customers; for they are the pauper's rendezvous, and offer lodgings to beggars of every grade. They seem to be always open for new comers, and in some way or other they can accommodate them. There are various neighborhoods of this kind in this city, and I have called your attention to the one named, that I may give you an illustration of the remarks I have made. In one of these houses, in a garret, with sloping roof and low ceiling, one small, broken window, no bedstead, nor other bedding than a few bundles of rags upon the floor, I have found three families of men, women, and children: there they lived, and there they all slept. Now, if a woman accustomed to humble life, or decent poverty, be constrained to remove to such a place, what must be the effect on her mind, her morals, and her habits? At first, she will recoil from undressing in the presence of a strange man, but soon she will do it without a blush. Is she a wife? There are other wives and their husbands in the room, without even a curtain to hide the most private transactions. That which transpires cannot be unobserved, though seeking the darkest recess, and soon it will be imitated without secrecy and without scruple. Children, too, will see them, and think, and imitate—and thus become depraved in their thoughts, desires, and practices. Can any one doubt that there must be rapid declension in morals, in both parents and children? or that a bar is here opposed to moral or religious instruction? or that this state of things was consequent on the circumstances and condition of life? Beside this, persons living thus, are almost necessarily drunkards, whether men or women. Drunkenness, probably, reduced them to this state, but if it did not, the landlord would hardly allow them to remain in the house, or their fellow lodgers, in the room, unless they became such. If questioned upon this subject, they are accustomed to reply that they do drink, but not too much; yet the question, what quantity is too much, is one upon which their opinion and mine would not agree. When the visitors from the City Tract Society, with whom I am accustomed to act, succeed in awakening in the minds of such persons a sense of their degradation, their first care is to cut them off from the society that misery loves. If, then, they can be induced to break off from their de-based habits and associations, and to keep themselves and the clothes they give them, clean—and especially, if they can be induced to work, then some hope is entertained that they will listen with attention to religious instruction; but not till then.

4th, 5th, and 6th. As to the remedy proposed for these evils, I think there can be no doubt that if *the love* of cleanliness could be instilled into their minds by *moral means*, all the good you suggest would result from it, and real good would result if cleanliness were secured by *any* means; but I think it very problematical whether this could be obtained by coercion. Unless the will assents, there must be constant evasion, and but little will be accomplished. There is that in the nature of man which will induce him to respect advice, if it be given with evi-dent kindness, respect, and disinterestedness, but to reject real benefits if they be forced upon him against his will. The poorer classes often imagine that they possess rights which they do not, and no persons are more jealous of what they deem their rights than these persons are, or more ready to resent and oppose any infringement of them. I hold it to be a sound principle that no one has a right to do wrong; but many would dispute this, or if they admitted it, the question would arise, what is wrong? I regard it as wrong for any family, by neglect of cleanliness, to surround itself with a fetid atmosphere; but there are multitudes of the poor, or rather that class of the poor particularly in-terested, who imagine they have a right to do as they please in this matter, and that it would be a wrong that should be resisted, if any one interfered with this right. It seems therefore necessary, as a pre-liminary measure, to correct the judgment, for it is not that which a man ought to believe, but that which he does believe, that regulates his conduct. If this be not done, will he not regard what you propose, as a high-handed measure of the rich for the oppression of the poor? And if the poor man's shanty be visited more frequently than the rich man's mansion, will he not regard the law as partial and unjust, and probably as unconstitutional? And if this estimation of the law prevail, can it be carried into effect? It requires something more than legisla-tion to convince the judgment, and no legislation, though based upon the soundest principles, will be generally respected, if it be opposed to popu-lar error. I can imagine that there are many who would be glad to receive the visits of a health officer, *if he* were gentle, kind, and un-officious—if he had the confidence of the family, and if he caused all clean-ing and improvement to be done without expense or inconvenience to the tenant—*but not else.* I have been accustomed to visit the poor during the last forty years, and experience convinces me that if a wealthy individual, when bestowing a gift, find fault with the dirtiness of a place, he must do it with gentleness, and with due regard to feelings, and with no assumption of superiority, or he will exclude from the mind all sense of gratitude for the gift bestowed. Or if the person com-municating kindness be known as the almoner of others, everything like scolding, and bluster, and importance, will be still more offensive ; and though regard for the yet ungiven dollar that he holds between his fingers, may preserve the peace until he leaves the room, then will there be a bursting forth of pent-up indignation ; and though at his future visits he may be received with civility, it will be the civility of hypocrisy. How then can we expect that the official intrusion, without a peace-offering, of a public officer into the place which, however poor, the poor man calls his castle, will be received with favor ? He may, indeed, be clothed with legal authority to enter the place, and there to look into holes and corners, enforce the scrubbing of the floor, the liming of the walls, and the cleansing of the furniture, and oblige the woman to wash herself and her children, comb their hair, and scour their clothes ; and all this may be important to the welfare of the family, and the health of the neighborhood—but it will be more likely to cause a breach of the peace, than to be regarded as a kindness.

There is a power somewhat similar in England, given to the governors of the poor ; but in that country, under monarchial government, rights are often proportioned to property ; laws are made to benefit or coerce distinct classes, and strength is given to the government by clothing it with vast powers to be used whenever discreet—that is, in cases of urgency. So with the law ; the spirit of Englishmen would not submit to the every day enforcement of the power it gives, and therefore it is not to be found in every day life, but in the Statute book, ready for use in case of pestilence, or other apparent necessity. *Then* such a law would be really valuable. They have it in reserve for such a season, and it might be well if we had a similar law to be used under similar circumstances ; for then, the judgment of every one showing its importance and necessity, it would be enforced without difficulty. Of this we have an illustration in the operation of quarantine laws. The great plague of London, caused by the arrival in the port of an infected cargo of hides, and various other cases, have impressed on the minds of men the horror of a plague, and the great danger of its being so introduced into a city or nation. Hence, every one sees and feels the necessity of a ship being inspected ; yet that inspection is not hailed with pleasure, but submitted to as a necessary evil. Such, at least, I have found to be the case ; and I was one of about 160 persons who terminated a tedious and almost suffocating voyage at this port, while cholera was raging both here and in Europe. The same acquiescence in domestic inspection could be secured, I presume, only in the same way—that is, by the judgment being convinced that the measure is just and necessary. But how is the judgment of men to be so convinced, and especially in a season of general health ? Not by the enactment of a new law giving new powers ; but by moral means. If we had an awful pestilence, and all the physicians united in declaring its cause to have been the filthiness of the dwellings of the poor, it would no doubt produce an impression—though perhaps even then conviction would not be produced unless dicta were sustained by demonstration.

Yours, very truly,   ISAAC ORCHARD,

Sec. of C. T. Society, and Missionary of 15th Ward.

There is one other aspect in which the relations of the state or community, to its citizens, are to be viewed, which cannot be omitted here, without doing both parties injustice, especially as in this connexion, the relation is very intimate, as well as important. 1 refer to the dependence of the community upon the labors of its members, for its prosperity, support, and advancement. The influence exerted by a single individual upon the character and capacity of a government, is well marked and freely acknowledged, when men of commanding intellect step out from the common ranks. No one, for example, can measure the degree of influence exerted upon the character of this country, or of mankind, by Washington, Franklin, or Fulton, or upon the prosperity of this state by the genius of Dewitt Clinton. And so on downwards through the various gradations, and the ever varying abilities, physical and mental, of the masses of individuals, to the most insignificant, it is impossible not to see that each one possesses more or less influence upon the condition of the community, and by his peculiar labors, adds to it, or saves for it. How many conflagrations have been prevented by the devotion to his calling of the sooty and despised chimney sweep? while thousands of dollars have been rescued from filth and nothingness, by the industry of the degraded Chiffonier.*

Now, a great part of the wealth of the community consists in its physical labor. " Labor is wealth." The manufacturer, the artisan, the builder, *all*, depend upon the skill and strength of those employed to do their work. Who then will say that labor of the most insignificant kind should not be protected, improved, and facilitated, that the laborer of the smallest capacity should not be strengthened to the utmost, by careful training and education? It very often happens that almost the minutest muscles of the human body (those of the hands and fingers) are those which perform the most important and delicate work; so do we frequently find the most essential part of a magnificent structure, as of an engine, or a building, requires the labor of the poorest and roughest operative. Sound vigorous health is an essential pre-requisite to the proper performance of all labor.

The following passage, from an author before quoted,† written for an analogous subject, is so directly applicable, so appropriate to my purpose, and so forcible, that no apology will be required for its length.

" This subject has merits which should command the attention of the statesman and political economist. All investments to preserve or increase the public health, would be reimbursed many fold, in an increased capacity for production. One of the most important items in a nation's wealth, consists in the healthfulness and vigor, enjoyed by its people. All agriculturists and manufacturers must feel the force of this remark in regard to their own workmen; and they would feel it still more, if

---

* As an instance of the perseverance and frugality of this class of operatives, I was lately informed of one who, by his dirty trade, has amassed $400, which he was about investing in Western lands. Hundreds of these people derive a good support from the business in this city.

† Hon. Horace Mann.—Sixth Annual Report of the Board of Education of Massachusetts.

they were obliged at their own expense to support those workmen during all periods of sickness or incapacity to labor ; and this is the relation in which the state stands to its citizens. It has been said by some writers on political economy, that from one-seventh to one-eighth of all the wealth of a country originates in the *labor of each year.* Hence, if any nation or community should cease from production for seven or eight years, the whole of its wealth,—houses, lands, goods, money—would be consumed. What a forcible idea of the value of labor, is presented by this fact ! Yet, what a sick workman or operative would be to a capitalist who was obliged to maintain him, a sick citizen is to the republic. Every sick man, every man rendered unserviceable by general debility, or specific ailment, must be subtracted from a nation's available resources. He not only adds nothing to the common stock, but he draws his subsistence in some form—and often, too, a very expensive subsistence—from the storehouse which the industry of others has filled. Omitting all considerations of personal and domestic suffering, of the extinction of intellectual power, and of those moral aberrations which originate in physical derangement and disease—and considering the race under the mere aspect of a money making power—in this respect it is clear that the health and strength of one community, if set in opposition to the debility and infirmity of another, would be sufficient not only to determine the balance of trade, but to settle all other points of relative superiority. Let such information be diffused through the public, as all the children in our schools might easily acquire, and a single generation would not pass away, without the transfer of immense sums to the other side of the profit and loss account in the national leger. Of course, I do not mean that all diseases could be abolished at once, even by a universal diffusion of a knowledge of their causes ; or that the era foretold by the prophet would be ushered in, when " the child shall die a hundred years old," and when there shall be no " old man that hath not filled his days." The violation of those beautiful and benign laws which the Creator has inwrought into our system, has been too heinous, and too long persevered in by the race, to be expiated or atoned for in a single age. Disease and debility transmitted through a long line of ancestors, have acquired a momentum by the length of the descent, which cannot at once be overcome. But I do mean, if this subject were generally understood, that such a change would be wrought in a single generation, that a broad and deep current of wealth would be made to change its direction ; and instead of millions annually flowing outward from the common treasury, to defray the various expenditures of sickness, that treasury would be replenished by an equal number of millions, coined from the mint and from the ore, of labor-loving health. Yet amid all our pecuniary speculations, this grand financial operation, of substituting health and strength for sickness and debility—that is, immense gains for immense expenditures—has been unheard of.

" In the army and navy, where the expediency of giving battle has been discussed in a council of war ; or afterwards when the causes of defeat have been explained by the vanquished, the state of the sick list has been made the subject of inquiry. The historian, too, in his account of campaigns, recognizes health and sickness as among the grand causes of success or disaster. But the manly health and vigor of a people engaged in the arts of peace—as among the most essential items in a nation's valuation, as a capital ready for profitable investment, in any industrial enterprise, and therefore as a prolific source of public revenue, as well as of private wealth, have been overlooked by statesmen and law-givers, in all their schemes for national aggrandizement.

"The pecuniary merits of this subject may be presented under another aspect. Children at different ages, and under different circumstances, may be regarded as representing investments of different sums of money. These investments consist in the amount which has been expended for their nursing, rearing, clothes, board, education, and so forth, and in the value of the time of others which has been appropriated to them. Though differing exceedingly in regard to different persons, yet, in this country, the aggregate expense with its accruing interest, of the great majority at the age of twenty, or twenty-one years, can hardly be estimated at less than from five hundred to a thousand dollars, after deducting the value of all the services performed. Now if half mankind die by the time they arrive at this age, or before it, and half these come to their untimely end, through the ignorance of their parents or themselves, (and I may add through the inattention of government to their condition,) what an amazing price does our ignorance (and inattention) cost us? With what reckless prodigality do we continue to cherish it! What spendthrifts we are, not only of the purest source of affection and domestic happiness, but of wealth!"

Such being the condition of a great part of the population of this city, such the physical, and such the moral evils, which flow in a continually deepening and widening stream of misery, pollution, and death, it remains for me now to point out, in conclusion of the plan with which I commenced this paper, the means by which the sources of the current may be dried up.

To secure the community against invasion by disease from abroad, we have a well organized and efficient "Cordon Sanitaire." This consists of the Health Officer, residing at the Quarantine station, and the Resident Physician and Health Commissioner, residing in the city. These together form a board known as Health Commissioners, and in conjunction with the Board of Health, (composed of the Mayor, Aldermen, and Assistant Aldermen,) constitute the external Health Police. No vessel can reach the city without an inspection by the Health Officer, who has full power to determine whether she has on board any material, or comes from a port in such a state of health, as might produce disease in the city after arriving at our wharves. Should he discover good cause to suspect her to be in a condition dangerous to the public health, he is empowered to detain her at the Quarantine, a length of time sufficient to overcome all danger therefrom. The law is imperative, unless the Board of Health, for good and sufficient reasons, choose to permit the vessel to approach the city. The Health Officer has full control over the persons of the officers, crews, and passengers of vessels

6

suspected of infection, and over the cargo, and all the properties of the vessel and passengers. Certain articles may be destroyed by him, and he may order bedding and clothing to be purified and washed, before being brought up to the city.

These officers are all appointed by the Governor of the State. The city authorities have no voice in their selection, though the Resident Physician is to a certain extent, subject to the direction of the Board of Health. The only medical duty prescribed for him by the law, is to " visit all sick persons reported to the Mayor, or to the Board, or Commissioners, of Health, and perform such other duties as the Board of Health shall enjoin." " The Health Commissioner, under the direction of the Board of Health, shall assist the Resident Physician in the discharge of his official duties."

These officers, it will thus be seen, belong exclusively to the external, and not to the internal Health Police of the city, except so far, or at such times, as the Board of Health may direct. With the investigation and removal of causes of disease, and the suppression of epidemics generated, and existing within the city, they have nothing to do, unless ordered specifically by the Board of Health. Under present circumstances, the Board having no municipal officer upon whose knowledge and judgment in such matters they could depend, the state officers, would undoubtedly have plenty to do, should occasion for extra services unfortunately arise.

This I repeat is our *external* Health Police ; and it will be generally conceded to be well arranged, ample, and efficient. All the incumbents are medical men, and care has generally been taken to appoint those in good standing in the profession, and possessing sufficient age and experience. This is the more commendable, as nearly all the duties of some of the officers are merely financial, yet the incumbents may be, in the event of an epidemic, called upon to exercise their professional judgment and skill.

It cannot be denied that from within the confines of the city, more serious danger is to be apprehended than from without. In the pent up courts, the crowded tenements, the narrow streets and alleys, the damp dark cellars, in the destitution, filth, and misery of a large part of our population, are the germs of disease, which will readily account for a large proportion of the weekly average of nearly 200 deaths, announced in the bills of mortality.

In geographical position, in climatic placement, and in geological structure, no site perhaps could be selected for all the purposes of a great city, of a more salubrious character, than Manhattan Island. And yet whence this great mortality ? It is not from without—disease is forbidden to approach our wharves. It can only be then, from within, the people meet with such abundant destruction. Many of the immediate causes of this I have endeavored to point out. The remedy and preventive, are next to be considered, and I will now invite attention to our *Internal Health Police*. This consists of an officer entitled City Inspector, an Assistant City Inspector, an Assistant to the Board of Health, and eighteen Health Wardens. For 15 or 20 years past, it has been deemed important that the City Inspector, (who stands in the relation of a head to this corps of officials,) should possess medical attainments and qualifications, inasmuch as many of his duties prescribed by ordinance, and many others not prescribed, are of a character requiring that kind of knowledge for their performance. In the last appointment, however, to this office, this principle was repudiated for reasons not very clearly set forth ; it might have been considered as an oversight, had not an opportunity been given for a revision of the act, by the presentation of a memorial on the subject, by a very large number of medical practitioners, which set forth in a clear light, the true nature of the office, and the necessity of a medical education in its incumbent, and which memorial was not only responded to favorably, but its principles denied in the report of a committee appointed to consider the subject. The propriety of the appointment was insisted upon, and the sentiment was expressed, that not only is a medical, or even a literary education in the officer, unnecessary, but that without it, in the language of the report, " he is likely to prove equally, if not more, capable and efficient." I have no wish to criticise this remarkable exposition of a principle which must strike every one who observes it, as entirely out of character with the present advanced state of intelligence. I will, however, endeavor in the proper place, to show that a medical education is essential to the proper discharge of the duties of an officer of health, of whatever grade, and of this one especially, and that the greatest care should be exercised in selecting those best qualified for this duty. The Assistant City Inspector, and Assistant of the Board of Health, need not possess medical qualifications, as their duties are more strictly clerical ; yet such an education would often be useful, as they sometimes are obliged to act in the absence of the chief officer.

Nor has it ever been deemed necessary that the Health Wardens should be medically qualified. Indeed, had it been, medical men could not readily have been obtained for the duty, as conjoined therewith, is an office whose duties are of a totally different character, and entirely irrelevant to the habits and educational capabilities of a physician. I allude to the office of Dock Master, and lately, the office of Street Inspector has been added to it, in some of the wards.

Being one of the poorest offices in the gift of the Common Council, the post of Health Warden has rarely been sought for, or filled, by any other than the most ignorant and incompetent among the office-seekers. Its salary being the smallest of all, the most shameful collusions have been, and are daily, practised, for the purpose of increasing the emoluments, whereby a large amount of money is irregularly and improperly taken from the pockets of citizens.* Another serious objection to the present arrangement is, that during the prevalence of

* By the City Inspector, in 1842, a fraud was detected, which, had it proved successful, would have swindled householders of a large amount of money. It consisted of the printing of two hundred forged notices to empty sinks, which some night scavenger had ordered, and which would have yielded] him from ten to thirty dollars each. This was but one operation, and there is reason to believe that such acts are frequently committed, with the connivance of the Health Wardens.

epidemic or contagious diseases, in large numbers or single cases, the timid apprehensions of non-professional men, often wholly unfit them for the duties of officers of Health. They fear to approach a sick person, or even to enter a house where the disorder is said to exist, and they are more likely to increase, than allay, popular excitement. Some other equally injudicious matters, in this connection, might be stated, but these facts alone must be sufficient to convince any one of the utter inefficiency of the present system as a Health Police. *Not one of all the officers in that important branch of the City Government, is now occupied by a medically educated man.*

Allusion has been already made to a plan of a Health Police suggested nearly two years ago. There are three prominent principles upon which an organization for this purpose should be based.

In the *first place*, the incumbents should be men whose education, habits of investigation, and powers of judgment, would enable them to determine what constitutes a nuisance, and how far any particular matter is calculated to derange the healthy state of the atmosphere,—in short, they should possess a good knowledge of the doctrine of miasmata of all kinds, and their influence upon health.

2d. They should be men whose daily occupations, and, if possible, their *personal interests*, would aid them in the discovery and suppression or removal, of the causes of disease : whose general intelligence, and regard for the welfare of the city, and especially of its poorer inhabitants, would induce and urge them to give a regular and thorough examination of all suspected and doubtful places.

3d. They should possess the qualifications for reporting, when required, to the superior authorities, the sanitary condition of the various sections of the city ;—for recommending such measures as prudence and enlightened judgment may dictate, and the practical skill requisite for the application of preventive measures, such as vaccination and the like.

All these principles and aims would be answered by the adoption of the following plan of organization. I propose *first*, to abolish the office of *Health Warden*, (of whom there are usually eighteen ;) to divide the city in twelve districts, to each of which to appoint a respectable physician, to be entitled *Health Inspector*. These twelve, with the City Inspector and his office assistants, to constitute the "Health Police of the City of New York," the City Inspector, (also a respectable physician,) to be its head.

I need not enlarge here upon the benefits derivable from a reduction of the number of officers.

To obtain the advantages of the 2d principle, that is, to engage the *personal* and *private interest* of the proposed Health Inspector, (wherein we would have the best surety for the faithful performance of his duties,) I propose to make the boundaries of the Health districts identical with those of the present Dispensary districts, and to unite the offices of Health Inspector and Dispensary Physician, in the same individual.

The duties of the Dispensary Physician carry him in the very track of the nuisances which should be corrected, and while administering ʊ the relief of his patients, he would, as Health Inspector, cast about for the source of the evil, and apply the remedy. By the performance of his duty in one capacity, his labors in the other, would be materially lessened.

How great a proportion of the Rheumatisms, the Fevers, the Inflammations, the Pulmonary and other disorders, of all kinds, are attributable to the damp cellars, the filthy tenements, the foul yards, courts, and alleys, in which the poor are crowded, can be known only to the Dispensary Physician, who spends much of his time amid these wretched scenes, where he is now powerless for any preventive action that may occur to him.

But all are aware, for bitter experience has shown, that it is in those places the Cholera, Yellow Fever, Small Pox, Scarlet Fever, Measles, Typus Fever, and all other contagious and infectious disorders, are particularly abundant and malignant.

It has been customary upon the breaking out of an epidemic, for the public authorities to use great exertions and spend much money in cleansing and purifying these pestilential spots, in order to arrest the extension of the disease. Their previous neglect, or a false economy, has repeatedly sown a wide-spread desolation, which such preventive measures, as are now suggested, would to much extent have saved.

In addition to the duties now performed by the Health Wardens, the Health Inspectors should be required,

1st. To see that all persons are vaccinated, and for this purpose, to visit all houses, especially among the destitute, once a year ; to be constantly prepared, and to offer their services, to perform the operation gratuitously, and to urge it upon all who may require it.

2d. To be subject to the requisition of the Mayor, or any Alderman, or Assistant, to perform any professional duty they may justly require ; the Health Inspector, in whose district may be a Watch House or Police Office, to perform all the medical and surgical duties that may be required at those places, at the call of any officer attached thereto ; and to do all other things that may be required by the City Inspector.

The performance of the duties of this last section by a municipal officer, it will be at once seen, will relieve the Common Council of all the annoyance attendant upon the examination, and passage or rejection, of the numerous small bills now frequently laid before them.

It is evident that under such an arrangement as this, the duties of the Dispensary Physician would be performed with a greater degree of cheerfulness and care. The stimulus of a better remuneration, without the addition of any other duty than such as would tend to reduce the amount of his professional labors, and of a character not merely not incongruous with, but really in aid of, those labors, the duties of both offices requiring generally but a little more time than is now given to one, there could be obtained for the joint office, men of such character and age, as would not only prove a blessing to the poor, but a great assistance to the higher authorities, and give a profound satisfaction, and feeling of every possible security, to the whole community.

Not the least among the advantages derivable from the proposed combination, is this, that this corps of professional men, (selected as they are, and doubtless ever will be, by the trustees of the Dispensaries, as those best qualified, without the slightest reference to political opinion,) being *ex officio* Health Inspectors, though commissioned as such by another power, (the Board of Health,) if found competent, the Department would be at once raised above the corrupting atmosphere of partizanship, and we should then no more hear of public duties neglected for fear of making a politicel enemy, or through favor to a political friend : a practice too prevalent in this Department under its present organization.

In the protection of public health, as well as in private practice, party zeal should be entirely repudiated : it is incompatible with sound judgment and efficient action.

If any one Department, either of government or of private occupation, (and the remark has as much weight in one case as in the other,) should, more than another, be above the influence of political favoritism, and be sustained upon its intrinsic merits, it is that which has the care of the lives and health of the community, or of individuals.

From what has been related respecting the effects of the habitations of the poor, upon their health, lives, and morals, the evils are attributable to three things, viz., 1st, the living in damp, dark, underground, and other ill-ventilated apartments. 2d. The dirty and injured condition of the floors, walls, yards, and other parts of the premises. 3d. The crowding too many persons in single rooms of inadequate size and accommodations. To correct the first two of these evils, there appears but one way, and that is to place all the dwellings of the city under the inspection of competent officers, who shall have power *to enforce a law of domiciliary cleanliness.* For this purpose, those places known or suspected to be kept usually in improper condition, should be visited periodically, say once in one, two, or three months. The law should be so arranged as to make the cleansing bear upon the owner or lessee, and not upon the tenant directly, who is generally so poor, as to be unable to perform the necessary purgation and rectification of the premises.

The provisions of such a law should be similar to these.

1st. Every dwelling, or house, or room, court, alley, or yard, or other place used as a dwelling in the City of New York, shall be subject at any time, between sunrise and sunset, to the inspection of the Health Inspector in whose district it may be situated. If in opinion of said officer, it shall be deemed unfit for the purposes of a residence, by reason of dampness, darkness, dirt, filthiness, too low ceiling, ill-ventilation, being under ground, or any other good cause, he shall immediately report the same to the City Inspector, who shall, upon being satisfied that such report is true, serve a notice to that effect upon the owner, agent, or lessee, stating the reason therefor, and directing the same to be put in proper order and condition, within a specified time ; said room, house, or premises, to be outlawed, and forbidden to be occupied as a dwelling, until said order is complied with to the satisfaction of the Health Inspector.

2d. Should any room, cellar, dwelling, or premises, be found by the Health Inspector to be in a condition dangerous to the public health, by reason of emanations from the soil, or other places, or from any other cause, said officer shall report the same to the City Inspector, who shall upon being satisfied of its correctness, notify the owner, agent, or lessee thereof, directing him to cleanse and purify said place or premises, within a reasonable time; in default of a compliance with such order, it shall be the duty of the Health Inspector to cause such place to be purified and cleansed forthwith, and all the costs to be assessed upon the property so cleansed, and in addition thereto, a fine of fifty dollars.

3d. Should any owner, lessee, or other person feel aggrieved by the action of the Health Inspector or City Inspector, appeal may be made to the Mayor, or Board of Health, (sufficient time being allowed for the purpose,) who may reverse or confirm the decision of the City Inspector.

The power possessed by the City Inspector, or his assistants, is already sufficient for the general purposes of this proposition, such as entering and inspecting any premises, yard or dwelling, &c. But the essential points require some addition to the law, and I believe they are all embraced in the above proposed provision.

Can there be a doubt that such sanitary provisions, if well and discreetly carried out, would have the happiest effect upon the condition of large numbers of the poor of this city, and that they would prevent much of the devastation of health and life now made among them, by the manner in which they are compelled to pass their days by the negligent and unfeeling landlord?

The effect of such a law upon the habits of the tenant would not be *direct*,—his personal condition can only be reached by the moral law,—but the landlord, under this compulsory process, urged by the fear of having his premises out-lawed would, in letting them, stipulate with his tenants to keep them clean, to whitewash the walls and ceilings, wash the floors, remove the collections of dirt and garbage, and keep the yards and cellars in good order. And knowing that the health officer will pay them frequent visits, armed with the power of the law, it is altogether reasonable to suppose that the tenants themselve would be stimulated to maintain a better appearance of persons and domicils— that many would feel a pride in a good and cleanly aspect—that the smothered feelings of self-respect, love of praise, and desire for the comforts of cleanliness, would, in hundreds of bosoms, be re-awakened into life and energy.

Much of the good effect which might flow from the application of such a law, would depend upon the character and manner of the individuals appointed to enforce it. The exhibition of a regard for their health and comforts, a manner combining firmness, kindness, and patience, a disposition to instruct in the *manner*, as well as to require the *act*, giving an assurance while making the visit of inspection, that it is wholly for their advantage, would satisfy the tenants that their health, comfort, and protection, against the neglect of the landlord, were the chief objects of the law, and cause the visits of the inspector to be received with interest and pleasure. No person is more likely to be received with kindness, and welcomed as a friend, than he who comes to relieve suffering, or restore health. The plan I have suggested of uniting the offices of Dispensary Physician and Health Inspector in one individual, will effectually accomplish the object in view, in every particular.

The enforcement of a law to compel domiciliary cleanliness, may at first sight, appear to some as impracticable, to others as unconstitutional, (on the ground that a man's house is his castle, and his occupation of it cannot be interfered with without his consent,) and some may suppose it oppressive, as interfering with the rights of citizens to live as many in a room, in such manner as, and in whatever room they choose. An examination of this subject will expose the erroneousness of such views, and show that an inspection of dwellings will be as justifiable as the inspection of articles of food, or clothing, or of steamboat boilers.

We permit, without objecting, the examination of our houses by the fire wardens, to see that all is safe against fire. No one objects to the law limiting the number of passengers in a vessel crossing the ocean, and the confiscation of the vessel for its violation ; and the public voice would demand, in loud tones, the razing of a house in danger of falling upon the passers by. Chimneys are required by law to be swept every month, and if they take fire, a fine is imposed though no damage results. Cispools and sinks are now required to be emptied when the contents attain to a certain depth, under heavy penalty. Unsound beef, hides, skins, fish, or any putrid, or unsound or unwholesome substance, may be forthwith cast into the river by the officer. The fire law prevents the erection of wooden buildings within certain limits, and prescribes the mode in which brick buildings shall be built. All these instances, and many others that might be mentioned, may be said to infringe on the rights of citizens, with as much propriety as the amendments here suggested. Nay, further, with regard to nuisances, the statute expressly declares the right of the Common Council to *fill up* any lots, yards, or cellars which may endanger by their condition, the public health, and the same reason why a vessel without a clean bill of health, may not lie at our wharves, will apply to the dwellings in the city. Every house should be required to have a clean bill of health, or like the ships, be placed under the control of the proper officers.

To raise from the depressed and poor, the heavy necessity of living crowded in single rooms, the source as I have endeavored to show of great moral, as well as physical, evils, much aid cannot, I fear, be found in any legal enactment. If a family are so numerous as to require separate rooms, and so poor as to be unable to procure them, no law on the subject could be enforced, which would effectually prevent the evil. The remedy lies with the humane and philanthropic capitalists, by whom houses might be erected with all the comforts and conveniences of separate chambers, &c., which would yield a fair interest on their value, and make thousands of people happy. Here is a direction in which a fortune might be applied, which would produce an amount of happiness to the possessor, of good to the recipient, and benefit to the community, equal, I have no doubt, to all that could be possibly obtained by a new line of Atlantic steamers, though ever so successful.

This subject has two points of consideration of especial value with regard to the *temperance reformation*. An improvement in the condition of the home of the laborer, will remove one of the temptations to his frequent visits to the more comfortable and inviting grog shops, while the substitution of a more invigorating and stimulating atmosphere, will relieve in a considerable degree, the desire for artificial stimulus.

Atmospheric air is to the animal system, a powerful stimulant as well as nutrient substance. In sufficient purity and copiousness, it imparts a sustaining and vivifying power unequalled by any other substance. Its vitalizing operations present one instance of the wonderful adaptations of natural things to each other, but it is singularly striking, because of the immediate and incessant dependence of animals upon it, for life and strength. Air, when pure, gives a freshness and vigor, a tone to the nervous and muscular parts of the system, productive of the *highest degree* of mental and physical enjoyment. Without the tone thus imparted, the functions of the system become relaxed, and in addition, the animal spirits and feelings become depressed and uneasy. To relieve this condition, nature instinctively seeks some stimulating means. Many feed on mental excitement—the stimulus of business with some, with others of society, with some of hope and expectation, keep alive the energies. But the farmer feeds his nervous and general strength on fresh air and wholesome labor. Artificial stimulus is not required by him, he does not feel its want, and has comparatively little relish for it. But the dwellers in the cellars, courts, and ill-ventilated garrets, depressed and prostrated by the want of the stimulus given by nature, unable to enjoy the feelings guaranteed by an unfailing abundance of oxygen, *instinctively* feel the want of a substitute ; *they find it in alcohol.* The allurements held out by those dens of destruction, abounding on all sides, add temptation to instinct, and the child of ignorance and misfortune terminates his senses, and often his life, the victim of licentiousness and unnatural debauchery.

First take the drunkard from the cellar, give him the stimulus of a pure atmosphere, relieve the demands of nature in this particular, and the work of reformation is half done, and will then go on with increased vigor ; but as long as he is deprived of the sustaining power offered by nature, his artificial appetite will be less easily appeased.

The community is guilty of the double offence of cutting off from the destitute part of its members a proper supply of air, in other words, of exciting an appetite for a vile and destructive substitute, and then of presenting to them at almost every corner, opportunities for indulgence in the poison.

Very few members of the medical profession ever find a seat in the public council chamber. Legislative and executive bodies must, therefore, be dependent, in their ignorance of the subject, upon the knowledge and experience of the lay members of the profession, to enable them to make the proper laws, and exercise the proper authority for the pro-

7

tection of their constituents against the encroachments of disease. Is it not then, clearly the duty of the appointing powers, to fill the offices having the control and direction of sanitary matters, with men of the largest experience and most cultivated capacity in medical science, having regard to the important consideration that a man may be a good prescribing physician, without the kind of knowledge or the taste requisite for the due discharge of public duties of this character. This is a peculiar branch of the science, (though strictly medical,) and as distinct as the practice of surgery.

The judgment which should be exercised in seeking medical advisers for ourselves or our families, is equally, if not more imperative, when the protection of the 300,000 members of the community is concerned.

The necessity for a medical education in an Officer of Health, may be shown by instancing some of the practical duties which must be performed by him, whether a chief or subordinate. The question " what constitutes a nuisance ?" is one which now divides the scientific world. On either side are ranged the most acute and philosophic minds. Experiment upon experiment has been tried, the light of science and research has been profusely expended, in the endeavor finally and satisfactorily to settle this question, so important to the health and happiness of man. On the one hand, the public health is to be protected at whatever cost, and on the other, private property must not unnecessarily be destroyed. Can it be supposed that a decision of this frequently intricate question by an officer who has little or no knowledge of chemistry, nor physiology, nor the laws of miasma, nor any other science bearing on it, will be satisfactory to the public, or to the holder of the property destroyed by his order ? And is it reasonable to suppose that in such hands the public weal can be secure against the influence of disease—generating nuisances ? Such an officer should always be able to assign the most conclusive and satisfactory reasons for his acts. The severest acumen, and most rigid search, are frequently, for a time, at fault in detecting the source of a wide-spreading pestilence—this city has repeatedly been visited by endemic diseases, and has greatly suffered in reputation and interest in consequence of a want of energetic and capable officers early to detect and remove the latent cause of the disorder ; and where learning and experience have sometimes been baffled in the discovery, or right estimate, of the sources of general sickness, it is folly to suppose that ignorance and inexperience, though associated with moral worth, can infuse confidence in the community, or give to it safety or credit.

The nature of the products of decomposition must, therefore, be thoroughly understood, before a correct conclusion can be arrived at, for upon them it depends, whether the decaying matters are capable of generating disease in the human frame. And here we find the nicest distinctions necessary. For example, putrefying vegetable matter, in general, is believed to be a prolific source of disease, but there is a wide difference between different vegetables ; some are almost innocuous, while others are exceedingly baneful. Some, while decaying, give forth gases of the most offensive and deleterious character, and from others' in the like state, little will be observed. The difference between " decay" and " putrefaction," the two destroying processes which animal and vegetable matters undergo, and which are wide asunder in their nature and effects, should be well understood and never forgotten.

The following communication from my friend and colleague, Dr. R. K. Hoffman, exhibits in a striking light the vigilance and discrimination necessary on the part of those who have the care of the health of large numbers of persons.

From R. K. Hoffman, M. D., late Surgeon U. S. Navy.

22 Warren Street, August 30th, 1844.

MY DEAR SIR,—Your note of the 26th inst. reminds me of our conversation at the Hospital, in which I mentioned the occurrence of fever on ship board, from the decomposition of vegetable matter.

On referring to my Journal for the particulars you ask for, I find other causes combined, which alone may be considered sufficient to have originated and propagated the fever ; but I will state the circumstances from which you will make your own deductions.

In the summer of 1817, the U. S. sloop of war Ontario, commanded by Capt. James Biddle, was fitted out in this port for a voyage to the Pacific Ocean.   On the 24th of June, she left the Navy Yard and anchored in the North River, off the Battery.   The crew, consisting of 175, continued for a time as healthy as *usual for a new crew in port.*

Being destined to convey Mr. Rodney and Judge Prevost, as Commissioners to Buenos Ayres and Chili, a large supply of cabin stores, including the ordinary vegetables, was received on board, and stowed in rooms constructed for the purpose, on the berth deck, between the hatchways, obstructing ventilation, and encroaching on the space allotted to the men to sleep, while that under the top gallant forecastle was redolent of its new occupants—poultry and pigs.   The season was rainy, sultry, and damp ; and the state of the weather compelled the crew to sleep below, where the exhalations from decaying vegetables, especially in a calm night, rendered the air almost insufferably hot, and peculiarly offensive.

Such was the condition of the ship, when at the latter part of July, during the calm, sultry, rainy weather, a sudden increase of disease took place; it commenced with a sense of great debility, particularly of the limbs, aversion to all exertion, pains in the head, loins, and bones, anxiety and nausea—the skin generally moist and hot, tongue loaded with a yellow coat, bowels rather loose.   In some it assumed a Typhoid character in its progress, while its more ordinary type was that of bilious remittent.   There was a daily succession of cases, and from the 20th of July to the 15th of August, the average number was thirty.

Captain Biddle did not concur in opinion, with the surgeon, that local causes had the principal agency in producing the disease, but seeing no prospect of realizing the expectation of getting to sea, obtained from

Colonel Haidman, the commanding officer, a spacious and airy building on the south side of Governor's Island, to which at the date above mentioned, the sick were removed. On the 17th there were three new cases; on the 18th, two; on the 19th, none; on the 20th, two; on that evening the wind came from the north, the air was cool, and three more sickened, preceded by a chill. These cases were transferred in succession to the hospital on the Island. With the change in the weather, which continued comfortably cool, with fresh breezes, the fever gradually disappeared, no new cases occurring after the 24th.

I would add that in the course of the voyage, when all on board were healthy, the first Lieutenant, who occupied the forward state room, sickened with symptoms of fever. On searching for the cause, some rotten potatoes were found in a locker adjoining his room, from which it was separated only by a board partition.

The state of health in the city was good during that season. None of the men died.   I am, sir, yours truly,

RICHARD K. HOFFMAN.

The subject of *sewerage* is destined to be one, which of necessity must ere long occupy the attention of the people and the government, and upon which an intelligent and judicious officer of health may throw much light. It will, I am satisfied, be found not only the most economical, but the *only* mode, in which the immense mass of filth daily generated in this large city, can be effectually removed. In some foreign cities, underground sewerage on a regular uniform plan throughout, the sewers constructed on the most scientific and substantial plans, has been carried out in the completest manner, with the most decidedly beneficial results upon the general health and comfort. We are annually giving proofs of our belief in their necessity, by the construction of single sewers in various places, as they are demanded by circumstances, but it is done without reference to any uniform plan, and it is feared that thus much confusion and great additional expense, will fall upon the treasury when ever it shall be deemed proper to project and carry out over the whole city a complete and uniform system; and I believe, " to this complexion must we come at last." One thing especially brings this conviction; since the introduction of the Croton, the rain water cisterns being useless, the bottoms of them have in many instances been taken out, and they have been converted into cispools, into which the refuse matter of the houses is thrown. Great trouble is thus saved to families and domestics, but it needs no prophetic vision to perceive, that an immense mass of offensive material, will thus be soon collected, its decomposition polluting the air, in the immediate precincts of our chambers and sitting rooms, and generating an amount of miasmatic effluvia, incalculably great and injurious. Discharge all the contents of our sinks and cispools, through sewers into the rivers, and we will avoid two of the most powerful causes of sickness and early death.

The great quantity of water from the sky, the hydrants, the unused wells, &c., now accumulating beneath the surface, must find its way into many basements and cellars, rendering them very damp and unhealthy, and for which sewers constitute the only remedy.

Another mooted sanitary question, is the influence of *grave-yards, vaults,* and other burial-places, in large cities, upon the health of the inhabitants. Some acute men are now endeavoring to maintain that no specific bad results have ever been, or can be, justly attributed to them, while others, among whom is Chadwick, regard them as highly objectionable, and on this side appears the most direct and positive evidence. In this city are some places of interment, which, whatever may be said of their effects on health, are certainly crowded and offensive to a high degree; their condition and influence, as certainly, demand an intelligent and careful investigation.

While writing this communication, there applied to me for medical advice, a young man, who had gone, in good health, into a vault of a church in a densely populated part of the city, to see the coffin containing the remains of a relative; he had been in but a few moments when the effluvia was so offensive and powerful, as almost entirely to overcome him. He immediately retired, returned home, and when I saw him, three hours after, he was laboring under a considerable degree of fever, and other disordered symptoms, which he said had all come on since his visit to the vault. He thinks the vault must have contained not less than 200 bodies. The place has before been complained of, and it is difficult to avoid the belief that more or less injury must be inflicted by it on the health of the neighborhood.

Not the least important of the results which should be obtained from the appointment of an officer to superintend the affairs of public health, is that of keeping a constant watch upon the progress of diseases, drawing the proper inferences obtainable from a careful inspection of the mortality returns, and giving them to the public in a suitable form and manner. Living as we are in constant subjection to attacks of bodily disease, induced by the circumstances of life, the lances of death held constantly "in rest," by a thousand unseen hands, waiting only the stirring of the breeze to thrust them at our unconscious frames, such an officer should be as a sentinel upon the tower, watching with an intelligent and never closing eye, the manœuvres of the wily enemy, and with a ready pen, alert to send the alarm to every quarter, and prepare the city for a defence against his approaches. The inhabitants may be, some, reckless of danger, and careless of life, others may affect to despise the warnings of the watchman, and scoff at the " Philosophy of Diseases," but it is no less the duty of the faithful magistrate and officer, to see that at all points the constituency are guarded, with whatever of science *and* virtue they can find.

There is in this city but one officer in the receipt of the certificates of death—the only source of knowledge of the diseases which prevail. He is the City Inspector. It is by law made his duty to publish every Tuesday, a list of the deaths occurring during the preceding week, and in January, " to publish the whole number of deaths which shall have occurred in the city of New York during the preceding year, with the sexes, ages and diseases of the persons so dying." This is the *letter* of the law, and any boy, who has the *quantum sufficit* of reading, writing, and arithmetic, with a fair proportion of patience, may make out the tables in the unscientifically alphabetical mode in which it has usually been done. But of what use is this? we learn by it that 9,000 or 10,000 deaths, occur annually ; we are informed of the diseases which cause the *deaths*, (if the arangement is worthy of dependence, which it is not always,) but of the *causes of the diseases* we are told nothing. To derive the proper and full advantage from the returns of mortality, we must look beyond the mere name of the diseases, and ascertain the *sources of those diseases.* *Now!* the reports are useful for little more than to satisfy ordinary curiosity, or to enable the preacher " to point a moral " —but if properly analyzed, and their whole bearing and influence exposed and elucidated, they would become valuable aids to the private physician, and to the public officer of health, in studying the liabilities of New York, and the influences of its climate, position, temperature, and other circumstances in producing diseases.

If I may be allowed to illustrate this point, by referring to a result of my own study of some of the Annual Reports, I will recall attention to the discovery, that in this city there is less consumption among the native residents, than in Boston or Philadelphia. This is proved by a calculation, the corectness of which may be tried at any time, which has not yet been questioned, and which turns the tables completely, as they were before set down, by those who would make New York a comparative Golgotha.

This officer should study the influences of seasons, localities, and many other circumstances, on the aspects of disease, and he should keep a record of the Barometric, Thermometric, Hygrometric, and Pluvial changes. An improvement in the certificate of death, is also much needed ; a more clear designation of medical terms, inquiries into the condition and physical circumstances of the decedent, the length of his residence in this country, if a foreigner, and the influence of the change of climate upon the cause of death, and many other points, are necessary to obtain correct and specific conclusions, respecting the diseases of New York ; while a thorough knowledge of the wants of science, and of what has been done abroad, in countries where the subject has constituted the labor of the lives of the most gifted individuals, is highly desirable. All this knowledge can only be obtained, and the improvements properly urged and applied, by an individual of good medical education, and one who has a taste, and willingness for the work. A capable Health Officer would be well employed, and it should be made his interest, to devote his time and talents to the dissemination of sound precepts concerning the preservation of health and life, among the people, to whom knowledge on these snbjects is now almost inaccessible. To a vast number, for whom instruction as to the best method of regulating their internal and external domiciliary, and their personal arrangements, is most desirable, it could be given in such forms as would certainly arrest attention and be productive of incalculable benefits. The circumstances of life, which have influence in producing disease, are endless in number, and yet the sufferers, in too many instances, are wholly ignorant of their power, or even of their existence. This is true to a great extent of the rich and educated, as every physician knows, but it is emphatically the case with the destitute and ignorant, to whom the laws of health and life, are a sealed book.

These labors I regard as answering to the *spirit* of the law, and, in nearly the words of an able writer on poverty and crime, " The wisest civil regulations that can be devised, will avail but little for the advancement of society, if the officers who execute them, look not beyond the letter of their commissions, and fail to communicate what they learn of the causes, the remedy, and the prevention of diseases."

To this subject the language of an inspired penman may be literally applied ;—" the letter killeth, but the spirit giveth life."

A sanitary police, composed of such individuals as are herein suggested, would constitute an efficient corps of *Health Missionaries.* Their time would be principally devoted to the purpose of teaching the poor the rules which should regulate their household operations ; and the value of fresh air, ventilation, cleanliness, temperance, &c., would form constant themes for them. The circulation of Tracts on Health, distributed with the same freedom as religious tracts now are, by hands equally interested in the comforts and condition of the poor, would form a powerful addition to their means of usefulness. The Dispensary Physician wields for these purposes, a power possessed by no other class of men.

To the habits of life of many of the laboring classes, to their confinement in small apartments, and to *their ignorance of the laws of life and health,* by which especially, even their contracted arrangements are unnecessarily kept in a bad condition, we are to look for no inconsiderable amount of the injury which they sustain. The moisture, filth, and confined atmosphere of the courts and alleys, are also prolific sources of disease ; in the occupations of many lurks the enemy. But if we restrict our attention to them, we shall overlook a very large proportion of the causes of mortality, and with all our efforts to improve the sanitary condition of our city, we should fail in some of the most essential points. A well regulated and efficient Health Police might do much towards correcting the existing evils, but to carry the desired reform to the utmost limit, and with a greater permanency, measures which no police can carry out, are necessary. And as these evils are not confined to the laboring and destitute part of our population, but afflict also the wealthier portion, a more healthy state of public opinion is absolutely necessary, to effect the desired results.

This can best, if not only, be done, by making Physiology, as applied to the laws of life, and the prevention of diseases, a subject of study in all our private, public, and common schools. The children who attend these, especially the latter, are the individuals by and with whom, the important change of opinion and habit, is to be wrought, if at all. It is needless to say to an ignorant adult, apparently free from sickness, that he lives, works and sleeps, in too confined an atmosphere—he will answer that he is well enough, a change would be irksome, and cost money, and he will not believe what you say, for he cannot be easily made to understand the importance, or even the right use, of air.   But bring up his child in a knowledge of the value and necessity of pure fresh air, by teaching him the relations which it bears to the blood, the digestion and other functions—teach him never to fear it, that it is his immediate and incessant source of life and health, give him a knowledge of the diseases and dangers to which its absence will subject him, and think you he would not avoid its impurities, as he would poison or the pestilence ? In his school-room, his sitting-room, his chamber or his work-shop, he would seek for a pure clear atmosphere, as when thirsty he would seek the cool water, as the weary "hart panteth after the water brook." "Ventilate, Ventilate," would be his natural demand, in tones of earnestness proportioned to the necessity which his expansive lungs, and ever freshened feelings, would readily discover.   The humble tenement of the laborer, would then, though but a single room, be no longer shut night and day, unvisited by the refreshing air of heaven ; the workshop would then no longer be a close receptacle of foul effluvia of human and other origin, and our churches, public rooms, and lecture halls, be no more unventilated.   (En passant, what a strange inconsistency is it, in the refined and polished, to object to sip a mouthful of water from the same glass as an other, in which there could be no possible contamination, and yet swallow over and over again, the breath of others shut up in the same apartment, and which has passed through hundreds of lungs, perhaps diseased, and over teeth in every stage of decay.)

So with their food and drink, their exercise, personal cleanliness, and all other things pertaining to health and longevity ; when once instructed in the principles which should be observed with regard to them, how great would be the difference in the habits of life.   If it is admitted that many of the improprieties of life are due to an ignorance of its laws, then a knowledge of those laws would cause a diminution of the improprieties.

And I submit, whether a more powerful aid of temperance can be found, than instilling into the youthful mind a knowledge of the structure and functions of his system, and the poisonous results of alcohol upon them.

The general introduction of this subject as a branch of school learning, would, I hesitate not to say, have a greater meliorating influence upon the human condition, than any other.   Already has it been introduced into many private schools, and given delight to both teachers and pupils.   The abundance of material, and the facilities for its illustration, put it on a par with Chemistry and Natural Philosophy, in attractive interest, while for real usefulness to the concerns of life, it is far in advance of Astronomy, and many other studies, now generally taught, and for which it might be advantageously substituted, should any change be necessary.   The operations of a living machine must necessarily possess a degree of interest to the student and observer beyond those of inanimate bodies, and when once the study of the animal machine is divested of its ancient and unnatural feelings of superstitior and of its exclusive and unnecessary confinement to the physician, (which I think are rapidly disappearing,) it will be found to yield a degree of entertainment, as well as usefulness, unsurpassed.

Now where are the advantages of this study most needed? among what classes of the community are its precepts and laws, its vital and saving influences, its checks and guards against disease and danger, most required? Is it among those who live in high-ceiled rooms, who have plenty of time and means to go abroad and seek fresh air in the country, who can afford to live on the choicest delicacies, and dress in the most comfortable manner, who have no fear of want, and are not compelled to study the most economical mode of living? or to seek out, from a very limited field, the best they can do for themselves? No! indeed, such need comparatively little aid. They may turn night into day, and dissipate their time and strength in debauchery and folly, but they are not compelled to reside in cellars, and chambers ill ventilated, or to associate with filth, in foul air. *They* are to be reached only by *moral* teaching. But those whom penury subjects to the necessity of living in the cheapest rooms, who must submit to the hardest extortions, or live in the street, and whose gross ignorance prevents them improving their condition as much as they might, had they a knowledge of the true mode—these constitute a large class for whom humanity demands that we should employ every means in our power for bettering their physical, as well as their moral, condition. Of what use is science, if it cannot be applied to the *practical* purposes of life, or employed to improve the character and condition of our fellow creatures. It can no longer be shut up in monkish cells, nor yet will I believe that its absence in an Officer of Health, will, by the community, be regarded as a qualification for office.

These pages have become extended to a number entirely unexpected at the commencement, yet no allusion has been made to many matters of sanitary value, which cannot be omitted in the consideration of the general subject, without leaving it in a state of incompleteness. The present condition and wished for improvement of the destitute part of our population, have been my specific objects of attention. An extract from the latest (English) work upon the subject of ventilation, recently put into my hands, places this whole subject in its true light. " The " dwellings of the extremely poor present scenes of misery, desolation, " and woe, which it is afflicting to witness, where the sensibilities are " not hardened against the sufferings of humanity. They must be seen " to be understood, and to draw out that amount of individual sympa- " thy, which they imperiously demand, in a civilized and christian com- " munity. The station of this country in arts, literature, and science, " is acknowledged throughout the globe, as well as its naval, military " and commercial power; and, latterly, its exertions against the slave- " trade, have given a noble example in the cause of humanity, and " soften the recollections of former times. But the regeneration of its " own population, or rather the placing of them in that condition which " the progress of religion and philanthropy demands, is perhaps a task

8

" of more moral grandeur, and of still more difficult execution than " any which it has attempted."

To this I will only add, in conclusion, (what has been before briefly referred to,) that respecting the Laws of Health and Life, it may be said, though the remark may seem so extraordinary as apparently to amount to a libel on human nature, on no other subject connected with the interests, happiness, or longevity of man, is the darkness of ignorance so profound and so universal.

THE

RIGHTS OF LABOR.

BY

CALVIN COLTON,

AUTHOR OF "THE LIFE AND TIMES OF HENRY CLAY," "JUNIUS TRACTS,"
"FOUR YEARS IN GREAT BRITAIN," ETC., ETC.

NEW YORK:
PUBLISHED BY A. S. BARNES & CO., 51 JOHN STREET.

MDCCCXLVI.

CONTENTS.

THE RIGHTS OF LABOR.

CHAPTER I.

ATTRIBUTES OF LABOR, AND ITS POSITION IN THE SOCIAL STATE.

§ 1. *Definition.*

LABOR is the application of the powers and devices of man, to supply the wants and gratify the desires of the race.

§ 2. *Who are Laborers.*

It will be seen by the above definition, that laborers are a very comprehensive class. They are not confined to those who engage in manual toil; who dig, or who plough the land or ocean; who are occupied in the various branches of agriculture, manufactures, and commerce; in the mechanic, useful, or fine arts; who construct canals and railroads, build houses or ships; who make hard hands and hard fists, by striking hard blows; who wipe the sweat from the brow of toil, in any vocation, in doors or out, on land or water;—but all who apply their powers and faculties, of body or mind; their hands, or their heads, or their fingers; their invention, or their skill; their hearts, or their intellect, to supply the wants of society;—the learned professions, teachers of every class, artists, authors, devotees of science and literature; legislators, magistrates, judges, clerks, and many other classes, more than can be named or thought of; yet, being devoted to productive industry and improving pursuits, necessary to society, and to the supply of the wants and desires of the race;—all these are properly ranked among LABORERS.

§ 3. *Labor is Capital.*

The position which is usually awarded, in political science, to what is called capital, as if labor were not capital, and capital of the most important kind, has tended to degrade labor, and to strip it of its essential attributes as the producer of all adventitious wealth, or of that state of things which distinguishes civilized society from barbarism. It has also tended to cloud one of the most important branches of political science in obscurity, and led to much embarrassment in the consideration of others. The natural order of things is thus reversed; that which ought to be first, is put last; the cause stands in place of the effect; the agent is taken for the instrument; the producer for the thing produced.

Although it will be convenient in this work, in order to avoid frequent repetition and unnecessary circumlocution, to employ the customary phrase, capital and labor, in the usual sense, it is due to a just consideration of the comparative claims of these two things, to assert the prior and paramount rights of labor, as to the position to which it is entitled in a system of political science. Labor is capital of its own kind, not as a subject to be acted upon for the increase of its own value, but as an agent that imparts value to every other kind of capital which it employs as an instrument, or takes in hand for improvement. It is doubtless true, that the faculties or powers of labor are subjects of culture and use, for the increase of their skill and effectiveness, and in this sense are subjects of action for the increase of their value. In this particular, the faculties or powers of labor occupy the position of any other kind of capital, as subjects of improvement by labor itself. It will be observed, however, that it is not labor, but the faculty of labor, the value of which is thus increased.

§ 4. *The fundamental Error of European Economists, as to the Rights of Labor.*

Ricardo says: "The produce of the earth—all that is derived from its surface by the united application of labor, machinery, and capital—is divided among three classes, viz., the proprietor of the land, the owner of the stock or capital necessary for its cultivation, and the *laborers* by whose industry it is cultivated. The *proportions* of the whole produce of the earth which will be allotted to each of these classes, under the names of *rent, profit,* and *wages,* will be *essentially* different. To determine the laws which regulate this distribution is the *principal problem* in political science."

It should be observed, that European economists, for the most part, if not universally, regard labor as a mere power, like horse power, or any other brute force; and what Ricardo means above, by "the *proportion* of the whole produce of the earth allotted" to labor, is simply that which is necessary for its subsistence, as for that of a horse, an ox, or any other

155

brute. His three chief elements of political economy are "rent, profit, and wages." It must be seen, that a system of political science, constructed on such principles, is entirely unsuited to American society, and though its doctrines in the abstract may often be correct, its whole must be totally inapplicable to a state of things radically, fundamentally, and essentially different from that for which such a system is designed. It is morally impossible, from the social position of European economists, that they should be able to adapt a system of political economy to American society, not having thought it incumbent on themselves to make any other provision for labor, than to save it from starvation, and to get the greatest profit out of it, as the owner does out of his ox or his horse; and believing, as they do, that system the best, which will secure this end most effectually. There can be no redeeming quality with Americans, for a system of political science, one of the fundamental principles of which is of this kind, pervading it throughout, imparting its character to it, and constituting a part of its very essence. The three words, "rent, profit, and *wages*," in the sense in which they are employed by European economists, as representing the three comprehensive parts of this system, are sufficiently declaratory of its character, and look back to a feudal state of society. The things here intended are not to be found in this country, and are not tolerated by its institutions.

The Hon. Nathan Appleton, of Boston, suggests, that this system is based on that part of Mr. Malthus's theory, which supposes a surplus population, bidding against each other for bread with the lowest wages possible to live upon, and that this natural strife, being identical with the love of life, may be relied upon by capitalists. This extreme point of human necessity, Mr. Appleton says, is taken by the modern school of political economists, such as M'Culloch, Ricardo, and others, " as the natural rate of wages. This low and abject state of labor is the *original principle*, from which they have drawn most important conclusions as to the foundation of their system, it being admitted, that profits go wholly to the owners of capital employing labor, and no part of the accumulation to the laborers themselves." Such is the system of political science adopted as a text in American colleges, and made a guide to legislation by American statesmen!

§ 5. *Wherein Labor Capital is vested.*

It is not vested in the effect of the faculty or power of labor, but in the power itself. The laborer himself is the original, fundamental, most indispensable capitalist of the world.

§ 6. *Labor Capital is of indefinite Value.*

It has no measure but that of the ability and life of the agent, which are always indefinite.

§ 7. *Labor Capital is reproductive.*

It is true that other capital is called productive, and reproductive, figuratively; but its power of reproduction is not, like that of labor, in itself. It is the action of the labor of man upon it—or of his skill, which is the same thing—which makes it productive. Labor—which here and elsewhere is used metaphorically as the agent—can do the same thing one moment, one day, one year, which it had before done, other things being equal; and so on, to the end of life.

§ 8. *Labor Capital is the Parent of all other Capital.*

Other capital is chiefly, if not altogether, the creature of civilization, though the same thing, in substance, may be found in the savage state. But as a subject of political science, it is regarded as one of the things receiving its definite form and measure from the hand of civil polity. It will be found, indeed, that the entire structure of civilization owes its existence to labor, and of course those parts of it which derive their tangible value from its forms, and which are regulated by them. Civilization itself is secondary and ministerial, in relation to all the capital which labor creates, and comes in to define and protect it. It was in part the value of these products of labor which made civilization necessary, that it might receive a definite form, and be made secure. No man can apply his hand or point his finger to a thing regarded as capital, which is not the product of labor. All intrinsic values are but fictions of the imagination, always impalpable, vanishing as they are approached. The diamond and the pebble are of equal value in the eye of the barbarian, and would be equivalents in every other eye, but for the existence of that capital, the product of labor, which is able to purchase the diamond at a high price.

§ 9. *Labor more Profitable than any other Capital.*

Labor is not only the parent of all other capital, bringing it into existence, or preparing it for use; but the use of itself, in the discharge of these functions, is many times more profitable, for a given amount of value, than any other capital. In the United States, the laborer would think he did badly, if he could not lay up 50 per cent., or half of his wages. Labor, therefore, as capital, in this country, may be said to be worth 50 per cent. Frugal laborers often make it worth more than that, and soon obtain, in addition to their capital of labor, other capital, laid up and put to use, constituting the nucleus of a fortune—the foundation of wealth. Six per cent. is considered good use for money and other vested capital;

whereas, the savings of labor are often from 50 to 75 per cent. of its wages, besides the faculty and chances of the laborer to husband his acquisitions as the foundation and means of future wealth.

§ 10. *Labor Capital the Gift of God.*

This is evident from the fact, that it is vested in those powers and endowments which man receives from the hand of his Creator. It is not dug from the earth; it is not the handy-work of man; but it is the handy-work of God. Like God, it is endowed with intelligence, and as such is worthy of great respect.

§ 11. *Labor Capital the Source of all Wealth.*

It is true that the world, untouched by the hand of man, is rich in its resources. But all that which is commonly called wealth, and which constitutes the wealth of civilized society, is adventitious—the result of human labor. The precious metals are obtained at great cost of labor; and the forms given to them for the various purposes of use and ornament to which they are applied, require much additional labor. Estates, buildings, roads, canals, improvements of every kind, public and private; farms and plantations; utensils and products of agriculture, of manufacture, of commerce, and of art; carriages of burden and of pleasure; ships and navies; instruments of war and of peaceful vocations; towns and cities; states and empires; means of luxury and of usefulness; means and products of the intellectual, moral, and physical culture of the human race; laws and government; civil, literary, religious, and social institutions; the entire and comprehensive forms and values of human society, are severally and collectively the product and result of human labor. All that is prized by money, and bought with it, is obtained at the cost of labor. The immense and exhaustless material of wealth, as it exists in the resources of nature, receives all its value from the hand of labor. "Whatever," says Mr. Appleton, "exists under the name of property, wealth, or capital, is the result or representative of previous labor."

§ 12. *Labor Capital the Property of the Laborer, and inalienable.*

It may, indeed, be justly held under restraint or duresse, as a punishment for crime. But even that condition does not alienate the right of property in the agent. Its use and the avails thereof are forfeited to the law for a season; but when the law is satisfied, the offender that was, being free, is entitled to reassert his property for his own use and benefit. Labor may be bound under civil regulations, for an equitable quantum of its avails, to satisfy indebtedness incurred; but the faculties or powers of labor are not and can not be alienated. They are an inheritance from God, not transferable. The claims of parents for the services of children, during a minority fixed by the civil code, if the parents choose to assert them, are for the payment of a just debt, incurred by the expenses of infancy and childhood. But the rights of independence consequent on this period, as recognised by Divine and human authority, presuppose man's inalienable right of property in himself, and in his own powers.

§ 13. *Labor is bound to share in the Burdens of Society.*

It has been seen, that labor is indebted to society for its position and its value as capital; that it is capital of the most important and profitable kind; that, in this country, it occupies a dignified place in civil and social organization; and that, without civilization, it would be of little or no value. It is but reasonable, therefore, that it should sustain an equitable share in the expenses or burdens of society. But—

§ 14. *Labor has a Claim to Protection from Society.*

If labor is an important interest in and to itself, it is no less true, as already seen, that it constitutes the vitality of all other interests which are valuable in civilized society. It behooves society, therefore, as well from what it owes to labor, as from a regard to its own best interests, and to all its interests, to secure to labor those privileges and advantages, which will promote its greatest prosperity, and which are indispensible to it. What are those privileges and advantages? The answer is found in four words: EMPLOYMENT AND FAIR WAGES. This is the only protection which labor asks, and it is what it has a right to demand.

CHAPTER II.

SLAVE LABOR.

§ 1. *Position of Slave Labor in Political Science.*

IT occupies the position of a power simply, as horse power, or any other productive agency, that is the property of its owner, and subject to his will. Slave labor has no political rights in itself, and when the rights of labor are spoken of in this work, the labor of slaves

6

does not come into consideration, any more than that of horses. This is not said to disparage a slave as a human being, but simply to determine the position of his labor in political science, which has nothing to do with slavery as a moral, social, or political question. Nor does this determination of the position of slave labor contemplate either a positive or relative disadvantage to the interests of slaveholders on that account. The object is to make the same distinction in science, which actually exists, between free and slave labor.

§ 2. *Whether Slave and Free Labor are hostile to each other under a common System of Political Economy for the United States.*

It has been supposed by some, that they are hostile to each other, and that they come in conflict on the question of a protective policy. This supposition assumes, that, as it is the policy of the European states to force labor to its task without reward, that is, by allowing it barely enough for subsistence, so a like policy is necessary to a system of involuntary servitude, wherever it exists, the two states of society being the same in substance, though different in form, and labor in both occupying a similar position. The fact, however, that European states, for the most part, have always maintained a protective policy, in relation to each other, and to all foreign nations, is against this assumption. It can not, therefore, be alleged, that the slaveholding interest of the United States is actuated in its opposition to the protective policy, so far as it is manifested, by such a principle. It may further be observed, that a protective system for the United States is as much a question between slaveholders themselves as between slaveholders and non-slaveholders; and it appears, that the advocacy of a protective policy is gaining ground faster, perhaps, in the slave than in the free states. None will deny that protection is of vital importance to sugar-growers, that is, to the state of Louisiana; nor are the people of that state insensible of it. A convention of one hundred and four cotton-planters in Mississippi, in 1845, passed a series of resolutions in favor of the protective policy, of which the following are extracts:—" That they are in favor of the tariff of 1842, because it affords, as they believe, adequate protection to all kinds of domestic labor, and renders it independent, not only in name, but in fact; because it will induce, at the north, large investments of capital, and the employment of a large number of laborers, in the manufacture of cotton goods; that it will extend the consumption of manufactured articles, and thereby increase the demand for the raw material; that it will give the growers of cotton two markets instead of one, and one of these a home market; because it protects indirectly the growers of small grain, and gives them a home market; because it protects indirectly the hemp-growers, and keeps the large amount of capital now invested in that business from being employed in the culture of cotton; because it protects indirectly the breeders of hogs, horses, and mules, and gives them a home market; because it protects the producer of sugar, gives him a home market, and prevents the vast amount of capital and labor invested in the culture of cane from being directed to the already redundant production of cotton; because all experience proves that its ultimate tendency is to reduce the price of manufactured goods, and thereby benefit consumers of all classes; because no one great interest of the country can be adequately protected, without in some degree extending protection to all other interests, and that none derive more essential benefit from the general prosperity of other pursuits than the cotton-grower; because the interests of the manufacturers of cotton goods at the north are identified with the interest of the grower of cotton at the south, and that as strength is added to these two great interests, the one at the north and the other at the south, so will strength be added to the bands which bind this glorious Union together."

Georgia is becoming a manufacturing state, and feels the need of protection. North Carolina decidedly, and Virginia probably, is in favor of the protective policy; to which may be added Maryland and Kentucky as strongly in favor of it, and Tennessee is reckoned among the number. Considering the position which the slave states generally occupied on this question, fifteen years ago, there appears to have been a much greater proportionate increase of favor for the protective policy at the south than at the north. The opinion, therefore, can hardly be sustained, that the opposition at the south to a protective policy, arises from the existence of slavery, or from a belief that the interests of free and slave labor conflict with each other.

There may have been, and probably is, to a considerable extent, an impression, instinctive or other, both at the north and south, that these two interests are hostile to each other. But in a system of political economy for the United States, in relation to foreign nations, it would be difficult, if not impossible, to find any ground for it. In this respect, both interests are in the same boat, and the same foreign commercial policy that is good or bad for one, is good or bad for the other.

It must, however, be confessed, that a recent fact, entirely new, may possibly excite a deep interest in the state of Pennsylvania, viz., that under the tariff of 1846, slave labor in Virginia, at a cost of $120 per annum, seems likely to undermine free labor in the former state, which costs $300 per annum, in the production of iron; inasmuch as it is alleged, that, at the cost of slave labor, the making of iron in Virginia can go on and prosper, under the tariff of 1846, while in Pennsylvania, at the cost of free labor, it must stop. As slave labor at the south has been chiefly employed in the production of the staples of cotton, rice, and sugar, not grown at the north, there has been but little, if any occasion heretofore, for a collision between free and slave labor; and it is not easy to see how such a collision is possible, so far as these slave-grown staples are concerned.

It is not, indeed, probable, from past experience, that free and slave labor will ever clash in agricultural pursuits; at least, free labor, in this field, is not likely to be jealous of slave labor, as its skill and efficiency more than counterbalance the less cost of its antagonist. They have worked together under the same system, for the same markets, during the whole history of the country, in the production of wheat, Indian corn, tobacco, and other agricultural staples, without jealousy or complaint. In the production of iron and coal, possibly in manufacturing, a collision may arise, under a low, anti-protective system of duties.

CHAPTER III.

POLITICAL POSITION OF LABOR IN THE UNITED STATES AS COMPARED WITH THAT OF LABOR IN EUROPE AND OTHER COUNTRIES.

§ 1. *Labor considered as an Independent Agent.*

It is supposed, and will doubtless be conceded, that the design of the government and institutions of the United States, was to establish individual, as well as national, independence. The latter is of little, may be of no value, without the former. The most absolute despotisms on earth enjoy national independence. It was individual, private, and personal rights which the fathers of the American revolution fought and shed their blood for; and for none more especially, more distinctly, or more emphatically, than that the people should not be taxed without representation. In this claim was involved the personal right of every man to the enjoyment and disposal of the avails of his own industry and labor, as also his protest against any portion of them being taken for the uses of the commonwealth, without his consent in a representative capacity. By the establishment of this principle, at great hazard, and at the cost of much blood and treasure, personal or individual as well as national independence was acquired. This was a substantial independence, and from that time to this, the laboring classes of the United States have occupied a strong *political position.* Labor, for the first time, in the history of modern political society, has become an INDEPENDENT AGENT.

§ 2. *Labor considered as the Agent of Power.*

The last two words of the preceding section, in connexion with the heading of this, are designed to represent the difference between the *political* position of labor in the United States and that of labor in Europe and other foreign countries—the former as an *independent agent* and the latter as the *agent of power.* It should be observed that labor is never *independent,* when it has no *alternative;* that is, when it is not strong enough in its own position to accept or reject the wages offered to it in a given case, if unsatisfactory, and when, in such a case, it can not turn away, and live and prosper. When it can do this, it not only has a voice in its wages, but the parties in contract, the employer and the employed, stand on a footing of equality. This principle is equally applicable to the producer of commodities of any description, as proprietor of a farm, workshop, or any other producing establishment, over which he presides, and where, perhaps, he labors with his own hands, as to him who works for hire. The time has never yet been in the history of the United States as an independent nation, when labor was not in this sense an *independent agent*—when it could not reject an unsatisfactory offer, and yet live. It is not pretended that labor has been able to dictate its own terms. That would be equally improper and unjust, as for the employer to do it. But it has always had an *alternative.* As a last resort the American laborer can at any time go to the back woods. His independence is never necessarily sacrificed.

This wide, back-woods field for American labor, is a security for its independence for ages to come, if not for ever, which no European economist could ever appreciate. It was for want of this light, that Malthus stumbled, and all his followers stumbled after him, not excepting M'Culloch, who was doubtless influenced by the theory of Malthus. They have never been able to see how labor could be independent, and have planned their system on the assumption that it must for ever remain the *agent of power,* and be satisfied with a bare subsistence.

It is this independence, in connexion with the means of supporting it, that has sustained the wages of American labor, and kept them so far above the rates of wages in Europe and other foreign countries.

In the light of this contrast, the condition of European and other foreign labor is one of absolute bondage. In the first place, it is for the most part deprived of all political influence. This is the primary cause of its misfortunes. In the next place, and also for the most part, it has no voice in its wages. There is no *alternative* left to it. It must work for what is offered, and work hard, or perish in want; and the wages doled out are measured by so nice an estimate for bare subsistence, as to be often insufficient for that. In all those countries, labor is the *agent of power.* Power dictates its wages, controls it, enslaves it.

§ 3. *The Cause of the Difference between the Wages of American and the Wages of Foreign Labor, and between the Value of American and that of Foreign Capital.*

It is a *political* cause, clearly revealed, in the foregoing statements. The high position of American labor, is the award of freedom; the wages of American labor, are freedom wages; they are true and just; and when they fall, it will only be because freedom has fallen. The high value of American capital, is a freedom value; and when that shall be brought down to a common level with capital in Europe and elsewhere, freedom will be buried in the overthrow. High wages, and a high value of every species of property, as compared with those of Europe, are identical with freedom. The spirit of man falls with his wages—with the reward of his industry, toil, and care. Crush the latter, and he is crushed. Possibly he may rise from the impulse of despair, and make a new effort. He may succeed; but the chances are against him. Who can break the yoke on the neck, and the chains on the hands of the labor of Europe, and of other portions of the world? Can the oppressed break them?—No. Will the oppressors do it?—No.

§ 4. *The Power and Aims of Governments which oppress Labor.*

Their power is immense, arising from this source, at home and abroad, in moral and physical means. Suppose that two thirds of the fair reward of the labor of Europe is extorted and appropriated by its kings, princes, courts, nobility, gentry, and manufacturing and commercial millionaires. Two thirds of a fair value, is, in fact, about the average proportion of deprivation of right, which is perpetrated on the labor of that part of the world by the classes above named. It will be seen, that such a fraction of the rightful reward of the labor of Europe, or twice as much as it actually realizes, is an immense power. It is a great power in any single state, nation, kingdom, or empire. No small portion of this goes into the public exchequer, to be disbursed for the augmentation and exertion of power. It is all appropriated directly or indirectly for these objects. The adjuncts and props of power are an essential part of it. The nobility that surrounds a throne, is one of its chief supports. All wealthy proprietors of land or other capital, rich manufacturers, rich merchants, and gentry, have their security in the stability and strength of the government, and can afford to contribute largely from their large incomes derived from oppressed labor, for the support of the government which protects them. A crown is usually wealthy in itself, and costly to the people; a throne is costly; a nobility is wealthy, and its income great; wealthy proprietors of land, great manufacturers, rich merchants, rich tradesmen, rich bankers, rich holders of funded capital, rich gentlemen, and a variety of classes coming under the category of rich—all occupy a position in a state of society where labor is oppressed, that is interested in the support of power, and in the depression and hard fate of the laboring classes. The power that keeps them down is sustained by robbing them of the reward of their toil. They have neither the spirit to assert, nor the means of vindicating, their rights.

But the power thus derived, is not only efficacious at home, to sustain itself, but it is influential abroad, to diffuse itself. It is morally influential, by its political connexions, in extending and fortifying the empire of its principles; and physically so, if needs be, in propagating them by the force of its arms. It can afford sacrifices, in expectation of a valuable return, which, as is seen by the party concerned in such cases, will in the end yield ample indemnification.

CHAPTER IV.

FARTHER CONSIDERATION OF THE POLITICAL POSITION OF AMERICAN LABOR.

§ 1. *All other Interests of Civilization, having a Commercial Value, are indebted to Labor for that Value.*

A THING of commercial value can only be exchanged for money, or for a quid pro quo that is prized by money. There are privileges, rights, and affections, in the social state, which can not be thus prized—which are indeed priceless. These, too, are the fruits of care and pains, public and private, except such as are the spontaneous product of nature, which are also susceptible of improvement by culture. But they are too sacred to be classed among things of commercial value. Though they may have cost money, they can not be exchanged for it.

But, it will be found, that all things of a proper commercial value, are usually the products of labor. Accident, or good luck, may put a person in possession of a valuable exchangeable commodity, that cost little or no trouble. But such exceptions do not impair the general rule. Labor, therefore, in civilized society, occupies an elevated, important, commanding position—a position that supplies the wants of man, and gratifies his desires. It may, therefore, justly be denominated the great interest of civilization. But—

§ 2. *Labor is especially the great Interest of the American People.*

This republican empire was founded on labor, and was intended to be sustained by it. The fathers of the country were working men. The mothers and their daughters worked. They claimed the right of supplying their own wants, by their own arts, industry, and toil. This right was denied by the mother-country. They asserted it by force, and acquired it by victory. The policy of their oppressors was to keep the wages of American labor down to the European level, by prohibiting the manufacturing arts and profitable commerce, and by confining the people of the colonies to as few vocations as possible, chiefly agricultural, thus making and holding them *dependent*. The great object of the American revolution was *to vindicate the rights of labor*, which, with the American fathers, comprehended all other valuable rights.

§ 3. *The Rights of Labor, therefore, are Political Rights.*

And they are political in relation to a foreign state of political society to which they are opposed. This is the great practical point of this subject, which claims special attention and the gravest consideration.

That state of political society, to which the rights of American labor, as acquired in the establishment of American independence, are opposed, and which is for ever hostile to these rights, is that already referred to in European nations—it may be found elsewhere—which always has kept, and still keeps down the wages of labor to a bare subsistence, the average of which is not more than *one third* of its fair reward. This is the state of society on which European systems of political economy are founded, which gave birth to them, which they are designed to perpetuate, not even meditating any change in favor of labor; and labor, in those systems, is a principal and fundamental element. The consequence is, a political result, originally the cause—a seeming paradox, that a thing should be father to itself—a result, planned by those who framed and who maintain the system, viz., that the working classes live and die, as they were born, poor and dependent. It is impossible it should be otherwise, in such a state of things. The laboring classes have no chances to improve their condition, and to rise; it is not intended they should. They have no pride, no courage, no ambition, no hope. These sentiments are extinguished by the severity of their doom. They were born, they live and die, slaves to political tyranny.

In the meantime, American political society, *founded on the rights of labor*, has grown up —has established itself—has secured to labor a fair reward—and the practical operation of it has demonstrated to the world that any man, though born poor, may die rich; and that his personal qualities, and not his birthright, give him consideration in society.

In the meantime, also, that old political system, which depresses labor, and holds it in bondage, has maintained and fortified its position; though it has changed its modes of warfare against the rights of labor, it has not given up the contest; what it could neither arrest, nor subdue, by force of arms, it has undertaken to conquer by policy; and the great political contest of the age is, whether THE RIGHTS OF LABOR, as established on American soil, and nourished by American blood, shall be maintained, and extend their empire; or whether they shall be crushed by political devices—no man rising to say he will die for them—and the world fall back to where it was two centuries ago?

§ 4. *In what this Strife consists.*

It consists in the array of the money and labor of Europe, as producing powers—of the money and labor of all those countries with which we have commercial intercourse—the average joint value or cost of which is ONE, *against* the money and labor of the United States, as opposing producing powers, the average joint value or cost of which is TWO. It needs no prophet to predict the result. In a contest of arms, one may chance to beat two—a small force may rout a much larger one. But in the peaceful pursuits of trade, a merchant can never stand before a rival in the same market, who can afford to sell cheaper—and a good deal cheaper. The case settles itself, and the result is an absolute certainty.

The wages of labor in Europe, and in other countries foreign to the United States, have been kept down by oppression—by force—and money, and all capital, derived from it, cost in proportion to what is paid for labor. The wages of labor in the United States, as the result of political freedom, have risen to *three for one* of labor in Europe; and money, and all other capital here, cost in proportion. Now, it is proposed to put the products of the money and labor of the United States in open competition with the products of the money and labor of Europe. Does not every one see what will be the result, and that American labor must come down to the same price, before it can compete with the labor of Europe? In other words, that European policy and oppression shall govern the prices of American labor?— Such is the question, and such, on a free-trade platform, must be the result, unless it can be shown, that men will give *two* for that which they can buy for *one*, or for *one and a half*, or for *one and three fourths*, or for *one and nine tenths*. No matter what the difference is, they who can sell lowest, will have the market.

It must be seen, that this is an infallible commercial principle, destined, everywhere and in all cases, to control results, on the basis of free trade. It does not follow, however, that foreigners will sell us cheaper, as a matter of course. They will do it only to gain and hold the market; and it will yet appear, that a free-trade system is the most costly to the people of the United States, even in the very things proposed to be obtained cheaper by it; much more in the general result.

§ 5. *But it is said, " Let those stand who can, and those fall who must, by Free Trade."*

If that which is technically called "*free trade*," were *fair* trade, as is generally supposed by those who take the position defined above, there would be some reason in it. But " free trade," as now used, means, let foreigners come into this country and trade, and bring what they please to sell, without being taxed, and without paying anything for the privilege. This manifestly would be unjust to the whole community, who are taxed for the support of a government, which secures such immunities to foreigners. It would be an additional and double injustice to those American citizens, who might wish, and who are entitled, in preference to foreigners, to have this trade, because they are taxed for it, while deprived of it. It would also be a double injustice to those citizens who might wish to *make* and sell the same things. It would be another injustice to the whole community for depriving it of the profits of the business of making and vending these things, and for the draft it would make on the money of the country to foreign parts. Indeed, the injustice can not be estimated, in all its relations and bearings. The only thing that can be said as an offset to these numerous wrongs, to numerous parties, and to the whole community, is, that it is a benefit to the consumers, and that he who wants a thing, has a right to get it where he pleases, and as cheap as he can. It will be shown, by-and-by, that the consumers, in such cases, are not benefited, either by cheapness, or in any other way. That they have a right to do wanton wrong to so many parties, or to any party, is at least questionable.

When it shall be seen what is the scope, and what would be the consequences of the proposal, " Let those stand who can, and let those fall who must, by free trade," its inconsiderate and reckless character will be appreciated. It will be found, that it dooms Liberty to her grave, and consigns the country to the hands of strangers.

CHAPTER V.

THE FACTS WHICH CONSTITUTE THE NECESSITY OF A PROTECTIVE POLICY IN THE UNITED STATES.

§ 1. *The Main Proposition an Axiom.*

It is remarkable, considering how much and how long the protective policy has been debated in the United States, that the fundamental proposition which comprehends the whole, should never have been stated as an *axiom* in political economy, as it undoubtedly belongs to that category of propositions; and much more remarkable, that it should never have been stated at all in a definite and tangible form. It is perfectly understood by all who have given attention to the subject; and the argument, based upon it, has been eloquently made in various forms. It is founded on a principle that governs the whole commercial world—competition in trade—and it is determined by arithmetical quantities, and can not, therefore, but be infallible and imperative. To be seen and felt to be true, it needs only to be stated. It is as follows : *Protection must have respect to the difference in the joint cost, or price, or value, of money and labor in the United States and in the countries with which we trade.*

It will be found upon examination, that this rule can not be set aside, or got over; that the principle of it controls the whole subject; and that it is the only safe rule in graduating protection. It is not pretended that there are no exceptions to it; or that protection in all cases, or in any case, must be precisely measured by it; or that the interests of the country may not be well taken care of, with an average of protection considerably below this standard. The political and commercial position of the people of the United States, their moral energy, their enterprise ; a variety of facts inherent in the people and in the country, and a variety of facts relative to other nations, give to the people of this country advantages under which they can afford to dispense with some of their just claims in the application of this rule. Some interests are already so strong in their position, that they require little, some no protection, while others require a protection higher, some much higher, than the rule. It is the undoubted right of the people of the United States to have a system of protection, the average of which may be fully equal to this rule; and it is absolutely necessary, for the security of their interests and the preservation of their rights, that the protective policy of the country should *approximate* toward this standard, and be based on this principle. No country would have a right to complain, if it should be brought and held entirely up to it.

§ 2. *The Terms of the Rule.*

Authentic statistics, many years published, and not disputed, show that the average cost of labor in Europe, as compared with that in the United States, is about as 33 of the former to 100 of the latter, or as ONE to THREE. As labor is the producer of all wealth, it will be obvious, that the cost of capital, in these two quarters of the world, money or other, must be in a proportion corresponding with the difference in the cost of labor. It appears, however, that the average interest obtained for money in Europe—which determines its value—is somewhat higher, as compared with the average of interest for money in the United States, than the relative cost of European labor as compared with American. Money is more valuable than other capital of equal cost—the cost being measured by labor —because it is always more ready and effective for use. This, doubtless, is the reason why the average interest of money in Europe is higher, compared with interest in the United States, than the average cost of labor in the same comparison. It is proposed, therefore, to allow, that the value of money in Europe, as compared with its value in the United States, is as 67 for the former to 100 for the latter, or as 2 to 3. This makes the European value somewhat more than it actually is. It will be seen, therefore, that the joint value, or cost, or price of money and labor in Europe, as compared with that of these two things in the United States, is as 100 to 200, or 1 to 2; or the difference is 100 per cent., *at least.*

§ 3. *Influential Position of these different Values.*

These are great, stupendous facts, as elements of political economy, and there is no escape from their influence, their potency, their absolute control, as to the matters and result in the question under consideration. Here are TWO TO ONE in the producing power of Europe at the same cost—it is more than that in fact—against the producing power of the United States! It is "a FIXED FACT." Does not every one see the inevitable fall, the unavoidable ruin, the complete overthrow, of the producing power of the United States, in an open and unrestricted market with the producing power of Europe, when the difference in the cost of the two things which constitute that power, is at least 100 per cent. in favor of that of Europe, and against that of the United States? No matter, if the difference were only 50, or 25, or 10, or even 5 per cent.; no matter, indeed, if it were only a half cent per cent., or one fifth of that, a single mill, the principle and result would still be the same, other things being equal. There must be a protection somewhere, in some shape—a real, effective protection—equal to the difference, whatever it may be, 100 per cent. or 5 per cent., or one mill per cent.; or else the party and the interests against which the difference stands, will fall before the other. Such is the power, and such the result of competition in trade, and there is no escape from it. It is the same between nations, as between merchants, side by side, in the same city; the party that can undersell, however small the fractional difference, will beat the other. The fate of the cotton manufactories of Great Britain, in 1845, depended on the removal of half a penny a pound duty on raw cotton. It was in fact only five sixteenths of a penny. They may at any time depend on a far less trifle than that. What is called protection, or is intended for it, must be fully adequate, or it is no protection at all.

It is a remarkable fact, that this removal of duty on raw cotton in England, done as an indispensable measure of protection, was vaunted forth in this country, and over the world, as an approximation toward free trade, in the same manner as is the abolition of the British corn laws, which is also a measure of protection—not indeed to that specific interest, but to the manufacturing interest—to the empire. It was a choice of evils.

§ 4. *An Objection Answered.*

If it should be said, that the great variety of duties imposed for protection on different articles, and no duties being required for some, are inconsistent with the exact terms of this rule, if duties are imposed on its claims, it may be answered, first, that the facts which constitute the rule, are nevertheless true; next, that such various measures of protection, required for different articles, would be expected for the reasons stated in the first section of this chapter; and thirdly, that the protection required by this rule, is asserted as necessary, only in proportion to the accidental influences which affect the position of each article. It must be seen, that the rule is based on undeniable facts, and that it results from them on the well-known commercial principle of competition in trade.

But, fourthly, the answer to this cavil—it is nothing more—is found in the fact, that this

100 per cent. power against the United States, is not all employed for competition, as it is unnecessary, and would be a waste. It would subvert the European policy of keeping down wages, which is, that the spoils may be realized by the powerful at home. This difference of 100 per cent. is chiefly appropriated by those who create it, and they employ for competition only such a portion of it as may be necessary to secure the market. That fraction, in application to a given article, may be one hundredth, or one fiftieth, or one twentieth, or one tenth, or one fifth, or any other fraction, of the margin left for competition. Consequently, the protection of any given article, to be effective, must always exceed the power that is employed against it for competition, be it a larger or smaller fraction of the difference in the cost of money and labor in the two opposite fields. Ordinarily, the power thus employed is but a small fraction of the difference, because that is sufficient. It must be seen, however, that this fractional power is always arbitrary, and may be extended to any limit within the absolute difference—not, however, without regard to the habits of society, and the wants of power in that quarter. There is no danger that Europe will employ the whole of this power against the United States; for then the power would be all wasted, without benefit to those who have usurped it. Europe, however, may use a large part of this power, or even the whole of it, on specific articles, for a season, to gain a subsequent advantage. It is, therefore, the duty of the American statesman always to keep his eye, first on the actual difference in the cost of money and labor in the United States and foreign countries; and next on those points where that power is brought to bear against the interests of the American people, and on the amount of power thus employed. This knowledge is indispensable to ascertain *where, and to what amount*, protection is required. Otherwise, American labor is left to chance, and may thank its own stars, if it is not prostrated by this overwhelming influence, which always exists, and which always occupies a menacing position.

CHAPTER VI.

WHAT WOULD BE THE EFFECTS OF FREE TRADE ON THE PEOPLE AND GOVERNMENT OF THE UNITED STATES.

§ 1. *The Inequality of Free Trade.*

It has been supposed, that if all nations, having commercial intercourse with each other, would come to the practice of free trade, it would at least be fair, probably best. This conclusion is arrived at, without considering, first, that all other things in the nations entering into this compact, should be equal, to make the arrangement just. Secondly, that, in fact, all other things are not equal, but some very unequal. Thirdly, that the very object of the tariffs of different nations is to equalize existing inequalities, which makes them not only necessary but just.

Every nation, of course, must be the best and the sole judge of what regulations in its commercial intercourse with other nations, are necessary for the protection of its own interests, in the same manner as every individual person is as to the terms on which he will have intercourse or trade with his neighbors. There is not probably a private person living—none certainly in a prosperous condition—who has not a tariff of duties to protect his own interests. This he finds to be necessary in consideration of the fact, that his position, his circumstances, and his interests, are very different from those of his neighbors. If, for example, a land owner chooses to leave his fields unenclosed, rather than be at the expense of fences, because he has other interests to attend to, and turns out his cattle to graze upon them, can he rightfully claim of his neighbors, who live by their crops, to pull down their fences, that his cattle may go and feed there?

As no two persons can be found, whose interests are exactly the same, and who do not find it necessary, each for himself, to take care of his own interests; so neither can any two nations be found, whose interests are the same, and which do not find it necessary, each for itself, to watch over and protect its own interests. The regulations necessary for this end, whether for private persons or for nations, are in either case *tariff or protective duties.* It is absurd to suppose that such parties can do without them.

§ 2. *Difference in the Cost of Wages in Europe and the United States, as it affects this Question.*

The average cost of labor in Great Britain and in Europe, as compared with the average in the United States, is as 33 to 100, or as one to three. Would it be fair to open a competition on the basis of free trade, between the labor of Great Britain and Europe, at 33, and that of the United States, at 100, and thus reduce the latter to 33? That such would be the consequence, is as certain as that water, when unobstructed, will find a level. The water in one pond, which is higher than the water in another, will not maintain its level, when the dam between the two is broken away, but it will come down to that of the other, if both have one source and one outlet.

§ 3. *The Unfairness of forcing American Labor down to a Level with European.*

This will appear, first, from the fact, that the wages of labor in the United States, are a political right, purchased at great cost of blood and treasure : secondly, because, depriving the American laborer of this right, is doing him the greatest possible injustice ; and thirdly, because it is reducing him to the same abject condition with the European laborer, who is an *agent of power*, and not an *independent agent.*

The great political right of a fair and full reward of labor, is the primary, the chief, and the only distinction, between the government and institutions of the United States and those of European nations, which can be of any value after this shall have been destroyed. With free trade, that right must necessarily perish. It could not for a moment be maintained on that basis. The result is both a moral and mathematical certainty : mathematical, because it is a question of figures ; and moral, because a competitor in trade, who has the largest margin to reduce prices, will break down his opponent, and then have his own price. The United States are the last nation that could afford to go on a platform of free trade, and would be the first to suffer by it ; because, in that case, its industry, labor, and enterprise, would be worth no more than the same things in Europe and elsewhere. Heretofore, except when the protective policy has been impaired, labor and capital of every description, in this country, have had a freedom price—a freedom value—that is to say, a fair value. But it is impossible in the nature of things to keep them up, when unprotected from the effect of low wages and low priced capital, in countries where labor is an agent of power and not an independent agent.

§ 4. *Political Consequences of Free Trade.*

Not only will there be a commercial leveling in lowering the value of wages and property in the United States, to that of foreign countries, by free trade, but the political, moral, social, and physical condition of the people, and their political rights, will also come down to the same level. The change will all be on one side, and all for the worse—none for the better. Free trade would not bring up the rest of the world, in ameliorating the condition of the laboring classes, raising their wages to a fair value, and giving them freedom ; but it would carry down the people of the United States to their level, in all particulars, political, social, moral, and physical. That is to say, the people of the United States would lose all they have gained in the achievement of their independence, and in their subsequent political career. No people can be free and happy who can not realize fair pay for their labor, and have control of the proceeds. Such pay, and such control of their own affairs, is the essence of freedom.

§ 5. *The Moral Effect of Low Wages.*

It is to demoralize, to debase, to degrade man, and render him unfit to aspire to freedom, and unfit to enjoy it. Working ever for a bare subsistence, and hardly that, without hope of a better condition, leaves no place for pride, self-respect, and ambition. That debasement of mind, which is everywhere observable among the laboring classes of Europe, whose task is hard, and whose prospect of an improvement in their condition is hopeless, is the necessary effect and uniform concomitant of such a doom. Reduce those dependent on labor in the United States—which comprehends a majority of the people—to such low wages, by the establishment of free trade, which would be the inevitable result, and the moral effect would be the same. The character of the people would be entirely changed. The government would be changed—all would be changed. Labor would then be the *agent of power*, and not an *independent agent.*

CHAPTER VII.

ABOLITION OF THE BRITISH CORN LAWS.

§ 1. *The Abolition of the Corn Laws a great and comprehensive Measure of National Policy for purposes of Protection.*

THE corn laws were abolished ostentatiously, at one swoop, to make an impression on the world—especially on the people of the United States—as if the British government were approximating to the principles of free trade—whereas, they have never yet made an abatement of imposts, except on the principle of protection, or to obtain an equivalent, or more than an equivalent, in some other way. They were forced, in 1845, to remove the duty of half a penny a pound on raw cotton—for what ?—not for free trade, as was pretended, but to protect their own manufacturers against those of the United States and of the continent. It was absolutely necessary, as a measure of national policy, to make food as cheap in England, as in other manufacturing nations. It was a *national* necessity ; and therefore it was done.

Previously, however, by some ten years, to the abolition of the duty on raw cotton, the manufacturers in the north of England, disturbed and menaced by the trades-unions and the system of strikes for higher wages, removed, by a negotiation with the poor law commissioners, 10,000 paupers from the southern counties, into their mills, and thus defeated the unionists and the strikers, and kept down wages.

It now appears, that the primary and chief object of the league for the abolition of the corn laws, was for the benefit of the manufacturing system of Great Britain, and that the former interest was sacrificed—if sacrificed—to save a greater one—one more vital to the British empire—and to keep down wages. The same men, manufacturers (see first annual report of poor law commissioners), who were engaged in 1834 in dragging paupers, against their will, from the south of England, to immure them in the manufactories of the north, professedly, as appears from their letters to the commissioners, to counteract the trades-unions and keep down the strikes—in other words, to keep down wages—were afterward enrolled among the most influential leaders of the league for the abolition of the corn laws; and Sir Robert Peel, naturally sympathizing with that system, which had been to him " the goose that laid the golden egg," (his immense fortune was made in manufacturing), and not less as a great statesman, put the finishing stroke to the third great measure for the conservation and protection of the British manufacturing system. The first step was forcing the paupers of England, in 1834, into the manufactories; the next was the removal of duties on raw cotton, in 1845; and the third was the abolition of the corn laws in 1846 :—all done on the principle of protection, and to maintain the system of low wages, without which British manufactures, the soul and bulwark of the empire, must have fallen. It is now confidently expected and predicted, that, as soon as decency will permit, the wages of operatives in British manufactories will be reduced, by a measure equal to the cheapening of their bread, that the benefit of the abolition of the corn laws may accrue, not to the laborers, but to their employers; in other words, to the government; for the government support these great interests, that they may support the government. The amount of wheat used for paste in the cotton factories, is said to be equal to the supply of all the mouths of the operatives. Eight hundred thousand bushels are used annually for paste by members of the anti-corn law league, from the tax on which they are already relieved.

This great measure, therefore, which has been bruited far and wide, to the great astonishment of mankind, as a free trade measure—or the movement of a great nation in a philanthropic career, to give the poor cheaper bread—turns out to be the movement of British manufacturers, to bar the necessity of raising the wages of their operatives, and in the end to cheapen them;—and of the British government to sustain and protect the British manufacturing system, as the great bulwark of the empire ! Sir Robert Peel saw, that the British corn laws, or the manufacturing system, must fall, and he wisely sealed the doom of the former, to save the latter.

It will be seen, then, what this flourish of British free trade amounts to, viz., that at bottom, in principle, and in its ultimate practical design, it is directly the opposite of free trade, and that it is one of the most comprehensive and most effective measures of protection ever devised by a statesman. It was also a bold stroke of public policy, both in its domestic and foreign aspects : in its domestic, because it *seemed* to sacrifice one great interest, to save, strengthen, and fortify, another of far greater importance. In its foreign aspects, because it could be and *was* ostentatiously held up and proclaimed to the world as a great example of free trade, challenging other nations to follow. The United States were the first to swallow the bait, and be caught ! They thought at least, that the abolition of the British corn laws would open a market for American bread-stuffs. It will be seen, by-and-by, what is likely to be realized from this expectation.

§ 2. *A curious and instructive Item of Evidence on this Point.*

It is shown in Fisher's National Magazine (Sept., 1846), that, before the late changes in the British tariff, and as a cause, it was discovered by the labors of a select committee of the house of commons, on import duties, appointed in 1840, that " 94½ per cent. (or 21,700,630l.) of the total revenue from customs (22,962,610l.) was obtained from 17 articles;" that corn, or breadstuffs, was one of them; that the duty raised on that was less than one twentieth (1,098,779l.) of the revenue from customs; and consequently, if lost, it might easily be made up in other ways; or at most, it was no great loss. This much-vaunted act, therefore, viewed in the light of a generous measure of the government, dwindles into insignificance when scrutinized.

§ 3. *Farther Evidence on the same Point.*

To show farther, that the late changes in the British tariff were made for protection, and not on the principle of free trade, it is also proved, in the National Magazine, as above, by a minute display of statistical evidence, derived from authentic British records, first, that the changes were chiefly made to abate duties on raw materials, and articles partially manufactured, such as are used by British manufacturers, and in other ways to help them; secondly, that the manufacturers were actually benefited by this legislation—not reckoning the great relief derived from the abolition of the corn laws—in the annual value of about six millions of dollars; and thirdly, that the revenue, on the unchanged articles, was at the same time augmented in the excess of $2,436,000, over what was lost by the abatement of duties—being, by so much, as Mr. Williams, the author of this article, facetiously calls it, "an advance *backward* from free trade." The other articles (besides the 17), on which the small fraction of 5½ per cent. of the revenue from customs was raised, amounted to *eleven hundred*. It was on a part of these, that the abatements of duty were made—and they were all made for *protection*. There is no one of the recent or latest alterations in the British tariff, which, when examined, has even the aspect of free trade in it, except it be the reduction of duties on imported manufactured articles; and Mr. Williams, in the above named article, informs us, that the deputations of manufacturers who attended the board of trade in 1839 and 1840, expressed their willingness to dispense with all protection, except those engaged in manufacturing glass and silk. Their skill and perfection had placed them beyond the danger of competition. The duties from all imports of manufactured articles in 1839 were only 443,355*l.*, of which duties on silks made more than one half. The duties on manufactures, after reduction, only rose about 8 per cent., showing a small increase of imports. The British government have never abated duties, to operate against manufacturers, without their consent, but have uniformly protected them. Mr. M'Gregor, an eminent British authority, says: "We might, in every manufacture we now possess, meet foreign countries in every market in the world, and in most instances undersell them." The only thing in which they are still beaten, is silk, which yet enjoys 15 per cent. protection.

There is one potent reason which prevailed with the British government, for the abolition of the corn laws, deserving of notice, viz., to equalize at home the cost of breadstuffs with the cost on the continent. It was found, that British manufacturers were emigrating to the continent, setting up, and rivalling those at home, with great success, by the greater cheapness of food; and that there was no way of encountering this alarming competition, except by the abolition of the corn laws. This done, and the evil got over, Great Britain, apparently, could bid defiance to the world.

There is another small item of history, casting light on this point, viz., that the British government, jealous of manufactures on the continent, for a long time rigidly prohibited the export of machinery to that quarter, till they found, that, in spite of these laws and penalties, the manufacturers of the continent were obtaining their machinery from the United States. Then the British government made a virtue of necessity, repealed their laws against the export of machinery, and called it free trade! It was because they could not prevent this supply of machinery on the continent, that they were forced to repeal the corn laws, that food might be as cheap in England as with their competitors; and they call *this* free trade!

CHAPTER VIII.

AXIOMS.

IT is proposed, in this chapter, to state and illustrate some propositions, which may claim to be admitted as AXIOMS.

§ 1. *Government was not intended to prove how much a People can endure.*

Of course, this will be admitted as an *axiom*, or self-evident truth—a proposition that needs no proof. And yet, in a very considerable portion of the history of this country, it would seem, from the action of government, that this axiom should be reversed, and that the government had supposed itself commissioned to prove how much the people can endure. The mother-country first proved it. She would not let the people of the colonies supply their own wants, and they rebelled. The consequences were the revolution and independence. The articles of confederation answered precisely the same purpose : they proved how much the people could endure under a system of *perfect free trade*. Then came the federal constitution, enacted for the purpose of establishing a protective policy. For most of the next twenty years, the wars and misfortunes of Europe opened a field for American enterprise in unwonted channels, till the war of 1812 itself operated as a system of protection to American labor. After the peace, the tariff of 1816 was worth something, though defective, and of a short term. Then came free trade, in the shape of low duties, till 1824, which the people could endure no longer, and the tariff of that year was established to bless the land. The protective policy continued, till the bad administration of the compromise tariff of 1833— which act was devised to vindicate the principle of protection for future use, when the storms of that day should have passed over—brought on another term of free trade, and the people, suffering till they could suffer no longer, rose in 1840, and vindicated their rights. Then came the tariff of 1842. The British crown, the articles of confederation, and the subsequent free-trade periods, have alike proved how much the people can endure.

§ 2. Government was instituted for Protection.

Is not this an *axiom ?* Will anybody deny it ? What use, then, in having a government ? It is scarcely possible to conceive of any other use. All the functions of government, legislative, judicial, executive, and whatever, in all their branches and acts, resolve themselves into this—to protect the persons and rights of the people. What else has a government to do ? For a government to disclaim protection, is monstrous. And it is not only the duty of the government to protect the people in their persons and rights, relative to each other, but in all their rights as a body politic, relative to other bodies politic—that is, relative to other states and nations. No one will dispute this axiom, or the comprehensive construction here put upon it. PROTECTION is the appropriate function of government. It has no other. Any other is a usurpation. This axiom, as will be seen, leads to a *result*, in the great question now in debate.

§ 3. The People have a right to demand Protection.

This will scarcely be rejected as an axiom in a country that boasts of freedom. The people know best what they want, and it is enough if they think they want it. It is not for the government to say, we have a theory, and by that your request, if granted, would lead to a bad result. This is impertinence. The only just ground of refusal would be, that the request, granted, would interfere with the rights of other parties, or with the general good, which is the same thing. And the reason of the refusal should be made good. Else it is the denial of a right. It has been seen, that the protection of labor neither invades, nor impairs, anybody's rights, but benefits all in the commonwealth. Whatever art, therefore, or industrial pursuit, or enterprise, or whatever calling, a person may choose to devote himself to, for a living, or for the hoped-for acquisition of wealth, he has a right to protection in it from the government; and it can not with justice be refused.

§ 4. The Protection of Labor consists in the Protection of that which gives it Employment.

Will this be denied as an axiom ? It would be hard to make the denial good. Everybody sees it is true, and that is enough. Government can not strike at that which employs labor, without striking labor itself; it can not weaken and distress the former, without affecting the latter in the same way. It might well be asked, why it should do either, since both have equal claims to protection ?˜ The life of labor is in employment. The union is vital. That which touches one, touches the other, and violence to one is violence to both. It is *through* labor alone that the capital which employs it can be wounded ; it is over the dead body of labor only that its employer can be killed. Why a government should propose to do either, might seem very strange. It can not be denied, that it would be a violation of axiom No. 2.

§ 5. The Profit of Capital is the Profit of Labor.

This is asserted of the state of things in the United States, where labor is an independent agent, and not of the state of things in Europe and other quarters, where labor is the agent of power. It may be, and is contested, in the same manner as numerous of the plainest axioms are, by unreasonable minds. Nevertheless, everybody knows, that, in the United States, where capital finds encouragement by protection, there labor finds employment and reward.

§ 6. The greater the Profit of Capital, so much greater and more secure the Profit of Labor.

This, too, applies to the state of things in the United States, and is equally true, and for the same reasons true, as axiom No. 5. Politicians, demagogues, have, for the last quarter of a century, or less, set up a hue and cry in the country against the profits of capital, under the name of *monopolies ;* and they who have joined in the chase, were not aware that they were hunting down labor. It was by the dishonest application of a *misnomer* to a class of facts, that this fatal political row was excited. Everybody knows, when told, that a *monopoly* is an exclusive privilege, such, for example, as the New Jersey railroad, or any other corporate body with exclusive rights, which, under the laws enacting it, will not allow of competition. But it is well known that there is not a manufacturing or mechanic art in the country, except in patent-rights, that is an exclusive privilege ; and patents, which have never been subjects of complaint, only apply to the *instruments* of art, and not to art itself. All the arts, manufacturing and other, are open to all. Not one of them is exclusive—not one of them is patented, or chartered. If any specific application of capital, in manufacturing or other arts, is making large profits, at any given time, there are two results from the fact : one, that labor is employed, and well paid ; and the other, that more capital rushes into the business, employs more labor, and reduces the profits of the capital, while it does not reduce those of labor. It extends the field, and augments the benefits of labor, by increasing a demand for it. Wherever there are good profits of capital, labor never wants employment; and good profits of capital always invite larger investments where they are realized, to reduce such profits, and augment the employment and profits of labor, by increased demand. Good profits of capital, vested in the manufacturing and other arts, is an evidence of prosperity, and nothing is benefited more than labor by such a state of things. No matter how large the profits: the more the better. Capital will immediately rush where profits are great, and reduce them. The chief benefit always accrues to labor, in such cases, because it is certain to extend its field, and increase the demand for it. The consumers of the products are also benefited, because it augments supply relative to demand, and cheapens prices.

All this hue and cry, therefore, about *monopoly*, in application to pursuits which are open to all, is the trick of demagogues. Every intelligent honest man knows there is no foundation for it, nor a word of truth in it—knows that the counter-proposition is the only true one, in application to the facts, viz., that it all works for the benefit of labor, and not against it. That it does not work for the benefit of capitalists, and of other interests, is not pretended. The greater benefit of labor is dependent on this common benefit to all the other interests of the country. It is a COMMON-WEALTH, *common prosperity;* and in this great aggregate, there is no interest that derives so great a proportionate benefit in the United States, in prosperous times, as that of labor; and it is the profit of capital that makes prosperous times. The greater its profits, so much greater the prosperity. If capital gets 10 per cent., labor, as before seen, if frugal, realizes 50 per cent. on itself as capital.

The word, " *monopoly,*" has been put in the mouths of people who don't understand its meaning. They think of nothing but " *those rich men,*" and are taught to envy them; ten to one of whom began life poor, and by hard work, virtue, frugality, tact, and enterprise, have become rich as *the reward of their own labor;* and now they are not only able, but willing, to employ labor, and to help others along in the same path, to the same eminence. The wheel of fortune, in such a state of society, is for ever rolling round, and they who-are at the bottom now would soon be at the top, if mischievous persons did not put their hand on the wheel, and stop it. They point the finger to those at the top, and stop it with the cry of " *Monopoly !*"—and then those at the bottom are sure to stay there. The moment free trade comes, the wheel turns round no more. It is impossible. These demagogues are like the dog in the manger, which, not being able to eat hay, will not let the laboring ox have any.

It might be well, if these sagacious observers, who see men getting rich by their frugality and enterprise, and making others rich all around them by creating chances, could see a little farther, and descry the effect abroad of breaking down home manufactures and home labor, and of putting obstacles in their path. These princely fortunes, as they call them, are chiefly made by working men, who began life poor, and worked their way up; and all this wealth is in the country, giving employment to labor, that others, beginning in the same way, may rise in the same way. But stop this progress; arrest these acquisitions at home; and what is the consequence? The same wants, which produced this domestic wealth, must be supplied, so long as the money lasts; and who supplies them?—Who gets the money?—Who, then, makes the princely fortunes? The foreigner. But this rolling in wealth abroad, amassed by the sweat of the American laborer's brow, and by extorting the last penny from his pocket, that neither he, nor any other American, can any more use it as capital—for it has gone abroad—*that* wealth, *those* riches, *that* splendor, thus acquired, away off in England, or somewhere else, are not seen in this quarter. Nevertheless, the fortunes are made, and made at the expense of the American people! Since, then, money must and will be made, in the supply of these wants, is it not better that it should be made at home, be realized at home, and remain at home, as a part of the working capital of the country, that the laboring poor may have a chance to get rich by it? They who think they are breaking down American aristocracy, which, if there be such a thing, is always under control of American legislation, do not imagine, that, by the same act, and with American labor, they are building up foreign aristocracies, supporting foreign princes, and adding fresh glitter to the pomp of kings, and more lasting security to their thrones.

CHAPTER IX.

PROTECTIVE DUTIES NOT TAXES.

§ 1. *What is meant by this.*

It is not meant, that protective duties are never, in any case, taxes; but that, as a system, they are neither taxes on the country, nor on consumers; that, in the comprehensive operation of the system, no party or person is taxed; and that it is a benefit to all, rich and poor, without exception. This will be demonstrated by facts; and more than this, that it rescues the country, and all the parties and persons in it, from a system of foreign taxation.

§ 2. The Effect of Duties which are not Protective.

It is doubtless true, that imposts on articles which can not be produced at home, such as coffee, tea, spices, and numerous other foreign products, are taxes, though not of course to the exact amount of the duty, as is commonly supposed. The duty itself sometimes cheapens them for a transient, and even a protracted period; though ordinarily it is a tax. But whether the tax will be greater or less than the duty, depends on supply relative to demand, at any given time. These results, so various, and always shifting, demonstrate, that no certain reliance can be placed, even in such cases, on the amount of duty as a measure of taxation. The duty, however, may ordinarily be assumed as the average measure.

§ 3. Facts showing that Protective Duties are not Taxes.

Cotton goods which cost 85 cents a yard before the tariff of 1816, have been reduced to 7 cents. Cotton shirtings have fallen, under the system of protection, from 25 cents a yard to 5; sheetings, from 32 to 7; checks, from 32 to 8; striped and plain ginghams, from 26 to 8; printed calicoes, from 20 in 1826, to 9 in 1844;—each of the above being supposed to be of the same quality at the high and reduced prices. The fact, that the British government have been obliged to enact differential duties for their eastern dependencies, first of 5 per cent., then of 8½, next of 10½, and finally of 15, to exclude American cotton goods, is conclusive evidence, that the American manufacturers can and do sell cheaper than the British. This is a great, a stupendous result.

From 1809 to 1814, before cotton was manufactured in the United States, the British duty on the raw material was 25s. 6d. per cwt., or 5½ cents a pound. From 1815 to 1819, it was 8s. 6d. per cwt., or nearly 2 cents a pound. At last it got down to 2 farthings a pound, and that was taken off, as before shown, for protection against American competition. But for American cotton manufactures, the American cotton-grower would have been in the power of the British government at this moment, with a duty against him in England of 5½ cents a pound on cotton, more or less.

There is no doubt, if this domestic and world-wide competition had not been brought into the field by the American protective system, the prices of cotton goods, though reduced, would yet have been kept up much above what they are at present. But this is not the most important question. It is rather, whether England shall be made rich as producer, by monopolizing production, while we grow poor as consumers, not being able to produce for want of protection?

Woollen jeans, which sold in 1840 at 65 cents a yard, were reduced under the tariff of 1842, so as to be sold in 1846, in any quantity—the more the better—and of superior quality, at 35 cents a yard. A correspondent of the Journal of Commerce, understood to be one of the editors, found a Yankee trader, at Cleveland, Ohio, in the summer of 1846, who had settled in Canada, buying satinets and other low-priced woollen goods, who said he could pay the duties, on entering Canada, and make more on them, than to get British goods at Montreal.

The price of window-glass, in 1824, when a duty of $3 per 100 feet was imposed, was $10 50 per 100 feet. In 1828, price $6 50. In 1846, price of 8-by-10, most used, $2 25, under a duty of $2. The cut-glass works at Wheeling, Va., were forced to stop before the tariff of 1842. Under that tariff, they had more orders than could be supplied, and sold for 25 per cent. less than before. The flint glass works of the United States, in 1832, were in number 17; reduced to 5 in 1842; rose to 19 under the tariff of that year; labor in them rose 25 per cent., and the articles produced fell 25 per cent. So generally in the glass business.

In a report of the committee on manufactures (house document 420, 1st session 28th congress), it was proved, that the depression in the prices of 23 different kinds of manufactured iron, under the tariff of 1842, ranged from 10 to 46 per cent.—average reduction 23 per cent.; that, in a list of 22 different and chief materials of shipbuilding and rigging, such as had been imported, the fall of prices, from 1842 to 1844, ranged from 2 to 35 per cent.—average reduction 17½ per cent.; that, in a list of 9 articles of hardware, protected by increased duties in the tariff of 1842, the fall of prices ranged from 13 to 30 per cent.—average reduction 15 per cent.; and that, in a numerous list of other manufactured articles of various kinds, exhibited in the tables of that report, the reduction of prices, under the tariff of 1842, which afforded them the protection of increased duties, had been effected in some such measures as above cited. The evidence presented in that report, of the tendency and effect of protection to reduce prices of manufactured articles, was uniform, decided, and unanswerable. No one has ever yet been able to point to a single manufactured article, in extensive demand, enjoying protection for home production, the price of which has not been reduced; and the higher the duty, the greater the reduction of prices.

"Every production," says a "Southern Planter," in his "Notes on Political Economy"—(a most remarkable book, by-the-by, considering the quarter from which it came—the author being a grower of cotton, and owning slaves)—"Every production," he says, "the result of protection. in the country, has been brought cheaper and better into the market, than before such protection."—"Practical men," said Mr. Clay, in the senate, in 1832, "understand very well this state of the case, whether they do or do not comprehend the causes which produce it. I have, in my possession, a letter from a respectable merchant, well known to me. After complaining of the operation of the tariff of 1828, on the articles to which it applies, some of which he had imported, and that his purchases having been made in England, before the passage of that tariff was known, it produced such an effect upon the English market, that the articles could not be resold without loss, he adds, ' for it *really appears*, that, when *additional* duties are laid upon an article, it then becomes *lower*, instead of *higher*.' "

The effect of protection on brown sugar, in reducing prices, is remarkable, as shown, in part, by Mr. Secretary Walker's own tables, in his report (pp. 720–21). The variations there found correspond with what would be expected from the two causes of competition and amount of the home crop. In 1816, when we were dependent on the foreign product, the prices of brown sugar ranged from 14½ cents a pound to 16½. In 1820, after protection had begun to produce its effect, it was down to 8½ to 12½ cents. In 1825, it was down to from 7½ to 10 cents. In 1831, to from 5 to 7 cents. In 1834–'5, to from 5½ to 6. This year was a large crop. Mark how the price was affected in 1835–'6, when the crop fell short of the year previous by about one third. It rose to from 10 to 11 cents, not because there was no supply in the foreign market, but because we were *dependent*. From that time to 1842–'3, the home crop being good, and gradually increasing, prices gradually fell, when that year the home crop was unusually large, and the price was reduced to from 3¾ to 4 cents. In 1843–'4, the home crop was small, and prices rose to from 5½ to 6½ cents. Again, in 1844–'5, with a large home crop, prices were from to 3⅜ to 4⅜ cents. It should be remarked, that all this while, nearly twenty years, a part of the supply was from abroad, and the foreign and domestic products were brought into competition, the consequence of which was the reduction of prices. But the moment the competition was diminished, by the falling off of the home crop, up went prices.

All know what a clamor was raised among cotton-growers about duties on hemp and cotton-bagging. Mr. Calhoun proved by figures—claimed to have proved—when the tariff of 1842 was under debate, that it would be a tax on the cotton interest of $1,422,222 a year. Mr. Toombs, of Georgia, of the 29th Congress, who, as a Southern man, would naturally sympathize with Mr. Calhoun on this subject, in view of the facts, *also proved by figures*, while the tariff of 1846 was under debate, that Mr. Calhoun had been entirely wrong in his calculations and predictions, and that the protection given to hemp and cotton-bagging, by the tariff of 1842, had not only lowered prices, but lowered them more even than Mr. Calhoun predicted it would raise them! " Since the introduction of the business of making cotton-bagging in Kentucky," said Mr. Toombs—" since our own countrymen have come into competition in producing it—the price of bagging has fallen to less than *one third* of its average price before that period. . . . We now make good bagging in Kentucky more than 5 cents per yard less than it cost in Dundee, in 1842, and for 3 or 4 cents a yard less than the present price in Scotland"—(See National Intelligencer, Aug. 29, 1846). The price of cotton-bagging, in 1838, ranged from 18 to 20 cents per yard; in 1841, from 25 to 27; in 1846, from 8½ to 9½. Bale rope, in 1838, from 7 to 8 cents per pound; in 1841, from 11 to 12; in 1846, from 3 to 4. And yet Mr. Secretary Walker, in the face of these facts, being guided by his theory, represents the duties of the tariff of 1842 on these articles, as " an enormous tax that inures to the benefit of about thirty manufacturers"! He is forced, however, to call the facts " a mystery." " We are unable," he says, " to get any key to this mystery, from the *actual* prices since the duties were imposed"! If Mr. Calhoun had not predicted that the prices would rise, and put down the rise in figures, so that there is no getting away from them, then Mr. Walker might have solved the " mystery," by saying, it is true that prices have fallen, but they would have fallen as much more as the duties, without them. He does indeed give this reason in another part of his report; but he hardly had courage enough to give it in juxtaposition with a recognition of these facts, and therefore he called them a " mystery."

Iron, if not the greatest interest of the country, all things considered, is the most important. It enters into every person's wants, and into his constant use, and no one can do without it, in a variety of forms. It constitutes the most prominent necessity of war, of peace, of agriculture, of manufactures, of commerce, and it may be said, of every pursuit of life. It enters even into the finest embellishments of the arts. Time, that most momentous of all movements, carrying with it the destinies of all nations, and of all men, can not be accurately measured in its progress, without it.

By the wise arrangements of Providence, the necessities of man and of society, are abundantly provided for, in this particular, in the mineral wealth of the United States. The iron beds of this country have already been ascertained to be inexhaustible ; and what is not of less importance—greater indeed—the qualities of iron produced from the ores found here, are the best in the world. The question is, whether this immense and boundless field of American wealth, shall be protected and husbanded; or whether it shall be abandoned to everlasting repose, for the sake of giving profit to British producers and manufacturers of this article, and income to the British exchequer ? It is alleged, that free trade in this article, will bring it cheaper to the people of the United States. Suppose it should; that which is nominally cheaper, is not always the cheapest. The main proposition, however, is flatly and confidently denied, with the additional averment, that adequate and permanent protection for the home product and manufactures of this article, will afford it, in all forms, at lower prices to the people, than could be obtained from any other quarter, besides the advantages to the country of the home trade. The prices of the British market to-day, or this year, are no rule for to-morrow, or next year. They are as variable as the winds, and as fickle in their disposition—governed chiefly by their chances of obtaining the American market, or for want of it. When it is gained, and the American product is suppressed, their prices are sure to be high; and when it is wanted, they are low.

The protective system over iron and its manufactures, began in the United States when prices were very high, and the consequence has been a uniform and gradual reduction of prices. Take for example the following extract from the report on iron of the convention of the friends of domestic industry, held in the city of New York, November, 1831, signed "B. B. Howell, Secretary" (see Fisher's National Magazine for June, 1845):—

"STATEMENT B.—Showing the effects of a tariff of protection on the article of iron at Pittsburg and Cincinnati: In the years 1818-'19-'20, bar iron in Pittsburg sold at from $190 to $200 per ton.—Now the price is $100 per ton. In the same year, boiler iron was $350 per ton.—Now at $140 per ton. Sheetiron was but little made in those years, and sold for $18 per cwt.—Now made in abundance, and sold for $8.50 per cwt. Hoop iron, under same circumstances, was then $250, and is now $120. Axes were then $24 per dozen, and are now $12. Scythes are now 50 per cent. lower than they were then —as are spades and shovels. Iron hoes were in those years $9 per dozen—now a very superior article of steel hoes at $4 to $4.50. Socket-shovels are made at $4.50 by the same individual who, a few years ago, sold them at $12 per dozen. Slater's patent stoves, imported from England, sold in Pittsburg at $350 to $400.—A much superior article is now made there and sold for $125 to $150. English vices then sold for 20 to 22 1-2 cents per lb.; now a superior article is sold at 10 to 10 1-2. Brazier's rods in 1824 were imported, and cost 14 cents per lb., or $313.60 per ton.—Now supplied to any amount of 1-4 to 3-8 diameter, at $130 per ton. Steam engines have fallen in price since 1823 one half, and they have one half more work on them. The engine at the Union rolling-mill (Pittsburg), in 1819, cost $11,000—a much superior one of 130 horse-power, for Sligo mill, cost, in 1826, $3,000. In 1830, there were made in Pittsburg 100 steam-engines. In 1831, 150 will be made. averaging $2,000; or $300,000 in that article alone. A two-horse-power engine costs $250; six-horse, $500; eight to nine horse, $700. These last are the prices delivered and put up. At least 600 tons of iron made in Pittsburg are manufactured into other articles before it leaves the city, from steam-engines of the largest size, down to a threepenny nail. Eight rolling and slitting mills, of the largest power, are in the city of Pittsburg, five of which have been erected since 1828. Thirty-eight new furnaces have been erected since 1824 in the western parts of Pennsylvania, and that part of Kentucky bordering on the Ohio river, most of them since 1828. The quantity of iron made at Pittsburg was, in 1828, 3,291 tons, 19 cwt.; in 1829, 6,217 tons, 17 cwt.; in 1830, 9,282 tons, 2 cwt. Being an increase of nearly 200 per cent. in two years. The above facts were furnished by members of the committee residing at Pittsburg, who vouch for their accuracy."

"Prices of iron at Cincinnati.—In 1814 to 1818, bar iron $200 to $220 per ton; now $100, $105, $110. The fall in prices has been nearly as follows: In 1826, bar iron, assorted, $125 to $135; in 1827, $120 to $130; in 1828, $115 to $125; in 1829, $112.50 to $122.50; in 1830, $100 to $110; in 1831, $100 to $110. Castings, including hollow-ware, 1814 to 1818, $120 to $130 per ton; present price, $60 to $65, and the quality much improved."

It appears from the same document, that hammered iron, at a duty of $22.40 per ton, sold at less than it did at a duty of $9. It also increased the revenue from that source, which, under the law of 1816, at a duty of $9, was two millions and a half; and under the law of 1828, at a duty of $22.40, was five millions and a half. These are by no means remarkable facts. It is the uniform operation of the protective system, to cheapen the protected articles, and to augment the revenue. Under such a system, foreign producers can no longer have their own prices, because they alone have not the market, but are obliged to sell under the effects of competition; and the domestic producers meeting with foreign competition, are also influenced in the same way, all for the benefit of consumers.

Under the system of low duties, in the latter stages of the operation of the compromise act, down to the tariff of 1842, as is well known, the iron interest, in its raw products and manufactures, suffered greatly in Pennsylvania and elsewhere; and it is equally well known, that it revived again, in an astonishing degree, under the tariff of '42, cheapening manufactured articles in proportion as the manufactories were multiplied, and competition extended. These facts are so recent, and coming so directly within the observation and experience of the public, as not to require a detail of evidence. They demonstrate the general truth, that home products of manufacture, under protection, tend invariably and uniformly to reduce the prices of the articles. That the prices of the raw material should be well sustained, is as desirable as that those of agricultural products should be; and that some of the forms of iron manufacture, such as railroad iron, had not got down to the lowest British prices, results from the two-fold consideration, first, that immense capital was required to establish them, and next, that the policy of protection was not regarded as sufficiently secure to incur the risk. But the experiments made in this and other branches of iron manufacture, hitherto, in their incipient stages, and embarrassed as they have been for want of confidence in the disposition of the government, demonstrate, satisfactorily, that, under a system of permanent and secure protection, every branch of iron manufacture would afford its products at lower prices than to depend on imports. American railroad iron, in 1846, had got to be lower than the British product was in 1836, free of duty.

It is remarkable, that Mr. Secretary Walker should himself have given the strongest possible evidence, in his report, of the cheapening of American manufactured articles, under protection, as follows :—" The receipts of the first quarter of this year are less, by $2,011,885, than the receipts of the same quarter last year. Among the *causes* of decrease is the *progressive diminution* of many highly-protected articles, *and the substitution of rival domestic products.*"

It is marvellously singular, how, for want of fact and sound argument, the strongest evidence of reduced prices by protection, has been seized upon to decry protection as producing a contrary effect, as in the case of minimums, which have invariably reduced prices. When the price was reduced, the duty, on the minimum principle, would appear to rise— did rise, in respect to the real value; and therefore it is said to be an exorbitant duty! In this way, a minimum duty, beginning, say at 50 per cent. ad valorem, has sometimes mounted, by reduction of prices, to an ad-valorem duty of 200, or 250, or 300 per cent. " Behold !" says the sage member of Congress—for this argument has been used by that class of persons, in public debate—" behold !" he says, " what enormous duties ! what enormous prices ! what enormous profits !" Is it not mortifying to an American citizen, to be obliged to witness such ignorance or such dishonesty—for one or the other it must be— in the legislators of the nation ? This very 300 per cent. ad-valorem duty, on an article bearing a minimum duty equal to 50 per cent. ad valorem, when the law was passed, and still the same, is arithmetical demonstration, that the price has been reduced to *one sixth* of what it was when the duty was imposed ! The higher ad-valorem duties rise by the operation of minimums, so much greater the reduction of price ; and *vice versa*. But it is, or ought to be, enough, that everybody knows by experience, that manufactured articles in extensive use and demand, are cheaper under protective duties, than under low duties, or free trade ;—and that a protective tariff, like that of '42, enables the people, more especially the poor, to supply their wants, as a whole, at less cost, while they do better in all their pursuits, and are more prosperous. You can not convince the poorest and most ignorant man, who buys his shirt for less than the duty on that species of goods, that he *pays* the duty. It was the duty that cheapened it ; and if he were to believe, that he is taxed with the duty, he must believe, that, without the tax, he should have got his shirt for as much less than nothing as the difference between the duty and price ! and that the tradesman who sold him the goods, should not only not have *sold* them, but *given* them to him, and the difference between the duty and price *to boot !* In that way the tradesman, at least, would pay the duty. But the truth is, nobody pays it, if it is a domestic product, as in such a case it must be.

§ 4. *Reasons why the Doctrine deduced from the above Facts is a correct one.*

The doctrine is, that protective duties on manufactured articles in the United States, do not augment prices to consumers, and therefore are not taxes to them. The facts leading to this conclusion, have very much puzzled the advocates of free trade, and not being able to deny them, they still say, " It is manifestly an absurd conclusion, notwithstanding the facts. If the duties had not been imposed, the prices would have been reduced still lower, and as much lower as the amount of duties." In other words : " It is true, that your duties have reduced prices ; but they have not reduced them low enough !" This appears to be the substance of the answer to the facts.

Since, however, the *facts* are not satisfactory, it is possible that the *reasons* will have some weight, if they agree with and support the facts.

There are several reasons that tend to solve this difficulty, and show how the facts occur, and why they should be expected.

When a duty is imposed on an imported manufactured article from Great Britain, or elsewhere, to encourage its domestic production, it is pre-supposed, that the home producer could not compete with the foreigner without the duty, and consequently could not stand. It must be seen, then, in such a case, that the foreign producer has the market, and will have his own price. There is nothing to limit his price, but the competition from foreign quarters. That competition can not give the American consumer the benefit of cheap foreign labor ; for that is chiefly absorbed in an enormous system of taxation, which is never relaxed, except in the political competitions of the commercial policy of nations. Then it is made to bear with tremendous energy on the prices of wages and capital in the United States ; and a small fraction of the great difference in the cost of money and labor in these two quarters, will answer all the purposes of such a policy, when the American laborer and producer are not protected by their own government.

But in ordinary private competition, in foreign quarters, for the market in the United States, cheap foreign labor is no benefit to the American consumer. He saves not a penny on that score. Even in the action of the commercial policy of foreign nations, his benefit is small, which is more than counterbalanced by other facts under the control of foreign powers and foreign factors, so long as home production can not come into the field of competition. When it does, of course he is benefited; and that is the object contended for by protection. So long, therefore, as foreign producers of manufactured articles, which might be produced at home, under a system of protection, can command the market of the United States, these articles will always come at the highest prices that can be commanded by the advantageous position of the producers, which amounts to absolute control, except in their competition with each other. Being together interested to make money, and to make the most possible, they will not sell at loss, but only at profit.

In the first place, then, all the difference between the cost of money and labor in the United States and those quarters—not less than 100 per cent.—is absorbed by the system of taxation where the goods are produced, and more too—far more, as a part of government policy, when it is known that there is no competition to operate against them, in the market where the goods are going. That system of taxation is enormous, and for Great Britain, was once described by Henry, now Lord Brougham, as follows :—

" Taxes on every article that enters the mouth, or covers the back, or is placed under the feet ; taxes upon everything that is pleasant to see, hear, feel, smell, or taste ; taxes on everything on the earth and the waters under the earth—on everything that comes from abroad, or is grown at home ; taxes on the raw material, and on every new value that is added by the art and labor of man ; taxes on the spices that pamper man's appetite, and on the drug that is administered to his disease ; taxes on the ermine that decorates the judge, and on the rope that hangs the criminal ; taxes on the rich man's dainties, and on the poor man's salt ; taxes on the ribands of the bride, and on the brass nails of her coffin ;— at bed, or at board, lying down or rising up, WE MUST PAY. The school-boy spins his taxed top ; the beardless youth manages his taxed horse, on a taxed saddle, with a taxed bridle, on a taxed road ; and the dying Englishman, pouring his medicine, which has paid 7 per cent., into a spoon that has paid 15 per cent., flings himself back on his chintz bed which has paid 22 per cent., makes his will on a stamp that has paid eight pounds (sterling), and expires in the arms of an apothecary, who has paid 100 pounds (sterling) for the privilege of putting him to death. His whole property is then taxed from 2 to 10 per cent. in probate, and large fees are demanded for burying him in church. His virtues are handed down to posterity on taxed marble, and he is gathered to his fathers to be taxed no more."

No, not so. For if the marble that perpetuates his name and celebrates his virtues, can last so long, he is taxed till the morning of the resurrection ! Taxed for the privilege of coming into the world, taxed all the way through it, taxed on his passage out of it, and taxed EVER AFTER !

This immense, comprehensive, stupendous system of taxation, falls, in varied and complicated forms, on the English producers of the manufactured articles consumed by Americans, and enters into the price of them as a principal part, when there is no protection to guard against it ; and that price, in such cases, is higher, always and much higher, than it would be, if the articles could be produced at home, under a system of adequate protection.

To all this must be added the profits of the commercial agents or factors, engaged in the sale of these goods, the charges of clearance, transportation, and entry, and a variety of expenses accumulated in such transactions between remote countries. Is it a matter of surprise, then—should it not be expected—in view of all these facts, that the same goods which can be produced at home, under protection, will be afforded to the consumers cheaper, while the laborers, and all the parties concerned in the business, are well paid, on the American system of wages and other values ? Such, evidently, is the aspect of the facts, and the reasons are obvious—demonstrate the facts, which, being facts, need no other proof.

The American consumer of foreign manufactured articles, therefore, which might be produced at home, under protection, though he obtain them free of duty, derives not the smallest fraction of benefit from foreign cheap labor ; nor is he in any manner or degree taxed by protective duties which oblige him to supply his wants at home. He gets them cheaper. There may be, and doubtless are, exceptions to this rule, as, for example, in the infancy of a domestic production, which has received protection for the sake of starting it ; or in the slow progress of another, the protection of which is inadequate, or too insecure by political agitation, to invite sufficient capital to give it strength and vigor, and to open a wide field of domestic competition. In some such cases, the prices may be augmented temporarily ; not permanently, however, when the policy of protection is considered as settled. The moment a product of manufacture has received adequate protection, considered as secure, capital rushes into it, to fill the market, and cheapen prices by competition to the lowest point of a fair profit. And all experience in the United States proves—the above-cited facts prove—that all interests engaged in domestic manufactures, capital, wages of labor, prices of raw materials of home production, the wages of all the variety of employments which they create, pay of agents, carriers, and profits of merchants engaged in the trade, can all be sustained, and well sustained, on the American system of wages and profits, when the consumers obtain them at a lower rate than they would be afforded by importation. In the case of importation without competition, the consumers are in the power of foreigners, and of a foreign system of enormous taxation; and they can not escape from the burden, in the shape of high prices, resulting therefrom. In the case of home production, under the American system of society, which costs little, and might be entirely sustained by protective duties alone, at the same time that they cheapen the articles protected, the consumers are rescued from the power of foreigners, and all parties engaged in supplying their wants are well paid, while these wants are supplied at a lower rate, and with a better article. If a person or party, here or there, may have to pay a little more for the supply of a particular want, in the first stages of home production, before competition enters the field, the benefits such a party receives from the general system, much more than counter-balance this alleged tax, so that, on the whole, it is not a tax.

§ 5. *A Misfortune.*

It is a great misfortune to this subject, that political enonomists first, the schools next, statesmen third, the press fourth, and the public fifth, like a flock of sheep, that jump with a leader, have all consecutively, and in the end together, been accustomed to take for granted, that all duties are *taxes.* Who can resist such a common error, and turn men's minds back to reason, when the very persons, statesmen, conductors of the press, and others, who know it is an error, and are doing all they can to correct it, are yet so much the creatures of habit, as to call *all* duties taxes, without discrimination? Hence the advantage of their antagonists—both parties call the same thing by a *misnomer.* To allow that they are *taxes,* is giving it up. There can be no argument after that, except in the following form, which is indeed unanswerable:—

"So that a thing is made and supplied at home, it matters little whether it costs more or less. This is broad ground, and needs some illustration, because, if true, it does away all the objection that can be offered to a protecting tariff. It makes all the difference to the country, taking in its rounds and interchanges of labor, whether a dollar is laid out at home, or abroad, in buying an article. When it goes to a foreign country to buy a thing, *it is gone for ever,* and becomes the capital or dollar of that country, after it makes one operation only. Whereas, if you lay out that dollar at home, in the neighborhood, or next village, or next state, or district, for an article, it remains in the country, and is still a part of the capital of the country. It does infinitely more than that, because it circulates, and repeats its operation of buying an article perhaps one hundred times, possibly a thousand times, and in its rounds serves the purposes of a hundred or a thousand dollars, as the case may be. In the grand rounds of its circulation, it touches as many springs of industry, as it does hands, and is all the time doing good. When it shall have done all this, or while it is doing it—for the thing never ends—it is still a dollar, and counted properly among the dollars or the capital of the country. Figures can't calculate the difference. therefore, in expending a dollar at home or abroad; even the geometrical ratio can't accumulate fast enough to realize this difference. It outstrips everything but the human imagination in its progress. If the article should cost 10 per cent. more than the foreign, it is ten times made up in this grand round we have alluded to by the rapid repetition of the thing. It is again made up in the way that prices tally. or adapt themselves to each other. If the seller of the article gets a little more, he in his turn pays a little more to the laborers, and they a little more to the farmers, they a little more to the hands, and so on all round the circle, until a perfect equilibrium is not only restored, but kept up between all, and all prices quadrate into a perfect system, that. in the rounds, can not make the least difference as to the cost or difference of price."—[*Notes on Political Economy by a Southern Planter.*]

Is not this plain—conclusive—even if prices are raised? Some may say, that this benefit does not reach all; that it is partial in its distribution, being a tax to some, while it is a help to others, which is the evil complained of. With such minds, there is no reasoning. The above description is precisely the operation of the protective system, when, in some cases, and for a season, under a prohibitory duty, the manufacture of a protected article is starting, and before home competition has reduced prices, the prices are a little higher. The consumer, no matter who he is, is benefited in so many other ways, under a protective system, by cheapening most of the protected articles he has occasion to use; by giving him employment, if he lives on wages; or whatever be his calling or position, by making it better and more productive to himself, in a prosperous state of society, that it is impossible he should not participate in the general welfare, so as to more than compensate for this *supposed* burden, which, however, is only imaginary. When the duty is not prohibitory, the protected article is never dearer, but always cheaper necessarily, by bringing home competition into the field against foreign. The prices current in a foreign market prove nothing against this, however they may seem to do so; for the moment these protective duties are removed, as in the tariff of 1846, the foreign prices rise, just in proportion to the prospect of obtaining the American market, and when once they shall have gained it by breaking down the American producer, they will have their own prices, which will be higher than under a protective system. Even prohibitory duties reduce prices in the end, in the case of articles in general demand, if the system of protection is reliable, and capital dare venture into the business to a sufficient extent, as it always will, if protection is secure.

Such are the superior qualities of American iron, for example, and such the exhaustless beds of its ore, that nothing is required but permanent, secure protection, to afford every manufactured iron article demanded by the wants of society, cheaper than they could be obtained from England, or from any other quarter. Many of them had already begun to be cheaper under the tariff of 1842. But it requires time, confidence, and immense capital, to perfect all the manufactures of iron; and while marching to perfection, the prices would be satisfactory, beneficial to the country, and beneficial to all parties. If iron manufactures are discouraged, and languish in this country for want of protection, England will take advantage of it, and raise her prices higher than they would have been under an American system of protection, giving poorer iron, as she must, and poorer articles. The moment the tariff of 1846 passed, iron rose in England, and fell in the United States, proving that the lion was roused for his prey, and that his victim could not resist. If it proves that American prices, in this case were higher, it proves also, that English prices will not keep down. The level to which they tend, will be at the cost of this country, not only in the destruction of its labor, its business, and its capital, on an immense scale; not only in drawing off its cash; but in the augmentation of the prices of the articles imported. The same may be said of coal, though not falling under the head of manufactures. Iron and coal are among the greatest and most important interests of the United States, the working of which was yet in a state of infancy, when the tariff of 1846 came to cripple giant twins, and strangle them in the cradle. They had begun to scatter their blessings with a liberal and profuse hand. No one felt himself to be taxed—no one was taxed; none were poorer; all were richer; even though prices current in England might be quoted to prove, that prices were lower there. It proves nothing, exeept that England waits for another and better market, that she may *raise* her prices on her victims, which she will certainly do, when rivals are out of her path.

CHAPTER X.

FREE TRADE A SYSTEM OF FOREIGN TAXATION ON THE PEOPLE OF THE UNITED STATES.

§ 1. *What has been Proved, leading to this Result.*

IT is something to have cleared the way, in the preceding chapter, for the consideration of this important branch of the subject, by showing that protective duties are not taxes, but the contrary, viz., that they cheapen manufactured articles. This result naturally and necessarily incorporates itself with that part of the subject now to be considered, because, if protection cheapens prices, as demonstrated, the want of it is a tax. But—

§ 2. *It is a System of Foreign Taxation.*

It can not but be seen, that the money and labor of the United States which cost 2, brought into open competition, as producing powers, with the money and labor of Great Britain and Europe which cost 1, can be taxed by the latter *ad libitum*, and must fall before them.

§ 3. *The Manner of this System of Taxation.*

It is indirect and furtive, but not less real. The very and only ground of objection to the American system of protective duties, is, that it is an indirect and furtive mode of taxation, and all the prejudices against it have been sown by this charge. But since it is proved, that this is a false charge in the mouths of those who bring it, and a mere fiction in the imagination of those who are duped into the belief of it, it may perhaps prepare the way for the consideration of those grave and painful realities, in the shape of indirect and furtive taxation, which result from free trade; and they will not be less grave, nor less painful, when it shall be seen, that they are imposed by the hands of foreigners, of depredators on the rights of labor, of oppressors of the poor, of tyrants of the human race.

§ 4. *The Amount of this Taxation.*

When all its comprehensive influences are considered, it will be found to be stupendous and alarming. But there is a fraction of it, not small, nor of trifling import, that is more directly palpable, and which may be measured with some degree of accuracy. That alone ought to be enough to excite an indignant feeling of remonstrance, of solemn and determined protestation, in every American bosom. It will be indicated by the following extract from a public document, house of representatives, No. 296, 3d sess., 27th Congress, pp. 500–501 :—

" England levies no *direct* taxes upon her colonies, or rarely is it done. But by *indirect taxes* they give *four fifths* of their productive wealth to the mother-country. It was that support which she derived from the thirteen [North American] colonies, and it was for that alone she resisted their independence. She desired to *produce*, and that they should be forced to *consume*; and of all that they consumed [of imports from the mother-country], at least *four fifths* went into the national treasury at home, after supporting her farmers and mechanics. . . It is generally alleged, that a man pays 15 shillings for the use of government, out of every 20 shillings he spends in England. Some have stated the public tax at 17 shillings in the pound. Let us take one instance in the article of beer. The land pays a tax; the barley, when malted, pays an excise of 6 pence per bushel; hops pay one penny a pound; the beer, when brewed, pays an excise in some cases greater than the original value.; all the persons who labor in the premises, contribute to the national revenue, by their sundry consumptions, to the amount of *three fourths* of the whole price of their labor. It follows, then, that the people of this country [the United States] contribute in like proportion to the support of foreign governments, upon all that they purchase. In 1836, we imported more than $70,000,000 worth of foreign articles *free of duty*. The effect was, that they who purchased [consumed] these articles, paid not one cent to the support of our own government, while at least *four fifths* [$56.000,000] of that amount went into the treasuries of foreign governments, to support kings on their thrones, parliaments that make laws prohibiting our productions, and foreign armies and navies!"

Fifty-six millions of dollars of tax on the people of the United States, *in one year*, for the support of foreign governments, foreign institutions, foreign oppressors, foreign tyrants, who rob labor of *two thirds* of its fair reward, and tax the remaining third *three fourths* of its amount, on the necessaries of life consumed for the bare subsistence of the laborers!

But this is not the end of it. It is only the beginning. In the first place, it is a view of only one year's operation of this system of foreign taxation. It continued for many years, and ceased not, till it was, in some measure, arrested by the tariff of 1842—so far arrested, as to be no longer ruinous, that the people could bear it, and prosper. But it never *ceases* to be a tax imposed by foreigners, so long as the people of the United States import what they could produce, and produce cheaper, under a system of protection. But, secondly, it deprives home labor of so much employment and profit, by thus employing foreign labor at the expense of American. It deprives American labor of a political right. Even if American labor could not produce them cheaper, it might still be a political right. For every government is doubtless bound to protect the interests of the people against foreigners. But it has been shown that American labor *could* have produced them cheaper. Thirdly, it deprives the country, embracing numberless classes of all the profits of the business which would be created, in producing these things at home. And that is a tax. The great secret of taxation is to make it impalpable—" by indirection, to make direction sure." To be deprived of employment is, in fact, a more grievous mode of taxation, than to have employment itself taxed. The latter may be borne, when the former can not. But, fourthly, it is a positive and ruinous draft of money from the country, and in that way a system of *direct* foreign taxation—by indirect means indeed—but *direct* in the draft, and to an immense amount. By this means, the country, for years previous to the tariff of 1842, was impoverished—bankrupted. There was no money in it to do business with. It was gone—taken away by foreign taxation—swallowed up by the capacious mouths and never-satisfied throats of foreign exchequers and foreign vaults. American labor, and every species of business in the country, suffered incalculable and long-protracted sacrifices, and were relieved only by the tariff of '42. It was not a loss of *tens* of millions, nor of *scores* of millions. HUNDREDS OF MILLIONS ALONE would comprehend the sacrifices incurred under this stupendous system of foreign taxation—ALL THE EFFECT OF FREE TRADE!

§ 5. *The Commercial History of the Country as it relates to this Question.*

A few reminiscences will bring it all up. In the first place, the war of the Revolution originated in this species of taxation, and national independence was bought with a prodigal expenditure of blood and treasure, in order to be rescued from it. It was because the mother-country would not tolerate manufactures in the colonies—would not allow them to supply their own wants. After independence was acquired, it was found that the articles of confederation provided no powers to protect American labor, and the states went halting onward, without money (for it all went abroad to pay for manufactured goods), without credit, every year running deeper in debt, and ready to forfeit their position among the nations of the earth, from weakness and inability to maintain it. The constitution of 1789 was planned, framed, and adopted as a remedy for this defect of the articles of confederation, and the second act of the first Congress was entitled " An ACT for the encouragement and *protection* of domestic manufactures," &c., by duties on imports, General Washington, the president, appearing in a *domestic suit*. Such was the necessity and spirit of the country. It was found that, under the confederation, without the power of establishing a protective system, the people were entirely in the grasp of foreign taxation—more so, indeed, than they were before the Revolution. It was a perfect system of FREE TRADE.

This protective measure of the first Congress began to work a remedy, and wherein that was deficient was afterward made up for many years by the belligerent state of Europe, which gave to the United States, as a neutral power, a large portion of her carrying trade, and to a considerable extent the supply of her markets. Such was the state of the commercial world during the protracted wars of Europe, and finally during the war of 1812 between the United States and Great Britain, that no opportunity was given for a fair experiment of an American protective system, such as a time of general peace requires. The tariff of 1816 was the first trial of such a policy, though a defective one. It established the American system of manufactures; but being of short duration, the failure of the tariff measure of 1820, in the midst of general distress already accumulated, brought universal devastation, not less upon the commercial, than upon the manufacturing interests of the country; and as all other interests depend chiefly upon these, it brought on a period of universal embarrassment and general ruin. Nearly all the manufacturing capital was sunk, and the establishments were either broken up, or changed hands, by the bankruptcy of the original owners. " If," said Mr. Clay, in a speech in the senate (1832), " I were to select any term of seven years, since the adoption of the present constitution, which exhibited a scene of the most wide-spread dismay and desolation, it would be exactly that term of seven years, which immediately preceded the tariff of 1824." He also said, at the same time, " If the term of seven years were to be selected, of the greatest prosperity which this people have enjoyed since the establishment of their present constitution, it would be exactly that period of seven years which immediately *followed* the passage of the tariff of 1824." Such is the contrast of the effect of free trade and the effect of protection on the interests of the country.

If Mr. Clay were to rise again in the senate of the United States now, in 1846, he might with the greatest truth and force, use precisely the same language, with the following slight alterations: " If I were to select any term of *five* years, since the adoption of the present constitution, which exhibited a scene of the most wide-spread dismay and desolation, it would be exactly that term of *five* years, which immediately preceded the tariff of **1842**." For this *five* years so much transcended the *seven* years previous to the tariff of 1824, in " wide-spread dismay and desolation," that the former period will not deserve mention in comparison. Mr. Clay might also, with equal truth and force, repeat in 1846 the second extract, with the following alterations : " If the term of *four* years were to be selected, of the greatest prosperity which this people have enjoyed since the establishment of their present constitution, it would be exactly that period of *four* years which immediately followed the passage of the tariff of **1842**." For the prosperity of this period of four years, under the tariff of 1842, so much transcends that of the seven years subsequent to 1824, that the one should not be mentioned with the other. Such is the commercial history of the country, in regard to the effects of FREE TRADE AND PROTECTION.

CHAPTER XI.

BENEFITS OF THE BUSINESS WHICH THE PROTECTIVE POLICY GIVES TO THE COUNTRY.

§ 1. *Every new Art, or new Calling, an Increase of National Wealth.*

WHEN any person finds encouragement, by legislative protection or otherwise, for a new art, or a new business of any kind, not before attempted in the community, it takes him off from some other calling, and gives to those engaged in it all the business he would have had by continuing therein. It is a benefit to them. He becomes a new customer for the supply of all the wants arising out of his new vocation, which affords additional business to several classes, it may be to many. His products, whatever they may amount to, are so much augmentation of the general wealth. He has made the business which he left for his new pursuit, and every other business with which his new wants have any connexion, better; and he has set up a new business which increases the general stock of valuables. Here is a new and substantial element of the commonwealth, that did not exist before, diffusing its benefits in numerous quarters—it may be extensively.

§ 2. *Benefits of an Aggregation of new Pursuits in the Community.*

If one new art, or calling, is so beneficial, then two, other things being equal, would double the benefit; three would triple it; four, quadruple it; and so on. Suppose these cases of new arts and new callings, each occupying a like position of importance in its relations, are multiplied indefinitely in a great community—that they go on in endless progression of increase as to number—and that each becomes a nucleus of indefinite, ceaseless aggregation. Their power of augmenting national wealth, then, becomes equally indefinite, boundless, interminable, immeasurable.

The new arts and new callings that have grown up in the United States, under the protective policy, can scarcely be counted, and the growth of some of them has become gigantic in their interests, and in the ramifications of their influence on other pre-existing interests, to put them forward with equal strides, and to raise them to a corresponding importance.

§ 3. *Examples of Aggregation.*

It has been ascertained and well certified, that the Glenham woollen factory, at Fishkill, New York, with a capital of $140,000, gives profitable employment to $1,422,000 worth of other American capital, chiefly agricultural, in items as follows: 66,000 sheep, $2 a-head, $132,000; 22,000 acres of pasture land, to feed the sheep, supposed to be worth in that county, $50 an acre, $1,100,000; farms employed to the extent of 2,600 acres, worth $70 an acre, $182,000; other capital, to furnish teazles, firewood, coal, provender, &c., &c., $8,000. Total, $1,422,000. To this should be added the sum of the wages paid to the operatives and agents of the factory, which would considerably increase the amount of capital employed. Nor is this the end of the calculation. All the persons employed in and about this establishment, all employed to tend the sheep and cultivate the farms, to furnish teazles, fuel, and provender, and to supply any and all other demands, are withdrawn from other pursuits, to afford them a better chance of profit, and become customers to a variety of callings, and to a great extent, where they would otherwise have been themselves employed.

The city of Lowell, Mass., is the sole creation of the protective policy. In 1821, the ground on which it stands was used for ordinary agricultural purposes, and was then bought by the Merrimack company. In 1845 it had a population of 30,000, of which nearly one third were operatives in the mills, consisting of 3,620 females, and 2,915 males. The capital invested in manufacturing and mechanical enterprises, was $12,000,000. The annual consumption of cotton, 61,100 bales; (wool not given, but great;) of coal, 12,500 tons; of wood, 3,270 cords; of oil, 67,842 gallons; of charcoal, 600,000 bushels; of starch, 800,000 pounds. Of course, these are only the leading and principal articles of consumption. More than a million and a half of dollars a year are paid for labor, and the profits are about the same.

Here, then, are 30,000 persons, withdrawn from other occupations of the country by means of these establishments, and concentrated on this single point, all living by them, and giving so much better chances for those occupying the places which they would otherwise have filled, both parties becoming customers of each other, directly or indirectly. To this population must be added that employed to supply the raw cotton, the wool, the coal, the wood, the oil, the starch, the food and clothing for 30,000 persons, the building materials, the erection of the buildings, the furnishing of the houses, and the thousand articles of consumption that can not be named. If it be supposed that the capital of $12,000,000 invested at Lowell, employs other capital of the country, in proportion to that invested at Fishkill, N. Y., as above noticed, that other capital, thus employed, would amount to $121,885,714! Nor does the vast benefit to other pursuits of the country, in preventing over-production, and in supporting the prices of their products, by withdrawing from them these 30,000 persons at Lowell, and the very great additional population occupied in charge of the one hundred and twenty millions of other capital employed by Lowell, come into this reckoning.

There are invested in the iron works of the United States, exclusive of iron manufactories, upward of $20,000,000. (See Fisher's National Magazine, June, 1846.) Say $20,000,000. At the same rate of calculation, demonstrating the result in the case of the Glenham factory, at Fishkill, this $20,000,000 invested in the iron works of the United States, employs other capital, of all kinds, to the amount of $203,142,857, not reckoning the capital of labor employed in these works, and the beneficial effects on other species of labor from which this is withdrawn.

The Hon. Mr. Ramsey, of Pennsylvania, gave to the house of representatives some instructive statistics on the coal trade. (See National Intelligencer, Sept. 1, 1846.) A part of them, bearing on the point now under consideration, lead to the following result: That the investment of capital for the coal business, in the single county of Schuylkill, in canals, boats, horses, railroads, cars, locomotives, collieries, landings, working capital, coal land, &c., &c, amounted to $26,856,000; that $9,330,000 of this was added under the tariff of 1842; that the agricultural products consumed, in 1845, by those engaged in the coal business of that county, such as wheat, flour, corn, rye, buckwheat, oats, hay, straw, beef, pork, potatoes, poultry, butter, lard, eggs, fruit, vegetables, &c., &c., amounted to $965,000; that the amount of the same products consumed in 1841, was only $588,000; showing an increase, in four years, of $377,000; that the merchandise of various kinds consumed, same year (1845), amounted to $1,758,000—increase on 1841 of $840,000; that many articles of considerable amount were omitted in this reckoning; that the farms, in the county, had doubled in value, and the value of those in adjoining counties was much increased by the same cause; that the amount of anthracite coal taken to market, had risen from 360 tons in 1820, to 2,000,000 in 1845; to all which should be added the navigation interest to be found in the coal fleet, engaged in this trade, a part of which, some scores of vessels, is constantly seen waiting for and taking in cargoes, at the depot on the Delaware, above Philadelphia. The employment which this trade gives to labor, the increased value which it imparts to both labor and property, and the wide-spread commercial activity which it creates, bringing profit to all parties, are but one instance of the power and benefits of *aggregation*, which a single great interest, like this, carries along with it.

The whole manufacturing capital of the United States was estimated some years ago at $300,000,000. The Hon. Chas. H. Carroll, of N. Y., in a speech in Congress, 1846 (see National Intelligencer, Aug. 7, 1846), puts the minimum estimate, for the present time, at

$500,000,000. It will be sufficient for the present purpose, however, to take the first-named estimate of $300,000,000. If this aggregate be supposed to employ other capital of the country, in the same proportion as the Glenham factory, without counting itself, or the wages of labor employed in the establishments, it puts in active operation, and profitably sustains, other property to the amount of $3,047,142,857 ! This, as must be admitted, is an astonishing result !

Some manufactories may employ less, some more, of other capital, in proportion to their own investments, than that at Fishkill, New-York. No accuracy, however, derivable from the minutest information of facts, could vary this general result, so as to affect the lesson which it teaches, in showing how new arts and new callings, in the aggregate, under a protective system, promote private, general, and national wealth.

§ 4. *General Jackson's Policy, as developed in a Letter to Doct. Coleman on this subject, in* 1824.

It will be found in the following extract :—

"Heaven smiled upon and gave us liberty and independence. That same Providence has blessed us with the MEANS of national independence. . . . He has filled our mountains and plains with minerals—with lead, iron, and copper—and given us a climate and soil for the growing of hemp and wool. These being the great materials of our national defence, they ought to have extended to them adequate and fair protection, that our manufacturers and laborers may be placed in a fair competition with those of Europe. . . . I will ask, what is the real situation of the agriculturist? Where has the American farmer a market for his surplus produce? Except for cotton he has neither a foreign, nor a home market. Does not this clearly prove, when there is no market at home or abroad, that there is too much labor employed in agriculture, and that the channels for labor should be multiplied? Common sense at once points out the remedy :—Draw from agriculture this superabundant labor; employ it in mechanism and manufactures; thereby creating a home market for your breadstuffs—distributing labor to the most profitable account; and benefits to the country will result. Take from agriculture, in the United States, 600,000 men, women, and children, and you will at once give a market for more breadstuffs than all Europe now furnishes us with. In short, sir, we have been too long subject to the policy of British merchants. It is time we should become a little more *Americanized*, and instead of feeding paupers and laborers of England, feed our own ; or else, in a short time, by continuing our present policy, we shall be paupers ourselves. . . . The experience of the late war ought to teach us a lesson, and one never to be forgotten. If our liberty, and republican form of government, procured for us by our Revolutionary fathers, are worth the blood and treasure by which they were obtained, it is surely our duty to protect and defend them. . . . It is, therefore, my opinion. that a careful and judicious tariff is much wanted, *to pay our national debt* [a high and strong tariff that], and afford us the means of that defence within ourselves on which the safety of our country and liberty depends; and last, though not least, *give a proper distribution to our labor*, which must prove beneficial to the happiness, independence, and wealth of the community."

§ 5. *General Jackson's Policy carried out, and his Prediction fulfilled.*

It should be observed, that this letter to Doct. L. H. Coleman, of North Carolina, was written before the tariff of 1824 had gone into effect, and when the whole country was suffering so much for want of it. Precisely the thing here proposed by him has been carried out, and more than he predicted has been fulfilled in consequence. He proposed to take 600,000 men, women, and children, from agriculture, and put them to manufacturing. It has been done. The latest official return of operatives in the manufactories of the United States, is 850,000, who have been turned from other employments to these since 1824. These 850,000 *operatives* do not of course include the vast population, amounting probably to four millions (see Niles' Register, vol. 44), counting their families, to whom the American manufacturing system has opened new and profitable pursuits, on which they are dependent, and which otherwise would have had no existence. It was the *principle* of the policy, rather than any specific mode of its application, that led to such important, prolific results. Its application was left to circumstances which developed its amazing power.

General Jackson predicted, that this transfer of men, women, and children, to manufacturing pursuits, " would at once give a market for more breadstuffs than all Europe now [1824] furnishes us with." This has been much more than fulfilled—vastly more—as will appear from the following facts :—By the latest reports of the United States treasury department, of the 29th Congress, it appears, that England and Ireland, in 1845, took of the breadstuffs of the United States, of all kinds, only $223,251, and that our agricultural exports, other than cotton and tobacco, for the same year, to all the world, were only $11,195,515. But the state of Massachusetts, alone (as will be found by consulting the official statistics of that commonwealth), after exhausting her own supplies of breadstuffs, consumes annually of flour from other states, $4,000,000 ; of corn and other grain $2,800,000 ; in all $6,800,000 ; and her entire annual consumption of the agricultural products of other states, amounts to $42,000,000. After deducting *seven millions* for cotton, there is $23,804,485 in *excess* of the demand for the same agricultural products in all quarters of the foreign world, as officially reported for 1845 ! In 1845, Massachusetts took 1,000,000 barrels of flour from other states, being more than all the foreign world took. This great and growing consumption in Massachusetts, of the agricultural products of other states, arises chiefly from its manufacturing establishments and mechanic arts. Massachusetts alone, by executing the plan proposed by General Jackson in 1824, has not simply "created a market for more breadstuffs than all Europe then furnished us with;" but more than all the world has ever called for, down to the present time. Less than one third of the manufacturing capital of the United States is in Massachusetts. What, then, must be the aggregate result, in this particular, of such an amount of capital, so invested, and thus swallowing up the agricultural products of the entire Union!

The Hon. Andrew Stewart, M. C., of Pennsylvania, estimates all the agricultural productions of the United States, exclusive of cotton and tobacco, at *one thousand millions of dollars a year.* According to the last census, the annual products of the labor and industry of the people of the United States, of every description, were about $2,000,000,000. (See Senate, doc. 340, 2d sess., 27th Congress.) The average annual exports of the United States, of every description, do not commonly exceed $100,000,000. The average annual exports of agricultural products, other than cotton and tobacco, is not much over $10,000,000. What, then, becomes of the remaining fraction of $1,000,000,000, that is, deducting cotton and tobacco, about $900,000,000?—It is consumed at home, of course. The home market, then, is worth about one hundred to one of the foreign market of all the world for these agricultural products! The foreign market, indeed, is hardly worth counting, in comparison. And a very large proportion of this home demand is created by the manufacturers, as already seen in the case of Massachusetts, and in the examples of aggregation presented in this chapter. It will also be seen, that the home market is the chief dependence for all other home products, not less than $1,000,000,000.

CHAPTER XII.

THE EFFECTS OF THE PROTECTIVE AND ANTI-PROTECTIVE SYSTEMS OF DUTIES ON THE CURRENCY, BUSINESS, AND LABOR OF THE COUNTRY, CONTRASTED.

§ 1. *Amount of Cash wanted for Use.*

IT is generally supposed, that eighty millions of cash, or specie, is necessary for domestic exchanges and common business purposes. At least this amount is demanded, perhaps more. Possibly one hundred millions, for present population and business, in an ordinary state of things, would be convenient. There is no use in having more cash in the country than its business or trade requires, as more would be idle. That amount is important—is indispensable for the convenience and prosperity of the people. Its chief function is to constitute the basis of the currency, the bulk of which is always paper in a civilized, active, commercial community. But the cash, or specie, must be in the country, in abeyance to demand; else the currency is unsound, being irredeemable.

§ 2. *Nothing but the Protective Policy can keep the necessary Amount of Specie in the Country.*

This is evident from what has already been, and will yet farther be, proved. "History is prophecy." The past proves what the future will be. There never was a time of no duties, as under the confederation; or of low duties, as for the few years previous to the tariff of 1824, and previous to that of 1842; when the specie did not leave the country, and the currency break down. The reason is, that low or anti-protective duties always run the country in debt to foreign parts, buying more than is sold; and no foreign balances against the country can be settled, except by cash, weighed in the scales. Consequently, the specie is required, and must go; and unless the banks suspend, to stop it, it must continue to go, till these balances are settled. One hundred millions of balances of this kind against us, would at any time drain the country of all the specie in it, as there is never more than that, if so much, at one time. It is commonly supposed, there is not more than eighty millions. But the commercial history of the country demonstrates, that a short period of low, anti-protective duties, will run up more than a hundred millions of balances against us. That is the reason, and the sole reason, of all the currency troubles of the country, in times past.

A man of business, in a sound state, as to his own private finances, can not fail, if he should try, so long as he does not buy more than he sells. It is the same with a nation. Having once in its bosom cash enough for its business, or trade, domestic and foreign, it will always have enough, till it begins to buy of foreign parts more than it sells to them, take the foreign trade as a whole. Then the cash must go, to settle the balances, whatever be the amount. If they be equal to half of the specie in the country, then half of it must go; if equal to the whole, the whole must go; or the debts must be protested; or be arranged; in any case, if the whole does not go, the debts must remain unpaid.

The foreign debts of the United States are at this moment more than three times as much as the amount of specie in the whole country; and they were all created in a time of low duties, and by reason of them. But those which were not settled by private bankruptcy and state repudiation, thus returning home from inability or bad faith, have been arranged, and the nation pays, through the debtors, from twelve to fifteen millions annually, in the shape of interest, with the principal hanging over its head. It is so much foreign debt against the country; and if justice is done, the interest must always be paid.

But the nation has never run in debt to foreign parts, under the existence and action of a protective policy; and it has never paid any foreign debts except by that policy. Such are the facts. It is not intended to say, that no foreign engagements have ever been met, under a system of low, anti-protective duties; but only, that foreign engagements, in the aggregate, have never been liquidated, but always increased, under that system; and that the aggregate has only been lessened, and credit revived only, under the action of a system of protective duties.

§ 3. *The Currency can never fail, will always be sufficient, and can never be unsound, under an adequate System of Protective Duties.*

Nothing more is meant here by the term, *adequate*, than that the system shall be strong enough to prevent foreign commercial balances accumulating against the country; and it is supposed, that a tariff based on the principles of that of 1842, and as a whole equally protective, will be sufficient. It is also supposed, that the legislation for the regulation of the currency, shall be ordinarily prudent and effective. A bank, here and there, might fail, from mismanagement, or other cause; but such an event, rarely occurring, could no more disturb or impair the general system, than the failure of a merchant, in the city of New York, could shake the commercial fabric of this great emporium. So long as no foreign commercial balances are accumulating against the country, the specie in it would remain as the basis of the circulating medium, and a part of it. And the small balances in favor of the country, annually accruing, as under the tariff of 1842, showing that the country is selling more than it buys, would gradually enlarge and fortify the basis and body of the currency. It could neither fail, nor be insufficient, nor unsound, any more than a private individual could fail, who has once started strong, and never buys more than he sells, but always sells more than he buys. All the money, and more too, is in the country—is always here; and therefore the currency is always sound, and must remain so. All the talk about overtrading, and about the alternate inflations and contractions of the currency, has arisen entirely from, and only applies to, a state of things, which the want of a protective system brought about. Nothing but bad government can injure trade. It is absurd, because it is a paradox, to suppose that trade will injure itself. Its very nature and essence are to take care of itself. Its instinctive sagacity discerns every peril, and fortifies its position; and there is no power that can injure it, but that of government. All that trade wants from government is a protection of those interests with which trade is connected, and by which it flourishes. It will always take care of itself, and is alone competent for that function.

As to inflations and contractions of the currency, they were all produced by changes in the policy of government. Banking is trading in money, and the same principle of self-preservation controls this branch of trade, as all others. It will not commit suicide, as would be the case, by a voluntary sacrifice of the confidence of the public. It is only the irresistible pressure of a superior power, that of government, which leads to such a result.

All the currency troubles of the country, all bank suspensions, all bank troubles of a serious nature to the wide community, all insufficiency and unsoundness of the circulating medium, and such like, have occurred ONLY in the absence of a protective policy of the government over the commercial interests of the people. *Such is history.* It is, therefore, fair to say, that these troubles came *in consequence* of such defect. If it had been only once, or twice, or three times, the evidence would be less strong. But it has been *many times, without a single exception to the rule.*

§ 4. *The Tax of all these Misfortunes fell on the Business and Labor of the Country.*

That was inevitable from the position they occupied in relation to these calamities. They crushed business, and paralyzed the arm of labor, by depriving it of employment and sustenance. All these misfortunes resolve themselves in making labor the chief victim—a helpless sufferer. It may yet appear, that the government of the United States has undertaken to master a power, which, in its dying agonies, may prove the strongest, and turn on the smiter, to vindicate its rights, with recovered health, vigor, and independence.

CHAPTER XIII.

EFFECTS OF THE PROTECTIVE AND ANTI-PROTECTIVE SYSTEMS OF DUTIES ON FOREIGN COMMERCE, CONTRASTED.

§ 1. *The Farmer who protects himself.*

A FARMER who keeps up good fences, pastures only his own cattle, and keeps his crops from cattle that run at large, so that they can not break in, will be likely to have not only enough for home consumption, but something for market. And if he takes care to sell more than he buys, he will grow rich. If, by such economy, his annual income is greater than his expenses, it is impossible he should fall into bankruptcy; it is impossible he should not increase in wealth. He has then a substantial capital on which to trade, and if he follows up the same principles of economy, in all his business, he will be able to do more and more business, and will become richer and richer. As he grows rich, his wants increase. He will buy more, because he is able to buy, partly for taste, partly for comfort, and partly to augment the value of what he has. It was the tariff of duties which he imposed on himself and his neighbors—with no wrong to them, and certainly with great benefit to himself—it was this tariff, with which he started in life, that has made him a rich man, and able to trade largely with others; and it is the same tariff, continued, that fortifies his position, still increases his wealth, and still extends his business. Such a man can never fail. It is impossible. But let him lay aside these habits of self-protection and economy; let him throw away this tariff; let him begin to buy more than he sells; let his fences go down, and all cattle running at large feed in his pastures and on his crops—does it need a prophet to tell what will become of him?

§ 2. How this Principle applies to a Nation's Foreign Trade.

It is alleged, that the protective policy diminishes foreign commerce. It ought not to be so, according to the above illustration, and facts will show that it is not so. Though there may have been, for a time, larger importations in periods of low duties, or no duties, there was not really more foreign trade, nor in fact so much, as during the periods of protective duties, take those periods, respectively, through and through. Like the well-to-do farmer, who begins to buy more than he sells, and soon gets out of money and out of credit—who does indeed for a little while trade largely, to his own ruin—so has it always been with this country in times of free trade. The moment duties were relaxed, importations increased, and there seemed to be a more active foreign trade. Really, however, there was no more request for navigating craft—nor so much—inasmuch as the additional importations were costly manufactured goods, of little weight. As soon as the country got in debt, lost credit, and was forced to buy less, the navigating craft had less employment, and was much of it hauled off, and laid up. The foreign commerce of the country was injured and diminished. Whereas, under the protective system, in all cases, foreign commerce has been more uniform, uniformly increasing; shipping has had better and more employment, and navigation has rejoiced in its business and profits—never more than for a few years after the tariff of 1824; and never more than under the tariff of 1842. All the boasted increase of foreign trade, under low duties and no duties, has been the ruinous increase of a spendthrift, that brings debt, loss of credit, poverty, want, distress, in its train—beginning with flushed hope, and ending in disappointment.

It appears by the treasury documents, that the aggregate of dutiable imports from 1821 to 1824, inclusive, four years of low duties, were $264,960,000, an average of sixty-six millions annually. The average rate of duty on these articles was about 34 per cent.; and the aggregate revenue for this term of four years, was over ninety millions. By the tariff of 1824, the average duty was raised to 38 per cent.; the aggregate imports of dutiable articles for the first four years, were $301,550,000, being an annual average of about seventy-five millions. It will be seen by these facts, that, with increased duties, there were increased importations, by a difference of nine millions. By the tariff of 1828, the average duty was raised to about 41 per cent., and the amount of dutiable imports for the next four years was $297,330,000, with an annual average of $74,330,000—scarcely varying from the preceding four years. As both periods were under a protective policy, the results ought to be similar. The next nine years, from 1833 to 1841, inclusive, under the compromise tariff, was a very remarkable period of bold and excessive importations, exceeding the exports for that time by about two hundred and thirty-one millions. The population of the country, too, had increased; and if low duties increase foreign trade, it should have been very much augmented during this period, when the average duty, from beginning to end, was about 31 per cent., being 3 per cent. lower than the first, 7 lower than the second, 10 lower than the third, of the abovenamed periods. But what were the facts? The aggregate of dutiable imports for this period of nine years was six hundred and thirty-one millions, giving an annual average of seventy millions against seventy-four millions, when duties were 10 per cent higher. But this does not fully exhibit the difference in the effects of high and low duties on foreign commerce, without considering, that the exports of this period were two hundred and thirty-one millions less than the imports. That makes the difference in the comparative amount of trade, startling. Under the tariff of 1842, it is sufficient to say, that the imports, free of duty, fell off from thirty millions in 1842, to twenty-two millions in 1845—the fall having been gradual—and those paying duty (commonly stated at an average of 40 per cent., whereas the average duty of the tariff of 1842 was only 34.64 per cent.), rose from sixty-nine millions in 1842, to ninety-five millions in 1845; and that the revenue from duties which had descended to less than thirteen millions in the last year of the compromise tariff, rose to an annual average of over twenty-six millions, under the tariff of 1842. The facts, that during this period, the amount of imports free of duty decreased, and those paying duty under a well-adjusted system of protection, continued to increase in amount, relatively and positively, take the period as a whole, and doubling the revenue, are conclusive as to the effects of protective and anti-protective duties on commerce and revenue. The inference is fair, that protection gave the people the ability to purchase the protected articles, which they got cheaper in consequence of competition between home and foreign producers, benefiting themselves as consumers, benefiting labor by giving it employment and good wages, benefiting commerce and navigation, benefiting the country, on the largest and most comprehensive scale, and benefiting the government, by paying its debts, restoring its credit, and filling its treasury.

But there is another class of facts bearing on this question, also derived from the treasury documents. In 1840, when free-trade had brought down the country to the lowest depths of commercial ruin, still running down, the total tonnage of the United States amounted to 2,180,764 tons; in 1841, to 2,130,744; and in 1842, to 2,092,300, showing a falling off in three years, before the passage of the tariff of 1842, of 88,464 tons, instead of a gradual increase as it ought to have been. After the enactment of the tariff of 1842, the tonnage rose, in 1843, to 2,158,601 tons; in 1844, to 2,280,095; and in 1845, to 2,417,002, being a gain in three years, under the tariff of 1842, of 258,401 tons. The tonnage built in the United States, in 1845, was greater by 28,000 tons than the average of the three preceding years, showing an increasing demand.

From the same official records, it appears that the tonnage which entered the ports of the United States, and cleared, in 1841, was 4,639,458 tons; and in 1842, when the duties were down to the lowest ebb, 4,519,841 tons. But in 1844, two years after the passage of the tariff of 1842, it had risen to 5,812,168, and in 1845, to 5,930,303. These figures show a falling off from 1841 to 1842, when duties were lowest, of 219,617 tons, and an increase, in one year, from 1844 to 1845, under what are called high duties, of 118,135 tons. The tonnage which entered and cleared in 1845, was 1,410,462 tons more than in 1842, before the tariff of that year, dated August 30, had begun to take effect. It is unnecessary to go farther into the shipping and tonnage statistics—all of which lead to the same result—to demonstrate, that a system of low duties is injurious to the foreign trade of the country, and to its navigating interests; and that a system of protective duties is beneficial—highly so.

A system of low duties, besides lessening foreign commerce, tends to take what there is out of the hands of Americans, and put it into the hands of foreigners. It is stated by Mr. Hudson, that, in 1842, at the lowest duties of the compromise act, and before the tariff of that year went into effect, 74 per cent. of the imports into the city of New York, and 19 per cent. of those into Boston, were on foreign account; and foreigners, of course, had all the profits; whereas, in 1845, from the same source of evidence, it appears that by the operation of the tariff of 1842, the importing business in New York, on foreign account, had been reduced to 44 per cent. of the whole, and in Boston to 9 per cent.

Illustration: Under the tariff of 1842, American boot and shoe makers were protected, giving rise to large importations of hides—a heavy article—which, in 1845, amounted to near *four millions of dollars*, giving employment to American shipping, as well as to American boot and shoe makers. This one fact will illustrate scores of other like cases, which operated in the same way under the tariff of 1842, giving, at the same time, employment to American shipping, and to American labor. It is the raw material that makes freight. Manufactured goods make little. It may be well to remark, however, in this place, that our exports of boots and shoes, under the tariff of 1842, had risen, in 1845, to the amount of $330,000, and the exports of articles of American manufactures, of the same year, to about $12,000,000, being more than one tenth of all our exports, also augmenting foreign trade in the best way possible, substituting exports of our own products for imports of foreign and for re-exportations of foreign.

But beside statistical evidence, it stands to reason, that a protective system will give, not only a better, but a more extended, more comprehensive, larger, and more diversified foreign commerce, than a free trade system. Look to the case of the farmer, in the first section of this chapter, who takes care of his home interests. Is he not able to buy and trade more, than if he had neglected his system of economy? Free trade makes a nation poor—especially the United States—as has been shown. How can a poor man, or a poor nation, *buy*? The protective system makes a nation rich—none more than the United States. It makes the people rich. It gives to every man the ability to purchase foreign luxuries. When a man grows rich, he has new wants, and those wants must be satisfied. When a nation grows rich, its wants will comprehend the productions of all parts of the globe, will increase in number, and in the aggregate, and in the same proportion will enlarge its foreign commerce. Go to Lowell, Mass., and see what ranges, what whole streets of stores, full of foreign luxuries, and foreign products, are required to satisfy the wants of the ten thousand operatives in the manufactories of that city, and of the other population connected with them; and let it be remembered, that they are not only able to buy them, but to grow rich on their wages.

From this cause the importations of cotton goods, of the finer sorts, paying the highest duties, were augmented, under the tariff of 1842, and for three years, ranged from 10 to 13 *millions*. The operatives of Lowell support a savings bank in that city by their deposites, and many of them become stockholders, and even corporators in the establishments where they work. In one company, $100,000 of the stock is owned by operatives; in another $60,000; and so on.

Lowell, in these particulars, is but a picture of the whole country under the protective system. The people were all well off, and were able to indulge in foreign luxuries, and to gratify a thousand wants, which could only be supplied by foreign commerce.

§ 3. *Foreign Commerce, under a Protective System, may be made to supply all the Wants of the Government, in a Time of Peace, without taxing the People.*

That it may be made to supply all the wants of the government, in a time of peace, is proved by the tariff of 1824, 1828, 1832, and 1842; and that it will not tax the people, is proved from the fact, already established in these pages, that protective duties are not only not taxes at home, but that they are a rescue from an enormous system of foreign taxation. These points being established—as they are beyond controversy—it is clear, that a protective system, properly adjusted, without imposing duties on foreign articles that can not be produced at home, might be made to supply all the wants of government, in a time of peace; and therefore, without taxation, since protective duties are not taxes.

Much more than this is probably true—though it can not be asserted with so much confidence—viz., that a protective system, without imposing duties on articles which can not be produced at home—except, perhaps, some luxuries, and other articles not indispensable to the poorer classes—might be so adjusted, as to liquidate a very heavy national debt, in addition to defraying the ordinary expenses of government—all, of course, without a tax upon the masses, since protective duties are not taxes. Such are the resources of the country, such the amount of its home products and home trade, and such the ingenuity, skill, industry, enterprise, and physical ability, of the people, that, under an adequate system of protection, there are no assignable limits to the possible increase of the general wealth, or to the ability of the people to consume foreign products, subject to protective duties. Protect the people, let them grow rich, and they will buy largely from abroad, to raise an indefinite amount of revenue—enough, probably, to meet any future contingent wants of the government, even though the war with Mexico should cost one or two hundred millions—all, of course, for the reasons before stated, without a tax, in any form, direct, or indirect, since protective duties are not taxes.

§ 4. *Foreign Commerce, under a System of Low Duties, not amounting to Protection, ruinous to the Country; but under a Protective System, highly beneficial.*

The most important view of foreign commerce, under the two systems, respectively, of low anti-protective and protective duties, remains to be considered. It is this :—that the former system leads directly and uniformly to excessive importations, or excessive buying, leaving a balance against the country, to be settled by drawing away its money, and leaving the people without a currency. It was so under the colonial system ;—the money all went to England. It was so under the confederation : the money all went abroad, chiefly to England, to settle balances, because we bought more than we sold. The states, severally, then, possessed the only power to establish a protective policy, each for itself; and being unable to do it, without collision of interests, it resulted in a system of *perfect free trade*, and of complete commercial ruin. It appears, by Mr. Secretary Woodbury's annual report to Congress, of 1840, that the imports into the country, for the first two years after the peace of 1814, exceeded the exports by $126,466,059. How could the country pay such a balance, already deeply in debt as it was, when, in its best estate, there was not half so much money in the country ? The tariff of 1816, in its most important protective provisions, defective at best, and of a brief term, did but little toward the settlement of the immense balance that had previously accumulated against the country; and by the failure of the tariff of 1820, the country was doomed to run on again, under a system of low anti-protective duties, till the tariff of 1824 arrested it. According to Mr. Secretary Woodbury's report to Congress, in 1840, the balance of foreign trade against the country for 1815, was sixty-one millions of dollars; in 1816, it was sixty-five millions; in 1817, twelve millions; in 1818, more than twenty-eight millions; in 1819, seventeen millions; in 1820, about five millions; in 1821, two millions in our favor; in 1822, eleven millions against us; in 1823, about three millions against us; and in 1824, nearly five millions.

What country could stand up against such odds ? And all this in uninterrupted succession, without any chance to pay. The nation writhed and groaned under it. Its money gone abroad to pay debts; banks suspended ; the circulating medium become scarce, nobody knowing what it was worth, for it was irredeemable ; business of all kinds, in trouble; property of every description depreciated ; and labor unemployed and starving. Who that is old enough to remember those years, will not certify to Mr. Clay's picture of them cited in a preceding chapter, as " exhibiting a scene of the most wide-spread dismay and devastation" ?

3   185

But, from the date of the tariff of 1824, when the protective policy was for the first time, in the history of the country, well established, and from which time it continued till the duties went down again under the compromise act of 1833, the prosperity of the country was restored; labor found employment and reward; private and public wealth increased; the entire national debt of *one hundred and sixty millions of dollars*, left at the end of the war of 1812, was at last paid off in 1836, and *thirty-seven millions* of surplus funds in the national treasury were distributed among the states !

But, behold the contrast, as the duties under the compromise act descended below the protective standard, and approximated toward a system of free trade, till finally they came down to a maximum of 20 per cent. The excessive importations commenced as soon as President Jackson began to show his hostility to the protective policy, and continued down through the administration of Mr. Van Buren, who " followed in the footsteps of his illustrious predecessor." The balance accumulated against the country in its foreign trade, in nine successive years under General Jackson and Mr. Van Buren—including three of the latter's administration—according to the records of the treasury department, was more than two hundred and fifty millions of dollars ! The largest balance was in 1836, being sixty-one millions. The next largest was fifty-nine millions, in 1839; the next in comparative magnitude, was twenty-eight millions, in 1835; twenty-three millions, in 1837; twenty-two, in 1834; and so on. Nor is this all. It appears, by Fisher's National Magazine, for August, 1845, p. 279, that, for fifteen years, from 1830 to 1844, inclusive, the unenumerated articles of imports amounted to *one hundred and fifty millions of dollars*, being an average of ten millions a year, which, fairly, should be added to the above balances. That these balances were real, and not fictitious, is proved from the fact, that, at the end of this disastrous period, the foreign debts of the country, actually ascertained, were found to be upward of two hundred millions of dollars, most of them public. The state debts— most of them abroad—were reported to Congress by the secretary of the treasury, in 1842, as $200,855,793 ! A vast amount of other foreign debts, no small fraction of them private, and paid by bankruptcy, were unascertainable, swelling the aggregate much above the common estimate. " A Southern Planter," in his " Notes on Political Economy," estimates the foreign debt of the people and states of the Union at *four hundred and fifty millions*, viz., two hundred millions of state debts; two hundred millions of bank, and corporation, and national stocks ; and fifty millions of private debts—all owned abroad—drawing the interest annually from the country, for all that bankruptcy and repudiation has not kept back. He says, " it is enough to weigh down our industry for the next fifty years."

Here, then, is another result of a protracted period of low, anti-protective duties—a result of stupendous magnitude, impoverishing the people, the country, and the government, till neither had credit abroad, or at home, and till all were plunged in one common ruin. Who does not know this ? Who could ever forget it ? And will any one arraign the assigned cause as questionable, when he always finds the same results after the same antecedents ?

And behold the effects of the protective duties of the tariff of 1842. The balance of trade instantly whirls about, and is in favor of the country; twenty millions of specie return in one year, in excess of the exports of it; private and public prosperity is revived; business and credit revive; labor everywhere finds employment, and meets with a satisfactory compensation; the ruin of many years is repaired in four : all are prosperous, all happy, all satisfied, and the nation is advancing with rapid strides, in wealth, greatness, and strength. Will any one doubt what is the cause ?

The Hon. Simon Cameron, " democratic" senator, from the " democratic" state of Pennsylvania, said in his speech " on the reduction of the tariff of 1842," July 22, 1846 :—

" The individual cases of distress, which pervaded the country for a period preceding the law of 1842, were absolutely heartrending. Rich men not only lost their fortunes, but poor men lost their means of living. Our furnaces, and our forges, and our workshops, were emptied; our merchants were ruined ; and our farmers, our substantial yeomanry, many of them with abundance of products, for want of a market, found themselves in the hands of the sheriff. Not a section of the whole country but afforded abundant evidence of the truth of this picture. . . . I remember, and you, Mr. President [Dallas], doubtless know, that, in the organization of a new court in Philadelphia, there were over 500 applicants for the place of a *tip-stave !* Healthy, vigorous men sought this station, to get bread for their families ! . . . Do gentlemen desire these scenes renewed ? Will men never learn wisdom by experience ? How is it now [under the tariff of 1842] ? How changed the scene ! If a magician's wand had been waved over our country, the result would hardly have appeared more like enchantment, than the reality now before us. No man is idle who is willing to work. Contented, smiling faces are everywhere to be seen. The busy hum of industry gladdens the ear in all directions. Everybody is prosperous, and everybody happy."

CHAPTER XIV.

IMPORTANCE OF THE HOME TRADE.

If the aggregate annual product of the Union, of all kinds, be estimated at $2,000,000,000 —it was that in 1840, as appears by senate document, No. 340, 2d session 27th Congress— and if the average annual export of the same be $80,000,000, allowing $20,000,000 for re-exportation of imports, which is about the average for twenty-five years past—it will be seen, that only about *one twenty-fifth* of the entire product leaves the country, and that the rest is consumed or used at home. As there are no certain data by which to determine what portion of this is the subject of home trade, it may, perhaps, be safely put at $1,000,000,000, less or more. The amount, then, is more than ten to one of that which is the subject of foreign trade. Its comparative importance, however, is indefinitely, but vastly greater, than would be represented by this difference. That which is exported, is the subject of one com-mercial transaction, but ever after dead to the country. A large portion of that which re-mains, enters into the substantial capital of the country, and becomes reproductive, in end-less progression, and by a ratio not exceeded by the geometrical. Foreign trade, as before seen, may and will injure the country, if not carefully guarded by a protective system. Do-mestic trade can never injure, is always beneficial. The more of it, and the more active, so much the better. Foreign trade, as a whole for a nation, is always a delicate operation, and for the benefit of any country, should be so regulated, as not to buy more than is sold, taking all that goes and comes into consideration; and the sales ought to be something in excess. Whether they can be too much in excess, is perhaps a question. There is a natural limit. In Great Britain the average annual balance in favor of home, is upward of two hundred millions of dollars. This does not all appear from the usual display of her exports and im-ports. It comes in other ways; and if it comes, it is no matter how. Great Britain is the great capitalist of the world—owes nobody but herself, and everybody owes her, and must at least pay interest, as we do—*except what is repudiated.* Her subsidies, and compensa-tions, extorted from vanquished nations, is one great item. For the last fifty years she has been perpetually draining the heretofore richest portion of the world—the East—where gold was piled up in heaps, and silver was as stones. Was not China beaten, and forced to pay? —the Seikhs, and forced to pay? The national debt of Great Britain, all owned at home, is no otherwise a difficulty with the government, than the financial task of raising more money to pay interest. The nation, as a whole, is no poorer on that account. In the United States, under the tariff of 1842, the balance in our favor had got to be some six or seven millions average—just enough to save us from commercial bankruptcy in foreign trade.

But, in domestic trade, there is no such delicacy—no such danger. The more work there is done on an estate, the better; and the United States is only a large estate. Our home trade is, and must for ever be, the basis of our fortunes. In foreign trade, we have almost always been losers, and the loss, as before seen, has been immense. Individuals have prof-ited, at the expense of the public. Hence the seductions of foreign traffic, and the necessity of taking care of it, that the state receive no damage. The branches of foreign commerce are like the tenders of a fleet, the scouting parties of an army, the roving agents of a great commercial house; if licensed with privileges, care should be taken, that they *serve*, not *in-jure*, the main bodies. Every merchant in the foreign trade, sails under the flag of his country. It is loaned to him, protects him, secures to him all his benefits. Besides being a merchant, wherever he goes beyond the bounds of his country, he is a public political agent. Mr. Laing, an eminent British authority, says :—

"In every country, the home market is the great and steady basis of its prosperity. Commerce itself, if it be not founded on home comsumption—if it be merely a carrying trade between distant producers and distant consumers, has proved itself, as in the Hanse-Towns, in Genoa, Venice, and Holland, to be unstable, evanescent, and unattended with any well being and improvement in the condition of the mass of the people. The export trade is but the overflowings of the cup of our in-dustrial production. Its fulness is all within its own rim."

The "Southern Planter" says :—

"Commerce has as deep an interest in securing the home market and supply as manufacturers can have. Commerce has no patriotism in it, when based upon foreign supplies. All its profits are inci-dental, and have reference to its basis and support. Like the light of a satellite, the profits of com-merce are borrowed and reflected, not inherent as the centre sun of business—not creative, as the producers are."

The coasting trade, as appears from official documents, amounts to about half the tonnage of the country. And when the short and frequent voyages of this part of our commercial craft are considered, as compared with the part engaged in foreign commerce, the business it does in the home trade must be many times greater than the foreign. From the official records of Massachusetts, it appears, as stated by Mr. Hudson in his speech in Congress, June 29, 1846, from whom many of our facts are derived :—

" That the number of vessels which entered the port of Boston, alone, in 1845, from other ports of the United States, beyond the bounds of Massachusetts—not counting fishing-craft, nor the wood, lumber, and hay coasters from Maine—was 5,481, with an aggregate of 900,620 tons, or nine tenth's of all the registered tonnage of the country. Of these, 170 were from New Orleans, 39 from Mobile, and 35 from Florida—making 244 from the Gulf of Mexico. These 244 vessels, with a register of 118,600 tons, brought into the city of Boston, from the quarters mentioned, cotton, flour, corn, hemp, hides, feathers, lead, beef, pork, ham, lard, sugar, molasses, staves, tallow, wood, and tobacco, to the amount of $9,500,000—not to speak of grass-seed, castor-oil, linseed-oil, beeswax, furs, peltry, beans, peas, wheat, cornmeal, whiskey, buffalo-robes, copper, iron, leather, butter, and a great variety of other articles of domestic growth, amounting to millions. This includes only the freight from the gulf to Boston. If we add the freight from Boston to the gulf, and all the foreign products which were transported both ways, which are not included in the above estimate, it would amount to more than one fourth of our whole export to all foreign parts. The internal trade which comes to the Atlantic through the Hudson river, is equal to nearly half of our foreign commerce. The freight brought to the Hudson, in 1845, by the Erie and Champlain canals, was valued at $45,454,000, and the amount which entered these canals, at Albany and Troy, amounted to $55,454,000—showing a total of $100,906,000, being more than all exports to foreign nations, for the same year, of the growth or prod-uce of the United States. The transportation on the New York canals, in 1845, was 1,977,565 tons, being but 3 per cent. less than the whole amount of American tonnage which entered our ports the same year, from all foreign ports."

The following extract from an article in Fisher's National Magazine, Sept., 1846, contrib-uted by Lot Clark, Esq., of Lockport, on the New York canals, is pertinent here :—

" The tons of products and merchandise moved on these canals the past year, were 1,977,565 ; the total tonnage, clearing from all the ports of the United States, coasters and all, in the year 1844, as appears from the report of the secretary of the treasury, was 2,010,924 tons ; the difference, only 43,359 tons. The tonnage entering all the ports of the United States was 1,977.438 tons, being twenty-seven tons less than the tons of movement on the canals. If we compare values, the contrast is not less striking. The value of all the products and merchandise carried on the canals the year past, as appears from the trade and tonnage report of the commissioners of the canal fund, was $100,629,859 ; the whole amount of all the exports of products and merchandise from the United States, as appears by the secretary's report for the year 1844, was $99,715,179 ; difference in favor of canal commerce, $914,680. Again, if we compare the tons moved on the canals with the tonnage entering and arri-ving at the port of New York, from and to all parts, we find how much greater is the canal naviga-tion : In 1844, the tonnage cleared from New York, foreign and domestic, was 498,254 tons ; and of all that entered that port, was 576,480 tons ; total, 1,074,734 tons ; being in all, 902,831 tons less than was carried on the canals. Again, the total value of all the exports from the city of New York, clearing from that port in 1844, to all places, was $32,891,540, while the value of the products carried to the tidewater on the canals the past year, was $45,452,321 ; so that whatever comparison you institute, you find that this internal navigation is by far the greatest interest of the state."

The commercial craft employed on the lakes is 100,000 tons, a sufficient evidence of the great amount of trade carried on over the bosom of these inland seas. The imports and exports of Cleveland, in 1844, amounted to $11,195,703. The tonnage of the Mississippi and its tributaries is estimated at 160,000 tons. The freight downward to New Orleans, in 1845, was estimated at $60,000,000. It is supposed that the upward freight could not be less—in all, $120,000,000. But it is found that the trade done at intermediate places be-tween the extreme points of any long internal line, by land or water, is greater than the through trade ; and the entire annual commerce of the Mississippi and its tributaries, is stated, in Fisher's National Magazine, at the value of $225,000,000.

To have a just idea of the short-route trade, constantly going on, one has only to observe the active movement of the people throughout the country, on errands of business. Nearly all this activity is trade. Bargains, or exchanges, all which are trade, are constantly going on between neighbors, for reciprocal benefit. It is stated in the National Magazine, that " on the Erie canal, for a number of years after it was finished, for the whole distance between Albany and Buffalo, the amount of merchandise carried through, was only about 2½ per cent. of the whole." The same, or like, is alleged of the passenger trade on the Hud-son. From every point of the United States, where there are people, more start on business for five miles than for ten ; more for ten than for twenty ; more for twenty than fifty ; and so on. This shows, that the great amount of home-trade is imperceptible and incalculable.

It can not but be seen, that this internal and coasting trade—of which the abovecited facts are only very limited and restricted examples—running on lines which cross each other at all points, making a complete net-work of the whole land, to facilitate exchanges, must be vastly comprehensive, and not less important.

The Hon. Abbott Lawrence, in a letter to the Hon. Wm. C. Rives, of Virginia, dated Boston, January 16, 1846, says : " We," of Massachusetts, " previous to the war of 1812, were an agricultural and navigating people. The American system [the protective policy] was forced upon us, and was adopted for the purpose of creating a home-market for the prod-ucts of the soil of the south and west. We resisted the adoption of a system, which, we honestly believed, would greatly injure our navigation, and drive us from our accustomed employments, into a business we did not understand. We came into it, however, reluc-tantly, and soon learned, that, with the transfer of our capital we acquired skill and knowledge in the use of it; *and that, so far from our foreign commerce being diminished, it was increased; and that our domestic tonnage and commerce were very soon more than* QUADRUPLED."

CHAPTER XV.

A NEW DISCOVERY.

IT is remarkable how time and inquiry bring forth new things, which are in fact only old truths. All that is new in such cases, is the discovery, the perception of the truth. It is sometimes said that society is indebted to the advent of a genius for these useful lessons, or facts, or newly-seen verities; and that one is enough to signalize an age, or a century. Be it what is commonly called genius or not, these surprising developments often come from unexpected, humble sources, and are the result of unpretending, plodding industry—of patient investigation.

William Brown, Esq., an English merchant, and a landholder, who was a leader of the anti-corn-law league, and devoted to free trade, as he calls it—though when his views are scrutinized, they do not tally with the common notions of free trade—arrived, in his sober, plain way of thinking, as a matter-of-fact man, to the discovery of a very important, practical truth, in political economy, which, indeed, had never been concealed. It might, perhaps, more properly be said, that he reduced it to form. With him it was all incidental, and he was aiming at a very different thing, viz., to reconcile John Rolf, Esq., a landholder, to the abolition of the corn laws, by showing him, first, that what he would lose in prices of corn, would be made up in the prices of other agricultural products; and secondly, that, in fact, he would ultimately find himself indemnified in the article of corn itself. No matter about the correctness of Mr. Brown, in these views, for our present purpose. In his way to his end, he dwells strongly on an obvious truth, viz., *that British agricultural products incorporate themselves with British manufactures, and go forth to all the world, in that form, to market.* As much as to say to John Rolf, Esq., "Sustain us in this enterprise for the benefit of the British manufacturing interest, and you will be yourself sustained. British manufactures can not go to market, except they carry along British agricultural products; and for the most part, we shall not be indebted to foreigners for corn." The following are some of his expressions, in his letter to Mr. Rolf:—

"In sending you my remarks on your Aversham speech, I wrote to you not only in the character of a merchant, who has had transactions all over the world, but in that of a landed proprietor, who, in common with other gentlemen interested in the soil, is desirous to support the rent rolls. . . .

I presume it will not be denied, that all interests in this kingdom, are so linked together, that none of them can suffer without others being injured. We must sink or swim together. Paradoxical as it may appear, *I think Great Britain is the largest grain-exporting country in the world,* although it is impossible to estimate accurately what quantity of grain, &c., is consumed in preparing £50,000,000 [$242.000.000] value of exports, by which you so greatly profit. *It is placed in the laboratory of that wonderful intellectual machine, man, which gives him the physical power, aided by steam, of converting it into broadcloth, calico, hardware, &c., and in these shapes, your wheats find their way to every country in the world.* Within this century, this county alone has had use for 1.500,000 more manufacturers, merchants, and those depending on trade, than at any previous period. These aided and assisted by our natural advantages, have found foreign markets for you everywhere. On the other hand, your prosperity is very important to the merchants and manufacturers, for they must cease to make and export goods, *or to be able to use the agricultural produce of the country*. unless they can find purchasers for their returns. . . Can anything be more clear, than that it is the interest of the manufacturers and merchants, that all landlords, farmers, laborers, &c., should be sustained, and made more affluent, by which they may become more extensive customers, *enabling* the merchants to increase their importations. Be assured, the great movers in the league. *are quite aware of this, and have these objects steadily in view*. . . . You fear dependence on foreigners. We are now dependent on foreigners, *for using your wheat in the shape of broadcloths, &c., and I wish we were more so*. . . . If wheat, the most convenient article of transport, is a little cheaper, other articles of agricultural produce would advance under a prosperous trade. Any wheat that would come here, would only help to keep at home our 100.000 *human machines* [emigrants], and sustain our 400,000 annual increase, and again be sent away *in the shape of the products of our industry*. . . . The fact is, instead of keeping our own people at home, to manufacture for the rest of the world, *and be your best customers at your own door, for the products of the soil,* our anti-commercial policy is forcing them to emigrate, to seek work elsewhere; *and other nations are employing their hands to do what we could have done better for them, and at a lower price*. . . . Nor need you be afraid of the United States. Their population is increasing still more rapidly than that of Europe, and their growth of wheat is not excessive. In 1844, it was under 12,000,000 of quarters. You are aware that our growth of wheat, is estimated at 18,000,000. I am afraid we could not get a very large supply of Indian corn —which is very desirable to feed your winter cattle—as the bulk, compared with value, would make it a very expensive article of import. . . . With the advantages we have in climate, capital, security of property, intelligence, machinery, improved agricultural implements, and above all, in the in-

creased and cheap supply of the moving power, coal, we can afford to give [you] higher prices for agricultural products, to sustain the rent-rolls of the landlords, and maintain England as the most powerful and prosperous kingdom, *and the principal work-shop of the world.*
"Richmond Hill, Liverpool." "WILLIAM BROWN.
(See the entire letter, in Fisher's National Magazine, January, 1846.)

It will be seen, that the plan of the "League," was all for England, for British manufacturers, and for British commerce; and that it did not propose to injure British agriculture, but to open and secure for it a wider market, *in the form of manufactured exports.* Nobody will be surprised at the great truth, reduced to form by Mr. Brown, so instructive to all nations, especially to the people of the United States, viz., *that agricultural products, to such a large extent, enter into manufactured goods, and go forth with them to market, in an occult form;* but all will rather wonder, that it had not before been more distinctly seen, and more fully appreciated, as it is so eminently practical in the political economy of all nations. Impressed with this great idea, the Hon. Mr. Stewart, of Pennsylvania, in his speech on the protective policy, May 27, 1846, employed it with irresistible effect :—

"With all the protection we now enjoy" [under the tariff of 1842], said Mr. Stewart, "Great Britain sends into this country *eight dollars' worth* of her agricultural productions to *one dollar's worth* of all our agricultural productions, save cotton and tobacco, that she takes from us. I assert, and can prove, that more than half the value of all the British merchandise imported into this country, *consists of agricultural products, changed in form, converted and manufactured into goods.* Take down all the articles in a store, one after another; estimate the value of the raw material, the bread and meat, and other agricultural products which have entered into their fabrication; and it will be found, that one half and more of their value consists of the productions of the soil—agricultural produce in its strictest sense. By reference to Mr. Walker's report, it will be seen, that, for twelve years back, we have imported from Great Britain and her dependencies annually 52½ millions of dollars worth of goods—call it 50 millions—while she took of all our agricultural products, save cotton and tobacco, less than *two and a half* millions of dollars worth. Thus, then, assuming one half the value of her goods to be agricultural, it gives us $25,000,000 of her agricultural produce to $2,500,000 of ours taken by her, which is just *ten to one;* to avoid cavil, put it at *eight to one.* . . . We have imported yearly, for twenty-six years—so says Mr. Walker's report—more than 10 millions of dollars worth of *woollen goods.* Last year we imported $10,666,176 worth. Now. one half and more of this cloth was made up of wool, the product of labor and agriculture. The general estimate is, that the wool alone is half. The universal custom among farmers, when they had their wool manufactured on shares, was to give the manufacturer half the cloth. Thus we import, and our people have to pay, for *five* millions of dollars worth of foreign wool, mostly the product of sheep feeding on the grass and grain of Great Britain, to the prejudice of the market for our own wool; and this is the policy gentlemen recommend to our farmers! Yes, sir; and not satisfied with *five* millions, they wish to increase it to *ten* millions a year for foreign wool. Will gentlemen deny this? They dare not. They supported Mr. Walker's bill, reducing the duties on woollens nearly one half, with a view to *increase* the revenue. Of course, the imports must be doubled, making the import of cloth *twenty* millions instead of *ten,* and of wool *ten* instead of *five* millions of dollars per annum. . . . What is true of cloth is equally true of everything else. Take a hat, a pair of shoes, a yard of silk or lace, analyze it, resolve it into its constituent elements, and you will find that the raw material, and the substance of labor, and other agricultural products, constitute more than one half of its entire value. The pauper labor of Europe employed in manufacturing silk and lace, gets what it eats, no more; and this is what you pay for, when you purchase their goods. The article of iron is a stronger case. Last year, according to Mr. Walker's report, we imported $9,043,396 worth of foreign iron and its manufactures, mostly from Great Britain, *four fifths* of the value of which, as every practical man knows, consist of agricultural produce—nothing else. What gives its value? The labor of horses, oxen, mules, and men. And what sustained this labor, but corn, oats, hay, and straw, for the one; and bread, meat, and vegetables of every kind, for the other? These agricultural products are purchased and consumed, and make up nearly the whole price of the iron, which the manufacturer receives and pays over to the farmers again and again, as often as the process is repeated. Is not iron made in England of the same materials that it is made of here? Certainly. Then is not *four fifths* of the value of British iron made up of British agricultural produce? And if we purchase nine millions of dollars worth of British iron a year, do we not pay six or seven millions of this sum for the produce of British farmers—grain, hay, grass, bread, meat, and other provisions for man and beast—sent here for sale *in the form of iron?* . . . Mr. Secretary Walker informs us, that the present duty on iron is 75 per cent., which he proposes to reduce to 30 per cent. [which is the duty of the tariff of 1846], *to increase the revenue.* To do this, must he not then double [more than double] the imports of iron? Surely he must. Then we must add 10 or 12 millions a year to our present imports of iron, and of course destroy that amount of our domestic supply to make room for it. Thus, at a blow, in the single article of iron, this bill is intended to destroy the American market for at least *eight millions of dollars* worth of domestic agricultural produce, to be supplied from abroad!"

Every American laborer will be able to apply this great truth, stated by Mr. Brown, the English merchant, and so forcibly illustrated by Mr. Stewart, to his own case, whatever American product he may be interested in, the rights of which are thus menaced, and actually invaded by the tariff of 1846.

A writer in the "Economist," the London Free Trade Journal, of December, 1845, says:

"Manchester, Birmingham, and Leeds, are the great merchants, who buy up the duke of Buckingham's wheat at 55s. per quarter, pay a bounty of 20s. with it, and then sell it abroad at 35s. per quarter. In fact, it is the *foreigner* who pays the farm laborer and the landlord's rent—and if the

Chinamen, and the *Yankees*, and the Germans, were to stop payment, what would become of mortgages and daughters' settlements ?"

Is not this cool, not to say impudent, for an English free-trader to insult the world with such a notice ? It is the "*Yankees*," then, who redeem their mortgages and furnish the daughters of the English landlords with settlements, by consuming their agricultural products, in the form of manufactured goods !

There is another form in which this truth may be stated, which is, perhaps, even more forcible than that in which it is presented above—at least more comprehensive, because it covers the whole, or nearly the whole, instead of a fraction of the importations of foreign products, manufactured, or other, that might be produced at home. It is not only true, as above demonstrated, that we import the agricultural products of foreign countries, in large amounts, in the form of manufactured goods; *but we import labor in the same disguise*, which comprehends nearly or quite the whole cost of the articles; for what was the raw material, before the hand of labor touched it ? Did not labor impart to it all its value, as it comes to us ? And if the raw material emanated from us, as in the case of cotton, even then we import labor to the amount of four, five, and six times the cost of the raw product, according to the kind and quality of the article. In all such cases, the thing which we import is practically *labor in a disguised form*. Is it said to be cheaper ? And is that the reason why we import it ? The thing we import, then, is *cheap labor;* and the reason is, *because* it is cheap ! American labor, then, can no longer be ignorant. There it stands, with its hands folded, in the full sun-light of its position, thrust from employment, by the importation of *cheap foreign labor !* Or it must sell itself at the same price ! And a little lower ! Is it not so ? There is nothing imported but labor. That comprehends the whole. Is American labor prepared to yield to such an invasion of its rights ?—To be driven from the field ?

CHAPTER XVI.

MR. SECRETARY WALKER'S MISTAKES.

§ 1. *A Mistake of some years standing—not Mr. Walker's.*

As matters go on, in the administration of the government of the United States, the utterances of the secretary of the treasury, in his report on the finances, are of course to be regarded as the echoes of the mind and will of the president; though, by the constitution and laws, the secretary is an agent of Congress, accountable to that body alone, should act in harmony with his legitimate masters, and in obedience to their instructions. This incongruity was established in 1833, when the president took charge of the treasury. As the report of the secretary of the treasury, of December 3, 1845, was made the basis of the tariff of 1846, in accordance with the views of the president (it is an echo of the message), an examination of the principles of the report will determine those of the new law.

§ 2. *The Revenue Standard.*

" Revenue !" " Revenue !" " Give us revenue !" This is a new sound in American ears, coming from the government, and savors of a regal taste. What do kings and despots want but " revenue" ? Is government a question of "revenue" ? Or, is it a question of the country's welfare ? It would be a sad mistake, however, if they who evince such an appetite for " revenue," should, in their eagerness to acquire more, get less. The Hon. Silas Wright made a speech in the senate against the tariff of 1842, but voted for it, because, he said, high duties were necessary for an adequate revenue. Now, the plan is, low duties, to get a high revenue !

But Mr. Walker has made a discovery, to wit, that imposts laid for any other purpose than revenue are unconstitutional. He says : " The whole power to collect taxes, whether direct or indirect, is conferred by the same clause of the constitution. The words are : ' The Congress shall have power to lay and collect taxes, duties, imposts, and excises.' " Assuming, first, that " taxes" are identical with " duties and imposts;" next, that all duties are taxes; thirdly, that protective duties are either partially or entirely prohibitory; fourthly, that power is identical with duty, that is, a " power to collect," means, *shall* collect; and fifthly, that a tariff of duties on imports is a mode of taxation for revenue *prescribed* by the constitution;—with such a string of assumptions—the honorable secretary arrives, with self-plumed honors on, to the logical achievement, that protective duties are unconstitutional. First, because protection is not authorized by that instrument. Next, because, if it were, when the duty amounts to prohibition, as it sometimes does, the duty can not be *collected;* or to a partial prohibition, as at least it must, a *part* of it can not be collected. Hence, none but duties imposed expressly, and only, for revenue, can be constitutional.

It must be evident, that if either of the abovenamed assumptions—the validity of all of

191

which is necessary to the conclusion—fails, the conclusion is foreclosed. Unfortunately for the secretary, the first requires proof, and is open to disproof; the second is disproved; the third is of no consequence; the fourth is an absurdity; and the fifth requires proof.

To assume that " duties and imposts" are identical with " taxes," or that the same thing is meant by the former as by the latter, amounts to an accusation of superfluity of language, in this concise and comprehensive document. The constitution manifestly names " duties and imposts" as a different sort of thing from "taxes"—as occupying their own peculiar position, and as discharging their own appropriate functions, as in fact they do, in political economy. They may be taxes; they may not be; they certainly are not always. It has been proved, that protective duties are rarely taxes—never as a whole; and that, as a system, they operate quite the other way. If it be asked, why, then, are the two words, " duties and imposts," used here ? The answer is, because they do not always mean the same thing. Though duties are imposts, prohibitory imposts are not duties, in the strict meaning of terms, because, in such a case, there being no entries, there can be no duties to discharge.

The second assumption is answered by the evidence in a former chapter, that protective duties are not taxes. The third is granted, but is of no consequence, while the others fail. It need not be said, that the fourth is a manifest absurdity. As to the fifth, it may be remarked, that a tariff is *not prescribed* in the constitution as a mode of raising revenue; next, that the design of a tariff, in all nations, and in all cases, is to regulate foreign commerce so as to protect the interests of the state and of the people, in foreign trade; thirdly, and consequently, that the revenue functions of a tariff are *incidental*, not primary, or necessarily inherent. If, in accomplishing the original and main design of a tariff, revenue can be raised, it is well; but it is *incidental*. If a sufficient revenue can be raised, and direct taxation avoided, so much the better. Still, this incidental result does not change the original design and character of the measure. No one will pretend that drawbacks and bounties are any part of a revenue measure, though they may be a very important part of a tariff. The whole of the secretary's argument on this point, therefore, is a total failure.

Nothing could exceed the confusion and derangement which the principle of this " revenue-standard" theory, reduced to practice, would occasion to the interests and business of the country, because that rate of duty on a specific article which would raise the most revenue, when imposed, would, almost invariably, by its operation, require to be changed every year—often every six months—to accomplish the same object.

A common error, both of the secretary and of the president, in carrying out their " revenue-standard" theory, seems to have been, in assuming, that every duty on articles of desired home production is protection. This is an important practical error, and has given rise to the false notion of " *incidental* protection," when, in fact, there can be no such thing as *incidental*, that is not *positive*, protection. On this point, the president says, in his message of Dec. 2, 1845: " If Congress levy a duty for revenue, of one per cent., on a given article, it will produce a given amount of money to the treasury, and will *incidentally* and *necessarily* afford protection or advantage to the amount of one per cent., to the home manufacturer of a similar or like article, over the importer." The entire fallacy of this doctrine of " *incidental* protection" will be seen at once, when it is considered, that the ability of the home-producer to *begin* and to *sustain* himself against foreign competition, depends altogether on his having *adequate* and *positive* protection, which is rarely, if ever, as low as one per cent.; may be five, or twenty, or fifty, or one hundred, or two hundred per cent. But he can never begin, and can never sustain himself, till he has a *positive* protection, equal to the ability of the foreign producer to undersell him in his own market. This idea, therefore, of " *incidental* protection" is a perfect fallacy—a *positive deception*. There never was—there never can be any such thing, measured out in the way the president proposes, as if it could be effective for the degree specified, when it fails to be adequate. And yet—strange to say—this phantom is the only basis on which the president and secretary build their scheme of protection for the people ! It is the only protection that is proffered to their hopes in the tariff of 1846 ! The Pennsylvanians are favored with an " *incidental* protection," not of *one*, but of *thirty* per cent., on iron and coal. Is that protection ? So of a vast many interests of the country—an " incidental protection" to their ruin ! Just enough to *miss* it !

§ 3. *Mr. Walker's great Assumption.*

" At least two thirds of the taxes imposed by the present tariff [that of 1842] are paid, not into the treasury, but to the protected classes. The revenue from imports last year exceeded twenty-seven millions of dollars. This, in itself, is a heavy tax; but the whole tax imposed upon the people by the present tariff is not less than *eighty-one millions of dollars* [!]; of which twenty-seven millions are paid to the government upon imports, and fifty-four millions to the protected classes [!], in enhanced prices of similar domestic articles. This estimate is *based upon the position*, that the duty is added to the price of the import, and also of its domestic rival."

This, surely, is not a very small matter for an assumption ! " This estimate is *based upon the position,"* &c. There was at least some prudence in acknowledging this to be an *assumption*. Let us see how this stupendous tax of eighty-one millions a year on the people can be reduced, and the proposition reversed, so as to find a benefit of eighty-one millions, and much more. In the first place, a secretary of the treasury, who made up the tables, should have paid so much respect to his own figures, as to debit some party, and credit another, in this account, with the small item of duties raised on unprotected articles, if it is to be understood that he is making out a bill of cost for protection, as seems to be his drift. Whether that item be one fourth, or one third, or one half, of the twenty-seven millions, is not, perhaps, much matter, since it will be easy enough to find a balance for the remaining fraction of this eighty-one millions, whatever it may be; though a man of figures, like the secretary of the treasury, ought to be exact, as well as accurate—more especially in the footing of so large an account, throwing upon one party an immense burden, and hold another responsible for it.

Prima facie, presumptively, one would think there must be a mistake in this, unless it can be shown, that the more a people are taxed, so much more prosperous, and so much more happy they are. Eighty-one millions of dollars is a heavy tax, in one year, even for twenty millions of people. Can anybody believe it? And they have been prosperous and happy under it, too—never more so, never so much so. Who has felt it? All have had work, good pay, and good living; and what is very remarkable, they have found these very taxed articles—the protected articles—coming into their hands cheaper than before! And by their increased prosperity, under this state of things, they were more able to buy them—more able to indulge in luxuries. Surely, there must be some mistake about this immense tax of eighty-one millions of dollars.

This problem has already been solved in the preceding pages of this work. It is established beyond controversy, that protective duties are NOT taxes. Then what becomes of the secretary's astounding proposition—his *assumption?* But more than this is proved: It is proved, that protective duties, in this country, if carried high enough, rescue the people from an enormous system of foreign taxation. This agrees with facts—with the actual state of the country under the operation of a protective system, and with the experience of the whole people; whereas, Mr. Secretary Walker's theory—for it is a mere theory—is contradicted by all facts, and no reflecting man can pay the least respect to it. The entire edifice of his report, and the tariff of 1846, are built on this *groundless assumption!*

§ 4. *Minimum Duties.*

The rule of minimum duties is, that a given quality of goods, valued at or below a given price, shall be assessed with a specific duty at that price.

There is a most inexcusable statement in Mr. Walker's report on this subject, which is the more important, as it constitutes one of the chief elements of his reasoning in the document, and went directly, as a component part, into the *great assumption* above considered. In the same manner as British factors were introduced into a committee-room of Congress, in the winter of 1845-'6, and invited to display their goods, in order to show how much better it would be for the American people to buy than to make them, so Mr. M'Kay, in framing his report (house document, No. 306, 1st session, 28th Congress), thought proper to fortify one of his positions, by citing a price current, published in Manchester, England, by Stewart, Thompson, and Lay, January 31, 1843. The price of "stouts or domestics," an imitation of a species of American cotton goods, was there given, with the additional statement, that they had to pay 100 per cent. duty in entering the United States, under the minimum rule. Mr. Walker, eagerly catching at this information found in Mr. M'Kay's report of the preceding Congress, as it suited his purpose, and taking for granted that these goods were actually imported under that duty, made the following statement: "This difference is founded on *actual importation*, and shows an average discrimination *against* the poor, on cotton imports, of 82 per cent. beyond what the tax would be, if assessed upon the actual value." Mr. Walker hastily—it is presumed not reluctantly—adopted the conclusion, that trade was actually going on in that way; whereas, this very species of goods was actually selling lower in Boston and New York, at the time this Manchester price current was published, than the prices there quoted for the English market!

Now, it is very well known to those who understand the subject, and who are acquainted with the facts, that the effect of the minimum duties, is to lower the prices of low-priced goods, chiefly used by the poor, and to pull down prices at higher points of the scale, in proportion as American manufacturing skill improves. And yet Mr. Walker has made a bugbear of minimums, to frighten the poor! Did he himself understand the subject? If so, he is open to a more grave impeachment than that of ignorance!

It is on this false principle, and false statement of facts—of which it is charitably supposed the honorable secretary was ignorant—that he arrives at the following false conclusions, first, *generally*, that "minimums and specific duties render the tax [which is no tax at all] upon the real value much higher upon the *cheaper* than upon the *finer* article;" secondly, and *specifically*, that, "by estimates founded on the *same document* [Mr. M'Kay's report], the discriminations against the cheaper article [under the tariff of 1842] must amount to a *tax* of $5,108,422, *exacted* by minimums and specific duties *annually* from the poorer classes"! And yet, *as a matter of fact*, the true proposition on the point, is, in both particulars, directly the *reverse* of this! Minimum duties were first introduced by southern statesmen, Messrs. Calhoun and Lowndes, in the tariff of 1816. It will be found, by an examination of senate document, No. 109, second session, 28th Congress (a document from the secretary of the treasury), that the application of the minimum principle to *woollens*, puts the tax (if indeed it were one, but it is not) on the costly goods worn by the rich, and is all in favor of the cheaper goods worn by the poor. The annual revenue from this source, under the tariff of 1842 (see same document), was over two millions of dollars. By the same authority, it appears, that the application of the minimum principle to cottons yielded annually to the revenue, under the tariff of 1842, upward of four millions of dollars, the chief burden of which (if burden it was, but it was not) falls on the finer goods worn by the rich. Even these are cheapened, such of them as are rivalled at home by the action of domestic against foreign competition; and those not rivalled at home are the finest and most costly, not used except by those who indulge in luxuries. That the low-priced cotton goods are greatly cheapened, is not only proved by the prices current, but is demonstrated beyond all contradiction by the facts, that they go forth into the widest field of competition, in all parts of the world, with British goods of the same description, and that the British government was forced to enact differential duties for their dependencies, in favor of British products, to keep out American.

The revenue raised in one year, under the tariff of 1842, by the application of the minimum principle, on cotton goods, as stated in the abovenamed document, was as follows: $1,121,000 from goods costing above the minimum, at a duty of 30 per cent.; $2,574,000 from printed and colored goods, at 9 cents square yard, or 43 per cent. duty; $544,000 from plain goods, at 6 cents square yard, or 45¼ per cent. duty; and $34,000 from velvets, &c., at 10½ cents square yard, or 35 per cent. duty; in all, $4,273,000, with an average duty of 38 per cent. If this minimum duty were a tax, it must be seen how it falls chiefly on those who bought the high-priced goods; and that the small amount collected on the low-priced goods was not a tax, is evident, as well from the positive reduction of prices, as from the fact, that they are sold against the same description of British goods in this country, and in all parts of the world. But it has been shown elsewhere, that none of these duties, imposed for protection, are taxes.

But one of the most stupendous effects of the application of the minimum principle of duty, is the opening of a vast market for American cotton fabrics—of course for the raw material—in eastern Asia, whence the same kind of goods formerly came to Europe and America. The cheap labor of China and the far east has been *undersold* by the high-priced labor of America, in the application of superior skill and economy of production, and a channel for an annual export of some millions, from the United States, has been opened by this course, destined to increase, almost without limit, under the same system.

South Carolina, in establishing the cotton minimums of 1816, laid the foundation for this turning back upon Asia the most essential production of the Southern states.

§ 5. *Specific and Ad-valorem Duties.*

The president said in his message: "I recommend to Congress the abolition of the minimum principle, and of specific duties, and the substitution in their place of ad-valorem duties." This recommendation constitutes the fifth fundamental article of Mr. Walker's report, and is carried out in the tariff of 1846. A specific duty is assessed by *measure* of the article; an ad-valorem duty, by an assumed value (for after all the ad-valorem is an assumed rule, which it aims to do away, and more often a false one, as will appear), and is reckoned *per cent.*, or by fractions of every hundred of the value, as 10, or 20, or 50 per cent. Minimums are one form of specific duties.

If one could not be surprised, in the midst of so many new things, one might yet be so, in view of a reason given by the secretary for the adoption of ad-valorem as a substitute for specific duties. He says: "Experience proves, that, as a general rule, a duty of 20 per cent. ad valorem will yield the largest revenue." Now, it happens, that all experience leads to the opposite conclusion, and that statesmen, heretofore, in all countries, wishing to raise the largest revenue, by imposts, have preferred the form of specifics. Great Britain has had, and still has, occasion for the highest possible revenue on certain articles, and she invariably, when it is practicable, having that object in view, adopts the specific form, as on teas, the duties on which are at least 200 per cent., and produced, in 1842, upward of $19,000,000. Her duty on sugar, for the same year, specific, produced upward of $24,500,000. The subsequent reduction of duty on sugar, was for relief, not for revenue. Her duties on wines and tobacco are specific, varying from 300 to 900 per cent., and produce a revenue of about $40,000,000. It is unnecessary to go farther for the experience of England. Our revenue for the year 1831, under the high tariff of 1828, the duties having been made specific, as far as possible, was $30,312,851 net, at rates of duty averaging 41 per cent. on dutiable articles. Our lowest tariff was in 1842, with an average duty of less than 24 per cent.—commonly supposed to be 20—on dutiable imports, and the net revenue for the year was $12,780,173! Is it *such* experience which Mr. Walker appeals to? Or where is it? Mr. Polk said, in a speech at Madison, Tennessee, in 1843, while canvassing for the office of governor : "It [the tariff of 1842] will not produce annually half the amount of revenue which would have been produced by the lower rates of the compromise act;" that is, by the tariff that was in operation when that of 1842 went into effect. This less than HALF, as will be seen, would have been less than $6,390,036 annual revenue for the tariff of 1842. But it actually produced an average of over $26,000,000 net. Was *this the experience* on which Mr. Walker came to his conclusion? *Twenty per cent.* was the commonly alleged maximum, at the time, which produced a revenue of *twelve millions and a half!*

The experience of our own, and of other governments, has, from the beginning, prompted the greatest possible pains to apply specific duties wherever practicable in the nature of the article ; and in accordance with this experience, the list of specific duties has been increased, and that of ad-valorems diminished, in all these quarters, at every new modification of the tariff, almost from time immemorial. England has always been aiming at this; many of the continental tariffs, the famous Zoll-Verein in particular, are wholly specific. Mr. Gallatin, when at the head of the treasury, earnestly recommended more specific duties ; so Mr. Dallas (Alexander J.); so Mr. Crawford; and under each of these secretaries, as well as under others, much has been done to accomplish the end—chiefly, indeed, to prevent frauds on the revenue, at the same time that specific duties have always been regarded as the best mode of increasing the revenue, if required; and Mr. Walker's opinion to the contrary notwithstanding, it will probably still be believed. He will be a lucky man, if, to his great disappointment and cost of reputation, he does not find it so.

But, though the amount of revenue can not be a trifling consideration, at a time when the public expenditures are running up to between fifty and a hundred millions a year (and it is proved, if anything can be, that specific duties are the surest reliance for revenue), yet the universal experience of frequent and great frauds, under a system of ad-valorem duties—frauds on the revenue, and frauds on American citizens and interests—presents considerations, which ought to bring every man to a pause, before he should consent, much less propose, by the sanction of legislation, to open such a door to immorality and crime—to legalize fraud, and offer the most seductive advantages to perjury! What does a European factor of merchandise care for a customhouse oath, who has been bred in a school which teaches, that the evasions of imposts, by whatever means, is equally a virtue and a duty, and who will glory in it, when beyond the reach of punishment? Such, notoriously, is the state of morals in Europe, on this subject. The writer of these pages has seen and heard it there, as openly proclaimed and boasted of, as the proudest achievements. Nor is this the worst of it. Customhouse officers can be bribed, as abundant experience demonstrates. The temptation to share in the spoils—and *such* spoils—is equally great to them, as to foreign factors, who, for the consideration they expect to realize, have been judicially proved, to have sworn in their false invoices, with as much indifference, as if they were making a fair trade! It puts the government, the people, and the interests of the country, on a stupendous scale, in the power of unprincipled villains of the blackest character.

A report of the secretary of the treasury, 1843 (senate document, No. 83, 3d session, 27th Congress), is replete with melancholy instruction on this subject, showing, by the action of the United States court, in the investigation of such cases, that frauds and perjuries, for a term of years, under ad-valorem duties, were habitually and systematically committed by foreign factors, with connivance of customhouse officers, involving great amounts of value; and as but one crime in many is usually detected, the inference is fair, that, aggravated and great as these frauds were, as proved in court, they comprehended but a small fraction of those which were successfully carried on, simultaneously with these, and escaped punishment. In the case of one British importer, "John Taylor, jr.," aided by a deputy collector of New York, whose name is given as "Campbell," the frauds committed, in the course of twenty-one months, amounted to $200,000! This was but one of many cases brought before the court, and each of the many was doubtless but one of many more that escaped exposure. Such is the system of duties adopted by the tariff of 1846, and such, inevitably, must be the consequences, in this country, or any other, while man remains the same. It was to avoid these crimes, as far as possible, that great pains have been taken, for generations, by all governments, to substitute specific for ad-valorem duties, without regard to the amount of revenue—though it appears, that specific duties are more favorable to that.

The law supposes that ad-valorem duties are assessed on the true value, and that is the intention. But when honest witnesses in court differ so widely, and scarcely any two ever agree, how shall an interested importer be controlled, or ordinarily convicted of his frauds? When the importer can afford to purchase the connivance and aid of a deputy collector, with a consideration, five, or ten, or twenty times as much as the officer's salary, the door to crime is wide open, and the temptations, with such chances of impunity, are irresistible. The greatest evil is not the robbery of the national treasury. That is one of the smallest, though the amount, in the aggregate, is very great. There is crime, corrupting the administrators of the law, and poisoning the fountains of commercial integrity. Neither American merchants, nor American manufacturers, can stand before such a torrent of iniquity. The former are supplanted, and the latter are ruined. The very foreigner, who, in his own market, has sold a New York merchant goods at one price, comes here, under the screen of his false invoices, and undersells him in the very same articles! How can the American merchant stand, or the American manufacturer live?

The following extract from a memorial to the senate of the United States, signed by 48 firms, or houses, comprehending all the importing drygood merchants of Boston, is pertinent here:—

" To the honorable senate of the United States:

" The undersigned, your memorialists, would respectfully represent, that they are importers of foreign goods into the city of Boston, and as such they have examined with alarm and consternation, the bill recently passed by the house of representatives, to change, in a great measure, our system of collecting duties on imports. Should the bill referred to become a law of the land, we are fully convinced that we shall be compelled to abandon our business into the hands of unscrupulous foreigners, who have little or no regard to our customhouse oaths. From long experience, we are fully satisfied, that we can not compete with this class, when duties are based merely on the ad-valorem principle."

§ 6. *The Wages of Labor.*

Mr. Walker says: " The wages of labor have not augmented since the tariff of 1842, and in some cases they have diminished." " The wages of labor did not increase in any corresponding ratio—or in any ratio whatever." " Have not augmented ;" " in some cases have diminished." What does he mean? Take this by itself, it means—wages of labor reduced ; taken in connexion with the sympathy everywhere affected throughout the report for the poor as suffering great wrongs under an oppressive tariff, it would appear to be a decided averment of a fact. Or perhaps the secretary means what the president says in his message : " It," the tariff of 1842, " does not benefit the laborers whose wages are not increased by it." Did neither of these gentlemen ever think, that it is a blessing to labor to have work? Suppose its wages are not increased, if they are sufficient and satisfactory. Will Mr. Polk or Mr. Walker find fault with this, if the laborer himself does not? If these gentlemen had dared to say, that there was no employment for labor, under the tariff of 1842, they would have had a decided case. But one says, wages did not increase ; and the other ventures to say, that in *some* cases they diminished. Did not increase from what standard? That *before* the period of the tariff of 1842; or that which this period established? This is a point of at least some, not inconsiderable, importance. If it could be known where these gentlemen mean to take up their position, one could not refuse a fair challenge on this question. Everybody knows that, in 1840, labor went begging for bread, and could not always get it. The Hon. Simon Cameron, of Penn., tells us, as before cited, and calls the president of the senate, Mr. Dallas, to witness, that, in 1840, " there were over five hundred applicants—healthy, vigorous men—for the place of *tip-stave*," in a court of Philadelphia, " to get bread for their families" ! It is also a fact, that an ex-governor of Pennsylvania wept, when General Harrison was obliged to refuse him an office in that commonwealth, because, he said, " he was poor and needed it" !

If Mr. Polk and Mr. Walker mean to say, that the wages of labor, under the tariff of 1842, did not rise above the level of wages in 1840, one would be very much surprised ; and if they mean to say, that they did not rise above the standard of the period of the tariff of '42, it is a simple truism ; it is saying that a thing is equal to itself !

Since, however, these gentlemen have raised the question about wages of labor, they must meet the FACTS. First, then, they do not pretend, that labor could not find employment under the tariff of 1842. Doubtless, they would have said this, if they had dared. This point, settled, is a very important one. It was not necessary, then, under the tariff of 1842, for " five hundred healthy and vigorous men," to go begging for the office of " tipstave" in a court of Philadelphia, " to get bread for their families," and for 499 of them to return to their families disappointed; nor is it likely that an ex-governor of any state will shed unavailing tears, because he was impoverished by the hard times of that era. Messrs. Polk and Walker, apparently, did not think of this ; they do not seem to have well considered, how much it is worth to labor, to be secure of employment ; nor have they been well advised about the wages of labor, under the tariff of 1842, as the following facts will show :—

For some two or three years before the tariff of '42, most of the manufacturers of the country were obliged to compound with labor, at low wages, in hope of better times, or suspend operations.

The Hon. Abbott Lawrence, in his second letter to the Hon. Wm. C. Rives, of Virginia, dated Boston, January 16, 1846, says :—

" I will give you an example of the rate of wages under low duties, and under the tariff of 1842. In 1841-'2, the depression in all kinds of business became so oppressive, that many of the manufacturing establishments in New England were closed, and the operatives dismissed, the mechanical trades were still, and every resource for the laboring man seemed dried up. In the city of Lowell, where there are more than thirty large cotton-mills, with from six to sixteen thousand spindles each, it was gravely considered by the proprietors, whether the mills should be stopped. It was concluded to reduce the wages. This was done several times, until the reduction brought down the wages from about $2 to $1.50 per week, exclusive of board. This operation took place upon between 7,000 and 8,000 females; the mills ran on; no sales were made of the goods; the south and west had neither money, nor credit; and finally, it was determined to hold out, till Congress should act upon the tariff. The bill [tariff of 1842] passed, and of course the mills were kept running, which would not have been the case if the act had been rejected; and now the average wages paid at Lowell—taking the same number of females for the same service—is $2 per week, exclusive of board. Yet, Mr. Walker says, labor has fallen. Where are wages of labor, I ask, lower than they were in 1842? Who is to be benefited by the adoption of a system that gives up everything, and gives no reasonable promise of anything?"

The same is true at the large manufacturing towns of Manchester and Nashua, New Hampshire. (See certificates on this subject, with details, in Fisher's National Magazine, May, 1846.) The Hon. Mr. Ramsey, of Penn., in his speech on the tariff, house of representatives (see National Intelligencer, Sept. 1, 1846), represents, that, from 1837 to 1842, a large portion of the miners and laborers in the mining regions of that state, were out of employment; that the laborers who got work, received only from $3.50 to $4 a week—and miners only from $5 to $6—generally paid in goods, equal to 15 or 20 per cent. discount; and that in 1845–'6, laborers got from $5 to $6, and miners from $8 to $10, cash—average increase, 30 per cent.

This, in amount, is generally, if not universally, true of the manufacturing establishments of the country, of every description; and it is equally true in every department of life, that employs labor. Employment was never wanting under the tariff of '42, and wages *did* increase—an average of full 25 per cent. higher than they were before.

Everybody knows what savings-banks are instituted for, viz., to afford to labor a safe deposite for its savings. They now exist in many parts of the country, and are a great blessing to the laboring poor. There are two items in the history of these institutions, which are probably better evidence of the employment and prosperity of labor, than any or all other that could be given, viz., the comparative number of depositors and the comparative amount of deposites in a course of years. In the state of Massachusetts, the banks of savings are obliged by law to make annual returns to the legislature, of which the following are quotations for three years:—In 1841, the number of depositors was 39,832; the amount of deposites, $6,485,424. In 1842, depositors 41,102; deposites $6,675,878. In 1845, depositors $54,256; deposites $9,214,954. The first two years were under the disastrous period that preceded the tariff of '42; the last was the third year of the operation of that tariff. The comparison is instructive, and to the point. The increase from 1841 to 1842, was about 3 per cent. on depositors, and about 3¼ per cent. on amount deposited. The difference between 1842 and 1845, was about 32 per cent. on depositors, or nearly 11 per cent. per annum; and about 38 per cent. on amount deposited, or nearly 13 per cent. per annum. The amount of deposites in the savings bank at Lowell, was, in 1841, $448,190; in 1842, $478,365; in 1843, $462,650; in 1844, $591,910; in 1845, $730,890. At Portsmouth, N. H., in 1842, $220,636; in 1846, $336,960. At Saco, Maine, in 1842, $29,667; in 1846, $48,157. (*See Fisher's Magazine, March and June*, 1846.) It is believed that these facts require no comment, as it is well known for whom these institutions were established, and what classes of persons use them. Like results, no doubt, could be obtained from every savings-bank in the Union, proving the same thing, viz., that labor was never so prosperous, and never laid up so much, in a given time, as under the tariff of '42. The following is from Fisher's National Magazine, for March, 1846:—

" Within the past year 200 houses have been built in Pawtucket, and the adjoining village of Central Falls, all by the hands employed in the manufactories of the two places, some of which have cost upward of $2,000.

" The deposites in the Pawtucket savings-bank, amount, on an average, to $70,000.

" The following are the prices paid for wages, in the years 1842 and 1845. They all relate to the same hands who were employed in both years:

Wages for Dec. 1842.	Dec. 1845.	Wages for Dec. 1842.	Dec. 1845.
Female Weavers, - - - - $11 12	$17 03	Female Weavers, - - - - $11 30	$18 64
" " - - - - 11 16	18 80	Engineer, per day, - - - 1 33	1 75
" " - - - - 10 76	17 80	Machinist, - - - - - - 1 33	1 75
" " - - - - 12 60	21 85	Firemen, - - - - - - - 75	1 00
" " - - - - 13 32	17 27	Spare girls, per week, - 18 to 21s.	4 00

" Before the protective duty was enacted, the best workmen could only obtain one dollar per day; the same men now receive one dollar and a half per day."

Another important item of evidence on this subject will be found in the same magazine for May, 1846:—

" Mr. R. FISHER: Sir—In answer to your queries on the subject of labor in the following years, we state as follows :—

The Price of Wages per day, for Masons and Laborers, in the month of May, in the following years :

1832 ... Masons, 13 shillings, ... Laborers, 7 shillings,

1835	"	14	"	"	8	"
1836	"	17	"	"	10	"	After the great fire in New-York.
1837	"	15	"	"	8	"
1838	"	13	"	"	7	"
1839	"	13	"	"	8	"	Great expansion of the currency.
1840	"	12	"	"	6	"
1841	"	12	"	"	7	"
1842	"	11	"	"	7	"
1843	"	12	"	"	7	"
1844	"	13	"	"	8	"
1845	"	14	"	"	8	"

" In addition to the rise in the wages, from 1842 to 1845, there have been employed from 50 to 75 per cent. more men than there were from 1838 to 1842.

"JOSEPH TUCKER,   AMOS WOODRUFF,   } Mechanics of the city
" WM. TUCKER,   JAMES WEBB,   }   of New-York."
" JAMES HARRIOT,   SAMUEL OLLIVER, }

The wages of labor in the mechanical trades, on railroads and canals, in agriculture, in common job-work of cities and towns, and in every pursuit throughout the land, in the two periods under consideration—the former universally known as disastrous, and the latter as prosperous—are too well known to those concerned to require certificates from other authorities; and there can be but one voice from all these quarters, which, for one reason we are sorry to say, is most remote from verifying the statements of Mr. Polk and Mr. Walker, on this subject. All the world know it is not so, and it ought not to have been necessary to adduce evidence on the point.

§ 7. *The alleged Power of Capital over Labor.*

If bad blood is not engendered in the heart of labor against capital, it will not be because Mr. Secretary Walker has not tried hard to do it; and it is a pity that a corresponding effort should be found in a message of the president to Congress. Mr. Walker says : " When the number of manufactories is not great, the power of the system to regulate the wages of labor is inconsiderable ; but as the profit of capital invested in manufactures is augmented by the protective tariff, there is a corresponding increase of power, until the control of such capital over the wages of labor becomes irresistible."

Now, exactly the opposite of this is the truth. If manufactures were *monopolies*, as they are sometimes falsely called, that is, if they had exclusive privileges—for nothing else can be a monopoly—then there might possibly be some foundation for such a statement as this of Mr. Walker. But the more manufactories are encouraged, multiplied, and extended, under a protective tariff, and the more capital there is vested in them, so much greater are the chances of labor, and so much greater is its relative power. When the manufactories are few, and the competition between them small, their power relative to labor is greater ; but when they become numerous as competitors, and rich in capital, their rivalship with each other is all for the advantage of labor. In the former case, labor pays court to them, and is obliged to *receive* terms : in the latter, labor *dictates* terms, and becomes the object of courtship. Is it not singular that a man, in so eminent a position, should hazard an official statement so opposed to common sense, and so inconsistent with all experience ?

§ 8. *Mr. Walker's Agricultural Project for the United States.*

Mr. Walker says: " We have more fertile lands than any other nation, can raise a greater variety of products, and, it may be said, could feed and clothe the people of nearly all the world. Agriculture is our chief employment. It is best adapted to our situation. We can raise a larger surplus of agricultural products, and a greater variety, than almost any other nation, and *at cheaper* rates. Remove, then, from agriculture, all our restrictions, and by its own unfettered power, it will break down all foreign restrictions, and, ours being removed, would feed the hungry and clothe the poor of our fellow-men, through all the densely-peopled nations of the world. . . . Foreign nations can not for a series of years import more than they export."

This is a great country—is it not ? Big enough to let all the rest of the world sit down, or play. We can feed and clothe them all—why not ? But Mr. Walker forgot one country —*Utopia*—where one would think he was born and educated ; and where, it might be supposed, he had been intimate with their greatest sages, brought away the cream of their philosophy, and must know how much of our agricultural products they will want. He should have added this to the sum of benefits we are to receive by adopting his *Utopian* theory.

Alas ! to be obliged to hold controversy with an immigrant sage from such a country ! It is hopeless, more because, by his flying so high, so fast, and so far, he is hard to catch, and when caught, hard to hold still, by any logic which ordinary men are used to, than from any other cause. What can the man mean?

But, coming down from this loftiness, and setting aside all this nonsense, let us look at *facts*. Mr. Walker evidently dreams of our feeding and clothing all the world, and the inhabitants of Utopia besides. It is not less true, as a fact, that every nation takes care to feed and clothe itself, than that Mr. Walker proposes to do it for them; and so long as they refuse to avail themselves of our kind offers, we must find other employment, else, as General Jackson said, in his letter to Dr. Coleman, in 1824, but in different words, we shall soon need their charity. Mr. Walker's proposal to turn this nation all back to agriculture, as hardly need be said, is a violation of General Jackson's theory, the carrying out of which, as shown elsewhere in these pages, laid the foundation of the wealth, greatness, and power of the American people.

" I will ask," said General Jackson, " what is the real situation of the agriculturist? Where has the American farmer a market for his surplus products? *Except for cotton*, he has neither a foreign nor a home market. Does not this clearly prove, when there is no market either at home or abroad, that there is too much labor employed in agriculture, and that the channels for labor should be multiplied? Common sense points out, at once, the remedy. Draw from agriculture this super-abundant labor; employ it in mechanism and manufactures, thereby creating a home market for your breadstuffs, and distributing labor to the most profitable account; and benefits to the country will result. Take from agriculture in the United States 600,000 men, women, and children, and you will at once give a home market for more breadstuffs than all Europe now furnishes us with. In short, sir, we have been too long subject to the policy of the British merchants. It is time that we should become a little more *Americanized*, and instead of feeding the paupers and laborers of England, feed our own; or else, in a short time, by continuing our present policy, we shall all be rendered paupers ourselves."

Mr. Walker proposes to *reverse* this policy, and bring the people back to agriculture. " If not depressed by the tariff," he says, " it would be the most profitable." He has only three steps to his end : First, break down the protective policy here; next, the corn laws of England will be abolished; thirdly, these two events will force open all the ports of the world to free trade; which, being accomplished, *the world is ours!* The American protective system and the British corn laws are now out of the way. But other predicted results do not all coincide with Mr. Walker's prediction.

Lord Ashburton, in a speech at Winchester, England, Jan. 19, 1846, looking into the future, even under the abolition of the corn laws—for it was then decided as an event to be —said :—

" The supply [of breadstuffs] must not be expected from America, and we could not have a better proof of it than the fact, that at this moment, American corn could come here from Canada, at a duty of 4 shillings; and yet, if the returns were examined, it would be found. that *nine tenths* of the foreign corn consumed in England, was from the Baltic, though the duty on the corn from its shores was 15 shillings a quarter. This was entirely owing to the *low price of labor* in the north of Europe." Again Lord Ashburton said, on the 29th January, ten days later. in parliament : " The British farmer must not have his hands tied behind him. Did he meet the foreigner on equal terms? The farmer on the shores of the Baltic had his labor at *six pence a day*, to compete with the farmer of this country (England) with his labor at *two shillings a day*. It required no skill in political economy to discover that these two parties did not meet on equal terms."

Does not the American farmer see by this, that " his hands are tied behind him," when he is doomed, even under the abolition of the British corn laws, to meet in the British market, the farmer of the north of Europe, whose labor costs him only *six pence* (sterling, or 12½ cents) *a day?* And that the farmer of the north of Europe, being near, will be in the British market first, and at less cost?

Corn laws or no corn laws, it could make no difference, except it would be better for the American farmer, in such a competition, that the corn laws should not have been abolished, as before that event, he could get to the English market, through Canada, with four shillings duty, when his competitor, in the north of Europe, had to pay fifteen shillings; but now, the corn laws being abolished, the farmer, in the north of Europe, has as much greater advantage over the American farmer, than in the former state of things, as the difference between fifteen and four. At best, the abolition of the corn laws can be no advantage to the American farmer.

The transient effect of the news of the failure of the potato and grain crops of Europe, in 1846, in raising the prices of American breadstuffs and provisions, will not at all affect this argument, when the result of the whole shall have transpired. There is, doubtless, a greater failure than in 1845. But the same rage for speculation prevailed then as now, and the result this year may be expected to be as the last, a subsequent depression—a full year only will be full proof, or till another good crop in Europe.

The following table will show what are the chances of the American producer of breadstuffs, in the British market, as the competition, on both sides, will be equally benefited by the abolition of the corn laws, except, as above noticed, the loss is on the side of the American :—

Importations of Wheat into Great Britain, from the principal wheat countries for 1841, 1842, *and* 1843, *in bushels, together with the sum total from each country.*

Countries.	1841.	1842.	1843.	Total.
Russia..........	498,205	1,824,688	269,368	2,592,261
Denmark.......	1,915,279	617,656	565,248	3,098,183
Prussia..........	7,134,400	5,938,065	5,311,000	18,383,465
Germany........	5,295,674	1,626,172	1,027,224	7,949,070
Holland.........	815,964	73,979	6,864	896,507
France	1,643,932	4,216,100	29,248	5,889,280
Italy and Island..	901,600	4,878,597	24,840	5,805,037
N. A. Colonies..	2,333,354	3,729,690	2,790,504	6,853,548
United States....	1,107,840	1,195,873	749,601	3,053,278
Other countries..	866,859	1,816,340	272,407	2,955,606

These three years, 1841, 1842, and 1843, were years of the largest importations of bread-stuffs into Great Britain, averaging 18,300,000 bushels; whereas, the average from 1829 to 1843, including fifteen years, was only 10,964,896 bushels.

A glance at the above table will show whence Great Britain has been accustomed to obtain, and will continue to obtain, the chief amount of the bread-stuffs she may require. It is only when prices are low, that the American farmer sends bread-stuffs to England and Europe. Will that suit him? He has to contend with the cheap labor of the countries named in the above table. "His hands are tied behind him," as Lord Ashburton says; and the end of the whole is, that this competition falls on American labor, and brings that down toward the level of wages in these rival quarters. That result is inevitable. This, indeed, appears to be the main object of Mr. Walker, in order to keep up the price of cotton, as is betrayed by him in many forms of phraseology found in his report: "While bread-stuffs *rise* in England, cotton almost invariably *falls.*"

It is the low price of cotton that he complains of, and he has conceived the notion, that the only way to raise it is to depress the prices of other agricultural products of the country, which he considers of less importance. He would, therefore, have the whole country go to farming, that they may produce enough to bring down the prices of agricultural products, *other than cotton,* as would, doubtless, be the result. But Mr. Walker mistakes in supposing that cotton is the only great interest of the country, and the only interest worth sustaining. He mistakes, even in supposing, that in sustaining the interests of cotton, it is necessary to depress other interests. All stand or fall together; and it is impossible to injure one without injuring all, directly or indirectly.

That American bread-stuffs can not go to England, to any considerable extent, except at low prices, appears from the fact, that Russia, Denmark, Prussia, Germany, Holland, France, Italy, the Islands, and other European and Asiatic countries can feed her, whenever she wants more than she produces, at lower rates than American labor will be satisfied with—for all depends on the price of labor. The following tables and facts, from the Hon. Chas. Hudson's speech in Congress, of February 26, 1846, are pertinent here :—

" The following table will show the prices of wheat per bushel in the principal marts of trade on the continent, from 1830, to 1843, inclusive :—

	Dantzic.	Hamburg.	Amsterdam.	Antwerp.	Odessa.
1830,	$1.07	93	1.13	95	68
1831,	1.18	1.19	1.15	1.07	71
1832,	93	90	1.10	90	62
1833,	83	70	89	55	61
1834,	70	67	66	50	77
1835,	61	65	70	68	57
1836,	70	79	76	70	52
1837,	73	76	81	99	50
1838,	94	79	1.20	1.48	65
1839,	96	1.15	1.33	1.37	79
1840,	1.07	1.30	1.11	1.48	71
1841,	1.23	99	1.09	1.45	74
1842,	1.10	1.11	1.11	95	65
1843,	76	82	78	76	48
Average,	91	90	99	98	64

" Here we have the prices of wheat, at five great marts of the wheat trade, for 14 years, showing a general average of 88 cents per bushel.

" The prices at our seaports during the same period, run as follows:—

In 1830,	-	-	-	-	-	$1.15	In 1837,	-	-	-	-	-	$1.83
1831,	-	-	-	-	-	1.18	1838,	-	-	-	-	-	1.54
1832,	-	-	-	-	-	1.15	1839,	-	-	-	-	-	1.42
1833,	-	-	-	-	-	1.13	1840,	-	-	-	-	-	1.10
1834,	-	-	-	-	-	1.08	1841,	-	-	-	-	-	1.03
1835,	-	-	-	-	-	1.19	1842,	-	-	-	-	-	1.16
1836,	-	-	-	-	-	1.44	1843,	-	-	-	-	-	1.00

" The general average of the aforenamed prices is $1.25; being 37 cents more than the average per bushel at the aforementioned ports on the Black sea and Baltic. This shows demonatratively, that, in the first cost of the grain, we are not able to come into fair competition with our trans-Atlantic wheat-growers. And how is it with reference to freight? By official documents laid before Parliament, it appears that the freight on the highest calculation can not exceed, on an average, 13 cents per bushel. By the report of the Hon. Mr. Ellsworth, commissioner of patents, laid before Congress in 1843, where he examines this subject somewhat minutely, it appears that the average freight from New York to Liverpool is 35 or 36 cents per cwt. We can not estimate wheat at less than 56 pounds per bushel; and hence the freight must amount to 17 or 18 cents per bushel. The difference in the freight and first cost would make a balance against us of 41 cents per bushel. But as the year 1837 was one of uncommonly high prices in this country, I will omit that year in my estimate, which will reduce this balance down to about 36 cents; and from this I will deduct, for the difference of exchange, 10 cents, which will bring the difference down to 26 cents per bushel.

The English consul, writing from Odessa, at the close of 1842, says: Under present circumstances, extraordinary low freight and favorable exchange, a shipment of the best wheat could now be made and delivered in England on the following terms, viz:—

									s. d.	
First cost	-	-	-	-	-	-	-	-	22 6	per quarter.
Charge of loading	-	-	-	-	-	-	-	-	2 5	"
Freight	-	-	-	-	-	-	-	-	6 7	"
Insurance and factorage in England	-	-	-	-	-				4 0	"
					Total	-	-		35 6	"

" This reduced to our currency would amount to 97 cents per bushel delivered in England. And in 1843 there was a still further reduction; so that wheat from the Baltic could be delivered in England without duty at 87 cents, and from the Black sea at 78 or 80 cents per bushel. A price much less than our wheat could be purchased at in our own ports."

It will be found, that the British government never expected to be supplied with breadstuffs from the United States in case of the abolition of the corn laws, from the following facts, stated by Mr. Hudson:—

" In 1840 the British government called upon their consuls, at some of the principal marts of the corn trade, to inform them what amount of grain could be sent to the English market in case the English duty were reduced to a nominal sum. The substance of their replies will be seen in the following table, submitted, with their report, to Parliament, in 1841:—

								Bushels.
St. Petersburg	-	-	-	-	-	-	-	1,540,000
Liebau	-	-	-	-	-	-	-	240,000
Warsaw	-	-	-	-	-	-	-	2,400,000
Odessa	-	-	-	-	-	-	-	1,200,000
Stockholm	-	-	-	-	-	-	-	8,000
Dantzic	-	-	-	-	-	-	-	2,520,000
Konigsburg	-	-	-	-	-	-	-	520,000
Stettsic	-	-	-	-	-	-	-	2,000,000
Memel	-	-	-	-	-	-	-	47,712
Hamburgh	-	-	-	-	-	-	-	4,304,000
Elsinore	-	-	-	-	-	-	-	1,400,000
Palermo	-	-	-	-	-	-	-	1,600,000
								17,779,712

" From these twelve ports it appears that a supply of 17,779,712 bushels of wheat could be obtained annually; and it further appears that 7,298,000 bushels of rye. 6,820,500 bushels of barley, and 6,445,700 bushels of oats, could be supplied. In this list is not included Riga, Rotterdam, Antwerp, and several other important ports for the corn trade."

The above promises of supply are more than 8,000,000 bushels in excess of the annual average of imports of foreign corn into Great Britain, from 1829 to 1843, inclusive, 15 years; and of course demonstrate an absolute independence, as to any necessary supplies from the United States. Nor could the grain, alias corn growers, in the United States, have any chances in such a market, except on the basis of wages of labor and prices of products, corresponding with the wages and prices of the countries above named; or in a year of short crops in Europe. Will the American laborer and farmer be satisfied with that? Then in what are they or can they be benefited by the abolition of the British corn laws, and Mr. Walker's theory?

The first considerable abatement of duties on corn, in Great Britain, was by a law which took effect in April, 1842, reducing the duties at once about one half. Great results were expected, similar to those predicted to follow the entire abolition. What did they prove to be ? Directly the reverse of what was anticipated, as the following facts will show. The average annual importation of wheat into Great Britain for the three years previous to this reduction, was 20,692,000 bushels, and the importation for the first year after the reduction was only 9,540,000 bushels. All that is pretended to be proved by these facts, is, that other causes controlling these results, being more potent than the law, not only disappointed legislation, but made things go directly the other way from what was intended. And if the abatement of half the duties on the corn laws was followed by such a result, what certain evidence can be placed on the consequences predicted for their entire abolition ? One thing is put beyond doubt, by the facts above exhibited, that this event can not, in any probability, be of the slightest benefit to the producers of breadstuffs in the United States. It would be a calamity to those producers, if the prices of their products should be so low as to compel them to go to the same market which the producers of breadstuffs on the Baltic and on the shores of the Mediterranean resort to, and which these latter chiefly monopolize by the low wages of their labor, and the consequent low price of their products. It is an ascertained fact, that the small amount of bread-stuffs which has heretofore gone directly from the United States, to the English market, has been exported rather for freight and remittances than for profit, and only when the prices were not regarded by the producers as a remuneration.

" Every practical man," says Mr. Hudson " knows that, between two great commercial nations, an article will be exported from one to the other, when the prices in the two countries seem to forbid. The wheat that we have sent direct to Great Britain is, to a considerable extent, the result of accidental causes. A merchant is indebted abroad, and must send forth something to discharge his debt, and not being able to meet the demand in specie, he sends forward a quantity of flour. Or, a vessel is going out without a full cargo, and will take grain for a mere trifle. Or, a speculator has a large amount of flour on hand, bought perhaps on six months, and is obliged to send it out at a sacrifice. Our grain goes to England mainly in the shape of flour, by which a saving of 10 or 15 per cent. over the export of wheat is realized. These are the causes, more than anything else, which enable us to supply the English market to the small extent we now do. Ask our merchants who have had experience in this trade, and they will generally tell you that it is a precarious business, and one in which much more has been lost than made."

The wheat crop of the United States in 1840, was 84,823,000 bushels; and in 1844, it was 95,607,000 bushels. For fourteen years previous to 1846, the average annual export of wheat from the United States, to all parts of the world, was 5,505,000 bushels; in 1836, only 805 bushels; in 1838, 41,475 bushels; in 1837 we imported 4,000,000 bushels; deduct the imports, and the average of fourteen years was about 5,000,000. What is this to the whole product of nearly one hundred millions of bushels, all which found a home market, except the above fraction of a little more than *one twentieth ?* How much better would it have been for the American growers of wheat, if General Jackson's great principle, in his letter to Doct. Coleman, had been carried a little farther, by withdrawing more people from agriculture into manufacturing and other pursuits, so as to have created a home demand for the entire product of wheat during those fourteen years, and so as to have kept up the prices to a full and satisfactory remuneration of the producers, that they should not have been obliged to send so small a surplus to compete with the low wages and low prices of Europe, and thus bring down the prices at home ? For such was the inevitable effect of this small surplus. It brought down prices at home, and left both the laborer and his employer without a fair remuneration, simply because they were obliged to compete with the low wages and low prices of Europe.

This all-controlling principle of *supply and demand* seems not to have been understood by Mr. Walker; or else he has done an atrocious wrong to the country—a wrong in any case. It is a grand fundamental principle of political science, without a knowledge of which no man could begin to be a statesman, or to know what a tariff should be. There is an annual surplus of agricultural products in the United States, and Mr. Walker proposes, that those engaged in manufacturing and other pursuits, should turn to agriculture, and become producers instead of consumers, for the benefit of those already engaged in agriculture ! and for the benefit of the country ! Is this man a statesman ?

Let us illustrate the principle of *supply and demand.* A given number of houses and other buildings are wanted for a small business town; and so long as that number is not exceeded, they will rent for a fair remuneration. But if one tenth or one twentieth more than are wanted should be built, the owner or owners of these surplus buildings, rather than not have them occupied, will offer them at a lower rate than the others are hired for. Then down comes the rent of the whole; and so long as there is a surplus, rent will continue to fall to 50 per cent. of a remunerating price, or lower. Wherever it stops, there is still a surplus, and the effect of it will be ruinous to all the owners. Thus a small surplus of anything in market may annihilate half or more of the fair value of the whole. The *supply*, in such a case, exceeds the *demand.* Reverse the case, and let the demand exceed the supply, and the contrary effect will be produced.

" Supply and demand must ever be the governing rule of prices. Increase or diminish the supply one per cent., and prices may fall or advance 50 per cent., below or above the cost of production;

which, the moment the equilibrium is deranged, ceases to influence prices, which are then ruined by speculation."—*National Magazine.*

There is no need, indeed, of going farther than General Jackson's letter to Dr. Coleman, for all that is necessary to illustrate this point. If agriculture, or any other pursuit, ceases to be remunerative, in consequence of surplus production, " common sense," says General Jackson, " at once points out the remedy." Diminish the number engaged in it, by turning a part of them to pursuits not overstocked with laborers, that each party may become consumers, directly or indirectly, of the products of the other; and the greater the diversity of productive pursuits, in any community, so much greater its prosperity and common stock of productive wealth.

The European market for an American product, agricultural or other, that has a rival there, presents a distinct question in political economy, which can never be separated from a consideration of the wages of labor in that quarter, as compared with American wages; and that American statesman, who proposes to find a market in Europe, in England or on the continent, to any considerable extent, for American products of any kind, encountering competition there, proposes what no power can accomplish, with a satisfactory remuneration to, and without impairing the rights of, American labor. For all such products, the true policy of the American people and government is, to create a market at home, which shall adequately remunerate the labor of the country. Whenever there is a surplus production, a supply above demand, in a given pursuit, " common sense," as General Jackson said, " at once points out the remedy." Withdraw, diversify, distribute labor from that point, and make it bear on others not crowded. But Mr. Secretary Walker proposes to crowd that pursuit still more, if it happens to be agriculture; to turn the nation into it, and *force* the world to let us supply all their wants; to let us " feed the hungry, and clothe the poor of our fellow-men throughout all the densely-peopled nations of the world !" This, surely, is a magnificent scheme, magniloquently propounded, considering that it appears in a financial document ! But, if there is common sense in it, there was little, and none to spare, in the man, whose name this honorable secretary once professed, and would doubtless now be thought, to honor.

But one of Mr. Walker's reasons for the policy he proposes is, that " foreign nations can not, for a series of years, import more than they export." This was very safely, very prudently, very sagely said. It will, doubtless, be " a series of years" before they will feel able to afford it. But since WE can afford to import some forty, or fifty, or sixty millions a year more than we export—that appears to be the plan of the secretary, and the scope and bearing of the tariff of 1846—we shall then be able to take the field, get ahead of all other nations, and " feed the hungry and clothe the poor of all the densely-peopled nations of the world !" The apparent simplicity and gravity with which the secretary announces the axiom, that " foreign nations can not, for a series of years, import more than they export," brings one to a pause as to what could have been the state of his mind—whether he was really dreaming that WE could afford it *now,* and that other nations, " after a series of years," would follow our example !

It can not be denied, that Mr. Walker is candid in disclosing two objects, which he appears to have had in view, viz., to raise the price of cotton by lowering that of other agricultural products. It is believed he made a mistake, as to the effect of his plan on cotton ; but let that go. He evidently foresees that the effect of his plan will greatly reduce the prices of American agricultural products, other than cotton, and assumes it. He says, " we can raise a larger surplus of agricultural products, and a greater variety, than almost any other nation ; *and at cheaper rates.*" It was impossible, in the nature of things, that his plan should go into operation, without bringing down the wages of American labor to the European standard, when the essence of his plan was to bring its products, without restriction on either side, into direct and open competition in the same markets. He, therefore, proposes to put the whole nation to agriculture, to make up in surplus production, what may, in consequence, be wanting in price ! The greater the surplus, of course, the greater the reduction of price. But, it being assumed that we can " sell *at cheaper rates* than almost any other nation," it is also assumed, that we can drive them all from the field, and have the market of the world ! This appears to be the secretary's plan ; and it is absolutely necessary it should succeed, to rescue it from the imputation of the greatest folly that was ever conceived by man, however it may fail to save the people from the greatest disasters that ever befell a nation.

§ 9. *The position of Cotton as one of the great interests of the Country.*

" The cotton planting interest," says the secretary, " is the great exporting interest, and suffers from the tariff in the double capacity of consumer and exporter. Cotton is the great basis of our foreign exchange, furnishing most of the means to purchase imports, and supply the revenue. It is thus the source of two thirds of the revenue, and of our foreign freight and commerce, upholding our commercial marine and maritime power. It is also a bond of peace with foreign nations, constituting a stronger preventive of war than armies or navies, forts or armaments. At present prices, our cotton crop will yield an annual product of $72,000,000, and the manufactured fabric, $504,000,000, furnishing profits abroad to thousands of capitalists, and wages to hundreds of thousands of the working classes, all of whom would be deeply injured by any disturbance, growing out of a war, to the direct and adequate supply of the raw material. If our manufacturers consume 400,000 bales, it would cost them $12,000,000, while selling the manufactured fabric for $84,000,000 ; and they should be the last to unite in imposing heavy taxes on that great interest, which supplies them with the raw material, out of which they realize such large profits."

The most impressive feature of the above passage, from the report of the secretary of the treasury, is the sympathy and concern which he seems to manifest for British capitalists and laborers, as contrasted with his feelings toward American capitalists and laborers. To the former he is more than courteous; to the latter, here and throughout the report, he is somewhat severely censorious. It is not a little remarkable, that he should be able so clearly to see the dependance of these " hundreds of thousands" of British " working classes" on their position, in connexion with their employers, and that he should so feelingly depre-cate " any disturbance" of that position, by which they might be " deeply injured ;" and yet not be able to see the importance of not disturbing the same position of American laborers. The secretary seems to have great satisfaction in contemplating the growing wealth of British capitalists, and is apparently ready to vindicate their utmost prerogative. The slightest exposure of the British " working classes" to injury, very sensibly affects him. This does not appear to be the charity that begins at home ; but that which roams abroad for beneficiaries.

The secretary is right, that there is a great American staple, worth annually $72,000,000, more or less. It will probably increase ; but there are also other great staples, other great interests ; and the aggregate of the whole leaves even cotton in the shade. It appears by senate document, No. 340, 2d session, 27th Congress that the annual products of the United States of all kinds, amounted, in 1840, to $2,000,000,000. Now they are, doubtless, con-siderably in excess of that. The consideration, therefore, due to this $72,000,000, as an American interest, for the attention and care of the government, as a fraction of the general interest of $2,000,000,000, on republican principles of equality, can be easily ciphered out by the terms above given. Can it rightfully claim anything more ? It is by no means the largest, even of the agricultural interests of the country. The Hon. Mr. Cameron, of Penn-sylvania, stated in the senate, that the hay crop was worth twice as much as the cotton crop. The Hon. Edward Everett, when minister to the court of London, is reported to have said at an agricultural meeting, held at Derby, in 1843, Earl Spencer in the chair, that al-though the commerce between Great Britain and the United States is twice as great as be-tween England and any other country, yet the whole of the products, passing to and fro, was not worth so much as the oats and beans raised in Great Britain, as proved by their agricultural statistics ; and that the entire value of the products employing British navigation, all the world over, was not equal to the grass grown in Great Britain. Mr. Cameron also stated, that the wheat crop was worth full 40 per cent. more than that of cotton ; that oats were worth about two thirds as much : potatoes more than half as much ; and so on. The amount of Indian corn produced in 1840, was 377,000,000 of bushels—doubtless half a million, or more, in 1846. This, at 50 cents a bushel, would be $188,500,000 ; that is, $116,500,000 more than Mr. Walker's valuation of the cotton. Neat cattle, in 1840, num-bered 15,000,000, which, at $10 a head, would be $150,000,000. Swine were 26,000,000, at $4 each, $104,000,000. Horses and mules were estimated at $170,000,000, and the trifling article of poultry at $9,000,000. All these have increased in six years. The prod-ucts of the dairy are probably worth more than cotton. The annual products of manufacture have been stated at $300,000,000. Boots and shoes, in the state of Massachusetts alone, mount up to $14,000,000. There are many interests in the Union, great in the amount of their products, and of great importance to those concerned in them. Every interest of every man, has a claim to respect and protection.

But the secretary ascribes some very pretending *political* attributes to the cotton interest, for which he seems to think it merits the special care of the government. " Cotton is the great basis of our foreign exchanges, furnishing most of the means to purchase imports, and supply the revenue. It is thus the source of two thirds of the revenue, and of our foreign freight and commerce, upholding our commercial marine and maritime power. It is also a bond of peace with foreign nations, constituting a stronger preventive of war than armies or navies, forts or armaments."

It can not be denied that this is a high pretension, an extraordinary claim, put forward on the basis of eminent political considerations ; and these, apparently, are some of the reasons why the secretary thinks that all other interests of the country should give way to that of cotton, and that the public policy should be shaped for this. Believing in these facts, as he has stated them, his position and course, as a public officer, may be easily explained. How could he do otherwise ?

But if, after all it shall appear, that the position of this interest of $72,000,000, so far as its claims to protection are concerned, is purely a commercial one ; that it is an interest of so many dollars, and no more, in the pockets of the growers of cotton ; that so far as it has any political importance, it is so much additional commercial value to itself, and therefore can only be regarded as a basis of commercial speculation—and a very strong one it is; then, what becomes of these high and superior claims set up for it by the secretary?

It appears by one expression in the passage now under consideration, viz. : " cotton suffers from the tariff in the double capacity of consumer and exporter," that the secretary holds to the old " forty bale theory," which has been so long and so thoroughly exploded, that no one has dared, for years, to propound it, under the original terms. But here, manifestly, is its ghost again. It is this assumption on which the secretary has erected the entire scheme of his anti-protective policy. It was this, partly, though not alone, that led him to ascribe such paramount importance, political and other, to the cotton interest.

Mr. Clay treated this theory, at the time it was first propounded in 1832, as follows :—" It is alleged that the import duty is equivalent to an export duty, and falls on cotton, The framers of our constitution, by granting the power to Congress to lay imposts, and prohibiting that of laying an export duty, manifested that they did not regard them as equivalent. Nor does the common sense of mankind. An export duty fastens upon, and incorporates itself with, the article on which it is laid. But an import duty on a foreign article, leaves the exporter of the domestic article free,—first, to import specie ; secondly, goods which are free from the protecting duty ; or thirdly, such goods as, being chargeable with the protecting duty, he can sell at home."

Again : " The case has been put in debate, and again and again in conversation, of the South Carolina planter, who exports one hundred bales of cotton to Liverpool, exchanges them for one hundred bales of merchandise, and when he brings them home, being compelled to leave at the custom-house forty bales in the form of duties. The arrangement is founded on the *assumption* that a duty of 40 per centum amounts to a *subtraction* of forty from the one hundred bales of merchandise. The first answer to it is, that it supposes a case of *barter*, which never occurs. If it be replied, that it nevertheless occurs in the operations of commerce, the answer would be, that, since the export of Carolina cotton is chiefly made by New-York or foreign merchants, the loss stated, if it really occured, would fall upon them, and not upon the planters.

" But, to test the correctness of the hypothetical case, let us suppose, that the duty, instead of 40 per centum, should be 150, which is asserted to be the duty in some cases. Then, the planter would not only lose the whole hundred bales of merchandise, which he had gotten for his hundred bales of cotton, but he would have to purchase, with other means, an additional fifty bales, in order to enable him to pay the duty accruing on the proceeds of the cotton! Another answer is, that, if the producer of cotton in America exchanged against English fabrics, pays the duty, the producer of the fabrics also pays it, and then it is twice paid ! Such must be the consequence, unless the principle is true on one side of the Atlantic, and false on the other ! The true answer is, that the exporter of an article, if he invests his proceeds in a foreign market, takes care to make the investment in such merchandise as, when brought home, he can sell with a fair profit."

When a doctrine or theory—for this is nothing but a theory—is proved *absurd*, as above, that is enough. No reasoning can stand before a plain palpable absurdity, like this. The cotton-planter usually sells his cotton, out and out, to a New-York broker, or to a merchant somewhere, at the market price, puts the money in his pocket, *and there it is*. But Mr. Walker's theory supposes *it is not there!* Or, that, by some unaccountable process, 40 per cent. of it is afterward abstracted ! If Mr. Walker, having the money for his cotton once in his own desk, lets a part of it go, it must be his own fault. There is no such thing as *barter* in these transactions. The exporter of cotton pays the cotton-grower cash, and if he imports merchandise with its proceeds, instead of cash, it is because he expects more cash in the end, by profits on his imports, duties or no duties.

But admitting the truth and validity of the " forty bale theory," or of what Mr. Walker calls " cotton suffering in the double capacity of consumer and exporter by the tariff "—it would be hard to *believe* it—but *admitting* it, it has been demonstrated in another part of this work, that protective duties, in this country, are not taxes, in the operation of the system, to any party or person ; that protected articles are generally cheaper—in the aggregate always cheaper ; and that the system relieves the people from a heavy burden of foreign taxation. Then where is this " suffering," this loss, to be found ? It has vanished ; it is turned into a positive gain, in all cases, and with all parties in the country—producers, consumers, buyers, sellers, exporters, and importers. And thus the whole of Mr. Walker's theory falls to the ground.

It was on the basis of this theory that nullification rose in 1832—disturbed the repose, and menaced the integrity of the Union. The South-Carolinians were made to believe that they were taxed millions a year, " in the double capacity of consumers and exporters." Mr. Clay, in his reply to General Hayne, in February, 1832, proved very satisfactorily, that, on their own principle, their tax, as a state, could not exceed $333,000, which was only about one third of their fair proportion of the public burden, when the revenue from customs was twenty-five millions. But even this burden is removed by the proof, that protective duties are not taxes.

As to the political importance of the cotton interest, stated by Mr. Walker, in maintaining peace, whatever of truth there is in it—and there is doubtless a good deal—nevertheless, it all redounds to the commercial advantage of that interest, rendering it always more secure, more available, more productive. As to the credit claimed for the cotton interest, in affording the basis for two thirds of the public revenue, the fact is not apparent. England must have the cotton, and the planter is glad to sell it. *These* are facts. But why does the exporter of the cotton bring back merchandise ? Because the people want it, and because he can double his profits by the operation. It is the wants of the people, then, that constitute the basis of the public revenue, and not cotton. If it should be said, the cotton pays for the merchandise, to the extent specified, this fact is not inconsistent with another contingent one, to wit, that, in the absence of cotton, something else would be found to pay for it. As to the aid of cotton in providing a maritime force, by employing a commercial marine, that, too, rests on a similar foundation to the other pretension, and if it should be granted, would it not be fair to balance the account, and bring the cotton interest in debt to the country, by charging back upon it five or six millions a year for the expense of a navy to protect it, on its passage to market ?

What now remains of the secretary's glorification of cotton ? No doubt it is a great blessing to itself. It is also a blessing to mankind, as food is. Nor is it intended to disparage its fair relative importance, as one of the great interests, though not the greatest, of the Union. But it can hardly be allowed as entitled to the claim that every other interest of the country should make obeisance to that, crouch to it, be its slave, be sacrificed for its advantage.

§ 10. *The Profits of Manufacturers and of Cotton-Growers compared.*

Mr. Polk, in his message, says : " While it [the tariff of 1842] protects the capital of the wealthy manufacturer, and increases his profits, it does not benefit the operatives or laborers in his employment, whose wages have not been increased by it." How far the last part of this proposition is true, has been considered in the sixth section of this chapter. Mr. Walker says : " The profit of capital invested in manufactures is augmented by the protective tariff." It may be so, ought to be, doubtless is, as one object of the tariff is to encourage and sustain manufactures. But Mr. Walker maintains, that this is done at the expense of laborers and the poor—and done to an exorbitant amount. He has applied to the tariff of 1842 the epithets, " unjust," " unequal," " exorbitant," " oppressive," meaning that the manufacturers got all the benefit, and other classes, especially the laborers and the poor, all the wrong, which he reiterates in many different forms.

So serious an allegation as this, involving so important a question, and emanating from such a quarter, should have been substantiated by the evidence of *facts*. There can be no apology for this defect of duty, inasmuch as it was perfectly in the power of the secretary to prove it, if it was true. He did, in fact, open a correspondence in all quarters for that purpose; and yet, not a single fact to the point is forthcoming ! He complains, that the manufacturers would not give evidence to convict themselves ! But there were thousands of disinterested and well-qualified persons whom he might have put under oath. Their certificates would have been influential, for or against the secretary. The fact that he has not produced them, is the strongest evidence that they could not be obtained for *his purpose*.

The secretary does indeed say : " It seems strange, that while the profit of agriculture varies from 1 to 8 per cent., that of manufactures is more than double." This, certainly, is a very equivocal mode of expression, unexplained. If he means that the profit of manufactures is more thau double of 1, that is not saying much. Or if he means that it is more than double of the medium between 1 and 8, that is, of 4—it is perhaps fair to conclude this was his meaning—even that is not very extravagant, and is probably about what he meant to allow for agriculture. But whatever he meant is unsupported by evidence.

Assertion is at least as good on one side as the other, and when, in replication, it happens to correspond with known facts, it is simply a reference to the most valid evidence—is evidence. It will not be denied that more capital has been sunk, entirely and for ever lost to the original stockholders, in starting manufactories in the United States, than in any other business whatsoever. Nearly all that was invested during the war of 1812, and under the tariff of 1816, down to 1824, was sacrificed; and the amount was very great. Hundreds, not to say thousands, of families, who were rich before their all was thus hazarded here, were for ever ruined by these misfortunes. It is not less true that, in the history of manufacturing in the United States, down to this time, frequent failures, some for great amounts, have been constantly taking place. On these ruins, others following, and taking the same establishments, at a large discount on the cost—50 or 75 per cent., sometimes more, sometimes less—have, for a season, been able to make large dividends, not on the first cost, but on the last. What was their good luck, had been the ruin of others. In the same manner, handsome profits have sometimes been realized by the first establishments in a new business, till other capital, waiting for employment, rushed into it, and reduced the profits to an unsatisfactory level, as is generally the result in such cases, till one reaction after another brings it to a moderate and fair business—all for the benefit of labor, as before shown.

The Hon. Mr. Evans, of Maine, whose scrupulosity and accuracy of statement in such matters are not questioned by his opponents in the senate of the United States, or elsewhere—much less are his statements often disturbed—replied to Mr. M'Duffie, of South Carolina, on this point, in a speech delivered January 23d, 1844. His conclusion was : " I venture to affirm, that the profits of capital invested in cotton manufactures [these are the most profitable] from the commencement to this time, have not averaged 6 per cent." Mr. M'Duffie asked, "What are they now?" "I can not certainly inform the senator," said Mr. Evans; "but I am assured that, altogether, they will not average 12 per cent." It has been since proved that they did not average so much; and it is doubtless true, that "they have not averaged 6 per cent. from the commencement." No others have done so well, and some have suffered great disasters.

The Lowell factories have, undoubtedly, done better than the average of cotton-mills in the country. The Hon. Nathan Appleton states that, of the nine companies there, five made no dividend during the year 1842, and that the average of the dividends of all the Lowell companies, for the years 1842, 1843, 1844, and 1845, of the net profits, was $10\frac{1}{2}$ per cent. per annum. These statements are, of course, open to verification, and if they could be proved incorrect, it would have been done, as there was no want of disposition.

"I am very sure," said Mr. Evans, "that in other branches of manufacture much less [profit] still has been derived. How is it with the woollens? The profits there, we know, have been very low; great losses have been sustained; and the stock has been, generally, far under par. In the iron business, the senator from Pennsylvania [Mr. Buchanan] has told us that many of the furnaces have ceased to operate. . . . With plain and conclusive facts like these," said Mr. Evans, "with what justice or propriety can the act of 1842 be stigmatized as an act to legalize plunder and oppression [so Mr. M'Duffie called it], or the policy, as a policy to enrich the manufacturer and capitalist at the expense of the laborer?' These are charges, sir, easily made; but they are not sustained, and can not be sustained by any proof drawn from experience, or the practical operation of the system."

But what are the profits of the cotton-growers? In Mr. Clay's reply to General Hayne, in February, 1832, he said:—

" The cotton-planters of the valley of the Mississippi, with whom I am acquainted, generally expend about one third of their income in the support of their families and plantations. On this subject I hold in my hand a statement from a friend of mine, of great accuracy, and a member of the senate. According to this statement, in a crop of $10,000, the expenses may fluctuate between $2,800 and $3,200." Again: " If cotton-planting is less profitable than it was, that is the result of increased production. But I believe it to be still the most profitable investment of capital of any branch of business in the United States; and if a committee were raised, with power to send for persons and papers, I take it upon myself to say, that such would be the result of the inquiry. In Kentucky, I know many individuals who have their cotton plantations below, and retain their residence in that state, where they remain during the sickly season; and they are all, I believe, without exception, doing well. Others, tempted by their success, are constantly engaging in the business, while scarcely any come from the cotton region to engage in western agriculture. A friend, now in my eye, a member of this body, upon a capital of less than $70,000, invested in a plantation and slaves, made, the year before last, $16,000. A member of the other house, I understand, who, without removing himself, sent some of his slaves to Mississippi, made, last year, about 20 per cent. Two friends of mine, in the latter state, whose annual income is from $30,000 to $60,000, being desirous to curtail their business, have offered [cotton] estates for sale, which they are ready to show, by regular vouchers of receipts and disbursements, yield 18 per cent. per annum. One of my most opulent acquaintances, in the county adjoining that in which I reside, having married in Georgia, has derived a large portion of his wealth from a cotton estate there situated."

So far as this evidence goes—and it is large and comprehensive—it proves a great deal; proves what agrees with common report and observation, viz., that cotton-planting has been one of the most lucrative, money-making pursuits in the United States; that fortunes have been made quick and easy by it; that it has been uniformly profitable; that vast estates have been amassed in this calling; that men have grown so suddenly and greatly rich as to be satisfied, and willing to sell out, when the business was worth 18 per cent.; that it is a business which is not liable to fluctuation, and never fails; that the average profit can hardly be less than 20 per cent. on the capital invested, when it has, probably a long time and extensively, been very much better than that; that, if prices have fallen from the enormous profits of former years, it has been owing to the natural tendency of capital where so much money could be made, resulting in over-production; and that the business is still one of the best in the whole country. All but the last of these statements are verified by Mr. Clay's evidence; and for the last, to wit, that this business is still the best, it is now proposed to introduce a witness, whose evidence, considering the quarter from which it comes, as well as for its forcible and convincing character, will, perhaps, be somewhat surprising. In 1844, Leavitt, Trow, & Co., New York, published a remarkable book, pp. 304, entitled, "NOTES ON POLITICAL ECONOMY, AS APPLICABLE TO THE UNITED STATES, BY A SOUTHERN PLANTER." Among the many remarkable things contained in it (it was written by a master hand), are the following:—

" Let us now calculate what cotton can be grown for when prices get down to a mere support for master and slave. With the proper economy, by the owner living on his place, deriving his household and table expenses from it, and clothing and feeding his own slaves, his annual expenses, consisting of salt, iron, medicine, taxes, wrapping for his cotton. and overseer's wages, do not exceed 2 cents a pound on the product or crop. All over that is a profit in their sense, that is, over and above annual expenses. I will give the details to make this clear. A plantation of fifty hands. makes the average of seven bales to the hand, weighing four hundred and fifty pounds. This is three hundred and fifty bales. Suppose 2 cents for expenses. This amounts to $3,150 on the crop. This crop, say, sells for 4 cents a pound, net, and, clear of charges for transportation, insurance, and commission for selling, leaves $3,150 profit for the luxuries of the owner, who gets his necessaries out of the plantation by living on it. This is a very pretty sum ; and half of it would be ample for him, which would reduce cotton to three cents. As to insurance, unfortunately, the slaves not only insure themselves, but give a large increase, which grows up with the owner's children, and furnishes them with outfits by the time they need them. Now, I will go into a calculation to show that two cents a pound cover the annual expenses. Here follow the items, taking a plantation of fifty hands as a basis : For overseer, $500 ; for salt, $20 ; iron, $30 ; medicines, $20 ; doctor's bill, $100, for you can contract by the year, and it is often done, at $2 a head ; bagging and rope to wrap it, at 12 1-2 cents for the one, and 5 cents for the other, amounts to $300 ; taxes, $100 ; sundry small things, $100 ; all told. The writer speaks from experience, for he is a planter of cotton, and owns slaves. All this amounts to $1,170, much below the allowance of 2 cents a pound, amounting, as we have seen, to $3,150. I only wish to show, that we can grow cotton *for 3 cents a pound, and have a living profit.* . . . The cotton culture, then, is sure to go on in this country, at any price, from 3 cents up, that the market warrants, and with increased energies. These facts warrant us in asserting, which we do broadly and unqualifiedly, that we can grow cotton cheaper than any other people on earth, not even excepting the Hindoos. The consequence of this will be, that we will take the market of the world, and keep it supplied with cotton. . . . I am not speaking hypothetically, when I say the United States can grow all the cotton wanted—have slaves and land enough to do it, and even overdo it. [This was written before there was any serious expectation of the annexation of Texas.] This country can raise 3,000,000 of bales, when that much is wanted, and then keep ahead of the consumption far enough *to prevent any advance in the price.* . . . If we keep cotton down, not to its minimum price, but to five or six cents, it will cease to come around the cape of Good Hope, and the United States will have the market of the world, just as certainly as at three cents. . . . England can not decline taking our cotton, because it is cheapest, and because she has built up her manufactories on the minimum price of the raw material, and buys it wherever cheapest, and has conformed all prices of labor and goods to that principle. She has, in France and Germany, as well as in us, rivals to her cotton manufactures, and such skilful rivals, too, that she dare not pay more for the raw material than they do. If she were to pay two cents a pound more for cotton than we do, or than the continent of Europe does, she would lose her hold on the cotton manufacture, and her opponents would take her markets. *The halfpenny-a-pound duty now levied in England will have to give way to insure her success.* [This duty was taken off in 1845, the next year after this remarkable prediction was uttered.] . . . According to the opinions of our most deserving and most skilful commission merchants and factors, our own [American] spinners are now worth fully *two cents a pound* to the cotton market, each and every year, by the competition they create with the Europeans. . . . Fears have been expressed that, should we get under way by the stimulus of a protective tariff, we would not only pass the dead point, but go ahead beyond our own consumption, so as to aim at supplying the whole world with manufactures. Such arguments cut like two-edged swords, and show how much might be done under protection."

The above extracts are a little more comprehensive than what is strictly pertinent to the point of the comparative profits of manufacturing and cotton-growing. Nevertheless, they exhibit some practical suggestions of great importance relative to the subject. One of them is a maximum price of cotton, five to six cents, that will be best for the country, though not, perhaps, for individual growers, except as it might prove to be their interest thus to command the market of all the world. It is clear that the prices can not be kept up as high as they have been, so long as the business is so profitable, and so attractive to capital. It may, therefore, be better for each, as it would be better for the aggregate interest, that prices should come down to that point, which will secure an exclusive market in all quarters. The idea suggested by this writer, that, in such a case, it would be policy to *prevent* the rise of prices above that point, is doubtless repugnant to the complaint, that they have already fallen too low. But it will be hard to disturb his reasoning. The clearness with which he has set forth the position of England, in her absolute dependance on American cotton, will be appreciated. It will be seen that it disposes of the argument, that England would purchase less of American cotton under an American protective system, and proves that she would rather be forced to purchase more, to keep her own markets, which would be exposed to American and other competition. In any case, these rival interests would necessarily enlarge the field of demand for manufactured cottons, and the world *must* be supplied, which necessarily increases the demand for the raw material. With those who wish to sustain and raise the price of American cotton, the *two-cents-a-pound* sustaining power, imparted to it by American spinners—admitting the fact—could hardly be unwelcome to them ; and it will be difficult to avoid the conclusion, that the fact is so.

With the facts afforded by the "Southern Planter," as to the expense of raising cotton, it is only necessary to find what have been the prices of cotton, during the history of its production in the United States, down to the present time, and its price now, to have a just idea of the profits of the business. In a variety of instructive and useful statistics on cotton, published in the "National Intelligencer," Sept. 8, 1846, which had been prepared with great care by a Virginia gentleman, is a column of the average price of cotton per pound, for each year, from 1790 to 1838, as follows :—

Years.	Cents.	Years.	Cents.	Years.	Cents.
1790	14½	1807	21½	1823	10 and 12
1791	26	1808	19	1824	15
1792	29	1809	16	1825	21
1793	32	1810	16	1826	11
1794	33	1811	15½	1827	9½
1795	36½	1812	10½	1828	10¼
1796	36½	1813	12	1829	10
1797	34	1814	15	1830	10
1798	39	1815	21	1831	9¼
1799	44	1816	29½	1832	10
1800	28	1817	26½	1833	11
1801	44	1818	34	1834	13
1802	19	1819	24	1835	16½
1803	19	1820	17	1836	16¾
1804	20	1821	16	1837	14⅛
1805	23	1822	16½	1838	10⅛
1806	22				

By a table in the report of the secretary of the treasury, Mr. Walker, on page 612, these average prices are brought down to 1844, inclusive. It begins with 1833 :—

Years.	Cents.	Years.	Cents.	Years.	Cents.
1833	11	1837	14	1841	10
1834	12	1838	10	1842	8
1835	16	1839	14	1843	6
1836	16	1840	8	1844	8

The slight variation in six concurrent years, from 1833 to 1838, inclusive, in these two authorities, establishes at least the fidelity of the first, if it should suggest that there may have been a motive in the second (it was sent to the secretary from South Carolina, in answer to one of his circulars), for making the price as low as fairness would allow. Both are doubtless worthy of confidence, and in any case are accurate enough for the present purpose.

It is proper to remark, that the higher prices of former years do not determine the question of comparative profits in the business at different times. The advantages of experience and sundry improvements, might make the prices of latter years more profitable than those of the former. The right of using Whitney's cotton-gin, was open to all, in 1800. It will be seen that the prices have never yet come down to the maximum, five to six, which the "Southern Planter" thinks would be best for the interest, and that, for the last twenty of these years, from 1825 to 1844, inclusive, they amount to an average of 11 1-5 cents (taking Mr. Walker's prices as far as they go), leaving nearly four times a living profit, which is three cents. The average prices of the first thirty-five years, from 1790 to 1824, inclusive, were twenty-four cents, or eight times the living profit of the present period.

There is enough in all this, to show, in connexion with the evidence of Mr. Clay, and the practical statements of the "Southern Planter," first, that cotton-growing in the United States, has not only been a very profitable business, down to this time, but by far the most profitable of any in the country; secondly, that it has never seen a day of adversity; and thirdly, that it occupies a commercial position, in relation to the wants of mankind, and to the rest of the world, which, for an indefinite future period, apparently for ever, is very sure to command uninterrupted prosperity and great profits.

And this is the interest which complains of the profits of manufacturing, when the latter, in its best days, never did so well as cotton-growing in its poorest days; when cotton-growing never failed—can't fail, except as the crop fails, and then the price, ordinarily, will make it up—whereas, manufacturing has broken down many times—has sunk more money, and ruined more fortunes, than has happened to any other interest in the land.

§ 11. "The Protected Classes."

Mr. Polk, in his message, speaks of the tariff of 1842, as a system of duties laid "for the protection merely of a *favored interest*." Mr. Walker speaks of the protection afforded by this tariff as "a tax on all consumers for the benefit of the *protected classes*;" "to increase the resources of the *protected classes*." He is opposed to "legislation for *classes*." "His opposition is to the *protective system*." "Equal rights and profits look to the whole country, not to *classes*." "The number of manufacturing capitalists, who derive the benefit from the heavy taxes extracted [extorted ?] by the tariff from twenty millions of people, does not exceed 10,000. The whole number, including the working-classes engaged in our manufactures, deriving any benefit from the tariff, does not exceed 400,000, of whom not more than 40,000 have been brought into this pursuit by the last tariff."

What is said in the above extracts, about "a tax," and "taxes," having been disposed of in this work, as being no tax and no taxes at all, but the contrary, the object here is to

58

call attention to the "*protected classes*," against whom the secretary, the president, and the tariff of 1846, are arrayed. The secretary sets down one class at 10,000, and another at 400,000—in all 410,000. What are they among 20,000,000 ? It is admitted, that these 10,000 capitalists, and these 400,000 other supposed beneficiaries of the tariff of 1842, whoever they may be, are not of so great consequence as nineteen and a half millions, being only about one fortieth of the whole population of the country ; but it will be observed, that the aims of the president and secretary, in devising the tariff of 1846, were, by their own confession, directed against the "*protected classes.*" "His," the secretary's, "opposition is to the *protective system.*" The president appears to be with him, or rather the leader ; and there is very little doubt, that the tariff of 1846 will answer all their purposes in breaking down "the protective system."

But the question is, whether the president and the secretary have not made a mistake, and broken down the classes which they did not intend; whether they have not hit those whom, taking their own word for it, they did not aim at ? The question is, who are the "*protected classes*" ? After all that has been proved, in the preceding chapters of this work, it is presumed there will be very little difficulty in deciding this question. Doubtless the 10,000 capitalists—their number is probably much greater than that—and the 400,000 other beneficiaries of the tariff of '42, though somewhat difficult to tell who are meant by this larger number—yet, doubtless, both these classes had an interest in the protective system. But the capitalists, however they may be injured, can not generally be broken down by the tariff of 1846. They are able to make shifts, take up a new position, and accommodate themselves to the new state of things. It is also probable that the other 400,000 in the eye of the secretary, are classes in such intimate connexion with the capitalists, that they, too, will be able to save themselves from the general wreck. These 410,000 persons will, no doubt, for the most part, protect themselves, in spite of the new tariff. They had no just claim for the benevolent regrets of the secretary and president, or for the eminent position assigned them in this matter. They should have been forgotten, and may now be set aside for ever, in comparison of the numerous other classes, and of the immense aggregate of those classes, over whom the tariff of 1842 threw its protecting shield, and who are destined, under the tariff of 1846, to feel and rue the want of it. Not to speak of the whole country, dependent as it has been shown to have been, for its prosperity and happiness, on the tariff of 1842, those more immediately connected with it, including their families, and to whom it had opened the means of living, and of comfort in life, are not probably less than four millions. It is charitably supposed, that the president and secretary did not understand who constituted "the protected classes," most worthy of consideration, and having the strongest claims for it, in the change which they proposed to make, and have made, in the tariff policy of the country. They need not have bestowed one thought or feeling, of kindness or of unkindness, on those whom they have made so prominent as "protected classes," as if there were no other. These were not worthy of notice, in comparison of the countless hosts of laborers of every class ; of the wives and children dependent upon them; of mechanics of every kind, and their families ; of the husbandman who ploughs the earth, and the sailor that ploughs the ocean ; of the miner that seldom sees the light, and the smith that burns his coal ; of the woman that plies her needle, and the girl that tends the loom ; of widows and orphans that could not afford to be deprived of a precarious subsistence ; and of all the industrial pursuits of twenty millions of people, provided with a competency, contented and happy. *These* were "the protected classes," whom it behooved the president and secretary to think of, when they made war on protection, and resolved to strike it for ever from the statute book !

§ 12. *Mr. Walker's "true question."*

"The true question," says Mr. Walker, "is, whether the farmer and planter shall, to a great extent, supply our people with cheap manufactures, purchased abroad with their agricultural products ; or whether this exchange shall be forbidden by high duties on such manufactures, and their supply thrown, as a monopoly, at large prices, by high tariffs, into the hands of our own manufacturers."

Not to speak again of the barter principle here assumed as the basis of this operation, which is never practised in the commerce of the civilized world—certainly not in this case—this question, which the honorable secretary dignifies with the eminence of " THE TRUE QUESTION," all falls to the ground at once, by what has been proved in this work, to wit, that prices are cheapened by protection. Without seeming to have the first elemental idea of the philosophy of trade, of commercial competition, and of the doctrine of supply and demand (one is loath to speak so irreverently of such a high dignitary, who is bound to understand these things), the honorable secretary, with all the simplicity of a man who has first opened his eyes on the world, reads the prices current in England, compares them with prices-current in the United States, and jumps to the conclusion announced in his report, as follows : "The truest comparison is between the present price of the same article at home and abroad ; and to the extent the price is lower in the foreign market than in our own, the duty, if equal to that difference, must to that extent enhance the price, and in the same ratio

210

with the lower duty." Ought not this secretary of the treasury to know, that the moment a foreign producer of a manufactured article encounters the check of an impost duty in the United States, or in any other market which he had been accustomed to monopolize at his own prices—a duty imposed for protection—his prices must fall, first, by the law of competition, brought into action by the duty, if it is not prohibitory; and next, if the duty be prohibitory, because he has lost a market, and must do as well as he can with his surplus productions, and in competition wiih domestic rivals, in a more limited field? Here are two principles, that reduce prices on both sides—that of a more extended competition, and that of supply, or ability to produce, above demand. And ought not the honorable secretary to know—he has at least been instructed by the fact, since the passage of the tariff of 1846—that the moment these duties are taken off, or lowered, in the United States, prices instantly rise in England, and other foreign parts? Up went iron—up went everything—in England, on the first intelligence, for which a prospective increased demand was opened in this country, by this new measure; and the secretary reads a different story in the foreign prices-current! The secretary is made wise too late—if, indeed, he is capable of being made wise. The British house of lords did him the compliment to order his report to be printed, because it answered their purposes; and the British manufacturers have laughed at his folly in opening to them a door for an increased demand for their products, and consequently for higher prices. Now Mr. Walker will find, that "the cost of production," which he lays down as a rule of price—guided, doubtless, by Ricardo, and others of that tribe—has little to do with it, and that it is controlled by supply and demand. He will find, not only that his cheap foreign prices have vanished, but that, as soon as the British manufacturers shall have silenced the music of the American hammer, and the rattle of the American loom, they will have their *own* prices, and make the American people sweat for it! So they had their own prices when these states were British colonies; so they have always had them, when the American protective system was not high enough to reduce them; and so they always will have them, when this system of protection lies prostrate—bleeding in the dust.

§ 13. *Free Trade between the States of the Union.*

The blessings of universal free-trade, Mr. Walker says, "are clearly illustrated by the perfect free-trade which exists among all the states of the Union, and by the acknowledged fact, that any one of these states would be injured by imposing duties on the products of the others." Probably the secretary meant, the others would be injured. But that is no matter. This illustration halts in the way to its end, first, for lack of analogy; and next, by begging the question. The United States, so far as this question is concerned, are *one* family, and *the* family out of whose position, relative to other families, the question is raised. There can, therefore, be no analogy in the relations between the different branches of this family, whose political interests are one, and in the relations between this and other families, whose political character and structure, as well as interests, are diverse. It is, therefore, begging the question to assume this example as an illustration. But, since it is brought forward, it is fair to take advantage of all that may be learned from it. Suppose that Ohio were free, by the constitution, to impose duties on the products of the adjoining state Kentucky, or Indiana, or Pennsylvania, and should do so; can it be imagined, that either of these other states would lie still under it, and not impose countervailing duties? That is precisely the case between the United States and other nations, and ought to settle the question. But there is more in it than that. Even if all other nations should propose free-trade with us, there are differences between their political structure and ours, as has been shown in this work, which would amount to a system of duties on their part against us, and which would still compel us to countervailing measures; or else, we should inevitably be dragged down to their level, in the depression and dependence of our labor. All other things must be made equal, before such parties, so diverse in their character and interests, can safely come to stand on the same commercial platform.

It has been seen how the only country in the world pretending to offer us free-trade, Great Britain, has advanced *backward* in giving it. Whence are we to look for it? American flour in Cuba pays a duty of about $10 a barrel; in Rio Janeiro, $5 to $6; and in many other foreign parts, the duties on this article range from 50 to 150 per cent. In return, we take coffee without duty. This is free trade! We have reciprocity treaties with several foreign powers, the effect of which has already been to take away about one third of our carrying-trade. And this is free-trade! The effect of our reciprocity treaty with Great Britain has been, that while, in 1830, American bottoms carried exports from this country to that, to the amount of $19,876,000, and British bottoms to the amount of $5,897,000, the British carrying had increased in 1844 to $18,716,000, against $29,078,000 in American bottoms, showing an increase, in fifteen years, in favor of British bottoms, of over 300 per cent., against an increase in American bottoms, of less than 50 per cent. And this is free trade! (*See Fisher's Magazine for May*, 1846, p. 1113.) When Americans began to export their goods to Hindostan, the British government imposed a duty there against us, first of 5, next of $8\frac{1}{2}$, then of $10\frac{1}{2}$, and finally of 15 per cent., which, it is supposed, will be an exclusion. And this is free trade! It is worthy of remark, that on the single staple of tobacco, which she receives from the United States, Great Britain levies an amount of duties about equal to the total amount of customs collected on all articles imported into the United States from all foreign countries; and also about equal to the total annual expenditures of our government. And this is free trade! The Hon. P. Triplett, of Kentucky, made a communication to the committee on manufactures, in the 27th Congress, from which are deduced the following facts: that American products consumed in Europe pay duties on entering there, equal to *half* of their entire value; whereas, European products consumed in the United States pay duties here equal to *one fifth* of their value. And this is free trade! In 1841, imports into the United States were $127,945,000, and exports, $91,000,000. The duties raised from these imports amounted to $14,487,000, being about $11\frac{1}{2}$ per cent.; whereas, the duties which foreign countries obtained from exports from the United States, of that year, amounted to $113,500,000, or 124 per cent.! The average of exports of tobacco from the United States to Europe, for 1839 and 1840, was $9,225,000 for each year; and the average duties imposed for each year by European governments, was $32,463,000, or 350 per cent.! The duties on American tobacco in Europe have been as high as $35,000,000 a year. And this is free-trade!

§ 14. *The Subtreasury and Warehousing System.*

The sub or independent treasury has been too long before the public, to demand much notice here. It can not, however, but be seen, that it has a very important relation to the *rights of labor*, in claiming cash for the uses of government, and turning off labor with a currency which the government pronounces bad, and which its practice tends to make bad.

But the warehousing system is a new thing. Unfortunately for the labor and trade of the country, both seem now doomed to fall into a new gulf of perdition, dark and deep—dark, because nothing is known about it here, and deep, because no one can fathom it. That it will prove destructive to both, can hardly be doubted, if it be considered who wants it—to whom, chiefly, it will operate as an accommodation—a facility. It is indeed a marvellous grant, a most seductive facility to foreigners. It is not only permitting, *inviting* them to come with their goods, and wait for the chances of the market, to supplant American merchants and American labor, but it provides them with house and storeroom! It is taxing American labor with the means of destroying itself! Forcing it to extend a gratuitous, prodigal hospitality, to a deadly foe; to give that foe a position and a power to pull down the house over the head of American labor, and to carry away its bread! That foe would do all this—has done it, on a large scale, even when forced to pay duties on entrance; but now, having no duties to pay till he can find a market, and those duties so small, that American labor can not compete with him, the field is won! The victory is complete! The door is now thrown wide open, with no obstacle in the way; means of accommodation are provided; and the invitation is given to the holders of all the surplus manufactured products of Europe, and of any other parts where they may exist, to come and make their deposites, free of tax, in the storehouses provided by the government of the United States, to be brought out and sold when they can best do it, or to be re-exported at their pleasure. Surpluses of every species of manufacture are constantly accumulating abroad, by overproduction and bankruptcy, which must be disposed of, at whatever sacrifice. Nothing was wanted but the warehousing act of the United States to answer all their purposes, and, with other concurrent causes, to involve American labor in overwhelming distress and irretrievable ruin!

CHAPTER XVII.

PRESIDENT POLK A CONSISTENT ANTI-PROTECTIONIST.

SOME have supposed, that Mr. Polk's practice as president, has been inconsistent with his letter to Mr. Kane, when he was a candidate in 1844. Observe what he says in that letter: " My opinions on this subject have been *often* given to the public. They are to be found *in my public acts, and in the public discussions* in which I have participated. I am in favor of a tariff *for revenue*—such a one as will yield a sufficient amount to the treasury to defray the expenses of the government economically administered. In adjusting the details of a *revenue* tariff, I have heretofore sanctioned such moderate *discriminating* duties as would produce the amount of revenue needed, and at the same time afford *reasonable incidental protection* to our home industry. I am *opposed* to a tariff *for protection merely*, and not for revenue. Acting upon these general principles, it is well known that I gave my support to the policy of General Jackson's administration on this subject. . . . In my judgment it is the duty of the government to extend, as far as it may be practicable to do so, by its *revenue* laws, and all other means within its power, fair and just protection to all the great interests of the whole Union, embracing agriculture, manufactures, the mechanic arts, commerce, and navigation."

As this letter could not, from its brevity, contain an exposition, Mr. Polk very fairly gives the rule of interpretation : " My public acts, and the public discussions in which I have participated."—" The policy of General Jackson's administration on this subject." Although General Jackson went strong for protection in his letter to Dr. Coleman, in 1824, as before seen, and recommended it in his early messages to Congress ; although he gave his sanction to the tariff of 1832, a strong protective measure, advocated and passed by a " democratic" Congress, George M. Dallas saying, in support of the bill, " I am inflexible, sir, in nothing but adequate protection ;" nevertheless, it is equally well—much better—known, because more recent and more notable, from the prominency of the facts and the gravity of their consequences, that General Jackson was the leading, potential man, who arrayed all the power of the government, seconded by all the power of an overwhelming party, for the destruction of the protective policy, as advocated by Mr. Clay, and as now advocated by all protectionists. No one doubts, that this is precisely " the policy of General Jackson's administration" referred to in Mr. Polk's letter to John K. Kane, to which, he says, " it is *well known* that I gave my support." Mr. Polk did not refer to General Jackson's letter to Dr. Coleman, in 1824 ; nor to the corresponding doctrine of General Jackson's early messages to Congress ; but to the *distinguishing* " policy of General Jackson's administration," to wit, the destruction of the protective system, which existed and was in operation when he came into power. No one could suppose, that Mr. Polk, in this reference, was lending his sanction to Mr. Clay's views as opposed to General Jackson's, but to General Jackson's as opposed to Mr. Clay's. But Mr. Polk has himself determined what he meant by " the policy of General Jackson on this subject," in his address to the people of Tennessee, dated April 3, 1839, in which he says : " In repeated instances, he [General Jackson] recommended *modifications and reductions* of the tariff, *with a view* to the final ABANDONMENT *of the odious and unjust system.* So effectual were these recommendations, and so rapid the change in public opinion, that the friends of the tariff, and Mr. Clay, its reputed father, seized on a favorable moment, *to save the whole from* DESTRUCTION *by a timely* COMPROMISE [the act of 1833]. By yielding a PART, he [Mr. Clay] *prevented the destruction of* THE WHOLE."

But, if there had otherwise been any possible room for doubt, as to Mr. Polk's meaning in this letter, he put it out of question by appealing directly to his " public acts and public discussions" on this subject. He himself points to two of those acts : his vote for the bill of 1832, and his support of Mr. Verplanck's bill. It must be confessed, that these two acts neutralize each other; but the latter demonstrated the bent of his mind. General Jackson himself voted for, that is, *signed* the act of 1832; George M. Dallas advocated it in the senate, and voted for it ; every " democrat" of that Congress voted for it. The plan of destroying the protective system made its first appearance in the executive *projet* of Mr. Verplanck's bill, and was defeated only by the compromise act of 1833.

Apart from the equivocal act of voting for the tariff of 1832, which he says he did because it " contained modifications of the objectionable provisions of the act of 1828," Mr. Polk's public course and public discussions are most remote from being equivocal " on this subject." In the journal of the house of representatives, it will be found, that, on the 10th of February, 1827, Mr. Polk voted three several times, as follows : against protection for wool and woollens; against protection for carpet manufactures ; and against protection for woollen blankets. April 7, 1828, he voted five times, as follows : against protection for worsted stuff goods and bombazines; against protection for cotton-bagging; against protection of hemp and flax manufactures; and twice against duty on distilled spirits. April 9, 1828, he voted thrice, as follows : against protection of iron manufactures ; against protection of oil-cloths, oil-carpeting, patent and other, floor matting, &c. ; against protection for pig lead, lead sheets, shot, &c. April 22, 1828, after having opposed in detail, by votes and speeches, the protective features of the tariff of that year (a part of which, sanctioned by Martin Van Buren and Silas Wright, was doubtless objectionable, as being too stringent), Mr. Polk voted against it as a whole. February 26, 1829, he voted against the repeal of tonnage duties on ships and vessels of the United States and certain foreign vessels. May 11, 1830, he voted, first, against protection of wool and woollens; and then against protection of iron, hemp, flax, cotton-bagging, molasses, cotton goods, &c. December 13, 1830, he voted against protection of sugar. December 14, 1830, against protection of iron, wool, woollens, and cotton-bagging. June 22, 1832, he voted seven times, as follows : against protection of woollen manufactures ; of woollen yarns; of cabinet wares; of hats and caps, made of fur, leather, or wool ; of whips, bridles, saddles, and all manufactures of leather not otherwise specified ; of carriages and parts of carriages ; and of blank books. June 26, 1832, he voted against protection, by drawbacks of duty on iron used for ploughs, axes, hoes, wagons, carts, and all other implements of agriculture. June 27, 1832, he voted four times, as follows : against protection for mits, gloves, bindings, blankets, hosiery, &c. ; against flannels and baizes ; against carpets; and against hemp. July 10, 1832, against duty on merino shawls and other manufactures of wool. February 18, 1833, he voted against a comprehensive measure for protection of woollen manufactures, part of it designed for revenue. February 20, 1833, against duty on raw cotton. February 21, 1833, he voted three times, as follows: first, against protection of linseed, hempseed, and rapeseed oils; next, to retain duty on coffee; and third, to retain duty on tea.

In all Mr. Polk's public course in Congress, to which he appeals in his letter to Mr. Kane, he proved himself a consistent *anti-protectionist*, as a member of the house, of the committee of ways and means, in his speeches, by his votes, in whole and in detail of all public measures, passed or attempted to be passed while he was there, relating to the protection of home interests and home labor. It is enough, that, as a member of the committee of ways and means, he voted for Mr. Verplanck's bill, and subsequently to 1832, supported " the policy of General Jackson's administration on this subject," the great aim of which was to destroy the protective system.

Mr. Verplanck's bill, which will be found to be the 14th document in the volume of reports of committees, at the second session of the twenty-second Congress, was to reduce duties as follows—all assessable *on the foreign valuation*:—On *woollens*, to 15 per cent.; on all not exceeding 35 cents the square yard, 5 per cent.; on worsted stuff goods of all kinds, 10 per cent.; on worsted and woollen hosiery, gloves, nets, bindings, and stockinets, 10 per cent.; on all other cloths, merino shawls, flannels, baizes, and cassimeres, carpetings and rugs of all kinds, 20 per cent.; on clothing ready-made of all descriptions, 20 per cent; on all *cotton goods*, 20 per cent., except Nankins from India, on which Mr. Polk's duty was 15 per cent.; and cotton hosiery, gloves, mitts, and stockinets, on which his duty was 10 per cent.; as well as upon cotton twist, yarn, and thread; on all manufactures of *flax and hemp*, or sail-duck, and cotton-bagging, 15 per cent.; on all manufactures of tin, japanning, gilt, plated, brass, and polished steel, 20 per cent.; on common saddlery, 10 per cent.; on earthen and stoneware, 20 per cent.; on all side and fire arms, rifles and muskets, 20 per cent.; bridle-bits and glass-ware, 20 per cent.; on manufactures of iron and steel generally, a duty of 20 per cent.; on salt and coal, 5 per cent.; on everything produced by the farmer in the middle and northern states, Mr. Polk, who is a cotton-grower, recommended, in this bill, one unvarying standard of only 15 per cent.; 15 per cent. on potatoes; 15 per cent. on oats; 15 per cent. on wheat and wheat-flour, butter, bacon, beef, and pork.

The Hon. John M. Clayton remarked, in a speech at Wilmington, June 15, 1844, on the above items, which are borrowed from him, that " by reducing the duty on wool to 15 per cent., it put the knife to the throat of every sheep in the country. By a duty of 20 per cent. on ready-made clothing of all descriptions, it struck down a whole class of the most industrious and useful mechanics of the nation. If it had been a bill purposely designed to set fire to most of the mechanic shops in the country, it would hardly have had a worse effect upon the laboring classes. It would have fed us on potatoes from Ireland; and, at those periods when the farmers of the middle and northern states were suffering most from the pressure of the times, our bread-stuffs would have been grown on the borders of the Baltic and the Black sea, instead of on our own soil."

Mr Polk says, in his letter to Mr. Kane, " as a member of the committee of ways and means of the house of representatives, I gave my assent to a bill reported by that committee in December, 1832," &c. This was Mr. Verplanck's bill, which would have become a law, but for the introduction of Mr. Clay's compromise bill.

But Mr. Polk's appeals to his " public discussions on this subject," referring, doubtless, to those before the people of Tennessee, when he was candidate for governor, are worthy of some attention. In his public address to the people of Tennessee, dated Columbia, March 15, 1843, in reply to sundry questions sent him by Messrs. G. W. Smith, R. E. Titus, C. Stewart, and others, he says—" Your second interrogatory is as follows : ' Are you in favor of restoring the principle of the compromise tariff bill of 1833 ?' I answer that I am !'" This principle was understood and claimed by these parties as a maximum duty of 20 per cent., as carried into effect, under Mr. Polk as president, in the tariff of 1846. Mr. Polk says again, in the above named address, " Your *eleventh* interrogatory is as follows, to wit: ' Are you in favor of the tariff act [the act of 1842], now in force, passed by the last Congress ?' I answer that I am not ' in favor of the tariff act now in force, passed by the last Congress.' It is, in my opinion, in many of its provisions, highly *protective*, and not designed as a *revenue* measure."

In another document from the hand of Mr. Polk, of the same date as the above, made public by him, and addressed to Messrs. Wyatt Christian, J. P. Leath, and others, he says : " Your 5th and 6th interrogatories are in the following words, to wit : ' 5th, are you in favor of a tariff or direct taxes for the support of the general government ? 6th, If a tariff, do you approve of such a tariff as would give protection to home industry against foreign industry ?' I answer, that I am opposed to a system of direct taxation, and am in favor of a *moderate scale of duties*, laid by a tariff on imported goods, for the purpose of raising the *revenue* which may be needed for the economical administration of the government. In fixing the rates of a tariff, my opinion is, that the object in view should be to raise the revenue needed by government, *leaving* the interests engaged in manufactures to enjoy the *incidental* advantage which the levy of such duties will afford them. If by 'giving protection to home industry,' you mean to assert the *distinct principle,* that a tariff is to be laid solely, or in any extent not for revenue, but for protection of capitalists who have made their investments in manufacturing establishments, &c., then I say, that I am opposed to such a principle, and to any tariff which recognises it. . . . I am *opposed* to the tariff act of the late Congress [act of '42], considering it to be in many respects of this character—and indeed *so highly protective* upon some articles as to prohibit their importation into the country altogether. *I am in favor of* REPEALING *that act,* and of restoring the compromise tariff act of March 2, 1833, believing as I do, that it would produce more revenue than the present law, and that the *incidental* protection afforded by the 20 per cent. duty, &c., will afford sufficient protection," &c.

In another communication to the public, dated, Columbia, May 17, 1843, Mr. Polk says: " ALL who observed my course, KNOW, that I have *at all times been* OPPOSED *to the 'protective policy.'* . . . I am in favor of a tariff for *revenue,* and opposed to a tariff for *protection.* I was a member of Congress when this subject excited greatest interest. I was opposed to the protective tariff of 1828, and voted against it. I voted for the act of 1832, *because* it reduced the tariff of 1828 to lower rates. That made *some* reduction, though not *as much* as I desired to have made. I voted for the act of March 2, 1833, commonly called the compromise act, which reduced the rates of the act of 1832 to still lower rates, and finally brought the rates of the act of 1832 down to a point, at which no article, after the 30th of June, 1842, was to be subject to a duty higher than 20 per cent. This was the law when the whig Congress came into power. By the tariff act of the 30th August, 1842, the compromise act was violated and repealed. *I am opposed to the act of* 1842, not regarding it to be a revenue tariff, but in many of its provisions *highly protective* and oppressive in its character. I am in favor of the restoration of the compromise act of 1833."
Again :—

" *To the people of Tennessee*—
" The object which I had in proposing to *Governor Jones,* at Carrollville, on the 12th of April last, that we should each write out and publish our views and opinions on the tariff, was, that our respective positions might be *distinctly* known and understood by the people. That *my* opinions were *already* fully and distinctly known, I could not doubt. I had *steadily,* during the period I was a representative in Congress, *been opposed to a protective policy, as my* RECORDED VOTES *and public speeches prove.* Since I retired from Congress, I had held the same opinions. In the present canvass for governor, I had *avowed my opposition* to the tariff act of the late whig Congress [act of '42], as being *highly protective* in its character, and not designed by its authors as a revenue measure. I had avowed my opinion in my public speeches, that the interest of the country, and especially of the producing and exporting classes, REQUIRED ITS REPEAL. " JAMES K. POLK.
" *Winchester, May* 29, 1843."

In Mr. Polk's inaugural, March 4, 1845, and in his first message to Congress, Dec. 2, 1845, he advances the same doctrine. This evidence might be greatly extended ; but it will probably be regarded as sufficient to establish Mr. Polk's consistency, in all his public life, as an *anti-protectionist.* It was not Mr. Polk's fault, if those who undertook to interpret his language, *imagined* that they found in the words, " discriminating duties," and " incidental protection," enough to prove him a *protectionist,* or to afford any pledge of the kind. " Discrimination"—for what ? For *revenue,* Mr. Polk says; and has never said anything else. " *Incidental* protection"—and what is that ? Protection when it is not possible to prevent it, in getting a revenue. But Mr. Polk appealed to his " public acts," and " public discussions." Was not that enough ?

CHAPTER XVI.
TARIFF OF 1846.

THE fundamental principles of the tariff of 1846, have been fully considered in the preceding pages. It remains to take some notice of its practical operation on the great and minor interests, on the business and labor, of the country.

§ 1. *The Responsibility of agitating this Subject, when the Country was doing well.*

It will not be denied, that the state of the country under the tariff of 1842, as regards this department of public policy, was tranquil, generally satisfactory, and greatly prosperous. If " let well alone," be a useful maxim in private affairs, how much more in public ? From what quarter, what state, what body, what party, what individual person, did a petition go in to Congress, proposing to disturb the tariff of 1842 ? Not from one.

Is not this a remarkable fact? But there were many parties, from many quarters, who did send in petitions and memorials, remonstrating against disturbing that measure. Do we live where the will of the governors is to govern? Or in a republican country? Was there not a great responsibility in originating an agitation of this subject, unsolicited by the people?

From the effects of tariff regulations, none can escape. The weal or the wo of the country is in them. It was thought that the public weal had been promoted by the tariff of 1842. Nobody, indeed, thought otherwise. The evidence was too strong to be resisted. The people were prosperous and happy.

§ 2. *Instinct and Panic.*

Reason is fallible; but instinct never errs. The instincts of animal tribes are the guidance of the Divinity within them. Man, too, is endowed with instinct, but in an imperfect degree, compared with animals. Reason, a higher and nobler attribute, was given him, to preside over instinct; but reason is often unfortunate in its dictations.

If the convicts of all the state-prisons in the United States were put to making shoes, and the state should throw them into market at a small advance on the cost of the materials, and the subsistence of the convicts, would it be necessary for the free laborers engaged in this pursuit to study and understand political economy, before they could appreciate the effects of this measure on themselves? Their *instincts* would leap to the conclusion with the speed of lightning. They would be excited, alarmed. The riotous disposition manifested in the city of New York, a few years ago, for using the Sing-Sing marble, quarried and dressed by the convicts, and called the " state-prison monopoly," which was sold at prices to paralyze the arm of free laborers, is directly in point. In the same manner, all the free laborers of the United States know, that Europe is but a prison-house for labor, forcing it to toil for bare subsistence, and that it is equally unfair and wrong to force them into a competition with such a power, as to force shoemakers or stonecutters to compete with the convicts of state-prisons. And all the business pursuits of the country sympathize with each other. One can not be wronged, but all are injured; and if labor, the great power of the country, on which all depend, is depressed, all feel it. Any measure of the government that begins to *look* like an invasion of the rights of labor, startles the wide community, and people are alarmed. Nor is there any mistake in it; what all see, is truth; it is impossible that such instincts should err.

This is what is called a PANIC. It is an error to say, it is *got up*. Trade never commits suicide; it never does that willingly, which is injurious to itself; but it will keep off a panic as long as possible. Nor can a few interested persons, like the bears in Wall street, make a general panic. If they succeed in depressing stocks a little one day, they will rise the next. Such a thing as a general panic was never known, in any country, without cause. It is the quick operation, the infallible foresight, the premonition of the instincts of the wide community.

In this manner, the inaugural address of President Polk, on the 4th of March, 1845, startled the country. The people were enjoying great blessings under the tariff of 1842. Labor everywhere found employment and reward, and the nation had risen from a long period of suffering and calamity, produced by the reign of free-trade principles, to an unexampled and rejoicing career of prosperity. To have such a condition menaced, from such a quarter, was alarming. Nevertheless, a sanguine people will still hope on, and though timid from instinctive dread, with confidence trembling in the eye of the winds, they waited for the message of December 2, 1845, from which time till the passage of the tariff of July 30, 1846, the commercial business of the whole country was paralyzed with apprehension. It was the operation of the public instincts. Ships, in large numbers, ready, or nearly ready, or preparing, to sail, freighted with wealth, were stopped; voyages were delayed; orders for goods were countermanded, and others kept back; many, and some vast, schemes of domestic enterprise, with a corresponding capital ready to be invested for the employment of labor, were arrested; and all these great transactions, connected by a thousand channels, and a thousand links, with all the other great and minor interests of the country, were held in suspense for eight long and tedious months, waiting for the blow that was so seriously apprehended, the falling of which only demonstrated that these instincts of the people were infallibly just. One hundred millions of dollars would not fully indemnify the people of the United States for all the injury done to their vast and complicated interests during this agitation, till the consummation of the scheme which it proposed to fasten upon the country, and under which it now groans. What, then, must be the sequel?

§ 3. *The Sequel.*

The sequel, it is true, is, for the most part, yet in the future. But enough has already transpired, in connexion with the experience of former years, under the two antagonist systems of protective and anti-protective duties, to prognosticate, with a sufficient degree of certainty, the coming results. Not less, probably, than a hundred millions of capital, waiting for the decision of this great question, and ready to be invested in a great variety of enterprises for the employment of labor, and for the increased production of private, public, and national wealth, have already been locked up, or turned to employments not productive of the general good. "Capital," says the Southern Planter, "when not permanently invested, merely seeking interest annually, is almost sure to do more harm than good, because those branches most depressed and in debt are the first to come forward to take offered loans, to pay their old debts, under the hope that business will revive so as to justify the transaction. Alas! soon they become convinced, that the capitalist will absorb all, and end in a break-up for both." Such, all know, was the result of the great revulsion of 1836–'7. While there was no encouragement for the investment of capital in those establishments, and enterprises, manufacturing and other, which employ labor and promote the general good, it turned itself to secure mortgages on the distressed, and made vastly more profits in the end than it could have done in any other way, in the ruin of the thousands that asked its aid. "Capital," says Mr. Lawrence, in his second letter to Mr. Rives, "has usually had the power to take care of itself, and does not require the aid of Congress to place it in any other position *than to put the labor in motion.* Congress should legislate for the *labor,* and the capital will take care of itself." Here is disclosed a great principle, apparently not discerned by those who have sought, by legislation, to depress capital, and impair its position relative to other interests. They only elevate and strengthen it, positively in some cases, relatively in all. They create the very monopoly, the very power, of which they complain. Before, it was no monopoly—no undue influence, as shown in these pages. But under the tariff of 1846, the strong manufacturing establishments which are able to stand, will be strengthened by the breaking down of the weak, and the consequent greater business they will have. Lowell will not suffer, except, perhaps, in its printing establishments and woollen factories. Lowell will stand in spite of the world, and rise and flourish on the ruins of all around; and the greater the general ruin, so much greater at least its *relative* strength, and so much firmer its *relative* position. It is the weak that will be stricken down by the tariff of 1846; it is the labor of the country that will suffer first and most. Capital will always take care of itself. Some of it, being so invested, as to be assailed by legislation, may suffer; but it will make shifts, and live; while that which is ready to take advantage of the change, will double, or triple, or quadruple itself, in a short period of general distress. But labor can not take care of itself; it is dependent on employment; it will fall before the first rude blast of the storm. He who has contributed, by legislation, to silence the music of the hammer, the noise of the shuttle, the whistle of the ploughman, the song of the boatman and sailor, and the varied harmony of industry, has taken away the bread of dependent wives and children, clothed them in rags, left them to shiver in winter's cold, and drag out a life of sorrow and pain. Says Mr. Lawrence to Mr. Rives:—

"In less than twelve months, after the new plan shall have been in operation, this whole country will be literally surfeited with foreign merchandise (if it be not so, the revenue will fall short of the wants of the government); we shall then owe a debt abroad of millions of dollars, which must be paid in coin. The exchanges go up to a point that makes it profitable to ship specie; money becomes scarce in the Atlantic cities; yet bills on England and France do not fall; the loans made to the south and west are called in; demands for debts due from those sections of country, are made; exchange can not be obtained—produce is purchased and shipped; and when it arrives at the north, it will not command the cost in the west: a paralysis will have struck the business of the country; produce will no longer answer to pay debts due at the north, and the next resort is to coin, which is to be collected and sent down the Mississippi, or over the mountains, to Baltimore, Philadelphia, New York, and Boston. Western and Southern credits are cut off, as the people of those sections can no longer promptly meet their engagements. The new states, and the outer circle of the republic, are the weak points; and the first giving way of the banks is heard from those places, where there is the least amount of capital. We see the storm approaching like a thunder-shower in a summer's day; we watch its progress, but can not escape its fall. It at last reaches the great marts of trade and the exchanges, having swept everything in its course; and the banks of the Atlantic cities, after a violent effort to maintain their credit and honor, are forced to yield to this Utopian experiment. I have no hesitation in stating that all this will take place within the space of eighteen months from the time this experimental bill goes into operation; and not a specie-paying bank, doing business, will be found in the United States."

Possibly all this may not take place. All classes of the people are afloat in one ship, and though tossed and pelted by a merciless tempest, they will try hard to bring the vessel into port again. They will endeavor to accommodate themselves to their position. The weak will fall, and the laborer will find it hard to get bread. The great improvements and enterprises of the country will be checked for years. The nation, probably, will not go backward; neither will it go forward. All classes will be obliged to stand it as well as they can. This country, thank God, has too many resources, for the people to be reduced to absolute want, to starvation, before they will see the cause of their misfortunes, and be able to apply a remedy. But why should such a country suffer such misfortunes, if government was not instituted to prove how much the people can endure? They have gone through it all once, and but recently. Why should they be compelled to go through it all again?

Doubtless the government, frightened at the consequences of their measure, will undertake to tinker and mend the act. But wrong in principle, at the foundation, throughout, it is impossible to mend it. If parts of it should be altered, to appease such a state as Pennsylvania, it will only aggravate the injustice to other states, and other portions of the Union. The relief of one interest, for party purposes, will only rivet tighter the chains fastened upon others. It would be ignoble, it would be wanting in that magnanimity which bound together the revolutionary fathers, for one state to consent to be relieved, while others are held in bondage. To find so late, that this Union is not a grand republican fraternity, to stand or fall together, would be a painful discovery.

§ 4. The great Question.

It is a question of the *rights of American labor.* If American labor will be contented with the wages of European labor, there is no doubt that American capital can do as well on a platform of free trade as European capital. American capital, comparatively, is worthy of little consideration in determining and establishing a system of foreign commercial policy. It is chiefly the protection of American labor, against the low-priced labor of Europe and elsewhere, that demands the solemn consideration of American statesmen, and their scrupulous and unceasing care. The great doctrine of this work, derived from and founded upon the difference between the cost of money and labor in the United States, as heretofore maintained, and in the countries with which we trade—a difference at least of 100 per cent.—is a doctrine, which controls this whole subject as certainly, as inevitably, and as irresistibly, as the presence of the sun makes day, and its absence, night. No contrivance or power of man, and no policy of nations, here or elsewhere, can step between this cause and this effect, to disturb the connexion, or modify the result. The stronger power will overcome the weaker, and the wages of American labor must come down, unless they are protected.

§ 5. *Probable Operation of the Tariff* of 1846 *on Capital and Labor.*

It is not exactly safe to set up as a prophet of the future; but there are certain causes which may be relied upon for the production of certain effects, by the teachings of experience. The Hon. Abbott Lawrence, as already seen, has ventured on a prediction. And he is a gentleman of no ordinary experience and sagacity in such matters. The fall in the prices of labor will not probably be so early, or so great at an early period, as some have apprehended; but the final result can not be avoided under such a system. It has not been easy, down to this time, to obtain a full supply of labor for the manufactures of the country, because the demand calls laborers off from other pursuits, and requires an apprenticeship. All those manufacturers, therefore, who have any hope of standing, or who are obliged for the present to continue, will also be obliged to keep up the wages of labor as long and as high as they can—even after their business may have become a losing one—in hope of a favorable change. The disastrous effects of the new tariff will fall first, and continuously, on the weak, to make them weaker, and on the poor, to make them poorer; while the strong will grow stronger—at least relatively, in some cases positively—and the rich richer.

When weak manufacturers, and other employers of labor who are comparatively weak, are obliged to suspend their business, there will then be a surplus of labor seeking employment; and as in every other case of surplus, no matter what, prices will fall. They may fall rapidly and greatly. Such will unavoidably be the effect, when there is much labor out of employment. It is in such a state of things, when the weak break down, and the poor are suffering for want of something to do, that the rich grow richer, and the strong stronger, because they are able to take advantage of cheap commodities, cheap labor, and of the necessities of those who are trying to get along by borrowing money at exorbitant rates, most of whose estates fall at last into the hands of their creditors.

Such are the prospects of the country under the tariff of 1846, if it remains unaltered. Either the expected increase of importations must come, or the finances of the government will be in a bad plight. If the former fails, the people may be in some measure saved. It is a singular position of affairs, that the bankruptcy of the government is necessary for the protection of the people! For, if the expected importations come, to supply the wants of the government, it will subtract so much from American labor and trade. Either the government or the people must be in a bad case, since the country can not consume enough to make both do well, under the existing system. And how will the people, made poor for want of work, be able to pay for the importations necessary to supply the government with an adequate revenue? Or, if resort be had to direct taxation, as now begins to be talked of, that, too, will be hard for an impoverished nation.

It is quite probable, that the increased demand from Europe for American breadstuffs and provisions, on account of the failure of crops in that quarter, will suspend for a season the natural and worst effects of the new tariff. It may bar them off till the next good European crop of the necessaries of life, by such large exports as may in some measure balance the imports. The moment, however, it is known that the crops of Europe are good again,

67

American agricultural labor, so far as it depends on the European market, will necessarily have to compete with European prices, and must fall, with the fall in the prices of its products. It will take some years before the full effects of such a great and comprehensive measure, as the tariff of 1846, can be known; though it can hardly fail to develop some of its most important results in one or two years.

§ 6. *Discriminations of the Tariff of* 1846 *against Labor, Manufactures, and the Arts.*

It has been pretended that England and the United States are marching, with equal strides, toward the goal of free trade. It has, in several parts of this work, been shown, that the recent alterations of the British tariff, alleged to be of this character, have been made on the principle of protection, generally or specifically. When the Manchester and other British manufacturers ask for what is there called free trade, they ask it to fortify their own position in relation to the rest of the world, hoping their example will be followed by other nations, and believing themselves strong enough, for the most part, to defy and break down competition on this pretended basis of free ports. It is remarkable, however, that they do not ask for the remission of the differential duties in their favor, in supplying the wants of British dependencies. Mr. Williams, in an article before alluded to, in Fisher's National Magazine, for September, 1846, has clearly shown, that the late abatements of duty in the British tariff, vaunted so loudly as free trade reductions, if so nominally, are quite the other way in their practical operation. He has proved, in the first place, that the revenue sacrificed, is trivial, and that they gain on that score more thán they lose. But secondly, the most important point established is, that these numerous changes, except that of the abolition of the corn laws, have been made directly—abolition of corn laws indirectly—for the protection of British manufactures and arts, by the abolition of duties on raw materials, and partially manufactured articles imported for their perfection by British skill and labor. Whereas, the American tariff of 1846 has imposed duties in these very quarters where the British tariff has taken them off, not only withdrawing protection from American skill and labor, but taxing them, as the following comparative table, prepared by Mr. Williams, and representing, in these particulars, the tariffs of 1846 and 1842, with the British tariff for the same, will show :—

	New Tariff of 1846.	Tariff of 1842.	British Tariff.
Coarse wool	30 per cent.	5 per cent.	free
Raw hides and skins	5 "	5 "	free
Wood, mahogany. &c.	20 "	15 "	free
" other kinds, except timber	30 "	free	free
Antimony, crude	20 "	free	free
Barilla	10 "	free	free
Bark of the cork tree	15 "	free	free
Berries used for dying	5 "	free	free
Brimstone, or sulphur	20 "	free	free
Dye woods	5 "	free	free
Ebony	20 "	free	free
Cochineal	10 "	free	free
Crude saltpetre	5 "	free	free
Burr stones, unwrought	10 "	free	free
Brass, old	5 "	free	
Gum Arabic	10 "	free	free
India rubber	10 "	free	
Kelp	10 "	free	
Kermes	5 "	free	
Precious stones	10 "	7 per cent.	free
Pearl, Mother of	5 "	free	free
Ivory, unmanufactured	5 "	free	free
Madder	5 "	free	free
Palm-leaf, unmanufactured	10 "	free	free
Ratans and reeds, do	10 "	free	free
Shellac	5 "	free	free
Sumac	5 "	free	free
Weld	5 "	free	free
Tin, in sheets or plates	15 "	2½ per cent.	
Tin, in pigs, bars, or blocks	5 "	1 "	
Tortoise shell	5 "	5 "	free.

" We might extend this list, but enough is given to show the comparative legislation of the American and British governments, with regard to raw materials and other articles essential for the use of manufactures and in the arts. While the British parliament are removing all duties on articles required for the use of their manufacturers, our American Congress have increased the burdens of our manufacturers, by additional duties on the raw materials imported for their use ; at the same time that they have reduced the protective duties. Was there ever a parallel case of injustice in the history of legislation in any country ?

219

" Several classes of articles used in manufactures which pay small specific rates of duties by the tariff of 1842, have been changed by the new tariff, and on most of them the ad-valorem rates will be higher than the specific rates now paid. The following will serve as specimens, taking the duties actually paid on the last importations, by the report of the secretary of the treasury:—

	Rates of Tariff of 1842.		Equal to.		New Tariff.
Indigo - - - -	5 cts. per lb. - - - -		6½ per cent. - - -		10 per cent.
Bristles - - - -	1 " - - - -		2 " - - - -		5 "
Flax - - - -	$20 per ton. - - - -		10 " - - - -		15 "
Paper rags - - -	25 cts. per 100lbs. - - -		6½ " - - - -		5 "

" On all the previously-named articles, it will be observed, the duties are increased, except rags, on which there is a small apparent reduction on those of the quality imported last year.

" The importance in amount of raw materials and other articles imported for our manufactures, is shown by the following statement of the value of part of those articles imported, for the year ending June 30, 1845—(the last returns). Let it be borne in mind that while our government withdraws a large proportion of the protection to our manufactures, by reducing the rates of duties on articles imported coming in direct competition with them, it taxes them with additional duties on the raw materials used; as if intentionally to deprive them of the ability of competing with the British manufacturer, who obtains the like raw materials free of duty.

" *Value of Articles Imported, principally for the use of manufactures, in the year ending June* 30, 1845.

Articles paying Duty.	Amount.
Coarse wool - - - - - - - - - - - - - -	$1,553,789
Mahogany - - - - - - - - - - - - -	261,292
Rose wood - - - - - - - - - - - - -	18,912
Satin and cedar wood - - - - - - - - - - -	18,878
Indigo - - - - - - - - - - - - -	862,700
Bristles - - - - - - - - - - - - -	172,076
Flax - - - - - - - - - - - - -	90,509
Rags - - - - - - - - - - - - -	421,080
Block tin and other articles, at 1 per cent. duty - - - -	212 975
Tin, in plates or sheets, &c., at 2½ " " " - - - -	1,690,460
Raw hides and skins, &c., at 5 " " " - - - -	1,975,103
	$7,277,674

Articles free of Duty.

Dye-wood, in sticks - - - - - - - - - -	$603,408
Wood, unmanufactured - - - - - - - - - -	87,315
Burr stones, unwrought - - - - - - - - -	32,624
Brimstone and sulphur - - - - - - - - -	108,619
Bark of the cork-tree - - - - - - - - -	8,812
Barilla - - - - - - - - - - - -	22,917
Nuts and Berries, used in dyeing - - - - - - - -	132,490
Clay, unwrought - - - - - - - - - -	14,670
Articles, not enumerated - - - - - - - - -	2,958 563
Total - - - - - - -	$11,247,092

" It is within bounds to say, that the additional taxes imposed on the manufacturer by the new tariff, on raw materials alone, will amount to at least ten per cent., or over one million of dollars, unless we suppose that the operation of this new law should reduce or destroy, as it probably may, some branches of manufactures, and thus diminish the tax imposed on them. Compare this effect with the new British tariff, which, as we have already stated, releases the more favored manufactures of Great Britain from taxes on raw materials formerly paid, amounting to more than five millions of dollars.

" The great leading interests of national industry which will be most affected by our new tariff, are the manufactures of iron, cottons, woollens, leather, paper, machinery, lead in its various branches, glass, ready-made clothing, and cordage. Many other branches of manufactures might be mentioned, which will be affected directly or indirectly. Indeed, we apprehend all classes, who depend on their daily labor for subsistence, will suffer by this blow at our protective system; for while the great manufacturing interests we have mentioned are prostrated, the country can not be prosperous; and if the condition of the people will not sustain the present or recent demand for articles of consumption, how can those classes of mechanics, manufacturers and others, who seem to be protected by the new tariff, flourish, with a diminished and constantly-decreasing market for their fabrics?

" We might also notice those branches of industry which have recently sprung into existence, or have exhibited signs of life and excited hopes for the future; but which infantile manufactures must be checked or destroyed, under the operation of the new tariff. Among these the important interest of silk should be named as the most prominent. The tariff of 1842 wisely fixed specific and other protective rates of duty on manufactures of silk, which were considered absolutely necessary to sustain this new branch of industry, and under those auspices it has been fast growing into importance, exciting the most lively interest in many parts of the Union. The new tariff repeals the specific duties on silk, and fixes a low rate of ad-valorem duties, leaving the enterprising and industrious citizens who have engaged in its cultivation and manufacture, at the mercy of foreign competition.

" Thus, then, we see that the present approaches to what is erroneously called ' Free Trade,' is in England one thing and in the United States another. In England, it is, to lay the heaviest duties on the great articles of tobacco, tea, coffee, distilled spirits, sugar and wines; not one of which is produced in the realm, but which are largely imported, and which pay two thirds of the whole customs revenue, and to remove the duty from every species of material that enters into manufactures of any kind; thus sustaining the industry of her working classes. While in the United States, what is called ' Free Trade,' or an approach to it, is to reduce the duty on all manufactured goods, and to increase it to the destruction of the working classes, on many raw materials, as we have already shown.

" Does not this establish, beyond all dispute or cavil, what we have asserted in another place, that no such thing as ' Free Trade' now exists, or can exist? and that while England, our great rival, is doing everything she can to foster and sustain her superiority in manufacturing, our present rulers are playing most completely into her hands, and rendering us more and more tributary to her, while lessening our ability to pay for every foreign production imported into this country?

" The plain truth is, and it is folly to attempt to conceal it, that the worst evil, the skill, capital and labor of this country have to contend with, is its own present government, who, not content with demanding specie in all payments made to them by the people, have, by the enactment of the tariff of 1846, legislated *against* America, and *in favor* of England."—*National Magazine, September*, 1846.

These are the "*discriminating* duties," spoken of in Mr. Polk's letter to John K. Kane, that is, discriminating *against* protection, *for* revenue. It has been before shown, that Mr. Polk is a consistent anti-protectionist.

The following table, prepared by the Hon. Mr. Stewart, of Pennsylvania, while the tariff of '46 was under debate, requires no alteration, as the bill, as to these items, passed precisely as it stood then, and is now part of the law :—

" The operation of this bill," said Mr. Stewart, " upon the national industry will be seen from the following examples, assuming that the reduction of wages will always be in proportion to the reduction of *protection*, and that as home consumption can not be increased, home production must be diminished to the extent of the increased importations :—

Employments, &c.	Importations under the Tariff of '42.	Estimated increase of importations under Tariff of '46.	Duties of Tariff of '42, as per Mr. Walker's report, table C.	Duties of Tariff of '46.
Shoemakers........................	$42,250	$45,000	45 pr ct.	30 per ct.
Tailors............................	1,173,028	200,000	50 "	30 "
Blacksmiths	—	200,000	61 "	30 "
Hatters...........................	16,646	110,000	49 "	30 "
Tanners...........................	128,277	100,000	40 "	20 "
Iron-makers	4,489,553	1,185,000	75 "	30 "
Miners of coal....................	223,919	5,150,000	67 "	30 "
Glass-makers......................	106,905	100,000	90 "	25 "
Paper-makers......................	51,724	150,000	75 "	30 "
Hemp, cordage, &c.................	355,875	275,000	65 "	25 "
Lead..............................	—	—	92 "	20 "
Pins..............................	45,078	50,000	70 "	20 "
Nails and spikes	—	—	66 "	20 "
Manufactures of wool..............	10,057,875	2,000,000	40 "	30 "
Do. cotton.................	—	—	90 "	25 "
Do. silk...................	—	—	42 "	25 "
Salt..............................	898,663	1,000,000	76 "	20 "
Sugar.............................	4,780,555	630,000	75 "	30 "
Brandy and spirits distilled from grain, &c. .	—	—	180 "	100 "
Wool..............................	1,689,794	200,000	40 "	30 "
Blankets..........................	—	—	30 "	20 "
Potatoes..........................	58,949	150,000	36 "	20 "

This table might be extended much farther; but it is sufficient to exhibit the practical operation of the new tariff on labor, so long as that measure answers any purpose for revenue; and on labor and the currency, when the revenue shall fail; for the act, as a revenue measure, will not fail entirely, till, and only because, labor and the currency are both broken down.

The various branches of American labor named in the above table, will of course see the amounts, respectively, by which their occupations are to be curtailed, in the operations of the new tariff. They read their doom in the second column. That is the amount of business, of which they are to be deprived. They are Mr. Secretary Walker's own figures. He openly proposed, in his report, to *substitute* the products of European labor for those of American; and this is the way and the measure of his doing it! Mr. Stewart says :—

" The question, then, is distinctly presented to all these mechanics, manufacturers, and farmers, whether they are prepared to submit to these reductions in their prices and wages, or give up the market to foreigners? One or the other they must do—and why? Mr. Walker says, to increase the revenue; but this is manifestly not true; for when you take all the increase of imports Mr. Walker himself estimates, and assess on these the proposed reduced duties, there will be, on his own showing, a loss instead of a gain of revenue. Then why the proposed reduction? To substitute *foreign* for *American* fabrics, as declared in Mr. Walker's report. To favor *foreigners* by breaking down *American mechanics, manufacturers, and farmers.*"

§ 7. The Alternatives.

It is clear, that the tariff of 1846 must either fail of its object as a revenue measure, or cripple the labor of the country and destroy its currency. It will undoubtedly do the last, and to a great extent accomplish the first. That it will do the last, is proved from experience. No system of low, anti-protective duties, has ever been in operation in this country, without these results, as has been abundantly demonstrated in these pages. Importations, in all such cases, flood the country, as long as there is money to pay for them; and when that is gone, to the breaking point of credit. Of course, and uniformly, the money being gone, and credit failing, the currency fails, and labor is prostrate, first on account of low wages, and next for want of employment. Cheap foreign labor has done that which American labor ought to have done—has superseded the latter, by being imported in the shape of manufactured goods—has surfeited the market, and produced universal stagnation. When trade languishes, for want of money and credit, labor is the first and chief sufferer.

The tariff of 1846 is doubtless sufficient to accomplish these objects, in its experiment as a new revenue system; and before it shall have half done it, it will itself fail for purposes of revenue. It will indeed fail in the outset, in comparison with the revenue system of the tariff of 1842. It is impossible it should produce as much, because to do that, it would require an amount of importations, which neither the money, nor credit of the country could stand for six months. When money and credit are gone, no one can tell what it will produce; but the product must be very slender. When duties were on the same scale, in the last year of the compromise act, called the fiscal year of 1842, the revenue from customs run down to about twelve millions and a half, which is less than half the average product of the tariff of 1842. There is little reason to suppose, that the tariff of 1846 will do better than this, after the first year.

§ 8. A new way of invading the Rights of American Labor.

There is one mode, some time in use, in disposing of surplus accumulations of manufactured goods in England and Europe—and it applies to all kinds of manufactures—which is not commonly observed, and which is the worst of all for American interests of manufacture, trade, and labor, besides being extremely difficult to control. These surpluses are constantly accumulating in Europe, not only by regular production, in the hands of manufacturers, but by bankruptcies. They are dead property at home, and must be disposed of in some foreign market, *at whatever sacrifice.* The inquiry, in all such cases, is, what market is the best? And the uniform answer is, the United States—New York; and hither they are shipped and consigned, with orders to be sold by private negotiation, or by auction. Sold they must be and will be, *at whatever price they will bring*, generally at a sacrifice on the cost of production in Europe. A house in New York received a large consignment of goods in this way, in 1846, and sold them at an average of less than 50 per cent. of the original cost of production. This business, as is known to the merchants of New York, is done on a large scale. It is *forcing* off the goods. Nor is this mode of sale limited, either as to quantity or time, but unlimited. It is a regular, uninterrupted, systematic trade, carried on for more than twenty years, to dispose of surpluses on hand in Europe. As the sources are inexhaustible, embracing all kinds of manufactures, without the application of a legislative remedy, the flood is destined, apparently, to increase, and to overwhelm the labor and manufacturing interests of the country, together with American importing merchants. It will naturally be vastly augmented by the low duties of the tariff of 1846. Nor can any remedy be found, short of a union of state and federal legislation. So long as the laws of the state of New York impose but 1½ per cent. duties on foreign goods sold at auction, the practice can never be arrested. In this way, all the regular manufacturing and importing business of the country is endangered, and American labor is doomed to fall with it, necessarily and unavoidably; for, in such a case, American labor has to compete, not with the low-priced labor of Europe at par, but at a discount, sometimes of 50 per cent.; that is, with the pauper labor of Europe at half price, the average of which is about one sixth, or 17 per cent. of the average price of American labor. American merchants and manufacturers are first injured; but it all ends in depriving American labor of its rights.

It may, perhaps, be said, that this is all for the benefit of consumers. But it does not operate so. It is the sole benefit, first, of those holders of these surpluses in Europe, who can not otherwise dispose of them; next, of the jobbers, who make the first purchase, and thirdly, of the retailers. Before they get into the hands of consumers, the prices are up to the ordinary level. The whole tendency of the operation is to injure the regular trade and the labor of the country.

§ 9. *Cause of Fluctuation of Prices.*

"This matter of price," says the Hon. Mr. Evans, "is very elastic. A light weight sinks it below the level which the additional burden would naturally occasion; and the removal of the pressure gives it an upward spring, beyond what it would otherwise have reached." A better description of this fickle, evanescent, impalpable power, was perhaps never given, than the above. Sudden and frequent changes of prices suddenly make and lose the fortunes of speculators, and are injurious to the wide community, since nothing can long retain a market value much above or much below its worth. Steadiness and firmness of prices is that state of things most desirable to the country. In the same manner, as a short crop of an agricultural staple, in general use and demand, will naturally raise the price, so a surplus will naturally depress it. The same remark is applicable to products of every description. It is the principle of *supply* relative to *demand*, which produces these changes; and its character may be farther described, beyond Mr. Evans's apt illustration, by raising a quiet pendulum from its perpendicular direction to any given point, and letting it fall. It will then pass to nearly the same point on the other side. Arresting the comparison here, it shows how prices tend to extremes, when once their regularity is disturbed by extraordinary events.

§ 10. *The Effect of Short Crops in Europe on the Prices of American Agricultural Staples.*

The effect of the potato-rot, and an extensive failure of the wheat crop, in Europe, in 1846, is obvious. It immediately raises the price of American bread-stuffs, and of all provisions which man requires for his sustenance. It is only at such a time, which ordinarily happens only once in a series of years, that American agricultural labor can obtain a fair remuneration in European markets. It is the profit which one part of the world derives from the calamities of another. But no wise statesman would venture to found a public policy on such an extraordinary and unreliable basis. If American agricultural labor profits by the calamities of Europe, under one commercial system, it would profit under any other, because necessity has no law, and hunger will break through stone walls. It would be a great error to suppose that better prices of breadstuffs, and of other supplies of man's mouth, in the fall of 1846, is owing to legislation, in this country, or elsewhere. It is owing to Providence, in the destruction of potatoes, and in a general short crop of grains, in foreign parts. Legislation has nothing to do with these transient fluctuations of prices, any more than it has with the profits of an epidemic to the medical profession. Every reflecting person must be sensible of the want of wisdom in establishing a system of public policy for extraordinary and uncertain events, in disregard of the ordinary course of things.

CHAPTER XIX.

SOME OF MR. CLAY'S VIEWS ON THE PROTECTIVE POLICY, WITH REMARKS.

§ 1. *Mr. Clay a Protectionist from the Beginning of his Public Life.*

MR. CLAY's *debùt* as a statesman, in this cause, was made in 1808, at the age of twenty-five, in the legislature of Kentucky, when he moved a resolution in that body, that the members, as an example to the people, and as an expression of patriotic duty in giving countenance and support to domestic manufactures, should clothe themselves, from head to foot, in articles of domestic fabric and production. The first speech made by Mr. Clay in Congress on the protective policy, was in the senate, April 6, 1810, while in all the freshness of his youth as a statesman. The following is an extract:—

"The opposition to manufacturing institutions recalls to my recollection the case of a gentleman, of whom I have heard. He had been in the habit of supplying his table from a neighboring cook and confectioner's shop, and proposed to his wife a reform, in this particular. She revolted at the idea. The sight of a scullion was dreadful, and her delicate nerves could not bear the clattering of kitchen furniture. The gentleman persisted in his design: his table was thenceforth cheaper and better supplied, and his neighbor, the confectioner, lost one of his best customers. In like manner, Dame Commerce will oppose domestic manufactures. She is a flirting, flippant, noisy jade, and if we are governed by her fantasies, we shall never put off the muslins of India and the cloths of Europe. But I trust that the yeomanry of the country, the true and genuine landlords of this tenement, called the United States, disregarding her freaks, will persevere in reform, until the whole national family is furnished by itself with the clothing necessary for its own use.

"It is a subject no less of curiosity than of interest, to trace the prejudices in favor of foreign fabrics. In our colonial condition, we were in a complete state of dependence on the parent-country, as it respected manufactures, as well as commerce. For many years after the war, such was the partiality for her productions, in this country, that a gentleman's head could not withstand the influence of solar heat, unless covered with a London hat; his feet could not bear the pebbles, or frost, unless protected by London shoes; and the comfort or ornament of his person was only consulted when his coat was cut out by the shears of a tailor 'just from London.' At length, however, the wonderful *discovery* has been made, that it is not absolutely beyond the reach of American skill and ingenuity, to provide these articles, combining with equal elegance greater durability. And I entertain no doubt, that, in a short time, the no less important fact will be developed, that the domestic manufactories of the United States, fostered by government, and aided by household exertions, are fully competent to supply us with at least every necessary article of clothing. I therefore, sir, *for one* (to use the fashionable cant of the day), am in favor of encouraging them, not to the extent to which they are carried in England, but to such an extent as will redeem us entirely from all dependence on foreign countries. There is a pleasure—a pride (if I may be allowed the expression, and I pity those who can not feel the sentiment)—in being clad in the productions of our own families. Others may prefer the cloths of Leeds and of London, but give me those of Humphreysville."

The British colonial system, commonly so called, as it applies to the United States, has been of serious consequence to the navigating interests of this country, over which the government is equally bound to extend its protection, as over other interests of the people. It is a branch of the protective policy. After the peace of Ghent, Great Britain adopted measures to exclude the navigation of the United States from the British West Indies and her other American colonies, comprehending a trade estimated at six millions of dollars; but by a clause in the second article of the convention of London, the right of a countervailing policy was left open to the United States. On the basis of this right, an effort was made in Congress, in 1816, and 1817, to exclude from the ports of the United States all foreign vessels, British or other, trading with those British possessions, from which American vessels were excluded, and Mr. Clay supported the measure on the principle of retaliation, with a view to force Great Britain to a reciprocity, and to recover those rights of navigation for American shipping. He said :—

"The policy of Great Britain was deeply laid in selfish considerations—a policy which she had never relaxed, except in periods of war when it became her interest to do so. The question was, whether the total exclusion of our ships from the colonial ports of Great Britain, was such a measure as we ought to fold our arms and submit to ? The effect was to deprive us of the advantages, in the augmentation of our commerce, and in the increase of our seamen, which would result from the carriage of our own produce, to the amount of six millions of dollars. With regard to the importance of encouraging our own navigation, he said, he need not resort to argument. Some measure ought to be devised, by which the navigation of Great Britain should be prevented from enjoying peculiar advantages over us, in a trade wherein reciprocity had been solemnly promised by the convention of London."

The measure, however, failed. In 1818, a like attempt was more successful; in 1820, the act of 1818 was superseded by a new one; and so again in 1823—the design of each of which was to bring Great Britain to terms. Attempts at negotiation were made under the administration of Mr. John Q. Adams, but the death of the British prime minister, Mr. Canning, put the question into new hands, and deferred a settlement. In 1829, Mr. Louis M'Lane was sent to London by General Jackson, with instructions on this subject; the question was claimed to be advantageously settled, and the transaction much lauded; the practical operation of which, however, made it worse than it was before, and it has never yet been satisfactorily arranged. Nothing has proved more deceptive, or more injurious to the navigating interests of the United States, than these commercial treaties, professedly based on principles of reciprocity—a mock reciprocity. The great commercial nations, such as England, France, Russia, Sweden, Portugal, Holland, and Belgium, have taken good care not to be caught in the American trap, and have sprung it on the trappers, by loaning their own craft to the flags of the small and non-commercial states, such as Denmark, Hamburgh, Bremen, Prussia, Brazil, Tuscany, Rome, and Greece, which had nothing to lose, and everything to gain, by arrangements of this kind, with the United States. Thus the larger commercial powers have *stolen* the benefit, and escaped from the obligation of reciprocity !

With this exception, the navigating interests of the country have received a very fair protection from the government. It is not, perhaps, commonly considered by those engaged in this pursuit, that if this protection were taken away, the American commercial marine would not only be chiefly driven from the seas by foreign competition, but even the coasting trade of the United States would be carried on by craft built and manned in the north of Europe, at about half the expense of American shipping, and at half the wages of American seamen. On the basis of free trade, it would be impossible for the navigation of the United States to compete with foreign craft.

§ 2. *History of the Protective Policy from* 1812 *to* 1824.

The peace of Ghent left the manufactures of the United States, which had been reared during the war to answer the necessities of the country, and of which the war itself was a sufficient protection, in a defenceless condition. The products of British and other European manufacture, poured into the country at a rate to threaten the existence of American establishments, and the ruin of the currency, by the withdrawal of specie to pay for them. The tariff of 1816 was not enacted to go into operation till a year and a half after the peace ; and when it came, it proved equally inadequate to protect American manufactures, and to check the alarming balances of trade which were heaping up against the nation, by the influx of foreign products. Mr. Clay had labored faithfully in 1816 to get a tariff that would answer the necessities of the country; but in vain. The disappointment and distress which he predicted, followed. As the nation was constantly buying more than it sold, the money of the country was necessarily required to pay the balance ; and like a private individual who does the same thing, and precisely for the same reason, the country grew poorer and poorer, till it was compelled to stop payment by a general bank suspension—for that is the only mode in which a nation stops payment, and to which it is necessarily compelled, when, for a length of time, beyond what it can bear, it continues to buy more than it sells. The balance is demanded in specie, which is drawn from the banks, till, in self-defence, they close their vaults. And that is the insolvency of a commercial nation. Nor is it an abuse of the monetary system, as some aver. It is real poverty. The money is gone, and has to be made again, by living within means, and by hard work.

The general distress consequent on the defects of the tariff of 1816, led to an attempt in Congress to get up a new one in 1820 ; and on the 22d of March, of that year, Mr. Baldwin, of Pennsylvania (afterward judge of the supreme court of the United States, and since deceased), reported a bill from the committee of the house on manufactures, to supply the deficiencies of the existing tariff. The bill passed the house by a vote of 90 to 69, but was lost in the senate by 22 to 20. The following is an extract from a speech of Mr. Clay on that bill in the house of representatives, April 20, 1820 :—

" Mr. Chairman, whatever may be the value of my opinions on the interesting subject now before us, they have not been hastily formed. It may possibly be recollected by some gentlemen, that I expressed them when the existing tariff [of 1816] was adopted ; and that I then urged, that the period of the termination of the war, during which the manufacturing industry of the country had received a powerful spring, was precisely that period when government was alike impelled. by duty and interest, to protect it against the free admission of foreign fabrics, consequent upon a state of peace. I insisted, on that occasion, that a less measure of protection would prove more efficacious. at that time, than one of greater extent at a future day. My wishes prevailed only in part ; and we are now called upon to decide whether we will correct the error which, I think, we then committed.

" In considering the subject, the first important inquiry that we should make is, whether it be desirable that such a portion of the capital and labor of the country should be employed in the business of manufacturing, as would furnish a supply of our necessary wants ? Since the first colonization of America, the principal direction of the labor and capital of the inhabitants, has been to produce raw materials for the consumption or fabrication of foreign nations. We have always had, in great abundance, the means of subsistence, but we have derived chiefly from other countries, our clothes, and the instruments of defence. Except during those interruptions of commerce arising from a state of war, or from measures adopted for commercial rights, we have experienced no very great inconvenience heretofore from this mode of supply. The limited amount of our surplus produce, resulting from the smallness of our numbers, and the long and arduous convulsions of Europe, secured us good markets for that surplus in her ports, or those of her colonies. But those convulsions have now ceased, and our population has reached nearly ten millions. A new epoch has arisen ; and it becomes us deliberately to contemplate our own actual condition, and the relations which are likely to exist between us and the other parts of the world. The actual state of our population, and the ratio of its progressive increase, when compared with the ratio of the increase of the population of the countries which have hitherto consumed our raw produce, seem, to me, alone to demonstrate the necessity of diverting some portion of our industry from its accustomed channel. We double our population in about the term of twenty-five years. If there be no change in the mode of exerting our industry, we shall double, during the same term, the amount of our exportable produce. Europe, including such of her colonies as we have free access to, taken altogether, does not duplicate her population in a shorter term, probably, than one hundred years. The ratio of the increase of her capacity of consumption, therefore, is, to that of our capacity of production, as one is to four. And it is manifest, from the simple exhibition of the powers of the consuming countries, compared with those of the supplying country, that the former are inadequate to the latter. It is certainly true, that a portion of the mass of our raw produce, which we transmit to her, reverts to us in a fabricated form, and that this return augments with our increasing population. This is, however, a very inconsiderable addition to her actual ability to afford a market for the produce of our industry."

The unsuccessful attempt to make a new tariff in 1820, was a very important and eventful point in the political history of the country. Its failure doomed the people to four years of incalculable loss, and great distress, from which they did not begin to emerge till they were rescued by the tariff of 1824.

" If you want to find an example of order," said Mr. Clay, in advocating the bill of 1820, " of freedom from debt, of economy, of expenditure falling below rather than exceeding income, you will go to the well-regulated family of a farmer. You will go to the house of such a man as Isaac Shelby [governor of Kentucky] ; you will not find him haunting taverns, engaged in broils, prosecuting angry lawsuits ; you will behold every member of his family clad with the produce of their own hands, and usefully employed—the spinning-wheel and the loom in motion by daybreak. With what pleasure will his wife conduct you into her neat dairy, lead you into her storehouse, and point you to the tablecloths, the sheets, the counterpanes, which lie on this shelf for one daughter, or on that for another, all prepared in advance by her provident care for the day of their respective marriages. If you want

74

to see an opposite example, go to the house of a man who manufactures nothing at home, whose family resorts to the store for everything they consume. You will find him perhaps in the tavern, or at the shop at the cross-roads. He is engaged, with the rum-grog on the table, taking depositions to make out some case of usury or fraud. Or perhaps he is furnishing to his lawyer the materials to prepare a long bill of injunction in some intricate case. The sheriff is hovering about his farm to serve some new writ. On court-days—he never misses attending them—you will find him eagerly collecting his witnesses to defend himself against the merchant and doctor's claims. Go to his house, and, after the short and giddy period that his wife and daughters have flirted about the country in their calico and muslin frocks, what a scene of discomfort and distress is presented to you there! What the individual family of Isaac Shelby is, I wish to see the nation in the aggregate become. But I fear we shall shortly have to comtemplate its resemblance in the opposite picture. If statesmen would carefully observe the conduct of private individuals in the management of their own affairs, they would have much surer guides in promoting the interests of the state, than the visionary speculations of theoretical writers.

"This maxim [let things alone], is indeed everywhere proclaimed," said Mr. Clay, "but nowhere practised. It is truth in the books of European political economists. It is error in the practical code of every European state. It is not applied where it is most applicable; it is attempted to be introduced here, where it is least applicable ; and even here its friends propose to limit it to the single branch of manufacturing industry, while every other interest is encouraged and protected according to the policy of Europe. . . . America presents the image of a fine, generous-hearted young fellow, who has just come to the possession of a rich estate—an estate, which, however, requires careful management. He makes nothing—he buys everything. He is surrounded by a parcel of Jews, each holding out his hand with a packet of buttons, or pins, or some other commodity, for sale. If he asks those Jews to buy anything which his estate produces, they tell him, ' No—it is not for our interest—it is not for yours.'—' Take this new book,' says one of them, ' on political economy, and you will there perceive it is for your interest to buy from us, and to let things alone in your own country.' "

Here is the misfortune—the trick, as it might, with more propriety and truth, be called : Great Britain is the Jew, that has furnished other nations with books on political economy, to suit herself—not such as she follows, but such as she wishes them to follow; and they are quoted in argument by American free-traders, who are, by this means, Jewed.
Hundreds of millions were lost to the country in the loss of the bill of 1820.

§ 3. Epoch of the Tariff of 1824.

In 1824 the country was ripe for ruin or rescue. It was impossible, that the evils of the past should be longer endured. The tariff of 1816 had utterly failed to protect the great interests of the country. Onward rolled time, and onward the car of commercial desolation. In 1824 most men had waked up, necessarily to the distress, and apparently to some sense of the perils, of the republic, whose very vitals were being consumed by the vulture-maw of foreign policies and foreign factors.

"The creation of a home market," said Mr. Clay, on the bill of 1824, "is not only necessary to procure for our agriculture a just reward of its labors, but it is indispensable to obtain a supply of our necessary wants. If we can not sell, we can not buy. That portion of our population (and we have seen that it is not less than four fifths) which makes comparatively nothing that foreigners will buy, has nothing to make purchases with from foreigners. It is in vain that we are told of the amount of our exports supplied by the planting interest. They may enable the planting interest to supply all its wants; but they bring no ability to the interests not planting ; unless, which can not be pretended, the planting interest is an adequate vent for the surplus produce of the labor of all other interests. It is in vain to tantalize us with the greater cheapness of foreign fabrics. There must be an ability to purchase, if an article be obtained, whatever may be the price, high or low, at which it is sold. And a cheap article is as much beyond the grasp of him who has no means to buy, as a high one. Even if it were true that the American manufacturer would supply consumption at dearer rates, it is better to have his fabrics than the unattainable foreign fabrics, because it is better to be ill-supplied than not supplied at all. A coarse coat, which will communicate warmth and cover nakedness, is better than no coat. The superiority of the home market results, first from its steadiness and comparative certainty at all times ; secondly, from the creation of reciprocal interests; thirdly, from its greater security, and lastly, from an ultimate and not distant augmentation of consumption (and consequently of comfort), from increased quantity and reduced prices. But this home market, highly desirable as it is, can only be created and cherished by the PROTECTION of our own legislation against the inevitable prostration of our industry, which must ensue from the action of FOREIGN policy and legislation."

One of the greatest errors or oversights which American statesmen, averse to the protective policy, have betrayed in political economy, is perhaps shutting their eyes to the importance of artificial power in its positive influence in promoting a nation's wealth, and in its relative influence in enabling the United States to keep pace with rival nations, especially with Great Britain. Mr. Clay had occasion to notice, as long ago as 1824, that some British authorities estimated the machine power of Great Britain as equal to two hundred millions of men. The number of operatives to apply this machinery has never yet amounted to one million. Here, then, is a nation with a population of some twenty-five millions, with a producing power of two hundred millions. Its capabilities of producing wealth by artificial means, is so great, that its natural power is scarcely worthy of being brought into the account. To this cause chiefly is attributed her prowess in her struggles against the

226

colossal power of Napoleon, and her ability at that period to afford such constant and essential aid to her continental allies. One man at home did the work of two hundred, less or more. With or without allies, she was able to contend against the power of France, till the victory of Waterloo gave her repose, if indeed she needed it.

Setting aside, therefore, the considerations arising from the necessities of the protective system, as a part of political economy, national pride, wealth, and greatness, are concerned in concerting and securing an equally rapid growth in power, for the great political ends of the United States in relation to rival nations. It is too late to question the advantages of art, and its potency in overcoming the obstacles of nature, in all the pursuits of individuals and of states. Science, which makes one man as powerful as two hundred, or a thousand, left to their natural powers, will and must prevail against numbers. That nation which cultivates the useful, mechanic, and manufacturing arts, all which have their foundation in science, and which excels in them, other things being equal, will excel in strength, and maintain a superiority. Great Britain at this moment is probably ten to one stronger than the United States, by reason of these advantages. It is obvious, that, with a constant liability to war with that power, sound national policy would dictate the encouragement of those arts, even at expense and sacrifice, which so rapidly augment national strength. How much more, when all the great interests of the commonwealth are shielded and promoted by the same means ? A nation, whose arts, in the present state of the world, are not adequate to supply its own necessities, is poor, weak, and vulnerable. It will be despised, and may be humbled.

In Mr. Clay's speech of 1824—now more than twenty years since—he answered most triumphantly the objection of the cotton-planting interest, that the tariff would cut off the market for cotton, not only by showing a tacit compact between the cotton-grower and the British manufacturer, which put the former in the power of the latter, but by the exhibition of the fact, as it then stood, that, out of the five millions sterling worth of the raw material bought by British manufacturers of American planters, after supplying the home consumption of the British empire with cotton fabrics, they sold to foreign parts to the amount of twenty-one millions and a half sterling, only one million and a half of which came to the United States. It was therefore absurd to suppose, that the British manufacturers would not continue their demand for the raw material, to the extent of their market for the manufactured products ; and if the American tariff should operate to supply the American demand, to the amount of a million and a half sterling, the raw material would of course come from the American planter, and the country would save the increased value of many to one, in the fabrics, in which the American planter would have his share. In confirmation of the validity of this argument, such, since that time, have been the results of actual experience. Mr. Clay also showed very clearly, that navigation is second in the order of nature to agriculture and manufactures, and can only prosper as they do.

It was objected to the tariff of 1824, that it would be a failure. Nature, it was contended, as Mr. Walker now contends, had indicated the natural occupation of man in North America, to wit, a culture of the soil. As if nature had not given the same hints in other quarters of the world; as if the countless rivers, streams, and waterfalls of the United States, had given no advice on this point; as if the lakes, bays, and other inland water-channels, did not invite trade, which could have no occupation without the arts ; as if this great continent, abounding in all the resources of nature, were to afford no other sustenance to the human family, but the milk of its own breasts ; as if all its tenants, like the aborigines, served by woman in slavery, were destined to vegetate on corn, and decay for want of employment ; as if the Anglo-Saxon race, transplanted to another and better country, would consent to fall behind the rest of the world, or allow their brethren of the original stock to outstrip them in art or enterprise ; as if that people, known to all the world as Americans, and who alone are thought of in Europe under this name, would willingly be dependent ; as if they would for ever sweat and toil in the field to supply the raw material for a more delicate and refined race, that would condescend to return them the wrought product, wrung in agony from their own slaves, at a cost five or ten times enhanced, and draw away all the earnings of the American laborer ; as if America were not a world in itself, and able by its ingenuity and skill to supply every luxury, as well as every necessity ; as if the lovers of freedom had turned their backs on the old world, to become greater slaves than they were before ; as if the powers of invention were native only to the European continent, or the Eastern world ; as if the moment a man crosses the sea from east to west, he is doomed to repress all the nobler faculties of his soul ; as if genius and art could not flourish in the western hemisphere ; as if, in short, America were fit only to be a dependent colony of Europe.

The question involved is neither less nor more than that of dependence or independence —whether America can do without Europe, or is to have connexions on fair terms, and equally honorable to both parties. A people without art are fit only to be slaves, and are easily made such. A nation that is only the producer of raw materials, can never claim equality with nations, which, by science and art, add many values to those materials, and send them back as a tax on those who consent to do such service. It is a state of dependence, and not of independence.

Another form of argument employed by the opponents of the tariff bill of 1824—one that is common at all times—was, that manufactures would rise of themselves, without the aid of protection. To this, Mr. Clay replied :—

" If I am asked, why unprotected industry could not succeed in a struggle with protected industry, I answer, the FACT has ever been so, and that is sufficient; I reply, that UNIFORM EXPERIENCE evinces that it can not succeed in such an unequal contest, and that is sufficient. If we speculate on the causes of this universal truth, we may differ about them. Still the indisputable fact remains. And we should be as unwise in not availing ourselves of the guide which it furnishes, as a man would be, who should refuse to bask in the rays of the sun, because he could not agree with Judge Woodward as to the nature of the substance of that planet, to which we are indebted for heat and light. If I were to attempt to particularize the causes which prevent the success of the manufacturing arts, without protection, I should say that they are, first, the obduracy of fixed habits. No nation, no individual, will easily change an established course of business, even if it be unprofitable ; and least of all is an agricultural people prone to innovation. With what reluctance do they not adopt improvements in the instruments of husbandry, or in modes of cultivation ! If the farmer makes a good crop, and sells it badly, or makes a short crop, buoyed up by hope, he perseveres, and trusts that a favorable change of the market, or of the seasons, will enable him, in the succeeding year, to repair the misfortunes of the past. Secondly, the uncertainty, fluctuation, and unsteadiness of the home market, when liable to an unrestricted influx of fabrics from all foreign nations ; and thirdly, the superior advance of skill, and amount of capital, which foreign nations have obtained, by the protection of their own industry. From the latter, or from other causes, the unprotected manufactures of a country are exposed to the danger of being crushed in their infancy, either by the design, or from the necessities of foreign manufacturers. Gentlemen are incredulous as to the attempts of foreign merchants and manufacturers to accomplish the destruction of ours. Why should they not make such attempts ? If the Scottish manufacturer, by surcharging our market, in one year, with the article of cotton bagging, for example, should so reduce the price as to discourage and put down the home manufacture, he would secure to himself the monopoly of the supply. And now, having the exclusive possession of the market, perhaps for a long term of years, he might be more than indemnified for his first loss, in the subsequent rise in the price of the article. What have we not seen under our own eyes ! The competition for the transportation of the mail, between this place and Baltimore, became so excited, that to obtain it an individual offered, at a great loss, to carry it a whole year for one dollar ! His calculation no doubt was, that, by driving his competitor off the road, and securing to himself the carriage of the mail, he would be afterward able to repair his original loss by new contracts with the department. But the necessities of foreign manufacturers, without imputing to them any sinister design, may oblige them to throw into our markets the fabrics which have accumulated on their hands, in consequence of obstruction in the ordinary vents, or from over-calculation ; and the forced sales, at losing prices, may prostrate our establishments. From this view of the subject, it follows, that, if we would place the industry of our country upon a solid and unshakable foundation, we must adopt the protecting policy, which has everywhere succeeded, and reject that which would abandon it, which has everywhere failed."

England commenced her war on American manufactures in 1699, and continued it to the war of the revolution. Lord Chatham said, in parliament, " He would not have the Americans make a *hobnail*." Another noble lord added, " Nor a razor to shave their beards." Mr. Brougham, now Lord Brougham, said, in the house of commons, in 1816, " It was well worth while, by this glut [excessive exports to America], *to stifle in the cradle* those rising manufactories in the United States, which the war had forced into existence." Mr. Robertson, another member, speaking of British policy, confessed, that it " was nothing more or less than for us [the English] to get a monopoly of *all markets* for our manufactures, and to prevent other nations, *one and all*, from engaging in them." The London Spectator, in 1843, said : " More general considerations tend to show, that the trade between the two countries most beneficial to both, must be what is commonly called a *colonial* trade—the new-settled country importing the manufactures of the old, in exchange for its own raw produce. In all economical relations, the United States *still stand* to England in the relation of *colony to mother-country*." Again : " Both England and the United States are suffering, because the *colonial* relation has been broken ; because the surplus capital of England does not find its way to America, along with the stragglers of its surplus population ; and because the raw produce of America, through the influence of restrictive duties, and for want of that capital, can not find its way to England."

This reasoning of British statesmen and British writers, is certainly plain enough to be understood and appreciated on this side of the Atlantic, and sufficiently evinces the correctness and validity of Mr. Clay's argument on this point. Immediately after the war, as stated by Mr. Clay in another part of this speech, " the influx of the Scottish manufacture of cotton bagging prostrated the American establishments. The consequence was, that the Scotch possessed a monopoly of the supply, and the price of it rose, and attained the year before last [1822], a price which amounted to more than an equivalent for ten years of protection of the American manufacture." This tempted the American manufacturers to resuscitate their establishments, which reduced the price, and they would have fallen again in the competition, but for the protection of the tariff of 1824. This case is an exact picture of all others.

The fallacy of what is called the *incidental* protection of a mere revenue tariff, was exposed by Mr. Clay at this time, and made obvious how it might be no protection at all, because inadequate.

As now, so also in 1824, it was urged, that Great Britain was relaxing her prohibitory and restrictive policy. But Mr. Clay showed, that, in every case of fact adduced in evidence, she relaxed in one point, only to gain a greater advantage in another—to extend and fortify her system; and it is the same now as then. It was also urged, that the continental powers were relaxing, which proved to be equally true as what was alleged of Great Britain. Russia, it seems, tried the relaxing policy for a short season, but soon got sick of it, and returned to a rigid system of protection.

Las Cases reports Napoleon to have said:—

" He opposed the principles of economists, which he said were correct in theory, though erroneous in their application. The political constitution of different states," continued he, " must render these principles defective; local circumstances continually call for deviations from their uniformity. Duties," he said, " which were so severely condemned by political economists, should not, it is true, be an object to the treasury; they should be the guaranty and protection of a nation, and should correspond with the nature and the objects of its trade. Holland, which is destitute of productions and manufactures, and which has a trade only of transit and commission, should be free of all fetters and barriers. France, on the contrary, which is rich in every sort of production and manufactures, should incessantly guard against the importations of a rival, who might still continue superior to her, and also against the cupidity, egotism, and indifference, of mere brokers.

" I have not fallen into the error of modern systematizers," said the emperor, " who imagine that all the wisdom of nations is centred in themselves. Experience is the true wisdom of nations. And what does all the reasoning of economists amount to ?"

"I will trouble the committee," said Mr. Clay, " with a quotation from Lowe; and from hearing which, the committee must share with me in the mortification which I felt on perusing it. That author says : ' It is now above forty years since the United States of America were definitely separated from us, and since, their situation has afforded a proof that the benefit of mercantile intercourse may be retained, in all its extent, without the care of governing, or the expense of defending these once-regretted provinces.' Is there not too much truth in this observation ? By adhering to the foreign policy, which I have been discussing, do we not remain essentially British, in everything but the form of our government ? Are not our interests, our industry, our commerce, so modified as to swell British pride, and to increase British power ?"

The above remark, cited by Mr. Clay from Lowe, discloses a grave and momentous truth, that is indeed humiliating to an American citizen. So feeble was the protection of American industry previous to 1824, that the advantages which accrued to Great Britain from her trade with the United States, were regarded by British statesmen and economists as greater than if the colonies had never severed, but retained their connexion with the crown! The American revolution and its results were at first regretted by the British government and people. They are now no longer regretted. And why ? Because they are saved the expense of government, and still have the market on terms as favorable as if they had the entire control ! They could not legislate better for themselves than the Americans did. They have discovered it, they avow it, they boast of it ! Such was the actual state of things down to 1824—embracing nearly fifty years from the declaration of independence. From the peace of 1783 to the adoption of the constitution in 1789, it was much better for Great Britain to have the United States independent of her politically, as she was able, in the absence of a protective system under the confederated states, to make them entirely dependent upon her commercially. It was not her concern that the United States thus consented to be ruined, and again enslaved. They were getting deeper and deeper in debt, and would soon have lost their political standing, if they had not adopted the new form of government under the constitution, to save themselves—the professed and main object of which was to establish a protective system, and rescue the country. But this was very imperfectly done, and still left to Great Britain and other foreign powers the greatest benefit. The European wars gave ome chances to the United States, but no protection to home industry. And the pursuit of these chances brought them into a collision with the belligerents, and finally into a war with Great Britain, inducing with it a protracted period of suffering and sacrifice, ending with a national debt of one hundred and sixty-eight millions ! The war of 1812 was itself a protection to home industry, but purchased with the expenses and hazards of the contest. Peace came, but no protection. The nation was still in the power of Great Britain and of other nations. The tariff of 1816 came late, and when it did come, was inadequate. The tariff bill of 1820 failed, in the midst of great national distress arising from the want of it. The nation was a victim of free trade. The tariff of 1824 brought relief and prosperity, which continued till the Jackson regime broke it all down again.

During the whole history of the country, therefore, down to 1842, with only one breathing spell for a few years subsequent to 1824, the commercial connexions of Great Britain with the United States, excepting the brief period of the war, have been more advantageous to her, and more ruinous to them, than if she had retained them as dependent colonies.

§ 4. *Epoch of* 1832.

" When gentlemen have succeeded," said Mr. Clay, in 1832, "in their design of an immediate or gradual destruction of the American system, what is their substitute ? Free trade ? Free trade ! The call for free trade is as unavailing, as the cry of a spoiled child in its nurse's arm's for the moon, or the stars that glitter in the firmament of heaven. It never has existed, it never will exist. Trade implies at least two parties. To be free, it should be fair, equal, and reciprocal. It is, indeed, possible, that our industry and commerce would accommodate themselves to this unequal and unjust state of things ; for such is the flexibility of our nature, that it bends itself to all circumstances. The wretched prisoner, incarcerated in a jail, after a long time, becomes reconciled to his solitude, and regularly notches down the passing days of his confinement.

" Gentlemen deceive themselves. It is not free trade that they are recommending to our acceptance. It is, in effect, the British colonial system that we are invited to adopt ; and if their policy prevail, it will lead substantially to the recolonization of these states, under the commercial dominion of Great Britain."

The opponents of Mr. Clay were much addicted to quoting foreign authorities especially British, in support of the doctrine of free trade. Whereupon Mr. Clay flung back the following citation from a speech of a member of parliament :—

" ' *It was idle for us to endeavor to persuade other nations to join with us in adopting the principles of what was called ' free trade.' Other nations knew, as well as the noble lord opposite, and those who acted with him, what we meant by ' free trade,' was nothing more nor less than, by means of the great advantages we enjoyed, to get a monopoly of all their markets for our manufactures, and to prevent them, one and all, from ever becoming manufacturing nations.* When the system of reciprocity and free trade had been proposed to a French ambassador, his remark was, that the plan was excellent in theory, but to make it fair in practice, it would be necessary to defer the attempt to put it in execution for half a century, until France should be on the same footing with Great Britain, in marine, in manufactures, in capital, and the many other peculiar advantages which it now enjoyed.' "

Joshua Gee, one of the standard oracles of British policy for a century past, undertook to show :—

" First, that manufactures, in American colonies, should be discouraged, or prohibited. * * * We ought always to keep a watchful eye over our colonies, to restrain them from setting up any of the manufactures which are carried on in Great Britain : and any such attempts should be crushed in the beginning ; for if they are suffered to grow up to maturity, it will be difficult to suppress them.

" Our colonies are much in the same state Ireland was in, when they began the woollen manufactory, and as their numbers increase, will fall upon manufactures for clothing themselves, if due care be not taken to find employment for them, in raising such productions as may enable them to furnish themselves with all their necessaries from us. * * * * *

" Secondly, the advantages to Great Britain, from keeping the colonists dependent on her for their essential supplies.

" If we examine into the circumstances of the inhabitants of our plantations, and our own, it will appear, that not *one fourth* part of their product redounds to their *own profit ;* for out of all that comes here, they only carry back clothing, and other accommodations for their families, all of which is of the merchandise and manufacture of this kingdom."

" All these advantages we receive by the plantations, besides the mortgages on the planters' estates, and the high interest they pay us, which is very considerable ; and therefore very great care ought to be taken in regulating all the affairs of the colonists, that the planters be not put under *too many difficulties*, but encouraged to go on cheerfully.

" New England and the northern colonies have not commodities and products enough to send us, in return, for purchasing their necessary clothing, but are under very great difficulties, and therefore any ordinary sort sells with them. And when they have grown out of *fashion* with us, they are new-fashioned *enough* there."

After having made liberal citations of this kind from this author, Mr. Clay says :—

" Sir, I can not go on with this disgusting detail. Their refuse goods, their old shop-sweepings, their cast-off clothes, good enough for us ! Was there ever a scheme more artfully devised, by which the energies and faculties of one people should be kept down, and rendered subservient to the pride and the pomp and the power of another ? The system then proposed differs only from that which is now recommended in one particular—that was intended to be enforced by power ; this would not be less effectually executed by the force of circumstances."

Coincident with these citations made by Mr. Clay from British authorities, the following historical facts are derived from Pitkin's Statistical View : In 1699, the British parliament prohibited the colonies from exporting wool, yarn, or woollen fabrics, and from carrying them coastwise from one colony and place to another. In 1719, parliament declared, that the erection of manufactories in the colonies tended to lessen their dependence on the mother-country ; and the English manufacturers memorialized parliament, that the colonies were carrying on trade, and erecting manufactories, with a view to obtain legislation to arrest it. In 1731, the board of trade were instructed to inquire as to the colonial laws made to encourage manufactures, as to manufactories set up, and as to the trade carried on in the colonies, and to report thereon. In 1732, they reported, that Massachusetts had passed a law to encourage manufactures ; that the people of New York, Connecticut, Rhode Island, and Maryland, had fallen into the manufacture of woollen, and linen for the use of their own families, and of flax and hemp into coarse bags and halters—all which interfered with the profits of British merchants. The board recommended, that the minds of the people of those colonies should be immediately diverted, and a stop be put to it, or the practice would be extended. The same year parliament prohibited the exportation of hats from the colonies, and trading in them from one colony to another, by ships, carts, or horses. No hatter should set up business who had not served seven years, nor have more than two apprentices, and no black person should work at the trade. Iron mills for slitting and rolling, and plating-forges, were prohibited, under a penalty of five hundred pounds. This system of prohibition and restriction continued to increase, till the colonies rebelled, and declared independence in 1776.

Not having space to cite from Mr. Clay's matchless effort of 1832, it must suffice to present what he claimed to have proved, in summing up:—

"First, that the policy which we have been considering ought to continue to be regarded as the genuine American system.

"Secondly, that the free-trade system, which is proposed as its substitute, onght really to be considered as the British colonial system.

"Thirdly, that the American system is beneficial to all parts of the Union, and absolutely necessary to much the larger portion.

"Fourthly, that the price of the great staple of cotton and of all our chief productions of agriculture, has been sustained and upheld, and a decline averted, by the protective system.

"Fifthly, that if the foreign demand for cotton has been at all diminished, by the operation of that system, the diminution has been more than compensated, in the additional demand created at home.

"Sixthly, that the constant tendency of the system, by creating competition among ourselves, and between American and European industry, reciprocally acting upon each other, is to reduce prices of manufactured articles.

"Seventhly, that, in point of fact, articles within the scope of the policy of protection, have greatly fallen in price.

"Eighthly, that if, in a season of peace, these benefits are experienced, in a season of war, when the foreign supply might be cut off, they would be much more extensively felt.

"Ninthly, and finally, that the substitution of the British colonial system for the American system, without benefiting any section of the Union, by subjecting us to a foreign legislation, regulated by foreign interests, would lead to the prostration of our manufactories, general impoverishment, and ULTIMATE RUIN."

§. 5 Instructive Facts.

A farmer in Illinois wrote a letter to his friend in the east, in 1842, complaining that he could get only 31 cents a bushel for his wheat, 25 cents for beans, 10 cents for corn, 1½ cents a pound for beef and pork, 2½ cents a pound for tobacco, &c., stating that he had to pay *five dollars*, or which is the same thing, 16 bushels of wheat, or 20 bushels of beans, or 26 bushels of corn, or 300 pounds of pork or beef, or 200 pounds of tobacco, *per yard* of British broadcloth to make him a coat! The cost of this yard of cloth at the manufactories in England, was probably about *three dollars*, three bushels of wheat, as sold in the market there. That is, the producer in England received for the cloth *one eighth* of what was charged to the farmer in Illinois. Who got the difference? If the manufacturer had been in Illinois, or anywhere in this country, the farmer might have got his yard of cloth by three bushels of wheat, instead of *sixteen*, and the manufacturer would have made a market for the farmer's beans, corn, pork, beef, &c., at a good price.

It appears from a report of the Hon. J. P. Kennedy, of the 27th Congress, from the committee on commerce, that, from 1820 to 1830, the aggregate imports of the United States amounted to $798,500,000, and the amount retained for domestic consumption to $568,900,000; and that, from 1830 to 1840, the imports were $1,302,500,000, and the amount retained for domestic consumption, was $1,103,100,000. Herein is revealed a great secret: As the effect of the protective policy established in 1824, and continued for a number of years, the nation paid off a debt of one hundred millions. Chiefly in the last half of the period from 1830 to 1840, a foreign debt of two hundred millions was contracted. It is accounted for in the abovecited imports for that period. About one hundred millions of the state debts were made in 1835 and 1836, and nearly all of them got into the foreign market about this time to settle balances for excessive importations.

CHAPTER XX.

THE PROTECTION OF LABOR NECESSARY TO FREEDOM AND A SOUND CURRENCY.

LABOR in Europe and other foreign parts is employed by its oppressors as a power—a tremendous agent to enslave the masses of mankind. This is the reason why American labor will for ever require protection against such an agency, so long as the present state of society exists in Europe, or in other parts of the world, with which the United States have commercial intercourse. The fact, that the substance of this doctrine has been, for so many years and so often, used in argument, by politicians and statesmen—and the fact, that the idea that "the pauper labor of Europe," brought into competition with American labor, invades and impairs the rights of the latter, has taken so strong a hold of a very large portion of the laboring classes of the United States, and is instinctively felt by them, as a matter in which they are deeply concerned—are strong presumptive evidence, that the doctrine is not without foundation. It is manifest, that politicians and statesmen have long had this idea in their heads, though perhaps not in a definite shape. It is not less manifest, that no inconsiderable fraction of the common mind is possessed of it. It only remains that the doctrine should be made palpable—that the plainest man should be able, forced to see, that "the pauper labor of Europe," and of other foreign parts, as an agency in the hands of oppressors, is hostile to the labor of American freemen; that the two things can never subsist together on the same platform; that, on the principles of free trade, one must yield to the other; that, in such a conflict, American labor will inevitably be deprived of its rights; and then the whole controversy, as a political question, is for ever decided.

The power of foreign pauper labor over the labor of American freemen, is not vested in isself, but in the arm of its oppressors. It is a mere agent of the latter. Nor can that power be abated, except by a change of political society in those quarters, for the emancipation of labor. So long as political society is the same there, and the same here, there can never be a time when "the protected arts" in the United States, "shall have acquired such strength and perfection as will enable them subsequently, unaided, to stand up against foreign competition." No matter what strength, no matter what perfection, they may acquire, they will never be strong enough, never perfect enough, to employ free labor at a fair price, in a field of competition with the same arts worked by forced labor at a price which barely supports existence.

The question, then—the great, practical, momentous question—is, shall European capital and labor, in a field of open and free trade, be permitted to bring American capital and labor, that is, American society, down to the same level? Or shall American society, by the American government, *protect* American capital and labor, and maintain the position to which the cost of American freedom has elevated them?

The great battle of the world is between freedom and despotism; and more than in anything, or all things else, the *form* under which that contest is now carried on, is between European capital and labor on one side, and American capital and labor on the other. On this pivot turns the destiny of nations. Sustain the position of American capital and labor, that every man may be secure of the fair reward of his exertions, however humble his birth and calling, and freedom will prevail all the world over. The American people, *united and resolved* in this great emprise, can beat the world—the *whole* world—and crumble into dust the bulwarks of despotic sway. But, let European capital and labor prevail against American capital and labor, for want of protection to the latter, and there is an end of freedom, till another cycle of ages, with its sad round of experience, shall burst the chains again, and they who succeed shall better appreciate their duty and their chances.

The battle for American freedom was only begun in the establishment of American independence. The commercial systems of Europe are more to be feared than all the power of European arms. A perpetual war would be less expensive and less perilous than the effects of this occult, silent, insinuating, all-pervading power, *if unresisted.*

Of all reasons that can be urged in favor of a protective policy, no one perhaps can be named of greater cogency, than its necessity for a good and adequate currency. The currency of the country—a sound currency—does not depend on banking, or the modes of banking, or whether banking be done by a national institution, or by state corporations, or by both, or by neither, though doubtless there is a choice in modes—a better way. There can be no sound currency, where there is no money; and there never can be money enough for the currency of a country which is constantly sending off more than it brings back—unless one of its products be money, as has been the case with Mexico, and some of the South American states. In that case, money is not th medium, but an article, of trade. But the United States do not produce money in any quantity sufficient to rely upon, either as an article, or basis, or medium of trade. They are obliged, therefore, to depend on getting and keeping money enough *by trade*, to answer the purposes of a currency.

A man may have a very large estate, well stocked, well worked, and be making extensive improvements; but if he buys more than he sells, his money, or active capital, is all the while growing less; and unless he has a great deal of it he will soon find himself embarrassed. When this state of things arrives, he is precisely in the condition of a nation that has been guilty of the same improvidence. Without money, neither he, nor a nation, can do business to advantage. An income is as necessary to a nation, as to a private individual; and the income of a nation is the money it gets by selling more than it buys. While this is the case, it is impossible that the currency of a nation should be bad or inadequate. A bank here, and a bank there, may fail, as private individuals do, and for like reasons of mismanagement, or misfortune; but there can be no such thing as a general bank suspension, when the public policy is such as to secure the coming in of more money than goes out; or, when there is enough in, to prevent more going out than comes in. These results, in one case or the other, are always contingent on the sufficiency or insufficiency of the protective policy.

The intimate and indissoluble relation of the protective policy to the currency of a country, commends it, therefore, as a point for consideration too important to be overlooked. No man can trade safely, and with a warrant of prosperity, except on the basis of a credit which solid capital affords, and with such means as that credit will constantly supply him. The moment his means, and with his means, his credit, fail, he is stopped. There is no use in his trying to go on; it is impossible, except by a transient career of fraud, which only makes it worse when he is found out.

It is precisely the same with a nation in its trade with the rest of the world. When, for the lack of an adequate protective policy—which is the same thing as the improvidence of a spendthrift—it is habitually buying more than it sells, and its money goes off to settle balances, its means of trade, domestic as well as foreign, are all the while growing less and less, and without a change, a reform, that nation must fail. Its insolvency is as inevitable, as that of an improvident individual, who conducts business on the same principle. The way in which the insolvency of a commercial nation shows itself, is, first, by a scarcity of money, which everybody feels; as a consequence, a general contraction in all monetary operations, by which business is carried on, necessarily drawing along with it commercial inactivity, dulness; diffidence in all credit transactions; and at last, if no relief comes, the banks suspend. This last act is the consummation of a nation's commercial insolvency. The banks, at the moment, and during the whole time of suspension, may be sound, as the specie in their vaults is not the exponent of their capital. Being allowed by their charters to issue more paper than they have specie, the heavy commercial exchanges against the country operate directly on their vaults, to draw off the specie into foreign parts, and they are compelled to suspend, or part with the last cent. Even then they must suspend, so long as they have more paper out, than specie in. It is the unfavorable state of foreign exchanges, the large commercial balances against the country, which occasion a general bank suspension. It is because there is not money enough in the country to pay its debts; and like a merchant, who finds himself in a like condition, to avoid complete and irretrievable ruin, that would incapacitate the country for all trade, the banks stop payment, to the injury of their own credit, and the credit of the country. They can not help it. They are forced into it by the effect of the policy of the government, which tempts the people to buy more than they sell, and the nation to do the same, till, after repeated and long-continued drafts on the money of the country, the pressure begins to be felt, and before the remedy can be applied—for it is too late when the effects of such improvidence have already come—the whole community is involved in the general calamity. It is only for the want of an adequate protective policy. So long as an industrious and producing nation does not buy more than it sells, it is impossible it should be involved in general commercial distress—absolutely impossible in the nature of things. A nation of such resources and wealth as the United States, with such an enterprising population, can bear a great deal of loss in its foreign trade, and yet prosper. Think of nine hundred millions of loss in fifty years, as appears from public documents—or reduce it even to five hundred millions—this has been more than the nation could bear; and hence its frequent calamitous vicissitudes. Under an adequate and uniform protective policy, such disasters could never come. There can not be an effect without a cause. Such a country as the United States—which is a world in itself—physically capable—and much more capable in the genius, arts, and moral energy of its tenants —of producing everything essential to the complete and perfect independence of a nation, in articles of luxury as well as necessity—a nation capable of an equal pace in science, and in all improvements of art, as any other people, not to say more so—ought never, by the improvidence of legislation, to be in debt to other nations. There is no apology for such a nation to be in the habit of buying more than it sells, which is the only cause of debt and embarrassment. There can be no other.

It has heretofore been set up in defence of the government, that such a state of things comes from the fault of the people. But this will not answer, so long as the government permits the foreign factor—who is not a citizen, and who has no other interest than to make his fortune, and then carry the money away—to bring his goods and merchandise, without paying for the privilege—or, if he pays, pays nothing adequate to protect American citizens in the same business—and thus tempts jobbers, and jobbers tempt retailers, and retailers tempt the people, till the latter are in debt, which can only be discharged by a remittance through the same channels backward—and the foreign factor departs with the money of the people in his pocket! The parties concerned in all the stages of the trade, have doubtless profited by it; but the people are ruined, because their money has gone out of the country, and they have little or nothing left to pay other debts, and do business with.

CHAPTER XXI.

It would perhaps be improper to call anything on this subject, done by a man so much at home in state matters, as Mr. Webster, *elaborate*. Nevertheless, the composition of such a speech, including the collection and arrangement of the matter which it contains, must have cost even *him* no small amount of research and toil. Besides the simplicity of thought, vigor of style, and force of argument, which his productions always carry with them, there is a *freshness* in this speech, adapted to the present moment, too glowing and too captivating, as well as too convincing, to pass it over unnoticed, in a work of this kind. It would be great presumption, indeed, to attempt to assist Mr. Webster; and inasmuch as the greatest portion of this work consists of the somewhat laborious efforts of the author, and inasmuch as Mr. Webster's speech will not of a certainty be read by many who may chance to peruse these pages, it is thought it may not be unacceptable, or altogether without some good effect, in presenting, in this chapter, some extracts from Mr. Webster's recent effort in the senate of the United States, in behalf of American labor.

§ 1. *Mr. Webster's introductory Observations, not without Argument.*

"It will be denied by none, Mr. President, that this subject is important in various respects. The bill before the senate is one which seriously affects, for good or for evil, the revenue of the country, and this in time of war. It also affects the interests, occupations, and pursuits of a vast number of the people of the United States. I may add, that the great principle on which it is founded as a revenue bill—that is to say, that hereafter all duties of customs shall be levied by an assessment *ad valorem*—is an entirely new and untried principle in this government. I may say, too, in respect to the principal practical measures of this bill, that its rates of impositions, and its distribution of duties upon the several articles of import, are quite new. And I suppose I may add, without offence to any gentleman or any party, what I think must appear evident to all who will examine the bill, that it is not drawn with remarkable care, either for the purpose of securing a just collection of the revenue itself, or for a proper distribution of taxes and assessments on importations, according to the principles of the bill itself.

"Mr. President, it appears strange, but after all we must admit the fact, that the appearance of this bill in the senate, with a prospect of its passage, has struck the country suddenly, and with surprise. It has brought about no small degree of alarm. The public expectation was not prepared for it. I do not say that there had not been enough of previous admonition or indication. I speak of the fact, and I think it must be the conviction of every person who hears me, who has observed the development of public sentiment since the appearance of this measure, that the country is surprised, greatly surprised, at any probability that it should receive the final sanction of Congress and the president. Now, sir, it seems to me, that, in this state of things, with such a measure before us, at this advanced season of the year, when there is no pressing necessity for immediate action, the true policy is to postpone its further consideration. If this were a measure to raise money to carry on a war, if it were a measure of taxation, for the contraction of loans, or the issue of treasury-notes, or any other measure which had for its object the supply of means to meet the necessities of government, why then the exigency of the case might be a very just motive for proceeding to its immediate consideration. But there is no man within the hearing of my voice, and I am happy that there are some within its hearing who are not of this chamber [referring to Mr. Secretary Walker, who was present, occupying the seat of one of the senators], who will say that the treasury will not be as competent, the ability of the government as great, its arm as well nerved to prosecute the war in which we are engaged three months longer, if this bill should not pass, as if it should."

§ 2. *Production relative to the Power of Consumption.—Over-Production.—Means of paying for Importations.*

"Those who indulge the hope of an augmentation to the extent stated from increase of exportations, seem to forget, to forget altogether, what is as common a truth as any other, that there can be such a thing as over-production. It has happened many times within my experience in public life. There may be produced in England, and in this country, more manufactured articles than both countries together, with all that they can sell to the rest of the world, can consume or dispose of, and that creates what is commonly called a " glut" in the market. Such instances have been frequent. That there is an indefinite power of consumption is necessarily assumed by all those who think that an indefinite extent of importation may be expected. The honorable member from Maine stated, with great truth and propriety, that the augmentation of imports, drawing after it, or supposing to draw after it, an augmentation of exports, went upon the ground of an augmented consumption on both sides. Now, be it for ever remembered, that there is a limit to the power of consumption, both on one side and the other. Over-production has happened frequently. It may happen again, and therefore it is that I hold it to be exceedingly uncertain and fallacious to rely for revenue, in time of war, upon a matter so theoretical as that we shall have a vast augmentation of importations, with capacity to pay for them, and a desire to consume them. I think that if such an importation should take place, which I do not expect, and can not anticipate, we could not pay for it. Sir, what are our means of paying for the importations of foreign manufactured articles in this country? They are two. They are our exports in the first place, and they are the earnings of freight, or of navigation, in the second place. For carrying out our exportations, we earn a freight. For bringing foreign commodities home, we earn a freight. Our ability, therefore, to discharge foreign debt incurred by importations, consists in the extent of our exports and of our earnings of freight. If there be a demand for means beyond these, it must be met by a drain of the common currency of the world, specie, to the extent that we possess it, or so far as may be necessary."

§ 3. Re-exportation to save Duties, and consequent Loss to Revenue.

" Well, now I will say a word upon this matter of expected importations, although I do not intend to go at any length into the subject. I beg the attention of the honorable member at the head of the committee on finance, and all others, to a consideration which I hope has been well-weighed. Has it been considered, or has it not, what will be the loss of revenue for the ensuing quarter, if this bill pass, by debenture and re-exportation? There is in the country a vast quantity of merchandise, imported at high duties. After the first day of December next, if this bill pass, all such commodities will come in at a greatly reduced duty. It is now all liable to re-exportation and debenture. Take the case of brandies—and there are many others in a memorandum furnished to me from a very respectable source in New York, quite friendly to the government, and wishing it all success—and look to probabilities. Brandies now pay one dollar a gallon; having been purchased at fifty cents per gallon : by the present bill the duty is reduced to 100 per cent. ad valorem ; that is to say, to fifty cents. There is then fifty cents to be made on every gallon of brandy in the United States, if it can be carried out of the country now, and brought in on the first of December next. Is there not? Sir, it will all go to Cuba, or to Canada, or elsewhere, and be returned when December comes. So of carpets, and many other articles."

§ 4. No means of Paying for the expected Excess of Importations.

" I say that we have no means of paying for this expected excess of importation, except by exports and freight. Now, how are we to increase our exports? Not in manufactured goods, which now constitute a considerable part of our exportations, because this bill is an axe laid to the root of that productive tree. It seeks to strike down at once the main interest which sustains these exportations. It is not, therefore, from manufactured goods that we can expect this increase. Well, then, from what can we expect it? Why, we have some national articles of export—cotton, tobacco, and some others of the nature of raw materials, or raw products. Now, does any body suppose that twenty, thirty, or forty millions of augmented exportation of cotton and tobacco can possibly take place? Allow me to put the question to those concerned, those practically concerned, in this great interest. As the product of cotton increases, the tendency in the price is downward; therefore, non sequitur [it does not follow], that if we produce so many more million pounds of cotton, just in that extent do our means of importation increase. The question is, whether there is any reasonable expectation, upon the face of the earth, that we shall so increase our exports of cotton, as that the value of the cotton exported shall amount to twenty, thirty, or forty millions of dollars additional? Does any man believe it?"

§ 5. The New Tariff against all Interests.—Nobody asked for it.—All protested against it.

" As to the freight, which, as I have said, constitutes one of our means of paying for foreign commodities, what chance is there for the increase of freight? Why, the effect of this bill is to diminish freights, and to affect the navigating interests of the United States most seriously, most deeply; and therefore it is that all the shipowners of the United States, without an exception,so far as we hear from them, oppose the bill. It is said to be in favor of free trade and against monopoly. But every man connected with trade is against it; and this leads me to ask, and I ask with earnestness, and hope to receive an answer, at whose request, at whose recommendation, for the promotion of what interest, is this measure introduced? Is it for the importing merchants? They all reject it to a man. Is it for the owners of the navigation of the country? They remonstrate against it. The whole internal industry of the country opposes it. The shipping interest opposes it. The importing interest opposes it. What is it that calls for it, or proposes it? Who asks for it?

Who ? Has there been one single petition presented in its favor from any quarter of the country ? Has a single individual in the United States come up here and told you that his interest would be protected, promoted, and advanced by the passage of a measure like this ? Sir, there is an imperative unity of the public voice the other way, altogether the other way."

§ 6. " *The Bill that vindicates itself.*"

" I must be permitted to say, with great respect for gentlemen on the other side, that I enter upon this discussion under some disadvantages. We do not hear from them. We hear no defence of this bill. An honorable member from South Carolina [Mr. M'DUFFIE] said that ' the bill vindicates itself.' That is so far true as this, that if it did not vindicate itself, it is not vindicated at all. Nobody here stands sponsor for it. Nobody here answers the objections which are urged against it. I see on the opposite side, sir, gentlemen of the highest character in this country, and of the longest experience in this government—gentlemen who have debated questions, great and small, for thirty years—gentlemen properly considered as being among those from whom selection is to be made for the highest honors in the gift of the people ; and yet on this question—as important, I will undertake to say, as any which has been discussed in Congress from the formation of the constitution—we hear from those gentlemen not a word ! not one single word ! They hear us patiently. They appear to be attentive and thoughtful. But they have ' charactered' in their memories at least one of the precepts of Polonius—' Give thy thoughts no tongue !' [Laughter.] They ' give their thoughts no tongue.' I trust they will remember the next, ' nor any unproportioned thought his act.' [Renewed laughter.] They are obedient to the instructive adage : ' Be checked for silence, but never taxed for speech.' They do not mean to be taxed for speech, whatever else they may be taxed for." [Laughter.]

§ 7. *Ad-Valorem Duties.*

After Mr. Webster had exhibited the political history of the country on this point, as already presented in these pages, he introduced the following certificates, which are a fit supplement to section 5 of chapter XVI. of this work :—

" My honorable friend from Maine (Mr. EVANS) must have satisfied the honorable chairman and the senate, as well as everybody else, of the number and the notoriety of the cases of fraudulent under-valuation, because he enumerated instances, and hundreds of instances, in which goods were seized and forfeited for under-valuation. I know no limit to that list of cases ; and, sir, since this subject has come up, and since persons out of doors have heard the declaration of the honorable chairman [that he did not know of any frauds of this kind], my desk has been laboring under the weight of cases and facts communicated from various portions of the commercial community. I will state only a few, out of hundreds. Here is one, and here is the proof :—

" 'A merchant orders goods to be shipped from France, and entered at New Orleans for the Western trade, with the understanding that he is to have them at the foreign cost, with the duties and charges added.

Francs.
A shipment was made with and forwarded to the purchaser, amounting to - - - - 6,829.93
At the same time the invoice forwarded with the goods to New Orleans was - - - 5,258.00

Difference - - - - - - - - - - - - 1,571.93
Or, $316.94 out of $1,300.94.

" ' The goods were valued, therefore, in the entry, at $316.94 less than they were to the purchaser, and the purchaser was actually charged for the duty on this $316.94 as paid to the government, amounting to $95.10. Both the government and the purchaser were therefore cheated out of that sum.
" ' This transaction occurred in the spring of 1846, and I send you a copy of the correspondence in which these facts are stated, and not denied ; but the French house attempts a roundabout justification for putting the foreign cost to the purchasers at a greater amount than the entry invoice.   J. D.'

" This transaction occurred this very year. And here, sir, is another, communicated by a most highly respectable merchant of my acquaintance. Hear the letter :—

" 'BOSTON, *July* 17, 1846.
" ' DEAR SIR : I am informed that a respectable house in this city received an invoice of European goods from a foreign house, the amount of which was about $2,000, and that, after entering the goods at the customhouse by the invoices, they received another invoice valuing the same goods at about $8,000, with a letter, stating that the first invoice was to levy duties by, and the second to sell by.
" ' The consignee here, who is also an importer, not being willing to be a party to the fraud, deposited both invoices at the customhouse, where they were yesterday.
" ' I have no doubt of the authority from which I received this information, but I do not wish to be quoted for it.
" ' I have thought that you might be pleased to know this fact, as the fraud is so great and the per-petrator beyond the reach of any penal statutes of this country.
" ' Your most obedient servant,
" ' Hon. D. WEBSTER, Washington.
" ' P. S. I hear that Mr. Lamson is the consignee.'

"Sir, one case more. A highly respectable firm in Boston (Messrs. George H. Gray & Co.), have been dealers many years in hardware, and in the habit of making importations of certain articles from the north. In these articles they found themselves constantly undersold by the dealers in New York. They could not understand the reason of this for a long time, but last spring the secret came to light. They had ordered a small amount of hardware to be sent to them, and in due time the goods came, and *two* invoices came with them. In *one* invoice the cost was stated at 958 thalers, in the *other* at 1,402. And the letter accompanying these invoices says: 'You find herewith duplicate invoices of the greatest part of your order, &c. The original I send by Havre packet. *You also find herewith an invoice made in the manner like* [that which] the most *importers of your country require—perhaps to save some duty.*'

"Now, sir, these original invoices, the false and the true, and the original letter which I have read, are now in my hand, and any gentleman who may feel disposed may look at them. Of course Messrs. Gray & Co. carried both invoices to the customhouse, because they were honorable merchants, and the duties were assessed on the higher invoice. And by this time these gentlemen were no longer at a loss to account for the low price at which this description of merchandise had been selling in the city of New York.

"But now, sir, take not a single case, but the results of long experience. I am about to read a letter, not addressed to me, but placed in my hands from a gentleman well known, I presume, to both the senators of New York and to other members. This letter, I think, will startle the honorable chairman. It must open to his mind quite a new view of things :—

"'TROY, JULY 14, 1846.

"'LE GRAND CANNON, Esq.—Sir: Agreeably to your wish, I avail myself of this opportunity to give you the benefit of my experience in mercantile and manufacturing business, hoping it may tend to an improvement of the bill now pending in the senate for the collection of duties. I hope, members of Congress will have the same views of the probable results which I anticipate, which are, that the system of ad-valorem duties does give the foreign importer and manufacturer a very undue advantage over the American importer. This will be apparent from my own experience, which I give you annexed. My brother and myself were brought up in the town of Manchester, and well acquainted with the manufacturers and manufacturing. At the age of twenty years it appeared very evident to me that we could finish goods and import goods into New York about ten per cent. lower than the American merchant; and with this conviction, I agreed to come out to New York, and dispose of the goods, and leave my brother to finish and forward the goods.

"'The result was equal to our expectations. We imported our goods ten per cent. cheaper than our competitors, and by the ad-valorem duties we paid nearly five per cent. less duties; so that in twenty-two years we made nearly a million of dollars, while nearly all the American merchants failed. Now, I reason, what has been will be; and, should the present tariff bill pass it will give the foreign manufacturer a decided advantage, and tend to reduce the rate of duties lower than is anticipated. And I can not avoid expressing my decided opinion in favor of specific duties, as then the foreign manufacturer would pay the same duties as the American importer.
"'BENJ. MARSHALL.'

"Can any man gainsay the truth of all this? Is there a merchant, foreign or American, in the United States who will express any contrariety of opinion? Is there a man, high or low, who denies it? I know of none; I have heard of none.

"Sir, it has been the experience of this government always that the *ad-valorem* system is open to innumerable frauds. What is the case with England? In her new notions favorable to free-trade has she rushed madly into a scheme of *ad-valorem* duties? Sir, a system of *ad-valorem* duties is not *free-trade*, but *fraudulent* trade. Has England countenanced this? Not at all; not at all. Sir, on the contrary, on every occasion of a revision of the tariff of England, a constant effort has been made, and progress attained in every case, to augment the number of specific duties and reduce the number of *ad-valorem* duties. A gentleman in the other house (Mr. SEAMAN) has taken pains—which I have taken also, though I believe not quite so thoroughly as he has—to go through the items of the British tariff, and see what proportion of duties in that tariff are *ad-valorem* and what are specific. Now, sir, the result of that examination shows that at this day, in this British tariff, out of 714 enumerated articles, 608 are specific, and only 106 are subject to ad-valorem duties. Everything that, from its nature, could be made specific is made specific. Nothing is placed in the list of *ad-valorem* duties but such as seem to be incapable of assessment in any other form. Well, sir, how do we stand then? We have the experience of our own government; we have the judgment of those most distinguished in the administration of our affairs; we have the production of proof on this most important point, in hundreds and hundreds of instances, of the danger of the *ad-valorem* mode of assessing duties. What is produced in its favor? Every importer of the United States, without exception, is against it."

§ 8. *Duties on Raw Materials used in Manufactures.*

The substance of Mr. Webster's argument, relative to the duties of the new tariff on raw materials used by American manufacturers, tending to their wide-spread injury and destruc-

tion, has already been made in these pages, except that Mr. Webster presents some very instructive certificates and statistics, which the want of space renders impossible to copy here. The following remarks, however, on this point, are worthy of citation :—
"Here, then, on one hand, the foreign agent prays for and urges the passage of Mr. M'Kay's bill; and on the other, the American manufacturer implores us to stick to the tariff of 1842, reject Mr. M'Kay's bill, and suffer him to go on and get an honest living, as heretofore. They have a directly opposite interest ; and as it is no matter of revenue of any considerable amount, how are we to interpret the fact that the former is so obviously protected at the expense of the latter ? How is it that, in this contest, the foreign manufacturer obtains the preference ? Are the suspicions of this gentleman [one of the correspondents adduced]—whom I know to be a highly respectable man of business—entirely unreasonable ? He says there must have been some one at work having an interest foreign and hostile to the interest of the American producer of this article, and similar articles; and judge you whether that be not the case. It is plain and manifest it is an English provision, favorable to English labor and prejudicial to American labor."

§ 9. *The Interests and Feelings of New England.*

"I may not permit myself to be supposed to be influenced, on these topics, by the interests of manufacturers around me, and among whom I live, and for whose prosperity and happiness I never can feel unconcerned. Driven from her original and chosen pursuit, to which she had been enthusiastically addicted—commerce—and compelled to enter upon the field of manufactures twenty-two years ago—if it be now the pleasure of this government—if it be the sense of the American people—if the south, and the middle, and the west say so— New England *can go back, and still live.* You can distress her—you can cripple her—you can cramp her—but you can not annihilate her industry, her self-respect, her capacity to take care of herself. A country of workingmen who are able, if necessity calls for it, to work fourteen hours a day, may bid defiance to all tariffs, and all miserable, false, partial legislation. They stand upon the strength of their own character, resolution, and capacity; and by this strength and that capacity they maintain themselves, do what you please. Not, sir, that there is one house in New England, at this moment, in which the proceedings of this day are not looked for with intense interest. No man rises in the morning but to see the newspaper. No woman retires at night without inquiring of her husband the progress of this great measure at Washington. They ask about it in the streets. They ask about it in the schools. They ask about it in the shoemakers' shops, the machine shops, the tailors' shops, the saddlers' shops, and, in short, in the shops of all artisans and handicrafts. They ask about it everywhere. And they will take whatever answer comes, as men should take it; and they will feel as men should feel when they hear it. I therefore leave, sir, to the senate, all these considerations. I will not suffer myself to be subjected to the temptation of being led away by causes which might be supposed to influence me; and turning from them, therefore, I proceed to the consideration of other subjects, in which, so far as New England is concerned, if she have any interest at all, it is in favor of this bill, and against protected interests. Does she mean the less to exercise her power, little or great, or whatever it may be, in favor of those whose interests are menaced by this bill ? No, sir—no, sir—never."

§ 10. *Iron and its Manufactures.*

As considerable attention has been given to this subject, in these pages, let it suffice to cite the following paragraph from Mr. Webster :—
"Sir, in my opinion, we have before us at this moment the general question, shall we give efficient protection to the American production of iron ? If we say we shall, then it is clear this bill ought not to pass. If it should pass, leaving iron, with all its manufactures and ramifications, at thirty per cent., they might just as well be put at five per cent. The trade would as soon have it so, as I understand. The manufacture declined under the old 'compromise act.' It rose in 1842, and the labor of persons employed rose in proportion. That law was certainly hailed in Pennsylvania as being conformable to all her views and opinions. Now, sir, let us come to a conclusion. Let us decide once for all. I am for protecting the domestic iron interests in the United States. Are you ? If you are, reject this bill. If you are not, say so, and pass the bill; and let every man along the branches, and up to the sources of the Susquehannah and the Schuylkill, and every man beyond the Allegany, in Pennsylvania, and every man in Maryland, Tennessee, Virginia, and every other state in which iron is produced, understand you. Let us have no more fighting under false colors. Enough of that. If you favor the domestic manufacture of iron, reject the bill. If you wish to destroy that domestic manufacture, pass the bill."
In regard to the coal interest, Mr. Webster's facts and figures lead to the same result as on that of iron, and may be expressed in his own words, as above, relating to iron : "If you favor the American coal interest, reject the bill; but if you would destroy it, pass the bill."

The following remarks of Mr. Webster, growing out of the history and results of the coal interest, are worthy of attention :—

"And here, sir, I wish to advert to a general fact, worthy to be recollected in all our political economy, viz. : The increase in the investments of capital in great works of this kind, tends to reduce the profits on that capital. That is a necessary result. But then, it has exactly the reverse action upon labor; for the more that capital is invested in the great operations, the greater is the call for labor, and therefore, the ratio is here the other way, and the rates of labor increase as the profits of capital are diminished. Well, is there anything *undemocratic* and unpopular in such a system as that—a system that causes a diminution of profits to the capitalists and an increase of remuneration to the hand of labor ?"

§ 11. *Effect of the New Tariff on the Interests of Navigation and Labor.*

The elaborate statistical evidence adduced by Mr. Webster, on the first of the above-named points, is too copious to admit of a place here, and it must suffice to present the results, in his own language, as follows :—

"Now, be pleased to notice these results. Fifty-eight millions of dollars of manufactured goods imported yield less than one million for freight. Twenty-two millions of dollars brought in articles to be manufactured here yield three millions and three quarters; being very nearly one half of all the freight earned on all our imports. Certainly this is a most important fact, and worthy of all attention.

" We propose, then, Mr. President [by this new measure] in the first place to diminish and discourage labor and industry at home, by taxing the raw materials which are brought into the country for manufacture. We propose, in the second place, to diminish the earnings of freight very materially, by diminishing the importation of bulky articles, always brought in our own ships. We propose, in the third place, to diminish the amount of exports of our own domestic manufactured goods, by refusing to take in exchange for them raw materials, the products of other countries. This is our present policy ! This is our notion of free trade ! Surely, surely, Mr. President, this enlightened system can not fail to attract the admiration of the world !

* * * * * * *

" Now, sir, taking the mass of men as they exist among us, what is it that constitutes their prosperity ? Throughout the country, perhaps more especially at the north, from early laws and habits, there is a distribution of all the property accumulated in one generation among the whole succession of sons and daughters in the next. Property is everywhere distributed as fast as it is accumulated, and not in more than one case out of a hundred is there an accumulation beyond the earnings of one or two generations. The consequence of this is, a great division of property into small parcels, and a considerable equality in the condition of a great portion of the people; and the next consequence is, that out of the whole mass, there is a very small proportion, hardly worthy of being named, that does not pursue some active business for a living. Who is there that lives on his income ? How many, out of millions of prosperous people between this place and the British provinces, and throughout the north and west, are there who live without being engaged in active business ? None : the number is not worth naming. This is, therefore, a country of labor. I do not mean manual labor entirely. There is a great deal of that; but I mean some sort of employment that requires personal attention, either of oversight or manual performance; some form of active business. That is the character of our people, and that is the condition of our people. Our destiny is labor. Now, what is the first great cause of prosperity with such a people ? Simply, *employment.* Why, we have cheap food and cheap clothing, and there is no sort of doubt that these things are very desirable to all persons of moderate circumstances, and laborers. But they are not the first requisites. The first requisite is that which enables men to buy food and clothing, cheap or dear. And if I were to illustrate my opinions on this subject by example, I should take, of all the instances in the world, the present condition of Ireland.

" Well, now, what is it ? Ireland is an over-peopled country, it is said. It has eight and a half millions of people, on an area of thirty-one thousand eight hundred square miles. It is, then, a very dense population ; perhaps a thicker population, upon the whole, than England. But why are the people of Ireland not prosperous, contented, and happy ? We hear of a potato panic, and a population in Ireland distressed by the high price of potatoes. Why, sir, the price of potatoes in this city is three times the price of potatoes in Dublin; and at this moment potatoes are twice as dear throughout the United States as throughout Ireland. There are potatoes enough, or food of other kinds, but the people are not able to buy it. And why ? That is the stringent question. Why can not the people of Ireland buy potatoes or other food ? The answer to this question solves the Irish case; and that answer is simply this, the people have not employment. They can not obtain wages. They can not earn money. The sum of their social misery lies in these few words—*there is no adequate demand for labor.*"

An Irishman, being asked if potatoes were not cheap in Ireland, said, " Chape! Only saxpence a bushel."—" How is it, then, you are starving there ?"—" Just becase we have no work, and can't get the saxpence."

" But, then," said Mr. Webster, " *how* is it that people in Ireland are so destitute of employment ? Mr. M'Culloch says that four fifths of the labor of Ireland is laid out upon the land. There is no other source of employment or occupation. This land, being under a ' rack-rent,' is frequently in little patches, sometimes of not more than a quarter of an acre, merely to raise potatoes, the cheapest kind of food. This is the reason why labor is nothing and can produce nothing but mere physical living, until the system shall be entirely changed. This constitutes the great difference between the state of things in Europe and America. In Europe the question is, How can men live ? With us the question is, How well can they live ? Can they live on wholesome food, in commodious and comfortable dwellings ? Can they be well clothed, and be able to educate their children ? Such questions do not arise to the political economists of Europe. When reasoning on such cases as that of Ireland, the question with them is, How can physical being be kept from death ? That is all.

" Sir, if I were not overwhelmed with topics, and if I were not conscious of having already occupied the attention of the senate quite too long, I would turn your attention to the contrasts, produced by the very causes which we are now considering, between Ireland and Scotland. The population of Ireland is eight millions and a half, on an area of 31,800 square miles. Scotland has a population less than three millions, and an area of 26,000 square miles, only one third of which is arable.

" But, nevertheless, the tonnage of Scotland is four hundred and twenty-nine thousand tons of shipping, employing twenty-eight thousand men, while that of Ireland is only one hundred and forty thousand, employing eleven or twelve thousand men. With regard to the agriculture of Scotland, though her climate is not so good, nor her soil so rich as that of Ireland, yet Scotland is a wheat-growing country, and the prices are high, and all agricultural business active. Why, sir, how has this come about ? This great reformation, it is said, has been accomplished within sixty or seventy years; and respectable authorities say that the growth of the manufacturing cities of Glasgow, Paisley, and Edinburgh, and the rest, by furnishing a market for the immediate sale of agricultural products, has doubled those products—raised them from a lower to a higher species of production, and changed the whole face of Scotland. I will not pursue this illustration farther. It is enough to say that Scotland has commerce, manufactures, and a variety of employments for labor. In Ireland there is little of commerce, and little of manufactures—*four fifths of the whole labor of the country being bestowed on the land*. These facts are enough to show why Scotland is that Scotland which we find her, and Ireland that Ireland which we find her.

" Now, sir, no man can deny that the course of things in this country, for the last twenty or thirty years, has had a wonderful effect in producing a variety of employments. How much employment has been furnished by the canals and railroads, in addition to the great amount of labor not only in the factories, rendered so odious in some quarters by calling them monopolies and close corporations, but in the workshops, in the warehouses, on the sea and on the land, and in every department of business ? There is a great general activity, and a great variety in the employment of men among us; and that is just exactly what our condition ought to be.

" The interests of every laboring community requires diversity of occupations, pursuits, and objects of industry. The more that diversity is multiplied or extended, the better. To diversify employment is to increase employment and to enhance wages. And, sir, take this great truth; place it on the title page of every book of political economy intended for the use of the United States; put it in every Farmer's Almanac; let it be the heading of the column in every Mechanic's Magazine; proclaim it everywhere, and make it a proverb, that *where there is work for the hands of men, there will be work for their teeth*. Where there is employment, there will be bread. It is a great blessing to the poor to have cheap food; but greater than that, prior to that, and of still higher value, is the blessing of being able to buy food by honest and respectable employment. Employment feeds and clothes and instructs. Employment gives health, sobriety, and morals. Constant employment and well-paid labor produce, in a country like ours, general prosperity, content, and cheerfulness. Thus happy have we seen the country. Thus happy may we long continue to see it!

* * * * * * *

" Sir, I beseech gentlemen to pause. If I were a friend of the administration—and I do not mean to call myself its enemy, for I have no unfriendly feeling to it—I would beseech it not to make this leap in the dark, in the early part of its career, unnecessarily, in the midst of a war—a war of which no man can see the end, and of which no man can now reckon up the expense. I would beseech it to stand firm on established ground—on the system on which our revenue now stands—and to lay aside all propositions for extensive and elementary change."

☞ The extracts in this chapter are taken, here and there, and the divisions into sections, are made by the author.

CHAPTER XXII.

HISTORY OF THE FREE-TRADE DOCTRINE.

THE doctrine of free trade is a fraud, imposed upon the world by pensioned writers, for the benefit of Great Britain chiefly, which originated the fraud, and has supervised it from the beginning down to this time. The British writers on political economy, down to Sir James Stewart and Adam Smith, running through about a century, were, for the most part, strenuous advocates of a protective policy; and they were doubtless, in some way, rewarded, with honor or profit, so far as their works were considered serviceable to the state. Joshua Gee, who wrote his book in 1730, entitled, " *The Trade and Navigation of Great Britain considered, showing that the surest way for a nation to increase in riches, is to prevent the importation of such foreign commodities as may be raised at home,*" &c., said he wrote " *by order of the lords of trade.*" This confession, leaking out, before the necessity of caution was thought of, is sufficient. A century of teaching and practice on the protective principle, had taught England the benefit of it. She had established her policy, and has never relaxed it, down to this moment, except in *form* for the very purpose of protection, as has been demonstrated in these pages, notwithstanding all that has been said of her approximation to free trade. Nothing could be more contradictory than the doctrine of British writers, since Adam Smith, including him, and the practice of the British government; and this social problem must some way be solved. Writers of such acknowledged ability, of such transcendent talents, could not have been so entirely disregarded in the practice of the government, without collusion. It was for the interest of Great Britain, that all the world, foreign to herself, should believe in free trade; and if, by pensioning the greatest talents, she could make that doctrine plausible, captivating to other nations, would she not do it? There is the doctrine of modern British writers, and there the practice of the British government, diametrically opposed to each other. If any one can give a better reason than the above, he is at liberty to do so. Our explanation accounts for the facts, while no other can.

Dr. Adam Smith's leaving the university of Glasgow, at the instance of Charles Townsend—" a man of lax principles"—to accompany the young duke of Buccleugh in his travels on the continent, " on conditions which assured the philosopher an ample, competent independence of fortune for his future life," and his subsequent appointment, under the corrupt Grenville administration, of which Charles Townsend was a member, to the office of commissioner of customs in Scotland, when the taxation of the North American colonies was on foot, are sufficient evidence, that he was not likely to engage in anything detrimental to the British exchequer, as his " Wealth of Nations" would be, if put in practice. Dr. Smith did not begin his " Wealth of Nations," till he was seduced from his high dignity at Glasgow, and stepped into the sunshine, and became a beneficiary, of the British government—first indirectly, afterward directly.

But, if it were possible to doubt this great conspiracy against mankind, from Adam Smith down to M'Culloch, including the latter, who is still living, the following extract from M'Culloch's own pen, proving at the same time his fidelity to his patrons, the British government, and his treason to all other nations, will be sufficient to settle the question :—

" Our establishments for spinning, weaving, printing, bleaching, &c., are infinitely more complete and perfect than any that exist elsewhere ; the division of labor in them is carried to an incomparably greater extent ; the workmen are trained from infancy to industrious habits, and have attained that peculiar dexterity and sleight of hand in the performance of their several tasks, that can only be attained by long and unremitted application to the same employment. Why, then, having all these advantages on our side, should we not keep the start we have gained ? Every other people that attempt to set up manufactures must obviously labor under the greatest difficulties, as compared with us. Their establishments can not, at first, be sufficiently large to enable the division of employments to be carried to any considerable extent; at the same time that expertness in manipulation, and in the details of the various processes, can only be attained by slow degrees. It appears, therefore, reasonable to conclude, that such new beginners, having to withstand the competition of those who have already arrived at a very high degree of perfection in the art, must be immediately driven out of every market equally accessible to both parties ; *and that nothing but the aid derived from restrictive regulations and prohibitions, will be effectual to prevent the total destruction of their establishments,*" &c.—p. 19.

The passage in italics tells the story, and discloses the doom assigned to us, and to all nations, which adopt the free trade commended to them by the *pensioned* economists of Great Britain.

The motive of the British government, for such a systematic and stupendous fraud, as is here supposed, was a potent one : It was to become the richest nation in the world—in that way, the most powerful—and to maintain that ascendency. England was *poor*, when she commenced her protective system, in the 17th century, under her first tutors, Child, Gee, and others, who wrote by " order of the lords of trade." But " England" *now*, says the Southern Planter, " stands at the head [of nations], both for wealth and manufactures. She lives in wealth and luxury, and has capital enough to buy the world, if offered for sale. In other words, she has as much money as all Europe besides. The question naturally arises, how did she acquire it? Not by her agriculture; for the utmost it ever did, was to feed and support her, and now does not do that much. Not by her fisheries; for they barely supplied her with the luxuries and products of the ocean. Not by working gold, silver, and diamond mines; for she has none of them. It is the fruit of her *labor*, her *manufacturing* labor and skill, and the commerce that is based upon it. England, her writers say, has a clear income in money, after supplying herself every year, of *two hundred millions*, to add to her capital."

An interesting and instructive table, directly in point, exhibiting the imports, exports, and balances of Great Britain, from 1700 to 1787, is given in Fisher's National Magazine, for October, 1845, pp. 389 and 390. In 1700, the British protective system had been in operation about half a century, and from this time to 1787, according to this table, not a single year failed to bring a balance of trade, in favor of Great Britain; and the aggregate balance for the period, was £289,321,713; or $1,388,744,226. But the gains of British policy and trade have of late been much greater, and were stated, in 1844, by the American Institute, New-York, to have averaged considerably in excess of $200,000,000 a year, for 1839, 1840, and 1841. (*See the explanation of this balance on page* 35 *of this work.*) The footing of accounts in the commercial history of the United States, in relation to foreign parts, presents a sad contrast to the above, in a balance of nearly a thousand millions against us!

Notwithstanding that attempts have been made to impair the force of the rule, commonly called the BALANCE OF TRADE, by stigmatizing it as a " detected fallacy," for the sake of annihilating the arithmetical certainty which it affords as a species of evidence in determining the gains and losses of a nation in its foreign trade, it is a means of information on this subject which, on account of its importance and the unerring result to which it leads, can not be surrendered. All the uncertainty arising from the application of this rule, results from failing to collect and put forward the facts which constitute the rule. It certainly would not be infallible to say, that a nation which has sold the value of one hundred millions, and bought the value of one hundred and eleven millions, is therefore eleven millions minus, without considering the place where and the rule by which the values were ascertained, and to what party or parties the profits of the trade belonged. But there can be no possibility of mistake when the commercial exchanges against a nation are making perpetual drafts on its money, instead of paying its debts by exports of other commodities, and when it finds itself growing poorer and poorer in pocket, till, like an unwise spendthrift, it has parted with all its cash; or is obliged to turn bankrupt or repudiate, because it can not pay. It is well known there have been times of commercial distress in the United States—want of money, loss of credit, and general embarrassment in all kinds of business—and it is found, that these times have always followed immediately after large balances of trade have fallen against the nation by its having bought more than it had sold. It is also found, that this excess of buying over the amount of selling, has always prevailed most when the protective policy was least stringent, and that the nation has uniformly been most prosperous when the tariff has been strongest, or highest. The balance of trade, in favor of a nation, is its income; the balance against it, is its loss, and will be its ruin, if continued; the same as it is with a private individual. The man that trades with a profit, grows rich; and it is only another truism to say, that he who trades with loss, grows poor. The " detected fallacy" is the doctrine that questions these self-evident truths—not less true in application to a nation, than to a private man.

The following extract from a report on the commercial intercourse of the United States and Great Britain, published by the American Institute, New-York, 1844, is not less instructive than pertinent in this place:—

" Without entering into a discussion of the question of the balance of trade, we deem it important *to* notice the operation of the system pursued by the British government, in fostering industry and trade, on their own commerce, compared with the policy of the United States. The total value of exports and imports of Great Britain and Ireland for three successive years was as follows:—

Year.	Exports.	Imports.
1839	£110,198,716	£62,004,000
1840	116,479,679	67,432,964
1841	116,903,668	64,377,962
	£343,582,061	£193,814,926

Balance in favor of Great Britain. £149,767,136, or an annual average of £49,822,378, equal to $237,227,414. It is her commercial policy, producing these yearly balances of two hundred and thirty-seven millions of dollars in her favor, which sustains her currency, enables her to do as she wishes, to spend as she pleases, to endure our defalcations, and, from her surplus, she is ready to lend us, and permit us to increase our indebtedness a few millions more. ' Money to let' is the fortune of those only who so manage their business as to have yearly balances in their favor.

"In contrast, the amount of imports into the United States from foreign countries, for the nine years from 1831 to 1839, inclusive, exceeded the total amount of exports therefrom by the sum of $235,278,605, as shown by the following statement:—

Year.	Imports.	Exports.
1831	$103,191,124	$18,310,583
1832	101,029,266	87,176,913
1833	108,118,311	90,140,433
1834	126,521,332	104,336,973
1835	140,895,742	121,693,577
1836	180,980,034	128,663,040
1837	140,989,217	117,419,376
1838	113,717,404	108,486,616
1839	163,092,132	121,028,476
Total,	$1,195,534,562	$960,255,957
	960,255,957	

Balance against United States, - $235,278,605

"It is not deemed necessary to search farther than a knowledge of these facts, to account for the loss of currency; for the large amount of indebtedness by states, corporations, and individuals of the United States, to the capitalists of Great Britain; nor beyond this, to seek for a principal cause for the insolvency and ruin of our banks and other corporations, as well as of individuals, the depreciation in the value of property, the decline of trade, and ending in the modern doctrine of repudiation."

Was not such success of more than a century's operation of a protective system, motive enough, with the British government to begin, toward the close of the 18th century, to put out their own lights, or throw them behind a screen, that the rest of the world should not see them; and to hold up other lights, to lead the nations astray, while England still continued to work by Sir Josiah Child and Joshua Gee?· That she has ever worked, and still works, by those early lights, since they began to shine, has been shown in these pages; nor is it less true, that new lights have blazed forth from her hearth on the world, which she has never deigned to follow, but commends them to others!

Too unfortunately for the United States, our schools, colleges, and universities, have respected this recommendation, adopted these new lights, and sent forth their graduates over the land, to become statesmen and teachers, indoctrinated in the principles of free trade! Common sense has ever been at war with these principles; nevertheless, *theory* has pressed its dictations on the public mind. Again and again, by such an influence, has the experiment of free trade, or an approximation toward it, been attempted in the United States by legislation; and as often has the nation been plunged in the deep abyss of ruin, dug for it by such a fraud! Not a single American writer on political economy, ever had the independence, the courage, the manliness, the patriotism—certainly not the discernment—to disengage himself from these shackles of foreign authority, thus imposed, till "a Southern Planter" came up to the task in 1844, dissipated the mists and clouds of deception, and put the whole subject in the sunlight of truth. One of the best popular arguments ever made on this subject, is contained in "the address of the Society of Tammany, New-York, 1819, to the several branches of the order throughout the United States." The only fault, perhaps, that could be found with it, if any, was, that it carried the doctrine of protection too far. Like the vibrations of the pendulum, that society has of late years been, and seems now to be, in the other extreme. But standing in the midst of the general distress and commercial ruin of that day (1819), they could not but be instructed by the facts around them.

Admitting that these foreign and borrowed authorities are worthy of more respect than is here ascribed to them; admitting that they were sincere and independent in their opinions; still they wrote for a state of society, and a state of things, entirely different from that of the United States; and it would be equally safe for a man in one kind of business, to adopt the principles and modes of a man in another kind of business, as for the United States to adopt European systems of political economy, though they might have some fitness for the state of things for which they were made. European political economists have never yet dreamed, that labor could be an independent political agent. They have devised nothing for it, but to occupy a position of bare subsistence, and to serve masters; and all their systems have been constructed in conformity with this humiliating view of human society. To borrow those systems, and to apply them here, is to fall back on the same political platform where we stood when we were subject colonies of the British crown. It is to go even farther back. No matter what definitions may be given to political economy, as a science, it is impossible to divorce it from political society. It enters deep into the foundation of such society, pervades its structure, and mounts to its highest pinnacle. Is not labor the great element, the moving power of both? And what is the position which foreign systems of political economy give to labor! Anything but that which would impart to it dignity and social importance.

Such, as above depicted, being the history of the doctrine of free trade, till it was shot forth from a British laboratory into the American mind, by the adoption of British authorities, manufactured for us, and not for themselves, it remains to observe, that a new edition of this theory—" the forty-bale theory"—was fabricated some fifteen years ago, on our own soil, with a view to raise and sustain the price of cotton. It was all a mistake, as has been shown. But nevertheless, it was a fact. And strange to say, after having triumphed once, and forced upon the country the compromise tariff of 1833—as the best thing that could be done to save anything—and at last run down the duties to a twenty per cent. maximum, without adopting the home valuation as the compromise stipulated, and thus bringing upon the nation the greatest misfortunes and distress, this very theory, after a short respite, has triumphed again, through Mr. Secretary Walker, and the president, by the instrumentality of an obsequious Congress! Such is the history of the doctrine of free trade, foreign and domestic.

CHAPTER XXIII.

WHAT IS SUGGESTED BY THE GENERAL ARGUMENT OF THIS WORK.

§ 1. *A Home Market for all Agricultural Products common to Europe and other Parts.*

It has been seen, in the progress of this work, that the agricultural products of the United States, which are common to Europe and other countries, can not go into the market of those parts, without coming into competition with their cheap labor, which usually reduces prices below that which is regarded as remunerative of American labor. There is no possibility of avoiding this result, and no exception to the rule, except in the cases of short crops in some of those foreign parts, the necessities of which would supersede all legislation, here or there; but, in an ordinary state of things, and in relation to cheap foreign labor, American labor feels itself borne down and oppressed, by an irresistible influence; and what it feels is a fact. And is there no remedy? There is one and one only: A HOME MARKET.

§ 2. *The Charm of a Diversity and Multiplication of Pursuits.*

It has been seen, by examples and by facts, how this operates. It falls within the scope of every one's observation. Who does not know, that of two producers of one thing wanted by both, neither can find a market with the other? What, then, are they to do, when they have nowhere else to go? Plainly, one must produce something else wanted by both, and each will then have a market, and be supplied. It is only necessary to multiply this diversity of pursuits, to the extent of human wants, and the end of political economy, as to this point, is attained. A surplus production, as a uniform result, is death to the profits of agricultural, or of any other pursuits. A squaw can raise all the corn that a wigwam requires, and her husband can find the game. What do they want more, so long as there is nobody to buy? This, apparently, is the primitive condition, to which Mr. Secretary Walker proposes to bring back the people of the United States! General Jackson saw, in 1824, that too many people were engaged in agriculture, and he proposed to withdraw 600,000, men, women, and children, and put them to manufactures and the mechanic arts. Has it not been proved in these pages, that he was right then, though he was wrong afterward? It is diversity and multiplication of pursuits, economized according to the wants of all, that affords a living for all; and in a great commonwealth, the greater this diversity, the better. The necessary wants of man from agriculture, are limited. How ever much is produced, no man can eat more than his full. So of any other wants supplied from this source. A surplus is a surfeit; appetite palls; demand is deadened; prices fall; and the producers are sacrificed. If the American agriculturist is forced to go to Europe for a market, he must sell his labor for what it costs there, except in a case of short crops in that quarter. Will that be satisfactory? To be sure of his reward, then, he must have a home *market*. And how can that be?

§ 3. *Manufacturing and other Arts create the only Market on which American Agricultural Labor can rely.*

Does not every one see this in the experience of the past? Look at a manufacturing village. How quick it raises the price of land in the vicinity, and turns farms into gardens, which are the most profitable species of agriculture. And not only is there this near benefit, but it branches out, and connects itself with the agriculture of the whole Union. Every new manufactory, of whatever kind, and in whatever place, gives life, activity, and profit, to agriculture, on a large scale. By these establishments, the workshops of Europe are brought to the door of American farmers—are planted alongside of their fields, and the two parties supply each other's wants without the costs of transportation over seas, the farmer getting as much, or nearly as much, at home, as his products would command abroad, thus saving the costs of transport, and the parties retain among themselves all the profits of manufacturing skill and labor, and all the additional values which are imparted by art and labor to the raw material.

The following history of a *pound* of cotton, from an English paper, will illustrate the values added by manufacturing : " There was sent off for London, lately, from Glasgow, a small piece of muslin, about one pound weight, the history of which is as follows : The cotton came from the United States to London; from London it went to Manchester, where it was manufactured into yarn; from Manchester it was sent to Paisley, where it was woven; it was sent to Ayrshire next, where it was tamboured ; afterward it was conveyed to Dunbarton, where it was handsewed, and again returned to Paisley, when it was sent to a distant part of the county of Renfrew to be bleached, and was returned to Paisley ; then sent per coach to London. It is difficult precisely to ascertain the time taken to bring this article to market, but it may be pretty near the truth to reckon it two years from the time it was packed in America till its cloth arrived at the merchant's warehouse in London, whither it must have been conveyed 3,000 miles by sea, and 920 by land, and contributed toward the support of no less than 150 people, whose services were necessary in the carriage and manufacture of this small quantity of cotton, and by which the value has been advanced 2,000 per cent. What is said of this piece, is descriptive of no inconsiderable part of the trade."

The following is another extract from an English journal, to the same point :—

"The quantity of *cast-iron* worth £1 sterling, becomes worth the following sums :—
When converted into ordinary machinery............................£4.00
Large ornamental work..... ....45.00
Buckles—Berlin work...660.00
Neck chains..1386.00
Shirt buttons..5896.00
"The quantity of bar iron worth £1 sterling, becomes, when formed into
Horse-shoe work...£2.10
Knives (table)...36.00
Needles...71.00
Penknife blades..657.00
Polished buttons and buckles............ ....897.00
Balance springs of watches...................................50,000.00"

The question with Americans is, whether these values, running up, in one instance, from 1 to 2,000 ; in another, from 1 to 5,896 ; and in a third, from 1 to 50,000, shall be created at home, and remain here as part of the capital of the nation; or whether they shall be created abroad, and this capital be lost to us? These are only three of hundreds of similar instances, involving, as the case may be, the loss or gain of uncounted private and public wealth, to one side or the other.

Here is the secret, not only of sustaining, but of raising, the prices of American agricultural products. With a home market, thus created, American agricultural labor can obtain a fair and satisfactory remuneration. The money that would otherwise go abroad, remains at home, and the currency is sound. All trade is cash, if required ; and all prices remunerative to all parties. Herein are the RIGHTS of American labor, as purchased by the blood and treasure of the American fathers.

§ 4. *Protection of Agriculture.*

The average protection extended by the tariff of 1842, to wool, hemp, beef, pork, hams, bacon, cheese, butter, lard, potatoes, flour, and wheat, was 50 per cent., being higher than the average protection afforded by that measure to manufactures. But, as seen above, the protection of manufactures is the best possible protection of agriculture, by affording the latter a home market. The difference in the end, in favor of agriculture, by an adequate protection of manufactures, is equal to the cost of transportation of agricultural products, always heavy and costly, to a foreign market, besides the effect of competition with cheap foreign labor. To this should be added the reciprocal benefit to all parties by the home trade.

The most important function of the protective policy on the interests of agriculture—so silent in its operation as scarcely to be noticed by common observers, but which, when mentioned, must strike every one with great force—is its effect in steadily SUSTAINING a demand for, and the prices of, agricultural products. Foreign markets for the agricultural products of the United States, except cotton and tobacco, are uncertain, continually fluctuating, and in a time of general peace the whole foreign world does not consume so much of them as the state of Massachusetts alone demands from other states, over and above the products of her own soil—and that solely in consequence of the existence of her manufactories and mechanic arts. It has indeed been found necessary to impose protective duties, to prevent the influx of foreign agricultural products to cheapen those of the United States—

a fact which shows that American farmers can not depend on foreign markets, and would be essentially injured by free trade in the products of their labor.

The prices of agricultural products are subject to more fluctuation than the products of manufacture, on account of excess or deficiency of supply by more or less favorable seasons. But the tables of Mr. Hudson's report, before cited, show that they generally and considerably improved under the operation of the tariff of 1842. The average fall in the prices of some products, from 1842 to 1844, had been 9½ per cent., while the average *rise* in the majority had been 25 per cent. But the saving to agriculturists in the prices of the products of manufacture, by reason of a protective tariff, should be added to this account for the true economical result, which, as will be seen, would very much enhance the benefit. The practical operation of a protective tariff, for the increase of prices of agricultural products, is very simple, and may be thus explained: All agricultural products are comparatively gross and heavy, and consequently more expensive in being carried to a remote market. Suppose the cost of transportation from the remote west to the eastern market be 100 per cent. In other words, that the products are only worth *half* as much in the place where they are grown as in the place where they are consumed. Add as much more for the expense of delivery in a foreign market, and the price to the producer is reduced to *one third* of the price at the place of destination. But bring the market half way toward the producer, and the price is raised *one third*. Bring it to his door, and his price is *tripled*. This is precisely the principle of the theory of protection, and its practical effect on agricultural interests. By encouraging and protecting domestic manufactures, the market is brought home, and the expense of transportation is saved. Farther: All who work at manufactures and trades established by a protective policy, are withdrawn from agricultural pursuits, and give to the residue employed in agriculture better chances for a ready market and high prices. The multiplication of useful crafts and vocations contributes to the profit of each, as well as to national wealth. A home market is more steady and more secure. The money paid for products of domestic manufacture, instead of going abroad, and thus impoverishing the nation, stays at home and enriches it. All know how the country prospered under the tariff of 1842.

§ 5. *The United States a World.*

This country has come to be a world in itself, and if all the rest of the world were sunk to-day, never to be found, we might feel the want of tea and coffee, and a few foreign luxuries, which can not be produced here; but the skill, science, art, industry, labor, enterprise, civilization, resources, and capabilities, still left behind, would amply supply the loss, and it would scarcely be felt. It would be far better than a system of free trade, as the world now is, holding us for ever in bondage. Let this country be put on its own resources and capabilities, and it would rise and march, with giant strides, to its own proper and legitimate destiny of unexampled wealth, greatness, and power. It requires nothing to accomplish this, but an adequate system of protection.

§ 6. *The Way for American Labor to sustain itself, and beat the World.*

Mr. Walker proposes that it should fall back on agriculture. It has been seen that his project will not do; and that it is a retrograde movement toward barbarism. The American aborigines practised on his theory, if hunting and fishing be added. The squaws raised the corn, and that was enough.

But there is a way for American labor to beat the world, and only one. It is based on the principle of General Jackson's letter to Dr. Coleman: Whenever too many people are engaged in agriculture, for the wants of the country, take them off, and put them to manufacturing and other arts; or, since they can not be forced, let them take themselves off, as they will do, if they know what is best, which they will naturally discover. It is of no use for them to raise corn for Europe and other parts, where labor is lower than they are willing to work for. They must soon get sick of that. Immutable laws have decided against it. But there is not a single manufacturing or mechanic art, if adequately protected, in which American skill can not equal that of Europeans, in a course of time. And if Americans can equal them in skill, they can beat them in all things else, and gradually acquire the market of the world; for European, and all foreign nations, labor under disadvantages, inherent in their institutions, from which the people of the United States are exempt. Even under the slender and inadequate protection extended to American arts heretofore, Americans, in some things, have entered into competition over the wide world, with the boasting mistress of the arts, that boasts of being mistress of the seas, and were rapidly gaining upon her under the tariff of 1842. That is conclusive evidence of what can be done. In this way, and in no other, can the prices of American labor be sustained. That devoted to agriculture would be kept up, because the policy supposes that it would, as near as convenient, have in view only the supply of the home market, which is always best, most uniform, and most secure. The prices of manufacturing and mechanic labor would be kept up, first, because experience proves it; next, because it could be afforded; and thirdly, because labor would occupy a position to demand it. And lastly, the prices of manufactured articles would be kept down, and reduced still lower, first, because experience proves that, too, as shown in these pages, however it may be a "mystery" to Mr. Walker; and next, because they *must* be reduced, in order to compete with the manufactured products of Europe. Nature, sound policy, and Providence, seem to have decided, that agriculture and manufactures, in the United States —anywhere indeed—should support each other, and that they together should keep commerce in motion, to distribute their products over the face of the earth; for, after all, the products of manufacture are but the products of agriculture in disguise, as before seen, and this is the only way in which the prices of American agricultural labor can be sustained at home and abroad. We are indebted to a British free trader for the lucid development of this stupendous practical truth. Let American agriculture find a market in American manufactures, and it has the market of the world at its feet, which otherwise it could never have —nor of the smallest part of it—at remunerating prices.

§ 7. *The Cause of the past Commercial Troubles of the Country.*

It is remarkable, that all the commercial troubles of the United States have occurred under a system of low, anti-protective duties, as has been several times proved, in the progress of this work; that the country has never prospered, except under a protective system; and that it has uniformly been most prosperous under the highest protective duties. These are historical FACTS. These fluctuations, from prosperity to adversity, and from adversity to prosperity, sometimes greater and sometimes less, in the history of the country, have been fully explained on the principles of the opposing systems of a protective and anti-protective policy, as having been graduated precisely as the one or the other of these has prevailed, the facts always harmonizing with the theory, that protection is favorable to prosperity, and the want of it unfavorable.

It follows, therefore, that nothing was necessary from the beginning of our history, as a nation, to have secured uninterrupted commercial prosperity, and an uninterrupted sound currency, but a uniform and adequate protective system. The state of the currency, as has been seen, always agrees with the presence or absence of protection, and the reasons have been explained. What, then, would have been the state of the country at this moment, comparatively, in wealth, greatness, and power, if it had not been so repeatedly broken down for want of protection? The answer will be found in the history of any two men, engaged in business, one of whom never failed, and the other of whom has failed many times. Look at the fortunes accumulated by Stephen Gerard, of Philadelphia, by John Jacob Astor, of New York, and by many other men of the same class, who never failed. If any of them had broken down a plural number of times, as the United States has, by an impolitic change in their habits, by an experiment, as enterprising men they might still have mended their fortunes by correcting their habits, after each disaster; but they would never have attained to great wealth. Thus might the United States have become, even by this time, the richest, greatest, most powerful nation on earth, if it had established at the beginning, and maintained throughout, an adequate and uniform protective system. That it would, at least, have become greatly rich, and greatly powerful, compared with its present condition, is as certain as that John Jacob Astor is a rich man. How can a man, or a nation, always engaged in large and prosperous business, and never coming to bankruptcy, but ever going farther from it, fail to be rich? How can a man, or a nation, whose annual income is greater than the expenditures, fail to accumulate? But let a man, or a nation, frequently fall into bankruptcy, by improvident habits, and that man and that nation will be always weak, always in trouble; or, if relieved by a new and more prudent start, by a like improvidence will break down again. Such, and for this reason, has been the ever-changing commercial history of the United States.

"The first duty of all good government," says the Southern Planter, "is to look to its labor—insure it not only full occupation, but the greatest productiveness. Political economy abhors idleness worse, if possible, than nature does a vacuum. It is worse than a vacuum, because gravity rushes forth to fill the vacuum; but idleness is a grave, where lies dead and buried the creative genius of man—the means given to him by the God of nature to improve his condition. . . . It would appear to one dropped from another world, unacquainted with all our interests and resources, that our whole Congress or national legislature were taken or subsidized by Europe to favor all their productions or operations exclusively —even to the total disregarding of those of this country. It would seem to such that Great Britain sat enthroned in all our legislative halls, and dictated all their enactments regulating industry and a tariff; and if told otherwise, could not be made to believe that some laws and most important regulations were not the results of bribes on the body politic by the superior wealth and foresight of older and wiser nations. Every idle finger will be pointed some day against those short-sighted and unpatriotic legislators, who left it in sloth, and to vice, and mischief, instead of stimulating it to proper action and usefulness. . . . This country, like a young giant, knows not its own strength, or its resources, because it has never exerted the one, or examined the other. Nothing is wanted to bring fo h all this, but a permanent policy, a certainty of protection, a security of the home market. All would then come forth and show themselves—capital, labor, raw materials, a market, wealth, comfort, elegance, taste, and independence. As soon as confidence was established, they would flash forth, as the gas-lights when touched by a match. No country is underlaid so universally with valuable minerals; and they lie in its extended fletz, or secondary formation, in horizontal strata, that can be followed into the thousands of hills and ridges, and, lying above the valleys, can be poured forth, without shafts or drainings, to the fertile plains, water-powers, and navigations, that are there found. Had this young giant, with its free limbs, hold of these mines of wealth, in the real skilful way, he could glut and monopolize all markets, both in the raw and wrought state. These hidden treasures need a protecting tariff to uncover them—its inducement to make them available, and wiser statesmen than we yet have, to put all in train, and on the certainty of the reality. . . . When the fulcrum is furnished by nature's God to this young Archimedes [the United States], it still fails to move the commercial world. Our commerce, if we demanded it, might double with England around the great capes of South America and Africa, and sweep the bays of Bengal and Bombay; might scour with her the West Indies; run with her through all her various colonies, and in every port, place, colony, and in the mother-country, be a part of herself as to the facilities secured by treaty. No nation could gainsay us, for we would be in possession of all seas. No nation could war upon us, for we would be full of resources and wealth. No nation could countervail us, for we would control all the productions necessary to her existence. We would stand on high and enviable ground, placed there by our own wisdom, that made use of natural advantages and resources too valuable to nations to be placed on any doubtful footing. This young Hercules, that strangled not the serpent in its early grasp, will fall, like Laocoon, in the foldings of its wrath."

248

THE END.

AMERICA FOR FREE WORKING MEN !

𝔐𝔢𝔠𝔥𝔞𝔫𝔦𝔠𝔰, 𝔉𝔞𝔯𝔪𝔢𝔯𝔰 𝔞𝔫𝔡 𝔏𝔞𝔟𝔬𝔯𝔢𝔯𝔰

READ !

HOW SLAVERY INJURES THE FREE WORKING MAN.

THE SLAVE-LABOR SYSTEM

THE

FREE WORKING-MAN'S WORST ENEMY.

By CHARLES NORDHOFF.

NEW YORK:

HARPER & BROTHERS, PUBLISHERS, FRANKLIN SQUARE.

1865.

PARTS OF THIS PAMPHLET HAVE APPEARED IN THE EDITORIAL COLUMNS OF THE NEW YORK "EVENING POST."

CONTENTS.

What Democratic Leaders think of Slavery.

"Speaking for myself, slavery is to me the most repugnant of all human institutions. No man alive should hold me in slavery; and if it is my business no man, with my consent, shall hold another. Thus I voted in 1851, in Ohio, with my party, which made the new constitution of my own State. I have never defended slavery; nor has my party."

Speech of Hon. S. S. Cox, of Ohio, in the House of Representatives, Jan. 12, 1865.

Mr. Brooks, of New York, in defending slavery, "did not pretend to speak for the democratic party. Indeed, he does not profess to speak for it, but rather as an old line Whig, having now his views independent of all machines of party. During the last session he held that slavery was dead. Gentlemen should not object to his eulogizing the deceased, but by so doing he does not intend, *nor does he if he intends*, commit any democrat to his moral convictions."

Speech of Hon. S. S. Cox, of Ohio, in the House of Representatives, Jan. 12, 1865.

" The democratic party of the free states are neither the advocates nor the apologists for slavery. Democracy and slavery are natural enemies. Impressed with the value of free labor, there is not a democrat in the North who would not resist the establishment of slavery in a free state."

Speech of Hon. William S. Holman, of Indiana, in the House of Representatives, Jan. 13, 1865.

" I have ever believed slavery wrong. The North have always believed it. Hardly one can at present be found who will claim that slavery is now, or has ever been, other than an evil. * * * The South, by rebellion, has absolved the democratic party at the North from all obligation to stand up longer for the defence of its 'corner-stone.' They are now using the very system which this amendment proposes to abolish, for the overthrow of our government, founded on the broad principles of right, justice, and humanity."

* * * * * * *

" I cannot but conclude, from the best light I can obtain, that the *operation of this measure will be most beneficial to the non-slaveholding white population of the Southern States.*. When these poorer laboring classes shall no longer have to contend with and struggle against and be degraded by slave labor, then, and not until then, will they come into the enjoyment of blessings such as are now fully enjoyed by the honest, toiling workingmen of the North.

" When labor shall be free at the South, then will it command and have the respect which is its just due. Then will millions of the white men of the North participate and share in the blessings thus secured. The masses of our native and foreign-born laborers, now toiling in the severer climate of the North, will be invited to enter upon these newly-opened fields, for their industry and occupation. The now hidden resources of the States South will be developed by the brain and muscle of the northern laborer.

" The existence in our country of antagonistic systems of labor has brought upon the nation the terrible calamity of a wasting civil war, with all its desolations. It has cost the country the lives of hundreds of thousands of its best and bravest sons, and has wasted her material resources.

" The day has come when this conflict of labor is to end, and the question is forced upon us by the South. They alone are responsible for it."

Speech of Hon. M. F. Odell, of New York, in the House of Representatives, Jan. 9th, 1865.

" I am opposed to the re-admission into the Union, with the rights of slave property of any State which our triumphant armies have subjected."

Speech of Hon. Elijah Ward, of New York, in the House of Representatives, Jan. 9th, 1865.

" I believe, and have ever believed since I was capable of thought, that it is a great affliction to any country where it prevails ; and, so believing, I can never vote for any measure calculated to enlarge its area, or to render more permanent its duration. In some latitudes, and for some agricultural staples, slave labor may be, to the master, the most valuable species of labor, though this I greatly doubt. In others, and particularly in my own State, I am convinced that it is the very dearest species of labor; and in all, as far as national wealth and power and happiness are concerned, I am persuaded it admits of no comparison with the labor of freemen; and, above all, disguise it as we may, if the laws of population shall not be changed by Providence, or man's nature shall not be changed, it is an institution, sooner or later, pregnant with fearful peril.

*　　　*　　　*　　　*　　　*　　　*　　　*

" I shall not stop to inquire, as I before intimated, whether the institution has produced the present war or not. However that may be, one thing, in my judgment, is perfectly clear, now that the war is upon us : *that a prosperous and permanent peace cannot be secured if the institution is permitted to survive.*

*　　　*　　　*　　　*　　　*　　　*　　　*

" As we at present are, I cease to hope that the government can be restored and preserved so as to accomplish the great ends for which it was established, unless slavery be extinguished.

*　　　*　　　*　　　*　　　*　　　*　　　*

" If suffered to continue, it will ever prove a fruitful topic of excitement and danger to our continuing peace and union. Terminate it, and the imagination of man, I think, is unable to conceive of any other subject which can give rise to fratricidal strife.

*　　　*　　　*　　　*　　　*　　　*　　　*

" I think the honor and good name as well as the interest and safety of the country require, the abolition of slavery throughout our limits."

Speech of Hon. Reverdy Johnson, of Maryland, in the United States Senate, April 5th, 1864.

" The question of slavery is rapidly diminishing in importance ; whether for good or evil, it is passing away."

Speech of Hon. D. W. Voorhees, of Indiana, in the House of Representatives, Jan. 9th, 1865.

Mr. Yeaman, of Kentucky, justified " anti-slavery measures " by quoting a letter signed by John J. Crittenden, William T. Barry, R. C. Anderson, J. Cabell Breckinridge, G. Robertson, John Rowen and B. W. Patton, all of Kentucky, urging the nomination of Henry Clay to the Presidency, and saying of Clay :

" We apprehend that no mistake could be greater than that

which would impute to him the wish to extend the acknowledged evils of slavery; for we are persuaded that no one entertains a stronger sense of its mischiefs than he does, or a more
ardent desire, by all prudent and constitutional means, to extir-
pate it from our land."

Mr. Yeaman added: " Shall a man be told that it is wrong
or disgraceful to hold opinions that have been sanctioned by the
minds and hearts of such men."
*Speech of Hon. George H. Yeaman, of Kentucky, in the
House of Representatives, Jan. 9th, 1865.*

"Slavery is the chief lever by which the rebel leaders have
wielded the Southern mind; and for that reason it has lost
nearly all the sympathy and support it once maintained."
*Speech of Hon. Austin A. King, of Missouri, in the House
of Representatives, Jan. 13th, 1865.*

" At the last session I voted against the proposed amendment,
but when the question is again taken, I intend to record my
name in the affirmative."
*   *   *   *   *   *
" We never can have peace until we in some way dispose of
the institution."
*Speech of Hon. James S. Rollins, of Missouri, in the House
of Representatives, Jan. 14th, 1865.*

"The demoratic party never advocated slavery as a moral institution.   That is a question which will not admit of discussion."
*New York Leader, (organ of Tammany Hall,) Jan. 7th,
1865.*

"The triumphs of our army and navy have put the rebels in
such straits that they no longer refuse to listen to propositions
of peace; and the plan of getting rid of slavery legally by a
constitutional amendment which shall recognise and respect the
rights of States, is a democratic measure, suggested by democrats, and it ought to be supported by democrats."
*New York Leader, (organ of Tammany Hall,) Jan. 14th,
1865.*

How Slavery Injures Free Workingmen.

The slave-labor system gives to the capitalist many unjust advantages over the poor free workman; it gives to a dozen slave-owners, with a thousand slaves, as many votes in the Legislature, and as great a political power in the State as is possessed by five hundred free workingmen; it discourages schools, prevents the formation of villages and towns; and gives to slave mechanics, slave shoemakers, slave blacksmiths, slave carpenters, slave wheelwrights, the labor, and to their wealthy masters the profits, which of right belong to the free workingman. To quote the words of the governor of a slave state, Governor Cannon, of Delaware, "Slave labor is uncompensated, white labor is compensated; when the two are brought into competition, white labor is crowded out. If capital owns its labor, the avenues to honest livelihood are forever closed to the white."

When a slave commits murder in Virginia, or any of the other Slave States, he is hanged, and his owner is paid for him the price he could have sold him for before the crime was committed. He is paid for the slave out of the treasury of the State; that is to say, *the tax-payers pay the slaveholder for his slave.*

When a farmer's bull does mischief and is killed, does the State pay the farmer? When a farmer's horse becomes unmanageable and is killed, does the State pay for him? Not at all. It is only the slave, the peculiar property of the rich, for whom the tax-payers are taxed. The poor man's horse or cow may be killed without payment to the owner.

FREE WORKINGMEN, AS SLAVE-GUARDS.

In the Slave States, whether in the city or in the country, a patrol of the white men is kept up at night—for what? To secure the persons and property of free workingmen? Not at all; but *to look after the slaves of the rich:* to prevent the slaves from running away; to keep them from visiting strange plantations; to catch them and bring them back, if they stray into the woods. "An ordinance organizing and establishing patrols for the police of slaves in the Parish Court of St. Landry, in Louisiana," which lies before us, describes minutely the organization of such patrols. "Every free white male person, between the ages of 16 and 60," is bound to do patrol duty. The parish (county) is to pay for "all books, blanks, papers, laws, &c., required for the organization of the patrols." Captains of patrols are to see that the enrollment for this duty includes every man; and anyone who neglects or refuses to serve, "at any hour of the day or night" which may be appointed, shall be fined or imprisoned. Six pages of the pamphlet are then taken up with defining the powers and duties of the patrols towards the slaves. They have no other duty to perform, as the title, indeed, asserts. They are "patrols for the police of the slaves." They are not to look out for horse-thieves, or to hunt for stolen cattle; it is made no part of their duty to guard the lives and property of the white workingmen of the county. "Every free white male, between 16 to 60," in the county is required to mount guard over the peculiar property of the few wealthy planters.

Now the parish of St. Landry had, in 1860, according to the census, 10,703 whites, and 11,436 slaves. According to the last census there were 3,953,587 slaves, and somewhat less than 400,000 slaveholders in the country—an average of ten slaves to each owner. At that rate the slaves in the parish of St. Landry would be owned by eleven hundred and forty-three of the 10,703 whites (for children and women own slaves as well as men); and *the whole free population of the county was taxed, in time, labor, and money, to care for the property of a little more than a tenth, and those the wealthiest part.*

Do not suppose that the white workingmen of the Slave States have not felt the oppression of this burden. Where they have been permitted, they have complained. Thus, in an address of Mr. Pierpoint, of Virginia, delivered in 1860, he remarked :

"The clerk or mechanic needs no protection of the law ; he is one of the sovereign *body guard to prote t and keep in subordination the master's slaves.* Yet his income—the labor of his weary hand and aching head, is *taxed two per cent.* to buy arms and erect armories in which to manufacture the munitions of war, *with which to equip himself, to defend the master in his right to his slaves.*"

An address to the working people of Virginia, in 1860, called attention to the fact that " if a bull or a steer of one of our farmers becomes vicious, so as to be a public nuisance, he is ordered by the law to be killed, and his loss falls upon his owner, and upon him alone ; but if it happens that a slave of one of the Eastern Virginia capitalists becomes vicious and commits crime, he is hanged or transported, and *it is provided by law that his owner shall be paid his assessed value out of the State Treasury.*"

The appropriation, by the Virginia Legislature, in 1856, for patrols, and as pay to slave owners for vicious slaves hanged or transported, amounted to over forty thousand dollars ! At the same time, every laboring man in the State, with an income above $250 per annum, had to pay a heavy income tax, while the slaves of the rich were almost totally exempted from taxation.

THE FREE LABORER AND THE SLAVE.

The system of bond-labor is *antagonistic to that of free labor*, and breeds in the masters a contempt for the workingman, as well as for his vocation. This is perfectly natural, and indeed unavoidable. *The slave-owner is a competitor in the slave-market against the free workingman.* He lives upon the labor of his slaves, and he regards with dislike the free laborers who come into the market to bid against him and the labor he controls.

This fact is notorious in the South. It has long attracted the attention of free white workingmen there, but they have been too weak to resist the powerful slave-holders. In 1860, Robert C. Tharin, of Alabama, once a law-partner of the notorious William L. Yancey, endeavored to set up a newspaper called the *Non-Slaveholder*, to urge the passage of a law forbidd.ng the employment of slaves except in agricultural labor and as servants. He thus sought to protect the free mechanics, and secure them employment. *For this Mr. Tharin was summarily driven from the State.*

Mr. Tharin, exposing the sopistries of William L. Yancey, writes:

"He had seen the rich man's negro 'come in contact' with the poor white blacksmith, the poor white bricklayer, carpenter, wheelright, and agriculturist. *He had seen the preference invariably given to the rich man's negro* in all such pursuits and trades; like me, *he* had heard the *complaints* of the poor white mechanic of the South against this very negro equality the rich planters were rapidly bringing about. These things he had heard and seen in Charleston, New Orleans, Mobile, Montgomery, and Wetumpka

"Have not the planters *for years condemned every mechanic in the South to negro equality?*" exclaims Mr. Tharin. "I never *envied* the planters of Wetumpka, or, indeed, of any part of the South. My *dislike* to them arose from their contemptible meanness, their utter disregard of decency, their supercilious arrogance, and their daily usurpations of powers and privileges at variance with my rights, and the rights of my class."

FREE WORKINGMEN MUST GIVE WAY TO SLAVES.

In 1853 the free mechanics of Concord, Cabarras county, North Carolina, held a meeting, at which they complained that the "*wealthy owners of slave mechanics were in the habit of under-bidding them in contracts.*" The free mechanic who led in this movement was driven from the town. A Long Island carpenter removed to a southern town; he was asked for an estimate for certain work in his trade. The person who proposed to have it done demurred at the price, and remarked that *he could do better to* BUY *a carpenter, let him do the work* and sell him again when it was done. The free carpenter, being a man of sense, packed up his tools and returned to New York, where a rich man cannot *buy* a carpenter and sell him again.

Olmsted relates, in his "Texas Journey," that at Austin, the capital of the state, the German mechanics complained that when the labor for building the state capital was given out, many of them came with offers, but *were underbid by the owners of slave-mechanics.* But when the free mechanics had left town, in search of employment elsewhere, the slave owners threw up their contracts, and, having no longer any opposition, obtained new contracts at advanced prices.

In the iron mines and furnaces near the Cumberland river, in Tennessee, before the war, several thousand men found employment—but almost without an exception they were slaves. One company had a capital of $700,000—and owned seven hundred slaves. *Of course an equal number of free workmen were robbed of employment,* and had either to starve, or emigrate to the Free States, as so many thousands have done.

THE "FAT" FOR THE SLAVE, AND THE "LEAN" FOR THE FREE WORKINGMAN.

Printers call that work which is most quickly and easily done, and which is the best paid, "fat;" that which is hard to do and poorly paid, they call "lean." Now, in all mechanical and other labor performed in the Slave States, the slave constantly gets the best, the easiest—the *fat;* the free mechanic or laborer, if he is employed at all, gets only the leavings of the slave, the *lean.* This comes about, because the slave-owner is a wealthy and influential man, who is able to select the lightest tasks for his slave; by this the slave-owner of course makes the greatest profit, and incurs the least expense. But the free white workingman must stand aside, or take that task which the slave-owner will not have.

In Virginia, a wealthy slave-owner told Olmsted that he used Hussey's reaper rather than McCormick's, because " it was more readily repaired by the *slave-blacksmith* on the farm." Another planter in Virginia employed a gang of Irishmen in draining some land. But mark the reasons he gave for this use of free labor. " It's dangerous work" (unwholesome), said he; "and *a negro's life is too valuable to be risked at it.* If a negro dies, it is a considerable loss, you know." This slaveholder did not care how many Irishmen died in his malarious ditches. So, too, on the southwestern steamboats, *slaves* are employed to do the *lightest* and *least dangerous labor ;* but *Irish and German free workingmen are employed to perform the exhausting and dan-*

gerous work. Thus, on the Alabama river, Olmsted observed that slaves were sent·upon the bank to roll down cotton bales, but Irishmen were kept below to drag them away. The mate of the boat said, by way of explanation, " The niggers are worth too much to be risked here; *if the Paddies are knocked overboard, or get their backs broke, nobody loses anything.*"

Alfred E. Matthews, of Starke county, Ohio, in his " Journal of his Flight" from Mississippi, in 1861, remarks: "*I have seen free white mechanics obliged to stand aside while their families were suffering for the necessaries of life, when slave mechanics, owned by rich and influential men, could get plenty of work;* and I have heard these same white mechanics breathe the most bitter curses against the institution of slavery and the slave aristocracy." In his journal at Columbus, Mississippi, he writes : " Business is very dull. Many of the free white mechanics have nothing to do, and there is a great deal of suffering amongst them. *Most of what little work is to be done is given to the slave mechanics.* An intelligent carpenter, an acquaintance of one of the persons in the office where I was engaged, came up one day and told his friend that his family were suffering for provisions; he had no money, and could not get work at anything. He assured me this was the case with others of his acquaintance." This was in a town of three thousand five hundred inhabitants.

SLAVES ARE TRAINED TO MECHANICAL PURSUITS.

On a rice plantation in South Carolina the planter showed Mr. Olmsted " shops and sheds at which blacksmiths, carpenters, and other mechanics—all slaves—were at work." Of course, *this planter employed no free mechanics.* Indeed, the writer of this pamphlet was told by a wealthy Alabamian in 1860, that *the planters* in his region were *determined to discontinue altogether the employment of free mechanics.* " On my own place," said this person, " I have now slave carpenters, slave blacksmiths, and slave wheelrights, and thus *I am independent of free mechanics.*"

These instances, culled from southern life, show the bearing of the slave system upon the free working population. The planters do not need the assistance of the free laboring class ; they despise it, and discourage it. What is the result ? Let "mudsill" Hammond, Governor of South Carolina, bear witness. In an address before the South Carolina Institute, some years ago, he said :

"According to the best calculations which, in the absence of statistic facts, can be made, it is believed that of the three hundred thousand white inhabitants of South Carolina there are not less than fifty thousand whose industry, such as it is, is not in the present condition of things, and does not promise hereafter, such a support as every white person in this country is and feels himself entitled to."

In another part of his address he said : "Eighteen or at most nineteen dollars will cover the whole necessary annual cost of a full supply of wholesome and palatable food, purchased in the market," for one person in South Carolina. It would seem, therefore, that so *completely had the slave system robbed the free workingman of the opportunity to make an honest livelihood, that one-sixth of the free white population of South Carolina could not earn even the paltry sum of eighteen dollars per annum !* So completely have the slaveholders monopolized the labor market for their slaves !

The bitter hatred of the "free white" in the South for the negro has been often spoken of. Does any one wonder at it, when he considers that these free men feel the wrongs they suffer, but are too ignorant to trace them to their sources? They hate the slaves, but if they were somewhat more intelligent they would hate the slaveholders, who are the authors of all their woes. It is because Mr. Lincoln, himself a southern man, and a son of one of the oppressed and expatriated free workingmen of the South, understands this, that he will not suffer the re-establishment of the iniquitous class of monopolists of labor, whose hatred for free workingmen has dragged the country into a civil war. He aims, not so much to free the slave, as *to free the workingmen.* He sees, as a stateman, that a system which degrades and discourages free labor, and whose supporters hate and refuse to employ free workingmen, is ruinous to the prosperity of the country, and is necessarily the parent of constant dissensions, the fruitful source of hatreds, jealousies and heart-burnings. He knows as a stateman, that the security of free government rests upon the virtue, intelligence and prosperity of the working class :

2

and that if we desire the perpetuity of our Union and liberties, we must sweep out of the way a system whose constant and necessary tendency is to impoverish and debase the free workingman.

WHY FREE WORKINGMEN HATE THE SLAVES.

They hate the slaves because slavery oppresses them. Turn where he will, the southern *free mechanic and laborer finds the negro slave preferred before him.* The planter has his slave blacksmith, his slave carpenter, his slave wheelwright, his slave engineer, if he needs one. It is now as it was in Marion's day, who said : " The people of Carolina form two classes—the rich and the poor. The poor are generally very poor, because, *not being necessary to the rich, who have slaves to do all their work,* they get no employment from them."

The slaveholders have the political power ; they look only to their own interests ; and even where they have established manufactures, they have given work by preference to slaves over free men and women. " *We are beginning to manufacture with slaves,*" wrote Governor Hammond of South Carolina, in 1845, to Thomas Clarkson. A writer in the Augusta *Constitutionalist,* quoted approvingly by De Bow, in 1852, said, " for manufacturing in the hot and lower latitudes, slaves are peculiarly qualified, and *the time is approching when they will be sought as the operative most to be preferred and depended on.* I could name factories in South Carolina, Alabama and Georgia, where the success of *black* labor has been encouraging." At the Saluda Factory, near Columbia, South Carolina, so long ago as 1851, one hundred and twenty-eight operatives were employed—*all slaves.* "Slaves not sufficiently strong to work in the cotton fields can attend to the looms and spindles," wrote the superintendent of this mill ; and he showed how these slaves underworked the free whites :

" Average cost of a slave operative, per annum.......... $75
" Average cost of a white operative, at least............ 106

    " Difference $31

" Or over thirty per cent. saved in the labor alone by using only the weakly and deformed slaves."

Free labor is killed by such unnatural competition. A writer upon manufactures in the South, in 1852, compared the wages paid to operatives in Tennessee with those in Lowell; " In Lowell, labor is paid the fair compensation of eighty cents per day for men, and two dollars per week for women, while in Tennessee the average compensation for labor does not exceed fifty cents per day for men, and one dollar and twenty-five cents per week for women." Another writer said : " A female operative in the New England cotton factories receives from ten to twelve dollars per month; *this is more than a female slave generally hires for in the southwest.*" This was twelve years ago. But he goes on to explain how *the slaveholder*, monopolizing the labor of his slaves, has the power to control the labor market and *underbid the free workman under any circumstances.* " It matters nothing to him (the slaveholder) how low others can produce the article ; he can produce it lower still, so long as it is the best use he can make of his labor, and so long as that labor is worth keeping." That is to say, a free white mechanic is at the mercy of his neighbor, the capitalist, in a slave state, because, *if the capitalist does not like his price, he can* " *go and buy a carpenter and sell him again when the work is done.*" Thus, while it is true that in the long run and on the average free labor is always cheaper than slave labor, the capitalist who monopolizes the slave labor is able to *drive out or starve out the free laborer,* over whom he and his slaves have an unfair advantage. The slaveholders used to boast that there were no " strikes" in the South—here we see the reason. The writer we have quoted adds :

" It is a fact that slaves learn blacksmithing, carpentering, boot and shoemaking, and in fact all handicraft trades, with as much facility as white men ; and Mr. Deering of Georgia, has employed slaves in his cotton factory for many years with decided success."

FREE WORKINGMEN ARE " PESTS TO SOCIETY.

Olmstead, when he asked in the slave states why the white laboring men were not employed, was told that they were not hired " because you cannot *drive* them as you do a slave." *The aristocratic slave-owner refuses to employ a workman whom he cannot flog and curse.* On a rice plantation in South Carolina he found a *slave engineer*, for whose education in that profession his owner had paid five hundred dollars to a steam-engine builder. This slave machinist, an able man, *lived better than any laboring free white man in the district.* His master, who also owned slave blacksmiths, carpenters, and other mechanics, *did not employ a single freeman*, except an overseer. But an estate of the same size and value in a free state would have given employment to twenty-five or thirty white mechanics of different trades, not to speak of a large number of free laborers.

By the census of 1850 it appears that the average wages of the female operatives in the Georgia cotton factories were $7 39 per per month; in Massachusetts it was $14 57 per month. New England factory girls were induced by the special offer of high wa es to go to Georgia to work in newly-established cotton factories, but they found the position so unpleasant, owing to the general degradation of the laboring class, they were very soon forced to return. Nor shall we wonder at this when we read the following sentiment, which appeared in the Charleston *Standard*, in 1855:

" *A large portion of the mechanical force that migrate to the South are a curse instead of a blessing ;* they are generally a *worthless, unprincipled class*, enemies to our peculiar institution (slavery), and formidable barriers to the success of our native mechanics (slaves). Not so, however, with another class who migrate southward—we mean that class known as merchants; *they* are generally intelligent and trustworthy, and they seldom fail to discover their true interests. They become slaveholders and landed proprietors; and in ninety-nine cases out of a hundred they are better qualified to become constituents of our institution than a certain class of our native born, who from want of capacity are perfect drones in society, *continually carping about slave competition.* * * * The *mechanics*, the most of them, are *pests to society*, dangerous among the slave population, and ever ready to form combinations against the interests of the slaveholder."

Is it strange that the ignorant, neglected, despised free white workingman of the slave states hates the slave? He feels that the slave injures him in every possible way; the slave robs him of work; the slave deprives him of bread and clothing for his children; the slave gets the easiest tasks, the free laborer the hardest and most dangerous; the slave steps before him whenever he looks for a job, and has the preference everywhere, *because he is the tool of a capitalist whose influence and wealth enable him to grasp*—for his own benefit—whatever might be of advantage to the free mechanic or laborer.

The capitalist, in a slave state, is a man with a hundred black arms, all bare, all eagerly seeking work, all ready to work for less than a free man can support his family decently upon. The capitalist is a hundred-armed workman, with enough social influence to command work for all his hundred arms, *to the exclusion of the honest free mechanic and laborer*. The slave, in the hands of this capitalist, is the most dangerous enemy the free workman can have. Suppose a job of work for twenty mechanics is to be given out in a southern town—twenty free men offer themselves—but a slave-owner comes, with the prestige of great wealth, with his social influence and his political power, and he gets the preference for his twenty slaves, *the profits of whose labor go to make him richer, while his free neighbors grow poorer.* It is not strange that the southern free workingmen resent this monstrous wrong—but it is lamentable that they make the error of hating the tools with which the wrong is done, and not those who use these helpless tools, and the iniquitous system which permits it. It is as though a martyr should abhor only the thumb-screws which torture him, but regard kindly the executioner who applies them; it is as though a western traveller should complain of the scalping knife, but love the Indian savage who uses it.

It is the slave-holder who wrongs the free workingman. It is the slave system which oppresses him. Make the slave free and he is no longer your fatal competitor; take the slaves away from the capitalist, and he has no longer the power to rob you of work and bread. Free the negroes, and you redeem the free white working-class from the domination of the selfish capitalists, and make the blacks themselves harmless to you. It is only while they are slaves that the negroes injure the white working men.

HOW FREE WORKINGMEN ARE OVERTAXED IN SLAVE STATES.

We have shown how the slave-labor system robs the free workingman, the free mechanic and laborer, of employment and bread, and thus keeps him poor and helpless—or drives him into the free states. But the subjection of free labor in slave states does not stop there. Not only is the free workingman condemned by the monopolists of slave labor to idleness and poverty, but his children are held in ignorance; his political rights are cunningly abridged; the products of his labor are forced to bear an *unequal* burden of taxation; and he—the non-slaveholding workingman—is compelled by the laws to mount guard over the slaves of his wealthy neighbor, or else to pay for such a guard. Thus he is injured in every interest, for the benefit of the slaveholder.

In the free states of the Union a poor man's vote counts as much as his wealthy neighbor's, and the millionaire enjoys no special political privileges over the carpenter who builds his house, or the blacksmith who shoes his horse. We are accustomed to think this a good system, but how is it in the slave states? Take Virginia as an example. There, while in one branch of the Legislature men are represented, in the other *money* and slaves have also a large representation.

So great was this political power of wealth, that before the war *ten thousand white men—slaveholders—in Eastern Virginia* had as much power—as many votes—in the Senate, as forty thousand white men—non-slaveholders—of Western Virginia.

How did the slaveholders, the aristocrats of Eastern Virginia, use this power? *They exempted a great part of their peculiar property from taxation*, and laid the burden of taxes upon the free workingmen of the state. They enacted a law by which all slaves under twelve years of age were exempted from taxation altogether—*but they taxed the calves, the colts, the lambs, of the farmers.* They limited the tax upon slaves over twelve years to one dollar and twenty cents per head; but they taxed a trader with a capital of only six hundred dollars, sixty dollars for his first year's license, and a heavy duty on his sales afterwards. The slave property of Virginia, before the war, paid about

$300,000 per annum taxes—but *if it had been taxed as other property was, according to value, it would have contributed one million three hundred thousand dollars per annum!* The odd million was raised by extra taxes on the earnings of the free laborers.

Not only this—the *products* of slave labor were also exempted from taxation. Tobacco, corn, wheat and oats were not taxed; but the product of free labor, consisting of cattle, hogs, sheep, &c., was heavily taxed; as were *also the earnings of free laboring men,* who were obliged to pay an income tax. It was asserted by Mr. Peirpoint, in 1860, that "upwards of two hundred and thirty million dollars of the Virginia slaveholders' capital in slaves was *exempted from taxation.*"

But while the slave owner was so protected, see how it fared with the free laborer? Every free mechanic, artisan, or laborer of whatever kind, who was in the employment of any person, was obliged, by a special law, to pay an income tax of *one-half of one per cent. if his income did not exceed* $250 : of one per cent. if his income was under $500; of one and a half per cent. if it was under $1,000, and two per cent. if he earned over $1,000. Our workingmen think the United States income tax onerous; but that, at least, exempts the man who earns less than $600. *The Virginia slaveholders exempted only themselves!* They taxed the poor, but left the the rich to pay nothing.

ENORMOUS AND UNEQUAL TAXATION OF FREE WORKINGMEN IN
VIRGINIA.

See how this act worked. In Wheeling there were employed in 1859 about 1,500 free men in the iron mills; these earned an average of $400 per annum each. On this they had to pay one per cent.—four dollars—making $6,000 per annum; besides eighty cents poll tax, $1,200 more; total $7,200, drawn from 1,500 free laboring men. Now *this tax was equal to that levied on six thousand slaves.* That is to say, each free workman was taxed four times as heavily as a slave. But take note of this: the owner of the slave was not only very lightly taxed for his property in him; *he paid no income tax at all.* That is to say, the net income from the labor of six thousand slaves might be reckoned in those times at $900,000 per annum. On this the masters, the capitalists, who received this sum, paid not a cent of income-tax ! Or, take another example : a foreman in a factory earned $1,100 per annum ; he had to pay $22 80 income tax to the State. But a slave-owning capitalist paid no more than that as his tax on nineteen slaves; *he trained them to mechanical work*—hired them out in such manner that they threw nineteen free mechanics out of employment—and on the proceeds of the labor of these nineteen slaves, amounting to $5,700 per annum, *he was taxed not a single cent !*

"There are many poor men in this State," said Mr. Pierpoint in 1860, " getting 75, 80, 90, and 100 cents per day, with families to support, who all have to pay, in addition to the income tax, for everything they own on the face of the earth, forty cents on a hundred dollars, while the slaveholder only pays 10 cents on the hundred dollars' worth of slaves ! " " The income tax levied by the slaveholders upon the small incomes of free mechanics," Mr. Pierpoint said, " will eat out the very vitals of all the manufacturing energy of the State." Nor were the free mechanics the only sufferers. " The farmer in Western Virginia (not a slaveholder) who 12 years ago paid his tax with 15 dollars, now pays $60, with little increase in actual value." *Only the slaveholders were exempted !*

Thus was slave labor encouraged and free labor made penal in the South. Thus, to use Marion's words, the poor became poorer and the rich richer. Thus free mechanics were driven out of the slave states, taxed out, starved out, until, in 1859, Charleston, one of the chief seaports of the South, had not left so much as a single ship-carpenter. Thus was brought about the unhappy condition of the free workingmen, described by Mr. Tarver, in " DeBow's Industrial Resources of the South and Southwest."

" The acquisition of a respectable position in the scale of wealth appears so difficult that they decline the hopeless pursuit, and many of them settle down into passive idleness, and become the almost passive subjects of all its consequences. An evident deterioration is taking place in this part of the population ; the younger portion of it being less educated, less industrious, and in every point of view less respectable than their ancestors."

HOW SLAVES OUT-VOTE FREE WORKINGMEN.

These are the effects of the slave labor system upon the unfortunate free laborers who are subject to its influence. Bear in mind that it is not only in Virginia that the free mechanic and laborer is thus wronged. In Louisiana, in South Carolina, in most of the slave states, slave property is represented and favored in some special manner. In Louisiana the representation, under the old system, was apportioned according to the whole population—free and slave. Thereby it happened that the thousands of free laborers of New Orleans were placed at the mercy of a few enormously wealthy slave-owning capitalists in the sparsely settled river parishes; and *a thousand votes of free mechanics had not so much power in the Legislature as two hundred and fifty planters' votes, whose slaves filled up a legislative district.*

South Carolina has always been called the model slave state. Her system was and is the admiration of the slaveholding class. There the free laborer was entirely debarred from influence, totally unrepresented. He could vote—but not for one of his own class; *only a slave owner could serve in the Legislature; only a slave owner could be governor; and the Legislature, composed exclusively of slave owners,* appointed the judges, the magistrates, the senators, the electors for President.

Not only this—the Legislature set apart the state Congressional districts; and it managed this in such manner that the slaveholding interest was alone represented in Congress. The lower part of the State, where the slaves were most dense, sent four out of the seven representatives to Congress. In the legislative apportionment the free workingmen of the State were still more outraged. Five-sixths of the white population, residing in those counties where there were but few slaves, had only seventy-eight out of one hundred and twenty-two representatives in the Legislature—a little more than one-half. The Pendleton district, with over twenty-six thousand white inhabitants, but few slaves, sent but seven members; the parishes of St. Philip and St. Michael, with less than nineteen thousand whites, but a heavy slave population, sent eighteen.

Now take notice of the results of this system upon the free

3

workingmen.   Governor Seabrook, of South Carolina, said, in a message a few years ago :

"Education has been provided by the Legislature *but for one class of the citizens* of the State, which is *the wealthy class.* For the middle and poorer classes of society it has done nothing, since no organized system has been adopted for that purpose. * * * * * Ten years ago twenty thousand adults, besides chi... en, were unable to read or write, in South Carolina. Has our free school system dispelled any of this ignorance? Are there not reasonable fears to be entertained that the number has increased since that period ? "

In the Charleston *Standard*, in November, 1855, was advanced by eminent South Carolinians the atrocious doctrine that the State should educate only its capitalists and the officers and overseers who, under the order of the capitalists, should command and direct the laborers.   Chancellor Harper, one of the foremost men of the State, said, in a public address printed by De Bow, and received with general approval :

"Would you do a benefit to the horse, or the ox, by giving him a cultivated understanding or fine feelings ? So far as the *mere laborer* has the pride, the knowledge, and the aspiration of a free man, he is unfitted for his situation, and must doubly feel its infelicity."

And what was the effect of this system upon the free workingmen of the State?   Let Governor Hammond, one of its chief citizens, reply.   Fifty thousand, he said, a sixth of the white population of the State, *were unable to earn their living*.   He added : "Most of them now follow agricultural pursuits, *in feeble but injurious competition with slave labor.*"   And another writer, whose essay on cotton and cotton manufactures at the South is printed by De Bow, remarks that " a degree and extent of poverty and destitution exist in the Southern States among a certain class of people, almost unknown in the manufacturing districts of the North. * * * Boys and girls by thousands, destitute both of employment and the means of education, grow up to ignorance and poverty, and too many of them to vice and crime."

Such are some—but not all—the disabilities under which the

free workingman labors, in a State where the slave-labor system prevails. Deprived of employment, left without education, misrepresented in the legislative halls by men whose interests are opposed to his, and before whom he is powerless, the free laborer grows poorer as his wealthy neighbor grows richer; and looking at these things we cease to wonder at the persistent emigration from the eastern slave states, westward, of which Mr. Tarver said, speaking of South Carolina, " That necessity must be strong and urgent which induces *thirty per cent. of the population of a State, in the short space of ten years, to break all the social and individual ties which bind man to the place of his birth, and seek their fortunes in other lands.*"

FREE WORKINGMEN FLY FROM THE SLAVE STATES.

The slave states are the most sparsely populated of the Union; their soil is rich, their climate kindly, they abound in mineral wealth; everything there favors the workingman—yet the workingmen of the free states refuse to go there; and a *constant and large stream of emigration has set for years, from the slave states into the free states.* The free workingmen of the slave states have fled from the oppression and blight of the slave institution, to the part of the Union where all labor is free and paid.

If we take the census report of 1850, we find that the slave states had sent nearly six times as many of their population into free territory as the free states had sent into slave territory. We find that Kentucky had sent on to free soil sixty thousand more persons than all the free states had sent into slave soil. Little Maryland had sent more than half as many persons into free territory as all the slave states had sent into slave territory. Virginia had sent sixty thousand more persons into free territory than all the free states had sent upon the slave soil. Kentucky and Tennessee were but little behind the other states we have mentioned.

This shows the course of emigration. But it is even more clearly shown in some interesting tables contained in the last census report—that for 1860. In a table of "Internal Migration" we find that there were in the country, and returned by the census-takers, 399,700 persons born in Virginia, but *living in other states ;* 344,765 persons born in Tennessee, but living in other states; 272,606 persons born in North Carolina, but living in other states; 137,258 persons born in Maryland, but living in other states ; 32,493 persons born in Delaware, but living in other states ; 331,904 persons born in Kentucky, but living in other states.

Now it is true that not all these 1,518,726 persons who had migrated from only the border line of slave states were living in the free states, but by far the greater number were. The " course of internal migration" is exhibited in a table of the Census Report. There we find that emigrants from Virginia have removed " chiefly" to Ohio, Missouri, Kentucky, and Indiana; from Kentucky they have removed chiefly to Missouri, Indiana, Illinois and Ohio. From Maryland they have removed chiefly to Ohio, Pennsylvania, Virginia and the District of Columbia. From Delaware they have migrated chiefly to Pennsylvania, Maryland, Ohio and Indiana. From Tennessee they have removed chiefly to Missouri, Arkansas, Texas and Illinois.

But this table shows us a far more remarkable fact. From the southern tier of slave states the migration was chiefly into other slave states, in a western or northwestern direction *towards the free states.* From the border slave states the migration was *chiefly into the free states,* and into that slave state (Missouri) which promised first to become free. But from the free states, which sent forth also a large stream of emigrants, there was *no* emigration to slave states; *all*, with insignificant exceptions, removed to *other free states.* 399,700 Virginians had removed chiefly to Ohio, Missouri, Kentucky and Indiana ; but of 582,512 Pennsylvanians, just across the line, it is recorded that they removed " chiefly" to Ohio, Illinois, Indiana, and Iowa. 331,904 Kentuckians had removed " chiefly" to Missouri, Indiana, Illinois and Ohio ; but 593,043 persons born across the river, in free Ohio, had removed chiefly to Indiana, Illinois, Iowa and Missouri. These contrasts hold good of the whole table. From no free state has there been emigration to the slave states ; but from every border slave state there has been a very heavy migration to the free states.

Observe, that this course of migration is unusual and unnatural.

The tendency, in all the history of the world, has been the other way. Tribes and families have fled from the bleak climate and barren soil of the North to the milder climate and more generous soil of the South. A French writer, the Count de Segur, says: "The human race does not march in that direction; it turns its back to the North; the sun attracts its regards, its desires, and its steps. It is no easy matter to arrest this great current." In other countries all emigration has turned to the Southward, by an instinctive movement; but with us the horror of slavery, the aversion of the free laborer to come in contact and competition with slave labor, has sufficed to conquer even this strong instinctive tendency.

Bear in mind, too, that the South has lost, by this migration, the best class of her citizens. The indolent masters remained; the slaves remained; those free whites who were too poor and helpless and ignorant either to desire or to be able to remove, remained; but there has been a constant drain of the yeomanry of the border slave states—the forehanded farmers and industrious mechanics, the class whom a state can least afford to lose. These men and their families have helped to fill our northwestern territories and states; and have taken the places of the thousands who removed from the border free states to the northwest. They have faced unwonted winters and harder conditions of life—why? Because *these free workingmen felt slavery to be a curse, a bar to all their efforts.* They were not abolitionists—they brought into the free states with them their curious hatred of the negro, as though it was the slave and not the master who was their oppressor.

SLAVERY EXTERMINATES FREE MECHANICS.

Charles J. Faulkner, of Virginia, said, in 1832, in the legislature of that state: "*Slavery banishes free white labor; it exterminates the mechanic, the artisan, the manufacturer, it deprives them of bread.*" And C. C. Clay, of Alabama, not less eminent in the South than Mr. Faulkner, said a few years ago: " Our wealthier planters, with greater means and no more skill, are buying out their poorer neighbors, extending their plantations and adding to their force. The wealthy few, who are able to live on smaller profits, and to give their blasted fields some rest, are thus pushing off the many who are merely independent. Thus *the white population has decreased, and the slave increased,* almost *pari passu* in several counties of our state. In 1825 Madison county cast about three thousand votes; now she cannot cast more than two thousand three hundred. In travelling that country one will discover numerous *farm-houses, once the abode of industrious and intelligent freemen, now occupied by slaves,* or tenantless, deserted, and dilapidated. He will see the moss growing on the mouldering walls of once thrifty villages, and will find 'one only master grasps the whole domain,' that once furnished happy homes for a dozen white families."

Thus southern men, themselves slaveholders, bear witness to the causes which lead to the great and constant migration of the most valuable class of citizens from the slave to the free states. The agriculturist and the mechanic alike, the blacksmith, the carpenter, the farmer, all are "pushed off," to use the expressive phrase of Mr. Clay, to make way for the masters and their slaves.

SLAVERY SHUTS THE SOUTH AGAINST GERMANS AND IRISHMEN.

If a considerable part of the white workingmen of the slave states have migrated to the free states, it is equally true that of the thousands of German, Irish and other workingmen who have, with their families, sought our shores, the southern states have received but an insignificant fraction.

To the industry and thrift of this part of our population a large share of our prosperity and wealth is owing; without the help of their strong arms, the free states, though thriving and populous, and receiving increase from the South, must have advanced much more slowly than they have. This fact has been generally recognized amongst us. Indeed, in the western states special inducements have been held out to immigrants, so strongly have the people there felt the need of their labor and the advantage of their presence. Consider, then, what has been the loss of the South, which has utterly failed to attract this class, while at the same time it was drained to a considerable extent of its own free working class.

If we compare free states with slave states, we find that while

South Carolina had in 1860 but 9,986 foreign born citizens. Massachusetts had 260,114; Virginia had but 35,058 foreigners, but Pennsyslania, her neighbor, had 430,505; Georgia, the empire state of the South, had but 11,671, but New York had 998,640; Mississippi had only 8,558, but Illinois had 324,643, Tennessee had 21,226, and Kentucky 59,799; but Ohio had 328,254, and Indiana 118,184. Little Rhode Island, with an insignificant territory and a dense population of 133 to the square mile, had attracted 37,394 foreign emigrants; but North Carolina, with a milder and more varied climate, a fertile soil, ready access by sea, and the advantage of a profitable fishery and several other special pursuits, not to speak of an immensely greater territory, had been able to attract to her borders but 3,299 foreign emigrants.

Nor must we fail to notice that in those states where slavery languished or had but a slender hold, emigrants at once increased in numbers. Maryland had 77,536, nearly seven times as many as Georgia; Delaware had 9,165, nearly three times as many as North Carolina; and Missouri had 160,541, as many within fifteen thousand as all the slave states east of the Mississippi, except Maryland and Delaware. That is to say, Missouri, which was in the popular belief certain to become a free state before many years, was able to attract to her soil nearly as many emigrants as Kentucky, Tennessee, Mississippi, Alabama, Georgia, North and South Carolina and Virginia together! Still, slavery told against Missouri when compared with the free states. With a milder climate, immensely greater mineral resources and a nearer and cheaper access to great markets, Missouri had attracted but 13.59 per cent. of foreigners, while Iowa had 15.71 per cent., Minnesota 33.78 per cent., and Wisconsin 35.69 per cent.

The census report shows that of the foreign born population the free states have received over eighty-six and one-half per cent., and the slave states less than fourteen. It shows the States which have received the smallest percentage of this accretion to be North Carolina, Arkansas, Mississippi, Georgia, and South Carolina—all slave states. And it shows also the singular fact, that while eight foreign emigrants have settled in the free states to one in the slave states, the number of slaves—if we add the insignificant number of free colored—gives just one to every eight of our population.

FREE WORKINGMEN KEPT OUT OF THE FINEST PART OF THE UNION.

Is it no matter to workingmen that they are thus driven out and kept out of the largest, most fertile, and pleasantest part of the Union by the slave-labor system, which there robs them of work, and attacks their rights? In the mild climate of the border slave states, the seasons are longer, the productions more varied; trades which can be pursued in the North during only eight or nine months, may be carried on there all the year round; food is or ought to be cheaper; the workingman and his family need fewer and less costly clothes; in many ways the conditions of life are easier, for the mechanic and laborer as well as the farmer, than in the colder North. *But that great region the slavemasters closed against the free working men,* and preserved for themselves and their slaves.

The climate is not too hot in any of those states for white men and women to labor in the fields. Governor Hammond, of South Carolina, said: "The steady heat of our summers is not so prostrating as the short but sudden and frequent heats of northern summers." White men work on the levee in New Orleans in midsummer, and have the severest labor put upon them at that. He who writes this has rolled cotton and sugar upon the levee of New Orleans in the month of July, and screwed cotton in Mobile Bay in August. Dr. Cartwright, the great apostle of slavery, rightly remarked: "*Here in New Orleans the large part of the drudgery—work requiring exposure to the sun, as railroad making, street paving, dray driving, ditching, and building is performed by white people.*" This severe labor was put upon the free white workingmen; the slave-owners reserved the light tasks for their slaves.

In Alabama, by the census of 1850, sixty-seven thousand, in Mississippi, fifty-five thousand, in Texas forty-seven thousand *white men, non-slaveholders, labored in the fields,* and took no hurt. Cotton was cultivated in Texas, before the war, with perfect success, by white men; the Germans managed even to raise more pounds to the acre, pick it cleaner, and to get a higher price for it, than the neighboring planters. Olmsted mentions an American in Texas who would not employ slave labor, and who, with white men as his help, "produced more bales to the hand than any planter around him."

The mortality reports of the census show that the southern states are not peculiarly unhealthful. In Alabama, the deaths, per cent., were less than in Connecticut; in Georgia they are 1.23 per cent., in New York, 1.22 ; in South Carolina they are 1.44 per cent., in Massachusetts, 1.76, which is precisely the same as in Louisiana, notoriously, till General Butler cleaned New Orleans and drove out the yellow fever, the most sickly state in the South.

Nothing, therefore, has kept free workingmen out of these states—nearer to the great markets of the world, having more abundant mineral wealth, and in every way more favorably situated than the cold Northeast and the far away Northwest—except the fatal competition of the slaveowners. To avoid that, millions of workingmen, native and foreign born, have removed to the northwest, until at last the tide of emigration has even trenched upon the inhospitable desert, and has spread beyond the extreme limits of arable land, and far beyond the profitable reach of markets. The Northwestern farmer has burned his corn because he could not afford to send it to the distant seaboard—*was it no loss to him that slavery kept him out of the fertile fields of Virginia and North Carolina?*

Even had slavery remained in full vigor, the time had come when free labor, seeking new outlets and greater opportunities, would have pressed hardly upon it. If slavery is swept away, free workingmen will hereafter have opportunity in the South, and to all that great region a boundless future of wealth and prosperity opens up. The abandoned farms, the mouldering villages, the empty cottages, will once more be filled with the busy and cheerful hum of the labor of freemen.

Their cunning will repair the waste of unskillful slave labor; their ingenious toil will redeem the barren fields of Virginia and other southern states. The tide of emigration, sweeping in that direction, may repeat in the South the marvellous results which it has accomplished during the last twenty five years in the Northwest ; Virginia will be another Minnesota, North Carolina a new Iowa, and in Tennessee will be repeated the story of Ohio.

4

HOW TO LESSEN THE BURDEN OF TAXATION.

When a man falls into debt, and is anxious to free himse'f of it, what does he do? He works harder, and lives more frugally, He tries to make a dollar more per week, and to live on a dollar less. In that way he may hope to get clear of debt. Well, as with a man, so it is with a nation: we have incurred a great debt; and henceforth, we must, as a people, live more economically, and use, to better advantage, our property and our strength. We can no longer afford to exhaust our soil, by "artless" methods of culture; we can no longer afford to employ half a dozen men to do one man's work; we can no longer afford to use poor tools, to do with a hoe the work of a plough, to reap by hand instead of by steam, to work by main strength and stupidness, instead of intelligently.

It is not enough that one part of the country shall do its best—the resources of all parts must be fully developed. It is not fair to the working men of the free states, that they shall pay heavier taxes, in order that slaveholders may indulge their fancy for dull, plodding, unskilled slave labor. It is not fair that we of the North should bear a heavy burden, more than our proper share of the common debt, when, by the use of proper means, by throwing the Southern states open to free labor, and to skilled labor, its resources can be rapidly developed to the point where those states will be as populous, and as wealthy, as the free states.

If we can discover a way to make the whole country populous, and to make the whole nation prosperous, the weight of taxation will be much lightened; increased numbers and increased wealth will enable us to bear, without suffering, burdens under which we might sink if these elements of strength were lacking.

WE CANNOT AFFORD SLAVERY.

We cannot afford to omit measures which will add to our ability to pay taxes. There was a time when we might live after a slipshod fashion, but hereafter it is important to every man in the country, and especially to the workingmen and their families, that the natural resources of the whole country shall be wisely and effectively developed. It is easy to show that the Southern states have enormous and inexhaustible wealth of iron, coal, copper, and many other things; but if that mineral wealth is to remain, in future as in the past, in the bowels of the earth; if Virginia, with the richest coal and iron deposits, is hereafter, as heretofore, to buy both coal and iron in Pennsylvania; if Tennessee, abounding in minerals, is to continue to be cursed with a slave-labor system, which forbids the development of her greatest sources of wealth; if we do not use the only means in our power, or any one's power, to bring out that wealth, and thus add enormously to the general wealth of the country—which can only be done by extirpating slave-labor, and substituting free labor in its place—why then, we may as well reconcile ourselves—we free working men of the North—to paying perpetually much the heaviest share of the national taxation.

A shrewd foreign traveller once remarked that the slave-labor system was such a costly economical blunder, that no European nation could afford it; only a country having no debt, and scarcely any expenses, could indulge in it. The time has come when we, too, can no longer afford it. *If the working men of the free states wish to lift from their backs some portion of the heavy burden of taxation, they must insist that the southern states shall be thrown open to free labor*, in order that this vast region shall be enabled to yield an equal share of the national revenue. It cannot do this till it is equally wealthy; but, as we shall proceed to show, the slave labor system has made it poorer instead of richer, for many years.

How are we to equalize the burden? By making Virginia as populous and wealthy as Pennsylvania, Kentucky as Ohio, Tennessee and Georgia as New York, South Carolina as Massachusetts, Mississippi as Iowa. The Lynchburg *Virginian* wrote some years ago:

" The coal fields of Virginia are the most extensive in the world; and the coal is of the best and purest quality; her iron deposits are altogether inexhaustible, and in many instances so pure that it is malleable in its primitive state; and many of these deposits are in the vicinity of extensive coal fields. She has, too, very extensive deposits of copper, lead, and gypsum. Her rivers are numerous and bold, generally with fall enough for extensive water power."

VIRGINIA AND PENNSYLVANIA COMPARED.

But these coal and iron and copper and lead deposits of Virginia, greater than those of Pennsylvania, and lying in a finer climate, are almost untouched. And because they are so, the whole industry of the state has suffered. The census of 1850 gave the following values to agricultural lands in the adjoining States of Pennsylvania and Virginia:

	In Virginia.	In Penn'a.
Number of acres of improved land in farms	10,380,135	8,626,619
Number unimproved	15,792,176	6,294,728

Cash value of farms in Virginia, *eight* dollars; in Pennsylvania, *twenty-five* dollars per acre.

Does any one need to be told which state is able to pay and will pay the largest amount of revenue to the government? Is it not easy to see that, with the same policy in Virginia which has prevailed in Pennsylvania, that state would in a very few years be as populous, as wealthy, and as great a source of revenue, as her neighbor? And is it not to the interest of every free workingman, every tax-payer, that this should be brought about?

The Southern states, if we include Missouri and Kentucky, have an area of 851,508 square miles; the free states have an area of only 612,597 square miles. The South has a milder climate, shorter winters, a far more fertile soil, immensely greater mineral wealth, more abundant natural water communications with the sea, than the North. Yet in 1850, by the census, the total value of the real and personal property of the free states was $1,161,081,000 *greater* than that of the real and personal property of the South, *including three millions of slaves.* But in 1860, according to the census of that year, the total value of real and personal property in the free states was $2,657,165,268 *greater* than that of the South. The wealth of the free states, excluding the territories, was in 1860, in round numbers, nine thousand two hundred and eighty-seven millions; that of the slave states, including Missouri, six thousand six hundred and thirty millions, also including the slaves!

Now if, by wise measures, by encouraging the mechanic arts, fostering free schools, developing mineral resources, and, in short, treating the South as we treated the Northwest, we can make it increase as rapidly, after the war, in free population, and in wealth, as the Northwest has, we may expect this difference to disappear in a very few years; we may expect the South to become as prosperous and as wealthy, in a few years, as the North is. In that case *it will contribute a revenue to the government greater than the whole North does at this time. That is to say, we can double our revenue without increasing our taxation, or we can raise the same revenue with half the taxes.*

But to do that we must do away with the wasteful and ruinous system of slave-labor which has made sterile the lands of the South, driven out her mechanics and artisans, made poor her people, and decreased her wealth. We cannot afford to waste anything; but Olmsted wrote to a Texan friend as the fruit of " a large class of observations :"

"The natural elements of wealth in the soil of Texas will have been more exhausted in ten years, and with them the rewards offered by Providence to labor will have been more lessened than without slavery would have been the case in two hundred. After two hundred years' occupation of similar soils by a free laboring community, I have seen no such evidence of exhaustion as in Texas I have after ten years of slavery."

TESTIMONY OF SLAVEHOLDERS.

In 1859 Charleston had not a single ship-carpenter. In 1859 Governor Wise, of Virginia, said to his people:

"Commerce has long ago spread her sails, and sailed away from you. You have not, as yet, dug more coal than enough to warm yourselves at your own hearths; you have set no tilt-hammer of Vulcan to strike blows worthy of gods in your own iron foundries; you have not yet spun more that coarse cotton enough, in the way of manufacture, to clothe your own slaves. *You have no commerce, no mining, no manufactures.* You have relied alone on the single power of agriculture, and *such agriculture!* Your sedge-patches outshine the sun. Your inattention to your only source of wealth has seared the very bosom of mother earth. Instead of having to feed cattle on a thousand hills, you have had to chase the stump-tailed deer through the sedge-patches to procure a tough beefsteak. The present condition of things has existed too long in Virginia."

Thomas Marshall, another slaveholder, said:

"Slavery is ruinous to the whites; it retards improvement, *roots out an industrious population, banishes the yeomanry of the country; deprives the spinner, the weaver, the smith, the shoemaker, the carpenter, of employment and support.*"

In little more than ten years Wisconsin lands became worth on an average nine dollars and fifty-four cents per acre; but after two hundred and fifty years those of Virginia, with all her natural advantages, were worth but eight dollars and twenty-seven cents per acre. Virginia, free, might have had as rapid an increase as Massachusetts; she would have had in 1850, that is to say, a population of 7,751,324 whites, instead of 894,800. Consider what would have been her wealth, with such an enormous population. Consider what would have been her ability, with her minerals, her water-power, her grain fields and her seacoast, to contribute to the national revenue.

If we want to lighten the burden of taxation, we must give the South the same opportunity for growth and increase which has made the West and Northwest so populous and rich in the last twenty-five years. But to do that, we must encourage free labor there—for it is the free workingman who makes the land rich—and the free man will not and cannot toil in competition with the slave.

THE WASTEFULNESS OF SLAVE LABOR.

The slave-labor system exhausts the soil, wastes its products, and contirbutes less—a very great deal less—to the national wealth, than the more skilful and intelligent free labor. The slave workman cannot be trusted with machinery; he cannot be trusted with the best tools; he must have—so the slaveholders themselves have said—the coarsest, rudest tools; anything else he breaks. Now every workingman knows that with heavy, rough tools he cannot accomplish as much as another man can with light, well-made, handy tools. Every working man knows that it makes a world of difference what sort of a plough, what sort of an axe, what sort of a plane, what sort of a hammer he uses. He wants the best; he knows that it pays him to have the best; and he knows, too, that if he can make a machine saw, or plane, or mortice, or do anything else for him, that is so much gained—so much more money made in a given time. But the slave laborer cannot be trusted with any of these helps. Is it a wonder that with *a system which thus prevents the use of the best tools and machinery, the South is poor?*

It is a fact, proved by the census, that *labor in Massachusetts is four times as productive as in South Carolina.* The average value of the product *per head* of the cotton factories of Massachusetts was in 1855, $725—ten times greater than the average value of the products of labor in South Carolina. The State of Massachusetts, with the help of skilled and industrious free labor, sent annually into the commerce of the world, *values greater than that of the entire cotton crop of the South!* Such is the enormous difference between slave labor and free labor.

Mr. Guthrie, in his report on the finances, in 1854–5, prepared a table from the census report, showing the average value of products per head in the different States. A comparison of some of the Free States with some of the Slave States, will show how much more productive is free labor than slave labor. In Massachusetts, with a bleak climate and a sterile soil, the average product per head of the population is valued at $166 60; in South Carolina but $56 91; in New York, $111 94; in Georgia, the Empire State of the South, $61 45; in Pennsylvania, $99 30; in Virginia, $59 42; in Ohio, $75 82; in Arkansas, $52 04; and in North Carolina, $49 38.

SLAVERY LOWERS THE VALUE OF LAND.

But this is not all; slave labor not only produces far less, and thus adds less to the taxable wealth of the community; it at the same time wastes and ruins the substance of the country. It ruins the soil. The cotton planters were continually removing westward, with their slaves, to new lands; and Olmstead reports that in Texas even, recently settled as it is, he already found the two curses of the planter—worn out and abandoned plantations and " poor whites." In North Carolina, six bushels of wheat to the acre is counted a fair crop. Compare Virginia and Pennsylvania, and we find, by the census report, that the actual crops per acre of corn were, in *Virginia eighteen*, and in *Pennsylvania thirty-six* bushels; of tobacco, in Virginia—whose speciality is tobacco—630 pounds per acre, in Pennsylvania 730 pounds. Under the slave-labor system of the South, according to Mr. Gregg, an accredited writer on the southern side, South Carolina had, before the war, one hundred and twenty-five thousand *white* persons " who ought to work and who do not, or who are so employed as to be wholly unproductive to the State."

Does anyone imagine that it is not the slave system, but the climate, which is to blame for this enormous and ruinous waste of labor and of the natural resources of the South? In Virginia, wherever, before the war, free labor got the upper hand, and slavery was driven out, there productions were at once largely increased. The Charleston *Standard* remarked, in 1857, " The Virginia journalists have frequently borne witness to the fact, that in many districts where large estates have been divided and sold to small farmers, the land is turning off from three to six times as much produce as it did a few years ago." In Cahill, Mason, Brooke, and Tyler counties, Virginia, which had, before the war, a free laboring population, with slaves but one in fifteen to the freemen, but no advantages of towns in or near them, land was worth, in 1855, $7 75 per acre. In Southampton, Surrey, James Town, and New Kent counties, in the same state, where the slave population was as 1 to 2, the *land was worth but half as much*, $4 50 per acre. In Fairfax county the slave population was much reduced within the last twenty-five years; free laboring men took the places of the slave laborers; and the County Commissioners reported officially:

" In appearance, the county is so changed, in many parts, that a traveller, who passed over it ten years ago, would not now recognize it. Thousands and thousands of acres had been cultivated in Tobacco, by the former proprietors, would not pay the cost, and were abandoned as worthless, and became covered with a wilderness of pines. These lands have been purchased by *northern emigrants ;* the large tracts divided and subdivided, and cleared of pines; and neat farm-houses and barns, with smiling fields of grain and grass, in the season, salute the delighted gaze of the beholder. Ten years ago, it was a mooted question whether Fairfax lands could be made productive; and, if so, would they pay the cost? This problem has been satisfactorily solved by many, and, in consequence of the above altered state of things, *school-houses and churches have doubled in number.*"

That is to say, slavery makes a rich country poor, free labor makes a poor country rich ; slave labor—improvident, wasteful, unskillful—rots out the heart of the land, and, finally, leaves the soil when it can no longer make a living from it : free labor comes in, and, in ten years, restores the soil, and works it at so great a profit that the face of the country is changed, and "churches and schools are doubled." *But mark ! until slave labor is driven out, free labor will not come in.* The two systems cannot work together. Which, then, shall we protect— the slavemaster, who impoverishes the country, or the free laborer who enriches it ?

The Wheeling *Intelligencer*, then published in a slave state, spoke out on this question, some ten years ago, in the following words :

"The present great and pressing want of our state, like that of the whole United States, is cultivation and improvement, not enlargement and annexation, and the obvious and the only mode of a rapid growth of our state or city is such a change of public policy as shall invite to our aid and co operation our Caucasian cousins, the intelligent, moral, and industrious artizans, mechanics, miners, manufacturers, and commercial men of Europe and the northern states, to share our taxation, develop our resources, and make ours a *white man's country*, with all the energy, education, love of order, of freedom, and of order characteristic of the Anglo-Saxon race. The history of the world, and especially of the States of this Union, shows most conclusively that *public prosperity bears an almost mathematical proportion to the degree of freedom enjoyed by all the inhabitants of the state.* Men will always work better for the cash than for the lash. The free laborer will produce and save as much, and consume and waste as little as he can. The slave, on the contrary, will produce and save as little, and consume and waste as much as possible. Hence states and counties filled with the former class must necessarily flourish and increase in population, arts, manufactures, wealth, and education, because they are animated and incited by all the vigor of the will ; while states filled with the latter class must exhibit comparative stagnation, because it is the universal law of nature that force and fear end in ruin and decay."

5

EFFECTS OF FREE AND SLAVE LABOR CONTRASTED.

In the newly settled free states we find villages, towns, churches, schools, and other conveniences of civilization springing up in the immediate track of the settlers; in the slave states, on the contrary, these are to a great extent lacking. The free workingman of Iowa, or Minnesota, may count upon being able to send his children to good schools, to attend church with his family, to enjoy the profits of a sale in an adjacent village for all the " small truck" of his farm, if he is a farmer; or if he is a mechanic, to obtain employment, through the gathering of the population in villages and towns, to afford him a comfortable living. In the slave states, on the contrary, even in the oldest settled of them, towns and villages are few and far apart; the small farmer can find no sale for his chickens, eggs, vegetables or fruits; the free mechanic is restricted to the few cities where alone he can find employment; all inducements to any methods of mechanical labor, or of farming, not practised in cities or upon great slave plantations, are lacking.

So few are the towns, even in the long settled states of Georgia and South Carolina, that a large part of the railroad stations are numbered—as station 1, station 2, station 14; and where, as at Millen, and other points, a name is given, there is, in most cases, no town or village, but only a dépôt for cotton.

SLAVERY LEAVES NO CHANCE FOR SMALL FARMERS.

Of course, in such a country, with such a state of affairs, the small farmer, and the country carpenter, blacksmith, wheelwright, &c., have no chance to live. The small farmer, with us in the free states, carries his chickens, eggs, feathers, turkeys, pigs, apples, and other minor produce to the " store," in the next village, and with this produce often clothes his family, and keeps up the supply of tea, coffee and sugar, while the staple of his farm, his grain or cattle, go to pay the cost of labor, and other expenses, and to form the balance of profit, which laid by, makes him yearly a more comfortable and independent man. But in the slave states this small farmer is surrounded by great plantations; no town or village is near him where he can sell the profitable "small truck;" he must neglect this important source of profit for the man of few acres; he toils away in the cotton field, and *his wife toils with him;* and they are no better off at the year's end than at the beginning.

Moreover, he does not enjoy the intellectual benefit of a weekly visit to a town or village; his children have no school provided for them; he and his wife cannot often go to church. He is deprived, too, of the numberless conveniences which the numerous villages and towns, even in the most recently settled free states, afford to the farmer there. If he needs the services of a carpenter, or tailor, or blacksmith, or wagon maker, of any mechanic, the farmer of the slave states must either set out on a long journey over bad roads, for fifty or sixty miles—or he must do without. In South Carolina, to this day, the country people are obliged, in this way, to make their own rude, heavy, inconvenient wagons, often without a tire on the wheels, which are not unfrequently of solid wood. They must make their own ill-fitting harness; they must build their own rude cabins; no mason, or plasterer, or carpenter, or skilled mechanic can be found to help them; on the rich plantations such mechanics are found—*but they are slaves.*

There is thus, in the condition of society which is created by the slave labor system, *no room, and no encouragement for the free mechanic and the small farmer,* who make up the bulk of our population in the free states, and whose industry, and thrift and intelligence make the country prosperous and happy.

Does any one ask why this is so? Why has slavery this singular and disastrous effect? Because the wealthy own slaves, and "do not need the services of the free workingmen," to quote once more the words of Marion. The rich planter living upon his estate, owns his slave mechanics, goes North or to Europe when he wants to amuse himself, and has no interest in the social advancement of the county in which he happens to be settled. *What should he care for schools? his children have tutors at home, or go to northern colleges.* Why should he seek to form or elevate society around him? When he wants "company" he goes to Charleston, or Savannah, or Mobile, or New Orleans, or New York. Why should he buy the small farmer's "truck"? *His own slaves raise all he wants.* Why should he employ free mechanics?   He prefers to *buy* a carpenter and sell him again when the work is done.   Moreover, he would not help to support the village store, if there was one— for *he buys his supplies at wholesale in the great city.*   He does not need the village tailor, for his clothes are made in New York.   His wife does not not employ the village milliner, for she gets her dresses from New Orleans, or New York, or Paris.

In short, the planter has no interest in the county where he happens to own soil, except to raise as much cotton off the land as possible ; he spends the proceeds away from homo.

WHY THE SLAVE STATES LACK CAPITAL.

But with this, there has been a singular complaint amongst the planters, which meets one in almost every essay printed by DeBow ; a complaint of a lack of capital.   " The south needs capital " was the constant cry.   " Our tanneries will not succeed, because of our limited capital," says a writer on the resources of Georgia.   " For the last twenty years, floating capital, to the amount of $500,000 per annum has left Charleston, and gone out of the state " complained Governor Hammond, in a famous essay on Southern Industry.   " Ninety millions of capital," he says in another place, " has been drained out of South Carolina in twenty years ;" and another writer, urging the establishment of manufactories in the south, admits that " we have not the capital to spare."   *We do not hear such complaints in the free states.*   Our workmen are not idle, our mines are not undeveloped, our manufactories are not stopped for want of capital.

But they would be, if the manufacturer—or mine owner—had not only to buy his machinery, *but also his workmen.*   No company, however wealthy, could afford to run a mill in Lowell, or work a coal mine in Pennsylvania, or keep up a furnace in Pittsburgh, if it had to provide means, not only to pay for its machinery but to buy also its working men and women.   All the industry of the free states would come to a stand still if this system should suddenly be forced upon us.   No wonder the manufacturing industry of the South was never set going " for lack of capital."

But this same mischief has injured the South in other ways. Look, for instance, at this : Take two men, both farmers ; let one remove to Texas, the other to Iowa; let each have his land purchased ; and have five thousand dollars over. Each needs a carpenter to build a comfortable house for him. The Iowan gives notice in the newspapers—which are glad to print such intelligence—that carpenters can get higher wages in his neighborhood than farther East; and he readily gets the services of an enterprising young mechanic. But the Texan ? He must *buy his carpenter ;* he must pay probably two thousand dollars for the man. He has but three thousand left—the Iowan has spent only the wages of a carpenter while he needed him.

That done, each requires three laborers to clear and cultivate the new land. The Iowan advertises, offers good wages, and gets his men without trouble ; *the Texan must pay out his remaining three thousand dollars for three slaves.* He has now all his money invested—the Iowan, however, has yet the greater part of his in hand. He is able to purchase the best implements —but the Texan must manage without or run in debt. He is able to contribute to the building of a school and church; but the Texan, in the first place, has no money left for such purposes ; and in the next place, the children of his slaves must not be educated. *Therefore, his own children have no school or church.* The Iowan, having still say two thousand dollars in hand, may set up a friend, in a mill, or a store—and both will be supported by the laboring population which he has gathered about him, who are earning wages and will purchase clothing and provisions. But the Texan has no money to loan for such enterprises ; and if he had, they could not succeed, for his slaves have no wages to spend, and he gets his supplies at wholesale, from his factor in New Orleans or Shreveport.

Let any one, farmer or laboring man, answer, who is the most comfortable, whose children have the best chance to grow up intelligent, who has the most money at command, the Texan slave owner, or the Iowan farmer ? who builds up around him the most quickly, a thriving community ? who gives employment to free mechanics ? whose skill and capital is most productive of wealth and progress, and happiness, to the neighborhood ?

We see by this instance, how it is that in the South they always "lacked capital." The Texan emptied his purse before he got fairly started; the Iowan had money in hand when his farm was thoroughly furnished. The Texan was condemned by the slave system to live in solitude—the Iowan at once, and necessarily, gathered a little company about him, of working-men, and mechanics, and their families, and if he selected his farm wisely, he saw within a year a little village spring up near him, with its schools, church, stores, and proper supply of mechanics of different kinds.

Mechanics and laboring men, remember, that the slave system leaves no room for you! It shuts you out! The Southern planter does not need you; he cannot bear your independent ways; he "buys a carpenter when he wants one." He and his fellow planters have, for half a century, shut up, against you and your families, the finest part of the Union; *while slavery lasts you can gain no foothold there, for every slaveholder is your enemy;* your children can have no schools there; you can have none of the conveniences of life; you cannot even get employment. But do away with the slave system, make all labor free, take away from the rich planter his fatal monopoly, let every man who works be paid wages according to his ability, and let every employer pay just wages to his workmen, and you can safely go to the South, and take with you the society, the schools, the churches, the frequent villages and towns, all the conveniences of civilization, which the slave labor system has not.

Slavery is the free workingman's worst enemy; let this truth be spread abroad amongst you, free workingmen of the North and South! Then, for your own sakes, and for the sake of your children, *whom you do not wish to grow up in the overcrowded North,* let slavery die. In the South, if slavery is abolished, *the wages of mechanics and laboring men must for many years to come be very high.* That whole vast region is almost without skilled labor; free mechanics have been driven from it. *A region greater than all the free states, as healthful, with a finer climate, more abundant mineral resources, cheaper lands and a richer soil, lies open before you and your families.* You have only to possess it, and with your skill and energy subdue it.

Then you will not feel the hard struggle which severe climate, and tenement houses, and lack of employment, and the oppression caused by an overcrowded labor market, subjected you to in the North. *But you can never enter that land of ease and plenty; without first striking down your fatal enemy, slavery!*

A SPEECH

ON

THE GREAT SOCIAL PROBLEM

OF

LABOR & CAPITAL,

DELIVERED AT

COOPER INSTITUTE, NEW YORK CITY,

On Monday, May 8, 1871,

BEFORE THE

LABOR REFORM LEAGUE,

BY

VICTORIA C. WOODHULL.

NEW YORK:

JOURNEYMEN PRINTERS' CO-OPERATIVE ASSOCIATION,

No. 30 BEEKMAN STREET.

1871.

THE GREAT SOCIAL PROBLEM;

LABOR AND CAPITAL.

Three great questions, each based in human equality, the immediate future must solve, namely, Political Rights, Social Order and Moral Responsibility. The first unattained, the second is impossible, and the third preposterous. The first attained, the second will be organized, and the third naturally follow. Every human being is entitled to certain inalienable rights, of which no constitution or law can dispossess him, but every human being is also subject to certain duties flowing from the possession of such rights, which he should no more evade than he should be deprived of their possession.

Therefore it is that we find humanity a body of interdependent persons, every individual of whom sustains certain dependent relations to the aggregate, and is entitled to certain protection from the aggregate, against infringement by others. The interest and rights of each individual are therefore merged in a community of interests and rights, and the legitimate functions of government are to maintain and protect, so that by no possibility may the community of interest be made subservient to individual interest, or to the special interest of any number of individuals less than the whole.

From this position, which principle and reason sustain, it follows that my first postulate is true; that social order cannot exist unless political right is equally possessed by all among whom it is sought to be maintained; for if a government is organized to maintain it, in which but a portion of the community participate—or worse still, in which a portion are denied participation—there is a departure from the principle of equality of right among the members of the community, which must ever prove fatal to humanity.

So long as inequalities exist among the members of a community, first made possible and afterward maintained by *law*, *so* long will there be inharmonies in the community. This is a self-evident proposition. And so long as there are inharmonies in the community, there can be *no* equality of Moral responsibility, because the inharmony arising from unequal distribution and exercise of rights, to which all are equally entitled, places those who are *below* equality at the mercy of those who have usurped this quantity, and who are thus *above* equality. In such condition, equal responsibility is not justice, and hence our second postulate is maintained.

As there are three great questions pressing for settlement, so, too, do these questions find their legitimate basis in three great principles, which should guide every action of individuals and communities, and by which all results should be tried, and these are: Freedom, Equality and Justice. With the first, the second should be maintained by the ruling of the third, which would be perfect government, since the purposes for which government is organized would be secured to every individual.

Is our government based in these principles, and is it administered according to this formula? If not, why not? What is lacking which is right and what is superabundant which is wrong? Dismissing whatever relates to the first and third of the great questions named, the second, the social problem, will be considered. The sub-question of labor and capital, or the causes of the very unequal distributions of material possessions which obtain under government as now administered, is but a part of the greater one of social order.

Under a government which expresses the will of those over whom its functions are exercised, there can be no question to settle as between such government and the people. But there *is* a question between this people and their government, and it must be settled, and the settlement falls upon the present age to perform.

I fear that the principles involved in this controversy are little understood by the masses who join in it. I fear that portions of the people array themselves against other portions, without comprehending what is the difficulty which they represent, and from which they profess to suffer and desire relief. I fear, while those who do suffer are looking among the leaves and branches of the wrong for its cause, the roots are taking deeper and firmer hold of the vitals of society, and its trunk increasing to still more formidable proportions, and that before they who suffer become conscious of it supreme control will have been obtained over them.

But, says the poor laborer : "What right has my neighbor to all his wealth to produce which he never lifted his hand, while I who did assist in its production, am year after year compelled to continue producing, only to see him obtain all the benefit." As between you, my friend, and him, as individuals, he may have all right to his accumulations; but as between you and him as equal members of the community, and the *community*, he can have none; because the right and interests of the individual cannot properly exist in antagonism to those of the community, of whom you and he are equally constituent parts. Special rights and interests cannot legitimately exist in, and be maintained at the expense of, the general welfare. The general welfare of a people consists in having the greatest possible amount of happiness, and general happiness is not possible where there is such cause of complaint as the one mentioned. So long as the general good of the whole is possible, the greatest good of the greatest number is the object to be obtained through government. Whatever the professions of government are, its practices secure the supposed good of the very select few at the direct expense of the common masses.

Hence, I predicate that so long as the attempt is made to remedy the ills of which society has just cause of complaint, by temporary policies, expedient make-shifts and trimming among effects, instead of leaving all these to take care of themselves, and going to the "Root of the matter," just so long success will not crown the efforts.

But how shall we get at the "Root of the matter?" There is but one way, and that is to go back to the beginning and build better, by putting no bricks in the walls of the edifice to be erected except such as have been trimmed, squared and tested by the principles upon which all government should be constructed.

The people who maintain the present government in this country are not aborigines. As a people they have no primordial right to the soil upon which they live, any more than they have to the air they breathe, which is fully as important to life as is the soil. How comes this distinction to be made by humans between the elements upon which human life depends? How is it, that, in an aggregate population of forty millions of individuals, that less than a fortieth part have usurped the right to all the soil which belongs by natural right to the whole? This is an inequality of most alarming proportions. Every fortieth person has usurped the natural rights of the other thirty-nine, and what is worse than all, they are protected in it by the government.

If a person have in his possession a stolen article, it matters not through how many hands it may have passed, it is nevertheless stolen property and may be reclaimed by the owner upon proof. Now let us try the professed ownership of the soil by this rule, never minding the practice by which it was obtained, which by the way reminds me of that which prevailed in the armies during the late war : a person would steal a horse and "swap" him, and thus obtain one of his own. Suppose a person were to go into the public domain—there is a great deal of unappreciated meaning in that word—and fence off three hundred and twenty acres of soil and call it his own, and should afterward sell the same to another person who should take possession thereof, and that not long thereafter Uncle Sam should pass that way and observe what had occurred, and the question of title should arise, could the party in possession *hold* as against Uncle Sam? Not a bit of it. Let me ask what *better* title *any* person has to any soil he may *profess* to own than this one would have. I do not care through how many generations it may have descended, traced far enough back, the title will be found to have been a *squatter's*, and that *that* squatter took possession of some of the public domain, which belonged to all the people as represented and organized in government.

The conditions of ownership of soil are founded on no *better* principles than that would be had the whole present population of this country been suddenly transplanted to its soil from some other country, and had "grabbed" their present possessions. In principles of human rights, I say, there would be *no distinction* between this process and that by which they do possess it. Whatever *legal* rights there may be they can never destroy *human* right.

The first government this country knew after its discovery held the public domain in trust for the people ; as they increased, the number for whom the government held the public domain also increased. It was neither the people nor government who owned the soil. It was landed upon, seized and retained. Such a procedure should be called stealing. Its people or government never had a just title to a foot of soil in this or any other country, and cannot convey such a title.

The soil upon which we stand is as *common* property as the air is by which we are surrounded. It is really a wonder that schemers have not before this set afloat some feasible plan for bottling the atmosphere. and dealing it out for considerations to those who should be so unfortunate as not to have " gobbled" some on their own account. For my part I can see no difference in principle between dealing in *air, soil* or *water.* They are are all composed of the same elements, and are constantly being converted into each other. Thus then we arrive at the *foundation* for all *material* monopolies. From *this* process of stealing the rights of the people all the other and *lesser* thefts have come, by which the great proportion of people are defrauded of their natural inheritance. *Two* wrongs can never make one right. If a few people have possession of the rights of the many, the many cannot reclaim them, and the few retain them. The few *must* give way to the many.

Every person whom this government represents has a *natural, human* right to the use of his *just* proportion of the public soil, and government should *secure* this right to all, they, individually, paying to the fund for its support a certain amount of the *proceeds* obtained by its use. *This* is the true use which should be made of the public domain.

But what use is government making of it. Hon. George W Julian, in a speech made in the last session of the 41st Congress, enumerated *twenty-three* bills that passed the Senate granting seventy-five million six thousand three hundred and twenty acres. Beside them there were then pending in the Senate bills granting one hundred and fifteen million, two hundred and eighteen thousand, five hundred acres. Adding these proposed donations to those already made to the various Pacific Roads, and the enormous aggregate of more than four hundred million of acres is found to have been diverted from *public* to *private* use, an area exceeding in extent that of any *ten* of the present number of States.

The enormity of thus defrauding the people of the public domain is beyond comprehension, and can only be appreciated when we are reminded that many of those who have thus betrayed the public interest are now reputed to be possessed of *vast* wealth. We do not pretend to charge that these gentlemen obtained personal benefit from their action upon these various bills. Not by any means. We only desire that the people should know how *easy* it is for their public servants to *acquire riches* while in their service, and to the contemporaneous fact that the proportionate increase of their wealth coincides very *remarkably* with the size of the successful Land-Grabbing Schemes.

If Land-Grabbing continue at the rate it has the past few years, how long will the people have any public domain? That already voted away would have given two million five hundred thousand familes 160 acres each. Does a conception of the magnitude of these plundering operations begin to dawn upon your minds? Two million five hun- dred thousand families might have been provided with homes and farms and removed from indigence and poverty by allowing them the use of these lands. They would have tilled and made them *productive*; where they will now be idle until the occupation of *contiguous* lands shall increase the market value to seven, ten and even *fifteen* dollars per acre, which these *same families* will be *obliged* to pay for them. If it were simply a scheme to develop that vast territory lying west of the States, so that it should prove a source of revenue to government and thus indirectly to the public, why did not the government *build* these roads and *retain possession* of them for the people instead of building them with the people's *money* and *property*, and then giving them to private individuals?

Hundreds of millions of dollars—*enough to pay the whole national debt*—have been swallowed up and forever lost to the people by the manner these Railroads have been subsidized and built. The develop- ment theory has set men wild, and with them *anything* is justifiable which will build a railroad into or through *unoccupied* territory. It is quite time that the people should set about devising means to *stop* this wholesale system of plundering the public, and I seriously mistake if in the next presidential election the voices of the people do not speak *in thunder tones* their disapproval of these practices.

Time does not permit me to dwell longer upon *this* part of the sub-ject. But let me advise every one of you to obtain and carefully read the speech of Mr. Julian, to which I have referred. Also, permit me to mention that Mr. Julian is one of those who retired from Congressional duty on the 4th of March possessed of as little worldly goods as when he entered upon his public career—a fact which speaks more for his honor and integrity than can any word of mine.

Corporate Monopolies are the *legitimate* offspring of Landed Mono-polies, and though perhaps not so *immediately* alarming in their audacity or mendacity, are nevertheless a *constant leech* upon *all* the producing interests of the country. Though in nearly every instance these are *theoretically* based in some supposed benefit to flow to the public, their *practice* is universally beyond their legitimate functions, and conse-quently detrimental. No government has any *legitimate* right to grant special privileges to *any* man, or any *set* of men, by which they may be enabled to acquire a superiority over other men, or by which they may be in position to *compel* others to pay exorbitant charges for the use they may desire to make of like privileges.

Special grants of, and protection to, corporate powers, are only per-missable upon the supposition that the *people* will be benefited by them. Take, for instance, our great system of Railroads. Everybody knows of what immense benefit they have been to the country in a general sense. Government foreseeing their *necessity*, and being pressed forward by the great results of the initial roads, thought only of granting all the powers and aid required to build and put them in operation, never stop-ping to think that the time *might* come when they would oppress the people.

That time *has*, however, come, and one of the great questions of the immediate future will be how to curb and control the rapaciousness of these obese corporations. Few people realize the enormity of the frauds practised by them. They know that the roads are kept in operation and that they are obliged to pay such and such prices to make use of their accommodations. Here their knowledge ceases. They look upon the immense array of figures put forth from time to time, *pretending* to be statements for information, but which are, in *most* cases, statements for *deception*. None but experts can ever arrive at their *real* significance. They perhaps inform us that the Directory have been able to pay a *ten per cent. dividend*. But they do not inform us what the basis of that per cent. is. They do not tell us that their stocks are worth, 50, 75, 100 or 125 per cent. of their par value, because they are able to pay two, four, six, eight or ten per cent. dividends upon such value. They do not inform us that the par value of all their stocks is a *hundred* millions of dollars, while the real value of, what it represents is perhaps no more than *ten* millions. Oh no; this information they wish concealed within the gorgeous parlors of the Directory. Permit me to point out how the producing interests of the country are *swindled* out of their hard-earned products by these *patents* upon their industry, by giving some cases in point. In 1891, the capital stock of the Cleveland, Painesville and Ashtabula Railroad was three million dollars; an eight per cent. dividend required that its patrons should pay to that road during a year two hundred and forty thousand dollars in excess of its actual working expenses. In 1867, or in six years, the capital stock was increased to three and a quarter times its original amount, or to nine millions seven hundred and fifty thousand dollars. To pay an eight per cent. dividend upon this increase, required that this Company should extort from its patrons the large sum of five hundred and forty thousand dollars, which, added to the dividend on its *original* capital stock, increased it to twenty-six per cent. So that upon every dollar of actual investment the holders of said stocks in the year 1857, and every year thereafter, received *twenty-six* per cent.

Is it to be wondered that everybody who knows anything about railroad management is *convinced* of the desirability of such stocks?

Again: From New York to Chicago, via the New York Central and Lake Shore Roads, is 982 miles. These roads were built at a cost of about eighty-four and a half millions dollars. The amount of their present stock, upon which there is paid eight per cent. per annum dividends, is one hundred and sixty-four million dollars. To pay the dividends npon their cost requires six millions seven hundred and fifty thousand dollars. To pay the dividend upon their present stock requires twelve millions eight hundred thousand dollars, or in other words, these Companies must *steal from the people* the *enormous* amount of six million dollars annually, that they may be able to pay to the holders of their stocks their regular dividends.

Allowing that there are fifty-five thousand miles of railroads in the country, and calculating them upon the basis of these last mentioned, at what enormous an array of figures do we arrive. The cost of all the railroads would be the sum of four billions seven hundred thousand millions. And supposing all their stocks to have been watered to the extent previously calculated, and that eight per cent. dividends are paid thereon, we find that there must be added to the charges collected from the people to pay operating expenses and legitimate interest upon their original cost, the enormous sum of *three hundred and fifty* millions dollars.

What think you, laboring, wealth-producing people of the United States, of a government which granted franchises to a few individuals by which they may be able not only to extract from your hard earnings some four hundred million dollars interest upon their actual investments, but also *to steal the further* sum of three hundred and fifty million dollars? When all of you realize the enormity of *these swindles* which are practiced upon you by the *sanction* of the government, do you think you will endure it patiently?

I would also call your attention to another interesting bit of fact. All these immense sums come either *directly* or *indirectly* from the laboring classes. Why so? Because the middle-men who transact all the business between the producer and consumer of the respective articles of commerce, must make their profits, whether the railroads swindle the people or not. None of it comes from them. Not at all They are beyond the reach of this rapaciousness. But the weary laborer when he contemplates the results of his year's *hard* work, which he has just shipped to market, *knows* that they will net him just so much less than the market price of them as these *railroads* are pleased to charge him for transportation.

Should government levy a tax of ten cents per bushel upon wheat or corn it would rouse the people to revolt, but these gigantic *Monopolies* may levy ten cents per bushel extra upon both wheat and corn, or five dollars a ton extra on coal, to enable them to pay dividends on fictitious stocks, and never a word is said. What applies to the producer of wheat and corn and coal also applies with *equal* force to all other producers. They realize just so much *less* for their products than they *should*, as they are compelled to pay *more* than they ought for costs of transportation.

Do you realize the magnitude of this matter? The government has placed these Railroad Companies in the position to filch from you an amount *equal to that required* to *maintain* itself, and *which*, if so aplied, would relieve you from *all* kinds of taxation.

By Section VIII., Paragraph 1, of the Constitution of the United States, government is granted the power to provide for the *general welfare*. Does the kind of legislation referred to provide for the general welfare? No, a thousand times no. The general welfare is by it *sacrificed*, and a few *railroad* managers made *money-kings*, who are ambitious to obtain the power to control *not only* the condition of the *producing* and *consuming* people, but also to dictate to the government which created them—a more unlimited, unwarrantable, unjustifiable and insolent ambition and contempt for the public than was that of an Alexander or a Napoleon.

Listen to what the Lancaster (Penn.) Intelligencer says of perhaps the most corrupt of all railroad monopolies, the Pennsylvania Central Railroad:

" The Pennsylvania Central have nominally bought up a majority of the members of the legislature, who have bound themselves to vote as they may be directed. The agents of the railroad could be seen at all times in the loby or on the floor of the two houses watching the course of legislation, and forwarding or checking the passage of bills. No men in Harrisburgh are better known and none have a more distinctive and well recognized avocation than these lobby agents of the Pennsylvania Railroad. They have learned by long experience how to ply their foul trade successfully, and are adepts in all the arts of intrigue, and skilled in every species of corruption and bribery."

Not long since, when the question of adjournment was before the legislature, a member rose and said in effect: " *If Thos. Scott has no more business with the legislature, I think we should adjourn.*" Now this Thos. Scott is the Vice-President and the active manager of the affairs of this road Mr. Scott lately became President of the Union Pacific, and thus virtually controls a line of railroad extending from New York to

San Francisco, by which immense power, it is said, he intends also to control the next Presidential Election. It *remains* to be seen whether the working men and women of this country will continue *criminally* blind to their interests and permit such a scheme to be consummated. Whatever party Thos. Scott supports, may be set down as certain to be entirely antagonistic to their interest, no matter by what professions they may seek to obtain support.

What is true of the Pennsylvania Central Railroad Company and its managers, is true to a greater or less degree of *every* railroad company in the country ; and not only of every railroad company but of *every other monopoly* which flourishes at the *expense* of the *productive* interests of the country, at whose expense *all monopolies must flourish*, if they flourish at all. The power these corporations possess is full of danger to the freedom of this country. Combined, they could control all legislation, and carry every election. The New York Herald not long since spoke editorially thus : " Now it is possible the American people may not be alarmed at the probable effects a combination of capital and influence of these vast railroad corporations may have upon the future of the country, upon the permanency of its institutions and the perpetuity of its political liberties ; but, in view of *possible* contingencies, we think we are justified in cautioning the people against the possible creation of a railroad oligarchy here who may prove as dangerous to the nation as was the Southern cotton oligarchy in times past."

"This subject is one of considerable interest to the American people, and the election of members to the next Congress should be graduated accordingly."

We know that the Pennsylvania Railroad Company controls the legislature of the State ; that the Central and Erie combined can control that of New York; the Baltimore and Ohio that of Maryland, that all the Railroad interests of *every* State can control the Legislatures of their respective States, and that the *combined* Railroad Interests of all the States can control Congress.

The National Banking System is another element of power which is *too powerful* to be ignored. Its representatives even now assume to *dictate* to Congress upon measures of finance. 'Tis true this system was inaugurated in an hour of national peril and necessity. It looked well, it worked well, and all was serene with the public, for plenty of money meant *quick* transit, *rapid* sales and facilities in exchange. But the public now begin to understand that the Bankers are *too* happy over their privileges, which permit a double means of obtaining the people's money. They obtain interest from the people on deposits of Government Bonds, and also from the people triple interest on their circulation which they obtain by means of their Bonds. It was a *good day* for the Bankers, and at that time it was the *best thing* the government could do. Every one was happy *then*. The times, however, are changed. Everybody is *not* happy now. The people are not happy over the payment every year of thirty millions of dollars to these banks, in consideration for their having stepped forward to the assistance of the government in its time of need. The people remember that they too stepped forward and offered their lives without consideration. The banks have been well paid, and should retire from their unequal privileges *satisfied* with their gains, and be no longer permitted to remain patented charges upon the industries of the country. The yearly profit of these Banks, which they make from the use of a currency for which the people are in a measure responsible, is sufficient to pay the entire expenses of our National Government. Thus we have two distinct monopolies, each of whose profits are equal to all the expenses of the Federal Government. Please think of that !

The interests of *all* monopolies are mutual. To attack *one* is to put them *all* on the defence. Should the Bank and Railroad Interests of the country *combine*—and there is an effort now being made to that end—what would not they be able to do ? This is a matter of the most *serious* import, which tends to a despotism *more* intolerable than that exercised by any of the monarchies of the old world.

The inquiry comes up : How shall this danger be averted or controlled ? Experience teaches that there can be *no* legislation limiting their privileges that can not be rendered impotent or be evaded by them. We may not hope for relief from *this* source. There is but one resort left. Since they *will trespass* upon the welfare of the *entire* people to their own aggrandisement, paying no attention and giving no thought to their rights, they must be dispossessed of their power. Primarily they were permitted for the public good. They were constructed and the public welfare was subserved. The public welfare now demands that they shall not become *hereditary* drains upon the vitality of the country.

But, says one, government has no right to take the railroads away from these thieving corporations. The government of the United States has the Constitutional right to do *anything* which the public welfare demands, and the Human Rights of the people *demand* that they shall not be made to pay twenty dollars to be transported from New York to Chicago when the cost is but five, the other fifteen going to promote the interests of a would-be-despotism, which is endeavoring to .fasten itself upon the country.

The same results which have followed the inauguration of our Postal System for the transportation of the people's letters would also follow a *like* system extended to the transportation of their merchandise and themselves. If government had the right to take the *former* from private hands, so also has it the power to take the *latter*, and the exigency is a thousand times more formidable and urgent.

Under a *proper* Civil Service the railroads of the United States would be managed with all the *regularity* which pertains to the mails, and, with the official intgerity which, as a rule, characterizes our Postal, Military and Naval Service.

We lay it down as a general proposition that *all* legislation of the *special order* kind, which grants rights or privileges to individuals or corporations, to do what they could not *without* such grant, is a *monopoly* to be *sustained* at the *expense* of the *industrial* or *productive* classes.

All special legislation, I do not care of what *kind* or *grade*, or what *interest* it is to *protect* or *maintain*, is a *direct* blow at the wealth-producing people, for in the *end* the entire benefit which accrues to such interest, comes home to *their* doors and is by *them* paid. Equality which the Constitution pre-supposes among the people, and which it was framed to maintain, is an *impossibility* under *any* such practices, and it is for *this* reason that I have entered my protest *against* everything of the kind which is in our present governmental systems.

I call the system of Protective Tariff a *huge* fallacy, gotten up by the *money* interests to compel *labor* to maintain pursuits which it is assumed could not otherwise exist. The *results* of this system tersely stated are these : It interferes with the natural demand and supply—the natural ebb and flow—of the products of the world, by imposing upon certain of them such tribute that it is impracticable for them to get to the locality of natural demand, so that a special few who inhabit that locality are enabled to produce the same by a greatly increased cost, which the consumer must pay in order to obtain them.

It does not matter how much this plain statement may be *twisted* and *bent* by the alluring sophistries and glittering generalities of the *Protected*, it can never be robbed of its force as a statement, and can *never* be gainsaid. If it be any general benefit for a thousand people to pay one person fifty per cent. more for a desired article than it could be obtained for from a *foreign* producer, simply because it is of *home* production, we should be most happy to hear the demonstration. The argument used is, that the *one* man being protected in the manufacture of *this* article can give employment to a certain number of laborers, who in turn become the consumers of the products of these thousand people. But to make this position tenable it must be proved that laborers *thus* employed, would not be able to apply themselves to *any other* labor than the production of the article in question. This investigation leads to such an intricacy of cause and effect, and of reactionary benefit, that those who attempt to make it, prefer to *accept* the declaration that protection is a good thing to have, *rather* than acknowledge themselves lost in the *fog* and *obscurity* which they are asked to explore to determine the fact of the case.

But, says the Protectionist, pretending to speak in the interests of the laborer, when it is his own which are in jeopardy, would you place the *laboring* classes of this country in competition with the *pauper* labor of Europe. Not by any means. But I will tell you, Mr. Protectionist, what you are doing. You are putting the laboring classes of this country in a *position* which will very soon reduce them to the *condition* which you call pauper labor of other countries, for your practice tends to build up monopolies to which labor becomes every year more and more subservient.

The same results will follow in this country which have obtained in England, which, of all countries of the world, has most thoroughly tested this matter—because the greatest manufacturing country of the world—and her experience is literally conclusive. Let us glance at this beautiful system as practiced there. Its history gives some reliable data more instructive than all the essays of a thousand political economists, with all their theories of what might, could, would or should be, if something were to occur which has not and never can. It is no doubt one of the most self-satisfactory things in the world to figure national prosperity, compelling the figures to fit the ends desired, and forgetting to-day the facts of yesterday.

Mons. Guizot speaking in the French Corps Legislatiff, in 1846, said that the free trade policy of England had three results.

1st. It *maintained* and *augmented* the amount of labor.

2d. It *lowered* the prices of the necessaries of life of the laboring classes.

3d. It *diminishes* the terrible oscillations to which those prices were exposed.

In the following year, in consequence of the free-trade *vs.* protectionist excitement, certain statistics were laid before the English House of Commons, more particularly as to plate-glass, the manufacturers of which had loudly declaimed that free-trade would ruin them, asserting that the continued existence of their business had only been insured by by protection. The statistics were as follows:

In the year 1819 the duty was 98 shillings per cwt., the price per foot was 25 shillings with weekly sales of 3,000 feet. In 1829 the duty was reduced to 60 shillings; the price fell to 12 shillings per foot, with weekly sales of 5,000 feet. In 1849 the duty was removed; the price fell to 5 shillings per foot, with weekly sales of 10,000 feet. In 1836, when the duty was 60 shillings per foot, there 2,500 hands employed and 250,000 pounds sterling invested in the manufacture. In 1849, when there was no duty, there were 12,000 hands employed and 1,000,000 pounds sterling invested in its manufacture.

There was no English plate-glass exported to the United States in 1846, while in 1847 more was so exported than *to all the rest of the world* in 1846.

Comment on the above figures seems altogether superfluous, for the reason that *nothing* that can be said can present a *stronger* case in favor of free trade. We may, however, point out that from 1819 to 1827, under a protective tariff, lowering the duty 30 per cent. reduced the price of the article 52 per cent., and increased its weekly sales 66 per cent. We deduce from this a consumption of 66 per cent. more under the 60s. per cwt. duty than under the 98s. per cwt. duty, and that there were 66 per cent. more laborers engaged in the manufacture under the *lesser* tariff than under the *greater.*

Pursuing still further the official figures, we find that in the year 1847, when *all* the duty was taken off, the amount of labor engaged in the manufacture increased 480 per cent., as compared with the year 1836, when the duty was 60s. per cwt.

It is also notable that the increase in consumption and productiveness followed *exactly* in the wake of the *reduction* in the tariff.

We will now turn to the repeal of the corn laws in England, which was made a test case as to the merits of free trade, the conflict lasting from 1842 to 1846. In 1842 there was a sliding scale of duties in force, that is to say, the duty varied according to the price of corn ; the average of the duty was, however, 16s. per qr. This scale of duties lasted until 1846, when it was lowered to an average of 4s. per qr. ; the average amount of duty collected under the first-named tariff being £372,500 per annum, while in 1849, under a nominal tariff, the duty collected was £615,814 per annum.

The commencement of the free trade agitation found Sir Robert Peel, the Duke of Welliignton and Mr. Gladstone protectionists. In 1846, Sir Robert Peel, speaking in favor of a reduction of the tariff on corn, renounced his protectionist ideas, and became a free trader. In his speech he said he claimed the principle of *yielding* both to the *force of argument* and *conviction,* and of *acting* on the results of *enlarged experience;* and that " he was about to review the duties which applied to many articles the produce and manufacture of other States; that for the last three years, since the policy of acting on the principle of repealing and reducing certain duties had been acknowledged, there had been *increased* productiveness of revenue, *increased* demand for labor, *increased* commerce, as well as *comfort, contentment* and *peace* in the country, and he was about to proceed on the assumption that the repeal of *prohibitory* and the relaxation of *protective* tariffs is in itself a wise principle."

In 1846, Lord Russell said, "He believed it would have been better for the English farmers if the duty on imported corn had been reduced still lower in 1842."

And the Duke of Wellington voted for the reduction of the duty on corn. In 1815 Mr. Bennett (member of Parliament for Wiltshire) said that "Farmers could not grow wheat under a less protective duty than 96s. a quarter, yet he had since supported a minister who proposed to levy 56s. a quarter."

Mr. Gladstone, who, in 1842, opposed Lord Morpeth's free trade measures, has since become one of the most prominent of free trade champions.

The Earl of Derby, who had been a strenuous opposer of free trade, said, in the House of Commons in 1852, "That after the decision of the country in the recent elections, in favor of free trade, he was prepared to bow to its decisions." And in the same year the Queen in her speech *congratulated* Parliament on the *beneficial* results of *free trade* legislation.

We thus gather that free trade has not only given satisfaction to the *people* wherever it has been practiced, but has absolutely *convinced* its very opponents. In the matter of corn, at the very commencement of the free-trade agitation, the duty was 96s. per quarter; at the close and triumph of free trade it was 1s. a quarter, the results of each reduction only paving the way for a still greater one; had the opponents of free trade been able to show injurious effects from any one reduction of the tariff, the downward movement would have ceased, and probably a reaction have set in.

But the *primary* and *insuperable* objection to the policy of protection is, that under it *equality* to all citizens is impossible. Whatever favorably *appearing* argument may be adduced in its favor, tried by *this* comprehensive principle, it will surely fall to the ground. There is a no more *fatal* idea than that *high* prices are an evidence of prosperity. The very *reverse* is really the case. Real wealth and prosperity do not consist in high prices, but in the *quantities* which are actually possessed. Prices under a protective policy, which, is at all times open to change, must *always* fluctuate with every such change. A person *rich* this year may become *poor* next. Disaster, destruction, ruin and general alarm and want of confidence have always followed changes in the protective policy in this country. Prices which, under protection, are stimulated to *undue* proportions, on the removal or reduction of tariffs, fall as far *below* the actual mean as they were *above* it. High prices at the expense of permanency *are not* the ultimatum to be sought by *any* people of *any* country. The true point to seek is, the employment of industries in *those* directions *where most* can be produced at *least* expense, in the accumulation of the products of which, the country must become more rapidly wealthy than in the production of the *least* at the *greatest* expense.

If by protection this country become *enriched* at the expense of England, there would be a chance for an argument for protection : but such is not the case. The total "impositions" made on importations is a *direct* tax upon *one* part of the people for the benefit of the other part, but which results in benefit to nobody. Those whom it is supposed to benefit would be better off were they engaged in some pursuits which would be *self-supporting* and which if they did not bring them so large *present* wages, would have the *greater* advantage of permanency. It is no particular object, and we consider it an *empty honor*, for this country to manufacture articles at a cost of one hundred per cent. over what the same are produced elsewhere for; the only object gained being, that we may be able to say that they are produced at home, and that we pay double price that they may be thus produced.

The fallacies of protection are well illustrated by supposing that a dozen individuals, possessed of a thousand dollars each, should attempt to get rich by gambling among themselves. The sum total of their funds would be no larger if it were finally in the hands of one of their number. To *add* to their money they must *win* from some *outside* party. Protecting industries works similar results. It compels *one* part of the people to gamble with *another* part and finally results in the accumulation of all the wealth of the country in the hands of the few. It is impossible to add to the wealth of the country by making its farmer pay large prices to its manufacturers. Large products over consumption sent to other countries are the desideratum, our own citizens being the agents for their transportation. If the various interests of a country only produce a sufficient amount to meet the demands among themselves, how can they add to the aggregate wealth?

What would the manufacturers of Massachusetts say, were it attempted to enforce protection to the *farmers* of the state by levying a fifty per cent duty on Western produce, in order that *they* might be able to compete with the Western farmer and thus supply *all* the subsistence there used? Or what would Illinois say, were everything which she requires of Massachusetts, compelled to pay an *equal* duty before it could reach her for consumption. It is true the Constitution prohibits such a thing, but what better *principle* is followed in applying that which is prohibited as between states to the Commercial intercourse between nations? Protection is a short-sighted unprincipled and unreasonable policy and like land-grabbing, tends to the establishment of monopolies.

In the great problem of the assimilation of the world's interests, which is being rapidly solved, it must be learned that the United States is as yet but *part* of the world, and that the *best* interests of *individual* nations are subserved when the *best* interests of *all* nations are consulted. The same rule holds good in this application that is true in regard to the individuals of a country; the best interests of each lie in promoting the best interests of all. Under this rule, carried to its *perfect* working, the industries of the world would localize, where *each* would produce the most of its peculiar products at the *least* average cost, which being given over to commerce, would be transported to such parts of the world as demand them in exchange for products produced by *its* localized industries in the *greatest* quantities at the least cost. Thus would be introduced a grand system of economy, which would result in fixed and unchangeable channels of commerce, and the employment of the industries of the whole world according to the *natural* law of demand and supply, which *cannot* produce alternate flood and dearth.

If tariffs for the protection of *industries* are not admissible upon the principle of equality, are they any less to be *deprecated* as systems of *revenue*? Here we touch a point upon which the people are very sensitive, and justly so. The levying of duties upon imported goods is an *indirect* way of taxing that portion of the people who *consume* such goods. The amount obtained by this most unequal and indirect manner of taxing the people was, for the last fiscal year, the large sum of one hundred and ninety-four millions four hundred and forty-eight thousand four hundred and twenty-seven dollars, *every dollar* of which was an *additional* tax gathered from the *individuals* who *finally* purchased and consumed such imports. This would not have been important had it fallen *equally* upon the *taxable* property of the country, upon which general taxes are levied; but one hundred millions of this was collected from woolens, cottons, sugar, molasses, coffee and tea, all of which the *poorest* laborers, who should pay no tax, in common with the *richest* landlords are nearly equal consumers. Thus every laboring man was compelled to pay his ten, twenty or fifty dollars to the government, in proportion to the num-ber of his family.

Working men and women of the United States! how like you this manner of filching your hard-earned dollars under the *fraudulent* name of raising a revenue? It is no wonder that your wages will scarcely meet your families' necessities, when you are thus compelled to pay such *sums* upon the most *common staple* articles of general con-sumption. It is no wonder you continue to be laborers, never being able to become producers upon your own account, when you who *should not*, and under general and just principles of taxation, *would not*, be called upon to pay a *single* dollar as a *direct* tax, are thus burdened.

Nor are the other means to which government resorts for support, entitled to much more consideration. There is *no* equality for the peo-ple in *any* of them, and it is quite evident that the system of revenue for the support of government *must* be remodeled so as to *fall* where it *properly* belongs—*upon the taxable property of the country.* This done, and a sound financial system inaugurated, the laboring classes would begin to be leveled up to a medium and the upper classes to be leveled down to the same basis of material prosperity.

A system of taxation for the maintenance of government should be devised by which one set of officials should collect all the monies which are to be gathered, and thereby introduce a *grand system of econ-omy* which would save at least *three-fourths* of the expense now incur-red by the almost innumerable methods which obtain the people's money without their realizing the amounts they pay. All these things the laboring classes must first understand and then rectify. They will *never* attain *anything* approaching equality in the manner through which government is now administered. Never will the laboring classes become *independent* of the *wealthy* classes, until the *freedom*, *equality* and *justice* which are the birthright of *every* citizen of the United States are possible of attainment under their government.

Having thus passed in review the Land, Protection and Revenue systems of the country, which, with the finance system, complete the *foundation* on which labor and capital build, the relations which these sustain to each other as represented in practice, can be considered.

A stream can never rise higher than its source except by artificial means. If artificial means are used to elevate the stream above its source, when they are removed, changed or decayed, it will fall to its natural level. This principle holds good in all the varied operations of mind as well as matter. The stability of everything which occupies *unnatural* and *inconsistent* positions through *artificial* and *extraneous* means is never assured—is at all times liable to change, and is ever in danger of present, and certain of ultimate dethronement.

Such is the position of *capital* to *labor* in this country. Labor is the *direct* source of *all* capital and has *produced* all capital. But by the means of *unphilosophic*, *unnatural* and *unequal* laws capital has *usurped* a position *higher* than its source, and not only *occupies* it, but assumes to *dictate* to and control labor. The responsibility for this condition should not be charged upon the representatives of capital; neither does its cause exist *in* capital or in the capitalist. It is further back than they. *It is in the people* who have *constructed* society and government upon *false principles*, which being administered, permit all the *ills* of which they complain.

If the Constitution and laws of a country make possible certain things, which may be seized upon by a few persons to the injury of all the rest, it can scarcely be expected but there will be those willing to take advantage of it. Were this audience shown that by pursuing a certain course, which would not be in conflict with any existing law— no matter how much there should be law to prevent it—that each one of them could in a given time accumulate a *fortune*, I do not think there are many who would forego the opportunity because it would be at the *expense* of others or of the country.

Therefore, when the labor interest cries out against the oppression of capital, it must remember that had their places been reversed the *labor ers* instead of the capitalists would have been the oppressing power. It is a great thing for people to be able to look at *both* sides of a question— to see how it would be were it "my bull which had gored your ox."

The cause being in the *people* they must *look to themselves* for the remedy, and they must apply it before they may expect to see their rights adjusted. Between the *real* interests of labor and capital there is an *entire harmony*. Their *true* interests lie in each rendering *complete justice* to the other. In the understanding of *this* point lies the *solution* of the present question. *Strife* may continue—*war* even, may come of strife, but for all that the settlement must follow from a proper adjustment of their relations upon principle.

I am sorry that there is class of self-styled reformers who perpetually stir up strife, making interests antagonistic, and thus more widely separating them. These persons prate with considerable volubility of the *terrible condition* into which things have fallen. As a rule they belong to that class who, being upon the outskirts of society, wait, Micawber-like, for something to turn up by which they may ride into position. But do they present *remedies* for the ills they picture so graphically? Do they tell *whence* they come or *whither* they should go? Let me warn the laborers to beware of such persons; they are wolves in sheep's clothing, who would make *use* of the occasion that they may suck their blood.

The true friends of humanity are they who *find the causes* of their ills and teach them their *remedies.* There is no such obscurity about the conditions of society as to make it impossible for its members to comprehend their defects. But the *laboring* classes being *compelled* to *continuous* industry by these defects, do not have the opportunity to search for the hidden causes. They see others fatten from their labor year after year, and without inquiry why these things are so, at once *jump* to the conclusion that they are the subjects of *personal* tyranny which is *determined* forever to keep them in this condition of vassalage. *This* drives the laborers to resistence; they set about forming themselves into combinations to control hours of labor and wages, not yet comprehending that these are but *remedies, not* cures. Society has tried *remedies* long enough. They require to be used continually. *Prevention* is what the people demand, and prevention they *must, will* and *shall* have. But the dose for the cure should not be administered in such large proportions as to prove *worse* than the disease. While endeavoring to *prevent* the ills of society, care must be taken that its *life* is not put in jeopardy.

The judicious architect provides the material for the new, before pulling down the old, and thus leaves no unnecessary interval for anarchy to step in and occupy. Before breaking up the *present* construction of society by *revolution*, which would end in anarchy and confusion, from which better condition might possibly spring, the better condition should be prepared and by general consent *substituted* therefor. Surely, there need be no alarm among the laboring classes. This is a republican form of government, in which *all men* at least, are equal in political power. Political power consists in a majority of votes cast. Of what have the male laboring classes to complain? They *outnumber* and can consequently *outvote* the capitalist class, *ten to one*, and *that* too without turning repeaters, though I am sorry to say the repeaters are generally laborers. Though this is lamentably true, it does not follow that all laborers are repeaters, any more than it formerly did that all Democrats were horse thieves, for insinuating which, a prominent Whig was once called to account. Said the Whig, I did *not* say that *all* Democrats were horse-thieves, but I *did* say that all horse-thieves were Democrats, and for authority I refer to the political statistics of prisons.

I ask the Labor Party of the United States of what have you to complain? I will tell you what. You have *yourselves* of whom to complain, and the *complaint* is a most *grievous* one—one which should ever stand in *condemnation* over you until you shall have *repented* in sack-cloth and ashes. You have permitted the government of this country to be *wrenched* from your grasp, and *year after year* you still permit the few who *hold* it to your detriment to continue their encroachments upon your *liberties* and *rights*. You have *made your own beds* and now you complain of others because you have not *better* ones in which to lie. Where are your friends—your leaders—who dare stand forth and tell you the *truth*? 'Tis true they make fine stump-speeches, but nothing comes of them.

The Labor Party need to *learn* some *wholesome* truths which will *teach* them *when* learned, to look for their redemption from an *entirely* different source to that they have been seeking. It will not avail you to attempt to deal with the contingencies of the present, resorting to small expedients to enable you to dodge along, merely escaping complete shipwreck, to be *again* forced, the next day week or year, to the *same*, to escape *like* shoals.

I have told you that the *foundations* upon which society is built are *imperfect*; of what use is it to continually reform the frame work, and the finish, so long as this foundation remains? Society expresses itself through government. Public opinion is capable of many things but it is *powerless* at present, to *redress* grievances, *correct* errors and *right* wrongs which come of law unless it direct that to be done by proper forms of law.

In proper legislation, then, must the preventative of existing ills be sought, and to *this* end should the Labor Party turn *all* its attention and waste *no more time* and *strength* in *vain* denunciations and foundationless recriminations. Proper *legislation* supposes proper *legistators* and these it is your duty to select and elect. Most of your present legislators State and National, have shown themselves *incompetent* to the work *you* require performed. Waste no more time upon them. *Leave* them to seek their level and *turn* you to others who will *not lose sight* of *your* *interests* and allow them to *sink* in the *allurements* which place and power present. You must not expect those who are not of you to appreciate your needs. Choose from among *yourselves* and you will not go *far* astray. There are most noble exceptions among those reared in luxury, whose hearts feel your conditions as keenly as you do. These will be your best advocates ; but *see to it* that *not a vote* is again worse than withheld.

Further, permit me to call your attention to an important fact: that quite four-fifths of your legislators are lawyers. While we must confess to entertaining the highest respect for them as lawyers, we must be permitted to question if all governmental sagacity is confined to them. They are rarely comprehensive, philosophical and progressive, but rather sticklers for the *specialties* and *forms* to which they were trained and to which, in their *practice* they confine themselves. They practice from *policy* to gain certain ends, and resort to all the quibbles possible to defeat their opponents. They do not practice *from principles* to demonstrate their justice. Consequently lawyers are *not* the best material for legislators, and *this* the Labor Party should specially remember. But I should fail in my duty as a professed friend of humanity, did I not endeavor to point out, that all the results which can be obtained through proper legislation are of but *secondary* importance, yea, of *no* importance except as *means* to be used that *greater* and *better* ends may be reached. One basal fact—one which is greater than all others within humanity— which is entirely ignored in all material practices, *must* be placed as the *foundation* of the perfect structure which you propose to erect. *That* fact is the fact of the COMMON BROTHERHOOD OF THE HUMAN RACE. If this recognition is wanting in your propositions, they had better never be made. This is the touch-stone by which all legislation, all administration and all action should be tested and directed, failing in which a fatal error is committed which will poison all action.

The first duty of every living being, in all things in which people meet and mingle, is to accept the fact that *every other* human being is the offspring of the *same* Almighty power, and *equally* entitled to human rights with himself, and that it can make *no* difference in *this* fact if his *skin* be black, if he be a *pagan* or a *Jew*, *Christian* or *infidel*, *spiritualist*, *materialist* or a *nothingarian*, or *even a woman*. In behalf of this latter class, permit me to express a growing hope for the labor party, grounded upon the fact that many of its prominent men acknowledge the equality of civil, political and social rights.

In the first instance, the question of labor and capital is one of material prosperity and equality; secondly, it reacts upon *all other* human interests—intellectual, moral, physical and religious. None of them can flourish among a people burdened by material want. Either extreme of material interest is deleterious to the *best* advancement of *all* other interests. In the *mean* between the two extremes—in calling up those below and leveling down those above—is found the *perfect* harmony of all.

Because material acquirement has *preceded* all other acquirement, the mistake is made of giving it the most *prominent* position among the several interests. This mistake is the bane of society; for it must be apparent to all *considerate* minds that *capital* being the *result* of labor, is nothing more than the *means* to *further* and *greater* ends. The attainment of great *wealth* will not be the principal aim of the people of the future. It will only be considered that by which *higher* purposes may be gained. It was not until quite recently that the fact of a continuous life was any more than *theoretically* accepted by a few people. The large majority of *all* people still accept it as a theory only. Their practices are such as would naturally obtain, were it *certain* that this life is *all there is* of existence, and that the death of the body is the end of man.

Whatever people may *profess* to believe, their *practice* shows that purely material ends are all they really seek—the gratification of physical desires, and obtaining material comforts and pleasures. A conviction—a real faith—is, however, stealing into the consciousness of humanity that what is termed *death* is only a *change* in the conditions of *life*, by which that portion of individuality which constitutes the veritable man or woman is entered upon a *broader* sphere of existence. As this faith, this knowledge, grows in the human soul, so also will there come a change in the purposes and aims of life. That wealth which will be of most use and benefit when the higher life is entered, will be sought and obtained.

Humanity, when *analytically* considered, is still in its *babyhood*. This becomes evident when we observe how *few* there are who seek the *higher* objects of attainment—intellectual, moral and spiritual wealth. These are the *only* kind of capital with which the pursuits of the future can be begun. Why, then, should humanity, in its greed for *material* wealth, lose all *sight* of, and *care* for, these. If our children are trained for the practical after life, so also should humanity adopt the philosophy of education and train for *their* after life. 'Tis true, this most important fact of life is ignored in government, and *here* is the cause of its failure to meet the requirements of humanity. People demand what they do not really comprehend, but still they know their real wants are unsupplied. Here do we also find that *no* government can be a perfect government which ignores any department of human life—which is not only physical, but mental, moral and religious.

In a *true* condition of society there would be *no such thing as individual* wealth. There would be the wealth of the *community* made use of for the *benefit* of the community. The *extreme* of individual wealth and poverty is in *direct* antagonism to a democratic government, which best expressed is: *the greatest good of the greatest number.* What is for the greatest good of the greatest number in the general sense is also for the *best* interests of every individual and of the whole number. No real benefit can flow to *any* individual by an *apparent* gain through *unjust* means.

Under a system of *exact* justice no person can ever possess what he did not himself produce, or which he did not obtain by a just exchange of something which he did produce. All great accumulations of wealth, in the *abstract* sense, were stolen from the producers. Thus *one* person may unjustly obtain what required a *thousand* persons all their lives to produce. What kind of justice is this to flourish as it does in these days when the religion of Jesus is the *external* garb worn by so great a part of humanity?

I tell you that the *first principles of life* have been *utterly* lost sight of, and that we are floundering about in the great ocean of material infidelity. If we would attain to better things we must stop short in our present course and come back to the point of departure, to wit : to the fact that we are a community of brothers and sisters, owning one Father, the Supreme Ruler of all, and build from that greatest of all human facts.

A party which would become successful and remain in power, must *plant* itself in *this* fact and never lose sight of it in its legislation. It must at all times be *firm* in the advocacy of *all* growth and reform which come from the *action* of fundamental principles. All *sectionalism*, all *favoritism*, all *specialism* must be swallowed in the greater interests of the whole. Whatever would detract from the good of the whole, no matter how much supposed *individual* or *local* benefit it promises, *must* be discountenanced.

If such a party is not shortly organized, conditions will develop which will make it a *necessity*, even *without* organization. It will arise as if by *magic* out of the exigencies of the times, and leaders will rise and come to the front as though heaven-directed, and they will be received by the people with acclamation. The trickery and fraud of elections even, may be suddenly dispensed with, and those will direct who have the inherent right to command, which will be recognized and hailed by the people, long sought and at last obtained. The whole sub. strata of society, in its social and political relations, is in ferment. The terrific strifes which *have* been and *are* being waged, lift the weight of *antecedents* and *customs* from the masses, and they begin to *rise*, demanding *such* recognition as has been and still is *denied* them. The Moses who shall divide the waters of the Red Sea that separates them from *their* Canaan will be their divinely appointed leader whom to oppose will be futile.

A *new order* of things is demanded, and a *new order* there will be, in which common honesty may be consistently sought. There are but *two* ways by which this can come. *One* through violent disruption and destruction of present systems, and temporary anarchy as the result; the other through the *scientific* organization and remodeling of society and *harmonized* conditions. The first will surely come if the people are not rapidly and properly instructed in the scientific needs of society. Nearly every result which is sought to be gained, except in government, is first tried by the tests of science. But in *this*, the most important feature of civilization, we blunder along either partially or totally blindfolded by custom or prejudice, which we so quietly and consistently lay aside in all things else.

There are a *variety of special* questions which arise from the *general* ones to which we have called attention remaining untouched, every one of which is of sufficient importance to command the earnest consideration of all people who have any comprehension of the changes which are to come to this people in the immediate future.

It may be objected to what I have said, that it contains more of destruction than of construction. This, perhaps, is true. It was not my purpose to propose forms by which better things can be had, but rather to call your attention to the principles which have been violated, the results of which are our present inequalities. I have said that these principles must be understood and given expression to through legislation that the present ills may turn to future good. Any other course than this lies through temporary anarchy, which I should regret to think a necessary cure.

In conclusion, I will but lay down a general rule, which can always be relied upon to guide the inquirer to correct conclusions, let the question be what it may, upon whatever subject. All questions which can arise are comprehended in the following:

They are questions of freedom; they are questions of equality, or they are questions of justice.

Reduced to these simple propositions, *every* person becomes a *competent* and, as nearly as may be, a *perfect* judge of all conditions to which society in its evolution is subject. They have but to ask is this compatible with freedom; is this consistent with equality, or is this just? If the mind relieve itself from the dominion of authority, custom and prejudice, it will encounter *no* difficulty in arriving at *legitimate* deductions whenever questioned.

Then let every person who would be counted among the consistent, plant himself upon the principle of human equality, and while demanding for himself all human rights, conceding to all others equal human rights. If but a nucleus of such persons is formed at first, their influence will be contagious, and will rapidly spread, until the time come when this people will have become repossessed of the rights of which they have permitted themselves to be unwarrantably robbed. Then may the ultimate of a republican form of government be attained, and its happy citizens labor together in harmony for the common advancement of humanity.

THE FOUNDATION OF THE LABOR MOVEMENT.

THE FOUNDATION OF THE LABOR MOVEMENT.

At the Labor-Reform Convention, which assembled at Worcester, September 4, 1871, Mr. Phillips presided, and presented the following resolutions, which were unanimously adopted. They are, indeed, a " full body of faith ; " and they show just where Mr. Phillips stood for the last thirteen years of his life.

PLATFORM.

We affirm, as a fundamental principle, that labor, the creator of wealth, is entitled to all it creates.

Affirming this, we avow ourselves willing to accept the final results of the operation of a principle so radical, — such as the overthrow of the whole profit-making system, the extinction of all monopolies, the abolition of privileged classes, universal education and fraternity, perfect freedom of exchange, and, best and grandest of all, the final obliteration of that foul stigma upon our so-called Christian civilization, — the poverty of the masses. Holding principles as radical as these, and having before our minds an ideal condition so noble, we are still aware that our goal cannot be reached at a single leap. We take into account the ignorance, selfishness, prejudice, corruption, and demoralization of the leaders of the people, and to a large extent, of the people themselves ; but still, we demand that some steps be taken in this direction : therefore, —

Resolved, — That we declare war with the wages system, which demoralizes alike the hirer and the hired, cheats both, and enslaves the working-man ; war with the present system of finance, which robs labor, and gorges capital, makes the rich richer, and the poor poorer, and turns a republic into an aristocracy of capital ; war with these lavish grants of the public lands to speculating companies, and whenever in power, we pledge ourselves to use every just and legal means to resume all such grants heretofore made; war with the system of enriching capitalists by the creation and increase of public interest-bearing debts. We demand that every facility, and all encouragement, shall be given by law to co-operation in all branches of industry and trade, and that the same aid be given to co-operative efforts that has heretofore been given to railroads and other enterprises. We demand a ten-hour day for factory-work, as a first step, and that eight hours be the working-day of all persons thus employed hereafter. We demand that, whenever women are employed at public expense to do the same kind and amount of work as men perform, they shall receive the same wages. We demand that all public debts be paid at once in accordance with the terms of the contract, and that no more debts be created. Viewing the contract importation of coolies as only another form of the slave-trade, we demand that all contracts made relative thereto be void in this country; and that no public ship, and no steamship which receives public subsidy, shall aid in such importation.

In presenting this platform, he enforced its far-reaching principles in a speech from which the following passages are taken : —

I regard the movement with which this convention is connected as the grandest and most comprehensive movement of the age. And I choose my epithets deliberately; for I can hardly name the idea in which humanity is interested, which I do not consider locked up in the success of this movement of the people to take possession of their own.

All over the world, in every civilized land, every man can see, no matter how thoughtless, that the great movement of the masses, in some shape or other, has begun. Humanity goes by logical steps, and centuries ago the masses claimed emancipation from actual chains. It was citizenship, nothing else. When that was gained, they claimed the ballot; and when our fathers won that, then the road was opened, the field was clear for this last movement, toward which the age cannot be said to grope, as we used to phrase it, but toward which the age lifts itself all over the world.

If there is any one feature which we can distinguish in all Christendom, under different names, — trades-unions, co-operation, Crispins, and Internationals, — under all flags, there is one great movement. It is for the people peaceably to take possession of their own. No more riots in the streets; no more disorder and revolution ; no more arming of different bands; no cannon loaded to the lips. To-day the people have chosen a wiser method, — they have got the ballot in their right hands, and they say, " We come to take possession of the governments of the earth." In the interests of peace, I welcome this movement, — the peaceable marshalling of all voters toward remodelling the industrial and political civilization of the day. I have not a word to utter, — far be it from me ! — against the grandest declaration of popular indignation which Paris wrote on the pages of history in fire and blood. I honor Paris as the vanguard of the Internationals of the world. When kings wake at night, startled and aghast, they do not dream of Germany and its orderly array or forces. Aristocracy wakes up aghast at the memory of France; and when I want to find the vanguard of the people, I look to the uneasy dreams of an aristocracy, and find what they dread most. And to-day the conspiracy of emperors is to put down — what ? Not the Czar, not the Emperor William, not the armies of United Germany ; but, when the emperors come together in the centre of Europe, what plot do they lay ? To annihilate the Internationals, and France is the soul of the Internationals. I, for one, honor Paris ; but in the name of Heaven, and with the ballot in our right hands, we shall not need to write our record in fire and blood; we write it in the orderly majorities at the ballot-box.

If any man asks me, therefore, what value I place first upon this movement, I should say it was the movement of humanity to protect itself ; and secondly, it is the insurance of peace ; and thirdly, it is a guaranty against the destruction of capital. We all know that there is no war between labor and capital; that they are partners, not enemies, and their true interests on any just basis are identical. And this movement of ballot-bearing millions is to avoid the unnecessary waste of capital.

Well, gentlemen, I say so much to justify myself in styling this the grandest and most comprehensive movement of the age.

. . . .

You do not kill a hundred millions of corporate capital, you do not destroy the virus of incorporate wealth by any one election. The capitalists of Massachusetts are neither fools nor cowards: and you will have to whip them three times, and bury them under a monument weightier than Bunker Hill, before they will believe they are whipped. Now, gentlemen, the inference from that statement is this : The first duty resting on this convention, which rises above all candidates and all platforms, is, that it should keep the Labor party religiously together.

The following address was delivered in Music Hall, Boston, October 31, 1871.

LADIES AND GENTLEMEN : We are sometimes so near an object that we cannot see it. I could place you so near the City Hall to-night that you would not know whether you were looking at a ton of granite or a wall of a large building. So it is with a fact. The men who stand the nearest to it are often the last to recognize either its breadth or its meaning. Perhaps the last men to appreciate a fact are the men nearest to whose eyes it passes ; and it is just so in government. We are hardly aware of the changes that are taking place about us ; our children will understand them distinctly.

There is a large class among our German fellow-citizens who advocate the abolition of the Presidency. The thoughtful in that class perceive, what the ordinary passer-by does not recognize, that we are daily abolishing the Presidency, and the movement of the country for fifty years has been toward the abolition of the Presidency. You see this tendency in a variety of circumstances. When we were first a nation, the greatest men among us were chosen President, and named for President ; but now we don't think of putting up a first-rate man.

There is another feature we don't see, — that the government is fast being monopolized by the House of Representatives. If we go on as we have done for half a century, there will be no government in this country except the House. Whatever defies the power of the great House will go down. Whether harmonious and beneficent results will follow our adoption of the system, depends upon whether the great mass of men and women, with universal suffrage as their sheet-anchor, can work out through these results one single tool like the House.

I have only gone into this statement to approach a second point; and that is, we stand on the moment when the people actually put their hands forth for power. We stand at an epoch when the nature of the government is undergoing a fundamental change. I have been speaking of machines, — whether we should operate through a Senate and President, or solely through a House. I have been speaking of the spindles and wheels. Below that lies the water-power. The water-power of Great Britain has been the wealth of thirty thousand land-holders, — thirty thousand land-holding families, perhaps seven hundred thousand or a million voters. With us, the water-power is to be the ballots of ten millions of adult men and women, scattered through all classes, — rich and poor, educated and ignorant, prompt and conservative, radical and timid, all modes and kinds and qualities of mind. Well, that brings me to the form which this great advance of the people takes. It is the working masses that are really about to put their hands to the work of governing.

It is no accident, no caprice of an individual, no mere shout of the political arena, that heralds to-day the great Labor movement of the United States.

But in the mean time, over the horizon, looming at first and now almost touching its meridian, comes up another power, — I mean the power of wealth, the inordinate power of capital. Our fathers, when they prevented entail, when they provided for the distribution of estates, thought they had erected a bulwark against the money power that had killed Great Britain. They forgot that money could combine; that a moneyed corporation was like the papacy, — a succession of persons with a unity of purpose ; that it never died ; that it never by natural proclivity became imbecile. The grandson of a king is necessarily one third an idiot; but the third generation of a money corporation is wiser for the experience of predecessors, and preserves the same unity of purpose.

This great money power looms over the horizon at the very moment when, to every thoughtful man, the power of the masses concentrating in the House of Representatives is to become the sole omnipotence of the State. Naturally so ominous a conjecture provokes resistance ; naturally a peril so immediate prompts the wealthy class of the community to combine for defence.

The land of England has ruled it for six hundred years. The corporations of America mean to rule it in the same way, and unless some power more radical than that of ordinary politics is found, will rule it inevitably. I confess that the only fear I have in regard to republican institutions is whether, in our day, any adequate remedy will be found for this incoming flood of the power of incorporated wealth. No statesman, no public man yet, has dared to defy it. Every man that has met it has been crushed to powder ; and the only hope of any effectual grapple with it is in rousing the actual masses, whose interests permanently lie in an opposite direction, to grapple with this great force ; for you know very well that our great cities are the radiating points from which go forth the great journalism, the culture, the education, the commercial influences, that make and shape the nation. The great cities are the arsenals of great wealth, where wealth manages every thing its own way.

Now, gentlemen, to me the Labor movement means just this : It is the last noble protest of the American people against the power of incorporated wealth, seeking

to do over again what the Whig aristocracy of Great
Britain has successfully done for two hundred years.
Thirty thousand families own Great Britain to-day ; and
if you multiply John Bright by a hundred, and double
his eloquence, it seems impossible that he should save
England from a violent convulsion in the great grapple
between such a power and the people who have determined to have their way.

Men blame us, the representatives of the workingmen of the nation, that we come into politics. The
other day it was my good fortune to meet that distinguished Frenchman, Monsieur Coquerel ; and he asked
me what was the motto of the working-men of the
United States. I said to him, " Short hours, better
education, co-operation in the end, and in the mean
time a political movement that will concentrate the
thought of the country upon this thing."

Now, here I take issue with the best critic which
the Labor movement has met : I refer to Rev. Samuel
Johnson of Salem, one of the thinkers who has spread
out before the people his objections to the Labor movement of this country. His first objection is, that we
will hurry into politics. Well, now, our answer to him,
and to the score of other scholars who have been criticising us, is this : Gentlemen, we see the benefit of going
into politics. If we had not rushed into politics, had
not taken Massachusetts by the four corners and shaken
her, you never would have written your criticisms. We
rush into politics because politics is the safety-valve.
We could discuss as well as you, if you would only give
us bread and houses, fair pay and leisure, and opportunities to travel. We could sit and discuss the question
for the next fifty years. It 's a very easy thing to discuss, for a gentleman in his study, with no anxiety
about to-morrow. Why, the ladies and gentlemen of

the reign of Louis XV. and Louis XVI., in France, seated in gilded saloons and on Persian carpets, surrounded with luxury, with the products of India, and the curious manufactures of ingenious Lyons and Rheims, discussed the rights of man, and balanced them in dainty phrases, and expressed them in such quaint generalizations that Jefferson borrowed the Declaration of Independence from their hands. There they sat, balancing and discussing sweetly, making out new theories, and daily erecting a splendid architecture of debate, till the angry crowd broke open the doors, and ended the discussion in blood. They waited too long, discussed about half a century too long. You see, discussion is very good when a man has bread to eat, and his children all portioned off, and his daughters married, and his house furnished and paid for, and his will made; but discussion is very bad when —

> " Ye hear the children weeping, O my brothers!
> Ere the sorrow comes with years ; "

discussion is bad when a class bends under actual oppression. We want immediate action.

We would fain save this issue from an outbreak of actual violence. Therefore we go into politics.

Well, then. our critic goes on to say, " What do you call yourselves Labor party for ? All men labor. Rufus Choate labors. Daniel Webster labors. Why do you confine your party to the men that work ? " Well, now, we confine it because thus there is no mistake. Now, suppose you should take up a book presenting the condition of the laboring classes of Great Britain. Mr. Gladstone works harder than any other man there ; Lord Brougham did more work than any other man there ; Lord Palmerston, up to his eightieth year, worked hard as any man there. But if you were to take up a book on the working-men of Great Britain, do you think you would find the condition of Lord Brougham there? If you took up a book on the British laboring class, or how much they eat, what kind of houses they live in, etc., do you think you would find Gladstone's income, and the number of rooms he had in his house, and how many children he had had the last fifty years? So if an Englishman came here, and said, " I want to know something about your working-men. Please let me hear it from some of themselves. Whom shall I go to?" Would you send him to Daniel Webster or Rufus Choate? But Daniel Webster did as much work as any man of his day. Would you have him sent to Rufus Choate? But Rufus Choate was a hard-working men. John Marshall and Lemuel Shaw did as much work as any men in Massachusetts or Virginia; but if George Combe had come to this country, and said, " I want to see a specimen of the laboring class of the United States," I doubt whether any man would have sent him to Lemuel Shaw. I ask the critics of the Labor movement, whether any man ever misunderstood this? Every man who reads of the Labor Question knows that it means the movement of the men that earn their living with their hands; that are employed, and paid in wages; are gathered under roofs of factories; sent out on farms; sent out on ships; gathered on the walls. In popular acceptation, the working class means the men that work with their hands, for wages, so many hours a day, employed by great capitalists; that work for everybody else.

Why do we move for this class? " Why," says Mr. Johnson, " don't you move for all working-men?" Because, while Daniel Webster gets forty thousand dollars for arguing the Mexican claims, there is no need of anybody's moving for him. While Rufus Choate gets five thousand dollars for making one argument to a jury, there is no need of moving for him, or for the men that work with their brains, — that do highly disciplined and skilled labor, invent, and write books. The reason why the Labor movement confines itself to a single class is because that class of work does not get paid, does not get protection. Mental labor is adequately paid, and more than adequately protected. It can shift its channels; it can vary according to the supply and demand. If a man fails as a minister, why, he becomes a railway-conductor. If that does n't suit him, he turns out, and becomes the agent of an insurance office. If that does n't suit, he goes West, and becomes governor of a Territory. And if he finds himself incapable of either of these positions, he comes home, and gets to be a city editor. He varies his occupation as he pleases, and does n't need protection. But the great mass, chained to a trade, doomed to be ground up in the mill of supply and demand, that work so many hours a day, and must run in the great ruts of business, — they are the men whose inadequate protection, whose unfair share of the general product claims a movement in their behalf.

Well, the third charge brought by Mr. Johnson against us is, that we are cruel, — we combine; we prevent this man from laboring there, and we won't let that man learn our trade; we form trades-unions. To be sure we do. We say to the Chinese, "Stay at home. Don't come here by importation; come by immigration." We say to the crowding millions who try to swamp our trade, "Stand aloof; we won't teach you." We say to the mills of Lowell, who have turned us out of doors, "We 'll starve you into submission." Well, " it 's a narrow contest. It 's an unjust, it 's a cruel, it 's an avaricious method." So it is. Where did we learn it? Learned it of capital, learned it of our enemies.

11

I know labor is narrow; I know she is aggressive; I know she arms herself with the best weapon that a corrupt civilization furnishes, — all true. Where do we get these ideas? Borrowed them from capital, every one of them; and when you advance to us on the level of peace, unarmed, we 'll meet you on the same. While you combine and plot and defend, so will we.

But Mr. Johnson says, " Come into the world with the white banner of peace." Ay, we will, when you disarm. How foolish it would have been for Grant to send home his Sharp's rifles to Springfield, and garner all his cannon in New York, and put all his monitors in the harbor of Norfolk, and go down to Virginia with eighty thousand unarmed men, to look her in the face! Labor comes up, and says, " They have shotted their cannon to the lips; they have rough-ground their swords as in battle; they have adopted every new method; they have invented every dangerous machine, — and it is all planted like a great park of artillery against us. They have incorporated wealth; they have hidden behind banks; they have concealed themselves in currency; they have sheltered themselves in taxation; they have passed rules to govern us, — and we will improve upon the lesson they have taught us. When they disarm, we will — not before."

Well, then, the fourth charge is found in the *Daily Advertiser.* We had a meeting at Framingham, and passed a set of resolutions; we adopted a platform; and the next day the *Daily Advertiser* granted us the condescension of an article, criticising our action, especially mine; and they described what we had adopted. They painted its horrible tendency. They said, " If you adopt that principle, it will lead you to that (and so on to that) till the final result will be — " I held my breath. I said to myself, " What will it probably be? Perhaps the stereotyped ghost of the French Revolution; that's what's coming." " The final result will be — " Horrible! I thought probably they would paint a millionnaire hanging on every lamp-post. " The final result — " Perhaps it will be Mormonism; society dissolved into its original elements. Horrible! I began to feel a faint sensation; but I concluded to read on: " The final result will be an equalization of property." Horrible, horrible! Actually, men will be almost equal! An equalization of property! Any man that does that ought to be hanged. Well, we do mean it; we do mean just that. That's the meaning of the Labor movement, — an equalization of property. The *Advertiser* has found us out, actually discovered our plot. He's let the cat out of the bag. We did n't mean to have told you, but it is so. What we need is an equalization of property, — nothing else. My ideal of a civilization is a very high one; but the approach to it is a New England town of some two thousand inhabitants, with no rich man and no poor man in it, all mingling in the same society, every child at the same school, no poorhouse, no beggar, opportunities equal, nobody too proud to stand aloof, nobody too humble to be shut out. That's New England as it was fifty years ago, the horrible creature that the *Daily Advertiser* fears. That's what Framingham proposes to bring about. But why is n't Framingham contented? Because the civilization that lingers beautifully on the hillsides of New England, nestles sweetly in the valleys of Vermont, the moment it approaches a crowd like Boston, or a million of men gathered in one place like New York, — rots. It cannot force the crowd; it cannot stand the great centres of modern civilization.

Our civilization cannot stand the city. One reason is, it has got some hidden disease. Another reason is, the moment it flows out into the broad, deep activity of the nineteenth century, it betrays its weakness, and copies Europe. The moment this sweet-scented, dew-smelling Vermont flows down into the slums of New York, it becomes like London. The moment the North gathers its forces, and goes down the Mississippi Valley into New Orleans, social science stands aghast. Modern civilization shrinks back at the terrible evil which she can neither fathom nor cure, just as she does in Europe.

What is our cause ? It is this: there are three hundred and fifty millions of human beings in what you call Christendom, and two hundred millions of them don't have enough to eat from January to December. I won't ask for culture, for opportunities for education, for travel, for society; but two hundred millions of men gathered under Christendom don't have even enough to eat. A hundred thousand men in the city of New York live in dwellings that a rich man would n't let his horse stay in a day.

But that is n't anything. You should go up to beautiful Berkshire with me, into the factories there. It shall be the day after a Presidential election. I will go with you into a counting-room, — four hundred employees. The partners are sitting down, the day after a Presidential election. They take the list of workmen, and sift them out; and every man that has not voted the ticket they wanted is thrown out to starve just as if he were cattle. That's Christian civilization ! that's Massachusetts ! I don't like that significant fact. I leap from that town into a large mill, with five hundred employees, and say to the master, " How about the dwellings of your operatives ? How many hours do they have at home ? " " Well, I hope they don't have any. The best-ventilated place they are ever in is my mill. They had better stay here sixteen hours out of the twenty-four; it keeps them out of mischief better than any other place. As long as they work, they are not doing worse. I cannot attend to their houses." I say to him, " It seems to me you do the same for your ox." That's another significant fact of our civilization. I go to Lowell, and I say to a young girl, wandering in the streets, " How is this ?" " Well, I worked here seven years, and I thought I would leave that mill and go to another; and the corporation won't give me my ticket. I have sued them in the Supreme Court, and I cannot get it; and here I am, penniless, in Eastern Massachusetts." That's Christian civilization. I am picking up, not individual facts, but significant rules, that were made for labor.

You say, " What does labor need in New England ? " It needs justice. Mr. Stewart, in New York, has bought a whole town; and he is going to build model houses, and house there all the labor he can get to go into them. Yet the civilization which alone can look the New Testament in the face is a civilization where one man does not depend on the pity of another man's building him a model lodging-house; the civilization which alone can look the New Testament in the face is a civilization where one man could not build, and another man would not need, that sort of refuge.

No, gentlemen, what we mean is this: The labor of yesterday, your capital, is protected sacredly. Not so the labor of to-day. The labor of yesterday gets twice the protection and twice the pay that the labor of to-day gets. Capital gets twice the protection and twice the pay.

Now, we mean a radical change, and in the few minutes that are left me, I want to indicate our object.

We mean certain great radical changes. I am not quite of the opinion of Mr. Secretary Boutwell, when he said here the other night, that fifty years hence the idea that a man could own land, and leave it to his children, would be ridiculous. I have not quite come to that. But then, you know there is a reason for it; he is a radical, and I have always been a conservative. There is a curious thing underlies lands. We are not quite certain that we have got the best system. Secretary Boutwell may be right. Seventy years ago a man offered to a relative of mine all the land between Federal Street and Hawley Street, between Milk Street and Franklin, for thirty-three hundred dollars. He came to him day after day, urging him to purchase; and the answer was, "I am not rich enough to have a cow-pasture at that price, and I could n't use it for anything else," — that tract of land which to-day, gentlemen, as you know, would sell for three million dollars. Now, labor goes about, like Socrates, asking questions. We don't assume anything. When we were little boys, and did our sums on the slate, and the answer came out wrong, we did n't break the slate. We went to the master; and he said, "Go back; there's a mistake somewhere; if you examine, you will find it." I come into a civilization in which two men out of three don't have enough to eat. I come into New York, where it is a rich man that supplies a lodging for houseless poverty. I say to myself, "That course is n't right; there's a mistake somewhere." Do unto others as you would have others do unto you. The end of things is New York. That does n't cohere. Where is the mistake? It is somewhere, and the Labor movement is trying to find it out.

Again, gentlemen, we have another doubt to express. Are you quite certain that capital — the child of artificial laws, the product of society, the mere growth of social life — has a right to only an equal burden with labor, the living spring? We doubt it so much that we think we have invented a way to defeat Tom Scott, of the Pennsylvania Central.   We think we have devised a little plan — Abraham Lincoln used to have a little story — by which we will save the Congress of the Nation from the moneyed corporations of the State.   When we get into power, there is one thing we mean to do. If a man owns a single house, we will tax him one hundred dollars.   If he owns ten houses of like value, we won't tax him one thousand dollars, but two thousand dollars.   If he owns a hundred houses, we won't tax him ten thousand dollars, but sixty thousand dollars; and the richer a man grows, the bigger his tax, so that when he is worth forty million dollars he will not have more than twenty thousand dollars a year to live on. We'll double and treble and quintuple and sextuple and increase tenfold the taxes, till Stewart, out of his uncounted millions, and the Pennsylvania Central, out of its measureless income, shall not have anything more than a moderate lodging and an honest table.   The corporations we would have are those of associated labor and capital, — co-operation.

We'll crumble up wealth by making it unprofitable to be rich.   The poor man shall have a larger income in proportion as he is poor.   The rich man shall have a lesser income in proportion as he is rich.   You will say, "Is that just?"   My friends, it is safe.   Man is more valuable than money.   You say, "Then capital will go to Europe."   Good heavens, let it go!

If other States wish to make themselves vassals to wealth, so will not we.   We will save a country equal from end to end.   Land, private property, all sorts of property, shall be so dearly taxed that it shall be impossible to be rich; for it is in wealth, in incorporated, combining, perpetuated wealth, that the danger of labor lies.

POVERTY:

BY IRA STEWARD.

'Barely they rise by Virtue's aid, who lie
Plunge in the depth of helpless poverty."—JUVENAL.

There is no Wealth but Life."—RUSKIN.

PUBLISHED BY
THE BOSTON EIGHT HOUR LEAGUE,
14 BROMFIELD STREET, BOSTON.
1873.

PREFACE.

THE following pages upon Poverty were published originally in the Fourth Report of the Massachusetts Bureau of Statistics of Labor. They are the beginning, merely, of a statement of the Labor question. If this statement is ever completed, it will establish the relation between less Hours for Labor, and *less Poverty;* and this is the great idea of the Eight Hour movement: less Poverty, or more wealth for the masses. People who have *time,* are more *deliberate* in their movements, than they can be without the proper amount of time. Deliberation tends to thought. Thoughtful people grow wiser, and wise people soon learn what belongs to them and how to get it. This does not mean, however, that Eight Hours is a panacea, or "a cure-all." It is simply an indispensable *first step,* like emancipation for the slave. To give slaves freedom, does not suppose that they will immediately become wise and happy ; but to deprive them of freedom, means a perpetual hinderance to wisdom and happiness. If the hours of labor are *not* reduced, laborers will never be able to consider the many measures necessary to wholly emancipate them from the slavery and ignorance and vices of Poverty.

POVERTY.

POVERTY is the great fact with which the Labor movement deals. The problems that now most disturb and perplex mankind will be solved when the masses are no longer poor.

Poverty makes the poor poorer, and independence impossible. It corrupts judges, ministers, legislators, and statesmen. It decides marriages, shortens human life, hinders education, and embarrasses progress in every direction. It gives rise, directly and indirectly, to more anxiety, suffering, and crime, than all other causes combined. Poverty crams cities, and their tenement-houses, with people whose conduct and votes endanger the republic. The "dangerous classes" are always *poor*.

There is a closer relation between poverty and slavery, than the average abolitionist ever recognized. Whether a man should own himself, or whether he should own enough else to supply his natural wants, are both questions concerning his natural and inalienable rights. The great motive for making a man a slave, was to get his labor, or its results, for nothing; and the abolition of slavery did not abolish this disposition. The motive for employing wage-labor, is to secure *some* of its results for nothing; and, in point of fact, larger fortunes are made out of the profits of wage-labor, than out of the products of slavery.

Poverty originated slavery; for in the older times, as the only and last refuge from utter destitution, men sold themselves into bondage. But poor people now accept the position of public paupers. The pauper's body cannot be sold, but how much is a human being worth to himself, or to society, who can call nothing his own but his body? Under certain circumstances, extreme poverty has resulted in death; and under the vilest system of bondage ever known, the slaveholder could do nothing worse than to kill his slave.

All the distinction it is possible to make between poverty and chattel slavery, is the difference between a natural right, and a natural necessity. We call liberty a natural right; and food and shelter, that we may not starve or perish, natural necessities; but whether a natural right is more or less sacred than a natural necessity, is a question that decides, when answered, how close the relation is between slavery and poverty.

The anti-slavery *idea*, was, that every man had the right to go and come at will. The Labor movement asks how much this abstract right is actually worth, without the power to exercise it.

An abstract right, admitted, is correct in theory, but the masses are not theorists; and so many theories fail, finally, that most people dispute or distrust them until they are reduced to practice. Those who write books may be able to tell precisely how much was done for the average laborer, when, for example, his right to go across the continent was finally conceded by emancipation; but the laborer himself will never give a satisfactory account of this "right," until he actually goes across the continent, obtains larger views, sees home with its many local and narrow considerations, from abroad, and, as it were, takes a new parallax of life.

The laborer instinctively feels that something of slavery still remains, or that something of freedom is yet to come, and he is not much interested in the anti-slavery theory of liberty. He wants a fact, which the Labor movement undertakes to supply.

The poverty of the middle classes, however, should excite the most anxiety, and the most searching inquiry. They are a large majority of the people, and their poverty is generally carefully concealed. All who have barely enough to keep up appearances, are just the ones to cover up the fact that they have nothing more. They are ranked among the middle classes; and their power to cover up their poverty, is made to argue that they are not poor.

The middle classes have the strongest motives for never making any parade or public complaint of their poverty. To advertise one's self destitute, is to be without credit, that tides so many in safety — to their standing in society — over the shallow places where ready resources fail. To be without credit and without resources, is to be dependent upon charity whenever employment fails, or sickness prevents employment, and to depend upon charity is an advertisement of one's destitution and poverty that the public is very slow to forget.

> "Dimes and dollars, dollars and dimes,
> An empty pocket's the worst of crimes."

To betray or confess the secrets of one's destitution, is also regarded, in some measure, as a sign of incapacity; for, as the world goes, the poor man is an unsuccessful man; unless, like Professor Agassiz, or William Lloyd Garrison, whose reputations are otherwise assured, he cannot afford to "stop to make money."

The poverty that publishes or argues one's incapacity, closes many a door to more profitable or advantageous situations or promotions.. The more expensive and superior style of living adopted by the middle classes, must therefore be considered in the light of an *investment*, made from the soundest considerations of expediency, — considering their risks and their chances, — and from motives even of self-preservation, rather than from the mere desire for self-indulgence, or because the middle classes are not poor. Very few among them are saving money. Many of them are in debt; and all they can earn for years, is, in many cases, mortgaged to pay such debt,— "debt that increases the load of the future, with the burden which the present cannot bear."

In the faces of thousands of well-dressed, intelligent, and well-appearing people, may be seen the unmistakable signs of their incessant anxiety and struggles to get on in life, and to obtain, in addition to a mere subsistence, a standing in

society. *If men have nothing but a bare living, they are in
a condition to believe, at any critical moment, that they have
something to gain from public disorder.*

The cheaper style of living of the pauperized class, does
not cost them as much as it costs to satisfy the pride, ambition, and changing fashions of the middle classes. But the
difference will be more than paid for by the taxable public,
in police, prisons, courts, and asylums. The dress and habits
of living of the lower classes are not cheap, in the broad and
comprehensive meaning of that word.

The cheapest fact of modern times is a *dear* man ; and the
dearest fact of our day is a *cheap* man ; and, within certain
limits, increasing the value of men will make them still
cheaper, while reducing their cost will make them dearer to
the public, through the terrible equivalents resulting from
their extreme poverty. "The dirt of the poor man's hovel
is the miasma of the rich man's parlor."

The poverty of the great middle classes consists in the
fact that they have only barely enough to cover up their poverty, and that they are within a very few days of want, if
through sickness, or other misfortunes, employment suddenly stops.

No one can describe the secret feeling of insecurity that
constantly prevails among them concerning their living, and
how it will be with them in the future ; and while actual
hunger and want may never be known, their poverty is felt,
mentally and socially, through their sense of dependence and
pride. They must work constantly, and with an angry sense
of the limited opportunities for a career at their command.

To travel, or change their situation or employment, from
considerations of health or independence, costs more than
they can afford ; and so they work on, silent and dissatisfied,
and for the most part hopeless, which is the most fatal fact
in connection with their poverty.

The story of many a self-made man's personal success,
derives all its interest and glory from the mere fact that it
was an escape from poverty ; that by pure force of character,
he has lifted himself up to the level where he no longer depends upon the goodwill of another for a chance to earn a liv-

ing. The compliments paid to self-made men, are not usually given with the avowed purpose of reflecting upon poverty, as a thing that ought not to be ; on the contrary, it receives a good word occasionally, in a patronizing way, from the wealthy, or from those who write in their behalf.

Admitting that it is a great hinderance, they claim that it acts as a stimulus in urging men to self-elevation, and is a great help to self-made men.

All that is properly meant by this, is that poverty supplies a strong motive for exertion and industry ; and it is true that it is better for a man to be so poor that he must do something, than to be so rich that he need do nothing ; that the exertion which poverty makes necessary, is better than the idleness which wealth makes possible.

But this is only another way of saying that poverty is better than something worse. To this sophism we reply, it is worse than something better ; and that it is better to have enough, than to have too little or too much.

To say that men succeed because they are poor, rather than in *spite* of their poverty, is as if we should say that a skilful mechanic has done perfect work because his tools are poor. Tolerably good work has been done, in spite of poor tools ; and poor workmen have failed, and will again fail, with the very best of tools ; but, as a rule, the most perfect causes or circumstances are necessary, to produce the most perfect results. Those who have succeeded in spite of poverty, might have done still better had they not had the hinderances of poverty to overcome.

But the most alarming fact concerning the poverty of the *native* middle classes in this Commonwealth, is, that for two or three decades past, marriages and births have so far decreased among them, that we are nearly or quite justified in saying that they are now dying faster than their children are being born ; and that it is to foreign sources (and to American born in other States), and to the lower class of native born, we must credit the present increase in our census returns. That the deaths exceed in number the births, among hose born and reared in Massachusetts, who belong to the middle classes, and who live in our large cities and towns, there can be no possible doubt.

The struggle of the more intelligent and ambitious to avoid poverty and its humiliating straits, is perfectly natural and honorable ; and one of the readiest ways is to marry late, or not at all. They have not indeed all studied Malthus and his theories, but have observed enough to learn that all the little mouths are not properly fed ; to say nothing of the more advanced considerations involved in the proper train-ing of offspring, and of a parent's pride in the rearing of a large family of well-behaved children. With the mass of intelligent people, early or late marriages, and few or no children, is largely a question of poverty and wealth.

That the sons and daughters of our New-England farmers are unwilling to stay at home, and follow the fortunes of their fathers and mothers ; that the farms are gradually passing out of the possession of those who have been the very hope and strength of New England, whose early schooling and sober training have given such character and stability to our self-managed institutions ; that the farms are being more rapidly sold than the public observes, to those whose habits of thought and living are foreign to our country, and to our most cherished ideas, — these lamentable results are due to the fact, most hateful to the middle classes, that the low pay and scant opportunities of a New-England farm, mean — poverty.

Poverty, however, falls the most crushingly on woman. In all countries and in all ages, among the middle and lower classes, she has worked harder, and for less pay, than men. A woman who has no resources for a living except from the labor.of her own hands, is tolerably sure in time, to become, either the poor man's slave or the rich man's plaything, — to marry for a home, or to do worse. To make prostitution unnecessary, is a part of the problem of social science ; but prostitution means getting a living. The science that will solve this problem, will easily dispose of war, intemperance, financial convulsions, and a dozen other evils that now dis-turb the peace of the race. Poverty is the mainspring of selfishness, for it is the destitution of the mass of mankind that prevents them from thinking and doing for others. As Mill says, " all their thoughts are required for themselves." It may be urged, however, that poor people are no more selfish than the wealthy ; in many cases this is true, and those who say it mean, that if it is poverty that causes selfishness, wealth, of course, ought to make people unselfish. But it is not true that the mere possession of wealth will make men unselfish, — no more than that mere knowledge, of itself, will ensure virtue, or wisdom, or happiness. How wealth is obtained, decides the selfishness or unselfishness of its owners. When none can secure wealth except by their own personal industry ; when all are intelligent enough to hold on to the profits and results of their own labor ; when (in other words) great wealth is no longer the *result* of more superior, intelligent, and successful selfishness, — its possession will mean a fair opportunity to think and do for those who, through no fault of their own, cannot manage for themselves.

The two classes most peculiarly open to the temptation of intemperance, are the very poor and the very rich young men ; and here I must follow briefly, at the risk of repetition, the exact line of thought first presented in print, in the Second Labor Report (1871), upon this subject (see p. 538). Those who through their poverty have little more than a place in which to sleep, eat, and work, and those, on the other hand, whose surplus wealth places them where they have nothing to do, cannot be observed too carefully ; for these are the circumstances that explain the secret beginnings of many a man's vices.

The steps of some young men turn finally to the light, warm, welcome saloon, not from force of appetite, for they have never yet drank enough to create the craving for stimulating beverages ; nor because it is fashionable, for their wages are not sufficient to lift them up to that level ; but because they are without homes, and are starving for society.

The sons of the wealthy have homes, and all that money can bring for their entertainment. But in many cases they have nothing whatever to do. They are corrupted by idleness ; and it is their extreme wealth that makes their hours of idleness possible. Who shall describe the sense of utter worthlessness that comes over a man from a simple waste of time, and because of precious faculties rusting from disuse! He lies down at night, tired though never having known the refreshing fatigue of honest work! All about him useful, and happy in their usefulness, — the very children glad to leave their sports if they can "help." The most terrible of all stagnations is idleness. It means moral and social rottenness; and intemperance is only a single manifestation of it A state of society which furnishes every year an increasing number of young men who have nothing whatever to do, — no idea, or hobby even, to pursue, — has created a force for profligacy that is sure to manifest itself in one or another form of dissipation. If by any miracle in legislation or in nature, the knowledge of distilling intoxicating beverages were to become one of the lost arts, and this form of vice was thereafter impossible, simply because men did not know how to distil, the infernal seed would spring up in other forms, claiming for its victims the same class who now fall victims to the dram-shop.

To banish the dram-shop, is one thing. To break the chain of circumstances that first turns men's faces towards any form of dissipation, is quite another thing. The presence of the wealthy at the enticing saloon, does much to make the business fashionable and reputable, and to keep in countenance the more humble resorts visited by the poor and homeless. The civilization, if not the temperance philosophy, of the future, will yet revolt at the idea of forcing out of society — through a poverty of culture, or a poverty of purse — any human soul, into temptations that lead down to the "first glass," and so on to the inebriate's untimely grave.

No one is fully educated, until the discipline of hard labor has been added to the culture of books, travel, and good society. And on the other hand, no one is educated who has had no chance to learn anything but to work hard and steadily, and to "know his place." Meantime, the poverty question appears in the reasons that impel a man to sell rum. It is his way of getting a living. He is asked to abandon his business, and earn his bread in some other way. But how easy, or how common is it, for men to change their occupations, and succeed!

Let those cast the first stone, whose honest convictions on any important question have never been smothered that their business might prosper, or who have never compromised, by silent or spoken falsehood, with crimes for any price. The policeman will not interfere, beyond a certain well-defined limit, with the dram-shop nuisance, because, if he did so, his situation would be endangered. The neutrality of the trading classes concerning the rum-drinking evil, is purchased through the difficulty involved in "getting a living"; and those who own the buildings, that make the traffic possible, are governed by the same considerations.

The "law of supply and demand," so often quoted as regulating wages and prices, means nothing more nor less than the great fact of the poverty of the poor, and the power and comparative independence of the wealthy. Whenever the supply of work fails, the masses are compelled, by the fact of their poverty, to demand labor immediately at any price. Starving men will always bid for wages at starvation prices. On the other hand, when trade is active, and there is a great demand for workmen, enough of the pauperized labor of Europe and Asia is at once imported, by wealthy employers, to keep wages down, — in other words, to manage or "regulate the law of supply," in the interest of capital. If there were no people on the earth poor enough to be imported, or none rich enough to import them, the operation of this law would be absolutely independent of wealth or poverty. As it is, however, wealth is the master and poverty is the slave of "the great law of supply and demand," and instead of saying that that law regulates wages, it will be more intelligible and more easily comprehended, to say that wages are regulated or ruled by the great fact of the wealth of the wealthy, and the poverty of the poor. "The rich man's wealth is his strong city; the destruction of the poor is their poverty." The law of supply and demand is said to regulate the price of commodities; but the "demand" is limited by the great fact of the poverty of the mass of consumers. There never was a market so overstocked with goods that it would have taken a day to empty it, if all the people had been able to pay for all they ought to have.

"A glut in the market" has never yet meant anything more, than that millions of people are too poor to pay for the food, clothes, houses, books, and opportunities that are waiting for customers. The demand for productions regulates the supply, but poverty regulates, or rather obstructs, the demand. In the last analysis, it is largely a question of poverty.

It is poverty that compels one man to borrow of another, and the price paid for the use of the money loaned, is what we call interest,— so that interest on money means poverty again.

The theory that justifies interest, is, that it is perfectly fair and proper for one whose bad habit of spending all or more than he earns, has forced him to borrow, to pay something for the use of the money loaned. The difficulty with this theory is, that little or no money is ever loaned under these circumstances; as those who are prudent and saving, are seldom imprudent enough to lend money to a spendthrift; and only the merest fraction of all the capital on interest, is the result of the personal earnings and savings of the lenders. It is the enormous profits made directly upon the labor of the wage-classes, and indirectly through the results of their labor, that, 1st, keeps them poor; and, 2d, furnishes the capital that is finally loaned back to them again. The theory upon which the capitalist, trading, and employing classes justify their enormous profits or compensation is, that intellectual, or brain work, is worth very much more than mere muscular or physical work; that the value of every worker may be increased to an indefinite extent by the organizing and inventive genius of a few leading minds; and that to thinking brains far more than to unthinking hands, is due the present rapid production of the world's wealth. Of course the productiveness and value of human labor depends, very largely, upon the intelligence with which it is directed; for ignorance is constantly attempting natural impossibilities, where knowledge would save the precious time of millions of workers wasted in such experiments ; and but for the modern organization and efficiency of the world's industry, mankind would still toil on as their fathers and their grandfathers did before them, in comparative poverty and want. The only reason the so-called brain-workers can ever give in behalf of extraordinary compensation, that can have any force whatever with the masses, is, the admitted fact that the present rapid increase in the world's wealth is largely due to the creative and organizing genius of a few leading minds ; for to increase the facilities for producing wealth, is to diminish the necessity that poverty should exist. Wealth is a blessing ; poverty is a curse. They are exact opposites. If brains are worth more than hands, it is because they mean more wealth or less poverty ! The claim for large compensation made by the professional classes is often based on the expense, time, study, and preliminary training necessary to the commencement of their work or practice, while the skilled mechanic gives substantially the same reason for claiming higher wages than are paid to a common laborer, who has spent no time in serving an apprenticeship. But these reasons do not cover the cases here contemplated. To say that the enormous compensation claimed by Peabody, Astor, Vanderbilt, Belmont, Stewart, or the Rothschilds, for their share of the world's work, is to make up for time and money lost in preparing for a profession or a trade, is of course absurd.

They were born with great natural money-gathering gifts, that never cost them anything, and it is a very grave question whether such gifts ought to be set up for sale. The gifts that friends receive from friends, are usually considered too sacred to be sold. Are the gifts of God less sacred?

The mere possession of extraordinary natural powers is a great compensation of itself. They are worth more than men know how to estimate in silver or gold ; and in the grander civilization yet to dawn upon us, the mere deference that the wisest will receive from the mass of mankind for the value of their opinions and counsel, will be more coveted than cities of wealth or mines of gold. However, we deal now with the only theory that can be urged in behalf of the enormous royalties or compensation secured by a few

men; and, strange as it may seem, when fully comprehended, the theory amounts to this, that the great managers of the world's industry should be rewarded with
extreme wealth to pay them for saving mankind from extreme poverty! No other reason can be given for paying
thinkers more than workers, than that their peculiar work
is worth more. But if it is worth more, it is because more
values are produced by it; and more production means, or
ought to mean, to somebody, — less poverty! Those who
have been saved from poverty, may be willing to concede
this price; but what of those who are still poor? The
enormous price charged, meantime, implies enough to establish all that we claim concerning the great curse of poverty.

It is clear that the large fortunes accumulated by the
wealthy can only be defended upon the theory that their
services are actually worth the compensation they receive.
" Are their services worth the price charged? " is, therefore,
the coming question.

Who can tell how much anything is actually worth? Upon
what principle is it decided that a rare order of intellectual
services of certain men are of more value, for instance, than
the united earnings of a thousand average laborers? That
the skilful organization of the mass of workers increases to
an incalculable extent their power to produce, is of course
admitted; but who knows, or can estimate, the relative value
of the services of these two parties, — the thinkers and the
workers? If it is fair to ask hands how much they could do
without brains, it is just as fair to ask brains how long they
could live without hands.

The alternative presented to mankind in case the services
of the managers are withdrawn, is, a reduced rate of production, which means poverty! But, on the other hand, the
alternative presented to those who manage labor, in case the
so-called brainless workers were withdrawn, is death, or
hard work with their own hands; for fields were never tilled,
nor houses reared, nor garments made, nor food cooked,
without manual labor. If Robinson Crusoe had had an
opportunity to profit by the labor and earnings of a hundred
thousand Fridays, he might have been wealthy, and have

called his fortunes his fair share of the work on his island. As it was, he did exactly what the Rothschilds would have done if placed in the same situation, — he worked with his own hands. The relation between those who plan and those whose hands perform the world's work, represents a simple " division of labor," in which each specialist is absolutely indispensable to the other. The army would be defeated without its officers, and the officers would never prevail without the men. We deny, therefore, the proposition that those who plan really earn millions of dollars more than those who execute ; that the labor of the brain should be paid so much more than the labor of the hands. In this theory, however, there are two propositions involved ; but thus far, for the sake of keeping each issue distinct and clear by itself, we have discussed only one of them. The first claim is, that brains are worth more than hands ; and upon this claim is based a second, — that the wealthy have the most brains ! The first claim is a matter of theory ; the second is a question of fact. We deny the extraordinary value placed on the services of the intellectual classes, and claim as a matter of fact that they are *not* the best rewarded. Those who are supposed to have worked their own way, unaided, from nothing, up to millions, are usually industrious, economical, and shrewd ; and these are the qualities that laid the foundations of their ultimate success. But they frequently confess that it was harder and took more time to obtain the first five hundred dollars, than the next five or ten thousand. This confession means, that their first money was actually earned by their own hands and brains. After a time, however, their wealth began to increase faster ; not because they were any more industrious, saving, or intelligent, but because the little capital already accumulated enabled them to profit by the labor of other hands and brains. Of course, such men learn fast, but they acquire faster than they learn. At fifty years of age, they may not be as capable of hard work and thought as at forty ; while their personal expenses are far beyond anything dreamed of in their early years ; yet their accumulations are swifter than ever, and their annual incomes may finally be reckoned by the hundred thousand

or the million. Brains do not explain why it should be so
hard to earn at first, or why it should be so easy to accumulate at last. But the two facts explain each other. The
first earnings were hard and slow, because some one else was
profiting by his labor. He was earning not only for himself,
but for somebody else besides. His last accumulations were
swift and easy, because he had changed places, and was now
making a profit by the labor of a large number of other
workers.

When no man can profit by the labor of another, all first
earnings of all workers will be more easily obtained, while
the enormous accumulations of later years will be impossible.
It is the poverty and destitution of the masses that make the
surplus capital of the capitalist profitable and desirable. By
the words " surplus capital," we mean all the wealth for
which the owner has no personal use ; whether for consumption, or for purposes of reproduction. The wealth
invested in a house to live in, clothes to wear, food to eat,
a library to read, a horse to drive, or in tools, in a farm, in a
profession or trade for the means to earn a living, — to earn
amusement, travel, education, leisure, and repose, — is not
" surplus " capital. Anything and everything that can add
to the convenience, beauty, and attraction of house and home,
is not surplus wealth. The best skill, taste, experience, and
science available should dictate its location, construction, and
appointments, from the pictures upon its walls, the statuary
in its spacious halls, the flower gardens and fountain for
summer, to the heat and ventilation for winter. A second
house by the seaside or in the country, for summer resort
and a change, is proper, if not absolutely necessary. Nothing that can minister to the comfort, health, education, or
happiness of a family, is too costly ; and none of these things
are contemplated in the words " surplus wealth." They add
to the knowledge and power of those who own them, without profiting upon any one else. It is proper, however, to
call the houses, tools, stock, money, etc., that are used by
those that do not own them, as the " surplus wealth " of those
who do own them. To pay a laborer or mechanic three dollars a day, and then to put tools, rent, and reputation enough

into his hands to enable those who employ him to charge five dollars a day, is a case of poverty on one side, and of surplus wealth on the other.

The capital of the capitalist is not simply the wealth he has somehow acquired, though this is indeed a very important part of his capital. The other part, without which the first would be worthless, and to which the political economist seldom or never refers, but to which we now call special attention, is the great and terrible fact of the poverty of the masses. It is their poverty, destitution, and consequent dependence that compel them, every day of their lives, to make the best terms possible with those who hold in their possession the surplus wealth of the world. Put the single element of poverty out of existence, and there is no power and no motive for the accumulation of surplus wealth by any individual.

What could a man do with wealth which he could not *use* himself, and which he could not loan to any one else, for the happy reason that all have enough of their own? What could any one do with a hundred houses, if all had houses of their own? And who shall dare to say that one man ought to be dependent upon another for a house and home? The owner of ninety-eight or ninety-nine surplus houses that can neither be let nor sold, would be obliged either to work most of his time, to keep them from going to decay, or else abandon them altogether : and thus demonstrate that enough is enough of anything, whether it be houses, clothes, food, or feasts. To raise in a single season a crop of potatoes twice or three times as large as can be eaten before potatoes could be raised again, would prove the folly and the waste of labor and production, that we are trying to illustrate. There is no motive, and no common sense, in raising a surplus of potatoes ! And what is true of them, is true of everything produced by human exertion, though clothes will last longer than food, houses longer than clothes, and monuments longer than either. But none of them will endure forever, however industriously man may toil to preserve them from the ravages of nature and time. There are natural and remorseless agents always and forever at war with the most enduring

3

monuments of human labor and ingenuity. They work day and night, summer and winter, with frost and sunshine, with rain and snow, with wind and dust, with weeds and webs, with damp and mould, with rust and decay; and before these restless and resistless forces, the proudest monuments of labor and of genius perish. Where are the monumental temples and columns of Greece and Rome? With the constant exertion necessary to repair natural decay, it is hardly possible for one man — in addition to the regular labor necessary to get a living — to keep whole and intact the value of a hundred thousand dollars, if it were put into the house, grounds, surroundings, and appointments necessary to a well regulated household.

It should not be supposed, however, that the actual labor involved in taking care of one's own house and property, must be performed by the owner himself, personally, with his own hands. In this, as in everything else, there may be that division of labor that accomplishes so much more efficiently and economically the world's whole work, than would be possible if every man attempted to be his own gardener or his own mechanic. In our social theory we are supposing poverty at an end; and all that poverty has made necessary or possible, to have also disappeared.

We are admitting the propriety and supposing the possibility of every family being in possession of a homestead worth a hundred thousand dollars, as property is now estimated; though we understand, as well as is necessary, that there is not wealth enough in the richest locality on the earth or in the whole world, to average that amount to each family.

In due season each of these difficulties will be disposed of. The point we desire to make now, is the fact that scores, if not hundreds of men, have an amount of wealth in their possession that could not possibly be preserved from ruin and decay, if the material or pecuniary independence of all around them left them free to serve only themselves.

The service that the painter renders to the blacksmith, editor, porter, clerk, or whoever has anything to paint; or the service performed by any specialist for those who demand his skill and experience, is recognized and welcomed in our philosophy.

But the service performed by a menial — in livery perhaps — disappears with poverty. Neither master nor servant have any place in the political economy that plans the annihilation of poverty. Men will be better served without servants; a better living will be earned without masters, when the knowledge that disposes of poverty has also harnessed into the service of man the great and obedient forces of nature. These are the services that can be rendered and accepted, without compromising the dignity and manhood of a single human being.

The claim that any one really earns millions of dollars, involves the additional claim that they have also earned the services of as many workers as are necessary to keep their property in good condition. For there would be neither reason nor decency in demanding an amount of production that could not be kept from natural destruction. One cannot do this work with his own hands, nor yet can he hoard for the mere wanton satisfaction of wasting that which he says is his own. Outside help must come from some quarter, if he has more of the results of labor than he has time and strength to keep in proper condition. These two claims,— that some men can earn vastly more than they can take care of, and that other men must help them do it, — involves a third claim, equally inadmissible : namely, that the masses ought not to have as much of the world's wealth as they can take care of ; for nothing but this fact — their poverty — makes it possible to hire them to help care for other men's wealth.

How could they serve any one else, if all the time they devote to labor were fully and profitably employed in serving themselves ? The proposition amounts to this,— that a large class ought to have so little wealth of their own, that they will be in circumstances to take care of the surplus productions that a select number of intelligent men ought to possess. Now if this ought to be, it justifies all that naturally follows. The greatest and most immediate hinderance to the rapid production of wealth, is the poverty of the masses. Their poverty serves a small class, but the world at large is vastly poorer for it. It is their poverty that creates the great limit to the otherwise extensive and natural demand for the products of labor. To limit the demand is to increase the labor of anything produced; the cost of an article depending almost entirely on the number manufactured. It pays to construct special machinery and tools to produce what everybody will buy; and those who make the manufacture a specialty, will improve the various processes and reduce the cost continually, especially if they are in competition with others equally anxious to share an increasing traffic. To double the demand for an article, does not mean doubling the expenses of its manufacture. It does not mean that the proprietor must now hire two high-salaried superintendents, or double the number of his overseers and mechanics.

Many of their duties can now be handed over to subordinates, whose pay is inconsiderable. But doubling the business does sometimes mean more self-acting machinery, operated by lower-priced help, with more perfect and rapid results. This, with a better division of labor, must bring down the cost of productions. The patronage of the few who are wealthy, is worth very little to large manufacturers. Take, for example, the seven rich men in New York City, whose united fortunes are said to amount to one hundred and fifty millions of dollars. For how many daily newspaper subscriptions does this vast wealth probably pay?

Sewing-machine manufacturers, who have invested largely in their business because so many are able to purchase a single machine, will be as much benefited by the humble patronage of seven poor seamstresses, each of whom can barely afford to buy one, as by the families of these seven rich men, representing a hundred and fifty millions of dollars. What is their patronage of the horse-cars worth, in comparison with that of the vast multitude, who can only afford six cents, once or twice a day, for a ride?

When a tradesman places a certain price on an article, we

are not obliged to prove that he asks too much, to excuse
ourselves from purchasing. It may or it may not be worth
all that is demanded; and yet our right to buy, or to wait,
or look elsewhere, is never questioned. And this same freedom we are at liberty to exercise in choosing the particular
workman whose services we require. If in purchasing, or
hiring, we make bad bargains, it may cost us a laugh or a
fortune; but our right to consult our own fancy, or prejudices even, in the premises, is thoroughly conceded by all
who have commodities or skill or labor to sell. Now suppose we admit — since we may never actually prove to the
contrary — that the services of certain managers are worth
from one to fifty millions of dollars. Does it follow, in their
case, any more than in any other, that we must buy or hire?
We may say to Messrs. Vanderbilt, Scott, Stewart, or to
Baron Rothschild, "Heretofore your services have been indispensable; they have made the world vastly richer, and much
more comfortable; you have organized its industry, and civilization has rapidly advanced through your share of the
world's work; but we now propose to employ some one else
for a time; we may lose by the change, perhaps, but we
mean to try!" What can they say in reply, except to concede the right of the public to employ whomsoever they
choose? And, if they are like most people who cannot get
all they ask, they will offer to work for less.

To propose to work cheaper, however, because there is
less of a demand for their services, involves a very important, if not a fatal, concession concerning their theory
of the relative value of brain-work, over mere muscular or
routine labor. They claim that the price of ordinary labor
is governed by the law of supply and demand; — meaning,
that when there is much work to be done, and there are but
few to do it, that the demand for workers will be greater
than the supply, and thus wage-prices will go up; and so,
vice versa. But concerning the price of their own labor, a
somewhat different theory is presented: namely, that brain-
work is *worth* more than mere muscular labor; that certain
men obtain millions of dollars, simply because they *earn*

them. While the price for ordinary labor is most accurately
determined by the prevailing demand, the superior value of
mental·exertion is of a more absolute and intrinsic character.
At any rate, there are two distinct and conflicting theories
concerning compensation; and the question now comes,
whether there ought to be more than one; whether, in other
words, the large compensation secured by railroad kings,
manufacturing chiefs, corporation presidents, and princely
merchants, is not as much subject to the law of supply and
demand as the starvation wages sometimes paid to hewers of
wood and drawers of water. Common laborers sometimes
insist that their work is worth two dollars a day, but fail,
finally, to obtain more than a dollar and seventy-five cents,
and are told by those who urge the theory of the superior
worth of brain-work, that a thing is worth what it will bring
in the market; and that rather than do nothing, they had
better accept the reduced price. For the common laborer
or mechanic, there is not much to choose between either of
these two theories. Neither of them will prevail finally; but
either one impartially applied to all who work for pay,— to
those who receive much, and to those who receive little,—
will do better than to adopt one rule for one class, and another rule for another class. If the great managers of the
world's industry insist upon the extraordinary value of their
services as the decisive point, it will be fair to offset against
their theory the opinions of the masses concerning the value
of their services. If, however, on the other hand, they claim
that the law of supply and demand must govern the compensation of the masses, that neither labor nor commodities
are worth any more than they can bring in a market where
all are free to buy or wait or look elsewhere, then let them
agree to the application of this theory to their own compensation. Upon the theory of supply and demand, mankind
are at perfect liberty to say to the management of the world's
railroads, manufactures, commerce, banks, and other industrial powers, — the Vanderbilts, Stewarts, and Peabodys, —
" Gentlemen, hereafter we propose to hire others, or pay you
less."

If they choose to work for the reduced rates, as millions

of laborers have before them, rather than change their business, or do nothing, then their theory about the extraordinary
value of brain-work is modified thus : it is worth all they
ask, *if* they can get it; but if they cannot, it is worth less.
And if the time ever comes when they cannot obtain any
more than other men, then they will not be worth more than
other men. Of course they are at liberty to reject a proposition reducing their large compensation, exactly as do work
ingmen when they dictate or propose a price according to
what they think their labor is worth, rather than according
to the prevailing demand; and their success will not prove
anything more than any successful strike against a reduction
of wages. It will not prove they are worth more, but that
the demand has enabled them to exact their present prices.
It will be quite as difficult to prove that one man's labor is
worth a thousand dollars a day, as to prove that another man's
is worth two dollars a day. These two theories concerning
compensation are deemed incontrovertible by just that class
which is most interested, pecuniarily, in proving that prices
are about as they ought to be. Their own pay is large and
is justified; and, as they are the wage-paying class, they
adopt another theory that clears them from all responsibility for paying very low wages. For if it is really true,
that the scanty wages of ordinary workers are purely the
results of natural causes, then those who pay wages are not
responsible; and meantime, if those who acquire vast fortunes actually earn them, as the just reward for their rare
genius and capacity, then how wrong again it is to complain
of this pleasant dispensation of Providence !

The idea upon which the vast compensation and accumulations of the wealthy are justified, amounts substantially to
this : that wealth goes exactly where it ought to go; that
men of great financial management secure large fortunes, and
that they ought to secure them. But the actual possession
of any exclusive advantage, with the power to hold it, has
always been confounded with the right to maintain it; and
this same logic has served Church and State in all ages,
whenever their monopoly of wealth, or political power, or of
education, even, has been challenged in the interest of a

more equal distribution. But too many public benefactors
have lived in penury and died in want; too many conspicuous exceptions can be cited in science, literature, and religion, to make this view of the matter perfectly conclusive.
It is not at all improbable that the most of these men would
thankfully accept five or ten millions of dollars in place of
ten or twenty millions formerly received for their labor, if
they could do no better; and the criticism upon this reasoning will not spring from any sense of hardship or of injustice, even, in reducing one-half, simply, their enormous
facilities or power to accumulate in the future, but rather
from the apprehension that its success may suggest still
further reductions to an unknown extent. The present tendency, however, must be considered also; for if the power
of individual capitalists to increase their wealth continues
as it has in the past, the next generation may see their enormous accumulations doubled again and again; so that men
who possess a hundred millions, will then be as common as
those who have now acquired one-quarter of that amount.
Large fortunes can be made now more easily than ever
before, because the present managers of the world's industry
have more pleasant, smoother, and far more profitable social
machinery than existed a century ago. And this improvement is steadily going on. The popular taste and general
intelligence so much more widely diffused now than even a
generation ago, are receiving quite as little appreciation from
capitalists, as many of their operatives and workmen give to
the improved and more profitable machinery of to-day, that
has abolished so much hard labor, and so many slow processes, in production.

When capital furnishes labor with machinery more easily
operated, and more agreeable for transportation, cultivating,
turning, weaving, or spinning, it claims larger rewards, if
not great consideration for its investments; and on this same
principle, the public may turn, to those who operate the
more easily managed social machinery of to-day, for the production and distribution of wealth.

This machinery may be described in much the same language that is used by inventors and owners about any labor

saving invention. It is more perfect in its operations, requires less attention, and is far more profitable. Never since the world began was there so much security for investments of capital, as now. Inventors are no longer mobbed, and inventions are not destroyed. The popular respect for law and contracts, and special legislation in every department of industry, all help the capitalist of our time, as he was never helped before; and this improved social and political machinery has cost more than treasures of silver or of gold. To emancipate slaves, — to make freedom mean the highest civilization, and thus multiply the motives for industry and skill, — to increase consumers who buy the products of capital and enterprise, — whole lives have been passed in poverty and persecution. Every step that has been taken, thus far, in the interest of the masses, has added to the security and profit of capital and enterprise. But each step has cost far more than wealth can ever repay; and the large fortunes a few have acquired, are no more due to the brains of to-day, than to the prophets and martyrs who have gone before. Indeed, emancipation and popular progress have been possible, only because they were found more productive and profitable to the ruling classes than slavery and ignorance. The intelligence and general conditions, however, that have accomplished so much, are the qualities that will ask for more; even as nations that produce the most perfect cannon and monitors, and war material, are the most likely to be the first to consider the conditions that will make war impossible. If it is fair to pay an intelligent manager so much more than an ignorant worker, is it not unfair to give wise and foolish men an equal vote, and the same pay, in a State government? There are as many difficulties, perhaps, in defending the justice and expediency of impartial or universal suffrage, as there are in the claim to a more equal distribution of wealth, or more equal compensation, but it is still more difficult to suggest anything better.

Certain men are very much wiser than the mass of mankind, and it does seem as if their opinions ought to prevail; but there is no way of deciding from year to year just who

4

these wise men are. If there is sufficient popular intelligence to have a republican form of government, and to preserve order, the average opinion of the masses, frequently
expressed, will prove safer and surer in the long run, than
the management of any one man, or class, that ever held
exclusive political and governmental power.

There is only this one fact in favor of despotism; it is preferable to anarchy. It was the iron hand of despotism that
first secured order and law, and opportunities for the masses,
and their final self-government is quite as much a matter of
preliminary development and progress, as of real natural
right.

While despotism is better than anarchy, the present industrial vassalage that makes a wealthy class possible, is far
better than the barbarism that made any considerable accumulations of wealth impossible. We are not obliged to choose,
however, between the present and something worse, but are
at liberty to choose between the present and something
better; which is a republicanization of labor, as well as a
republicanization of government.

Of course, it is neither possible nor necessary, nor even
desirable, to attempt to deal with the *present* possessions of
a single human being. With the millionnaires of our day,
there is, practically, a contract concerning the wealth they
have already secured, which society is bound by considerations of expediency, as well as of honor, faithfully to observe.

The attempt to redistribute their vast wealth by legislative
or arbitrary interference would be impossible, partly because
public opinion would never tolerate the idea, and partly because, if it would, the distribution could not be made permanent. The causes that operate now would continue in spite of
any arbitrary or unnatural intervention, and presently carry
the wealth back to nearly as few hands as held it before. It is
not even necessary to deal in this way with the vast accumulations of the wealthy, because there is another method which
is more natural and far better.

An interference with wealth already distributed would be
every way undesirable, because the very attempt would be
likely to disturb or unsettle the safe and legal habits of

thought and conduct of the masses, and leave them finally poorer than when they began. Nor is it possible even to manage or control to any practicable extent, or to any appreciable advantage to the masses, the wealth that has once passed into the possession of the monopolizing and speculative classes.

It was all the result of the labor of the masses ; but the wealth which they never knew enough to keep while it was in their hands, they will never succeed in controlling, after once allowing it to pass into the possession of others.

Possession is always nine points of law. There are always schemes enough in vogue to accomplish this, such as reducing the rates of interest on money, or abolishing interest altogether ; or plans to make money cheap by issuing it in large or in unlimited quantities ; or making its issue free to all who desire to do so ; or abolishing all banking legislation that seems to be exclusive in its advantages.

There is the idea of a sliding scale of taxation that will discriminate in favor of small property holders, and so tax away from the wealthy their vast possessions ; or, —

Of destroying all ownership in the land, so that upon the death of its possessor the State shall hold the title deed, as the National Government holds the right to the public lands of the West ; or, —

Of the National or State Government taking possession of certain railroad, telegraphic, or manufacturing monopolies, and conducting them more favorably to the interests of the people ; or, —

Of State aid to co-operative enterprises undertaken by workingmen, either through direct loans of capital, or by immunity for a period of time from taxation ; or, —

Of cheap railway transportation for the benefit of workingmen who live in the country and work in the towns ; or, —

Of repudiating public debts, as soon as the interest that has been paid upon them shall equal the amount of the principal, so that taxation, which labor always pays, shall be reduced ; or, —

Of compelling the banks to make loans more favorable to
the poorer classes ; or, —

Of furnishing employment at the expense of the public when
the masses are out of work, — these have each and all earnest
and numerous advocates, who believe the people would be
better off, if any or all of these measures prevail; and the
motives that prompt these suggestions entitle their advocates
to respectful consideration ; *but all of these plans deal with
wealth already distributed.*   They mean financial reform.
The distribution we propose concerns the wealth of the
future, — the wealth that human labor has yet to produce.
We plan for nothing whatever that was created and disposed
of yesterday, but for the productions of to-morrow, and the
days and the years and the generations that are to come.   It
not only means folly and knavery, and something worse than
sure failure, to undertake the redivision of property that
has already passed into hands through the present regularly
established and recognized channels of distribution, but the
fact that there is but very little reserved wealth that can be
apportioned to the needy, should not be forgotten.   Take,
first, all the property that is invested in railroad, steamboat,
canal, and ocean transportation ; and all that properly belongs
to telegraphic communication; and how little would be its
worth, in comparison to its cost when divided, if the masses
cannot co-operate in its management?   And when we
remember the thousands of millions of dollars, in practical
values, that would also be destroyed, from the mere loss of
transportation and of telegraphic facilities, it is hard to imagine and impossible to defend the folly that would suggest
such a distribution.

The only idea concerning property, thus invested, that
can be urged with any force, is, that its ownership by a few
capitalists increases unnecessarily the cost of transportation
and communication; and that the money thus paid helps to
support in luxury or idleness those who have never earned
it.   This is, of course, true, but as a purely pecuniary affair,
it is not so important as it seems to be.   The moral, social,
and intellectual consequences involved, it would be impossible to overestimate ; but their consideration can be enter-

tained to better advantage in another connection. We deal now with the single and simple point, that there is not wealth enough in existence to make a very great addition to each man's stock if it were equally divided; and that the amount that can be divided is very small. If railroad companies charge a cent a mile more than it costs to carry a passenger, and if the average number of miles each person travels is three hundred a year, then, as a matter of money, each inhabitant would realize through a complete readjustment or distribution of railroad wealth, less than one cent a day. It is true that if the cost of travelling were reduced one-third, more people would ride; but that fact belongs to to-morrow, not to yesterday, and should be considered in its proper place. We discuss now nothing but the idea of dividing wealth that has been, and not what will be created. The previous proposition was, that the wealth now produced ought not to be divided, and the present proposition is, that there is not much to divide, if it were attempted. That which ought to be done concerning a more equal distribution of the results of labor, will seem very much clearer, if we dwell long enough on what ought not to be done, to make the distinction marked and conclusive. It is not at all probable that there is cloth enough woven to-day, and held in reserve by the manufacturer or merchant, to furnish a single suit of clothes to one-quarter of those who now need them. It is said that American tourists spend abroad, in their pleasures and travels, more than two hundred millions of dollars every year. This wealth it would be possible to divide; but it would amount to only five dollars to each man, woman, and child, a very insignificant sum indeed, in comparison with their necessities. Whether a better distribution of large landed estates could not be safely effected by legislative enactments, is a question often enough suggested by those whose opinions are entitled to a more convincing and conclusive reply, than it will be possible to give in advance of the consideration of the natural causes that govern the distribution of all material wealth.

In the millennium of land reform, however, there will be no fences, and the farmers, like the coming mechanic or laborer in any industry, will be able to co-operate; and the law that could divide, and keep divided, into small farms, the land of the country, should be entitled "An Act to make co-operation on the farm impossible"; and without co-operation, mankind can never attain the highest civilization. The few co-operative successes of the present are feeble, sickly, hot-house exotics, — foreign to the age that makes extreme wealth and extreme poverty possible.

To recapitulate the points we have thus far attempted to establish by these considerations, will help to keep clear and distinct succeeding propositions.

1st. Brain work is not worth the large compensation claimed in its behalf.

2d. First-class brains do not receive the largest compensation.

3d. It is capital, not brains, that receives the largest rewards, and it is the poverty of the masses that gives capital its extraordinary power in this respect; so that the capital of the capitalist consists largely in the poverty of the poor.

4th. To make poverty impossible, will extinguish the motive for ever demanding compensation beyond a certain amount; as the work and care involved in keeping the results of labor, that are not required for present consumption, equal in condition to what they were when produced, can be employed to better advantage in producing only about as fast as they are wanted.

5th. The poverty of the masses is the great hinderance to production: a better distribution will stimulate production.

6th. Wealth is the master and poverty is the slave of the so-called law of supply and demand; and in a more equal distribution of wealth, there will be neither master nor slave.

7th. The skilful management of great financiers has no more to do with their vast accumulations, than the general progress of the masses.

8th. The public has the same right to plan for a more equal distribution of the future productions of labor, that employers have to plan concerning the wages they will pay to-morrow; and the more equal distribution we propose, means reducing, through natural causes, the future compensation of manufacturers, merchants, bankers, transportation and mining managers, etc.

9th. All of the wealth produced up to this hour has been distributed through generally recognized and accepted methods. It is neither possible, nor desirable, nor necessary, to propose its redistribution. Looking back upon the accumulations of the past, therefore, only for instruction, what do we now propose?

Through the gradual, peaceful, and perfectly acceptable operation of natural and permanent causes, we demand a more equal distribution of the *future* results of labor. How this can be done will seem clearer, if we first learn how wealth has been as equally distributed as it is. In other words, we must first discover how the masses obtain the food, clothes, shelter, and luxuries that they now possess, before we can intelligently suggest how their share of wealth in the future can be essentially and permanently increased. Through what channel of distribution the mass of mankind secure the little they now enjoy, is therefore the next question; and the answer will be found the same for all countries, wherever the organization of industry has advanced far enough to establish *a division of labor!*

FACTORY CHILDREN.

REPORT

UPON THE

Schooling and Hours of Labor of Children

EMPLOYED IN THE

MANUFACTURING AND MECHANICAL ESTABLISHMENTS
OF MASSACHUSETTS.

By GEORGE E. McNEILL,

DEPUTY STATE CONSTABLE.

"And whosoever shall offend one of these little ones . . . . it is better for him that a millstone were hanged about his neck, and he were cast into the sea."

BOSTON:
WRIGHT & POTTER, STATE PRINTERS,
79 MILK STREET (CORNER OF FEDERAL).
1875.

Commonwealth of Massachusetts.

BOSTON, MASS., January 11, 1875.

To His Excellency WILLIAM GASTON, *Governor of the Common-wealth of Massachusetts.*

SIR :—There are in this Commonwealth upwards of sixty thousand children, of school age, who are growing up in ignorance, contrary to the ancient policy of the State, and in open violation of the letter and spirit of existing laws.

To protect and provide for this vast and increasing body of illiterates, the legislature of 1867 authorized "the constable of the Commonwealth to specially detail one of his deputies." The Hon. Henry K. Oliver, of Salem, was the first appointee, serving two years, and making two official reports.

In August, 1869, the duties of the office were assigned to Capt. J. Waldo Denny.

After the establishment of the police commission, in 1871, no officer was detailed, but the following instructions were given to each member of the force :—

"Constables of the Commonwealth will, as far as practicable, ascertain by interviews with children employed, by examination of school certificates, or other evidence, if there is a compliance with the provisions of the law. Your attention is called to the statute of 1867.

"Officers will not incur extra expense in making investigations under the foregoing law, unless upon reliable and positive informa-tion of a violation of its provisions, when they will act as in any other criminal matter."

Upon the abolition of the police commission, it became the duty of the chief constable to detail an officer for this work.

At the request of Lieut. Governor Thomas Talbot, himself a manufacturer, I was appointed a state constable August 8, 1874, and detailed to carry into execution the laws relating to the employment and schooling of children.

In accepting the position, I stated to His Excellency and to the chief constable, that it was my purpose to prepare a plan of operations under which the intent of the law could be realized; that the present laws were confusing, conflicting; and that if the proper facilities could be granted me, I believed that the next legislature would so modify and improve its legislation as to make practicable and efficient a system of education that has been, since the earliest days of the Commonwealth, our chief glory and boast.

Immediately after accepting my commission, I commenced my investigations, and found the laws inoperative. In many places they were misunderstood; in others it was believed that the child-laws had been repealed; in others a desire was expressed for the adoption of some method by which the employer and child alike could be protected from misrepresentation as to age, schooling and previous employment.

To attempt the enforcement of law under these circumstances would seem oppressive.

In correspondence and conversation with some of our best educators and manufacturers, I have found, not only a willingness, but a desire to coöperate in any plan that should give to every child the benefit of a common school education.

I therefore desired to prepare and have printed the plan before referred to, together with the laws upon this subject. To do this required a room, stationery, etc. On the 21st day of November, I was assigned a room in the building formerly occupied by the state police, at No. 24 Pemberton Square. This gave me but about six weeks before the time of making the annual report. I therefore have deferred the publication of any plan or circulars until after the legislature had met and acted upon such recommendations as your Excellency might suggest, or the facts presented in this report, or the report of the Board of Education, or the Bureau of Labor Statistics, might inspire.

In addition to the visits made, I have occupied my time in the collection and compilation of such authentic statistics as the imperfect data of our system will permit, and the presentation of such matters of law and experience as will tend to the information of the general court.

Number of Children not attending School.

In the short time since my appointment, it has been impossible to obtain, by any system of visits or circulars of inquiry, the number of children employed in our manufacturing and mechanical establishments, or of non-attendance at school.

From the report of the Hon. H. K. Oliver (Senate Document No. 21, 1868), it appears that at that time there were 927 establishments, in 151 cities and towns, where children were employed between ten and fifteen years of age ; and in this connection he says :—

" Should the duties under this law be continued, it would seem to be necessary, in view of the fact of the wide extent of territory over which our manufacturing establishments are spread, to provide by law some definite and thorough means for obtaining exact information. It is clearly impossible for one person to travel through the State, canvass the whole area of each town, and visit each establishment, in order effectually to carry out the provisions of the statute. In the city of Boston alone there is a very large number of places wherein children are employed, though undoubtedly in much smaller number in each establishment than in those in large manufacturing towns, such as Lowell, Lawrence, and Fall River."

The number of children so employed was not obtained, on account of the fact that the proprietors, or persons in charge, refused or neglected to answer the inquiries contained in the circulars forwarded them. Of the 517 circulars of inquiries sent to these towns, only 100 responded. The next year, 343 responded. The same difficulties were met in the investigations of the Bureau of Statistics of Labor. So that it appears that no *voluntary* system can be made to accomplish the desired work.

Desirous of obtaining the nearest approximate number of unschooled children, I have analyzed the latest returns to the Board of Education, the printed proofs of which were furnished me by the kindness of S. C. Jackson, the state librarian.

Your attention is earnestly requested to the explanations of the accompanying tables, without which some of the returns may appear conflicting and confusing.

The data given by the school returns is as follows :—

Number of different scholars in the school during the school-year, 297,025 ; number of children in the State between five and fifteen, May 1, 1873, 292,481 ; number under five and over fifteen who attend public schools, 27,239 ; average attendance of all ages in the schools during the school-year, 210,248.

From this data, it appears that there are 4,544 more scholars registered as attending the public schools than there were children between five and fifteen years of age in the State, May 1, 1873. It also appears that there are 27,239 children under five and over fifteen who attend the public schools. This, subtracted from the number of different scholars registered as attending school, gives 269,786 registered scholars between five and fifteen years of age.

In the following table is given the data obtained from the school returns, and such other totals and averages as may be obtained therefrom, representing towns with populations of from 5,000 to 40,000. It will be observed that there are two sets of averages,—one representing the averages of attendance and non-attendance of children *registered* as attending school, the other representing the attendance and non-attendance of all the children in the several places between five and fifteen years of age.

The average attendance of those under five and over fifteen is obtained by subtracting from the total number of such children the same percentage of non-attendance as obtains in the per cent. of pupils of all ages. The average number of such attendants, subtracted from the average number attending of all ages, leaves the average attendance between five and fifteen. Subtracting this from the whole number between five and fifteen, gives the non-attendants of these ages. This formula gives the averages of the first set.

The average attendance of all the children between five and fifteen, in any given place is obtained by subtracting the average attendance of those between five and fifteen from the total number of such children in the place, on May 1, 1873, as for instance :—The total number of children in the State between five and fifteen was 292,481; the average attendance of the same age was 190,908; leaving *101,573* as the average number of non-attendants, or more than *one-third* of all the children between five and fifteen in the State non-attendants. Of this 101,573, 22,695 were not enrolled in the public schools, leaving 78,878 as the absentees of registered or enrolled scholars between five and fifteen years of age.

By personal examination, I find the actual per cent. of average *daily* non-attendance, from sickness and other causes, to be less than twelve per cent., not more than ten in most cases. But even allowing twenty per cent. of absentees from these causes, there would be *63,102* of the registered scholars between five and fifteen as habitual non-attendants. Adding to this the number not accounted for, gives *85,797* children practically receiving no benefit from the public schools.

Deducting the average number attending private schools, 13,144 (though their ages are not given), leaves 72,658 children, of school age, practically deriving no benefit from our school system.

By reference to Table I., it will be seen that, in several towns, the number of children between five and fifteen, *in school*, exceeds the number of children of the same age *in those places, May 1, 1873*, amounting in the aggregate to 1,251.

The cause of this excess may be found in the fact that the first is the registry of a whole year, the other is the enumeration of May 1. Many of those registered in school during the year may, on the first of May, have exceeded that age, or graduated, died or left town.

These errors do not invalidate the averages in Table II., nor do they the ratios in the 1, 2, 3, 4 columns of Table III., as both are based upon the registration of children in school. This is illustrated in the case of Fall River. There the number of different scholars registered in school is 7,581. The average attendance of the same ages is 3,821; non-attendance, 3,760. And the number between five and fifteen registered as in school is 7,361. Average attendance, same age, 3,711; non-attendance, 3,750.

TABLE I.

Number of Scholars in School, and not accounted for.

TOWN.	No. of children between 5 and 15, May 1, 1873.	No. of different scholars registered in public schools.	No. under 5 and over 15 in school.	No. between 5 and 15 in school.	No. between 5 and 15 not accounted for.
Attleborough, . . .	1,511	1,614	193	1,421	90
Amesbury, . . .	1,217	995	88	907	310
Beverly, ...	1,463	1,360	88	1,272	191
Danvers, ...	1,155	1,163	100	1,063	92
Marblehead, . . .	1,635	1,486	37	1,449	186
Westfield, ...	1,314	1,449	161	1,288	26
Brookline, ...	1,200	1,264	56	1,208	–
Dedham, ...	1,099	946	74	872	227
Quincy, ...	1,620	1,570	61	1,509	111
Plymouth, ...	1,143	1,003	60	943	200
Blackstone, . . .	1,149	1,297	90	1,207	–
Clinton, ...	1,115	1,244	53	1,191	–
Southbridge, . . .	1,063	984	114	870	193
Adams, ...	2,646	2,855	180	2,675	–
Pittsfield, ...	2,804	2,128	200	1,928	876
Haverhill, ...	2,659	2,860	262	2,598	61
Newburyport, . . .	2,414	2,456	120	2,336	78
Holyoke, ...	2,565	1,123	90	1,033	1,532
Northampton, . . .	2,191	2,403	250	2,153	38
Newton, ...	2,780	3,205	329	2,876	–
Fitchburg, ...	2,186	2,261	209	2,052	134
Fall River, . . .	7,096	7,581	220	7,361	–
New Bedford, . . .	3,790	3,671	233	3,438	352
Lawrence, ...	5,141	4,048	270	3,778	1,363
Lynn, ...	7,202	5,454	238	5,216	1,986
Salem, ...	5,420	4,125	294	3,831	1,589
Springfield, . . .	4,399	5,238	311	4,927	–
Cambridge, . . .	8,433	9,013	656	8,357	76
Lowell, ...	6,728	7,515	596	6,919	–
Worcester, . . .	7,681	9,990	670	9,320	–
Boston, ...	57,830	54,129	3,545	50,584	7,246
Totals, . . .	150,649	146,430	9,848	136,582	–
State, ...	292,481	297,025	27,239	269,786	22,695

TABLE II.

Average Attendance and Non-Attendance.

TOWN.	Average attendance of children of all ages registered as attending public school during the year.	Average non-attendance of children of all ages registered as attending public school.	Average attendance of children under 5 and over 15 registered as attending public school.	Average attendance of children between 5 and 15 registered as attending public school.	Average non-attendance of children between 5 and 15 registered as attending public school.
Attleborough, . . .	1,005	609	120	885	536
Amesbury, . . .	769	226	68	701	206
Beverly, ...	997	363	65	932	340
Danvers, ...	912	251	88	824	239
Marblehead, . . .	1,298	188	33	1,265	184
Westfield, ...	1,045	404	116	929	359
Brookline, ...	954	310	42	912	296
Dedham, ...	788	158	62	726	146
Quincy, ...	1,208	362	47	1,161	348
Plymouth, ...	829	174	50	779	164
Blackstone, . . .	699	598	49	650	557
Clinton, ...	950	294	41	909	282
Southbridge, . . .	648	336	76	572	298
Adams, ...	1,735	1,120	110	1,625	1,050
Pittsfield, ...	1,497	631	170	1,327	601
Haverhill, ...	2,255	605	207	2,048	550
Newburyport, . . .	1,554	902	76	1,478	858
Holyoke, ...	859	264	69	790	243
Northampton, . . .	1,721	682	180	1,541	612
Newton, ...	2,227	978	228	1,999	877
Fitchburg, ...	1,686	575	157	1,529	523
Fall River, . . .	3,821	3,760	110	3,711	3,650
New Bedford, . . .	2,868	803	182	2,686	752
Lawrence, ...	2,674	1,374	179	2,495	1,283
Lynn, ...	4,095	1,359	179	3,916	1,300
Salem, ...	2,833	1,292	203	2,630	1,201
Springfield, . . .	3,585	1,653	212	3,373	1,554
Cambridge, . . .	6,073	2,940	440	5,633	2,724
Lowell, ...	4,654	2,861	370	4,284	2,635
Worcester, . . .	6,134	3,856	409	5,725	3,595
Boston, ...	40,830	13,299	2,676	38,154	19,676
Totals, . . .	103,203	43,227	7,014	96,189	47,639
State, ...	210,248	86,777	19,340	190,908	78,878

2

TABLE III.

Ratio of Attendance and Non-Attendance.

TOWN.	Ratio of attendance of children of all ages to the number of different scholars registered as attending school.		Ratio of attendance of children between 5 and 15 to the number of scholars of same age registered as attending school.		Ratio of attendance of children between 5 and 15 to the number of children of same age in the town.	
	Attendance.	Non-Attendance.	Attendance.	Non-Attendance.	Attendance.	Non-Attendance.
Attleborough, .	62.26	37.74	62.28	37.72	58.57	41.43
Amesbury, . .	77.28	22.72	77.28	22.72	57.60	42.40
Beverly, . .	73.30	26.70	73.27	26.73	63.70	36.30
Danvers, . .	78.41	21.59	77.51	22.49	71.34	28.66
Marblehead, .	87.34	12.66	87.30	12.70	77.37	22.63
Westfield, . .	72.11	27.89	72.12	27.88	70.70	29.30
Brookline, . .	75.47	24.53	75.49	24.51	76.00	24.00
Dedham, . .	83.29	16.71	83.25	16.75	66 06	33.94
Quincy, . .	76.94	23.06	76.93	23.07	71.66	28.34
Plymouth, . .	82.64	17.36	82.60	17.40	68.15	31 85
Blackstone, . .	53.89	46.11	53.85	46.15	56.57	43 43
Clinton, . .	76.36	23.64	76.32	23.68	81.52	18 48
Southbridge, .	65.85	34.15	65.74	34.26	53.80	46.20
Adams . .	60.77	39.23	60.74	39.26	61.41	38.59
Pittsfield, . .	70.34	29.66	68.82	31.18	47.32	52.68
Haverhill, . .	78.84	21.16	78.82	21.18	77.02	22.98
Newburyport, .	63.27	36.73	63.27	36.73	61.22	38.78
Holyoke, . .	76.49	23.51	76.47	23.53	30.79	69.21
Northampton, .	71.61	28.39	71.57	28.43	70.33	29.67
Newton, . .	69.48	30.52	69.50	30.50	71.90	28.10
Fitchburg, . .	74.56	25.44	74.51	25.49	69.94	30.06
Fall River, . .	50.40	49.60	50.41	49.59	52.29	47.71
New Bedford, .	78.12	21.88	78.12	21.88	70.87	29.13
Lawrence, . .	66.05	33.95	66 04	33.96	48.53	51.47
Lynn, . . .	75.08	24.92	75.07	24.93	54.37	45.63
Salem, . .	68.67	31.33	68.65	31.35	48.52	51.48
Springfield, .	68.44	31.56	68.45	31.55	76.67	23.33
Cambridge, .	67.38	32.62	67.40	32.60	66.79	33.21
Lowell, . .	61.92	38.08	61.91	38.09	63.67	36.33
Worcester, . .	61.40	38.60	61.42	38.58	73.23	26.77
Boston, . .	75.61	24.39	75.42	24.58	65.97	34.03
State, . .	70.78	29.22	70.76	29.24	65.27	34.73

By these tables, it appears that the percentage of attendants of all ages (exclusive of Boston), is 67.57, non-attendants 32.43, and 67.36 per cent. of attendants between five and fifteen, and 32.64 per cent. non-attendants.

By personal examination of the statistics of a primary school having 472 registered pupils and an actual average daily attendance of 413, it appeared that there was 87.5 percentage of attendance and 12.5 per cent. non-attendance; while, according to the usual form of returns, the average attendance was 92.1 per cent., non-attendance 7.9 per cent., showing that there was an actual non-attendance of 4.6 per cent. more than given in the school returns. In the State, the percentage of attendance of pupils registered as in school, of all ages, is 70.78; non-attendants, 29.22; and the percentage of attendance between five and fifteen is 70.76; non-attendance, 29.24. Adding the 4.6, the per cent. of non-attendants would be respectively 33.82 and 33.84. The ratio of attendance and non-attendance of children between five and fifteen to the number of children of the same age in the State, is 65.27 attendants and 34.73 non-attendants, or about *one-third of the enrolled children habitual non-attendants.*

According to the United States census for 1870, the number of children in this State between five and seventeen inclusive, who did not attend any school, public or private, was 110,425. According to this table, the number between five and fifteen (supposed to be inclusive) is 101,570. If the attendance and non-attendance of those of and under seventeen years of age were given, it would doubtless more nearly agree with the census returns.

Making all deductions, and giving the most liberal allowance for errors, there would be above 60,000 children between five and fifteen years of age who are yet to be reached by some effective method of compulsory education.

Sixty thousand children growing up in ignorance! It is impossible for the mind to contemplate the terrible import of these figures. They are so astounding as to seem almost incredible, and will lead many to question the correctness of educational statistics. That our system is imperfect is confessed ; yet, as will be shown, that confession will not invalidate the truth of our statement.

At a meeting of the department of superintendence of the national educational association, held at Washington, in January, 1874, the subject of State and city school reports was fully discussed by some of the most practical and efficient superintendents in the country. The following brief synopsis will be found of interest, as showing the need of a better system of educational statistics :—

Hon. WILLIAM R. CREERY, of Baltimore : At the convention at St. Louis, I took strong ground against statistics generally, and pronounced them worthless for purposes of comparison, as they simply deluded the unwary. I used some plain language on the subject, which created a little feeling among my brother superintendents, who prided themselves on their splendid exhibits, the effort seeming to be in many cases to present school statistics in their best light, and not in the truest light. Superintendents are sometimes publicly attacked about the expenses of their schools. They must frequently defend themselves by using the statistics of other cities. How important is it, then, that these statistics should be made up in some generally known way. We should have a common language on statistics, that could be understood, on the mere reading, by any one of ordinary intelligence. When we read of the percentage of attendance and tardiness, we want to understand what is meant, and how the results are obtained. I am glad that my friend avoided the use of the phrase " the average number belonging." We hold that to belong is to be enrolled, and to have an actual membership, which cannot be changed every three days, at convenience. In making the percentage of attendance, we think it right to include all in the basis, not excepting the sick, or those temporarily absent from cause. Suppose that fifty is the number of a certain class, and five are absent from sickness, we estimate the attendance on the fifty, and not on the forty-five. The whole subject of school statistics is in need of reformation. Under existing circumstances, it is impossible to make intelligent replies to the many inquiries that are sent from city to city for information.

Mr. J. D. PHILBRICK, of Boston : The fundamental element which we want, I think, is the number of children who are due at school. What is the enumeration of the children who ought to go to school ? There is great diversity in regard to the age at which this enumeration is taken, and I hope General Eaton, our admirable national commissioner, will fix upon some age for the enumeration of the

children, which shall be recommended as the proper age for education in the public schools of the different States. If we can begin
by having the school age the same in all the States, we shall have
one element upon which we can begin our comparisons. The next
thing is the enrollment, or the number belonging. We use that
phrase, " the number belonging." My friend from Baltimore [Mr.
Creery] does not seem to fancy that. I should be very happy to
change that, and adopt a different phrase, if we can all agree upon
it. I find the word " enrollment" is used, but I do not understand
what is meant by that. I know what is meant by the number belonging, as we use it. We report the average number belonging for
six months, and the average number belonging for the year. We
know exactly what it means. We mean by that phrase simply
that, when a scholar comes to school, his name is placed on the
record-book, and that he is counted as one belonging to the school ;
and, if absent ten half-days, he is not so considered. We adopted
that practice in order to concur with suggestions from the West.
Mr. Weld made some plans, which were adopted by many cities, so
as to be, in certain respects, uniform. It made not the slightest difference whether we counted ten half-days or six half-days.

Mr. A. P. Marble, of Worcester : In case a pupil is absent ten
half-days, are these half-days counted among the absences?

Mr. Philbrick : Yes, sir. Now, see how perfectly easy it is to
obtain an average. You simply take the number " belonging," or
that are " enrolled" ; then, counting each day, and averaging for a
month or year, you will have the average number " belonging," or
" enrolled."

Mr. George L. Farnham : Suppose a pupil has left, and takes
his books, do you count him as belonging?

Mr. Philbrick : Of course not. If we agree on that point, the
rest will be easy. I learn that in the great State of New York
there are some 225,000 pupils. I look at the attendance, and I find
it is about 90,000. The enumeration is made up for a certain purpose, to meet certain requirements in regard to the distribution of
the educational fund. But, when we come to actual attendance, we
know what that is. There is no difficulty about actual attendance,
because it is the actual presence of the child ; and when I get that
from any State, I always feel that I am on *terra firma.*

Mr. R. W. Stevenson : In regard to the enumeration of children, the law of Ohio compels it to be made by those who are under
oath to make a fair and honest return of all children between the
ages of six and twenty-one. That is an item of our statistics upon
which we can rely.

Hon. J. P. Wickersham : We want to know, by some reliable

means, first, how many children there are to be educated; secondly, how many are enrolled in the schools; thirdly, the attendance.

Hon. M. B. HOPKINS: In Indiana, we have a law requiring an enumeration to be taken every year of all the children between six and twenty-one years of age; and we test that law every year. The results are decidedly satisfactory. I have no doubt that we have the matter as nearly right as we can get it. This enumeration is taken by the township trustees, and the regular increase from year to year shows that it must be about correct.

General EATON: We must know the number of children that are to be educated; for it is their education that we, as educators, are trying to accomplish. Now, we do not know that, and yet we are coming towards it with a certainty which is very encouraging, in spite of all the difficulties thrown in our way.

The result of this debate occasioned the recommendation of a system that will no doubt be presented to the proper committee of the general court.

With all the doubt that is thrown around statistics, they yet remain as the best authority for purposes of investigation, especially when they can be sustained by general observation and complete representative data.

That an immense army of uneducated and undisciplined children is growing up among us, is shown, not only by the State and United States statistics, but by the general observation of men interested in the welfare of children, the widest diffusion of education, and the perpetuity of our free institutions. The terrible fact is further revealed by the incontrovertible evidence of the organization and condition of our schools.

By the kindness of Francis Cogswell, superintendent of schools of Cambridge, I have been furnished with the following data, obtained from the registers of six of the grammar schools in that city :—

Number of pupils in the different Classes of Six of the Grammar Schools of Cambridge, October 17, 1874.

	First.*	Second.	Third.	Fourth.	Fifth.	Sixth.	Total.
Shepard, . . .	33	32	54	86	98	123	426
Washington,. . .	31	53	71	121	107	118	501
Harvard, . . .	61	75	120	158	100	144	658
Allston, . . .	29	37	76	123	138	165	568
Webster, . . .	33	55	96	102	147	171	604
Thorndike, . . .	25	34	68	80	91	172	470
Putnam, . . .	17	27	46	80	103	121	394
Totals, . . .	229	313	531	750	784	1,014	3,621

* The first is the highest class.

In the following table is given the per cent. of membership and average age of each class in six grammar schools :—

Per Cent. of Membership and Average Age in the Six Classes of Six Grammar Schools in Cambridge.

NUMBER OF CLASS.	Per cent. of membership.	Average age.	
		Years.	Months.
1 (highest), ...	6	14	6
2, ...	8	13	10
3, ...	15	13	–
4, ...	20	12	3
5, ...	21	11	6
6, ...	30	10	2

By this table, it appears that fifty-one per cent. are below twelve years of age, or eighty-six per cent. of and under thirteen years of age.

Mr. Philbrick, superintendent of the Boston schools, in his twenty-seventh semi-annual report, September, 1874, gives, on page 15, the following table of the grammar schools of Boston. The average ages of the different classes are not given :—

Classification of the pupils of the Grammar Schools at the close of the Summer term, 1873.

Classes.	No. Aug. 31, 1873.	Per cent.
First class (highest), ...	1,243	.07
Second class, ...	1,806	.10

	No. Aug. 31, 1873.	Per cent.
Third class, ...	2,526	.14
Fourth class, ...	2,996	.17
Fifth class, ...	4,181	.23
Sixth class, ...	5,144	.29

Ages.		
Under eight, ...	83	.005
Eight years, ...	981	.05
Nine years, ...	1,966	.11
Ten years, ...	2,872	.16
Eleven years, ...	2,958	.16
Twelve years, ...	3,144	.18
Thirteen years, ...	2,632	.15
Fourteen years, ...	1,828	.10
Fifteen years and over, ...	1,434	.08

Mr. Philbrick says :—

"These figures are extremely important, as showing the condition of our grammar schools. I confess that they do not look so well as I could wish. *There are too few pupils in the upper classes, and too many in the lower.* Taking the average of two or three years past, the number in the first class is about 28 per cent. of the number admitted from the primary schools. This proportion is far from being satisfactory. Then the number in the sixth class is, on the other hand, too large. It will be seen that it is larger, by some 800, than the number of pupils admitted during the year from the primary schools. This means that 800 pupils were more than one year engaged upon the studies of the sixth class. Again, if we compare the classification by ages with the classification by proficiency, the result is not so satisfactory as could be desired. The number in the two lower classes exceeds by upwards of 600 the whole number of pupils eleven years old and under. More than half of all the pupils in the grammar schools are found in the two lowest classes. *This showing ought to be radically changed.*"

By this table it appears that 66½ per cent. of the children in the grammar schools of Boston are under twelve years, and 81½ per cent. of and under thirteen years of age. In Cambridge, the total number of pupils in school January 1, 1874, was 7,379. Number in the primary schools, 3,954; number in the grammar schools, 3,420; number in the high school, 365. The number admitted to the grammar school in 1873 was

781. The number graduated, 156. Number admitted to the high school, 149. Graduated, 35.

In the report of the superintendent of schools of Worcester, for 1872, pages 109 and 110 City Document, Mr. A. K. Marble says :—

"Of the whole number registered in all the schools, except the evening schools, less than seventy-four per cent. (.738) is the average number belonging for the year. Of this average number less than ninety per cent. are in the schools daily. The cost of the schools for the year is $128,000. There has therefore been a pecuniary loss from absence of $12,800 ; or making allowance for unavoidable causes, a loss of $10,000. But dollars and cents cannot express the loss occasioned by this absence ; the interruption of classes and the loss of interest in school cannot be so computed.

The disparity between the whole number registered and the average number belonging to our schools shows two facts : First, that the law requiring the attendance at school of all children of school age three months in the year is pretty thoroughly obeyed ; and secondly, that about two thousand children are withdrawn from school at the end of that time. The first of these facts is a triumphant answer to the charge of some of our western friends, that the law of this State for compulsory attendance is a failure and cannot be enforced. The second proves the necessity for extending the time of attendance required, to the whole school year. The enforcement of the law would doubtless then be as complete as it now is, and less difficult. It is useless to repeat arguments on this subject. Thorough universal education is the recognized necessity of our institutions. Not more words, but a little healthy legislation, is the need of the hour."

The school committee of Fall River, in their report for 1873, page 1, referring to the same subject, say :—

"The number of scholars registered in our schools during the past year, supposing the returns to be correct, is 7,581, of which 220 were over fifteen years of age. From this statement it appears that nearly all the children of the city, between five and fifteen years of age, enter our schools some time during the year ; and yet the average attendance is only a fraction over fifty per cent., which shows that more than one-half of the children do not attend school long enough to receive a tithe of the benefits they are calculated to confer. How to awaken a deeper interest among all classes in public education, and especially to make parents realize the great necessity of requiring their children regularly and continuously to attend our public schools, are matters of pressing importance."

And again on page 5 :—

" The average attendance of children at our public schools in 1872—the latest date from which comparative statistics have been published—was a fraction over 58 per cent. of the number between five and fifteen years of age; which places us at the foot of the cities and towns in the county,—below Lowell, Lawrence, Worcester and other cities, and the three hundred and twenty-second out of the three hundred and fifty cities and towns which sent in their returns to the State. In our appropriation per scholar, our city stands the one hundred and thirty-ninth, and in the percentage of taxable property appropriated to public schools, the three hundred and twentieth in the list of cities and towns in the State; and the lowest but one of the nineteen in the county."

And on page 6 :—

" If most of the scholars which entered the primary schools passed through the succeeding grades in regular order, the labor of instruction would be greatly lessened, and a systematic method could be adopted, with a rational expectation of its being success-fully pursued. But when, as in our city, only a small fraction—as may be learned from the superintendent's report—of those who enter the primaries reach the grammar grade, and not one-quarter of the latter pass into the high school, the problem how to conduct the schools, so as to make them most efficient and useful, becomes somewhat complicated."

By the following table it appears that 49.6 per cent. of all the chidren registered in the Fall River schools are receiving, practically, no benefit from them. It will also be observed that the n mber of sittings or seats for pupils is 2,411 less than the number of registered scholars.

GENERAL STATISTICS—FALL RIVER SCHOOLS.

	This year.	Last year.
Whole number registered in schools, . . .	7,581	6,968
Average attendance, ...	3,821	3,545
Per cent. of attendance, based on enrollment, . .	50.4	51
Per cent. of attendance, based on average number belonging, ...	89.6	89
Per cent. of absence, ...	10.4	11
Number of sittings, ...	5,170	4,928
Number of pupils over 15 years of age, . . .	220	149
High School.		
Number of pupils registered in High School, . .	159	162
Average attendance, ...	144	150
Per cent. of attendance, based on enrollment, . .	90.5	93
Per cent. of attendance, based on average number belonging, ...	100	97
Number received during the year, ...	74	78
Number graduated, ...	21	29
Average age of those remaining, ...	17.3	17
Grammar Schools.		
Number of pupils registered in Grammar Schools, .	984	923
Average attendance, ...	628	591
Per cent. of attendance, based on enrollment, . .	63.8	64
Per cent. of attendance, based on average number belonging, ...	93.5	93
Average age of those remaining, ...	12.5	12.5
Intermediate Schools.		
Number of pupils registered in Intermediate Schools,	1,253	1,124
Average attendance, ...	762	684
Per cent. of attendance, based on enrollment, . .	60.8	61
Per cent. of attendance, based on average number belonging, ...	94.3	90
Primary Schools.		
Number of pupils registered in Primary Schools, .	3,758	3,106
Average attendance, ...	1,879	1,723
Per cent. of attendance, based on enrollment, . .	50	55
Per cent. of attendance, based on average number belonging, ...	88.1	90
Mixed Schools.		
Number of pupils in Mixed Schools, ...	376	435
Average attendance, ...	223	226
Per cent. of attendance, based on enrollment, . .	59.3	52
Per cent. of attendance, based on average number belonging, ...	76.1	84
Factory School.		
Number of pupils registered in Factory School, .	1,051	1,218
Average attendance, per term, ...	185	171

Further on the superintendent says :

" By referring to the summary of statistics, you will observe that the whole number of different persons enrolled in our schools is 7,581, while the average attendance is but 3,821, or 50.4 per cent. of the number registered.   The per cent. last year was 51.

"If we compare our average attendance with the number of persons in the city between five and fifteen years of age, we find the result to be nearly the same.   The number of persons in the city between the above ages, is 7,096.   The average attendance is 3,821, or 54 per cent. nearly of the children of school age within our limits.

" The per cent. of attendance in the county is nearly 69, while that of the whole State is 73.   Fall River, according to this exhibit, is 15 per cent. below that of the county, and 19 lower than that of the State.

" There is no subject connected with the schools of more importance than the attendance of the pupils.   There need be but little solicitude for those who attend, but the gravest alarm may very properly be felt for those children who are outside their walls.   It is encouraging to know that most of our children of school age have been enrolled in our schools, more or less of the time, during the year.   For this result much credit is due to the labors of our truant officer, and also to the coöperation of our mill agents in sending out those minors in their employ, of scholastic age, to attend school.

" But their attendance is not continuous, and they are not receiving the amount of schooling necessary to make them intelligent voters on the great questions agitating the country.   A republican form of government rests upon the intelligence of the people,— their power to exercise intelligently the elective franchise ; but if the necessary intelligence is not acquired, is not the stability of the government thereby endangered?   How are the wrongs to be righted, and the evils eradicated, which prevail on all sides, unless the children be trained and taught in our schools, so that they may grow up to be intelligent men and women?   How is the national or state government to become purified in character, or elevated in tone, unless the people, from whom the rulers are chosen, receive in our schools intellectual and moral training?   The subject is a very important one, and it should receive the attention of our citizens generally, for the amount of low attendance in our schools will tell upon our city morally, socially and intellectually.   Not only that, but our industries will be affected unfavorably.

" Many of our juvenile criminals begin their career by absenting themselves from school.   The next step is truancy, in its incipient stages, which soon becomes confirmed. After a very short time, usually, they commit some crime, and soon after we find them spending their time within the prison walls. This class is increasing in our midst, and in tracing many of these cases, non-attendance at school has usually been found to be their first offence.

"The following items taken from the summary of statistics for the year are interesting, and worthy of careful examination. They show, perhaps, in a more condensed form and forcible manner, the nature of our school attendance, than I am in any other way able to present:—

		Av. Attendance.
Pupils registered in High School, ...	159	144
in Grammar School, . . .	984	628
in Intermediate School, . .	1,253	762
in Primary School, . . .	3,758	1,879
in Mixed School, . . .	386	223

Time required to complete High School course, . . .	4 years.
to complete Grammar School course, . .	4 "
to complete Intermediate School course, .	2 "
to complete Primary School course, . .	2 "

"As there are 3,758 pupils registered in our primary schools, and but 1,253 in the intermediate grade, or three in the former to one in the latter, and the time required to complete each course the same,—two years,—it follows that every three pupils in the primary grade furnish but one for promotion to the intermediate schools. Or, in other words, two pupils out of every three leave our schools before promotion to the next higher grade. This may seem a startling announcement, but the results of this and many former years will bear me out in making this statement. Two-thirds, then, of our school population receive no instruction in school beyond the primary grade, except what they may receive in the factory or evening schools later in life.

"The course of study in the primary schools consists of qualifying the pupils to read in the third reader, to spell the words in their reading lessons, and in arithmetic to commit the tables, and perform simple exercises in the four fundamental rules, and the simplest operations in fractions. This is the maximum education which two-thirds of our children receive.

The government rests on the intelligence of the people, but will not such a meagre amount endanger its form, its grandeur and its perpetuity? Are we safe with such a state of affairs? Are we not 'like the foolish man who built his house upon the sand, and the rain descended, and the floods came, and the winds blew, and beat upon that house, and it fell, and great was the fall of it?'

"Having compared the number of pupils registered in our intermediate schools with those in the primary, let us now compare those in the grammar grade with the number in the intermediate schools.

"As the time required to complete the grammar course is four years, and there being registered 984 pupils, the average for each year of the course is one fourth of 984, or 246. The intermediate course requiring two years, and there being enrolled in those schools 1,253, gives an average for each year of the course of one-half of 1,253, or 626. Hence it follows, that every 626 pupils in the intermediate grade, furnish but 246 graduates for the grammar schools, or, in round numbers, five intermediate pupils furnish but two for promotion to the grammar grade. And it also follows that it requires 7½ primary pupils to furnish one for the grammar schools.

"Let us examine this subject a little farther, by comparing the high school with the grammar grade. The time required to complete either course is the same, hence the number of pupils registered in each will give the ratio : High school, 159 ; grammar schools, 984. The per cent. of enrollment in the high school is but 16 per cent. of that in the grammar grade, hence it takes six pupils of the lower grade to promote one into the high school, or 47 primary pupils to furnish one to enter the high school.

"Those pupils of the high school who intend to graduate at the close of the present term, being 24 in number, are but 15 per cent. of the enrollment, hence it requires 7 pupils of the enrollment to furnish one graduate ; or, to put this in another form, only about one-third of those who enter, graduate, and two-thirds leave before the completion of the course, and a very large percentage leave during the first year.

Now this low attendance upon our schools does not argue against the efficiency of the teachers or their instruction, any more than the poor attendance on churches on Sundays reflects upon the ministrations of the pulpits. It only shows us that the people do not fully realize the advantages of an education which our schools offer free to all. Poverty debars many families from giving their children as much schooling as they would like to have them obtain. There is no surer way of improving our city in every respect, materially, socially, intellectually and morally, than by increasing the attendance of pupils at school."

In relation to the factory school the superintendent says :

"The whole number registered for the year is 1,051, while the average attendance for each term is 185, a little better than last year.   Quite a number of children of this class, owing to the lack of room in the Anawan Street house, were permitted to attend in other schools the required time, according to law."

The following table gives the number of children sent from certain mills to the factory school in Fall River since 1869 :

Number of Children Received into the Factory School from each Mill, and Number of Cards Issued.

MILLS.	1869. Entered.	1869. Cards is-sued.	1870. Entered.	1870. Cards is-sued.	1871. Entered.	1871. Cards is-sued.	1872. Entered.	1872. Cards is-sued.	1873. Entered.	1873. Cards is-sued.
Merchants,	69	62	84	70	82	80	46	43	59	52
Granite,	47	45	45	43	48	46	68	61	72	64
Union,	86	80	89	77	90	83	58	57	51	43
Troy Manuf'g Co.,	63	57	50	48	53	51	50	47	45	36
Robeson,	28	26	25	24	33	29	27	25	24	21
Davol,	28	26	28	26	23	22	20	18	22	20
Durfee,	68	63	53	50	84	79	90	86	88	79
Tecumseh,	29	29	27	25	24	21	36	35	44	41
Woollen,	10	10	11	11	10	10	10	10	9	9
Pocasset,	43	41	53	48	34	31	22	21	28	24
Quequechan,	40	36	52	51	54	50	28	26	34	20
Watuppa,	26	26	26	25	33	33	29	26	29	25
Robeson Pt. Works,	36	35	32	30	33	32	20	20	11	10
Anawan,	30	26	24	21	19	17	9	9	17	14
Metacomet,	56	51	50	48	45	42	33	33	38	30
Linen,	143	134	138	132	108	108	68	67	76	65
Massasoit,	25	23	25	22	15	10	6	4	8	7
Globe Pt. Works,	29	26	19	15	15	13	7	4	12	9
Thread Mills,	3	3	3	3	5	4	3	3	3	3
Mt. Hope,	2	2	6	6	5	5	–	–	1	1
Amer Pt. Works,	3	3	65	59	71	68	75	75	88	83
F. R. Manuf'g Co.,	–	–	21	21	26	25	29	26	38	34
Cigar Manufactory,	–	–	2	2	–	–	–	–	–	–
Cooper's Shop,	–	–	2	2	–	–	–	–	–	–
Miscellaneous,	–	–	22	17	13	10	30	16	10	6
Harness Shops,	–	–	3	3	–	–	2	2	9	9
Wampanoag,	–	–	–	–	–	–	–	–	4	4
Stafford,	–	–	–	–	–	–	–	–	20	15
Crescent,	–	–	–	–	–	–	–	–	27	20
Borden,	–	–	–	–	–	–	–	–	33	26
Slade,	–	–	–	–	–	–	–	–	8	7
Mechanics',	–	–	–	–	–	–	–	–	1	1
	864	804	965	879	927	869	766	712	913	778

Mr. Geo. E. Hood, superintendent of schools in Lawrence, publishes a very instructive table, giving for the term from February 3, to June 27, 1873 (21 weeks), the whole number admitted; number received from other schools; number neither absent nor tardy; number under five years of age; number attending two weeks or more; number belonging twenty weeks; average number attending two weeks or more; average attendance; per cent. of attendance; number over fifteen years; average age; number promoted during or at close of term.

The whole number admitted was, . . .	4,138
From other schools, ...	90
Number belonging two weeks or more, . .	3,556
" " twenty-one weeks or full term,	2,140
Average number attending two weeks or more, .	2,760
Average attendance, ...	2,506
Number over fifteen, ...	130
Number promoted during or at close of term, .	918

The law of 1873 is printed in the superintendent's report, and the following comments made thereupon :—

" The frequent changes made by the legislature in relation to the attendance of children at school, and in relation to the employment of children in manufacturing and mechanical establishments, embarrass very much all that are affected by the law, and that desire to see its provisions complied with. If there were not other manifest sources of weakness in the law, these changes alone would almost defeat the object aimed at.

" A good law that has some degree of permanence is more serviceable than a better law that is continually being changed. These changes are sometimes made with so little reference to, and so out of harmony with, other existing statutes upon the same or kindred subjects, that if it were possible, one might think they were made hastily, and without consultation with those whose experience and observation upon the subject enables them to speak understandingly in reference to it. The educational interests of the children and of the public would be better served than they now are, if children were required to attend school throughout the entire school age, and could only be withdrawn from school during this time on account of their own ill-health, or because they had already obtained a certain fixed amount of knowledge. *The schools of this city, in common with those of other manufacturing places, are unavoidably disturbed to a considerable extent by the constant coming and going of the children between the schools and the mills.*"

On pages 23 and 24, twelfth annual report of the board of
education, Horace Mann, in giving the statistics of attendance and non-attendance, of the year 1849, says :—

"This is always a sad chapter in the year-book of the schools.
It presents a case where reason is not a remedy ; at least, reason
and argument have as yet failed to work a reform. Slight improvements are exhibited from year to year, but there is ground to fear
that the disease is too chronic and deep-seated to yield to anything
but more energetic treatment. My own belief and hope are, that a
government which has so far advanced in taking care of itself and
its people as to pass quarantine laws to prevent the importation of
physical disease, and the infections that result in natural death, will
soon be wise enough to practice that higher and more indispensable
form of self-preservation which consists in sanitary regulations
against spiritual distempers and the moral death, that come from
the ignorance and vicious abandonmeut of childhood and youth.
Until that time shall arrive, it will be the duty of all officers connected with the cause of education with stern fidelity to expose the
delinquencies of those parents who neglect to send their children to
the schools provided for them, however painful or humiliating to the
pride of the State such exposure may be.

"The average attendance for the last year's summer term was
123,046 ; and the average attendance for the last year's winter term
was 143,878. Take the whole number belonging to the State, who
were between the ages of four and sixteen (214,436), and subtract
from this the estimated number of those who attend academies and
private schools, and who do not depend upon common schools for their
education,—say 12,000,—and there will still remain 204,436 who
are wholly or mainly dependent upon the common schools for all the
education they will ever receive. The whole number registered as
belonging to the summer schools last year was 165,132, and the
whole number registered as belonging to the winter schools was 185,-
000. But of these, 3,656 were under the age of four years, and 9,977
were over the age of sixteen years. Deduct those under four from the
summer, and those over sixteen from the winter schools (because
those under four very rarely attend school in the winter, and those
over sixteen as rarely in summer), and it thus appears that the whole
number between four and sixteen, who belonged to the summer
schools, during any part of their term, was only 161,476, and the
whole number between the same ages who belonged to the winter
schools, during any part of their term, was only 175,023. Hence it
also appears, that of those supposed to be wholly or mainly depend-

ent upon the common schools for all the school education they will ever obtain, there was an unbroken and total absence in summer of 42,960, and in winter of 29,413,—that is, there was this number of children, who, respectively, during the summer and winter terms, were not brought for a day within the influences of our schools.

" But another and a scarcely less deplorable phase of the subject remains to be presented. Many of those whose names were enrolled upon the register book of the schools, have a flagrant amount of absences to atone for. The average attendance in summer was but 123,046, and in winter but 143,878. Hence, of the 204,436 children supposed to be dependent upon our common schools for their education, there was an *average* absence during summer of 81,390, and an *average* absence during winter of 60,558.

" In strictness, too, a still further reduction should be made from the number of attendants, both on account of the 3,656 children, under the age of four years, who were enrolled in the summer schools, and on account of the 9,977 above sixteen years of age, who were enrolled in the winter schools. But I forbear ; for it cannot be necessary to add another repulsive lineament to the deformities of a picture already so frightful."

ARGUMENT.

From the statistical testimony taken by the United States census marshals, by the returns of school committees, by the reports of superintendents, and from the organization of and condition of our schools, as well as from the general observation of educators, the fact is established beyond doubt that thousands of children here in Massachusetts, surrounded with the best educational facilities, are growing up in ignorance.

Before any method can be devised by which this growing evil may be overcome, the causes must be found, and, if possible, eradicated, or else some arbitrary power must intervene, and, by artificial processes, overcome the operating causes.

The incontrovertible cause toward which this combined testimony points, is the *poverty of the parents*. The love of one's offspring is one of the strongest of human passions. Parents, as a rule, will deny themselves of the necessities of life for the sake of their little ones. It is true that there are some so hardened by the crushing influences of poverty, or shrunken by the narrowing influences of avarice, that they will use the holy office of parent for the base purposes of gain.

The sale of their children by the peasantry of England in the fifteenth century, as well as the like conditions in our own sister States, under the demoralizing influences of chattel slavery, in the nineteenth, are evidences of the possibilities of human degradation, under circumstances wherein the baser nature rules the human, and not the natural operation of the human heart. We shrink with horror at every recital of child torture or outrage. ,In the annals of crime, there is nothing so appalling as those instances where the heart of the father or mother seems possessed with a hatred of its own, and wreaks upon its innocence outrageous physical torture or mental deformity.

This feeling is so strong, that many well-meaning men have answered my appeal for legal interference against the employment of children, with an outburst of indignation against those parents who would permit their little ones to spend their days of childhood amid the dangers to body, mind and soul, of a cotton or woollen mill.

During years of experience, investigation and observation, covering visits to nearly all of the manufacturing cities and towns in this Commonwealth, officially and unofficially, and in a way under both circumstances that gave me the entry to the homes of, and an opportunity to form an acquaintance with, the factory operatives, I have met with but few, as compared with the whole number, who did not hate the circumstances that compelled them to send their children to the mill.

The all-pervading power of custom in the old countries has somewhat checked the natural flow of human sympathies, so that it became half natural to expect to derive some help from the earnings of the child, and this feeling is fully stimulated by the selfish interests of the employers. "Men with growing families" is the standard demand in many of our manufacturing centres. Indeed, so well is this need understood, that it is made an excuse for the discharge of persons who have made themselves obnoxious to factory rule * by the

---

* Mr. Samuel Moores, a factory operative, sixty years of age, extolled by his overseer and by the superintendent as a very skilful, competent and faithful operative, was discharged, with the explanation that his employer "wished men with growing families."

advocacy of ten-hour legislation for minors and women, and half-time schools for children.

Yet with all this power of custom, demand and necessity, the factory operatives stand as a unit for reduced hours of labor for women and minors, and for the half-time system of England; and, whenever they are sufficiently congregated or free to act independently, they never fail to express themselves as freemen should, at the ballot box. Their poverty is the motive power that takes the child to the factory. Often the child is brought to the mill with the mother or father, for there is no one at home to care for him. When in Fall River recently, I visited many of the factory tenements, before school hours. In some, I found little children, two and four years of age, half dressed, father and mother at work, and the only care these little ones would have until the noon hour, if they receive any, would be the visit of some superannuated old lady.

In another place, I found a little babe, of less than two years of age, under the care of a girl of six. These are not exceptions, but the rule.

The testimony of a mule spinner, given before the Bureau of Statistics of Labor (p. 476, Senate Document 150—1871), gives so vivid a description of the usual factory life, and as that report is out of print, I reproduce it here, and vouch for the correctness of the description.

"Am English born, and have been a spinner since ten years of age; have a wife and two children; herself and a child, 12 years old, work in the mill, both weaving; the wife, with girl's help, tends ten looms, running 156 picks per minute; some tend eight, some seven, if without child help. Wife and child leave the house four days of the week at 6.20 in the morning, and do not return till about 7.30 at night. Wednesdays and Saturdays they leave home at 5.30 A. M., and on Saturdays get home at about 4.15 P. M., so that they are absent from home on four days of each week thirteen hours ten minutes; Wednesday of each week fourteen hours; Saturday of each week ten hours forty-five minutes, making for absence from home each week, seventy-seven hours and twenty-five minutes. Of this time they occupy about three hours going and returning, and four and one-half in eating dinner at the mill, as they never go home to do that.

"For breakfast we manage thus: I get up at 5 o'clock, and wife and children lie till I get the meal ready, then they get up, we eat and start for the mill. *Question.* Do you mean to say that you get the breakfast? *Answer.* Yes, sir. *Q.* Who gets the dinner? *A.* We make it and put it in the pails over night, because we have no time in the morning. I take my dinner to the mill and eat it there, then I run home and do a little choring, chop wood, and the like of that, to get ready for the night. I have bread and meat and a little pie, the same as wife has. I get home at seven o'clock, and help along supper until she gets home, and then it will take us both until half-past seven to get ready to commence on the supper, and we get through supper about eight o'clock. *Q.* In the summer time you have a little daylight, and in the winter none at all? *A.* Yes, sir. *Q.* Does what you now describe agree with your mill life in England, before you came here? *A.* No; in England we could go to our dinners. *Q.* Wife, child and all? *A.* The wife didn't work all the time. When she did, she went home to dinner. A good many there keep the old folks at home, and they generally do the work. *Q.* Is this the common way in which operatives in your city live? *A.* Yes, sir. *Q.* All of them? *A.* Yes, sir. *Q.* Through all the mills? *A.* Yes, sir; those that have wives that go to the mill. *Q.* They all live pretty much as you now describe? *A.* Yes, sir; all the difference will be, that some of them put up their dinners in the morning, and we put up ours at night. The dinner stands in the pails from the night time till the next noon. *Q.* What time do you get home on Saturday afternoon? *A.* Four o'clock; we leave off at quarter before four. *Q.* How do you employ yourselves on Sundays? Give a general description of the life of factory people on Sunday. *A.* Some different from others, of course; I generally lie in bed until about seven o'clock Sundays. Then we both get up and get the children ready for Sunday-school and send them to school, and then it takes wife and me about all the time to wash, clean and scrub up the house, and cook the extra dinner for Sunday, so we can have a comfortable meal. We have warm dinners on Sunday. In the afternoon we sometimes take a nap. Then I get supper and take a walk round and get myself ready for Monday morning again. *Q.* You describe the common factory life on Sunday? *A.* So far as I am concerned, it is about so. *Q.* Why do you not attend church on Sunday? *A.* I really have not time, because if I went to church, my woman would have all the work to do, and it would take her all the day Sunday, and that would be seven days' work, and I would be resting and she working, so I stay at home and help her, and we get through just in time for dinner, and then we take a nap and take a walk in the afternoon. *Q.* Was that your way in England? *A.* Yes, sir. *Q.* You didn't attend church there? *A.* No, sir. *Q.* Do the factory people of England, as a general thing, attend church? *A.* No, sir ; I do not suppose they do ; the majority do not, any way. They are too tired, I suppose, though when we had ten hours a day we had considerable more time than we have now. In England, we had even more, because we had no wood to chop. We burnt coals, and we could kindle them with paper, and then we had taps in the sink and got water from them, but here we have to fetch water ; we have to fetch it from one hundred to two hundred yards in some places. There we had taps on the sink for cleaning water and drinking. I don't think they have taps even in boarding-houses in our city. *Q.* Your children attend Sunday-school? *A.* Yes, sir. *Q.* When does your wife do the mending for the family? *A.* She does it at night after we have had supper. *Q.* Did you marry a factory girl? *A.* Yes, sir ; she was brought up in a factory from eight years of age. *Q.* What opportunities had she had at any time during her life to acquire a knowledge of household work? *A.* I don't know that she had much. Factory girls can learn cooking, washing, mending and household work after they get home from mill, and at no other time. I don't know as they are as apt at these things as out-of-mill girls who live at home or service. They cook plain food pretty well. My wife lets out the washing (she has to), at seventy cents a dozen. I have my youngest child at home ; she is ten years old ; she gets her own breakfast from what we leave for her on the table. Then she washes herself, or comes to the mill, and we wash her. At a little before nine o'clock she goes to school, and then comes to me at the house when I go from the mill after twelve o'clock to job round a little. She eats for dinner what is left in my pail. I go back to mill, leaving her at the house till about two o'clock, when she again goes to school. After school she comes to me at the mill and I give her the house-key. She goes home, unlocks and waits for us to come home. My wife has worked in a mill all the time since marriage, except when confined. Our children took care of themselves after about five years old. Before that, grandmother looked after them. That was when we were in England. She is now dead. *Q.* How near their time of confinement have you known pregnant women to work in a mill? *A.* To within six weeks, or much less, and to return to their looms in four weeks after confinement. But that is not common ; ten or twelve weeks is more common on each side of confinement. *Q.* At what age of children do mothers leave them to go back to the mill? *A.* English people leave them from five to twelve months old. *Q.* Is what you describe the general custom of factory parents? *A.* Yes, sir ; they leave them the same. The largest portion of English married people work in the mill and do as I do. *Q.* Do they do this all the year round? *A.* Yes, sir ; winter and

summer.   *Q.* But in the winter it is dark before five o'clock P. M.;
what does a child at home do till the parent gets home after seven
o'clock?   *A.*   It lights the lamp and waits; mine does.

This man is a kind father and good citizen, and hoped for
better times. *Will they come?* We fear not, for him. But
the children are the wards of the State. They can and must
be saved from the brutalizing influence of ignorance and
want, or else their testimony will be given in worse grammar, and not before a bureau of investigation, but before a
terrified and at last an awakened populace.

It may be easy to stigmatize this as the dream of a fanatic,
but clear eyes have long seen the danger. In another place
will be found the opinions of Horace Mann, as given in the
third annual report of the Board of Education, 1840.

As poverty cannot be abolished by any legislative decree,
it behooves the law-makers to devise some method that will
act as a counterbalance to its baneful influence. There are
two elements over which the general court has control:
" The hours of labor and the schooling of children." Legislation upon these subjects is no novelty. The founders of our
institutions recognized this principle, and, as early as 1650,
adopted the following :—

"Forasmuch as the good education of children is of singular
behoof and benefit to any Commonwealth; and whereas, many
parents and masters are too indulgent and negligent of their duty
in that kind, it is therefore ordered by this court and the authority
thereof, that the selectmen of every town in the several precincts
and quarters where they dwell, shall have a vigilant eye over their
brethren and neighbors, to see, first, that none of them shall suffer
so much barbarism in any of their families, as not to endeavor to
teach by themselves or others, their children and apprentices so
much learning as may enable them perfectly to read the English
tongue, and knowledge of the capital laws, upon penalty of twenty
shillings for each neglect therein."

In the May session of the general assembly of Connecticut for 1813, cotemporaneous with the incorporation of companies for manufacturing purposes, an act was passed to secure
the elementary instruction of children employed in factories
and manufacturing establishments, which, in the edition of the
statutes of 1838, is embraced in the seventh and eighth sections

of the act relating to masters and servants and apprentices, and of which the following is a synopsis :—

" Section 7 requires the president and directors of all factories, which are now or hereafter shall be legally incorporated, and the proprietor or proprietors of all other manufacturing establishments in this State to cause the children employed in such factory or establishment, in whatever manner bound, to be taught to read and write, and instructed in the first four rules of arithmetic, provided the term of services shall be of so long duration that such instruction can be given.

" Section 8 provides for a board of visitors, to be composed of the civil authority and selectmen, for and within such towns in which such factories or manufacturing establishments do or may exist, or a committee by them appointed, ' whose duty it shall be,' in the month of January, annually, or at such other time or times as they shall appoint, carefully to examine, and to ascertain whether the requisitions of this act * * * * * be duly observed ; any violation thereof, which may be discovered, to be reported ' to the next county court within the county within which the same shall have occurred ; and thereupon, such county court shall cause ' such reported offenders ' to appear before such court to answer in the premises' ; and if found guilty of not duly attending to the education of children by them respectively employed, as is by this act required, or that due attention is not paid to preserve the morals of such children, it shall be the duty of such court, and they are hereby authorized at their discretion either to discharge the indentures or contracts relating to such minors, and by which they may be bound to render services in such establishments, or they may impose such fine, or forfeiture upon the proprietor or proprietors of such establishments, as they may consider just and reasonable, provided the same shall not exceed the sum of one hundred dollars."

This is claimed to be the earliest legislative movement in behalf of children employed in factories and manufacturing establishments.

In his report on the school laws, the secretary of the board of commissioners of common schools, Connecticut, May, 1841, says :—

" The amount of instruction secured, or aimed to be secured, is altogether too small for any person, who, at the age of manhood, is to share in the privileges, duties and honors of society.   The health and physical education of all children under fourteen years of age, should be secured, by limiting the period of their daily employment to eight hours, and entirely prohibiting their employment at night."

Connecticut, though justly proud of her early attention to educational matters, is not alone in attempts to avert the danger of an *ignorant sovereignty.* Nearly all of the New England States have established precedents for further legislation in this direction. Massachusetts, under the inspiration of her great educator, Horace Mann, sought early to impress upon the people the full importance of their duty. In 1836, the Hon. Jas. G. Carter, chairman of the committee on education, made a report to the house of representatives of that year, in which, after referring to the growth of the manufacturing interest, and the consequent change of employment and condition of large classes of the people, says :—

" Two principal causes, founded upon the animal and imperious wants of our nature, and upon self-interest, that strongest of motives, politically speaking, are in constant operation to frustrate and prevent that universal education, which our institutions suppose and require, within the sphere of large manufacturing establishments. * * * * Labor being dearer in this country than it is in any other with which we are brought in competition in manufacturing, operates as a constant inducement to manufacturers to employ female labor, and the labor of children, to the exclusion of men's labor, because they can be had cheaper."

After describing the condition of the families who made up the factory population of that time, as those that have been unfortunate or from some cause unsuccessful in agriculture or other employments, and who despair of obtaining more than a comfortable support or a bare subsistence ; or of families formed around the establishments on the strength of the then present prospect of gaining a certain support; or by those young people who depend solely upon their daily wages and have nothing to expect but what they can obtain from day to day or from week to week, he says :—

" Of course, when such families, numerous and indigent, as they generally are, begin to increase, and when their wants begin to press hard upon their scanty means of comfort, or perhaps even of neces-

5

sary subsistence, there is a strong interest and an urgent motive, to seek *constant* employment for their children, at a very early age, if the wages obtained can aid them even but little in bearing the burden of their support.

"These two causes or principles of interest, in the *employer* on the one hand, and in the *employed* on the other, are operating, silently, perhaps, but steadily and powerfully, to deprive young females particularly, and young children of both sexes, in a large and increasing class in the community, of those means and opportunities of mental and moral development and cultivation, which are essential to their becoming the intelligent mothers and educators of the next generation, and good citizens of the republic."

This committee reported the following Act, which was passed in the same year, and amended in 1838 :—

AN ACT to provide for the better Instruction of Youth employed in Manufacturing Establishments.

SECT. 1. From and after the first day of April, in the year eighteen hundred and thirty-seven, no child under the age of fifteen years shall be employed to labor in any manufacturing establishment, unless such child shall have attended some public or private day school where instruction is given by a teacher qualified [*i. e.*, qualified to instruct in "orthography, reading, writing, English grammar, geography, arithmetic, and good behavior,"] according to the first section of the twenty-third chapter of the Revised Statutes, at least three months of the twelve months next preceding any and every year in which such child shall be so employed.

SECT. 2. The owner, agent or superintendent of any manufacturing establishment, who shall employ any child in such establishment contrary to the provisions of this act, shall forfeit the sum of fifty dollars for each offence, to be recovered by indictment, to the use of common schools in the towns respectively where said establishment may be situated. [*Approved by the Governor, April 16, 1836.*

The following is the amendment :—

AN ACT in addition to an Act to provide for the better Instruction of Youth employed in Manufacturing Establishments.

No person shall be liable to the penalty provided in the act passed the sixteenth day of April, in the year one thousand eight hundred and thirty-six, entitled "An Act to provide for the better instruction of youth employed in manufacturing establishments," who shall in each year, before employing any child under the age of fifteen years, as in said act mentioned, obtain and preserve a certificate signed by the instructor of the school where such child attended at least three months out of the twelve months preceding, as in said act is provided, that such child has received the instruction in said act intended to be secured ; the truth of which certificate shall be sworn to by the said instructor before some justice of the peace for the county where such instructor resides ; and upon said certificate shall also be certified the fact of such oath or affirmation by such justice."

The report of the Hon. Horace Mann, secretary of the Board of Education, January, 1840, contains the following observations upon this law :—

" It is obvious, that the consent of two parties is necessary to the infraction of this law, and to the infliction of this highest species of injustice upon the children whom it was designed to protect. Not only must the employer pursue a course of action, by which the godlike powers and capacities of the human soul are wrought into thorough-made products of ignorance, and misery and vice, with as much certainty and celerity as his raw materials of wood or cotton are wrought into fabrics for the market by his own machinery ; but the parent also must be willing to convert the holy relation of parent and child into the unholy one of master and slave, and to sell his child into ransomless bondage for the pittance of money he can earn. Yet, strange to say, there are many parents, not only of our immigrant, but of our native population, so lost to the sacred nature of the relation they sustain towards the children whom they have brought into all the solemn realities of existence, that they go from town to town, seeking opportunities to consign them to unbroken bodily toil, although it involves all the deprivation of all the means of intellectual and moral growth ;—thus pandering to their own vicious appetites, by adopting the most efficient measures to make their offspring as vicious as themselves."

In 1842, the hours of labor for children under twelve years was limited to ten per day with a penalty of fifty dollars. In 1865, eighteen weeks' schooling was allowed to all under twelve, and twelve weeks to all between twelve and fifteen. In 1866, the following law was passed. It was by far the best law we have ever had :—

AN ACT in relation to the Employment of Children in Manufacturing
Establishments.
Be it enacted, &c., as follows:

SECT. 1.   No child under the age of ten years shall be employed
in any manufacturing establishment within this Commonwealth, and
no child between the age of ten and fourteen years shall be so employed, unless he has attended some public or private day school
under teachers approved by the school committee of the place in
which such school is kept, at least six months during the year next
preceding such employment; nor shall such employment continue
unless such child shall attend school at least six months in each
and every year.

SECT. 2.   The owner, agent or superintendent of any manufacturing establishment, who knowingly employs a child in violation of
the preceding section shall forfeit a sum not exceeding fifty dollars
for each offence.

SECT. 3.   No child under the age of fourteen years shall be
employed in any manufacturing establishment within this Commonwealth, more than eight hours in any one day.

SECT. 4.   Any parent or guardian who allows or consents to the
employment of a child, in violation of the first section of this act,
shall forfeit a sum not exceeding fifty dollars for each offence.

SECT. 5.   The governor, with the advice and consent of the
council, may, at his discretion, instruct the constable of the Commonwealth and his deputies, to enforce the provisions of chapter
forty-two of the General Statutes, and all other laws regulating the
employment of children in manufacturing establishments, and to
prosecute all violations of the same.   [*Approved May 28, 1866.*

This law remained upon the statute-book until the spring
of 1867, when it was repealed by the passage of the following :

AN ACT in relation to the Schooling and Hours of Labor of Children employed in
Manufacturing and Mechanical Establishments.
Be it enacted, &c., as follows:

SECT. 1.   No child under the age of ten years shall be employed
in any manufacturing or mechanical establishment within this Commonwealth ; and no child between the ages of ten and fifteen years
shall be so employed, unless he has attended some public or private
day school, under teachers approved by the school committee of
the place in which such school is kept, at least three months during
the year next preceding such employment: *provided*, said child
shall have lived within the Commonwealth during the preceding six

months; nor shall such employment continue, unless such child shall attend school at least three months in each and every year; and *provided*, that tuition of three hours per day in a public or private day school, approved by the school committee of the place in which such school is kept, during a term of six months, shall be deemed the equivalent of three months' attendance at a school kept in accordance with the customary hours of tuition; and no time less than sixty days of actual schooling shall be accounted as three months, and no time less than one hundred and twenty half-days of actual schooling shall be deemed an equivalent of three months.

SECT. 2. No child under the age of fifteen years shall be employed in any manufacturing or mechanical establishment more than sixty hours in one week.

SECT. 3. Any owner, agent, superintendent or overseer of any manufacturing or mechanical establishment who shall knowingly employ, or permit to be employed, any child in violation of the preceding sections, and any parent or guardian who allows or consents to such employment, shall, for such offence, forfeit the sum of fifty dollars.

SECT. 4. It shall be the duty of the constable of the Commonwealth to specially detail one of his deputies to see that the provisions of this act, and all other laws regulating the employment of children or minors in manufacturing or mechanical establishments, are complied with, and to prosecute offences against the same; and he shall report annually to the governor all proceedings under this act; and nothing in this section shall be so construed as to prohibit any person from prosecuting such offences.

SECT. 5. Chapter two hundred and seventy-three of the acts of the year eighteen hundred and sixty-six is hereby repealed: *provided*, this act shall not affect any proceedings now pending.

SECT. 6. This act shall take effect sixty days from its passage.

The following is the law of 1873 :—

AN ACT relating to the attendance of Children at School.

Be it enacted, &c., as follows :

SECT. 1. Section one of chapter forty-one of the General Statutes is amended to read as follows :

Every person having under his control a child between the ages of eight and twelve years, shall annually cause such child to attend some public day school in the city or town in which he resides, at least twenty weeks; and for every neglect of such duty the party offending shall forfeit to the use of the public schools of such city or town a sum not exceeding twenty dollars; but if the party so neglecting, was not able, by reason of poverty, to send such child to school, or such child has attended a private day school, approved by the school committee of such city or town for a like period of time, or is regularly attending a public or private day school, known as a half-time school, also approved by them, or that such child has been otherwise furnished with the means of education for a like period of time, or has already acquired the branches of learning taught in the public schools, or if his physical or mental condition is such as to render such attendance inexpedient or impracticable, the penalty before mentioned shall not be incurred : *provided*, that no objection shall be made by the school committee to any such school on account of the religious teaching in said school.

SECT. 2.   The second section of chapter forty-one of the General Statutes is amended to read as follows :

The truant officers and the school committee of the several cities and towns shall vigilantly inquire into all cases of neglect of the duty prescribed in the preceding section, and ascertain the reasons, if any, therefor ; and such truant officers, or any of them, shall, when so directed by the school committee, prosecute, in the name of the city or town, any person liable to the penalty provided for in the preceding section.

Justices of police or district courts, trial justices, trial justices of juvenile offenders, and judges of probate shall have jurisdiction within their respective counties of the offences described in this act.

[*Approved May 12, 1873.*

The past thirty-eight years, since the passage of the first law upon the employment and schooling of children, have witnessed the great growth of the manufacture of textiles. Then, a native population filled our factory towns. The weaveroom was the Mecca of the ambitious farmer's daughter,—a Mecca to visit for a few months or years at most, and then return. The old New England pride of education was sufficient compulsory law for them. They were factory girls one day, teacher or wife the next. Theirs were longer days of labor, but they had more privileges and less discipline.

The agent and the spinner sat in the same church ; belonged, perhaps, to the same masonic lodge. The children went to the same school. The deacons of the church were overseers, and a certain public sentiment sustained the operative in a larger freedom.

The hands (workmen) were expected to vote as the head (agent) directed, but as both were generally more truly united in interest, it was in most cases less hardship than now.

Then, the spinner might leave, and become carpenter, teamster, blacksmith or grocer.   Now, we have that dreadful thing, a fixed factory population,—not fixed as to locality, but as to handicraft.   A hand!!   A hind!!   An operative!! Brought up in the mill from childhood; lulled to sleep by buzz of the spindles, or the incessant thud of the loom; short of stature, mostly without beard, narrow-chested, somewhat stooped; a walk not like the sailor's but equally characteristic; not muscular, but tough; flesh with. a tinge as though often greased; cheeks thin, eyes sharp,—a man pretty quick to observe, and quick to act, impulsive and generous, with a good deal of inward rebellion and outward submission.   A lover of freedom, but not to be humbugged with non-interference theories unless it touches his beer; an advocate of short hours by instinct.   *Except to obey*, the agent and overseer are nothing to him.   There is no public sentiment or societary influence to protect him except that of his fellows.   They have a union without organization, and are willing to deny themselves to help their class.   They know there is nothing before them, but to spin or weave.   If they marry, the wife may help, and if there are children, they will be of help, " if they can raise them."

Of course, this does not describe all, for there are different nationalties, each with their peculiar characteristics,—the Protestant English and the Catholic Irish and French-Canadian, the latter of whom are in one respect like the operatives of forty years ago; they work a year or two and then go home.   They are mostly very ignorant, yet their children, when they can be reached, learn quickly.

With such a population, having the past as a bitter memory of wrong, or the ever-present demoralization of want, their home for the most part within the factory walls, with no Yankee hobbies to ride, or to broaden the scope of their thought, they stand before us as the problem for our institutions to solve.   Let them understand they are free men with the largest liberty of speech and of action.   Let them under-

stand that their children are employed, not to help increase
their meagre earnings, but because they are *cheap;* that
there is no philanthropy that inspires the demand for "men
with growing families"; that an *education* will give their
children a better chance, and increase their own earnings.
Then no compulsion will be needed for the many, but only
for the few, whose souls have been made sordid by their
surroundings, and whose natures have been narrowed by
their limited opportunities.

To meet the wants of this population and these conditions,
we have practically, the same tenor of law and system of
education as that which obtained forty years ago. The law
of 1866 was a step in the right direction, inasmuch as it
established a minimum of age at which children could be
employed, gave six months' schooling, and provided a means
of enforcement.

But this law was repealed by that of 1867, and even that
so modified by subsequent law as to place the limit of age to
eight years instead of twelve or ten, and to limit its protection
to those between eight and twelve years of age. None of
these laws have ever been enforced, yet enough has been
done to establish possibilities of success under a law similar
to that of the English Factory Acts.

In Fall River the strong public sentiment in favor of the
ten hour law has caused the establishment of a factory school,
and it is often erroneously thought that this single school
provided for all of the children employed in the mills in that
city. By the report of the superintendent of schools, Mr.
Wm. Connell, it appears that the total number entering these
schools in one year was 1,051—probably not more than one-
third of the children employed.

At a clam-bake given the factory children by the manufacturers of that city, about three thousand participated,
one thousand each day of the three days' carnival.

The Naumkeag school at Salem, the result of the influence of
General Oliver, and of the kindness of Mr. Kimball, superintendent of the mills, from which the school derives its name,
serves, I fear, as a palliative, rather than as an effort to cure,
though it contains an important feature, that of the half-time
school, and is an evidence of the good intent of Mr. Kimball.

I have had no opportunity to visit the other schools at New Bedford and Indian Orchard.

But none of these schools meet the demands of the day. There must be a radical improvement in legislative enactments concerning this matter, before any creditable results can be reached. The manufacturers have a right to demand uniformity. The complaint has been, "the general disregard of the law," and although that cannot excuse any person for its infringement, they have a right to claim an impartial enforcement, such as the present laws do not provide.

In his second report, General Oliver says : —

"There is no power conferred whereby the party detailed to attempt its execution can determinately secure satisfactory evidence of its having been violated. No owner, agent, superintendent or overseer of any manufacturing or mechanical establishment, nor any parent or guardian, would be likely to criminate himself, if called on as testimony in any case that might be attempted under the statute, in which such party was concerned.

"No power to enter any such establishment in order to learn of any overt act under the law, is conferred upon any party whatever. Were the person detailed to see to its execution to be refused admittance to the premises of any party suspected, he could not move a step forward.

"It provides for no forms of certificates,—and these should be uniform throughout the State,—nor for other necessary papers to be used in determining either the age of a child employed, or the school attendance of such child, or length of time of employment in mill or elsewhere. It provides for no methods or books of registration to be kept by employers, setting forth the age and birthplace of the several children employed, the dates at which they commenced work, the amount of annual schooling, etc., etc., all of which, and many more, are essential to a perfect working of an exact and practical statute. In all these matters the English law is far preferable to ours.

"It makes it 'the duty of the constable of the Commonwealth to detail ONE of his deputies' to see to compliance with the provision of the Act. In my former report, I have attempted to show that, under my experience, *one man* is wholly insufficient for the perfect fulfilment of duties involving the great and severely important matters contemplated under this statute, a statute intended to protect Massachusetts against the terrible evils which have become manifest under a system which is a shame and a curse to England,

and which will be more calamitous to us here, unless its further progress is resolutely and thoroughly arrested."

In addition to these objections, it may be said that the word "knowingly" was introduced into this law against the protest of its friends. The only excuse that can be offered for its introduction into statute law is, that there was no protection to the employers against the misrepresentation of parents as to age or previous schooling.

What is needed is, a complete Factory Act, similar to that so long in successful operation in England ; an Act designating the minimum and maximum ages to be specially protected, the amount and kind of schooling, the hours of labor per day, etc., and this Act must specially designate the kinds of employment it shall cover; so that the several needs of the different employments may receive special and separate provisions.

It must not be understood that the manufacturers of textiles are alone guilty of wrong in this direction. Our cities are full of these little starvelings. It is estimated that over one hundred thousand children are at work in the various factories of New York City, including tobacco strippers 10,000, envelope makers 8,000, gold-leaf workers, burnishers, paper collar and paper box makers 8,000, twine makers, artificial flower makers 12,000. Many of these latter are children from five to seven years of age.

The author of the "Little Laborers of New York," Mr. C. L. Brace, in "Harper's Magazine," August, 1873, says :—

"What an immense population of children in this city are the little slaves of capital. How intense and wearying is their daily toil, and how much of their health and education is sacrificed in these early years and premature labor ! The evil in New York is evidently enormous, and most threatening to our future. These children, stunted in body and mind, are growing up to be our voters and legislators. There are already over sixty thousand persons in New York who cannot read or write. These little overworked operatives will swell this ignorant throng. Fortunately this great abuse has not escaped the attention of humane men."

The number of children so employed in Boston is not known, yet there are doubtless thousands, and none more in

need of the care of the State than the cash boys and girls of
our large retail stores.

The English Factory Acts.

We cannot give a more brief or condensed statement of the
causes that led to the passage of these Acts, than that contained in the article of Mr. Brace before alluded to.

"In Great Britain, the evil of this great army of infant workers
had increased to an alarming extent. Hundreds of thousands of
little. ones were found growing up without any education, except .the
petty practical experience of the small branch of factory labor in
which they were engaged, without any full development of body,
their little forms bent and rickety, their countenances pale, their
growth stunted by premature labor, and arriving at manhood utterly
unfitted either to be citizens or the heads of new families. Vast
numbers of them also died under this youthful slavery, and the
mines and factories were discovered to be an immense slaughter-
house for these unfortunate children.

"At length a band of devoted reformers and philanthropists
arose, who were determined that this burning shame of their country
should be wiped out; who felt that the wealth and culture of
England rested on a hideous foundation, when the labor of
oppressed children built up the structure. They began an incessant
agitation against the over-labor of factory children. They wrote
for the press, printed documents, held public meetings, petitioned
parliament, and sought in every way to rouse the public feeling and
conscience. They had against them the indifference of the poor
parents themselves, and an enormous factory interest which made
rich profits out of the toil of these unhappy children of poverty.
Everywhere the specious argument was brought forward, that the
poor themselves, most of all, needed the labor ; that the earnings of
the children supported the families of the laborers, and if these were
excluded from the factories, they would all come upon the unions
or the public almshouses. It was claimed that it was better to
support the children of the laborers even by their own overwork,
than to keep them in poor-houses.

"It was urged that it was an oppression on the parents who had
brought these children into the world, not to allow them to use their
earnings. The production of England would be diminished, it was
said, and she would lose in the markets of the world, if this great
source from children's labor were dried up. Even the education of
the factory was lauded, and it was claimed that the incessant labor

on one object was better for the child than the training it would get
in the streets. To direct the manufacturer where to procure labor,
and where not, was an interference with 'freedom of trade.' Capital
and labor, even child's labor, should be left to natural laws.

"Against all these sophistical arguments, however, the humanity
of England asserted itself. It saw it was the manifest duty of the
state to guard the children of the poor and unfortunate against the
greed of capital and the indifference of their own parents. It felt
that these little beings are the wards of the public ; that they ought
not to be dwarfed in body and cramped in mind by the covetous-
ness of others ; that they had a claim on the protection of the
fortunate. It was more and more seen, also, that it was not for
the interest of England that a great multitude of human beings
should grow up among the people, ignorant in mind, weakened in
body and unfit for the duties of manhood. There were ' dangerous
classes ' enough in the English cities, whom no reformation or legislation could reach, without adding to them this immense mass of
children, enslaved, as it were, in their early years. The interest of
the state was evidently in education, even if production were diminished. A greater evil than poverty was wide-spread ignorance.
It was clear, too, that this great class of children would produce all
the more hereafter if their minds could be trained in childhood.
The best condition for popular wealth is popular education. Moreover, it was not believed that the exclusion of the children from the
factories would drive the families to the almshouse. There was no
difficulty, evidently, in arranging for half-time schools and half-time
work. The one would help the other. The young laborer would
be the better for his school, and the young scholar for his toil.

"After incessant discussion and a long contest, the English
'Factory Bills' were carried through parliament, were repeatedly
amended, improved, and enlarged, until they form now a ponderous
blue-book. These Acts have been rigorously executed, and their
effect has been that hundreds of thousands of little ' white slaves '
have been redeemed from slavery, saved from premature toil and
sickness, and that a new class of English laborers is growing up,
better educated, healthier, happier, and of more value to their employers. The reform was one of the most glorious and beneficent
ever carried out in Great Britain."

These Acts have been so often referred to in the public
documents of the State for the past few years, it may be well
to give somewhat of their general plan. Quoting from "The
Factory Acts made easy, or how to Work the Law without

risk of Penalties," by Robert Baker, Esq., one of Her Majesty's Inspectors of Factories, 144 pp. 16mo, the following is a very brief synopsis of some of the main features.

FACTORY ACTS.

Accidents.

If any accident happens in a factory to any person employed therein, so that that person cannot return to his or her work by nine o'clock of the following morning, the occupier, or if he is not at the mill, the principal manager, must, within the next twenty-four hours after the accident, send a notice, in writing, of the accident, to the certifying surgeon of the district.

The following is a form to send to the surgeon, which might usefully be employed in case of such accidents :—

SEPTEMBER 1, 187

To Mr.   , *Certifying Surgeon,*

SIR :—An accident has happened this day [or yesterday] to
             , a person employed by us. She resides at   ,
whither she has been removed. [or, after the word us, " She has
been removed to   ."]

I am, sir,

For   Mill,

Manager.

The surgeon, having received notice of an accident, is to proceed as soon as possible to the factory, and make an investigation into the nature and cause of the injury, and report upon it to the inspector.

Actions for damages may be brought in behalf of any person injured by machinery (including mill-gearing) in a factory.

The certifying surgeon has a full right of entry into any factory, and into any room in any building into which a person to whom an accident has happened may have been removed, for the purpose of making an investigation into the nature of the accident : and he may question any person alone, if he likes, about it, or may do any other act that an inspector might do, such as the examination of the machinery by which, or the place where, the accident happened, so far as such an investigation may require it, but no further.

Alphabetical Index.

In all mills where more than twenty children or young persons are employed, an alphabetical index must be kept.

Certifying Surgeons.

A certifying surgeon must be a person registered to practise surgery or medicine, and he is to be appointed by an inspector, who is to make known the appointment to the mill occupiers of the district.

No surgeon occupying a factory, or having a beneficial interest in a factory, can be a certifying surgeon. The surgeon must register his visits to the factory, in the proper place in the register of workers, punctually, as in the following form :—

DATE OF VISITS.			Number of Persons presented for Examination.	Number of Certificates granted.	Signature of the Surgeon.
Months.	Days.	Years.			
June, .	12	1870	6	4	Edw. Wales.
June, .	19	1870	None.	None.	Edw. Wales.
June, .	26	1870	2	1	Edw. Wales.
July, .	2	1870	4	3	Edw. Wales.

Cleaning.

No shaft of any description, nor any drum, wheel, or pulley, by which the motion of the first moving power is communicated to any machine appertaining to any manufacturing process, must be cleaned by any child, female or young person, when the same is in motion.

The machines themselves may be cleaned when in motion; but no person, of the classes above mentioned, must be allowed to work between the fixed and traversing part of any self-acting machine while the latter is in motion.

Clock.

The time of beginning and ending work, and of meals, must be regulated by a clock, open to public view, which has been approved of in writing by the inspector or sub-inspector of the district.

A few minutes may be allowed before the engine or wheel starts, and after it ceases, for the hands to get in and out of the mill; but any work done by hand—such as weaving, slubbing, dusting the windows, cleaning, or oiling, or any-thing, in fact (unless by male persons above eighteen years of age), either voluntarily or by order, either before the moving power has commenced or after it has ceased, unless within the working hours, and exclusive of the meal hours,— is illegal, and may render the employer or his agent, as the case may be, liable to a penalty for wrong employment.

Employment.

A person is considered to be employed in a factory when doing any kind of work whatsoever within the outer gates or bounds of any factory, whether for or without wages, whether as a learner or otherwise—about or amongst any article made of cotton, wool, hair, silk, flax, jute, hemp, or tow, either separately or mixed.   And even if a person is found in a factory where any of these articles are used as materials, though not working, except when all the machinery is stand-ing, and no manufacturing process carried on, or when bring-ing food to the workers between four and five o'clock in the afternoon, such person is considered to be employed, unless evidence can be shown to the contrary.

Flax Mills.

Neither child, young person, nor woman, can be employed in a wet spinning-room, unless the workers are protected from being wetted; and where steam is used, unless where the steam is prevented from escaping.

Hours of Work.

Young persons and women cannot begin before six o'clock in the morning, nor work later than six o'clock in the evening (by the clock which has been approved and declared), on Mondays, Tuesdays, Wednesdays, Thursdays and Fridays, except from the first of October to the thirty-first of March, inclusive, when, on writing to say so to the inspector, stating for how long the alteration will be continued (such period being not less than a month), the hours of work may be altered, from seven in the morning till seven in the evening. But in no case is work allowed on Saturday after two o'clock, P. M.

Inspectors and Sub-Inspectors.

An inspector or sub-inspector may enter every part of a factory, either by night or by day, when any person is employed therein.

Either of them may, by day, enter any place which they may think to be a factory, or any school in which children employed in factories are educated; may take with them into any factory the surgeon, or any peace officer; may examine all documents; may annul the certificates of the surgeon; may give notice in writing of any dangerous machinery which they may observe in a factory; may summon any person to appear before the justices, either as principals or witnesses: they are protected in their office by the provisions of 24 Geo. III., c. 44, being extended to them. The inspector may appoint certifying surgeons, make rules for their guidance, and may also annul such appointments.

Lost Time.

When the number of hours lost is more than can be made up within the twenty-four of the same day, without working the hands more than ten hours and a half, then it may be made up at the rate of an hour a day within the next six months. But no lost time can be recovered on a Saturday afternoon.

Mill-gearing.

"Mill-gearing" comprehends every shaft, and every wheel, drum, or pulley, by which the motion of the first moving power is communicated to any machine appertaining to the manufacturing process.

"Machinery" comprehends all the various parts of the machines by which the processes of manufacture are carried on. (7 Vic., c. 15, S. 73.)

The gearing wheels of machinery constitutes its dangerous parts. They are first tó be observed, and then to be described in a notice to be served on the occupier, by the inspector or sub-inspector; after which notice, if an accident happens by them to any person for want of fencing, the penalty may be a hundred pounds, together with costs, however slight the accident may be; and unless the fences are kept secure continuously, heavy penalties may continuously be inflicted.

Meal-Times.

The time allowed for meals is an hour and a half, between half past seven in the morning aʋᵈ six in the evening.

No person under eighteen years of age, and no woman, can be employed more than five hours before one o'clock at noon, without an interval of thirty minutes.

Neither child, young person, nor woman, being a worker, must be allowed to remain in any room in which any machinery is then at work, or manufacturing process being carried on, during any meal hours.

Notices.

The following notices are required to be hung up at the entrance of the factory, on movable boards, and elsewhere, where the inspector or sub-inspector may direct :—

Name and address of the Inspector of this district :	A. B. Factory office.	Home Office, London.
Name and address of sub-Inspector of this district :	A. B.	[Place.]
Name and address of the Surgeon who grants certificates for this factory :	A. B.	[Place.]
Clock by which the hours of work are regulated :	at	Clock,

7

The Time allowed for Meals in this Factory.

DAYS OF THE WEEK.	BREAKFAST.		DINNER.		TEA.	
	From	To	From	To	From	To
Monday, ...	8	8.30	12.30	1.30	–	–
Tuesday, ...	8	8.30	12 30	1.30	–	–
Wednesday, ...	8	8.30	12.30	1.30	–	–
Thursday, ...	8	8.30	12.30	1.30	–	–
Friday, ...	8	8.30	12.30	1.30	–	–
Saturday, ...	8.30	9	–	–	–	–

Date.

Manager [or *Occupier*].

An abstract of this Act is to be also hung up at the entrance of a factory, and elsewhere if required.

The subjoined notice is required to be either given or sent: "When any person begins to occupy a factory, a notice must be sent to the 'Office of the Factory Inspectors, London,' within the first month of occupancy, under a penalty of from two to five pounds."

Parents.

If a parent (who must be assumed to know the age of his own child) takes such child when under the required age to work, either at eight or thirteen, as the case may be, and on the strength of the parent's assertion the child is employed, or is employed full time when by right it should only have been employed half-time, such parent may be liable to a fine of twenty shillings.

But if, on the representation of the parent, the surgeon grants a certificate of thirteen, the parent knowing that the child is not thirteen, then the parent is liable to imprisonment for six months. The parent is the person to cause his child who is a half-timer to attend school; which, if he neglects to do, he may be fined twenty shillings for every neglect.

Registers.

The registers are never to be kept locked up, but are to be at all times accessible both to the surgeon and the inspectors; and are to be produced, on demand, to an inspector or sub-inspector when the factory is at work.

The following is the form of registers and the mode of using them :—

For young persons between thirteen and eighteen years of age.

No. of reference to Age-Certificate Book, as required in Schedule A.	NAMES.		DATE OF FIRST DAY OF EMPLOYMENT OR RE-EMPLOYMENT.			Say "left" when left, and "18" when 18.
	Surname.	Christian Name.	Month.	Day.	Year.	
64	Jones, .	Mary, .	June	14	1866	Left.
65	Edwards, .	George .	June	16	1866	Eighteen.
66	Baxter, .	Samuel, .	June	18	1866	
XVI.	Lord, . .	Mary, .	June	20	1866	
67	Jackson, .	Grace, .	June	20	1866	
	Johns, .	Thomas, .	July	1	1866	
	Bell, . .	Mary, .	July	1	1866	
	Naylor, .	Sarah, .	July	1	1866	

Mary Lord is 16, and does not require a certificate, and "sixteen" is written where otherwise *the number* of her certificate would have been, and the last three are waiting for certificates till the surgeon comes.

Register of Children.

Names of the Children employed in this Factory before 12 o'clock, at noon, or the morning set.

No. of Reference to Age-Certificate Book, as required in Schedule A.	NAMES.		DATE OF FIRST DAY OF EMPLOYMENT OR RE-EMPLOYMENT.			When a Child ceases to be employed, say opposite its name 'left,' or if transferred to the afternoon set, 'changed,' or 'young person' when 13 yrs. of age.
	Surname.	Christian Name.	Month.	Day.	Year.	
605	Grace, .	Edward, .	June	12	1866	Left.
606	Smiles, .	Sarah, .	June	12	1866	Changed.
607	Baxter, .	Samuel, .	June	18	1866	Young Person.
608	Grace, .	Edward, .	June	20	1866	
	Teal, . .	Mary, .	June	24	1866	
	Worth, .	Sarah, .	June	24	1866	

We thus see that " Sarah Smiles," having changed, is transferred from the morning to the afternoon set ; and that Samuel Baxter is also transferred to the register of young persons.

Saturday.

No child, young person, or woman, can be employed in any factory later than two o'clock in the afternoon, on any pretence whatever.

School.

Every child employed in a factory must attend school ; and the person who receives any direct benefit from the wages of such child, is to take care it does attend. When children are working half-days, the schooling is to begin the day after a child has commenced work ; but when they are working on alternate days, schooling must begin the day before work.

There is no necessity for schooling on Saturdays. No school hours can be reckoned which are taken before eight o'clock in the morning, or after six o'clock in the evening.

The children must have three hours' schooling every Monday, Tuesday, Wednesday, Thursday and Friday, all the year round, when they are at school in the morning. The afternoon set must also have three hours' schooling, except between the first of November and the last day of February, when two hours and a half's attendance is all that is required in the afternoon.

When children work ten hours on alternate days, then the school attendance must be for five hours every other day, except Saturday, taking care that the school day precedes the working day.

When the school is on the factory premises, and the factory ceases to work the whole day, the schooling need not be carried on on that day.

The attendance is to be regular—sickness and other unavoidable causes, and holidays allowed by the Act, excepted.

To show the regularity of this attendance, the occupier is to obtain from the school-master, on Monday in every week, a certificate in the subjoined form, which he is to keep for six months, and produce to an inspector or sub-inspector on demand. Hence the necessity of having it always on the premises from Monday to Friday :—

Form of Certificate.

I hereby certify that the under-mentioned children employed in the factory of   , situated in   , have attended the school kept by me at   , for the number of hours, and at the time on each day. specified in the column opposite to their   names, during the week ending on Saturday, the   day of   , one thousand eight hundred and   , and that the causes of absence stated are true, to the best of my belief.

NAME OF CHILD.	MONDAY. Time.		TUESDAY. Time.		WED'SDAY.* Time.		THURSDAY. Time.		FRIDAY. Time.		Cause of Absence.
	From	To	From	To	From	To	From	To	From	To	
Jane Lee, .	9	12	9	12	–	–	9	12	9	12	
Ruth Wood,	9	12	a	a	–	–	9	12	9	12	Sick. and not at mill.
Jane West, .	1½	4½	1½	4½	–	–	1½	4½	1½	4½	
Ann Wild, .	1½	4½	a	–	–	–	{ 9	12	–	–	Kept at home by mother.
							1½	4½	1½	4½	

* Holiday.

(Signed),   *School-master* [or *School-mistress.*]
The   day of   18

Thus, the precise time that the children attended is entered, and the morning set and the afternoon set are each kept entered in their proper place. The names of the children may be written in the certificate, by anybody; but the time they attended school, and the signature of the school master, must be in his own hand-writing. The letter "*a*" shows that " Ruth Wood " was absent on Tuesday; but was sick at home and not at mill at all, and therefore the excuse was reasonable. On the contrary, "Ann Wild," who was "kept at home by her mother," was made to attend the whole day on Thursday, for that neglect.

School certificates may be given in the above form in loose sheets; but if so, they must afterwards be pasted in a book, to be called the " School-Certificate Book."

The case of "Ann Wild," wherein she makes up her lost school time of Tuesday on Thursday, is not a legal requirement, but a suggested arrangement, whereby the child's loss of wages is saved.

Legally, she could not have been employed during the following week for want of that one day's attendance; but having made it up, she may by consent.

Children often stay away from school, or are kept away, from the most unreasonable causes; such as "running errands," "sick"—although at work—"nursing," and a variety of other excuses; but as the law provides that if a child works any time at all during a week, it must go to school every day of that week, whether it is employed every day or not, unless it leaves the mill altogether during that week, it is clear that an absentee could not have the necessary certificate of attendance on the Monday morning of the following week, and therefore could not be employed. In order, therefore, to check these abuses, and thus to keep the children at work, they should be required to make up these absences. And this mode of curing absenteeism has been productive of the best results, and only requires a little coöperation between the overlooker of the mill, and the master or mistress of the school,—the one, to send a note of absence, on the evening of the absence, and the other to act upon it,—to make the school attendance regular, and it is a far more merciful proceeding than the infliction of fines.

The school book, made up in the form required by law, should be sent to the school every Friday afternoon, for the attendances to be marked therein, and should be returned from the school to the mill every Monday morning, in order that the clerk or overlooker may see whether every child has duly attended school on every day, or on every alternate day, the full number of hours during the week preceding, without which it cannot be legally employed.

The school certificates of a school master or mistress may be annulled by an inspector, by a notice in writing to the occupier, in which notice the reasons of annulment must be stated; these are,—

For incapacity to teach reading and writing.

For immoral conduct.

For being grossly ignorant.

For a want of books and materials to teach reading and and writing; and

For continued neglect to fill up and sign the school certificates.

Surgical Certificates.

Surgical certificates are required for all persons working in factories, from eight to sixteen years of age.

Certificate of Age.

The forms of certificate of age for children, and which are to be printed or written upon white paper, are as follows—

Firstly. Where the surgeon acts on his own opinion :

Factory Act.—Vic. 7, c. 15.
No.

Certificate of age for a child to be employed in the factory of   , situate at   , in the parish of

I,   , of   , duly appointed a certifying surgeon, do hereby certify, That   , son of and   , residing in   , has been personally examined by me this   day of   , one thousand eight hundred and   , and that said child has the ordinary strength and appearance of a child at least eight years of age ; and that I believe that the real age of the said child to be at least eight years ; and that said child is not incapacitated by disease or bodily infirmity from working daily in said factory for the time allowed by this act.

(Signed,)   , *Certifying Surgeon.*

Factories Regulation Act.—Vic. 7, c. 15.
No.   .

Certificate of age for a young person to be employed in the factory of   , situate at   , in the. parish of   .

I,   , of   , duly appointed a certifying surgeon, do hereby certify, That   , son of and   , residing in   , has been personally examined by me this   day of   , one thousand eight hundred and   ; and that the said young person has the ordinary strength and appearance of at least thirteen years of age, and that I believe the real age of said young person to be at least thirteen years ; and that the said young person is not incapacitated by disease or bodily infirmity from working daily in the above-named factory for the time allowed by this act.

(Signed,)   , *Certifying Surgeon.*

A surgeon may refuse to give a certificate of age. If he does, he may be required to give a certificate in writing for so doing

Workers.

Children, young persons, and women, are the persons of whom the law takes cognizance as regards work. Children are all persons between the ages of eight and thirteen years; but in the winding and throwing of raw silk, children become young persons at eleven years of age.

Young persons are all persons between the ages of thirteen and eighteen years.

Women of every age are treated the same as young persons. Lads of eighteen years of age are called men, and are therefore exempt from the provisions respecting "employment."

A child under eight years of age must not be allowed to work at all.

The surgeon is not bound to ask a child's age. He is to give a certificate of its having the ordinary strength and appearance of eight, and that he believes the real age to be eight, and that it is not incapacitated by disease or bodily infirmity from working seven hours. But if he is unable to satisfy himself on these points, he is bound to refuse the certificate, and the child must be sent home at once. If, however, the certificate is refused only for apparent want of real age, and if the parent knows that the child is really eight, and wishes to prove it, he may demand from the inspector or sub-inspector a requisition (gratis), on giving him the name of the child, and of both his parents, and the place where and the year in which he was born. The parent must then take the requisition to the person who has the care of the register of births where the child was born, and tender him a shilling when asking for the register. From him he will receive the register of real age, which must be taken to the surgeon, who will then, if the child is really eight years of age, give the required certificate.

When not making up lost time, a child may begin work in the morning at six, and continue working till one o'clock at noon, with an interval of thirty minutes for breakfast; or it may begin work at the usual afternoon time, and go on till six o'clock in the evening, on every day but Saturday. On Saturday, it cannot work later than two o'clock, on any pretence whatever.

Thus, the ordinary hours of work of any day but Saturday can only be between six in the morning and six in the evening, or, from October to April, between seven in the morning and seven at night.

If the usual dinner-hour of the young persons is twelve o'clock, and not one, the morning set of children cannot stay to carry on any manufacturing process after the young persons have gone away, because no child can remain during any meal-time in any room in which any manufacturing process is then going on. They cannot even clean the machinery during any part of the time noticed as meal hours.

No child can be employed unless it attends some school for three hours a day for all the year round, if in the morning, and also, if in the afternoon, except from the first of November to the twenty-eighth of February, during which four months two hours and a half attendance will do, but for the afternoon set only.

When the child is employed only half a day, the schooling may follow the employment; but when it works alternate days, it must precede it.

A child must attend school from the date of its first employment, whether it is only a learner or not; and so long as it works but five minutes in a week, it must go to school every half-day or every alternate day, as the case may be, reasonable excuses being allowed. It is a common supposition that if there is no work for a child on any day, that it is not bound to attend school on that day; but this is not so. So long as a child is considered a worker, its school attendance must be as regular as that of any other factory children at the same school.

Reasonable excuses are, sickness, and death of a near relative, or very wet days, when the school is far distant in country districts, and the ordinary holidays of the school. But staying at home to nurse or run errands, or any other such employment, renders their factory employment illegal.

Children working alternate days must attend school alternate days (except on Saturday) for five hours, between eight

8

o'clock in the morning and six o'clock in the evening, all the year round.

A child may be employed every alternate day, except Saturday, for ten hours, when the labor of the young persons is limited to ten hours also ; but not when the women and young persons work ten hours and a half. But a child cannot be employed ten hours for two days in succession, and schooled two days in succession ; nor even for ten hours a day on alternate days, until the master of the factory has sent a notice to the inspector, of his intention to work his young persons and children only ten hours, which notice must be repeated whenever ten hours a day, work having been discontinued, is about to be resumed.

A child must not be allowed to clean any part of the mill-gearing, when in motion for the purpose of propelling any part of the manufacturing machinery.

A child must not work between the fixed and traversing part of a self-acting machine while in motion by any mechanical power.

When the certifying surgeon is not employed to grant certificates, a child cannot be allowed to work without a certificate of age ; but when the certificates are granted by the certifying surgeon, a child may be allowed to be employed seven days without a certificate, if the mill is within three miles of the surgeon's residence, and thirteen days if beyond three miles.   The name of every child must be entered in the register of children as soon as it is employed.

The principal feature of the law to which I would call special attention, is that relating to half-time schools.   From all sources comes the testimony that they are in every way a success.   Here in Massachusetts we have the same class of operatives, the same conditions of life, and a stronger necessity for the adoption of the same system.

The Half-Time Factory Schools of England.

Mr. Richard Hinchcliffe, an overseer in a woollen mill, after an absence of twenty-eight years from England, returned during the past summer, and in answer to a request for his testimony upon this subject, writes as follows :—

" During a stay of two months in England the past summer I interested myself much in gathering facts in relation to the half-time system of schooling of English factory operatives. I visited factories in Leeds, Bradford, Rudsey, Farnley, Rochdale, and other important manufacturing centres ; conversed with factory owners and operatives ; all agreed as to the beneficial effects of the system. In a number of the factories I was permitted to call to the overseer's desk any child I saw at work, and I tested the extent of their knowledge of grammar, arithmetic and geography. I found that they would compare favorably with those who had had the opportunity of attending full time. Boys and girls, not over twelve years of age, were capable of properly working out difficult problems in common and decimal fractions ; many could write a fair hand, and in a few cases the penmanship was very creditable.

" Samuel Wray, of Armley, a half-timer, about twelve years old, gave me a beautiful specimen of his penmanship ; he has since been employed as a clerk in the Leeds Wholesale Coöperative Store.

" Robert Burnett, a school-teacher of Leeds, informed me that, as far as his experience went, he was convinced that the half-time scholars were but little, if any, behind those who had attended full time. James Corville, of Manchester, also a school-teacher, gave me similar testimony.

" The parents of factory children were generally satisfied with the half-time system, as it afforded an opportunity for gaining quite a respectable amount of education by the time they reached the age when they would be allowed by law to work full time.

" The half-time factory workers receive much larger wages than were paid to those of the same age who worked full time a quarter of a century ago, so that the half-time system has actually enlarged the *average* aggregate earnings of the factory operative's family.

" I am of opinion that the system is far preferable to the system of educating factory operatives in Massachusetts. Here they go three months to school, and afterwards work nine months in the factory, during which time they forget nearly all they have learned in school."

Protection of Children in Foreign Countries.

In France, many of the merchants and manufacturers of Mulhausen, the proprietors of very considerable establishments thereof, petitioned for the enactment of a law, limiting the age and hours of labor of children. As long ago as 1840, a law was reported by the Baron Charles Dupin, and observed favorably by the Duke de Praslin, the Count Chollet, M. Cousin, then the Minister of Public Instruction, the Marquis Laplace, M. Villemain and Baron de Gerando.

The limit of age was fixed at eight years, and the hours of labor for persons between eight and twelve, at eight hours per day. The greatest objection was to compulsory education. Upon this subject Baron de Gerando said :—

"Ought the law which is intended to afford protection to the children of the working classes to be confined to the protection of the bodily health, or should it be extended to the moral health also? Ought it to be a safeguard only to the physical powers of the child, without regard to the more noble moral and intellectual powers? Ought we to confine ourselves to the care of preparing a generation which will supply able soldiers to the government, or ought we not also to keep in view the importance of preparing good and virtuous citizens for the state, and estimable men for society? These were the questions which we proposed for our consideration; and I now state, openly and frankly, that the ruling sentiment in the committee was, that our object should be to improve not only the physical condition, but also, and more especially, the moral condition of the children of the working classes.

"There are many things to be done to improve the moral condition of the working classes; but the first in point of order, that which will be most powerfully efficacious, unquestionably, is the improvement of education in that class of society.

"But we are told that we wish to introduce the principle of compulsory education into the law. Now, I will declare in the name of the committee, that the idea of compulsion never once entered into our minds.

"I will not discuss the general principle. The distinguished individual who is at the head of the Ministry of Public Instruction entertains the same opinion with myself, at least I hope he does, that it is a salutary principle. It exists in the United States and in Switzerland, and I never heard any complaint of despotic rule, because parents are obliged to send their children to the primary schools. I could say much in favor of that principle. I could show that Article CCCLXXXV. of the Civil Code imposes upon fathers of families the very obligation that we are now contending for, inasmuch as they are required to give their children the benefit of education. Again, it is said that we are introducing into the law a principle of inequality. Our opponents are so sincere men, their objections proceed from such a right motive, that I do not at all fear to meet them on this point. There is no inequality in the law we propose; it is no more than a provision for a special object; it is not a general principle that we wish to establish, but we wish to provide for a special case; and with your leave *I will point out the principal reasons why children employed in factories form an exception, to meet which, separate provision must be made.*

"It is right to leave things to their natural course so long as there is no obstacle to impede it. We should never think of sending an engineer to examine the course of a river, unless something was obstructing its free passage. Now, what is the obstruction in this case? Why, that their working prevents the children from receiving instruction, and is an excuse to those who will not give them any. Parents send their children to the factories to derive profit from them; they find it more convenient to receive wages for their labor than to pay for their schooling; and thus the parent and manufacturer have a common interest. This is an obstruction that we wish to remove.

"There is another class of special circumstances which I wish to explain· to you, and I shall have need of all your indulgence in order that I may be rightly understood. Human labor is composed of two elements—material power and intellectual power. Now, what is, and what always must be, the tendency of human industry? Is it not this,—to endeavor to diminish the amount of the first element, the mechanical man, and exercise that of the second, the intellectual man? Assuming that principle to be admitted, what should be the effect of the invention and multiplication of machinery? Should it not evidently be to substitute a mechanical moving power for a human power? Consequently, to take away from a great number of individuals the necessity of using so much of their muscular powers, but conferring upon them, instead, the opportunity of a proportionate increase of intelligence.

But see what takes place in consequence of the progress of that manufacturing skill about which we boast so much. To what does that extreme division of labor tend? Is it not that an individual, even of mature age, is occupied incessantly in the same operation, in the same motions? You have read in Adam Smith how many work-people are required to make a pin. How does it happen that the making of a pin should require so many hands? Because the same individual performs the same single operation every day of his life, from year's end to year's end, and is thereby condemned to a mechanical and monotonous existence. It is against that tendency that we wish to interpose some obstacle.

"In proportion as the discoveries in arts multiply, and as we make progress in improvement, in like proportion ought the moral and intellectual condition of the species to rise. *The progress of civilization does not depend alone on the increase of wealth; it chiefly depends upon the improved moral and intellectual condition of the population.* All this has been often said, and much better said than I can pretend to do; but with your permission, I will offer some observations which, perhaps, may not yet have been made.

" It is important to draw a distinction between an apprenticed child and an operative child, and I beg you to attend to the distinction I make. The apprentice is in a course of instruction; I do not say that he is taught all he has occasion to know, but nevertheless his faculties are exercised in a variety of ways; he learns the elements of a process, and by and by he becomes more skilful: in short, he learns a trade. With the operative child it is very different. I will take a very simple instance, from the very subject upon which we are now engaged : A child that has passed ten years of his life as a piecer in a spinning-mill will have learned nothing; he will only have acquired the power of doing that which might be performed by a brute, for a tolerably docile ape might be taught to do as much.

" We desire, therefore, that the operative child, condemned to labor at a description of work that is calculated to reduce him to the condition of a brute, may have some compensation by receiving some moral and religious training.

" So far from our proposal being an act of tyranny, we dare to say that no provision in the law is more humane, or more advantageous either to the master or his work-people. We could read to you the very interesting testimony which we have received from one of the partners in one of the largest manufacturing establishments of France, one in which they employ from seventeen hundred to eighteen hundred people. He stated that, for the last twenty years, he and his partner had turned their attention to the moral condition of their work-people, and that they had gradually succeeded in raising it; and that in the same progression the produce of their industry improved in quality and quantity. And, in truth, gentlemen, there is no greater auxiliary to labor than sound morals. Those are the best workmen who have upright and honest sentiments. Improve the moral condition of the working classes, and you will improve their worldly condition."

But it was not until after the war with Germany, that France awoke to the importance of educating her citizens, and Jules Simon, Minister of Public Instruction, introduced a bill, of which the following is a synopsis; having previously expressed his opinion upon the subject in a letter to one of the *maires* of Paris, in which he says :—

" France can only be saved, the republic can only be firmly established, if, through unceasing exertions, we succeed in restoring the moral and intellectual grandeur of our country. That will be our work, our joy, the aim of our whole life, when this fearful and sanguinary tragedy will have passed away. We shall create a generation inaccessible to fear, enlightened with regard to public and private duties, freed from the old prejudices which enervate character and obscure reason,—a generation which, by its enlightened character, its patriotism, its virtue, has become worthy to put an end to the two great plagues of humanity—privilege and war ! "

Bill of Jules Simon.

" 1. Every child, male or female, between the ages of six and thirteen, must receive a minimum of education, either in the public or private schools. This minimum of education is to embrace the obligatory branches of instruction ; and its existence is, at the end of the period of schooling, to be certified by the ministry of public instruction through its subordinates in the departments. 2. A school committee, consisting of delegates from the canton, the maire, the clergyman, and three heads of families appointed by the municipal council, has to watch over attendance at school. 3. The government inspector in each district has a seat and vote in this committee. 4. If a child misses school three times during a month, without excuse, the father or guardian is summoned before the school committee, and is warned. If the case recurs, his name is placarded at the maire's office, and his family is deprived of all aid from the public funds. If this does not induce him to send his child to school, a fine not exceeding one hundred francs is imposed ; and finally, he can be deprived of his rights as a citizen for a period of three years. 5. The school committee issues certificates to children thirteen years of age, after having passed a public examination to which all must submit, whether educated in public or private schools. If, at this examination, it becomes evident that a child, who was supposed to receive private instruction, has in reality not received instruction in the obligatory branches, legal proceedings are instituted against the father or guardian. 6. From the 1st of January, 1880, no citizen twenty-one years of age will be registered as an elector who does not possess the above-mentioned certificate from his local school committee, or give sufficient proof of being able to read or write.   Articles 7 and 8 refer to the appointment of teachers, which is to be preliminary by the inspector of the academy, but definitely only after having passed an examination.   The inspector of the academy is also intrusted with the inspection of elementary schools."

In Switzerland, laws are provided and enforced to compel all children between the ages of six and fourteen to attend school. School teachers are furnished with the names of all the children in the districts, the roll is called every morning, and the absentees noted.   In Italy, a system has been adopted that is calculated to reach every class and condition of children.   Portugal, Russia and Austria are remodelling their school systems; even the Ottoman Empire has established a compulsory education.   The justices of the peace of the wards and villages are compelled to keep a register of the names of all the children who have reached the required age, as well as the names of the parents or guardians.

Conclusions and Recommendations.

It is the undoubted right and duty of the Commonwealth, through her law-making power, to educate all of the children within her borders, without regard to race, nationality or condition.   The refusal or neglect to do this, while at the same time she denies the franchise to those unable to read or write, is an unwisdom and an injustice unworthy of her past record, and dangerous to her future welfare.   Dr. Chalmers said : "It is, without question, both the duty and the right of the civil power to educate the people, such right and such duty resting on two distinct principles, one economic and the other judicial.   Education adds directly to the economic value of men, helping them under all circumstances ; helping them specially, when art brings forward new and better machinery, and science new and better methods, to accommodate themselves thereunto, and so increasing enormously the productive efficiency of their labor.

"That large portion of the people who are educated, and are also living by their own exertions of brain or hand, contributes with generous certainty to the wealth of the country, while a very large portion of those who are uneducated, not only contributes nothing thereto, but is a positive burden upon the community. Upon the fact that, by education, you can diminish the numbers that make up this last set, rests the economic principle. The judicial principle rests on the fact that the laws of a country are *written* laws ; written for the guidance of the people ; and to be guided by them, the people must be able to read them."

Upon the faithful performance of this duty the future welfare of the State depends.

"It is obvious," says Horace Mann, "that children of ten, twelve, or fourteen years of age, may be steadily worked in our manufactories without any schooling, and that this cruel deprivation may be persevered in for years, and yet, during all this period, no very alarming outbreak shall occur to arouse the public mind from its guilty slumber. The children are in their years of minority, and they have no control over their own time or their own actions The bell is to them what the water-wheel and the main shaft are to the machinery which they superintend. The wheel revolves, and the machinery must go ; the bell rings, and the children must assemble. In their hours of work, they are under the police of the establishment ; at other times, they are under the police of the neighborhood. Hence this state of things may continue for years, and the peace of the neighborhood remain undisturbed, except, perhaps, by a few nocturnal or Sabbath-day depredations. The ordinary movements of society may go on without any shocks or collisions,—as, in the human system, a disease may work at the vitals, and gain a fatal ascendency there, before it manifests itself on the surface. But the punishment for such an offence will not be remitted because its infliction is postponed. The retribution, indeed, is not postponed, it only awaits the full completion of the offence ; for this is a crime of such magnitude, that it requires years for the criminal to perpetrate it in and to finish it off thoroughly in all its parts. But when the children pass from the condition of restraint to that of freedom,—from years of enforced but impatient servitude, to that independence for which they have secretly pined and to which they have looked forward, not merely as the period of emancipation, but of long-delayed indulgence,—when they become strong in the passions and propensities that grow up spontaneously, but are weak in the moral powers that control them, and blind in the intellect which foresees their tendencies; when, according to the course of our political institutions, they go, by one bound, from the political nothingness of a child to the political sovereignty of a man,—then, for that people who so cruelly neglected and injured them, there will assuredly come a day of retribution."

To avert that day, I plead for the little ones. For years the voices of warning and entreaty have been raised. Every report from Europe and from our sister States, and every committee, commission, bureau, or other official department before whom this question has been brought, has urged in the strongest language the need of protective and effective legislation.

With the experience of the failure of past appeals, I enter here, even if for the last time, my solemn protest against the narrow policy that looks only to the material gain of the day, and leaves the future to the fate that comes from the neglect of the poor and helpless. Can nothing but calamity arouse us? Must "Granite Mills" burn down, and bury in their ruins the smouldering dust of mother and child, before the law will give to them the power of self-protection? Must children plead in vain? Shall we, with all the terrible warnings of the past, forget our duty? Shall Christian people shrink from Christians' duty, and infants' tears be shed in vain? Robbed of the innocent sports of childhood, weighed down with care, grown prematurely old,—

> "Ah! well may the children weep before you!
>   They are weary ere they run!
> They have never seen the sunshine, nor the glory
>   Which is brighter than the sun.
> They know the grief of man, without his wisdom,
>   They sink in man's despair, without its calm;
> Are slaves, without the liberty in Christdom;
>   Are martyrs, by the pang without the palm;
> Are worn, as if with age, yet unretrievingly
>   The harvest of its memories cannot reap;
> Are orphans of the earthly love and heavenly:—
>   Let them weep! let them weep!"

In these days of legislative interference, when the shield of the State protects the dumb beast from the merciless blows of his driver; when the overworked horse is remembered and released from his work; when capital expends the time of legislatures, taxes the people for any scheme that promises dividends to the stockholders; when monopolies have charters granted them,—then it would seem pitiable if childhood's want of leisure for rest of body and education for zest of mind should be denied them. Massachusetts is behind England, France and Germany, in legislation and in humanity upon this question. She goes on regardless of consequences; forgetful of the inevitable logic of events; protecting the strong, forgetting the weak and the poor,—and all under the false plea of non-interference with the liberties of the people. The children *have rights* that the State is bound to respect. Their right is to play and make merry; to be at school; to be *players*, not *workers.*

The argument that it would increase pauperism by forcing the parents to accept charity as a recompense for the loss of the child's earnings, comes mostly from those who have persistently sought protection through tariff laws. Why not have left our infant enterprises, our manufacturing interests, to the operation of natural laws?

But the argument has met its answer in the experience of England. It is the old objection, raised to blind thoughtless men. It has been the stale argument against all progress, and comes mostly from those who are earnest in the protection of their own selfish interests.

But even admitting that the wages of the factory operatives are so small that they would suffer for the necessities of life, if the earnings of the little ones were deducted from their income, would it not be better to pauperize the half-pauperized operative of to-day, rather than to multiply indefinitely the pauper class of the future? A hundred thousand children growing up in ignorance are not only a hundred thousand paupers in embryo, but they are in turn to be the parents of paupers.

But the prophesied evil of pauperism through the education of children, has no probability of fulfilment. Children are employed because they are cheap, and children's wages, like

those of adults, are governed by natural laws, though sometimes, and for a period, by artificial ones.

When the half-time system shall have been established, and
the minimum age at which children can be employed is placed
at twelve years, then wages will have taken care of themselves. Now the boy of eighteen bids against the father of
thirty, and the girl of sixteen against the mother of twenty-
five. The child of fourteen is now made to do the work of
the youth of eighteen, and at less price. The demand for
cheaper labor continues until the infant of eight is performing
the labor of the child of twelve. This has been the regular
and undeviating course for the past few years. Under proper
factory legislation, this *death-struggle* for an existence, *called
competition*, will have been righteously interfered with, and
the natural laws of God and humanity, instead of the unnatural laws of man and inhumanity, will rule. Wages will
increase, and the half-timers of 1884 will be the peers in
physical beauty, mental capacity and moral life of those
happy ones of this year who, at fourteen, are at school and
at play, making our hearts lighter and hopes brighter with
their presence. The old adage, " all work and no play," has
proved itself no less true than its counterpart, " all play and
no work." But the benefits that will follow this blessing
of the little ones, will accrue not only to them, but to all.
The toil-worn father, robbed in his youth of his birthright,
education, will find himself refreshed and *his home made
holier* through the improved discipline, the awakened culture,
and the higher tone that comes from the school-room. The
factory, with its noise and rude jests, its discipline that of
despotism, its culture and its tone, who shall describe it?
The influence of the Sabbath-school is believed to accomplish
much, not only for those who attend its sessions, but for the
parents of those who come under its Sabbath-day charge.
The day-school with its ten sessions each week, ought and
can be made to exert the most humanizing power of any instrumentality under government. But to reach the highest
possibilities, to receive the fullest results, radical changes
ought to be effected, both in the location and construction of
school-houses upon the basis of health, accommodation and
beauty, and the arrangement of studies not upon the idea that

every pupil is to be a college graduate, but that the majority
are to receive all they can hope to have of school education
by the time they are fifteen years of age.   School-houses,
pleasantly located in little parks of one or two acres,* with
play-grounds and fruits and flowers, school-rooms well ventilated and well *warmed*, not *heated*, the non-attendance for
ordinary causes will be diminished, and the discipline of the
school greatly enhanced.

The first thing that is needed, is regularity of attendance;
and, after that, the other great needs will come in their order.
Can any one doubt that material prosperity will follow?
Massachusetts is wealthy, not because of ignorant or cheap
labor, but because of the *Common Schools.   Common Schools
are an increase of wages;* an increase of wages is a better
distribution of wealth.

It has been said that ignorance and poverty are twin monsters, and that education is a means of removing poverty.
In his last report, Horace Mann dwells at length upon this
subject, in a manner masterly in its logic, as well as matchless in its beauty of diction.   No language of mine can por-
tray so forcibly the wonderful power of education over
material things, or give such warnings of the danger of
neglect.   The unrest of the laboring classes is beginning to
awaken some thinking minds, and the question that is
repeatedly asked, is, "What shall we do with them?"   The
question for statesmen to ask is not what shall be done with
the laborer of to-day, so much as what shall the laborer of
to-morrow be?

What kind of a constituency shall elect the president in
1900? or in the words of Horace Mann, "To what extent can
competence displace pauperism?   How nearly can we free our-

* " Observe the location of city school-houses, four or five stories high, crowded
into narrow streets, where neither sunlight nor pure air can reach them.   At recess,
when the pupils are allowed a few moments to escape the confined atmosphere of the
building, they are sent out into "pens," inclosed by high walls, and paved with brick.
Sir, I will venture the opinion that from two to five years would be added to the average life of the native population of cities, and the mortality among school children be
largely reduced, if public educational structures were required to be built not more
than two stories high, and each located upon a two or three-acre park.   And then, if
fewer hours of study and more hours of out-door physical exercise were required, a
more handsome, vigorous, healthy and intelligent race of men and women would
surely follow."—*From Speech of Hon. Joseph S. Potter, Mass. Senate,* 1873.

selves from the low-minded and the vicious; not by their expatriation, but by their elevation? To what extent can the resources and the powers of nature be converted into human welfare, the peaceful arts of life be advanced, and the vast treasures of human talent and genius be developed? How much of suffering, in all its forms, can be relieved; or, what is better than relief, how much can be prevented? Cannot the classes of crimes be lessened, and the number of criminals in each class be diminished?"

It is the blindest folly to contemplate men only as producers, to estimate only their productive capacity with that of perfected machinery; but even if we were to narrow our vision to this microscopic view of the real issue, we should see, upon scientific investigation, that education is the essential element of success in the accumulation of material prosperity. "It is a remarkable fact that human progress, even in regard to the worldly interests of the race, did not begin with those improvements which are most closely allied to material prosperity. One would have supposed, beforehand, that improvements would commence with the near, rather than with the remote. Yet mankind had made great advances in astronomy, in geometry, and other mathematical sciences; in the writing of history, in oratory, and in poetry; it is supposed by many to have reached the highest point of yet attained perfection in painting and in sculpture, and in those kinds of architecture which may be called regal or religious, centuries before the great mechanical discoveries and inventions which now bless the world were brought to light. And the question has often forced itself upon reflecting minds, why was this preposterousness, this inversion of what would appear to be the natural order of progress? Why was it, for instance, that men should have learned the course of the stars and the revolutions of the planets, before they found out how to make a good wagon-wheel? Why was it that they built the Parthenon and the Colosseum before they knew how to construct a comfortable, healthy dwelling-house? Why did they construct the Roman aqueducts before they constructed a saw-mill? Or, why did they achieve the noblest models in eloquence, in poetry, and in the drama, before they invented movable types? I think we have now arrived at a point where we can unriddle this enigma. *The labor of the world has been performed by ignorant men.*

"As soon as some degree of intelligence dawned upon the workman, then a corresponding degree of improvement in his work followed. At first, this intelligence was confined to a very small number, and, therefore, improvements were few, and they followed each other only after long intervals. They uniformly began in the nations, and among the classes where there was most intelligence. The middle classes of England and the people of Holland and Scotland have done a hundred times more than all the eastern hemisphere besides. What single improvement in art, or discovery in science, has ever originated in Spain, or throughout the vast empire of the Russias? But just in proportion as intelligence—that is, education—has quickened and stimulated a greater and a greater number of minds, just in the same proportion have inventions and discoveries increased in their wonderfulness, and in the rapidity of their succession. The progression has been rather geometrical than arithmetical. By the laws of nature, it must be so. If among ten well-educated children the chance is, that, at least, one of them will originate some new and useful process in the arts, or will discover some new scientific principle, or some new application of one, then among a hundred such well-educated children there is a moral certainty that there will be more than ten such originators or discoverers of new utilities; for the action of the mind is like the action of fire—one billet of wood will hardly burn alone, though dry as suns and north-west winds can make it, and though placed in the range of a current of air; ten such billets will burn well together; but a hundred will create a heat fifty times as great as ten; will make a current of air to fan their own flame, and consume even greenness itself.

"For the creation of wealth, then,—for the existence of a wealthy people and a wealthy nation,—intelligence is the grand condition. The number of improvers will increase, as the intellectual constituency, if I may so call it, increases. In former times, and in most parts of the world, even at the present day, not one man in a million has ever had such a development of mind as made it possible for him to become a contributor to art or science. Let this development proceed, and contributions numberless, and of inestimable value, will be sure to follow. That political economy, therefore, which busies itself about capital and labor, supply and demand, interest and rents, favorable and unfavorable balances of trade, but leaves out of account the element of a widespread mental development, is naught but stupendous folly."

The education of children, then, is the wisest means to secure material prosperity. Here in Massachusetts the danger is imminent, for here the population is more dense than the average of all our other States taken together, and density of population has always been the proximate cause of social inequality.

"If this be so, are we not in danger of naturalizing and domesticating among ourselves those hideous evils which are always engendered between capital and labor, when all the capital is in the hands of one class and all the labor is thrown upon another?

"Now, surely, nothing but universal education can counterwork this tendency to the domination of capital and the servility of labor. If one class possesses all the wealth and the education, while the residue of society is ignorant and poor, it matters not by what name the relation between them may be called; the latter, in fact and in truth, will be the servile dependants and subjects of the former. But if education be equally diffused, it will draw property after it by the strongest of all attractions; for such a thing never did happen, and never can happen, as that an intelligent and practical body of men should be permanently poor. Property and labor, in different classes, are essentially antagonistic; but property and labor, in the same class, are essentially fraternal. The people of Massachusetts have, in some degree, appreciated the truth, that the unexampled prosperity of the State —its comfort, its competence, its general intelligence and virtue—is attributable to the education, more or less perfect, which all its people have received; but are they sensible of a fact equally important; namely, that it is to this same education that two-thirds of the people are indebted for not being, to-day, the vassals of as severe a tyranny, in the form of capital, as the lower classes of Europe are bound to in the form of brute force?

" Education, then, beyond all other devices of human origin, is the great equalizer of the conditions of men—the balance-wheel of the social machinery. I do not here mean that it so elevates the moral nature as to make men disdain and abhor the oppression of their fellow-men. This idea pertains to another of its attributes. But I mean that it gives each man the independence and the means by which he can resist the selfishness of other men. It does better than to disarm the poor of their hostility towards the rich ; it prevents being poor. Agrarianism is the revenge of poverty against wealth. The wanton destruction of the property of others—the burning of hay-ricks and corn-ricks, the demolition of machinery, because it supersedes hand-labor, the sprinkling of vitriol on rich dresses—is only agrarianism run mad. Education prevents both the revenge and the madness. On the other hand, a fellow-feeling for one's class or caste is the common instinct of hearts not wholly sunk in selfish regards for person, or for family. The spread of education, by enlarging the cultivated class or caste, will open a wider area over which the social feelings will expand ; and, if this education should be universal and complete, it would do more than all things else to obliterate factitious distinctions in society.

" The main idea set forth in the creeds of some political reformers, or revolutionizers, is, that some people are poor *because* others are rich. This idea supposes a fixed amount of property in the community, which by fraud, or force, or arbitrary law, is unequally divided among men ; and the problem presented for solution is, how to transfer a portion of this property from those who are supposed to have too much, to those who feel and know that they have too little. At this point both their theory and their expectation of reform stop. But the beneficent power of education would not be exhausted, even though it should peaceably abolish all the miseries which spring from the co-existence, side by side, of enormous wealth and squalid want. It has a higher function. Beyond the power of diffusing old wealth, it has the prerogative of creating new. It is a thousand times more lucrative than fraud ; and adds a thousand-fold more to a nation's resources than the most successful conquests. Knaves and robbers can obtain only what was before possessed by others.

10

But education creates or develops new treasures,—treasures not before possessed or dreamed of by any one."

In conclusion, it is the imperative duty of the State to extend the privileges of her common schools to every child within her limits. To so legislate, that the rich shall feel the weight of their responsibility, and thus be made to insure the protection of their accumulated wealth by preventive measures ; that the poor shall feel the benign yet authoritative influence that protects their children against the terrible power of their cruel necessities ; that child-employers shall be brought into accord with law, and with that true political economy that looks at indirect as well as to direct causes ; that grasps at the deepest problems of life, seeking no favor and fearing no criticism,—a political economy that, while appealing to an educated self-interest, remembers that the golden rule of Christ is the wisest measure for our material, as well as for our spiritual welfare ; that the children who to-day—

" Are weary ere they run,"

shall bless the bounty and the wisdom of that State whose shores were consecrated to the establishment of a Commonwealth, whose every inhabitant should be secure in that freedom that is alone possible where education and wealth are as widely diffused, and as equitably distributed as the light of the sun that gives life, and the rain that brings forth the fruits in due season.

Recommendations.

As the subject-matter committed to my charge is that of the enforcement of the law relating to the employment and schooling of children employed in manufacturing and mechanical establishments, it might be deemed foreign to my duty to recommend any legislation not bearing directly upon this subject. But as indirect causes are sometimes more potent than direct, I take the liberty of suggesting—

First. That the school age shall include all from five years of age to eighteen.

Second. That all persons over five and under eighteen be enrolled annually, and their names, ages, addresses (and the places of employment of such as are employed) be entered in a register kept for that purpose ; said enrolment and registration to be made by such parties as the school committee may select.

Third. The establishment of a system of compulsory returns to schedules of inquiries, from school committees, assessors of towns and cities, and employers having children under their control as workers ; the schedule to contain such inquiries as, when answered, will give to the legislature and the public full information as to the number of children in the State, and in school, of six years and under ; that is, between five and six, between six and twelve, between twelve and fifteen, between fifteen and eighteen, over eighteen ; together with the actual attendance and non-attendance, with causes of all absence, where it exceeds ten half-days in any one month.

In addition to these suggestions, I would recommend : First. That a law be enacted similar to the Factory Acts of England, limiting the age at which a child can be employed in any cotton, woollen, flax, jute, silk, iron, glass, paper, boots and shoes, cordage and twine, hosiery, furniture, hats and caps, India-rubber, elastic goods, straw or tobacco manufactory, at twelve years, and not then unless such children have received the elements of a common-school education, and shall be physically qualified for such labor ; age, education, and physical condition to be matter of certificate provided for by law ; and every child between twelve and eighteen to receive twenty weeks' schooling each year, of ten sessions each week, or forty weeks of five sessions each week ; provided, that any child having graduated from the public grammar school, and being fifteen years of age, or upwards, and of good physical condition, may be exempt from further attendance ;—said act to limit the hours of labor to all children between twelve and eighteen to eight hours a day, except in the case of those children who attend half-time schools ; then the hours of labor shall be five per day. To provide for half-time schools ; to provide also for protection to life and limb, against accidents from unguarded belting and machinery, and for suitable fire-escapes. Second. The appointment, by the governor, of a factory inspector, with three deputies ; said inspector to report in print to the governor, on the first of January of each year, and to have such powers as are requisite to secure the impartial enforcement of all laws relating to the schooling, hours of labor and employment of factory children.

Respectfully,

GEORGE E. McNEILL.

Philadelphia Society for Organizing Charity.

ON THE RELATION OF EMPLOYERS AND EMPLOYED.

By Mrs. Josephine Shaw Lowell.

[A paper read at the Women's Conference of the Philadelphia Society for Organizing Charity, April 1st, 1885.]

I was very thankful when I heard that this Conference was to consider the relation of employers and employed, and very glad to have a chance to say a few words on the subject, because, while we, who have to do with the poor, say that usually the poverty and suffering of those who cannot take care of themselves is due to their own weaknesses and bad habits, yet we also see that these very weaknesses and bad habits are too often the result of injustices and wrongs commited against these people by their employers. Leaving aside the whole class of employers against whom all the world cries out, those who pay what are called "starvation wages," and who could find no one to accept such wages were there not workpeople partly supported by benevolent societies and individuals who in their mistaken zeal little dream that they themselves render possible the very cruelty against which they declaim, employers of a much better class are responsible for a great deal of the woe and misery that confronts us.

Those born without bodily health, who have no stamina, no power to take or keep their places in the battle of life, are the "hopeless cases" that come before such as try to relieve the poor—people without "back-bone" moral or physical. Nothing is more pathetic than to note the vast difference between even the children in different families, those of one stock, strong, alert, reliable, intelligent, full of energy and ability; sure to "get on," whatever may be their circumstances; those of another family, puny, limp, without force, without courage, unready for all the trials and struggles that are sure to confront them. And how can employers be responsible for such things? In more ways than one; first, by the over-work of mothers,—women who should be leading healthy lives, women who should be caring for their children,—working in factories in bad air working overtime, destroying their own health, turning off their children to be drugged and abused by careless, brutal nurses. What hope can there be for the health and strength of children so born and nurtured ? What hope for their characters, when they are left to run in the streets until they too are swept into the unrelenting grasp of these same dread factories ? Employers are responsible for the deterioration of the race because they allow such things. To show you the actual facts, I shall quote from the Second Annual Report (1884), of the Inspector of Factories of the State of New Jersey.

"The examination we have made in the leading districts of the State dishearten and distress. Nothing short of personal experience would have led us to believe in the frightful amount of ignorance which exists. The number of children who are being reared in ignorance, fitted for injuring society, in whom the natural feelings are destroyed, and who forget all the good they have ever learned, whose homes are too often habitations of wretchedness, and who seem to have no hope, is appalling. The condition of these children appeals to all who desire to save society from lawlessness and ruin, and who prefer prevention to punishment. The children of the toiling poor are not naturally disorderly or lawless. They were not born thieves, liars, prostitutes or murderers. They are as capable of good as the children who are more favored, and, with proper care and protection and nurture, they would make honest, honorable and intelligent citizens. With their wan faces and dwarfed forms and stunted minds, these little ones of our State outstretch their arms and appealingly implore the lawmakers of New Jersey to afford them the mental pabulum and physical protection which they so much need. Large numbers of children have been examined in all our manufacturing districts. The examinations were held either in factories or in private places selected for the purpose by the Inspectors. They were conducted with a view to reach correct conclusions in the interest of the State, the child, and society generally. Almost all the children examined were between the ages of 12 and 15. The average age at which these children went to work was 9 years. As a rule, they have been sent to school about their sixth or seventh year and taken away about two years later, for the purpose of being put to work. All of them had been accustomed to work ten hours a day, and many of them thirteen and more hours a day through overtime. One of the latter, a pale worn-out child of 14 years, said, when asked if she liked to work overtime, "No, but I am used to it now, but I don't feel well." A boy just turned 12 years of age, when asked, did he play, said "No ;" and another, when asked did he ever laugh, answered like an old man, "Not much." Such replies were not unfrequent. The general appearance of these children is worthy of note. Children who had been set to work at an early age were as a rule, delicate, puny and ignorant ; they know the least, having forgotten the little they had been taught before going to work. The most healthy and intelligent were those who had attended school till their 13th or 14th year. The boys in the glass works, who do no overtime and work about eight hours a day, looked stronger, livelier and healthier than any others. Many of the children, when questioned, answered that they did not remember when they first went to work, the time was so long past. Amongst the complaints made by children under 15 years of age, it was stated that a full dinner hour is not given ; that only fifteen or thirty minutes is allowed for supper during overtime ; that children who have long distances to go home, work overtime ; that boys and girls in stores and similar places are compelled to work twelve, fourteen and more hours a day, to their great mental and physical detriment, and that they are too tired after working ten or ten and a half hours to attend night school. As as an illustration of the evils of overtime for young persons, I may cite the case of a small girl under 15 years of age, but who looked no more than 13, whom I found at work with others at 10 P. M. in a badly ventilated factory where the thermometer stood above 100°. This child, after her thirteen and a half hours' toil, had to walk two miles over a country road before reaching home. The evil in such cases is not at all lessened by limiting the hours to sixty per week, or reducing the hours on Saturday. The great evil consists in working more than reasonable hours each day. Cases of this kind were found to be the rule, not the exception.

The examination of parents and children shows that the employment of children has increased with the reduction of wages, and that the employment of adults has decreased with the employment of children. It shows that there are thousands of children in the State who know no change but from the workshop to the bed and from the bed to the workshop. It shows that even ten hours labor in a factory for children is itself an overwork. It shows that overwork in the factory treadmill for women, not to mention children, is destructive not alone to their lives, but to the lives of their offspring. It shows that while the poor and even the criminal are responsible for their bad acts, they are not alone to blame, and that society which neglects and ignores their interests should not be acquitted of all responsibility. It is true that many of those who drive their children to work at tender ages, and who try to get them at work on some pretense, are unthinking, unscrupulous, debauched parents who have little regard for the mental, physical, and moral interests of their offspring. But it is also true that these same persons have been neglected in their youth and adolescence, and that the rights which we claim for the children of to-day were denied them. Therefore, our aim should be to save the youth of to-day from the ignorance and training through which so many parents have been ruined. Many of the worst kind of parents and guardians complained bitterly of the law. "They did not see what business the State had interfering with their children. What right had the law to compel their children to attend school ? They themselves got no schooling and they did not see what more their children wanted ! When they were little children they had to work, and why should not their children work ? Their children knew quite enough !"

That the State of New Jersey is not more negligent of her children than many other States, we know, and that this ruining of our people in their youth is a growing evil is proved by the census of 1880, which shows that in that year 1,118,356 children between 10 and 15 years were pursuing "gainful occupations," which is an increase of 379,192 over the number reported by the census of 1870. Here then we see that employers are guilty of a great crime, not only against their work people, but against the State, and this crime should be forbidden by law in every State in the Union, and the laws when passed, should be enforced.

And even with adults, who, theoretically, are supposed to be able to protect themselves, in how many ways do not employers contribute directly to their degradation ! By overwork, driving them to the use of stimulants ; by unhealthy surroundings, sapping their strength ; and by these and other means depriving them of all chance of being free and independent men. Corporations especially are acknowledged to be devoid of all conscience in their relations toward those who make the wealth which they divide ; the directors and officers convince themselves that their first duty is toward their stockholders, and that they are bound to make every dollar possible, regardless of the means by which it is done, the stockholders know nothing whatever of the methods adopted, and the workers go down in the struggle. All transportation companies, horse cars, steamboats and railroads, are peculiarly offenders in this regard, driving their men to work for sixteen hours in the day and often for seven days in the week. The mind and body cannot long hold out against such grinding, such unnatural labor. Here again legislation is required in the interest of the national health, to ensure that every man shall have at least one day in seven for his sabbath, his day of rest, essential both for his body and his soul.

The vast importance to us especially of the condition of our working people, is forcibly expressed by an English student of these subjects. Mr. Daniel Pidgeon in his book "Old World Questions and New World Answers," says: "The American Republic is founded upon the sovereignty of the people, and it will prosper or perish according as the mental and moral status of the sovereign people is high or low. The question whether labor in America will in future sustain, improve upon or degrade from its once high condition is one beside which every other national problem, social, religious, or political is a matter of trifling moment, for upon this depends the destiny of the greatest state, and the life of the most beneficent government which the world has ever seen." That it is for the interest of the employers as well as his duty to provide healthful and elevating surroundings for his work people is to be seen by the results that have been obtained by many men who have achieved great business success in this country and in Europe. It is delightful to read of such factories and villages as those of the Cheney Brothers in Connecticut, of the Fairbanks Company in Vermont, of the Willimantic Thread Company, where the employers try to give to their workmen some, at least, of the same kind of elevating and enjoyable surroundings that make their own lives valuable, and it is good to believe with Mr. Pidgeon that " every factory in Europe or America could be converted into a humanizing agency, such as Willimantic is, and it would pay owners, to say nothing of their hands, for them all to become so. Money mills of to day might all be "mills of God" to-morrow, producing intelligence and morality, with the least possible expenditure of civilizing effort, because of the assistance that association lends, whether to the making of morality or of cotton goods." In discussions concerning wages and the duty of the employer toward those they employ, it is common to say that the laws of business are not the laws of the gospel, and that it is unwise to mix up entirely distinct matters and to try to judge and settle business questions by gospel laws. Now, I do not agree that any province of life is outside the domain of the laws of the gospel : I hold that every relation of life should be governed by them, and that this is a duty, regardless of consequences. But this need not be here discussed, for the joyful discovery made of late by political economists and students of sociology is that the very objects which so-called business methods are supposed to help one to attain, can be much more readily and directly reached by following the laws of the gospel; that the real interests of employers and employed are always identical, and that even material interests are best served by not being pursued without regard to higher things. "Seek ye first the Kingdom of Heaven, and all these things shall be added unto you." In the growing recognition of this fact lies the hope that the "Kingdom of Heaven" is at hand. Students and theorists have discovered its truth,. and so have many practical men, both employers and employed, and it should be the duty of every one who wants to hasten the coming of the Kingdom, to insist upon this fact, and bring forward the proof of it, always and everywhere, in season and out of season. It is only showing that Jesus was true and that Christianity is right, but nothing so much requires to be taught as these two facts.

To take the question of wages, Mr. Atkinson, a business man, and an authority on social and economical questions has lately written a very interesting paper, called "The Distribution of Products," and he has shown conclusively that high wages make cheap products, and that in all industrial contests highly paid workmen can compete successfully with pauper labor. Mr. Atkinson says :

"Low rates of wages are not essential to a low cost of production, but on the contrary usually indicate a high cost of production, that is to say, a large measure of human labor and a large sum of wages at low rates. Conversely, high rates of wages may, and commonly do, indicate a low cost of production, that is to say, a small proportion of human labor and a small proportionate sum of wages at high rates in a given quantity of product * * Cheap labor, in a true sense, and low rates of wages are not synonimous terms, but are usually quite the reverse. The abuse of the word *cheap* eads to more mischievous fallacies than any other abuse of language. The cheapest labor is the best paid labor ; it is the best paid labor applied to machinery that assures the largest product in ratio to the capital invested. * * * In the long run, wages or earnings will be the highest in that country in which capital and labor co-operate to the fullest extent, thereby assuring tne largest production to the lowest labor cost. I have endeavored to separate the fundamental principle of wages from all side issues, and to prove, with as much scientific accuracy as may be possible, that the interests of the employer and the employed are absolutely identical, and that progress and poverty are not of necessity evolved together under the existing customs of the English speaking people."

It is then for the interest of the whole cummunity that wages should be high, and we may desire high wages not only for the good of the wage-earners, but for the good of the wage-payers as well, and it is well for us to bear in mind that we may help to make wages high by desiring that they should be so and believing that they ought to be so. Prof. Francis A. Walker in his "Wages Question" has made a good argument to show that public opinion has a great influence in fixing the rates of wages, and we ought to remember this, and be encouraged to freely express our sympathies.

Now, I ask, can it be doubtful that the respect and sympathy of the community must strengthen the wages class in their unceasing struggle for economical advantages; must give weight and force to all their reasonable demands; must make them more resolute and patient in resisting encroachment; must add to the confidence with which each individual laborer will rely on the good faith of those who are joined with him in his cause, and make it harder for any weak or doubtful comrade to succumb in the contest; and on the other hand, will not the consciousness that the whole community sympathize with the efforts of labor to advance its condition by all fair means, inevitably weaken the resistance of the employing class to claims which can be conceded; diminish the confidence with which each employer looks to his fellows to hold out to the end, and make it easier for the less resolute to retire from the contest and grant, amid general applause, what has been demanded? He must be more than human or less than human who is uninfluenced by the friendly or cold regards of men. And if such a disposition of the public mind must confirm the union and exalt the courage and sustain the faith of the party that hears everywhere approving words, meets everywhere looks of sympathy, and must tend to impair somewhat, at least, the mutual trust and common resolutions of their opponents, who shall say that wages may not be affected thereby?"

Passing, however, beyond the questions we have been discussing, where the wage-earners have been considered as dependent upon the wage-payers, we find that the experience of many men for many years has proved that there is a surer means for raising the character of working men, a means by which they shall have justice done them, and shall receive a fair share of the products of their labor, while, by the same means, these very products are increased, and also the profits of the employer. This means is what is termed "Profit-Sharing," under which title are included many different plans by which employers share with those they employ a certain proportion of the net profits of their joint labor. The practical results of many such enterprises justify us in looking upon "profit-sharing," as opening a possible, nay, a certain future of independence and self respect, of comfort and happiness for wage-earners, whenever they are sufficiently educated to accept its blessings, and their employers are sufficiently wise to offer them.

It is encouraging, it is exhilarating to learn of the success that has been reached by this means of distributing the results of the combined work of labor and capital. The first experiment was made by LeClaire, a Frenchman, born in 1801, the son of a poor shoemaker, who was taken from school at 10 years of age and put to work in the fields. When he was 17 he went to Paris, and penniless and friendless, apprenticed himself to a house painter. When he was 26 he started in business on his own account, and by his honesty and good work became successful, and in 1842 he told his workmen that he intended to divide with them a part of the profits of the last year's work. This he did, giving each one of forty-four workmen about $50 as his share, and so began an industrial partnership which has outlived its founder, and is to-day in successful existence. Mr. Sedley Taylor, writing of LeClaire in 1880, says:

The introduction of participation by workmen in the profits of employers admits of being recommended on purely economic grounds as a benefit to both the parties concerned. The increasing activity of the workmen, his greatest care of the tools and materials entrusted to him, and the consequent possibility of saving a considerable part of the cost of superintendence, enable profits to be made under a participating system which would not accrue under the established routine. If these extra profits were to be wholly divided among those whose labour produced them, the employer would still be as well off as he is under the existing system. But, assuming that he distributes among his workmen only a portion of this fresh fund, and retain the rest himself, both he and they will at the end of the year find their account in the new principles introduced into their business relations. It was on this tangible ground of mutual advantage that LeClaire by preference took his stand when publicly defending the system incorporated in the house. He constantly insisted that his conduct had been for his advantage, and that it was better for him to earn a hundred francs and give fifty of them to his workmen than to earn only twenty-five francs and keep them all for himself. 'I maintain,' he wrote in 1865, 'that if I had gone on in the beaten track of routine I could not have arrived even by fraudulent means at a position comparable to that which I have made for myself.'

This may be fully admitted as far as concerns the mere stimulation of the workman's energy by the prospect of increased gain; but the most superficial glance at the great institution reared by LeClaire suffices to show that his real aims were of an entirely different order from those of the self interested speculator with whom in his anxiety to avoid the dangerous reputation of an innovating visionary, he professed to identify himself. He was at bottom, as M. Robert, his biographer and successor assured me, and as indeed is evident from many passages in his published writings, an ardent social reformer, passionately desiring the emancipation of the wage-supported classes from the precarious situation in which the present relations between capital and labor held them bound as though by some inflexible law of nature. It was with an eye consciously fixed on this distant goal that he thought and wrote and labored in the immediate interests of his own workmen. As was the case with so many of those who have applied genius to philanthropy, the fountain of LeClaire's enthusiasm was essentially religious, though of a kind unconnected with the special dogmas of any particular Christian body. How intensely he held the 'great commandment' of Christian morality appears from the following words written in sight of death, when he felt 'sincerity' to be 'more than ever a duty.' "I believe in the God who has written in our hearts the law of duty, the law of progress, the law of the sacrifice of one's self for others. I submit myself to His will, I bow before the mysteries of His power and of our destiny. I am the humble disciple of Him who has told us to do to others what we would have others do to us, and to love our neighbor as ourselves; it is in this sense that I desire to remain a Christian until my last breath."

We have seen what one unaided man, imbued with this victorious spirit, was able to contribute towards the solution of the great social problem of our day—how, by bettering the relations between capital and labor, to assure to the toiling masses a self respecting present and a hopeful future. I cannot believe that this consummation will ever be reached through the conflicts of opposing self-interests; it can only be from "economic science enlightened by the spirit of the gospel," and pointing over the heads of lower antagonisms to a higher unity, that an ultimate solution is to be looked for? In another essay on "Profit-Sharing," after giving many examples of its success in raising the character of workmen, and in giving them a fair share of the results of their own labor, Mr. Taylor says:

"Trade conflicts and dictations *ab extra* are, however, merely symptoms of a deeper seated industrial malady, and can therefore be permanently got rid of only by a remedy capable of attacking the disease itself in its originating cause. That cause is evidently the widespread and profoundly erroneous conviction that the interests of employers and employed are in the nature of things essentially opposed to each other. Profit sharing attacks the root-evil in the most effective way, not by arguing against it, but by setting in active operation a system of remunerating labor based on the opposite doctrine. When employees have become convinced that the machinery of this system necessarily brings to them in virtue of its very construction a satisfactory portion of the net profits annually accruing, there will no longer be any motive for spasmodic efforts to drive up wages in order to secure some share of a perhaps but fleeting prosperity. Similarly, when all are directly interested in the results of production, and in improving to the utmost the technical processes by which it is carried on, the practice of seeking to control these processes by regulations emanating from an external body will naturally fall into desuetude. These great results, however, can be looked for only when extensive applications of the profit-sharing principle shall have won for it a strong body of public opinion. As Mr. Archibald Briggs has said with so much force, "its great advantages can only be secured by its becoming general, and gradually altering the whole tone of the relations between employer and employed, doing away with antagonistic combinations of one class against the other, and destroying the last remnants of the old feeling among the workmen, already I trust dying out in consequence of better education, that somehow anything tending to the disadvantages of the employer must be their gain.""

The practical success of profit-sharing is affirmed by many witnesses. Prof. Bohmert sums up a very full examination of the opposing arguments in the following words: "Most of the judgments pronounced against participation in profits emanate from men of business who have either never tried the system at all, or else only to an inadequate extent or for too short a time. The unfavorable judgments upon it coming from workmen originate likewise in circles possessing no knowledge derived from actual experience. On the other hand, it is precisely from those employers who have most thoroughly developed the system that we receive decidedly favorable judgments and experiences. The actually participating workmen likewise communicate their approval of the system in the liveliest terms. (Vol I. pp. 215, 216.) I cannot better close this paper than with a final quotation from Mr. Pidgeon's book : —"Each for all" instead of "each for each" will yet be the watchword of industry, and the device, let us hope, for that flag of discontented labour which still wants a motto. The long conflict between capital and labor draws to a close and the treaty of peace between these old foes will be a deed of industrial partnership."